THE COMPLETE
APOCRYPHA

PLUS:

ENOCH, JASHER, AND JUBILEES

MOSES ISRAEL

Orlando, FL 2023

Table of Contents

INTRODUCTION

The apocrypha is a selection of books which were published in the original 1611 King James Bible. These apocryphal books were positioned between the Old and New Testament (it also contained maps and geneologies). The apocrypha was a part of the KJV Bible for 274 years until being removed in 1885 A.D.

Many Israelite scholars believe it should never have been removed- that it was considered part of the Bible for nearly 2,000 years before it was recently removed a little more than 100 years ago. Many point to the verse in Revelation 22:19 that warns against taking away from the Bible "And if any man shall take away from the words of the book of this prophecy, God shall take away his part out of the book of life, and out of the holy city, and from the things which are written in this book." The word 'apocrypha' means 'hidden.' Fragments of Dead Sea Scrolls dating back to before 70 A.D. contained parts of the apocrypha books in Hebrew, including Sirach and   Tobit.

The Israelite people were continually wondering what God was saying to them during their difficult times. Out of their experiences arose the books of the Apocrypha. The following brief descriptions provide some background for the books in the collection. The individual Old Testament Apocrypha books are arranged in alphabetical order. The following listing shows the books as they are generally arranged in Bibles that contain the Apocrypha.

First Esdras: This is primarily an historical account of the return of the Israelite people from the Babylonian captivity and the reestablishment of the Temple and its worship. Its historical account is taken from 2 Chronicles 35:1; 36:23; Ezra 1:1-11, along with Nehemiah 7:73 - 8:12. It beams with the Passover celebration by King Josiah of Judah (640-609 B.C.) It discusses Josiah's death in the battle of Megiddo and continues with the events leading up to the fall of Jerusalem and the deportation of the Israelites to Babylon (586 B.C.)

Second Esdras: This book contains some visions and revelations of the early Israelite priests. It is helpful as a case history of Israelite thought and literature shortly before the time of Christ. It was probably written during the same time period as the Book of the Revelation (ca. 96 A.D.) by a Palestinian Israelite who was disillusioned over the destruction of the Temple in 70 A.D. He was puzzled by the evil in a world where God was supposed to be in control. This gloomy book is tied together with a thread of hope as deliverance for God's people is assured. God is ultimately in control of history His Word will never disappear.

Tobit: This is a narrative about good and evil spirits and teaches several lessons in morals. It is about Tobit, a Hebrew who was taken into captivity to Nineveh, the capital of Assyria, after the defeat of Israel in 722-721 B.C. Tobit was a strict observer of the Law who met with unfortunate circumstances. One night he was blinded when droppings from a swallow fell into his eyes. God heard the prayers of Tobit and another Israelite, Sarah, who lived in Babylonia or Media. God sent His angel Raphael, to help and save both Tobit and Sarah with the aid of Tobit's son, Tobias. The story ends happily as Tobias marries Sarah and defeats a demon named Asmodeus. Order was reestablished in their lives. Tobit was written to show the place of fasting and prayer in the lives of the faithful It teaches that God uses His angels to help people during difficult times.

Judith: This book is a narrative of a pious woman who murdered the Assyrian General Holofernes. Its aim is to show God's ability to deliver His people in dire circumstances. Judith was a wise and intelligent Israelite woman who was devoted to keeping the Law of Moses. The story takes place during the time when Holofernes was commander of the Assyrian army He was about to destroy the Israelite inhabitants of the city of Bethulia when Judith came to the aid of her fellow Israelite. The people prayed to God for help, allowing Him five days in which to help them or they would surrender. Judith went to the enemy camp, beheaded Holofernes, and took his head back to the Israelites of the city Terrified, the Assyrians fled and the Israelites were saved. The book of Judith appealed to Israelites living during a time of discouragement and defeat. It was probably written during the Hasmonean Period (142-63 B.C.). Judith exemplified the importance of faithfulness to the Law of Moses and the power of God in the lives of His people. The Additions to the

Book of Esther: The Old Testament Book of Esther does not mention the name of God or any worship rituals. These Apocryphal additions were written to connect the book of Esther to the traditions of Israel's faith in a more explicit way.

The Wisdom of Solomon: This is a collection of teachings in a system of moral philosophy, written in the style of Solomon. It reflects on the wisdom imparted in the Book of Proverbs.

Ecclesiasticus: This book should not be confused with the Old Testament Book of Ecclesiastes. The Apocrypha book was written in Hebrew around 180 B.C. and was translated into Greek for the Alexandrian Israelites. It deals with a wide variety of subjects from diet to domestic relationships. Ecclesiasticus upholds Israel's traditions as a channel through which God's Word is communicated. It indicates that a righteous person is rewarded by God, whereas a sinner will be punished.

Baruch: This book is attributed to the friend and scribe of Jeremiah. It offers encouragement to one in exile and is divided into three sections: a confession, a plea for mercy and pardon, and consolation and assurance.

The Letter of Jeremiah: The author of this letter, written around 300 B.C., is unknown. It is an impassioned sermon based on Jeremiah 11:10, in which Jeremiah showed the utter impotence of gods of wood, silver, and gold.

The Prayer of Azariah and The Song of the Three Young Men: The Prayer of Azariah was added to Daniel 3. It is the prayer spoken by Azariah from the Very furnace. The Song of the Three Young Men tells of their change as they walked about in the flames.

Susanna: This book relates the story of two Israelite elders in Babylon who falsely accused Susanna of adultery because she resisted their advances while she was bathing. She was condemned, but Daniel obtained a retrial and exposed her accusers.

Bel and the Dragon: This contains one of the world's oldest detective stories. Daniel plays detective to expose the priests of Bel for eating she food that they declared their god had eaten. The dragon was a serpent worshiped by the king until Daniel killed it by feeding it lumps of pitch, fat, and hair, thus exposing it as false.

The Prayer of Manasseh: This prayer is ascribed to King Manasseh of Judah, who, according to 2°Chronicles 33, was taken to Babylon, where he repented of the idolatry that had characterized the evil years of his reign. Some scholars believe that the prayer by Manasseh recorded in 2°Chronicles 33:19 is connected with this prayer.

The Books of the Maccabees: These two narratives contain much valuable historical matter about valiant priests, soldiers, and rulers of the Maccabean family. The first book is a history of the Israelites from the beginning of the reign of Antiochus Epiphanes to the death of Simon Maccabeus. The second book begins its account just before the time of the first book and relates much of the same material. However, it contradicts some of the first book and has less historical authenticity. There are three other Books of Maccabees, but they have never been recognized as canonical, except the third by the Greek Orthodox Church.

The Book of Enoch: is an ancient Israelite book, ascribed by tradition to Enoch, the great-grandfather of Noah. The first part of the Book of

Enoch describes the fall of the Watchers, the angels who fathered the Nephilim. The remainder of the book describes Enoch's visits to heaven in the form of travels, visions and dreams, and his revelations. The book consists of five quite distinct major sections: The Book of the Watchers (1 Enoch 1–36), The Book of Parables of Enoch (1 Enoch 37–71) (also called the Similitudes of Enoch), The Astronomical Book (1 Enoch 72–82) (also called the Book of the Heavenly Luminaries or Book of Luminaries), The Book of Dream Visions (1 Enoch 83–90) (also called the Book of Dreams), The Epistle of Enoch (1 Enoch 91–108).

The Books of Jasher: It's always good to get an understanding of what words mean and the same is true for the book of Jasher. The meaning of Jasher is from the he Hebrew "Yashar" and it means, "Upright", or "Righteous".

The book is also called the "book of the upright". When you read it you will find this to be true because of the more intricate details it gives us of patriarchs, such as Moses, Nimrod, Esau and Jacob…

If you have been led by organised religion all your life, the very thought of the book of Jasher most likely sounds very foreign to you. But the fact is, that it is mentioned in the scriptures twice…

Unfortunately, even with these mentions, there are still those that want to oppose this book, mainly due to ignorance and their resistance to change and repentance.

Here are scriptures that mention the book directly…

Joshua 10:13

"13 And the sun stood still, and the moon stayed, until the people had avenged themselves upon their enemies. Is not this written in the book of Jasher? So the sun stood still in the midst of heaven, and hasted not to go down about a whole day."

2 Samuel 1:18

"18 (Also he bade them teach the children of Judah the use of the bow: behold, it is written in the book of Jasher.)"

So in two places within the bible we see mention of the book of Jasher…

The Book of Jubilees: The Book of Jubilees, sometimes called Lesser Genesis (Leptogenesis), is an ancient Israelite book of 50 chapters. It covers much of the same ground as Genesis, but often with additional detail, and addressing Moses in the second person as the entire history of creation, and of Israel up to that point, is recounted in divisions of 49 years each, or "Jubilees". The elapsed time from the creation, up to Moses receiving the scriptures upon Sinai during the Exodus, is calculated as fifty Jubilees, less the 40 years still to be spent wandering in the desert before entering Canaan – or 2,410 years.

Four classes of Malak (angels) are mentioned: angels of the presence, angels of sanctifications, guardian

angels over individuals, and angels presiding over the phenomena of nature. Enoch was the first man initiated by the angels in the art of writing, and wrote down, accordingly, all the secrets
of astronomy, of chronology, and of the world's epochs.

1 ESDRAS

1 Esdras 1

[1] And Josias held the feast of the Passover in Jerusalem unto his Lord, and offered the Passover the fourteenth day of the first month;

[2] Having set the priests according to their daily courses, being arrayed in long garments, in the temple of the Lord.

[3] And he spake unto the Levites, the holy ministers of Israel, that they should hallow themselves unto the Lord, to set the holy ark of the Lord in the house that king Solomon the son of David had built:

[4] And said, Ye shall no more bear the ark upon your shoulders: now therefore serve the Lord your God, and minister unto his people Israel, and prepare you after your families and kindreds,

[5] According as David the king of Israel prescribed, and according to the magnificence of Solomon his son: and standing in the temple according to the several dignity of the families of you the Levites, who minister in the presence of your brethren the children of Israel,

[6] Offer the Passover in order, and make ready the sacrifices for your brethren, and keep the Passover according to the commandment of the Lord, which was given unto Moses.

[7] And unto the people that was found there Josias gave thirty thousand lambs and kids, and three thousand calves: these things were given of the king's allowance, according as he promised, to the people, to the priests, and to the Levites.

[8] And Helkias, Zacharias, and Syelus, the governors of the temple, gave to the priests for the Passover two thousand and six hundred sheep, and three hundred calves.

[9] And Jeconias, and Samaias, and Nathanael his brother, and Assabias, and Ochiel, and Joram, captains over thousands, gave to the Levites for the Passover five thousand sheep, and seven hundred calves.

[10] And when these things were done, the priests and Levites, having the unleavened bread, stood in very comely order according to the kindreds,

[11] And according to the several dignities of the fathers, before the people, to offer to the Lord, as it is written in the book of Moses: and thus did they in the morning.

[12] And they roasted the Passover with fire, as appertaineth: as for the sacrifices, they sod them in brass pots and pans with a good savour,

[13] And set them before all the people: and afterward they prepared

for themselves, and for the priests their brethren, the sons of Aaron.

[14] For the priests offered the fat until night: and the Levites prepared for themselves, and the priests their brethren, the sons of Aaron.

[15] The holy singers also, the sons of Asaph, were in their order, according to the appointment of David, to wit, Asaph, Zacharias, and Jeduthun, who was of the king's retinue.

[16] Moreover the porters were at every gate; it was not lawful for any to go from his ordinary service: for their brethren the Levites prepared for them.

[17] Thus were the things that belonged to the sacrifices of the Lord accomplished in that day, that they might hold the Passover,

[18] And offer sacrifices upon the altar of the Lord, according to the commandment of king Josias.

[19] So the children of Israel which were present held the Passover at that time, and the feast of sweet bread seven days.

[20] And such a Passover was not kept in Israel since the time of the prophet Samuel.

[21] Yea, all the kings of Israel held not such a passover as Josias, and the priests, and the Levites, and the Jews, held with all Israel that were found dwelling at Jerusalem.

[22] In the eighteenth year of the reign of Josias was this Passover kept.

[23] And the works or Josias were upright before his Lord with an heart full of godliness.

[24] As for the things that came to pass in his time, they were written in former times, concerning those that sinned, and did wickedly against the Lord above all people and kingdoms, and how they grieved him exceedingly, so that the words of the Lord rose up against Israel.

[25] Now after all these acts of Josias it came to pass, that Pharaoh the king of Egypt came to raise war at Carchamis upon Euphrates: and Josias went out against him.

[26] But the king of Egypt sent to him, saying, What have I to do with thee, O king of Judea?

[27] I am not sent out from the Lord God against thee; for my war is upon Euphrates: and now the Lord is with me, yea, the Lord is with me hasting me forward: depart from me, and be not against the Lord.

[28] Howbeit Josias did not turn back his chariot from him, but undertook to fight with him, not regarding the words of the prophet Jeremy spoken by the mouth of the Lord:

[29] But joined battle with him in the plain of Magiddo, and the princes came against king Josias.

[30] Then said the king unto his servants, Carry me away out of the battle; for I am very weak. And immediately his servants took him away out of the battle.

[31] Then gat he up upon his second chariot; and being brought back to Jerusalem died, and was buried in his father's sepulchre.

[32] And in all Jewry they mourned for Josias, yea, Jeremy the prophet lamented for Josias, and the chief men with the women made lamentation for him unto this day: and this was given out for an ordinance to be done continually in all the nation of Israel.

[33] These things are written in the book of the stories of the kings of Judah, and every one of the acts that Josias did, and his glory, and his understanding in the law of the Lord, and the things that he had done before, and the things now recited, are reported in the book of the kings of Israel and Judea.

[34] And the people took Joachaz the son of Josias, and made him king instead of Josias his father, when he was twenty and three years old.

[35] And he reigned in Judea and in Jerusalem three months: and then the king of Egypt deposed him from reigning in Jerusalem.

[36] And he set a tax upon the land of an hundred talents of silver and one talent of gold.

[37] The king of Egypt also made king Joacim his brother king of Judea and Jerusalem.

[38] And he bound Joacim and the nobles: but Zaraces his brother he apprehended, and brought him out of Egypt.

[39] Five and twenty years old was Joacim when he was made king in the land of Judea and Jerusalem; and he did evil before the Lord.

[40] Wherefore against him Nabuchodonosor the king of Babylon came up, and bound him with a chain of brass, and carried him into Babylon.

[41] Nabuchodonosor also took of the holy vessels of the Lord, and carried them away, and set them in his own temple at Babylon.

[42] But those things that are recorded of him, and of his uncleaness and impiety, are written in the chronicles of the kings.

[43] And Joacim his son reigned in his stead: he was made king being eighteen years old;

[44] And reigned but three months and ten days in Jerusalem; and did evil before the Lord.

[45] So after a year Nabuchodonosor sent and caused him to be brought

into Babylon with the holy vessels of the Lord;

[46] And made Zedechias king of Judea and Jerusalem, when he was one and twenty years old; and he reigned eleven years:

[47] And he did evil also in the sight of the Lord, and cared not for the words that were spoken unto him by the prophet Jeremy from the mouth of the Lord.

[48] And after that king Nabuchodonosor had made him to swear by the name of the Lord, he forswore himself, and rebelled; and hardening his neck, his heart, he transgressed the laws of the Lord God of Israel.

[49] The governors also of the people and of the priests did many things against the laws, and passed all the pollutions of all nations, and defiled the temple of the Lord, which was sanctified in Jerusalem.

[50] Nevertheless the God of their fathers sent by his messenger to call them back, because he spared them and his tabernacle also.

[51] But they had his messengers in derision; and, look, when the Lord spake unto them, they made a sport of his prophets:

[52] So far forth, that he, being wroth with his people for their great ungodliness, commanded the kings of the Chaldees to come up against them;

[53] Who slew their young men with the sword, yea, even within the compass of their holy temple, and spared neither young man nor maid, old man nor child, among them; for he delivered all into their hands.

[54] And they took all the holy vessels of the Lord, both great and small, with the vessels of the ark of God, and the king's treasures, and carried them away into Babylon.

[55] As for the house of the Lord, they burnt it, and brake down the walls of Jerusalem, and set fire upon her towers:

[56] And as for her glorious things, they never ceased till they had consumed and brought them all to nought: and the people that were not slain with the sword he carried unto Babylon:

[57] Who became servants to him and his children, till the Persians reigned, to fulfil the word of the Lord spoken by the mouth of Jeremy:

[58] Until the land had enjoyed her Sabbaths, the whole time of her desolation shall she rest, until the full term of seventy years.

1 Esdras 2

[1] In the first year of Cyrus king of the Persians, that the word of the Lord might be accomplished, that he had promised by the mouth of Jeremy;

[2] The Lord raised up the spirit of Cyrus the king of the Persians, and he made proclamation through all his kingdom, and also by writing,

[3] Saying, Thus saith Cyrus king of the Persians; The Lord of Israel, the most high Lord, hath made me king of the whole world,

[4] And commanded me to build him an house at Jerusalem in Jewry.

[5] If therefore there be any of you that are of his people, let the Lord, even his Lord, be with him, and let him go up to Jerusalem that is in Judea, and build the house of the Lord of Israel: for he is the Lord that dwelleth in Jerusalem.

[6] Whosoever then dwell in the places about, let them help him, those, I say, that are his neighbours, with gold, and with silver,

[7] With gifts, with horses, and with cattle, and other things, which have been set forth by vow, for the temple of the Lord at Jerusalem.

[8] Then the chief of the families of Judea and of the tribe of Benjamin stood up; the priests also, and the Levites, and all they whose mind the Lord had moved to go up, and to build an house for the Lord at Jerusalem,

[9] And they that dwelt round about them, and helped them in all things with silver and gold, with horses and cattle, and with very many free gifts of a great number whose minds were stirred up thereto.

[10] King Cyrus also brought forth the holy vessels, which Nabuchodonosor had carried away from Jerusalem, and had set up in his temple of idols.

[11] Now when Cyrus king of the Persians had brought them forth, he delivered them to Mithridates his treasurer:

[12] And by him they were delivered to Sanabassar the governor of Judea.

[13] And this was the number of them; A thousand golden cups, and a thousand of silver, censers of silver twenty nine, vials of gold thirty, and of silver two thousand four hundred and ten, and a thousand other vessels.

[14] So all the vessels of gold and of silver, which were carried away, were five thousand four hundred threescore and nine.

[15] These were brought back by Sanabassar, together with them of the captivity, from Babylon to Jerusalem.

[16] But in the time of Artexerxes king of the Persians Belemus, and Mithridates, and Tabellius, and Rathumus, and Beeltethmus, and Semellius the secretary, with others that were in commission with them, dwelling in Samaria and other places, wrote unto him against them

that dwelt in Judea and Jerusalem these letters following;

[17] To king Artexerxes our lord, Thy servants, Rathumus the storywriter, and Semellius the scribe, and the rest of their council, and the judges that are in Celosyria and Phenice.

[18] Be it now known to the lord king, that the Jews that are up from you to us, being come into Jerusalem, that rebellious and wicked city, do build the marketplaces, and repair the walls of it and do lay the foundation of the temple.

[19] Now if this city and the walls thereof be made up again, they will not only refuse to give tribute, but also rebel against kings.

[20] And forasmuch as the things pertaining to the temple are now in hand, we think it meet not to neglect such a matter,

[21] But to speak unto our lord the king, to the intent that, if it be thy pleasure it may be sought out in the books of thy fathers:

[22] And thou shalt find in the chronicles what is written concerning these things, and shalt understand that that city was rebellious, troubling both kings and cities:

[23] And that the Jews were rebellious, and raised always wars therein; for the which cause even this city was made desolate.

[24] Wherefore now we do declare unto thee, O lord the king, that if this city be built again, and the walls thereof set up anew, thou shalt from henceforth have no passage into Celosyria and Phenice.

[25] Then the king wrote back again to Rathumus the storywriter, to Beeltethmus, to Semellius the scribe, and to the rest that were in commission, and dwellers in Samaria and Syria and Phenice, after this manner;

[26] I have read the epistle which ye have sent unto me: therefore I commanded to make diligent search, and it hath been found that that city was from the beginning practising against kings;

[27] And the men therein were given to rebellion and war: and that mighty kings and fierce were in Jerusalem, who reigned and exacted tributes in Celosyria and Phenice.

[28] Now therefore I have commanded to hinder those men from building the city, and heed to be taken that there be no more done in it;

[29] And that those wicked workers proceed no further to the annoyance of kings,

[30] Then king Artexerxes his letters being read, Rathumus, and Semellius the scribe, and the rest that were in commission with them, removing in haste toward Jerusalem

with a troop of horsemen and a multitude of people in battle array, began to hinder the builders; and the building of the temple in Jerusalem ceased until the second year of the reign of Darius king of the Persians.

1 Esdras 3

[1] Now when Darius reigned, he made a great feast unto all his subjects, and unto all his household, and unto all the princes of Media and Persia,

[2] And to all the governors and captains and lieutenants that were under him, from India unto Ethiopia, of an hundred twenty and seven provinces.

[3] And when they had eaten and drunken, and being satisfied were gone home, then Darius the king went into his bedchamber, and slept, and soon after awaked.

[4] Then three young men, that were of the guard that kept the king's body, spake one to another;

[5] Let every one of us speak a sentence: he that shall overcome, and whose sentence shall seem wiser than the others, unto him shall the king Darius give great gifts, and great things in token of victory:

[6] As, to be clothed in purple, to drink in gold, and to sleep upon gold, and a chariot with bridles of gold, and an headtire of fine linen, and a chain about his neck:

[7] And he shall sit next to Darius because of his wisdom, and shall be called Darius his cousin.

[8] And then every one wrote his sentence, sealed it, and laid it under king Darius his pillow;

[9] And said that, when the king is risen, some will give him the writings; and of whose side the king and the three princes of Persia shall judge that his sentence is the wisest, to him shall the victory be given, as was appointed.

[10] The first wrote, Wine is the strongest.

[11] The second wrote, The king is strongest.

[12] The third wrote, Women are strongest: but above all things Truth beareth away the victory.

[13] Now when the king was risen up, they took their writings, and delivered them unto him, and so he read them:

[14] And sending forth he called all the princes of Persia and Media, and the governors, and the captains, and the lieutenants, and the chief officers;

[15] And sat him down in the royal seat of judgment; and the writings were read before them.

[16] And he said, Call the young men, and they shall declare their own sentences. So they were called, and came in.

[17] And he said unto them, Declare unto us your mind concerning the writings. Then began the first, who had spoken of the strength of wine;

[18] And he said thus, O ye men, how exceeding strong is wine! it causeth all men to err that drink it:

[19] It maketh the mind of the king and of the fatherless child to be all one; of the bondman and of the freeman, of the poor man and of the rich:

[20] It turneth also every thought into jollity and mirth, so that a man remembereth neither sorrow nor debt:

[21] And it maketh every heart rich, so that a man remembereth neither king nor governor; and it maketh to speak all things by talents:

[22] And when they are in their cups, they forget their love both to friends and brethren, and a little after draw out swords:

[23] But when they are from the wine, they remember not what they have done.

[24] O ye men, is not wine the strongest, that enforceth to do thus? And when he had so spoken, he held his peace.

1 Esdras 4

[1] Then the second, that had spoken of the strength of the king, began to say,

[2] O ye men, do not men excel in strength that bear rule over sea and land and all things in them?

[3] But yet the king is more mighty: for he is lord of all these things, and hath dominion over them; and whatsoever he commandeth them they do.

[4] If he bid them make war the one against the other, they do it: if he send them out against the enemies, they go, and break down mountains walls and towers.

[5] They slay and are slain, and transgress not the king's commandment: if they get the victory, they bring all to the king, as well the spoil, as all things else.

[6] Likewise for those that are no soldiers, and have not to do with wars, but use husbundry, when they have reaped again that which they had sown, they bring it to the king, and compel one another to pay tribute unto the king.

[7] And yet he is but one man: if he command to kill, they kill; if he command to spare, they spare;

[8] If he command to smite, they smite; if he command to make desolate, they make desolate; if he command to build, they build;

[9] If he command to cut down, they cut down; if he command to plant, they plant.

[10] So all his people and his armies obey him: furthermore he lieth down, he eateth and drinketh, and taketh his rest:

[11] And these keep watch round about him, neither may any one depart, and do his own business, neither disobey they him in any thing.

[12] O ye men, how should not the king be mightiest, when in such sort he is obeyed? And he held his tongue.

[13] Then the third, who had spoken of women, and of the truth, (this was Zorobabel) began to speak.

[14] O ye men, it is not the great king, nor the multitude of men, neither is it wine, that excelleth; who is it then that ruleth them, or hath the lordship over them? are they not women?

[15] Women have borne the king and all the people that bear rule by sea and land.

[16] Even of them came they: and they nourished them up that planted the vineyards, from whence the wine cometh.

[17] These also make garments for men; these bring glory unto men; and without women cannot men be.

[18] Yea, and if men have gathered together gold and silver, or any other goodly thing, do they not love a woman which is comely in favour and beauty?

[19] And letting all those things go, do they not gape, and even with open mouth fix their eyes fast on her; and have not all men more desire unto her than unto silver or gold, or any goodly thing whatsoever?

[20] A man leaveth his own father that brought him up, and his own country, and cleaveth unto his wife.

[21] He sticketh not to spend his life with his wife. and remembereth neither father, nor mother, nor country.

[22] By this also ye must know that women have dominion over you: do ye not labour and toil, and give and bring all to the woman?

[23] Yea, a man taketh his sword, and goeth his way to rob and to steal, to sail upon the sea and upon rivers;

[24] And looketh upon a lion, and goeth in the darkness; and when he hath stolen, spoiled, and robbed, he bringeth it to his love.

[25] Wherefore a man loveth his wife better than father or mother.

[26] Yea, many there be that have run out of their wits for women, and become servants for their sakes.

[27] Many also have perished, have erred, and sinned, for women.

[28] And now do ye not believe me? is not the king great in his power? do not all regions fear to touch him?

[29] Yet did I see him and Apame the king's concubine, the daughter of the admirable Bartacus, sitting at the right hand of the king,

[30] And taking the crown from the king's head, and setting it upon her own head; she also struck the king with her left hand.

[31] And yet for all this the king gaped and gazed upon her with open mouth: if she laughed upon him, he laughed also: but if she took any displeasure at him, the king was fain to flatter, that she might be reconciled to him again.

[32] O ye men, how can it be but women should be strong, seeing they do thus?

[33] Then the king and the princes looked one upon another: so he began to speak of the truth.

[34] O ye men, are not women strong? great is the earth, high is the heaven, swift is the sun in his course, for he compasseth the heavens round about, and fetcheth his course again to his own place in one day.

[35] Is he not great that maketh these things? therefore great is the truth, and stronger than all things.

[36] All the earth crieth upon the truth, and the heaven blesseth it: all works shake and tremble at it, and with it is no unrighteous thing.

[37] Wine is wicked, the king is wicked, women are wicked, all the children of men are wicked, and such are all their wicked works; and there is no truth in them; in their unrighteousness also they shall perish.

[38] As for the truth, it endureth, and is always strong; it liveth and conquereth for evermore.

[39] With her there is no accepting of persons or rewards; but she doeth the things that are just, and refraineth from all unjust and wicked things; and all men do well like of her works.

[40] Neither in her judgment is any unrighteousness; and she is the strength, kingdom, power, and majesty, of all ages. Blessed be the God of truth.

[41] And with that he held his peace. And all the people then shouted, and said, Great is Truth, and mighty above all things.

[42] Then said the king unto him, Ask what thou wilt more than is appointed in the writing, and we will give it thee, because thou art found wisest; and thou shalt sit next me, and shalt be called my cousin.

[43] Then said he unto the king, Remember thy vow, which thou hast vowed to build Jerusalem, in the day when thou camest to thy kingdom,

[44] And to send away all the vessels that were taken away out of Jerusalem, which Cyrus set apart, when he vowed to destroy Babylon, and to send them again thither.

[45] Thou also hast vowed to build up the temple, which the Edomites burned when Judea was made desolate by the Chaldees.

[46] And now, O lord the king, this is that which I require, and which I desire of thee, and this is the princely liberality proceeding from thyself: I desire therefore that thou make good the vow, the performance whereof with thine own mouth thou hast vowed to the King of heaven.

[47] Then Darius the king stood up, and kissed him, and wrote letters for him unto all the treasurers and lieutenants and captains and governors, that they should safely convey on their way both him, and all those that go up with him to build Jerusalem.

[48] He wrote letters also unto the lieutenants that were in Celosyria and Phenice, and unto them in Libanus, that they should bring cedar wood from Libanus unto Jerusalem, and that they should build the city with him.

[49] Moreover he wrote for all the Jews that went out of his realm up into Jewry, concerning their freedom that no officer, no ruler, no lieutenant, nor treasurer, should forcibly enter into their doors;

[50] And that all the country which they hold should be free without tribute; and that the Edomites should give over the villages of the Jews which then they held:

[51] Yea, that there should be yearly given twenty talents to the building of the temple, until the time that it were built;

[52] And other ten talents yearly, to maintain the burnt offerings upon the altar every day, as they had a commandment to offer seventeen:

[53] And that all they that went from Babylon to build the city should have free liberty, as well they as their posterity, and all the priests that went away.

[54] He wrote also concerning. the charges, and the priests' vestments wherein they minister;

[55] And likewise for the charges of the Levites, to be given them until the day that the house were finished, and Jerusalem builded up.

[56] And he commanded to give to all that kept the city pensions and wages.

[57] He sent away also all the vessels from Babylon, that Cyrus had set apart; and all that Cyrus had given in commandment, the same charged he also to be done, and sent unto Jerusalem.

[58] Now when this young man was gone forth, he lifted up his face to heaven toward Jerusalem, and praised the King of heaven,

[59] And said, From thee cometh victory, from thee cometh wisdom, and thine is the glory, and I am thy servant.

[60] Blessed art thou, who hast given me wisdom: for to thee I give thanks, O Lord of our fathers.

[61] And so he took the letters, and went out, and came unto Babylon, and told it all his brethren.

[62] And they praised the God of their fathers, because he had given them freedom and liberty

[63] To go up, and to build Jerusalem, and the temple which is called by his name: and they feasted with instruments of musick and gladness seven days.

1 Esdras 5

[1] After this were the principal men of the families chosen according to their tribes, to go up with their wives and sons and daughters, with their menservants and maidservants, and their cattle.

[2] And Darius sent with them a thousand horsemen, till they had brought them back to Jerusalem safely, and with musical instruments tabrets and flutes.

[3] And all their brethren played, and he made them go up together with them.

[4] And these are the names of the men which went up, according to their families among their tribes, after their several heads.

[5] The priests, the sons of Phinees the son of Aaron: Jesus the son of Josedec, the son of Saraias, and Joacim the son of Zorobabel, the son of Salathiel, of the house of David, out of the kindred of Phares, of the tribe of Judah;

[6] Who spake wise sentences before Darius the king of Persia in the second year of his reign, in the month Nisan, which is the first month.

[7] And these are they of Jewry that came up from the captivity, where they dwelt as strangers, whom Nabuchodonosor the king of Babylon had carried away unto Babylon.

[8] And they returned unto Jerusalem, and to the other parts of Jewry, every man to his own city, who came with Zorobabel, with Jesus, Nehemias, and Zacharias, and Reesaias, Enenius, Mardocheus. Beelsarus, Aspharasus, Reelius, Roimus, and Baana, their guides.

[9] The number of them of the nation, and their governors, sons of Phoros, two thousand an hundred seventy

and two; the sons of Saphat, four hundred seventy and two:

[10] The sons of Ares, seven hundred fifty and six:

[11] The sons of Phaath Moab, two thousand eight hundred and twelve:

[12] The sons of Elam, a thousand two hundred fifty and four: the sons of Zathul, nine hundred forty and five: the sons of Corbe, seven hundred and five: the sons of Bani, six hundred forty and eight:

[13] The sons of Bebai, six hundred twenty and three: the sons of Sadas, three thousand two hundred twenty and two:

[14] The sons of Adonikam, six hundred sixty and seven: the sons of Bagoi, two thousand sixty and six: the sons of Adin, four hundred fifty and four:

[15] The sons of Aterezias, ninety and two: the sons of Ceilan and Azetas threescore and seven: the sons of Azuran, four hundred thirty and two:

[16] The sons of Ananias, an hundred and one: the sons of Arom, thirty two: and the sons of Bassa, three hundred twenty and three: the sons of Azephurith, an hundred and two:

[17] The sons of Meterus, three thousand and five: the sons of Bethlomon, an hundred twenty and three:

[18] They of Netophah, fifty and five: they of Anathoth, an hundred fifty and eight: they of Bethsamos, forty and two:

[19] They of Kiriathiarius, twenty and five: they of Caphira and Beroth, seven hundred forty and three: they of Pira, seven hundred:

[20] They of Chadias and Ammidoi, four hundred twenty and two: they of Cirama and Gabdes, six hundred twenty and one:

[21] They of Macalon, an hundred twenty and two: they of Betolius, fifty and two: the sons of Nephis, an hundred fifty and six:

[22] The sons of Calamolalus and Onus, seven hundred twenty and five: the sons of Jerechus, two hundred forty and five:

[23] The sons of Annas, three thousand three hundred and thirty.

[24] The priests: the sons of Jeddu, the son of Jesus among the sons of Sanasib, nine hundred seventy and two: the sons of Meruth, a thousand fifty and two:

[25] The sons of Phassaron, a thousand forty and seven: the sons of Carme, a thousand and seventeen.

[26] The Levites: the sons of Jessue, and Cadmiel, and Banuas, and Sudias, seventy and four.

[27] The holy singers: the sons of Asaph, an hundred twenty and eight.

[28] The porters: the sons of Salum, the sons of Jatal, the sons of Talmon, the sons of Dacobi, the sons of Teta, the sons of Sami, in all an hundred thirty and nine.

[29] The servants of the temple: the sons of Esau, the sons of Asipha, the sons of Tabaoth, the sons of Ceras, the sons of Sud, the sons of Phaleas, the sons of Labana, the sons of Graba,

[30] The sons of Acua, the sons of Uta, the sons of Cetab, the sons of Agaba, the sons of Subai, the sons of Anan, the sons of Cathua, the sons of Geddur,

[31] The sons of Airus, the sons of Daisan, the sons of Noeba, the sons of Chaseba, the sons of Gazera, the sons of Azia, the sons of Phinees, the sons of Azare, the sons of Bastai, the sons of Asana, the sons of Meani, the sons of Naphisi, the sons of Acub, the sons of Acipha, the sons of Assur, the sons of Pharacim, the sons of Basaloth,

[32] The sons of Meeda, the sons of Coutha, the sons of Charea, the sons of Charcus, the sons of Aserer, the sons of Thomoi, the sons of Nasith, the sons of Atipha.

[33] The sons of the servants of Solomon: the sons of Azaphion, the sons of Pharira, the sons of Jeeli, the sons of Lozon, the sons of Israel, the sons of Sapheth,

[34] The sons of Hagia, the sons of Pharacareth, the sons of Sabi, the sons of Sarothie, the sons of Masias, the sons of Gar, the sons of Addus, the sons of Suba, the sons of Apherra, the sons of Barodis, the sons of Sabat, the sons of Allom.

[35] All the ministers of the temple, and the sons of the servants of Solomon, were three hundred seventy and two.

[36] These came up from Thermeleth and Thelersas, Charaathalar leading them, and Aalar;

[37] Neither could they shew their families, nor their stock, how they were of Israel: the sons of Ladan, the son of Ban, the sons of Necodan, six hundred fifty and two.

[38] And of the priests that usurped the office of the priesthood, and were not found: the sons of Obdia, the sons of Accoz, the sons of Addus, who married Augia one of the daughters of Barzelus, and was named after his name.

[39] And when the description of the kindred of these men was sought in the register, and was not found, they were removed from executing the office of the priesthood:

[40] For unto them said Nehemias and Atharias, that they should not be partakers of the holy things, till there arose up an high priest clothed with doctrine and truth.

[41] So of Israel, from them of twelve years old and upward, they were all in number forty thousand, beside menservants and womenservants two thousand three hundred and sixty.

[42] Their menservants and handmaids were seven thousand three hundred forty and seven: the singing men and singing women, two hundred forty and five:

[43] Four hundred thirty and five camels, seven thousand thirty and six horses, two hundred forty and five mules, five thousand five hundred twenty and five beasts used to the yoke.

[44] And certain of the chief of their families, when they came to the temple of God that is in Jerusalem, vowed to set up the house again in his own place according to their ability,

[45] And to give into the holy treasury of the works a thousand pounds of gold, five thousand of silver, and an hundred priestly vestments.

[46] And so dwelt the priests and the Levites and the people in Jerusalem, and in the country, the singers also and the porters; and all Israel in their villages.

[47] But when the seventh month was at hand, and when the children of Israel were every man in his own place, they came all together with one consent into the open place of the first gate which is toward the east.

[48] Then stood up Jesus the son of Josedec, and his brethren the priests and Zorobabel the son of Salathiel, and his brethren, and made ready the altar of the God of Israel,

[49] To offer burnt sacrifices upon it, according as it is expressly commanded in the book of Moses the man of God.

[50] And there were gathered unto them out of the other nations of the land, and they erected the altar upon his own place, because all the nations of the land were at enmity with them, and oppressed them; and they offered sacrifices according to the time, and burnt offerings to the Lord both morning and evening.

[51] Also they held the feast of tabernacles, as it is commanded in the law, and offered sacrifices daily, as was meet:

[52] And after that, the continual oblations, and the sacrifice of the Sabbaths, and of the new moons, and of all holy feasts.

[53] And all they that had made any vow to God began to offer sacrifices to God from the first day of the seventh month, although the temple of the Lord was not yet built.

[54] And they gave unto the masons and carpenters money, meat, and drink, with cheerfulness.

[55] Unto them of Zidon also and Tyre they gave carrs, that they should bring cedar trees from Libanus, which should be brought by floats to the haven of Joppa, according as it was commanded them by Cyrus king of the Persians.

[56] And in the second year and second month after his coming to the temple of God at Jerusalem began Zorobabel the son of Salathiel, and Jesus the son of Josedec, and their brethren, and the priests, and the Levites, and all they that were come unto Jerusalem out of the captivity:

[57] And they laid the foundation of the house of God in the first day of the second month, in the second year after they were come to Jewry and Jerusalem.

[58] And they appointed the Levites from twenty years old over the works of the Lord. Then stood up Jesus, and his sons and brethren, and Cadmiel his brother, and the sons of Madiabun, with the sons of Joda the son of Eliadun, with their sons and brethren, all Levites, with one accord setters forward of the business, labouring to advance the works in the house of God. So the workmen built the temple of the Lord.

[59] And the priests stood arrayed in their vestments with musical instruments and trumpets; and the Levites the sons of Asaph had cymbals,

[60] Singing songs of thanksgiving, and praising the Lord, according as David the king of Israel had ordained.

[61] And they sung with loud voices songs to the praise of the Lord, because his mercy and glory is for ever in all Israel.

[62] And all the people sounded trumpets, and shouted with a loud voice, singing songs of thanksgiving unto the Lord for the rearing up of the house of the Lord.

[63] Also of the priests and Levites, and of the chief of their families, the ancients who had seen the former house came to the building of this with weeping and great crying.

[64] But many with trumpets and joy shouted with loud voice,

[65] Insomuch that the trumpets might not be heard for the weeping of the people: yet the multitude sounded marvellously, so that it was heard afar off.

[66] Wherefore when the enemies of the tribe of Judah and Benjamin heard it, they came to know what that noise of trumpets should mean.

[67] And they perceived that they that were of the captivity did build the temple unto the Lord God of Israel.

[68] So they went to Zorobabel and Jesus, and to the chief of the families, and said unto them, We will build together with you.

[69] For we likewise, as ye, do obey your Lord, and do sacrifice unto him from the days of Azbazareth the king of the Assyrians, who brought us hither.

[70] Then Zorobabel and Jesus and the chief of the families of Israel said unto them, It is not for us and you to build together an house unto the Lord our God.

[71] We ourselves alone will build unto the Lord of Israel, according as Cyrus the king of the Persians hath commanded us.

[72] But the heathen of the land lying heavy upon the inhabitants of Judea, and holding them strait, hindered their building;

[73] And by their secret plots, and popular persuasions and commotions, they hindered the finishing of the building all the time that King Cyrus lived: so they were hindered from building for the space of two years, until the reign of Darius.

1 Esdras 6

[1] Now in the second year of the reign of Darius Aggeus and Zacharias the son of Addo, the prophets, prophesied unto the Jews in Jewry and Jerusalem in the name of the Lord God of Israel, which was upon them.

[2] Then stood up Zorobabel the son of Salatiel, and Jesus the son of Josedec, and began to build the house of the Lord at Jerusalem, the prophets of the Lord being with them, and helping them.

[3] At the same time came unto them Sisinnes the governor of Syria and Phenice, with Sathrabuzanes and his companions, and said unto them,

[4] By whose appointment do ye build this house and this roof, and perform all the other things? and who are the workmen that perform these things?

[5] Nevertheless the elders of the Jews obtained favour, because the Lord had visited the captivity;

[6] And they were not hindered from building, until such time as signification was given unto Darius concerning them, and an answer received.

[7] The copy of the letters which Sisinnes, governor of Syria and Phenice, and Sathrabuzanes, with their companions, rulers in Syria and Phenice, wrote and sent unto Darius; To king Darius, greeting:

[8] Let all things be known unto our lord the king, that being come into the country of Judea, and entered into the city of Jerusalem we found in the city of Jerusalem the ancients of the Jews that were of the captivity

[9] Building an house unto the Lord, great and new, of hewn and costly stones, and the timber already laid upon the walls.

[10] And those works are done with great speed, and the work goeth on prosperously in their hands, and with all glory and diligence is it made.

[11] Then asked we these elders, saying, By whose commandment build ye this house, and lay the foundations of these works?

[12] Therefore to the intent that we might give knowledge unto thee by writing, we demanded of them who were the chief doers, and we required of them the names in writing of their principal men.

[13] So they gave us this answer, We are the servants of the Lord which made heaven and earth.

[14] And as for this house, it was builded many years ago by a king of Israel great and strong, and was finished.

[15] But when our fathers provoked God unto wrath, and sinned against the Lord of Israel which is in heaven, he gave them over into the power of Nabuchodonosor king of Babylon, of the Chaldees;

[16] Who pulled down the house, and burned it, and carried away the people captives unto Babylon.

[17] But in the first year that king Cyrus reigned over the country of Babylon Cyrus the king wrote to build up this house.

[18] And the holy vessels of gold and of silver, that Nabuchodonosor had carried away out of the house at Jerusalem, and had set them in his own temple those Cyrus the king brought forth again out of the temple at Babylon, and they were delivered to Zorobabel and to Sanabassarus the ruler,

[19] With commandment that he should carry away the same vessels, and put them in the temple at Jerusalem; and that the temple of the Lord should be built in his place.

[20] Then the same Sanabassarus, being come hither, laid the foundations of the house of the Lord at Jerusalem; and from that time to this being still a building, it is not yet fully ended.

[21] Now therefore, if it seem good unto the king, let search be made among the records of King Cyrus:

[22] And if it be found that the building of the house of the Lord at Jerusalem hath been done with the consent of king Cyrus, and if our lord the king be so minded, let him signify unto us thereof.

[23] Then commanded king Darius to seek among the records at Babylon: and so at Ecbatane the palace, which is in the country of Media, there was found a roll wherein these things were recorded.

[24] In the first year of the reign of Cyrus king Cyrus commanded that the house of the Lord at Jerusalem

should be built again, where they do sacrifice with continual fire:

[25] Whose height shall be sixty cubits and the breadth sixty cubits, with three rows of hewn stones, and one row of new wood of that country; and the expences thereof to be given out of the house of King Cyrus:

[26] And that the holy vessels of the house of the Lord, both of gold and silver, that Nabuchodonosor took out of the house at Jerusalem, and brought to Babylon, should be restored to the house at Jerusalem, and be set in the place where they were before.

[27] And also he commanded that Sisinnes the governor of Syria and Phenice, and Sathrabuzanes, and their companions, and those which were appointed rulers in Syria and Phenice, should be careful not to meddle with the place, but suffer Zorobabel, the servant of the Lord, and governor of Judea, and the elders of the Jews, to build the house of the Lord in that place.

[28] I have commanded also to have it built up whole again; and that they look diligently to help those that be of the captivity of the Jews, till the house of the Lord be finished:

[29] And out of the tribute of Celosyria and Phenice a portion carefully to be given these men for the sacrifices of the Lord, that is, to Zorobabel the governor, for bullocks, and rams, and lambs;

[30] And also corn, salt, wine, and oil, and that continually every year without further question, according as the priests that be in Jerusalem shall signify to be daily spent:

[31] That offerings may be made to the Most High God for the king and for his children, and that they may pray for their lives.

[32] And he commanded that whosoever should transgress, yea, or make light of any thing afore spoken or written, out of his own house should a tree be taken, and he thereon be hanged, and all his goods seized for the king.

[33] The Lord therefore, whose name is there called upon, utterly destroy every king and nation, that stretcheth out his hand to hinder or endamage that house of the Lord in Jerusalem.

[34] I Darius the king have ordained that according unto these things it be done with diligence.

1 Esdras 7

[1] Then Sisinnes the governor of Celosyria and Phenice, and Sathrabuzanes, with their companions following the commandments of king Darius,

[2] Did very carefully oversee the holy works, assisting the ancients of the Jews and governors of the temple.

3 And so the holy works prospered, when Aggeus and Zacharias the prophets prophesied.

[4] And they finished these things by the commandment of the Lord God of Israel, and with the consent of Cyrus, Darius, and Artexerxes, kings of Persia.

[5] And thus was the holy house finished in the three and twentieth day of the month Adar, in the sixth year of Darius king of the Persians

[6] And the children of Israel, the priests, and the Levites, and others that were of the captivity, that were added unto them, did according to the things written in the book of Moses.

[7] And to the dedication of the temple of the Lord they offered an hundred bullocks two hundred rams, four hundred lambs;

[8] And twelve goats for the sin of all Israel, according to the number of the chief of the tribes of Israel.

[9] The priests also and the Levites stood arrayed in their vestments, according to their kindreds, in the service of the Lord God of Israel, according to the book of Moses: and the porters at every gate.

[10] And the children of Israel that were of the captivity held the Passover the fourteenth day of the first month, after that the priests and the Levites were sanctified.

[11] They that were of the captivity were not all sanctified together: but the Levites were all sanctified together.

[12] And so they offered the Passover for all them of the captivity, and for their brethren the priests, and for themselves.

[13] And the children of Israel that came out of the captivity did eat, even all they that had separated themselves from the abominations of the people of the land, and sought the Lord.

[14] And they kept the feast of unleavened bread seven days, making merry before the Lord,

[15] For that he had turned the counsel of the king of Assyria toward them, to strengthen their hands in the works of the Lord God of Israel.

1 Esdras 8

[1] And after these things, when Artexerxes the king of the Persians reigned came Esdras the son of Saraias, the son of Ezerias, the son of Helchiah, the son of Salum,

[2] The son of Sadduc, the son of Achitob, the son of Amarias, the son of Ezias, the son of Meremoth, the son of Zaraias, the son of Savias, the son of Boccas, the son of Abisum, the son of Phinees, the son of Eleazar, the son of Aaron the chief priest.

[3] This Esdras went up from Babylon, as a scribe, being very ready in the law of Moses, that was given by the God of Israel.

[4] And the king did him honour: for he found grace in his sight in all his requests.

[5] There went up with him also certain of the children of Israel, of the priest of the Levites, of the holy singers, porters, and ministers of the temple, unto Jerusalem,

[6] In the seventh year of the reign of Artexerxes, in the fifth month, this was the king's seventh year; for they went from Babylon in the first day of the first month, and came to Jerusalem, according to the prosperous journey which the Lord gave them.

[7] For Esdras had very great skill, so that he omitted nothing of the law and commandments of the Lord, but taught all Israel the ordinances and judgments.

[8] Now the copy of the commission, which was written from Artexerxes the king, and came to Esdras the priest and reader of the law of the Lord, is this that followeth;

[9] King Artexerxes unto Esdras the priest and reader of the law of the Lord sendeth greeting:

[10] Having determined to deal graciously, I have given order, that such of the nation of the Jews, and of the priests and Levites being

within our realm, as are willing and desirous should go with thee unto Jerusalem.

[11] As many therefore as have a mind thereunto, let them depart with thee, as it hath seemed good both to me and my seven friends the counsellors;

[12] That they may look unto the affairs of Judea and Jerusalem, agreeably to that which is in the law of the Lord;

[13] And carry the gifts unto the Lord of Israel to Jerusalem, which I and my friends have vowed, and all the gold and silver that in the country of Babylon can be found, to the Lord in Jerusalem,

[14] With that also which is given of the people for the temple of the Lord their God at Jerusalem: and that silver and gold may be collected for bullocks, rams, and lambs, and things thereunto appertaining;

[15] To the end that they may offer sacrifices unto the Lord upon the altar of the Lord their God, which is in Jerusalem.

[16] And whatsoever thou and thy brethren will do with the silver and gold, that do, according to the will of thy God.

[17] And the holy vessels of the Lord, which are given thee for the use of the temple of thy God, which is in Jerusalem, thou shalt set before thy God in Jerusalem.

[18] And whatsoever thing else thou shalt remember for the use of the temple of thy God, thou shalt give it out of the king's treasury.

[19] And I king Artexerxes have also commanded the keepers of the treasures in Syria and Phenice, that whatsoever Esdras the priest and the reader of the law of the most high God shall send for, they should give it him with speed,

[20] To the sum of an hundred talents of silver, likewise also of wheat even to an hundred cors, and an hundred pieces of wine, and other things in abundance.

[21] Let all things be performed after the law of God diligently unto the most high God, that wrath come not upon the kingdom of the king and his sons.

[22] I command you also, that ye require no tax, nor any other imposition, of any of the priests, or Levites, or holy singers, or porters, or ministers of the temple, or of any that have doings in this temple, and that no man have authority to impose any thing upon them.

[23] And thou, Esdras, according to the wisdom of God ordain judges and justices, that they may judge in all Syria and Phenice all those that know the law of thy God; and those that know it not thou shalt teach.

[24] And whosoever shall transgress the law of thy God, and of the king, shall be punished diligently, whether it be by death, or other punishment, by penalty of money, or by imprisonment.

[25] Then said Esdras the scribe, Blessed be the only Lord God of my fathers, who hath put these things into the heart of the king, to glorify his house that is in Jerusalem:

[26] And hath honoured me in the sight of the king, and his counsellors, and all his friends and nobles.

[27] Therefore was I encouraged by the help of the Lord my God, and gathered together men of Israel to go up with me.

28 And these are the chief according to their families and several dignities, that went up with me from Babylon in the reign of king Artexerxes:

[29] Of the sons of Phinees, Gerson: of the sons of Ithamar, Gamael: of the sons of David, Lettus the son of Sechenias:

[30] Of the sons of Pharez, Zacharias; and with him were counted an hundred and fifty men:

[31] Of the sons of Pahath Moab, Eliaonias, the son of Zaraias, and with him two hundred men:

[32] Of the sons of Zathoe, Sechenias the son of Jezelus, and with him three hundred men: of the sons of Adin, Obeth the son of Jonathan, and with him two hundred and fifty men:

[33] Of the sons of Elam, Josias son of Gotholias, and with him seventy men:

[34] Of the sons of Saphatias, Zaraias son of Michael, and with him threescore and ten men:

[35] Of the sons of Joab, Abadias son of Jezelus, and with him two hundred and twelve men:

36 Of the sons of Banid, Assalimoth son of Josaphias, and with him an hundred and threescore men:

[37] Of the sons of Babi, Zacharias son of Bebai, and with him twenty and eight men:

[38] Of the sons of Astath, Johannes son of Acatan, and with him an hundred and ten men:

[39] Of the sons of Adonikam the last, and these are the names of them, Eliphalet, Jewel, and Samaias, and with them seventy men:

[40] Of the sons of Bago, Uthi the son of Istalcurus, and with him seventy men.

[41] And these I gathered together to the river called Theras, where we pitched our tents three days: and then I surveyed them.

[42] But when I had found there none of the priests and Levites,

[43] Then sent I unto Eleazar, and Iduel, and Masman,

[44] And Alnathan, and Mamaias, and Joribas, and Nathan, Eunatan, Zacharias, and Mosollamon, principal men and learned.

[45] And I bade them that they should go unto Saddeus the captain, who was in the place of the treasury:

[46] And commanded them that they should speak unto Daddeus, and to his brethren, and to the treasurers in that place, to send us such men as might execute the priests' office in the house of the Lord.

[47] And by the mighty hand of our Lord they brought unto us skilful men of the sons of Moli the son of Levi, the son of Israel, Asebebia, and his sons, and his brethren, who were eighteen.

[48] And Asebia, and Annus, and Osaias his brother, of the sons of Channuneus, and their sons, were twenty men.

[49] And of the servants of the temple whom David had ordained, and the principal men for the service of the Levites to wit, the servants of the temple two hundred and twenty, the catalogue of whose names were shewed.

[50] And there I vowed a fast unto the young men before our Lord, to desire of him a prosperous journey both for us and them that were with us, for our children, and for the cattle:

[51] For I was ashamed to ask the king footmen, and horsemen, and

conduct for safeguard against our adversaries.

[52] For we had said unto the king, that the power of the Lord our God should be with them that seek him, to support them in all ways.

[53] And again we besought our Lord as touching these things, and found him favourable unto us.

[54] Then I separated twelve of the chief of the priests, Esebrias, and Assanias, and ten men of their brethren with them:

[55] And I weighed them the gold, and the silver, and the holy vessels of the house of our Lord, which the king, and his council, and the princes, and all Israel, had given.

[56] And when I had weighed it, I delivered unto them six hundred and fifty talents of silver, and silver vessels of an hundred talents, and an hundred talents of gold,

[57] And twenty golden vessels, and twelve vessels of brass, even of fine brass, glittering like gold.

[58] And I said unto them, Both ye are holy unto the Lord, and the vessels are holy, and the gold and the silver is a vow unto the Lord, the Lord of our fathers.

[59] Watch ye, and keep them till ye deliver them to the chief of the priests and Levites, and to the principal men of the families of Israel, in Jerusalem, into the chambers of the house of our God.

[60] So the priests and the Levites, who had received the silver and the gold and the vessels, brought them unto Jerusalem, into the temple of the Lord.

[61] And from the river Theras we departed the twelfth day of the first month, and came to Jerusalem by the mighty hand of our Lord, which was with us: and from the beginning of our journey the Lord delivered us from every enemy, and so we came to Jerusalem.

[62] And when we had been there three days, the gold and silver that was weighed was delivered in the house of our Lord on the fourth day unto Marmoth the priest the son of Iri.

[63] And with him was Eleazar the son of Phinees, and with them were Josabad the son of Jesu and Moeth the son of Sabban, Levites: all was delivered them by number and weight.

[64] And all the weight of them was written up the same hour.

[65] Moreover they that were come out of the captivity offered sacrifice unto the Lord God of Israel, even twelve bullocks for all Israel, fourscore and sixteen rams,

[66] Threescore and twelve lambs, goats for a peace offering, twelve; all of them a sacrifice to the Lord.

[67] And they delivered the king's commandments unto the king's stewards' and to the governors of Celosyria and Phenice; and they honoured the people and the temple of God.

[68] Now when these things were done, the rulers came unto me, and said,

[69] The nation of Israel, the princes, the priests and Levites, have not put away from them the strange people of the land, nor the pollutions of the Gentiles to wit, of the Canaanites, Hittites, Pheresites, Jebusites, and the Moabites, Egyptians, and Edomites.

[70] For both they and their sons have married with their daughters, and the holy seed is mixed with the strange people of the land; and from the beginning of this matter the rulers and the great men have been partakers of this iniquity.

[71] And as soon as I had heard these things, I rent my clothes, and the holy garment, and pulled off the hair from off my head and beard, and sat me down sad and very heavy.

[72] So all they that were then moved at the word of the Lord God of Israel assembled unto me, whilst I mourned for the iniquity: but I sat still full of heaviness until the evening sacrifice.

[73] Then rising up from the fast with my clothes and the holy garment rent, and bowing my knees, and stretching forth my hands unto the Lord,

[74] I said, O Lord, I am confounded and ashamed before thy face;

[75] For our sins are multiplied above our heads, and our ignorances have reached up unto heaven.

[76] For ever since the time of our fathers we have been and are in great sin, even unto this day.

[77] And for our sins and our fathers' we with our brethren and our kings and our priests were given up unto the kings of the earth, to the sword, and to captivity, and for a prey with shame, unto this day.

[78] And now in some measure hath mercy been shewed unto us from thee, O Lord, that there should be left us a root and a name in the place of thy sanctuary;

[79] And to discover unto us a light in the house of the Lord our God, and to give us food in the time of our servitude.

[80] Yea, when we were in bondage, we were not forsaken of our Lord; but he made us gracious before the kings of Persia, so that they gave us food;

[81] Yea, and honoured the temple of our Lord, and raised up the desolate Sion, that they have given us a sure abiding in Jewry and Jerusalem.

[82] And now, O Lord, what shall we say, having these things? for we have transgressed thy commandments, which thou gavest by the hand of thy servants the prophets, saying,

[83] That the land, which ye enter into to possess as an heritage, is a land polluted with the pollutions of the strangers of the land, and they have filled it with their uncleanness.

[84] Therefore now shall ye not join your daughters unto their sons, neither shall ye take their daughters unto your sons.

[85] Moreover ye shall never seek to have peace with them, that ye may be strong, and eat the good things of the land, and that ye may leave the inheritance of the land unto your children for evermore.

[86] And all that is befallen is done unto us for our wicked works and great sins; for thou, O Lord, didst make our sins light,

[87] And didst give unto us such a root: but we have turned back again to transgress thy law, and to mingle ourselves with the uncleanness of the nations of the land.

[88] Mightest not thou be angry with us to destroy us, till thou hadst left us neither root, seed, nor name?

[89] O Lord of Israel, thou art true: for we are left a root this day.

[90] Behold, now are we before thee in our iniquities, for we cannot stand any longer by reason of these things before thee.

[91] And as Esdras in his prayer made his confession, weeping, and lying flat upon the ground before the temple, there gathered unto him from Jerusalem a very great multitude of men and women and children: for there was great weeping among the multitude.

[92] Then Jechonias the son of Jeelus, one of the sons of Israel, called out, and said, O Esdras, we have sinned against the Lord God, we have married strange women of the nations of the land, and now is all Israel aloft.

[93] Let us make an oath to the Lord, that we will put away all our wives, which we have taken of the heathen, with their children,

[94] Like as thou hast decreed, and as many as do obey the law of the Lord.

[95] Arise and put in execution: for to thee doth this matter appertain, and we will be with thee: do valiantly.

[96] So Esdras arose, and took an oath of the chief of the priests and Levites of all Israel to do after these things; and so they sware.

1 Esdras 9

[1] Then Esdras rising from the court of the temple went to the chamber of Joanan the son of Eliasib,

[2] And remained there, and did eat no meat nor drink water, mourning for the great iniquities of the multitude.

[3] And there was a proclamation in all Jewry and Jerusalem to all them that were of the captivity, that they should be gathered together at Jerusalem:

[4] And that whosoever met not there within two or three days according as the elders that bare rule appointed, their cattle should be seized to the use of the temple, and himself cast out from them that were of the captivity.

[5] And in three days were all they of the tribe of Judah and Benjamin gathered together at Jerusalem the twentieth day of the ninth month.

[6] And all the multitude sat trembling in the broad court of the temple because of the present foul weather.

[7] So Esdras arose up, and said unto them, Ye have transgressed the law in marrying strange wives, thereby to increase the sins of Israel.

[8] And now by confessing give glory unto the Lord God of our fathers,

[9] And do his will, and separate yourselves from the heathen of the land, and from the strange women.

[10] Then cried the whole multitude, and said with a loud voice, Like as thou hast spoken, so will we do.

[11] But forasmuch as the people are many, and it is foul weather, so that we cannot stand without, and this is not a work of a day or two, seeing our sin in these things is spread far:

[12] Therefore let the rulers of the multitude stay, and let all them of our habitations that have strange wives come at the time appointed,

[13] And with them the rulers and judges of every place, till we turn away the wrath of the Lord from us for this matter.

[14] Then Jonathan the son of Azael and Ezechias the son of Theocanus accordingly took this matter upon them: and Mosollam and Levis and Sabbatheus helped them.

[15] And they that were of the captivity did according to all these things.

[16] And Esdras the priest chose unto him the principal men of their families, all by name: and in the first day of the tenth month they sat together to examine the matter.

[17] So their cause that held strange wives was brought to an end in the first day of the first month.

[18] And of the priests that were come together, and had strange wives, there were found:

[19] Of the sons of Jesus the son of Josedec, and his brethren; Matthelas and Eleazar, and Joribus and Joadanus.

[20] And they gave their hands to put away their wives and to offer rams to make reconcilement for their errors.

[21] And of the sons of Emmer; Ananias, and Zabdeus, and Eanes, and Sameius, and Hiereel, and Azarias.

[22] And of the sons of Phaisur; Elionas, Massias Israel, and Nathanael, and Ocidelus and Talsas.

[23] And of the Levites; Jozabad, and Semis, and Colius, who was called Calitas, and Patheus, and Judas, and Jonas.

[24] Of the holy singers; Eleazurus, Bacchurus.

[25] Of the porters; Sallumus, and Tolbanes.

[26] Of them of Israel, of the sons of Phoros; Hiermas, and Eddias, and Melchias, and Maelus, and Eleazar, and Asibias, and Baanias.

[27] Of the sons of Ela; Matthanias, Zacharias, and Hierielus, and Hieremoth, and Aedias.

[28] And of the sons of Zamoth; Eliadas, Elisimus, Othonias, Jarimoth, and Sabatus, and Sardeus.

[29] Of the sons of Babai; Johannes, and Ananias and Josabad, and Amatheis.

[30] Of the sons of Mani; Olamus, Mamuchus, Jedeus, Jasubus, Jasael, and Hieremoth.

[31] And of the sons of Addi; Naathus, and Moosias, Lacunus, and Naidus, and Mathanias, and Sesthel, Balnuus, and Manasseas.

[32] And of the sons of Annas; Elionas and Aseas, and Melchias, and Sabbeus, and Simon Chosameus.

[33] And of the sons of Asom; Altaneus, and Matthias, and Baanaia, Eliphalet, and Manasses, and Semei.

[34] And of the sons of Maani; Jeremias, Momdis, Omaerus, Juel, Mabdai, and Pelias, and Anos, Carabasion, and Enasibus, and Mamnitanaimus, Eliasis, Bannus, Eliali, Samis, Selemias, Nathanias: and of the sons of Ozora; Sesis, Esril, Azaelus, Samatus, Zambis, Josephus.

[35] And of the sons of Ethma; Mazitias, Zabadaias, Edes, Juel, Banaias.

[36] All these had taken strange wives, and they put them away with their children.

[37] And the priests and Levites, and they that were of Israel, dwelt in Jerusalem, and in the country, in the

first day of the seventh month: so the children of Israel were in their habitations.

[38] And the whole multitude came together with one accord into the broad place of the holy porch toward the east:

[39] And they spake unto Esdras the priest and reader, that he would bring the law of Moses, that was given of the Lord God of Israel.

[40] So Esdras the chief priest brought the law unto the whole multitude from man to woman, and to all the priests, to hear law in the first day of the seventh month.

[41] And he read in the broad court before the holy porch from morning unto midday, before both men and women; and the multitude gave heed unto the law.

[42] And Esdras the priest and reader of the law stood up upon a pulpit of wood, which was made for that purpose.

[43] And there stood up by him Mattathias, Sammus, Ananias, Azarias, Urias, Ezecias, Balasamus, upon the right hand:

[44] And upon his left hand stood Phaldaius, Misael, Melchias, Lothasubus, and Nabarias.

[45] Then took Esdras the book of the law before the multitude: for he sat honourably in the first place in the sight of them all.

[46] And when he opened the law, they stood all straight up. So Esdras blessed the Lord God most High, the God of hosts, Almighty.

[47] And all the people answered, Amen; and lifting up their hands they fell to the ground, and worshipped the Lord.

[48] Also Jesus, Anus, Sarabias, Adinus, Jacubus, Sabateas, Auteas, Maianeas, and Calitas, Asrias, and Joazabdus, and Ananias, Biatas, the Levites, taught the law of the Lord, making them withal to understand it.

[49] Then spake Attharates unto Esdras the chief priest. and reader, and to the Levites that taught the multitude, even to all, saying,

[50] This day is holy unto the Lord; (for they all wept when they heard the law:)

[51] Go then, and eat the fat, and drink the sweet, and send part to them that have nothing;

[52] For this day is holy unto the Lord: and be not sorrowful; for the Lord will bring you to honour.

[53] So the Levites published all things to the people, saying, This day is holy to the Lord; be not sorrowful.

[54] Then went they their way, every one to eat and drink, and make merry, and to give part to them that had nothing, and to make great cheer;

[55] Because they understood the words wherein they were instructed, and for the which they had been assembled.

2 ESDRAS

2 Esdras 1

[1] The second book of the prophet Esdras, the son of Saraias, the son of Azarias, the son of Helchias, the son of Sadamias, the son of Sadoc, the son of Achitob,

[2] The son of Achias, the son of Phinees, the son of Heli, the son of Amarias, the son of Aziei, the son of Marimoth, the son of Arna, the son of Ozias, the son of Borith, the son of Abisei, the son of Phinees, the son of Eleazar,

[3] The son of Aaron, of the tribe of Levi; which was captive in the land of the Medes, in the reign of Artexerxes king of the Persians.

[4] And the word of the Lord came unto me, saying,

[5] Go thy way, and shew my people their sinful deeds, and their children their wickedness which they have done against me; that they may tell their children's children:

[6] Because the sins of their fathers are increased in them: for they have forgotten me, and have offered unto strange gods.

[7] Am not I even he that brought them out of the land of Egypt, from the house of bondage? but they have provoked me unto wrath, and despised my counsels.

[8] Pull thou off then the hair of thy head, and cast all evil upon them, for they have not been obedient unto my law, but it is a rebellious people.

[9] How long shall I forbear them, into whom I have done so much good?

[10] Many kings have I destroyed for their sakes; Pharaoh with his servants and all his power have I smitten down.

[11] All the nations have I destroyed before them, and in the east I have scattered the people of two provinces, even of Tyrus and Sidon, and have slain all their enemies.

[12] Speak thou therefore unto them, saying, Thus saith the Lord,

[13] I led you through the sea and in the beginning gave you a large and safe passage; I gave you Moses for a leader, and Aaron for a priest.

[14] I gave you light in a pillar of fire, and great wonders have I done among you; yet have ye forgotten me, saith the Lord.

[15] Thus saith the Almighty Lord, The quails were as a token to you; I gave you tents for your safeguard: nevertheless ye murmured there,

[16] And triumphed not in my name for the destruction of your enemies, but ever to this day do ye yet murmur.

[17] Where are the benefits that I have done for you? when ye were

hungry and thirsty in the wilderness, did ye not cry unto me,

[18] Saying, Why hast thou brought us into this wilderness to kill us? it had been better for us to have served the Egyptians, than to die in this wilderness.

[19] Then had I pity upon your mournings, and gave you manna to eat; so ye did eat angels' bread.

[20] When ye were thirsty, did I not cleave the rock, and waters flowed out to your fill? for the heat I covered you with the leaves of the trees.

[21] I divided among you a fruitful land, I cast out the Canaanites, the Pherezites, and the Philistines, before you: what shall I yet do more for you? saith the Lord.

[22] Thus saith the Almighty Lord, When ye were in the wilderness, in the river of the Amorites, being athirst, and blaspheming my name,

[23] I gave you not fire for your blasphemies, but cast a tree in the water, and made the river sweet.

[24] What shall I do unto thee, O Jacob? thou, Juda, wouldest not obey me: I will turn me to other nations, and unto those will I give my name, that they may keep my statutes.

[25] Seeing ye have forsaken me, I will forsake you also; when ye desire me to be gracious unto you, I shall have no mercy upon you.

[26] Whensoever ye shall call upon me, I will not hear you: for ye have defiled your hands with blood, and your feet are swift to commit manslaughter.

[27] Ye have not as it were forsaken me, but your own selves, saith the Lord.

[28] Thus saith the Almighty Lord, Have I not prayed you as a father his sons, as a mother her daughters, and a nurse her young babes,

[29] That ye would be my people, and I should be your God; that ye would be my children, and I should be your father?

[30] I gathered you together, as a hen gathereth her chickens under her wings: but now, what shall I do unto you? I will cast you out from my face.

[31] When ye offer unto me, I will turn my face from you: for your solemn feastdays, your new moons, and your circumcisions, have I forsaken.

[32] I sent unto you my servants the prophets, whom ye have taken and slain, and torn their bodies in pieces, whose blood I will require of your hands, saith the Lord.

[33] Thus saith the Almighty Lord, Your house is desolate, I will cast you out as the wind doth stubble.

[34] And your children shall not be fruitful; for they have despised my

commandment, and done the thing that is an evil before me.

[35] Your houses will I give to a people that shall come; which not having heard of me yet shall believe me; to whom I have shewed no signs, yet they shall do that I have commanded them.

[36] They have seen no prophets, yet they shall call their sins to remembrance, and acknowledge them.

[37] I take to witness the grace of the people to come, whose little ones rejoice in gladness: and though they have not seen me with bodily eyes, yet in spirit they believe the thing that I say.

[38] And now, brother, behold what glory; and see the people that come from the east:

[39] Unto whom I will give for leaders, Abraham, Isaac, and Jacob, Oseas, Amos, and Micheas, Joel, Abdias, and Jonas,

[40] Nahum, and Abacuc, Sophonias, Aggeus, Zachary, and Malachy, which is called also an angel of the Lord.

2 Esdras 2

[1] Thus saith the Lord, I brought this people out of bondage, and I gave them my commandments by menservants the prophets; whom they would not hear, but despised my counsels.

[2] The mother that bare them saith unto them, Go your way, ye children; for I am a widow and forsaken.

[3] I brought you up with gladness; but with sorrow and heaviness have I lost you: for ye have sinned before the Lord your God, and done that thing that is evil before him.

[4] But what shall I now do unto you? I am a widow and forsaken: go your way, O my children, and ask mercy of the Lord.

[5] As for me, O father, I call upon thee for a witness over the mother of these children, which would not keep my covenant,

[6] That thou bring them to confusion, and their mother to a spoil, that there may be no offspring of them.

[7] Let them be scattered abroad among the heathen, let their names be put out of the earth: for they have despised my covenant.

[8] Woe be unto thee, Assur, thou that hidest the unrighteous in thee! O thou wicked people, remember what I did unto Sodom and Gomorrha;

[9] Whose land lieth in clods of pitch and heaps of ashes: even so also will I do unto them that hear me not, saith the Almighty Lord.

[10] Thus saith the Lord unto Esdras, Tell my people that I will give them the kingdom of Jerusalem, which I would have given unto Israel.

[11] Their glory also will I take unto me, and give these the everlasting tabernacles, which I had prepared for them.

[12] They shall have the tree of life for an ointment of sweet savour; they shall neither labour, nor be weary.

[13] Go, and ye shall receive: pray for few days unto you, that they may be shortened: the kingdom is already prepared for you: watch.

[14] Take heaven and earth to witness; for I have broken the evil in pieces, and created the good: for I live, saith the Lord.

[15] Mother, embrace thy children, and bring them up with gladness, make their feet as fast as a pillar: for I have chosen thee, saith the Lord.

[16] And those that be dead will I raise up again from their places, and bring them out of the graves: for I have known my name in Israel.

[17] Fear not, thou mother of the children: for I have chosen thee, saith the Lord.

[18] For thy help will I send my servants Esau and Jeremy, after whose counsel I have sanctified and prepared for thee twelve trees laden with divers fruits,

[19] And as many fountains flowing with milk and honey, and seven mighty mountains, whereupon there grow roses and lilies, whereby I will fill thy children with joy.

[20] Do right to the widow, judge for the fatherless, give to the poor, defend the orphan, clothe the naked,

[21] Heal the broken and the weak, laugh not a lame man to scorn, defend the maimed, and let the blind man come into the sight of my clearness.

[22] Keep the old and young within thy walls.

[23] Wheresoever thou findest the dead, take them and bury them, and I will give thee the first place in my resurrection.

[24] Abide still, O my people, and take thy rest, for thy quietness still come.

[25] Nourish thy children, O thou good nurse; stablish their feet.

[26] As for the servants whom I have given thee, there shall not one of them perish; for I will require them from among thy number.

[27] Be not weary: for when the day of trouble and heaviness cometh, others shall weep and be sorrowful, but thou shalt be merry and have abundance.

[28] The heathen shall envy thee, but they shall be able to do nothing against thee, saith the Lord.

[29] My hands shall cover thee, so that thy children shall not see hell.

[30] Be joyful, O thou mother, with thy children; for I will deliver thee, saith the Lord.

[31] Remember thy children that sleep, for I shall bring them out of the sides of the earth, and shew mercy unto them: for I am merciful, saith the Lord Almighty.

[32] Embrace thy children until I come and shew mercy unto them: for my wells run over, and my grace shall not fail.

[33] I Esdras received a charge of the Lord upon the mount Oreb, that I should go unto Israel; but when I came unto them, they set me at nought, and despised the commandment of the Lord.

[34] And therefore I say unto you, O ye heathen, that hear and understand, look for your Shepherd, he shall give you everlasting rest; for he is nigh at hand, that shall come in the end of the world.

[35] Be ready to the reward of the kingdom, for the everlasting light shall shine upon you for evermore.

[36] Flee the shadow of this world, receive the joyfulness of your glory: I testify my Saviour openly.

[37] O receive the gift that is given you, and be glad, giving thanks unto him that hath led you to the heavenly kingdom.

[38] Arise up and stand, behold the number of those that be sealed in the feast of the Lord;

[39] Which are departed from the shadow of the world, and have received glorious garments of the Lord.

[40] Take thy number, O Sion, and shut up those of thine that are clothed in white, which have fulfilled the law of the Lord.

[41] The number of thy children, whom thou longedst for, is fulfilled: beseech the power of the Lord, that thy people, which have been called from the beginning, may be hallowed.

[42] I Esdras saw upon the mount Sion a great people, whom I could not number, and they all praised the Lord with songs.

[43] And in the midst of them there was a young man of a high stature, taller than all the rest, and upon every one of their heads he set crowns, and was more exalted; which I marvelled at greatly.

[44] So I asked the angel, and said, Sir, what are these?

[45] He answered and said unto me, These be they that have put off the mortal clothing, and put on the immortal, and have confessed the name of God: now are they crowned, and receive palms.

[46] Then said I unto the angel, What young person is it that crowneth them, and giveth them palms in their hands?

[47] So he answered and said unto me, It is the Son of God, whom they have confessed in the world. Then began I greatly to commend them that stood so stiffly for the name of the Lord.

[48] Then the angel said unto me, Go thy way, and tell my people what manner of things, and how great wonders of the Lord thy God, thou hast seen.

2 Esdras 3

[1] In the thirtieth year after the ruin of the city I was in Babylon, and lay troubled upon my bed, and my thoughts came up over my heart:

[2] For I saw the desolation of Sion, and the wealth of them that dwelt at Babylon.

[3] And my spirit was sore moved, so that I began to speak words full of fear to the most High, and said,

[4] O Lord, who bearest rule, thou spakest at the beginning, when thou didst plant the earth, and that thyself alone, and commandedst the people,

[5] And gavest a body unto Adam without soul, which was the workmanship of thine hands, and didst breathe into him the breath of life, and he was made living before thee.

[6] And thou leadest him into paradise, which thy right hand had planted, before ever the earth came forward.

[7] And unto him thou gavest commandment to love thy way: which he transgressed, and immediately thou appointedst death in him and in his generations, of whom came nations, tribes, people, and kindreds, out of number.

[8] And every people walked after their own will, and did wonderful things before thee, and despised thy commandments.

[9] And again in process of time thou broughtest the flood upon those that dwelt in the world, and destroyedst them.

[10] And it came to pass in every of them, that as death was to Adam, so was the flood to these.

[11] Nevertheless one of them thou leftest, namely, Noah with his household, of whom came all righteous men.

[12] And it happened, that when they that dwelt upon the earth began to multiply, and had gotten them many children, and were a great people, they began again to be more ungodly than the first.

[13] Now when they lived so wickedly before thee, thou didst choose thee a man from among them, whose name was Abraham.

[14] Him thou lovedst, and unto him only thou shewedst thy will:

[15] And madest an everlasting covenant with him, promising him that thou wouldest never forsake his seed.

[16] And unto him thou gavest Isaac, and unto Isaac also thou gavest Jacob and Esau. As for Jacob, thou didst choose him to thee, and put by Esau: and so Jacob became a great multitude.

[17] And it came to pass, that when thou leadest his seed out of Egypt, thou broughtest them up to the mount Sinai.

[18] And bowing the heavens, thou didst set fast the earth, movedst the whole world, and madest the depths to tremble, and troubledst the men of that age.

[19] And thy glory went through four gates, of fire, and of earthquake, and of wind, and of cold; that thou mightest give the law unto the seed of Jacob, and diligence unto the generation of Israel.

[20] And yet tookest thou not away from them a wicked heart, that thy law might bring forth fruit in them.

[21] For the first Adam bearing a wicked heart transgressed, and was overcome; and so be all they that are born of him.

[22] Thus infirmity was made permanent; and the law (also) in the heart of the people with the malignity of the root; so that the good departed away, and the evil abode still.

[23] So the times passed away, and the years were brought to an end: then didst thou raise thee up a servant, called David:

[24] Whom thou commandedst to build a city unto thy name, and to offer incense and oblations unto thee therein.

[25] When this was done many years, then they that inhabited the city forsook thee,

[26] And in all things did even as Adam and all his generations had done: for they also had a wicked heart:

[27] And so thou gavest thy city over into the hands of thine enemies.

[28] Are their deeds then any better that inhabit Babylon, that they should therefore have the dominion over Sion?

[29] For when I came thither, and had seen impieties without number, then my soul saw many evildoers in this thirtieth year, so that my heart failed me.

[30] For I have seen how thou sufferest them sinning, and hast spared wicked doers: and hast destroyed thy people, and hast preserved thine enemies, and hast not signified it.

[31] I do not remember how this way may be left: Are they then of Babylon better than they of Sion?

[32] Or is there any other people that knoweth thee beside Israel? or what generation hath so believed thy covenants as Jacob?

[33] And yet their reward appeareth not, and their labour hath no fruit: for I have gone here and there through the heathen, and I see that they flow in wealth, and think not upon thy commandments.

[34] Weigh thou therefore our wickedness now in the balance, and their's also that dwell the world; and so shall thy name no where be found but in Israel.

[35] Or when was it that they which dwell upon the earth have not sinned in thy sight? or what people have so kept thy commandments?

[36] Thou shalt find that Israel by name hath kept thy precepts; but not the heathen.

2 Esdras 4

[1] And the angel that was sent unto me, whose name was Uriel, gave me an answer,

[2] And said, Thy heart hath gone to far in this world, and thinkest thou to comprehend the way of the most High?

[3] Then said I, Yea, my lord. And he answered me, and said, I am sent to shew thee three ways, and to set forth three similitudes before thee:

[4] Whereof if thou canst declare me one, I will shew thee also the way that thou desirest to see, and I shall shew thee from whence the wicked heart cometh.

[5] And I said, Tell on, my lord. Then said he unto me, Go thy way, weigh me the weight of the fire, or measure me the blast of the wind, or call me again the day that is past.

[6] Then answered I and said, What man is able to do that, that thou shouldest ask such things of me?

[7] And he said unto me, If I should ask thee how great dwellings are in the midst of the sea, or how many springs are in the beginning of the deep, or how many springs are above the firmament, or which are the outgoings of paradise:

[8] Peradventure thou wouldest say unto me, I never went down into the deep, nor as yet into hell, neither did I ever climb up into heaven.

[9] Nevertheless now have I asked thee but only of the fire and wind, and of the day wherethrough thou hast passed, and of things from which thou canst not be separated, and yet canst thou give me no answer of them.

[10] He said moreover unto me, Thine own things, and such as are grown up with thee, canst thou not know;

43

11 How should thy vessel then be able to comprehend the way of the Highest, and, the world being now outwardly corrupted to understand the corruption that is evident in my sight?

[12] Then said I unto him, It were better that we were not at all, than that we should live still in wickedness, and to suffer, and not to know wherefore.

[13] He answered me, and said, I went into a forest into a plain, and the trees took counsel,

[14] And said, Come, let us go and make war against the sea that it may depart away before us, and that we may make us more woods.

[15] The floods of the sea also in like manner took counsel, and said, Come, let us go up and subdue the woods of the plain, that there also we may make us another country.

[16] The thought of the wood was in vain, for the fire came and consumed it.

[17] The thought of the floods of the sea came likewise to nought, for the sand stood up and stopped them.

[18] If thou wert judge now betwixt these two, whom wouldest thou begin to justify? or whom wouldest thou condemn?

[19] I answered and said, Verily it is a foolish thought that they both have devised, for the ground is given unto the wood, and the sea also hath his place to bear his floods.

[20] Then answered he me, and said, Thou hast given a right judgment, but why judgest thou not thyself also?

[21] For like as the ground is given unto the wood, and the sea to his floods: even so they that dwell upon the earth may understand nothing but that which is upon the earth: and he that dwelleth above the heavens may only understand the things that are above the height of the heavens.

[22] Then answered I and said, I beseech thee, O Lord, let me have understanding:

[23] For it was not my mind to be curious of the high things, but of such as pass by us daily, namely, wherefore Israel is given up as a reproach to the heathen, and for what cause the people whom thou hast loved is given over unto ungodly nations, and why the law of our forefathers is brought to nought, and the written covenants come to none effect,

[24] And we pass away out of the world as grasshoppers, and our life is astonishment and fear, and we are not worthy to obtain mercy.

[25] What will he then do unto his name whereby we are called? of these things have I asked.

[26] Then answered he me, and said, The more thou searchest, the

more thou shalt marvel; for the world hasteth fast to pass away,

[27] And cannot comprehend the things that are promised to the righteous in time to come: for this world is full of unrighteousness and infirmities.

[28] But as concerning the things whereof thou askest me, I will tell thee; for the evil is sown, but the destruction thereof is not yet come.

[29] If therefore that which is sown be not turned upside down, and if the place where the evil is sown pass not away, then cannot it come that is sown with good.

[30] For the grain of evil seed hath been sown in the heart of Adam from the beginning, and how much ungodliness hath it brought up unto this time? and how much shall it yet bring forth until the time of threshing come?

[31] Ponder now by thyself, how great fruit of wickedness the grain of evil seed hath brought forth.

[32] And when the ears shall be cut down, which are without number, how great a floor shall they fill?

[33] Then I answered and said, How, and when shall these things come to pass? wherefore are our years few and evil?

[34] And he answered me, saying, Do not thou hasten above the most Highest: for thy haste is in vain to be above him, for thou hast much exceeded.

[35] Did not the souls also of the righteous ask question of these things in their chambers, saying, How long shall I hope on this fashion? when cometh the fruit of the floor of our reward?

[36] And unto these things Uriel the archangel gave them answer, and said, Even when the number of seeds is filled in you: for he hath weighed the world in the balance.

[37] By measure hath he measured the times; and by number hath he numbered the times; and he doth not move nor stir them, until the said measure be fulfilled.

[38] Then answered I and said, O Lord that bearest rule, even we all are full of impiety.

[39] And for our sakes peradventure it is that the floors of the righteous are not filled, because of the sins of them that dwell upon the earth.

[40] So he answered me, and said, Go thy way to a woman with child, and ask of her when she hath fulfilled her nine months, if her womb may keep the birth any longer within her.

[41] Then said I, No, Lord, that can she not. And he said unto me, In the grave the chambers of souls are like the womb of a woman:

[42] For like as a woman that travaileth maketh haste to escape the necessity of the travail: even so do these places haste to deliver those things that are committed unto them.

[43] From the beginning, look, what thou desirest to see, it shall be shewed thee.

[44] Then answered I and said, If I have found favour in thy sight, and if it be possible, and if I be meet therefore,

[45] Shew me then whether there be more to come than is past, or more past than is to come.

[46] What is past I know, but what is for to come I know not.

[47] And he said unto me, Stand up upon the right side, and I shall expound the similitude unto thee.

[48] So I stood, and saw, and, behold, an hot burning oven passed by before me: and it happened that when the flame was gone by I looked, and, behold, the smoke remained still.

[49] After this there passed by before me a watery cloud, and sent down much rain with a storm; and when the stormy rain was past, the drops remained still.

[50] Then said he unto me, Consider with thyself; as the rain is more than the drops, and as the fire is greater than the smoke; but the drops and the smoke remain behind: so the quantity which is past did more exceed.

[51] Then I prayed, and said, May I live, thinkest thou, until that time? or what shall happen in those days?

[52] He answered me, and said, As for the tokens whereof thou askest me, I may tell thee of them in part: but as touching thy life, I am not sent to shew thee; for I do not know it.

2 Esdras 5

[1] Nevertheless as coming the tokens, behold, the days shall come, that they which dwell upon earth shall be taken in a great number, and the way of truth shall be hidden, and the land shall be barren of faith.

[2] But iniquity shall be increased above that which now thou seest, or that thou hast heard long ago.

[3] And the land, that thou seest now to have root, shalt thou see wasted suddenly.

[4] But if the most High grant thee to live, thou shalt see after the third trumpet that the sun shall suddenly shine again in the night, and the moon thrice in the day:

[5] And blood shall drop out of wood, and the stone shall give his voice, and the people shall be troubled:

[6] And even he shall rule, whom they look not for that dwell upon the earth, and the fowls shall take their flight away together:

[7] And the Sodomitish sea shall cast out fish, and make a noise in the night, which many have not known: but they shall all hear the voice thereof.

[8] There shall be a confusion also in many places, and the fire shall be oft sent out again, and the wild beasts shall change their places, and menstruous women shall bring forth monsters:

[9] And salt waters shall be found in the sweet, and all friends shall destroy one another; then shall wit hide itself, and understanding withdraw itself into his secret chamber,

[10] And shall be sought of many, and yet not be found: then shall unrighteousness and incontinency be multiplied upon earth.

[11] One land also shall ask another, and say, Is righteousness that maketh a man righteous gone through thee? And it shall say, No.

[12] At the same time shall men hope, but nothing obtain: they shall labour, but their ways shall not prosper.

[13] To shew thee such tokens I have leave; and if thou wilt pray again, and weep as now, and fast even days, thou shalt hear yet greater things.

[14] Then I awaked, and an extreme fearfulness went through all my body, and my mind was troubled, so that it fainted.

[15] So the angel that was come to talk with me held me, comforted me, and set me up upon my feet.

[16] And in the second night it came to pass, that Salathiel the captain of the people came unto me, saying, Where hast thou been? and why is thy countenance so heavy?

[17] Knowest thou not that Israel is committed unto thee in the land of their captivity?

[18] Up then, and eat bread, and forsake us not, as the shepherd that leaveth his flock in the hands of cruel wolves.

[19] Then said I unto him, Go thy ways from me, and come not nigh me. And he heard what I said, and went from me.

[20] And so I fasted seven days, mourning and weeping, like as Uriel the angel commanded me.

[21] And after seven days so it was, that the thoughts of my heart were very grievous unto me again,

[22] And my soul recovered the spirit of understanding, and I began to talk with the most High again,

[23] And said, O Lord that bearest rule, of every wood of the earth, and of all the trees thereof, thou hast chosen thee one only vine:

[24] And of all lands of the whole world thou hast chosen thee one pit: and of all the flowers thereof one lily:

[25] And of all the depths of the sea thou hast filled thee one river: and of all builded cities thou hast hallowed Sion unto thyself:

[26] And of all the fowls that are created thou hast named thee one dove: and of all the cattle that are made thou hast provided thee one sheep:

[27] And among all the multitudes of people thou hast gotten thee one people: and unto this people, whom thou lovedst, thou gavest a law that is approved of all.

[28] And now, O Lord, why hast thou given this one people over unto many? and upon the one root hast thou prepared others, and why hast thou scattered thy only one people among many?

[29] And they which did gainsay thy promises, and believed not thy covenants, have trodden them down.

[30] If thou didst so much hate thy people, yet shouldest thou punish them with thine own hands.

[31] Now when I had spoken these words, the angel that came to me the night afore was sent unto me,

[32] And said unto me, Hear me, and I will instruct thee; hearken to the thing that I say, and I shall tell thee more.

[33] And I said, Speak on, my Lord. Then said he unto me, Thou art sore troubled in mind for Israel's sake: lovest thou that people better than he that made them?

[34] And I said, No, Lord: but of very grief have I spoken: for my reins pain me every hour, while I labour to comprehend the way of the most High, and to seek out part of his judgment.

[35] And he said unto me, Thou canst not. And I said, Wherefore, Lord? whereunto was I born then? or why was not my mother's womb then my grave, that I might not have seen the travail of Jacob, and the wearisome toil of the stock of Israel?

[36] And he said unto me, Number me the things that are not yet come, gather me together the dross that are scattered abroad, make me the flowers green again that are withered,

[37] Open me the places that are closed, and bring me forth the winds that in them are shut up, shew me the image of a voice: and then I will declare to thee the thing that thou labourest to know.

[38] And I said, O Lord that bearest rule, who may know these things, but he that hath not his dwelling with men?

[39] As for me, I am unwise: how may I then speak of these things whereof thou askest me?

[40] Then said he unto me, Like as thou canst do none of these things that I have spoken of, even so canst thou not find out my judgment, or in the end the love that I have promised unto my people.

[41] And I said, Behold, O Lord, yet art thou nigh unto them that be reserved till the end: and what shall they do that have been before me, or we that be now, or they that shall come after us?

[42] And he said unto me, I will liken my judgment unto a ring: like as there is no slackness of the last, even so there is no swiftness of the first.

[43] So I answered and said, Couldest thou not make those that have been made, and be now, and that are for to come, at once; that thou mightest shew thy judgment the sooner?

[44] Then answered he me, and said, The creature may not haste above the maker; neither may the world hold them at once that shall be created therein.

[45] And I said, As thou hast said unto thy servant, that thou, which givest life to all, hast given life at once to the creature that thou hast created, and the creature bare it: even so it might now also bear them that now be present at once.

[46] And he said unto me, Ask the womb of a woman, and say unto her,

If thou bringest forth children, why dost thou it not together, but one after another? pray her therefore to bring forth ten children at once.

[47] And I said, She cannot: but must do it by distance of time.

[48] Then said he unto me, Even so have I given the womb of the earth to those that be sown in it in their times.

[49] For like as a young child may not bring forth the things that belong to the aged, even so have I disposed the world which I created.

[50] And I asked, and said, Seeing thou hast now given me the way, I will proceed to speak before thee: for our mother, of whom thou hast told me that she is young, draweth now nigh unto age.

[51] He answered me, and said, Ask a woman that beareth children, and she shall tell thee.

[52] Say unto her, Wherefore are unto they whom thou hast now brought forth like those that were before, but less of stature?

[53] And she shall answer thee, They that be born in the strength of youth are of one fashion, and they that are born in the time of age, when the womb faileth, are otherwise.

[54] Consider thou therefore also, how that ye are less of stature than those that were before you.

[55] And so are they that come after you less than ye, as the creatures

which now begin to be old, and have passed over the strength of youth.

[56] Then said I, Lord, I beseech thee, if I have found favour in thy sight, shew thy servant by whom thou visitest thy creature.

2 Esdras 6

[1] And he said unto me, In the beginning, when the earth was made, before the borders of the world stood, or ever the winds blew,

[2] Before it thundered and lightened, or ever the foundations of paradise were laid,

[3] Before the fair flowers were seen, or ever the moveable powers were established, before the innumerable multitude of angels were gathered together,

[4] Or ever the heights of the air were lifted up, before the measures of the firmament were named, or ever the chimneys in Sion were hot,

[5] And ere the present years were sought out, and or ever the inventions of them that now sin were turned, before they were sealed that have gathered faith for a treasure:

[6] Then did I consider these things, and they all were made through me alone, and through none other: by me also they shall be ended, and by none other.

[7] Then answered I and said, What shall be the parting asunder of the times? or when shall be the end of the first, and the beginning of it that followeth?

[8] And he said unto me, From Abraham unto Isaac, when Jacob and Esau were born of him, Jacob's hand held first the heel of Esau.

[9] For Esau is the end of the world, and Jacob is the beginning of it that followeth.

[10] The hand of man is betwixt the heel and the hand: other question, Esdras, ask thou not.

[11] I answered then and said, O Lord that bearest rule, if I have found favour in thy sight,

[12] I beseech thee, shew thy servant the end of thy tokens, whereof thou shewedst me part the last night.

[13] So he answered and said unto me, Stand up upon thy feet, and hear a mighty sounding voice.

[14] And it shall be as it were a great motion; but the place where thou standest shall not be moved.

[15] And therefore when it speaketh be not afraid: for the word is of the end, and the foundation of the earth is understood.

[16] And why? because the speech of these things trembleth and is moved: for it knoweth that the end of these things must be changed.

[17] And it happened, that when I had heard it I stood up upon my feet,

and hearkened, and, behold, there was a voice that spake, and the sound of it was like the sound of many waters.

[18] And it said, Behold, the days come, that I will begin to draw nigh, and to visit them that dwell upon the earth,

[19] And will begin to make inquisition of them, what they be that have hurt unjustly with their unrighteousness, and when the affliction of Sion shall be fulfilled;

[20] And when the world, that shall begin to vanish away, shall be finished, then will I shew these tokens: the books shall be opened before the firmament, and they shall see all together:

[21] And the children of a year old shall speak with their voices, the women with child shall bring forth untimely children of three or four months old, and they shall live, and be raised up.

[22] And suddenly shall the sown places appear unsown, the full storehouses shall suddenly be found empty:

[23] And the trumpet shall give a sound, which when every man heareth, they shall be suddenly afraid.

[24] At that time shall friends fight one against another like enemies, and the earth shall stand in fear with those that dwell therein, the springs of the fountains shall stand still, and in three hours they shall not run.

[25] Whosoever remaineth from all these that I have told thee shall escape, and see my salvation, and the end of your world.

[26] And the men that are received shall see it, who have not tasted death from their birth: and the heart of the inhabitants shall be changed, and turned into another meaning.

[27] For evil shall be put out, and deceit shall be quenched.

[28] As for faith, it shall flourish, corruption shall be overcome, and the truth, which hath been so long without fruit, shall be declared.

[29] And when he talked with me, behold, I looked by little and little upon him before whom I stood.

[30] And these words said he unto me; I am come to shew thee the time of the night to come.

[31] If thou wilt pray yet more, and fast seven days again, I shall tell thee greater things by day than I have heard.

[32] For thy voice is heard before the most High: for the Mighty hath seen thy righteous dealing, he hath seen also thy chastity, which thou hast had ever since thy youth.

[33] And therefore hath he sent me to shew thee all these things, and to say unto thee, Be of good comfort and fear not

[34] And hasten not with the times that are past, to think vain things, that thou mayest not hasten from the latter times.

[35] And it came to pass after this, that I wept again, and fasted seven days in like manner, that I might fulfil the three weeks which he told me.

[36] And in the eighth night was my heart vexed within me again, and I began to speak before the most High.

[37] For my spirit was greatly set on fire, and my soul was in distress.

[38] And I said, O Lord, thou spakest from the beginning of the creation, even the first day, and saidst thus; Let heaven and earth be made; and thy word was a perfect work.

[39] And then was the spirit, and darkness and silence were on every side; the sound of man's voice was not yet formed.

[40] Then commandedst thou a fair light to come forth of thy treasures, that thy work might appear.

[41] Upon the second day thou madest the spirit of the firmament, and commandedst it to part asunder, and to make a division betwixt the waters, that the one part might go up, and the other remain beneath.

[42] Upon the third day thou didst command that the waters should be gathered in the seventh part of the earth: six parts hast thou dried up,

and kept them, to the intent that of these some being planted of God and tilled might serve thee.

[43] For as soon as thy word went forth the work was made.

[44] For immediately there was great and innumerable fruit, and many and divers pleasures for the taste, and flowers of unchangeable colour, and odours of wonderful smell: and this was done the third day.

[45] Upon the fourth day thou commandedst that the sun should shine, and the moon give her light, and the stars should be in order:

[46] And gavest them a charge to do service unto man, that was to be made.

[47] Upon the fifth day thou saidst unto the seventh part, where the waters were gathered that it should bring forth living creatures, fowls and fishes: and so it came to pass.

[48] For the dumb water and without life brought forth living things at the commandment of God, that all people might praise thy wondrous works.

[49] Then didst thou ordain two living creatures, the one thou calledst Enoch, and the other Leviathan;

[50] And didst separate the one from the other: for the seventh part, namely, where the water was gathered together, might not hold them both.

[51] Unto Enoch thou gavest one part, which was dried up the third day, that he should dwell in the same part, wherein are a thousand hills:

[52] But unto Leviathan thou gavest the seventh part, namely, the moist; and hast kept him to be devoured of whom thou wilt, and when.

[53] Upon the sixth day thou gavest commandment unto the earth, that before thee it should bring forth beasts, cattle, and creeping things:

[54] And after these, Adam also, whom thou madest lord of all thy creatures: of him come we all, and the people also whom thou hast chosen.

[55] All this have I spoken before thee, O Lord, because thou madest the world for our sakes

[56] As for the other people, which also come of Adam, thou hast said that they are nothing, but be like unto spittle: and hast likened the abundance of them unto a drop that falleth from a vessel.

[57] And now, O Lord, behold, these heathen, which have ever been reputed as nothing, have begun to be lords over us, and to devour us.

[58] But we thy people, whom thou hast called thy firstborn, thy only begotten, and thy fervent lover, are given into their hands.

[59] If the world now be made for our sakes, why do we not possess an inheritance with the world? how long shall this endure?

2 Esdras 7

[1] And when I had made an end of speaking these words, there was sent unto me the angel which had been sent unto me the nights afore:

[2] And he said unto me, Up, Esdras, and hear the words that I am come to tell thee.

[3] And I said, Speak on, my God. Then said he unto me, The sea is set in a wide place, that it might be deep and great.

[4] But put the case the entrance were narrow, and like a river;

[5] Who then could go into the sea to look upon it, and to rule it? if he went not through the narrow, how could he come into the broad?

[6] There is also another thing; A city is builded, and set upon a broad field, and is full of all good things:

[7] The entrance thereof is narrow, and is set in a dangerous place to fall, like as if there were a fire on the right hand, and on the left a deep water:

[8] And one only path between them both, even between the fire and the water, so small that there could but one man go there at once.

[9] If this city now were given unto a man for an inheritance, if he never shall pass the danger set before it,

how shall he receive this inheritance?

[10] And I said, It is so, Lord. Then said he unto me, Even so also is Israel's portion.

[11] Because for their sakes I made the world: and when Adam transgressed my statutes, then was decreed that now is done.

[12] Then were the entrances of this world made narrow, full of sorrow and travail: they are but few and evil, full of perils,: and very painful.

[13] For the entrances of the elder world were wide and sure, and brought immortal fruit.

[14] If then they that live labour not to enter these strait and vain things, they can never receive those that are laid up for them.

[15] Now therefore why disquietest thou thyself, seeing thou art but a corruptible man? and why art thou moved, whereas thou art but mortal?

[16] Why hast thou not considered in thy mind this thing that is to come, rather than that which is present?

[17] Then answered I and said, O Lord that bearest rule, thou hast ordained in thy law, that the righteous should inherit these things, but that the ungodly should perish.

[18] Nevertheless the righteous shall suffer strait things, and hope for wide: for they that have done wickedly have suffered the strait things, and yet shall not see the wide.

[19] And he said unto me. There is no judge above God, and none that hath understanding above the Highest.

[20] For there be many that perish in this life, because they despise the law of God that is set before them.

[21] For God hath given strait commandment to such as came, what they should do to live, even as they came, and what they should observe to avoid punishment.

[22] Nevertheless they were not obedient unto him; but spake against him, and imagined vain things;

[23] And deceived themselves by their wicked deeds; and said of the most High, that he is not; and knew not his ways:

[24] But his law have they despised, and denied his covenants; in his statutes have they not been faithful, and have not performed his works.

[25] And therefore, Esdras, for the empty are empty things, and for the full are the full things.

[26] Behold, the time shall come, that these tokens which I have told thee shall come to pass, and the bride shall appear, and she coming forth shall be seen, that now is withdrawn from the earth.

[27] And whosoever is delivered from the foresaid evils shall see my wonders.

[28] For my son Jesus shall be revealed with those that be with him, and they that remain shall rejoice within four hundred years.

[29] After these years shall my son Christ die, and all men that have life.

[30] And the world shall be turned into the old silence seven days, like as in the former judgments: so that no man shall remain.

[31] And after seven days the world, that yet awaketh not, shall be raised up, and that shall die that is corrupt

[32] And the earth shall restore those that are asleep in her, and so shall the dust those that dwell in silence, and the secret places shall deliver those souls that were committed unto them.

[33] And the most High shall appear upon the seat of judgment, and misery shall pass away, and the long suffering shall have an end:

[34] But judgment only shall remain, truth shall stand, and faith shall wax strong:

[35] And the work shall follow, and the reward shall be shewed, and the good deeds shall be of force, and wicked deeds shall bear no rule.

[36] Then said I, Abraham prayed first for the Sodomites, and Moses for the fathers that sinned in the wilderness:

[37] And Jesus after him for Israel in the time of Achan:

[38] And Samuel and David for the destruction: and Solomon for them that should come to the sanctuary:

[39] And Helias for those that received rain; and for the dead, that he might live:

[40] And Ezechias for the people in the time of Sennacherib: and many for many.

[41] Even so now, seeing corruption is grown up, and wickedness increased, and the righteous have prayed for the ungodly: wherefore shall it not be so now also?

[42] He answered me, and said, This present life is not the end where much glory doth abide; therefore have they prayed for the weak.

[43] But the day of doom shall be the end of this time, and the beginning of the immortality for to come, wherein corruption is past,

[44] Intemperance is at an end, infidelity is cut off, righteousness is grown, and truth is sprung up.

[45] Then shall no man be able to save him that is destroyed, nor to oppress him that hath gotten the victory.

[46] I answered then and said, This is my first and last saying, that it had

been better not to have given the earth unto Adam: or else, when it was given him, to have restrained him from sinning.

[47] For what profit is it for men now in this present time to live in heaviness, and after death to look for punishment?

[48] O thou Adam, what hast thou done? for though it was thou that sinned, thou art not fallen alone, but we all that come of thee.

[49] For what profit is it unto us, if there be promised us an immortal time, whereas we have done the works that bring death?

[50] And that there is promised us an everlasting hope, whereas ourselves being most wicked are made vain?

[51] And that there are laid up for us dwellings of health and safety, whereas we have lived wickedly?

[52] And that the glory of the most High is kept to defend them which have led a wary life, whereas we have walked in the most wicked ways of all?

[53] And that there should be shewed a paradise, whose fruit endureth for ever, wherein is security and medicine, since we shall not enter into it?

[54] (For we have walked in unpleasant places.)

[55] And that the faces of them which have used abstinence shall shine above the stars, whereas our faces shall be blacker than darkness?

[56] For while we lived and committed iniquity, we considered not that we should begin to suffer for it after death.

[57] Then answered he me, and said, This is the condition of the battle, which man that is born upon the earth shall fight;

[58] That, if he be overcome, he shall suffer as thou hast said: but if he get the victory, he shall receive the thing that I say.

[59] For this is the life whereof Moses spake unto the people while he lived, saying, Choose thee life, that thou mayest live.

[60] Nevertheless they believed not him, nor yet the prophets after him, no nor me which have spoken unto them,

[61] That there should not be such heaviness in their destruction, as shall be joy over them that are persuaded to salvation.

[62] I answered then, and said, I know, Lord, that the most High is called merciful, in that he hath mercy upon them which are not yet come into the world,

[63] And upon those also that turn to his law;

[64] And that he is patient, and long suffereth those that have sinned, as his creatures;

[65] And that he is bountiful, for he is ready to give where it needeth;

[66] And that he is of great mercy, for he multiplieth more and more mercies to them that are present, and that are past, and also to them which are to come.

[67] For if he shall not multiply his mercies, the world would not continue with them that inherit therein.

[68] And he pardoneth; for if he did not so of his goodness, that they which have committed iniquities might be eased of them, the ten thousandth part of men should not remain living.

[69] And being judge, if he should not forgive them that are cured with his word, and put out the multitude of contentions,

[70] There should be very few left peradventure in an innumerable multitude.

2 Esdras 8

[1] And he answered me, saying, The most High hath made this world for many, but the world to come for few.

[2] I will tell thee a similitude, Esdras; As when thou askest the earth, it shall say unto thee, that it giveth much mould whereof earthen vessels are made, but little dust that gold cometh of: even so is the course of this present world.

[3] There be many created, but few shall be saved.

[4] So answered I and said, Swallow then down, O my soul, understanding, and devour wisdom.

[5] For thou hast agreed to give ear, and art willing to prophesy: for thou hast no longer space than only to live.

[6] O Lord, if thou suffer not thy servant, that we may pray before thee, and thou give us seed unto our heart, and culture to our understanding, that there may come fruit of it; how shall each man live that is corrupt, who beareth the place of a man?

[7] For thou art alone, and we all one workmanship of thine hands, like as thou hast said.

[8] For when the body is fashioned now in the mother's womb, and thou givest it members, thy creature is preserved in fire and water, and nine months doth thy workmanship endure thy creature which is created in her.

[9] But that which keepeth and is kept shall both be preserved: and when the time cometh, the womb preserved delivereth up the things that grew in it.

[10] For thou hast commanded out of the parts of the body, that is to say, out of the breasts, milk to be given, which is the fruit of the breasts,

[11] That the thing which is fashioned may be nourished for a time, till thou disposest it to thy mercy.

[12] Thou broughtest it up with thy righteousness, and nurturedst it in thy law, and reformedst it with thy judgment.

[13] And thou shalt mortify it as thy creature, and quicken it as thy work.

[14] If therefore thou shalt destroy him which with so great labour was fashioned, it is an easy thing to be ordained by thy commandment, that the thing which was made might be preserved.

[15] Now therefore, Lord, I will speak; touching man in general, thou knowest best; but touching thy people, for whose sake I am sorry;

[16] And for thine inheritance, for whose cause I mourn; and for Israel, for whom I am heavy; and for Jacob, for whose sake I am troubled;

[17] Therefore will I begin to pray before thee for myself and for them: for I see the falls of us that dwell in the land.

[18] But I have heard the swiftness of the judge which is to come.

[19] Therefore hear my voice, and understand my words, and I shall speak before thee. This is the beginning of the words of Esdras, before he was taken up: and I said,

[20] O Lord, thou that dwellest in everlastingness which beholdest from above things in the heaven and in the air;

[21] Whose throne is inestimable; whose glory may not be comprehended; before whom the hosts of angels stand with trembling,

[22] Whose service is conversant in wind and fire; whose word is true, and sayings constant; whose commandment is strong, and ordinance fearful;

[23] Whose look drieth up the depths, and indignation maketh the mountains to melt away; which the truth witnesseth:

[24] O hear the prayer of thy servant, and give ear to the petition of thy creature.

[25] For while I live I will speak, and so long as I have understanding I will answer.

[26] O look not upon the sins of thy people; but on them which serve thee in truth.

[27] Regard not the wicked inventions of the heathen, but the desire of those that keep thy testimonies in afflictions.

[28] Think not upon those that have walked feignedly before thee: but remember them, which according to thy will have known thy fear.

[29] Let it not be thy will to destroy them which have lived like beasts;

but to look upon them that have clearly taught thy law.

[30] Take thou no indignation at them which are deemed worse than beasts; but love them that always put their trust in thy righteousness and glory.

[31] For we and our fathers do languish of such diseases: but because of us sinners thou shalt be called merciful.

[32] For if thou hast a desire to have mercy upon us, thou shalt be called merciful, to us namely, that have no works of righteousness.

[33] For the just, which have many good works laid up with thee, shall out of their own deeds receive reward.

[34] For what is man, that thou shouldest take displeasure at him? or what is a corruptible generation, that thou shouldest be so bitter toward it?

[35] For in truth them is no man among them that be born, but he hath dealt wickedly; and among the faithful there is none which hath not done amiss.

[36] For in this, O Lord, thy righteousness and thy goodness shall be declared, if thou be merciful unto them which have not the confidence of good works.

[37] Then answered he me, and said, Some things hast thou spoken aright, and according unto thy words it shall be.

[38] For indeed I will not think on the disposition of them which have sinned before death, before judgment, before destruction:

[39] But I will rejoice over the disposition of the righteous, and I will remember also their pilgrimage, and the salvation, and the reward, that they shall have.

[40] Like as I have spoken now, so shall it come to pass.

[41] For as the husbandman soweth much seed upon the ground, and planteth many trees, and yet the thing that is sown good in his season cometh not up, neither doth all that is planted take root: even so is it of them that are sown in the world; they shall not all be saved.

[42] I answered then and said, If I have found grace, let me speak.

[43] Like as the husbandman's seed perisheth, if it come not up, and receive not thy rain in due season; or if there come too much rain, and corrupt it:

[44] Even so perisheth man also, which is formed with thy hands, and is called thine own image, because thou art like unto him, for whose sake thou hast made all things, and likened him unto the husbandman's seed.

[45] Be not wroth with us but spare thy people, and have mercy upon thine own inheritance: for thou art merciful unto thy creature.

[46] Then answered he me, and said, Things present are for the present, and things to cometh for such as be to come.

[47] For thou comest far short that thou shouldest be able to love my creature more than I: but I have ofttimes drawn nigh unto thee, and unto it, but never to the unrighteous.

[48] In this also thou art marvellous before the most High:

49 In that thou hast humbled thyself, as it becometh thee, and hast not judged thyself worthy to be much glorified among the righteous.

[50] For many great miseries shall be done to them that in the latter time shall dwell in the world, because they have walked in great pride.

[51] But understand thou for thyself, and seek out the glory for such as be like thee.

[52] For unto you is paradise opened, the tree of life is planted, the time to come is prepared, plenteousness is made ready, a city is builded, and rest is allowed, yea, perfect goodness and wisdom.

[53] The root of evil is sealed up from you, weakness and the moth is hid from you, and corruption is fled into hell to be forgotten:

[54] Sorrows are passed, and in the end is shewed the treasure of immortality.

[55] And therefore ask thou no more questions concerning the multitude of them that perish.

[56] For when they had taken liberty, they despised the most High, thought scorn of his law, and forsook his ways.

[57] Moreover they have trodden down his righteous,

[58] And said in their heart, that there is no God; yea, and that knowing they must die.

[59] For as the things aforesaid shalt receive you, so thirst and pain are prepared for them: for it was not his will that men should come to nought:

[60] But they which be created have defiled the name of him that made them, and were unthankful unto him which prepared life for them.

[61] And therefore is my judgment now at hand.

[62] These things have I not shewed unto all men, but unto thee, and a few like thee. Then answered I and said,

[63] Behold, O Lord, now hast thou shewed me the multitude of the wonders, which thou wilt begin to do in the last times: but at what time, thou hast not shewed me.

2 Esdras 9

[1] He answered me then, and said, Measure thou the time diligently in itself: and when thou seest part of the signs past, which I have told thee before,

[2]Then shalt thou understand, that it is the very same time, wherein the Highest will begin to visit the world which he made.

[3] Therefore when there shall be seen earthquakes and uproars of the people in the world:

[4] Then shalt thou well understand, that the most High spake of those things from the days that were before thee, even from the beginning.

[5] For like as all that is made in the world hath a beginning and an end, and the end is manifest:

[6] Even so the times also of the Highest have plain beginnings in wonder and powerful works, and endings in effects and signs.

[7] And every one that shall be saved, and shall be able to escape by his works, and by faith, whereby ye have believed,

[8] Shall be preserved from the said perils, and shall see my salvation in my land, and within my borders: for I have sanctified them for me from the beginning.

[9] Then shall they be in pitiful case, which now have abused my ways:

and they that have cast them away despitefully shall dwell in torments.

[10] For such as in their life have received benefits, and have not known me;

[11] And they that have loathed my law, while they had yet liberty, and, when as yet place of repentance was open unto them, understood not, but despised it;

[12] The same must know it after death by pain.

[13] And therefore be thou not curious how the ungodly shall be punished, and when: but enquire how the righteous shall be saved, whose the world is, and for whom the world is created.

[14] Then answered I and said,

[15] I have said before, and now do speak, and will speak it also hereafter, that there be many more of them which perish, than of them which shall be saved:

[16] Like as a wave is greater than a drop.

[17] And he answered me, saying, Like as the field is, so is also the seed; as the flowers be, such are the colours also; such as the workman is, such also is the work; and as the husbandman is himself, so is his husbandry also: for it was the time of the world.

[18] And now when I prepared the world, which was not yet made, even

for them to dwell in that now live, no man spake against me.

[19] For then every one obeyed: but now the manners of them which are created in this world that is made are corrupted by a perpetual seed, and by a law which is unsearchable rid themselves.

[20] So I considered the world, and, behold, there was peril because of the devices that were come into it.

[21] And I saw, and spared it greatly, and have kept me a grape of the cluster, and a plant of a great people.

[22] Let the multitude perish then, which was born in vain; and let my grape be kept, and my plant; for with great labour have I made it perfect.

[23] Nevertheless, if thou wilt cease yet seven days more, (but thou shalt not fast in them,

[24] But go into a field of flowers, where no house is builded, and eat only the flowers of the field; taste no flesh, drink no wine, but eat flowers only;)

[25] And pray unto the Highest continually, then will I come and talk with thee.

[26] So I went my way into the field which is called Ardath, like as he commanded me; and there I sat among the flowers, and did eat of the herbs of the field, and the meat of the same satisfied me.

[27] After seven days I sat upon the grass, and my heart was vexed within me, like as before:

[28] And I opened my mouth, and began to talk before the most High, and said,

[29] O Lord, thou that shewest thyself unto us, thou wast shewed unto our fathers in the wilderness, in a place where no man treadeth, in a barren place, when they came out of Egypt.

[30] And thou spakest saying, Hear me, O Israel; and mark my words, thou seed of Jacob.

[31] For, behold, I sow my law in you, and it shall bring fruit in you, and ye shall be honoured in it for ever.

[32] But our fathers, which received the law, kept it not, and observed not thy ordinances: and though the fruit of thy law did not perish, neither could it, for it was thine;

[33] Yet they that received it perished, because they kept not the thing that was sown in them.

[34] And, lo, it is a custom, when the ground hath received seed, or the sea a ship, or any vessel meat or drink, that, that being perished wherein it was sown or cast into,

[35] That thing also which was sown, or cast therein, or received, doth perish, and remaineth not with us: but with us it hath not happened so.

[36] For we that have received the law perish by sin, and our heart also which received it

[37] Notwithstanding the law perisheth not, but remaineth in his force.

[38] And when I spake these things in my heart, I looked back with mine eyes, and upon the right side I saw a woman, and, behold, she mourned and wept with a loud voice, and was much grieved in heart, and her clothes were rent, and she had ashes upon her head.

[39] Then let I my thoughts go that I was in, and turned me unto her,

[40] And said unto her, Wherefore weepest thou? why art thou so grieved in thy mind?

[41] And she said unto me, Sir, let me alone, that I may bewail myself, and add unto my sorrow, for I am sore vexed in my mind, and brought very low.

[42] And I said unto her, What aileth thee? tell me.

[43] She said unto me, I thy servant have been barren, and had no child, though I had an husband thirty years,

[44] And those thirty years I did nothing else day and night, and every hour, but make my, prayer to the Highest.

[45] After thirty years God heard me thine handmaid, looked upon my misery, considered my trouble, and gave me a son: and I was very glad of him, so was my husband also, and all my neighbours: and we gave great honour unto the Almighty.

[46] And I nourished him with great travail.

[47] So when he grew up, and came to the time that he should have a wife, I made a feast.

2 Esdras 10

Why is 2 Esdras shown with the King James Bible?

[1] And it so came to pass, that when my son was entered into his wedding chamber, he fell down, and died.

[2] Then we all overthrew the lights, and all my neighbours rose up to comfort me: so I took my rest unto the second day at night.

[3] And it came to pass, when they had all left off to comfort me, to the end I might be quiet; then rose I up by night and fled, and came hither into this field, as thou seest.

[4] And I do now purpose not to return into the city, but here to stay, and neither to eat nor drink, but continually to mourn and to fast until I die.

[5] Then left I the meditations wherein I was, and spake to her in anger, saying,

[6] Thou foolish woman above all other, seest thou not our mourning, and what happeneth unto us?

[7] How that Sion our mother is full of all heaviness, and much humbled, mourning very sore?

[8] And now, seeing we all mourn and are sad, for we are all in heaviness, art thou grieved for one son?

[9] For ask the earth, and she shall tell thee, that it is she which ought to mourn for the fall of so many that grow upon her.

[10] For out of her came all at the first, and out of her shall all others come, and, behold, they walk almost all into destruction, and a multitude of them is utterly rooted out.

[11] Who then should make more mourning than she, that hath lost so great a multitude; and not thou, which art sorry but for one?

[12] But if thou sayest unto me, My lamentation is not like the earth's, because I have lost the fruit of my womb, which I brought forth with pains, and bare with sorrows;

[13] But the earth not so: for the multitude present in it according to the course of the earth is gone, as it came:

[14] Then say I unto thee, Like as thou hast brought forth with labour; even so the earth also hath given her fruit, namely, man, ever since the beginning unto him that made her.

[15] Now therefore keep thy sorrow to thyself, and bear with a good courage that which hath befallen thee.

[16] For if thou shalt acknowledge the determination of God to be just, thou shalt both receive thy son in time, and shalt be commended among women.

[17] Go thy way then into the city to thine husband.

[18] And she said unto me, That will I not do: I will not go into the city, but here will I die.

[19] So I proceeded to speak further unto her, and said,

[20] Do not so, but be counselled. by me: for how many are the adversities of Sion? be comforted in regard of the sorrow of Jerusalem.

[21] For thou seest that our sanctuary is laid waste, our altar broken down, our temple destroyed;

22 Our psaltery is laid on the ground, our song is put to silence, our rejoicing is at an end, the light of our candlestick is put out, the ark of our covenant is spoiled, our holy things are defiled, and the name that is called upon us is almost profaned: our children are put to shame, our priests are burnt, our Levites are gone into captivity, our virgins are defiled, and our wives ravished; our

righteous men carried away, our little ones destroyed, our young men are brought in bondage, and our strong men are become weak;

[23] And, which is the greatest of all, the seal of Sion hath now lost her honour; for she is delivered into the hands of them that hate us.

[24] And therefore shake off thy great heaviness, and put away the multitude of sorrows, that the Mighty may be merciful unto thee again, and the Highest shall give thee rest and ease from thy labour.

[25] And it came to pass while I was talking with her, behold, her face upon a sudden shined exceedingly, and her countenance glistered, so that I was afraid of her, and mused what it might be.

[26] And, behold, suddenly she made a great cry very fearful: so that the earth shook at the noise of the woman.

[27] And I looked, and, behold, the woman appeared unto me no more, but there was a city builded, and a large place shewed itself from the foundations: then was I afraid, and cried with a loud voice, and said,

[28] Where is Uriel the angel, who came unto me at the first? for he hath caused me to fall into many trances, and mine end is turned into corruption, and my prayer to rebuke.

[29] And as I was speaking these words behold, he came unto me, and looked upon me.

[30] And, lo, I lay as one that had been dead, and mine understanding was taken from me: and he took me by the right hand, and comforted me, and set me upon my feet, and said unto me,

[31] What aileth thee? and why art thou so disquieted? and why is thine understanding troubled, and the thoughts of thine heart?

[32] And I said, Because thou hast forsaken me, and yet I did according to thy words, and I went into the field, and, lo, I have seen, and yet see, that I am not able to express.

[33] And he said unto me, Stand up manfully, and I will advise thee.

[34] Then said I, Speak on, my lord, in me; only forsake me not, lest I die frustrate of my hope.

[35] For I have seen that I knew not, and hear that I do not know.

[36] Or is my sense deceived, or my soul in a dream?

[37] Now therefore I beseech thee that thou wilt shew thy servant of this vision.

[38] He answered me then, and said, Hear me, and I shall inform thee, and tell thee wherefore thou art afraid: for the Highest will reveal many secret things unto thee.

[39] He hath seen that thy way is right: for that thou sorrowest continually for thy people, and makest great lamentation for Sion.

[40] This therefore is the meaning of the vision which thou lately sawest:

[41] Thou sawest a woman mourning, and thou begannest to comfort her:

[42] But now seest thou the likeness of the woman no more, but there appeared unto thee a city builded.

[43] And whereas she told thee of the death of her son, this is the solution:

[44] This woman, whom thou sawest is Sion: and whereas she said unto thee, even she whom thou seest as a city builded,

[45] Whereas, I say, she said unto thee, that she hath been thirty years barren: those are the thirty years wherein there was no offering made in her.

[46] But after thirty years Solomon builded the city and offered offerings: and then bare the barren a son.

[47] And whereas she told thee that she nourished him with labour: that was the dwelling in Jerusalem.

[48] But whereas she said unto thee, That my son coming into his marriage chamber happened to have a fail, and died: this was the destruction that came to Jerusalem.

[49] And, behold, thou sawest her likeness, and because she mourned for her son, thou begannest to comfort her: and of these things which have chanced, these are to be opened unto thee.

[50] For now the most High seeth that thou art grieved unfeignedly, and sufferest from thy whole heart for her, so hath he shewed thee the brightness of her glory, and the comeliness of her beauty:

[51] And therefore I bade thee remain in the field where no house was builded:

[52] For I knew that the Highest would shew this unto thee.

[53] Therefore I commanded thee to go into the field, where no foundation of any building was.

[54] For in the place wherein the Highest beginneth to shew his city, there can no man's building be able to stand.

[55] And therefore fear not, let not thine heart be affrighted, but go thy way in, and see the beauty and greatness of the building, as much as thine eyes be able to see:

[56] And then shalt thou hear as much as thine ears may comprehend.

[57] For thou art blessed above many other, and art called with the Highest; and so are but few.

[58] But to morrow at night thou shalt remain here;

[59] And so shall the Highest shew thee visions of the high things, which the most High will do unto them that dwell upon the earth in the last days. So I slept that night and another, like as he commanded me.

2 Esdras 11

[1] Then saw I a dream, and, behold, there came up from the sea an eagle, which had twelve feathered wings, and three heads.

[2] And I saw, and, behold, she spread her wings over all the earth, and all the winds of the air blew on her, and were gathered together.

[3] And I beheld, and out of her feathers there grew other contrary feathers; and they became little feathers and small.

[4] But her heads were at rest: the head in the midst was greater than the other, yet rested it with the residue.

[5] Moreover I beheld, and, lo, the eagle flew with her feathers, and reigned upon earth, and over them that dwelt therein.

[6] And I saw that all things under heaven were subject unto her, and no man spake against her, no, not one creature upon earth.

[7] And I beheld, and, lo, the eagle rose upon her talons, and spake to her feathers, saying,

[8] Watch not all at once: sleep every one in his own place, and watch by course:

[9] But let the heads be preserved for the last.

[10] And I beheld, and, lo, the voice went not out of her heads, but from the midst of her body.

[11] And I numbered her contrary feathers, and, behold, there were eight of them.

[12] And I looked, and, behold, on the right side there arose one feather, and reigned over all the earth;

[13] And so it was, that when it reigned, the end of it came, and the place thereof appeared no more: so the next following stood up. and reigned, and had a great time;

[14] And it happened, that when it reigned, the end of it came also, like as the first, so that it appeared no more.

[15] Then came there a voice unto it, and said,

[16] Hear thou that hast borne rule over the earth so long: this I say unto thee, before thou beginnest to appear no more,

[17] There shall none after thee attain unto thy time, neither unto the half thereof.

[18] Then arose the third, and reigned as the other before, and appeared no more also.

[19] So went it with all the residue one after another, as that every one reigned, and then appeared no more.

[20] Then I beheld, and, lo, in process of time the feathers that followed stood up upon the right side, that they might rule also; and some of them ruled, but within a while they appeared no more:

[21] For some of them were set up, but ruled not.

[22] After this I looked, and, behold, the twelve feathers appeared no more, nor the two little feathers:

[23] And there was no more upon the eagle's body, but three heads that rested, and six little wings.

[24] Then saw I also that two little feathers divided themselves from the six, and remained under the head that was upon the right side: for the four continued in their place.

[25] And I beheld, and, lo, the feathers that were under the wing thought to set up themselves and to have the rule.

[26] And I beheld, and, lo, there was one set up, but shortly it appeared no more.

[27] And the second was sooner away than the first.

[28] And I beheld, and, lo, the two that remained thought also in themselves to reign:

[29] And when they so thought, behold, there awaked one of the heads that were at rest, namely, it that was in the midst; for that was greater than the two other heads.

[30] And then I saw that the two other heads were joined with it.

[31] And, behold, the head was turned with them that were with it, and did eat up the two feathers under the wing that would have reigned.

[32] But this head put the whole earth in fear, and bare rule in it over all those that dwelt upon the earth with much oppression; and it had the governance of the world more than all the wings that had been.

[33] And after this I beheld, and, lo, the head that was in the midst suddenly appeared no more, like as the wings.

[34] But there remained the two heads, which also in like sort ruled upon the earth, and over those that dwelt therein.

[35] And I beheld, and, lo, the head upon the right side devoured it that was upon the left side.

[36] Then I head a voice, which said unto me, Look before thee, and consider the thing that thou seest.

[37] And I beheld, and lo, as it were a roaring lion chased out of the wood: and I saw that he sent out a man's voice unto the eagle, and said,

[38] Hear thou, I will talk with thee, and the Highest shall say unto thee,

[39] Art not thou it that remainest of the four beasts, whom I made to reign in my world, that the end of their times might come through them?

[40] And the fourth came, and overcame all the beasts that were past, and had power over the world with great fearfulness, and over the whole compass of the earth with much wicked oppression; and so long time dwelt he upon the earth with deceit.

[41] For the earth hast thou not judged with truth.

[42] For thou hast afflicted the meek, thou hast hurt the peaceable, thou hast loved liars, and destroyed the dwellings of them that brought forth fruit, and hast cast down the walls of such as did thee no harm.

[43] Therefore is thy wrongful dealing come up unto the Highest, and thy pride unto the Mighty.

[44] The Highest also hath looked upon the proud times, and, behold, they are ended, and his abominations are fulfilled.

45 And therefore appear no more, thou eagle, nor thy horrible wings, nor thy wicked feathers nor thy malicious heads, nor thy hurtful claws, nor all thy vain body:

46 That all the earth may be refreshed, and may return, being delivered from thy violence, and that she may hope for the judgment and mercy of him that made her.

2 Esdras 12

[1] And it came to pass, whiles the lion spake these words unto the eagle, I saw,

[2] And, behold, the head that remained and the four wings appeared no more, and the two went unto it and set themselves up to reign, and their kingdom was small, and fill of uproar.

[3] And I saw, and, behold, they appeared no more, and the whole body of the eagle was burnt so that the earth was in great fear: then awaked I out of the trouble and trance of my mind, and from great fear, and said unto my spirit,

[4] Lo, this hast thou done unto me, in that thou searchest out the ways of the Highest.

[5] Lo, yet am I weary in my mind, and very weak in my spirit; and little strength is there in me, for the great fear wherewith I was afflicted this night.

[6] Therefore will I now beseech the Highest, that he will comfort me unto the end.

[7] And I said, Lord that bearest rule, if I have found grace before thy sight, and if I am justified with thee before many others, and if my prayer indeed be come up before thy face;

[8] Comfort me then, and shew me thy servant the interpretation and plain difference of this fearful vision, that thou mayest perfectly comfort my soul.

[9] For thou hast judged me worthy to shew me the last times.

[10] And he said unto me, This is the interpretation of the vision:

[11] The eagle, whom thou sawest come up from the sea, is the kingdom which was seen in the vision of thy brother Daniel.

[12] But it was not expounded unto him, therefore now I declare it unto thee.

[13] Behold, the days will come, that there shall rise up a kingdom upon earth, and it shall be feared above all the kingdoms that were before it.

[14] In the same shall twelve kings reign, one after another:

[15] Whereof the second shall begin to reign, and shall have more time than any of the twelve.

[16] And this do the twelve wings signify, which thou sawest.

[17] As for the voice which thou heardest speak, and that thou sawest not to go out from the heads but from the midst of the body thereof, this is the interpretation:

[18] That after the time of that kingdom there shall arise great strivings, and it shall stand in peril of failing: nevertheless it shall not then fall, but shall be restored again to his beginning.

[19] And whereas thou sawest the eight small under feathers sticking to her wings, this is the interpretation:

[20] That in him there shall arise eight kings, whose times shall be but small, and their years swift.

[21] And two of them shall perish, the middle time approaching: four shall be kept until their end begin to approach: but two shall be kept unto the end.

[22] And whereas thou sawest three heads resting, this is the interpretation:

[23] In his last days shall the most High raise up three kingdoms, and renew many things therein, and they shall have the dominion of the earth,

[24] And of those that dwell therein, with much oppression, above all those that were before them: therefore are they called the heads of the eagle.

[25] For these are they that shall accomplish his wickedness, and that shall finish his last end.

[26] And whereas thou sawest that the great head appeared no more, it

signifieth that one of them shall die upon his bed, and yet with pain.

[27] For the two that remain shall be slain with the sword.

[28] For the sword of the one shall devour the other: but at the last shall he fall through the sword himself.

[29] And whereas thou sawest two feathers under the wings passing over the head that is on the right side;

[30] It signifieth that these are they, whom the Highest hath kept unto their end: this is the small kingdom and full of trouble, as thou sawest.

[31] And the lion, whom thou sawest rising up out of the wood, and roaring, and speaking to the eagle, and rebuking her for her unrighteousness with all the words which thou hast heard;

[32] This is the anointed, which the Highest hath kept for them and for their wickedness unto the end: he shall reprove them, and shall upbraid them with their cruelty.

[33] For he shall set them before him alive in judgment, and shall rebuke them, and correct them.

[34] For the rest of my people shall he deliver with mercy, those that have been pressed upon my borders, and he shall make them joyful until the coming of the day of judgment, whereof I have spoken unto thee from the beginning.

[35] This is the dream that thou sawest, and these are the interpretations.

[36] Thou only hast been meet to know this secret of the Highest.

[37] Therefore write all these things that thou hast seen in a book, and hide them:

[38] And teach them to the wise of the people, whose hearts thou knowest may comprehend and keep these secrets.

[39] But wait thou here thyself yet seven days more, that it may be shewed thee, whatsoever it pleaseth the Highest to declare unto thee. And with that he went his way.

[40] And it came to pass, when all the people saw that the seven days were past, and I not come again into the city, they gathered them all together, from the least unto the greatest, and came unto me, and said,

[41] What have we offended thee? and what evil have we done against thee, that thou forsakest us, and sittest here in this place?

[42] For of all the prophets thou only art left us, as a cluster of the vintage, and as a candle in a dark place, and as a haven or ship preserved from the tempest.

[43] Are not the evils which are come to us sufficient?

[44] If thou shalt forsake us, how much better had it been for us, if we also had been burned in the midst of Sion?

[45] For we are not better than they that died there. And they wept with a loud voice. Then answered I them, and said,

[46] Be of good comfort, O Israel; and be not heavy, thou house of Jacob:

[47] For the Highest hath you in remembrance, and the Mighty hath not forgotten you in temptation.

[48] As for me, I have not forsaken you, neither am I departed from you: but am come into this place, to pray for the desolation of Sion, and that I might seek mercy for the low estate of your sanctuary.

[49] And now go your way home every man, and after these days will I come unto you.

[50] So the people went their way into the city, like as I commanded them:

[51] But I remained still in the field seven days, as the angel commanded me; and did eat only in those days of the flowers of the field, and had my meat of the herbs.

2 Esdras 13

[1] And it came to pass after seven days, I dreamed a dream by night:

[2] And, lo, there arose a wind from the sea, that it moved all the waves thereof.

[3] And I beheld, and, lo, that man waxed strong with the thousands of heaven: and when he turned his countenance to look, all the things trembled that were seen under him.

[4] And whensoever the voice went out of his mouth, all they burned that heard his voice, like as the earth faileth when it feeleth the fire.

[5] And after this I beheld, and, lo, there was gathered together a multitude of men, out of number, from the four winds of the heaven, to subdue the man that came out of the sea.

[6] But I beheld, and, lo, he had graved himself a great mountain, and flew up upon it.

[7] But I would have seen the region or place whereout the hill was graven, and I could not.

[8] And after this I beheld, and, lo, all they which were gathered together to subdue him were sore afraid, and yet durst fight.

[9] And, lo, as he saw the violence of the multitude that came, he neither lifted up his hand, nor held sword, nor any instrument of war:

[10] But only I saw that he sent out of his mouth as it had been a blast of fire, and out of his lips a flaming

breath, and out of his tongue he cast out sparks and tempests.

[11] And they were all mixed together; the blast of fire, the flaming breath, and the great tempest; and fell with violence upon the multitude which was prepared to fight, and burned them up every one, so that upon a sudden of an innumerable multitude nothing was to be perceived, but only dust and smell of smoke: when I saw this I was afraid.

[12] Afterward saw I the same man come down from the mountain, and call unto him another peaceable Multitude.

[13] And there came much people unto him, whereof some were glad, some were sorry, and some of them were bound, and other some brought of them that were offered: then was I sick through great fear, and I awaked, and said,

[14] Thou hast shewed thy servant these wonders from the beginning, and hast counted me worthy that thou shouldest receive my prayer:

[15] Shew me now yet the interpretation of this dream.

[16] For as I conceive in mine understanding, woe unto them that shall be left in those days and much more woe unto them that are not left behind!

[17] For they that were not left were in heaviness.

[18] Now understand I the things that are laid up in the latter days, which shall happen unto them, and to those that are left behind.

[19] Therefore are they come into great perils and many necessities, like as these dreams declare.

[20] Yet is it easier for him that is in danger to come into these things, than to pass away as a cloud out of the world, and not to see the things that happen in the last days. And he answered unto me, and said,

[21] The interpretation of the vision shall I shew thee, and I will open unto thee the thing that thou hast required.

[22] Whereas thou hast spoken of them that are left behind, this is the interpretation:

[23] He that shall endure the peril in that time hath kept himself: they that be fallen into danger are such as have works, and faith toward the Almighty.

[24] Know this therefore, that they which be left behind are more blessed than they that be dead.

[25] This is the meaning of the vision: Whereas thou sawest a man coming up from the midst of the sea:

[26] The same is he whom God the Highest hath kept a great season, which by his own self shall deliver his creature: and he shall order them that are left behind.

[27] And whereas thou sawest, that out of his mouth there came as a blast of wind, and fire, and storm;

[28] And that he held neither sword, nor any instrument of war, but that the rushing in of him destroyed the whole multitude that came to subdue him; this is the interpretation:

[29] Behold, the days come, when the most High will begin to deliver them that are upon the earth.

[30] And he shall come to the astonishment of them that dwell on the earth.

[31] And one shall undertake to fight against another, one city against another, one place against another, one people against another, and one realm against another.

[32] And the time shall be when these things shall come to pass, and the signs shall happen which I shewed thee before, and then shall my Son be declared, whom thou sawest as a man ascending.

[33] And when all the people hear his voice, every man shall in their own land leave the battle they have one against another.

[34] And an innumerable multitude shall be gathered together, as thou sawest them, willing to come, and to overcome him by fighting.

[35] But he shall stand upon the top of the mount Sion.

[36] And Sion shall come, and shall be shewed to all men, being prepared and builded, like as thou sawest the hill graven without hands.

[37] And this my Son shall rebuke the wicked inventions of those nations, which for their wicked life are fallen into the tempest;

[38] And shall lay before them their evil thoughts, and the torments wherewith they shall begin to be tormented, which are like unto a flame: and he shall destroy them without labour by the law which is like unto me.

[39] And whereas thou sawest that he gathered another peaceable multitude unto him;

[40] Those are the ten tribes, which were carried away prisoners out of their own land in the time of Osea the king, whom Salmanasar the king of Assyria led away captive, and he carried them over the waters, and so came they into another land.

[41] But they took this counsel among themselves, that they would leave the multitude of the heathen, and go forth into a further country, where never mankind dwelt,

[42] That they might there keep their statutes, which they never kept in their own land.

[43] And they entered into Euphrates by the narrow places of the river.

[44] For the most High then shewed signs for them, and held still the flood, till they were passed over.

[45] For through that country there was a great way to go, namely, of a year and a half: and the same region is called Arsareth.

[46] Then dwelt they there until the latter time; and now when they shall begin to come,

[47] The Highest shall stay the springs of the stream again, that they may go through: therefore sawest thou the multitude with peace.

[48] But those that be left behind of thy people are they that are found within my borders.

[49] Now when he destroyeth the multitude of the nations that are gathered together, he shall defend his people that remain.

[50] And then shall he shew them great wonders.

[51] Then said I, O Lord that bearest rule, shew me this: Wherefore have I seen the man coming up from the midst of the sea?

[52] And he said unto me, Like as thou canst neither seek out nor know the things that are in the deep of the sea: even so can no man upon earth see my Son, or those that be with him, but in the day time.

[53] This is the interpretation of the dream which thou sawest, and whereby thou only art here lightened.

[54] For thou hast forsaken thine own way, and applied thy diligence unto my law, and sought it.

[55] Thy life hast thou ordered in wisdom, and hast called understanding thy mother.

[56] And therefore have I shewed thee the treasures of the Highest: after other three days I will speak other things unto thee, and declare unto thee mighty and wondrous things.

[57] Then went I forth into the field, giving praise and thanks greatly unto the most High because of his wonders which he did in time;

58 And because he governeth the same, and such things as fall in their seasons: and there I sat three days.

2 Esdras 14

[1] And it came to pass upon the third day, I sat under an oak, and, behold, there came a voice out of a bush over against me, and said, Esdras, Esdras.

[2] And I said, Here am I, Lord And I stood up upon my feet.

[3] Then said he unto me, In the bush I did manifestly reveal myself unto Moses, and talked with him, when my people served in Egypt:

[4] And I sent him and led my people out of Egypt, and brought him up to the mount of where I held him by me a long season,

[5] And told him many wondrous things, and shewed him the secrets of the times, and the end; and commanded him, saying,

[6] These words shalt thou declare, and these shalt thou hide.

[7] And now I say unto thee,

[8] That thou lay up in thy heart the signs that I have shewed, and the dreams that thou hast seen, and the interpretations which thou hast heard:

[9] For thou shalt be taken away from all, and from henceforth thou shalt remain with my Son, and with such as be like thee, until the times be ended.

[10] For the world hath lost his youth, and the times begin to wax old.

[11] For the world is divided into twelve parts, and the ten parts of it are gone already, and half of a tenth part:

[12] And there remaineth that which is after the half of the tenth part.

[13] Now therefore set thine house in order, and reprove thy people, comfort such of them as be in trouble, and now renounce corruption,

[14] Let go from thee mortal thoughts, cast away the burdens of man, put off now the weak nature,

[15] And set aside the thoughts that are most heavy unto thee, and haste thee to flee from these times.

[16] For yet greater evils than those which thou hast seen happen shall be done hereafter.

[17] For look how much the world shall be weaker through age, so much the more shall evils increase upon them that dwell therein.

[18] For the time is fled far away, and leasing is hard at hand: for now hasteth the vision to come, which thou hast seen.

[19] Then answered I before thee, and said,

[20] Behold, Lord, I will go, as thou hast commanded me, and reprove the people which are present: but they that shall be born afterward, who shall admonish them? thus the world is set in darkness, and they that dwell therein are without light.

[21] For thy law is burnt, therefore no man knoweth the things that are done of thee, or the work that shall begin.

[22] But if I have found grace before thee, send the Holy Ghost into me, and I shall write all that hath been done in the world since the beginning, which were written in thy law, that men may find thy path, and that they which will live in the latter days may live.

[23] And he answered me, saying, Go thy way, gather the people together, and say unto them, that they seek thee not for forty days.

[24] But look thou prepare thee many box trees, and take with thee Sarea, Dabria, Selemia, Ecanus, and Asiel, these five which are ready to write swiftly;

[25] And come hither, and I shall light a candle of understanding in thine heart, which shall not be put out, till the things be performed which thou shalt begin to write.

[26] And when thou hast done, some things shalt thou publish, and some things shalt thou shew secretly to the wise: to morrow this hour shalt thou begin to write.

[27] Then went I forth, as he commanded, and gathered all the people together, and said,

[28] Hear these words, O Israel.

[29] Our fathers at the beginning were strangers in Egypt, from whence they were delivered:

[30] And received the law of life, which they kept not, which ye also have transgressed after them.

[31] Then was the land, even the land of Sion, parted among you by lot: but your fathers, and ye yourselves, have done unrighteousness, and have not kept the ways which the Highest commanded you.

[32] And forasmuch as he is a righteous judge, he took from you in time the thing that he had given you.

[33] And now are ye here, and your brethren among you.

[34] Therefore if so be that ye will subdue your own understanding, and reform your hearts, ye shall be kept alive and after death ye shall obtain mercy.

[35] For after death shall the judgment come, when we shall live again: and then shall the names of the righteous be manifest, and the works of the ungodly shall be declared.

[36] Let no man therefore come unto me now, nor seek after me these forty days.

[37] So I took the five men, as he commanded me, and we went into the field, and remained there.

[38] And the next day, behold, a voice called me, saying, Esdras, open thy mouth, and drink that I give thee to drink.

[39] Then opened I my mouth, and, behold, he reached me a full cup, which was full as it were with water, but the colour of it was like fire.

[40] And I took it, and drank: and when I had drunk of it, my heart uttered understanding, and wisdom grew in my breast, for my spirit strengthened my memory:

[41] And my mouth was opened, and shut no more.

[42] The Highest gave understanding unto the five men, and they wrote the wonderful visions of the night that were told, which they knew not: and they sat forty days, and they wrote in the day, and at night they ate bread.

]43] As for me. I spake in the day, and I held not my tongue by night.

[44] In forty days they wrote two hundred and four books.

[45] And it came to pass, when the forty days were filled, that the Highest spake, saying, The first that thou hast written publish openly, that the worthy and unworthy may read it:

[46] But keep the seventy last, that thou mayest deliver them only to such as be wise among the people:

[47] For in them is the spring of understanding, the fountain of wisdom, and the stream of knowledge.

[48] And I did so.

2 Esdras 15

[1] Behold, speak thou in the ears of my people the words of prophecy, which I will put in thy mouth, saith the Lord:

[2] And cause them to be written in paper: for they are faithful and true.

[3] Fear not the imaginations against thee, let not the incredulity of them trouble thee, that speak against thee.

[4] For all the unfaithful shall die in their unfaithfulness.

[5] Behold, saith the Lord, I will bring plagues upon the world; the sword, famine, death, and destruction.

[6] For wickedness hath exceedingly polluted the whole earth, and their hurtful works are fulfilled.

[7] Therefore saith the Lord,

[8] I will hold my tongue no more as touching their wickedness, which they profanely commit, neither will I suffer them in those things, in which they wickedly exercise themselves: behold, the innocent and righteous blood crieth unto me, and the souls of the just complain continually.

[9] And therefore, saith the Lord, I will surely avenge them, and receive unto me all the innocent blood from among them.

[10] Behold, my people is led as a flock to the slaughter: I will not suffer them now to dwell in the land of Egypt:

[11] But I will bring them with a mighty hand and a stretched out arm, and smite Egypt with plagues, as before, and will destroy all the land thereof.

[12] Egypt shall mourn, and the foundation of it shall be smitten with the plague and punishment that God shall bring upon it.

[13] They that till the ground shall mourn: for their seeds shall fail

through the blasting and hail, and with a fearful constellation.

[14] Woe to the world and them that dwell therein!

[15] For the sword and their destruction draweth nigh, and one people shall stand up and fight against another, and swords in their hands.

[16] For there shall be sedition among men, and invading one another; they shall not regard their kings nor princes, and the course of their actions shall stand in their power.

[17] A man shall desire to go into a city, and shall not be able.

[18] For because of their pride the cities shall be troubled, the houses shall be destroyed, and men shall be afraid.

[19] A man shall have no pity upon his neighbour, but shall destroy their houses with the sword, and spoil their goods, because of the lack of bread, and for great tribulation.

[20] Behold, saith God, I will call together all the kings of the earth to reverence me, which are from the rising of the sun, from the south, from the east, and Libanus; to turn themselves one against another, and repay the things that they have done to them.

[21] Like as they do yet this day unto my chosen, so will I do also, and recompense in their bosom. Thus saith the Lord God;

[22] My right hand shall not spare the sinners, and my sword shall not cease over them that shed innocent blood upon the earth.

[23] The fire is gone forth from his wrath, and hath consumed the foundations of the earth, and the sinners, like the straw that is kindled.

[24] Woe to them that sin, and keep not my commandments! saith the Lord.

[25] I will not spare them: go your way, ye children, from the power, defile not my sanctuary.

[26] For the Lord knoweth all them that sin against him, and therefore delivereth he them unto death and destruction.

[27] For now are the plagues come upon the whole earth and ye shall remain in them: for God shall not deliver you, because ye have sinned against him.

[28] Behold an horrible vision, and the appearance thereof from the east:

[29] Where the nations of the dragons of Arabia shall come out with many chariots, and the multitude of them shall be carried as the wind upon earth, that all they which hear them may fear and tremble.

[30] Also the Carmanians raging in wrath shall go forth as the wild boars of the wood, and with great power shall they come, and join battle with them, and shall waste a portion of the land of the Assyrians.

[31] And then shall the dragons have the upper hand, remembering their nature; and if they shall turn themselves, conspiring together in great power to persecute them,

[32] Then these shall be troubled bled, and keep silence through their power, and shall flee.

[33] And from the land of the Assyrians shall the enemy besiege them, and consume some of them, and in their host shall be fear and dread, and strife among their kings.

[34] Behold clouds from the east and from the north unto the south, and they are very horrible to look upon, full of wrath and storm.

[35] They shall smite one upon another, and they shall smite down a great multitude of stars upon the earth, even their own star; and blood shall be from the sword unto the belly,

[36] And dung of men unto the camel's hough.

[37] And there shall be great fearfulness and trembling upon earth: and they that see the wrath shall be afraid, and trembling shall come upon them.

[38] And then shall there come great storms from the south, and from the north, and another part from the west.

[39] And strong winds shall arise from the east, and shall open it; and the cloud which he raised up in wrath, and the star stirred to cause fear toward the east and west wind, shall be destroyed.

[40] The great and mighty clouds shall be puffed up full of wrath, and the star, that they may make all the earth afraid, and them that dwell therein; and they shall pour out over every high and eminent place an horrible star,

[41] Fire, and hail, and flying swords, and many waters, that all fields may be full, and all rivers, with the abundance of great waters.

[42] And they shall break down the cities and walls, mountains and hills, trees of the wood, and grass of the meadows, and their corn.

[43] And they shall go stedfastly unto Babylon, and make her afraid.

[44] They shall come to her, and besiege her, the star and all wrath shall they pour out upon her: then shall the dust and smoke go up unto the heaven, and all they that be about her shall bewail her.

[45] And they that remain under her shall do service unto them that have put her in fear.

[46] And thou, Asia, that art partaker of the hope of Babylon, and art the glory of her person:

[47] Woe be unto thee, thou wretch, because thou hast made thyself like unto her; and hast decked thy daughters in whoredom, that they might please and glory in thy lovers, which have always desired to commit whoredom with thee.

[48] Thou hast followed her that is hated in all her works and inventions: therefore saith God,

[49] I will send plagues upon thee; widowhood, poverty, famine, sword, and pestilence, to waste thy houses with destruction and death.

[50] And the glory of thy Power shall be dried up as a flower, the heat shall arise that is sent over thee.

[51] Thou shalt be weakened as a poor woman with stripes, and as one chastised with wounds, so that the mighty and lovers shall not be able to receive thee.

[52] Would I with jealousy have so proceeded against thee, saith the Lord,

[53] If thou hadst not always slain my chosen, exalting the stroke of thine hands, and saying over their dead, when thou wast drunken,

[54] Set forth the beauty of thy countenance?

[55] The reward of thy whoredom shall be in thy bosom, therefore shalt thou receive recompence.

[56] Like as thou hast done unto my chosen, saith the Lord, even so shall God do unto thee, and shall deliver thee into mischief

[57] Thy children shall die of hunger, and thou shalt fall through the sword: thy cities shall be broken down, and all thine shall perish with the sword in the field.

[58] They that be in the mountains shall die of hunger, and eat their own flesh, and drink their own blood, for very hunger of bread, and thirst of water.

[59] Thou as unhappy shalt come through the sea, and receive plagues again.

[60] And in the passage they shall rush on the idle city, and shall destroy some portion of thy land, and consume part of thy glory, and shall return to Babylon that was destroyed.

[61] And thou shalt be cast down by them as stubble, and they shall be unto thee as fire;

[62] And shall consume thee, and thy cities, thy land, and thy mountains; all thy woods and thy fruitful trees shall they burn up with fire.

63 Thy children shall they carry away captive, and, look, what thou hast,

they shall spoil it, and mar the beauty of thy face.

2 Esdras 16

[1] Woe be unto thee, Babylon, and Asia! woe be unto thee, Egypt and Syria!

[2] Gird up yourselves with cloths of sack and hair, bewail your children, and be sorry; for your destruction is at hand.

[3] A sword is sent upon you, and who may turn it back?

[4] A fire is sent among you, and who may quench it?

[5] Plagues are sent unto you, and what is he that may drive them away?

[6] May any man drive away an hungry lion in the wood? or may any one quench the fire in stubble, when it hath begun to burn?

[7] May one turn again the arrow that is shot of a strong archer?

[8] The mighty Lord sendeth the plagues and who is he that can drive them away?

[9] A fire shall go forth from his wrath, and who is he that may quench it?

[10] He shall cast lightnings, and who shall not fear? he shall thunder, and who shall not be afraid?

[11] The Lord shall threaten, and who shall not be utterly beaten to powder at his presence?

[12] The earth quaketh, and the foundations thereof; the sea ariseth up with waves from the deep, and the waves of it are troubled, and the fishes thereof also, before the Lord, and before the glory of his power:

[13] For strong is his right hand that bendeth the bow, his arrows that he shooteth are sharp, and shall not miss, when they begin to be shot into the ends of the world.

[14] Behold, the plagues are sent, and shall not return again, until they come upon the earth.

[15] The fire is kindled, and shall not be put out, till it consume the foundation of the earth.

[16] Like as an arrow which is shot of a mighty archer returneth not backward: even so the plagues that shall be sent upon earth shall not return again.

[17] Woe is me! woe is me! who will deliver me in those days?

[18] The beginning of sorrows and great mournings; the beginning of famine and great death; the beginning of wars, and the powers shall stand in fear; the beginning of evils! what shall I do when these evils shall come?

[19] Behold, famine and plague, tribulation and anguish, are sent as scourges for amendment.

[20] But for all these things they shall not turn from their wickedness, nor be always mindful of the scourges.

[21] Behold, victuals shall be so good cheap upon earth, that they shall think themselves to be in good case, and even then shall evils grow upon earth, sword, famine, and great confusion.

[22] For many of them that dwell upon earth shall perish of famine; and the other, that escape the hunger, shall the sword destroy.

[23] And the dead shall be cast out as dung, and there shall be no man to comfort them: for the earth shall be wasted, and the cities shall be cast down.

[24] There shall be no man left to till the earth, and to sow it

[25] The trees shall give fruit, and who shall gather them?

[26] The grapes shall ripen, and who shall tread them? for all places shall be desolate of men:

[27] So that one man shall desire to see another, and to hear his voice.

[28] For of a city there shall be ten left, and two of the field, which shall hide themselves in the thick groves, and in the clefts of the rocks.

[29] As in an orchard of Olives upon every tree there are left three or four olives;

[30] Or as when a vineyard is gathered, there are left some clusters of them that diligently seek through the vineyard:

[31] Even so in those days there shall be three or four left by them that search their houses with the sword.

[32] And the earth shall be laid waste, and the fields thereof shall wax old, and her ways and all her paths shall grow full of thorns, because no man shall travel therethrough.

[33] The virgins shall mourn, having no bridegrooms; the women shall mourn, having no husbands; their daughters shall mourn, having no helpers.

[34] In the wars shall their bridegrooms be destroyed, and their husbands shall perish of famine.

[35] Hear now these things and understand them, ye servants of the Lord.

[36] Behold, the word of the Lord, receive it: believe not the gods of whom the Lord spake.

[37] Behold, the plagues draw nigh, and are not slack.

[38] As when a woman with child in the ninth month bringeth forth her son, with two or three hours of her

birth great pains compass her womb, which pains, when the child cometh forth, they slack not a moment:

[39] Even so shall not the plagues be slack to come upon the earth, and the world shall mourn, and sorrows shall come upon it on every side.

[40] O my people, hear my word: make you ready to thy battle, and in those evils be even as pilgrims upon the earth.

[41] He that selleth, let him be as he that fleeth away: and he that buyeth, as one that will lose:

[42] He that occupieth merchandise, as he that hath no profit by it: and he that buildeth, as he that shall not dwell therein:

[43] He that soweth, as if he should not reap: so also he that planteth the vineyard, as he that shall not gather the grapes:

[44] They that marry, as they that shall get no children; and they that marry not, as the widowers.

[45] And therefore they that labour labour in vain:

[46] For strangers shall reap their fruits, and spoil their goods, overthrow their houses, and take their children captives, for in captivity and famine shall they get children.

[47] And they that occupy their merchandise with robbery, the more they deck their cities, their houses, their possessions, and their own persons:

[48] The more will I be angry with them for their sin, saith the Lord.

[49] Like as a whore envieth a right honest and virtuous woman:

[50] So shall righteousness hate iniquity, when she decketh herself, and shall accuse her to her face, when he cometh that shall defend him that diligently searcheth out every sin upon earth.

[51] And therefore be ye not like thereunto, nor to the works thereof.

[52] For yet a little, and iniquity shall be taken away out of the earth, and righteousness shall reign among you.

[53] Let not the sinner say that he hath not sinned: for God shall burn coals of fire upon his head, which saith before the Lord God and his glory, I have not sinned.

[54] Behold, the Lord knoweth all the works of men, their imaginations, their thoughts, and their hearts:

[55] Which spake but the word, Let the earth be made; and it was made: Let the heaven be made; and it was created.

[56] In his word were the stars made, and he knoweth the number of them.

[57] He searcheth the deep, and the treasures thereof; he hath measured the sea, and what it containeth.

[58] He hath shut the sea in the midst of the waters, and with his word hath he hanged the earth upon the waters.

[59] He spreadeth out the heavens like a vault; upon the waters hath he founded it.

[60] In the desert hath he made springs of water, and pools upon the tops of the mountains, that the floods might pour down from the high rocks to water the earth.

[61] He made man, and put his heart in the midst of the body, and gave him breath, life, and understanding.

[62] Yea and the Spirit of Almighty God, which made all things, and searcheth out all hidden things in the secrets of the earth,

[63] Surely he knoweth your inventions, and what ye think in your hearts, even them that sin, and would hide their sin.

[64] Therefore hath the Lord exactly searched out all your works, and he will put you all to shame.

[65] And when your sins are brought forth, ye shall be ashamed before men, and your own sins shall be your accusers in that day.

[66] What will ye do? or how will ye hide your sins before God and his angels?

[67] Behold, God himself is the judge, fear him: leave off from your sins, and forget your iniquities, to meddle no more with them for ever: so shall God lead you forth, and deliver you from all trouble.

[68] For, behold, the burning wrath of a great multitude is kindled over you, and they shall take away certain of you, and feed you, being idle, with things offered unto idols.

[69] And they that consent unto them shall be had in derision and in reproach, and trodden under foot.

[70] For there shall be in every place, and in the next cities, a great insurrection upon those that fear the Lord.

[71] They shall be like mad men, sparing none, but still spoiling and destroying those that fear the Lord.

[72] For they shall waste and take away their goods, and cast them out of their houses.

[73] Then shall they be known, who are my chosen; and they shall be tried as the gold in the fire.

[74] Hear, O ye my beloved, saith the Lord: behold, the days of trouble are at hand, but I will deliver you from the same.

[75] Be ye not afraid neither doubt; for God is your guide,

[76] And the guide of them who keep my commandments and precepts, saith the Lord God: let not your sins weigh you down, and let not your iniquities lift up themselves.

[77] Woe be unto them that are bound with their sins, and covered with their iniquities like as a field is covered over with bushes, and the path thereof covered with thorns, that no man may travel through!

[78] It is left undressed, and is cast into the fire to be consumed therewith.

THE BOOK OF TOBIT

Tobit 1

[1] The book of the words of Tobit, son of Tobiel, the son of Ananiel, the son of Aduel, the son of Gabael, of the seed of Asael, of the tribe of Nephthali;

[2] Who in the time of Enemessar king of the Assyrians was led captive out of Thisbe, which is at the right hand of that city, which is called properly Nephthali in Galilee above Aser.

[3] I Tobit have walked all the days of my life in the ways of truth and justice, and I did many almsdeeds to my brethren, and my nation, who came with me to Nineve, into the land of the Assyrians.

[4] And when I was in mine own country, in the land of Israel being but young, all the tribe of Nephthali my father fell from the house of Jerusalem, which was chosen out of all the tribes of Israel, that all the tribes should sacrifice there, where the temple of the habitation of the most High was consecrated and built for all ages.

[5] Now all the tribes which together revolted, and the house of my father Nephthali, sacrificed unto the heifer Baal.

[6] But I alone went often to Jerusalem at the feasts, as it was ordained unto all the people of Israel by an everlasting decree, having the firstfruits and tenths of increase, with that which was first shorn; and them gave I at the altar to the priests the children of Aaron.

[7] The first tenth part of all increase I gave to the sons of Aaron, who ministered at Jerusalem: another tenth part I sold away, and went, and spent it every year at Jerusalem:

[8] And the third I gave unto them to whom it was meet, as Debora my father's mother had commanded me, because I was left an orphan by my father.

[9] Furthermore, when I was come to the age of a man, I married Anna of mine own kindred, and of her I begat Tobias.

[10] And when we were carried away captives to Nineve, all my brethren and those that were of my kindred did eat of the bread of the Gentiles.

[11] But I kept myself from eating;

[12] Because I remembered God with all my heart.

[13] And the most High gave me grace and favour before Enemessar, so that I was his purveyor.

[14] And I went into Media, and left in trust with Gabael, the brother of Gabrias, at Rages a city of Media ten talents of silver.

[15] Now when Enemessar was dead, Sennacherib his son reigned in his stead; whose estate was troubled, that I could not go into Media.

[16] And in the time of Enemessar I gave many alms to my brethren, and gave my bread to the hungry,

[17] And my clothes to the naked: and if I saw any of my nation dead, or cast about the walls of Nineve, I buried him.

[18] And if the king Sennacherib had slain any, when he was come, and fled from Judea, I buried them privily; for in his wrath he killed many; but the bodies were not found, when they were sought for of the king.

[19] And when one of the Ninevites went and complained of me to the king, that I buried them, and hid myself; understanding that I was sought for to be put to death, I withdrew myself for fear.

[20] Then all my goods were forcibly taken away, neither was there any thing left me, beside my wife Anna and my son Tobias.

[21] And there passed not five and fifty days, before two of his sons killed him, and they fled into the mountains of Ararath; and Sarchedonus his son reigned in his stead; who appointed over his father's accounts, and over all his affairs, Achiacharus my brother Anael's son.

[22] And Achiacharus intreating for me, I returned to Nineve. Now Achiacharus was cupbearer, and keeper of the signet, and steward, and overseer of the accounts: and Sarchedonus appointed him next unto him: and he was my brother's son.

Tobit 2

[1] Now when I was come home again, and my wife Anna was restored unto me, with my son Tobias, in the feast of Pentecost, which is the holy feast of the seven weeks, there was a good dinner prepared me, in the which I sat down to eat.

[2] And when I saw abundance of meat, I said to my son, Go and bring what poor man soever thou shalt find out of our brethren, who is mindful of the Lord; and, lo, I tarry for thee.

[3] But he came again, and said, Father, one of our nation is strangled, and is cast out in the marketplace.

[4] Then before I had tasted of any meat, I started up, and took him up into a room until the going down of the sun.

[5] Then I returned, and washed myself, and ate my meat in heaviness,

[6] Remembering that prophecy of Amos, as he said, Your feasts shall be turned into mourning, and all your mirth into lamentation.

[7] Therefore I wept: and after the going down of the sun I went and made a grave, and buried him.

[8] But my neighbours mocked me, and said, This man is not yet afraid to be put to death for this matter: who fled away; and yet, lo, he burieth the dead again.

[9] The same night also I returned from the burial, and slept by the wall of my courtyard, being polluted and my face was uncovered:

[10] And I knew not that there were sparrows in the wall, and mine eyes being open, the sparrows muted warm dung into mine eyes, and a whiteness came in mine eyes: and I went to the physicians, but they helped me not: moreover Achiacharus did nourish me, until I went into Elymais.

[11] And my wife Anna did take women's works to do.

[12] And when she had sent them home to the owners, they paid her wages, and gave her also besides a kid.

[13] And when it was in my house, and began to cry, I said unto her, From whence is this kid? is it not stolen? render it to the owners; for it is not lawful to eat any thing that is stolen.

[14] But she replied upon me, It was given for a gift more than the wages. Howbeit I did not believe her, but bade her render it to the owners: and

I was abashed at her. But she replied upon me, Where are thine alms and thy righteous deeds? behold, thou and all thy works are known.

Tobit 3

[1] Then I being grieved did weep, and in my sorrow prayed, saying,

[2] O Lord, thou art just, and all thy works and all thy ways are mercy and truth, and thou judgest truly and justly for ever.

[3 Remember me, and look on me, punish me not for my sins and ignorances, and the sins of my fathers, who have sinned before thee:

[4] For they obeyed not thy commandments: wherefore thou hast delivered us for a spoil, and unto captivity, and unto death, and for a proverb of reproach to all the nations among whom we are dispersed.

[5] And now thy judgments are many and true: deal with me according to my sins and my fathers': because we have not kept thy commandments, neither have walked in truth before thee.

[6] Now therefore deal with me as seemeth best unto thee, and command my spirit to be taken from me, that I may be dissolved, and become earth: for it is profitable for me to die rather than to live, because I have heard false reproaches, and

have much sorrow: command therefore that I may now be delivered out of this distress, and go into the everlasting place: turn not thy face away from me.

[7] It came to pass the same day, that in Ecbatane a city of Media Sara the daughter of Raguel was also reproached by her father's maids;

[8] Because that she had been married to seven husbands, whom Asmodeus the evil spirit had killed, before they had lain with her. Dost thou not know, said they, that thou hast strangled thine husbands? thou hast had already seven husbands, neither wast thou named after any of them.

[9] Wherefore dost thou beat us for them? if they be dead, go thy ways after them, let us never see of thee either son or daughter.

[10] Whe she heard these things, she was very sorrowful, so that she thought to have strangled herself; and she said, I am the only daughter of my father, and if I do this, it shall be a reproach unto him, and I shall bring his old age with sorrow unto the grave.

[11] Then she prayed toward the window, and said, Blessed art thou, O Lord my God, and thine holy and glorious name is blessed and honourable for ever: let all thy works praise thee for ever.

[12] And now, O Lord, I set mine eyes and my face toward thee,

[13] And say, Take me out of the earth, that I may hear no more the reproach.

[14] Thou knowest, Lord, that I am pure from all sin with man,

[15] And that I never polluted my name, nor the name of my father, in the land of my captivity: I am the only daughter of my father, neither hath he any child to be his heir, neither any near kinsman, nor any son of his alive, to whom I may keep myself for a wife: my seven husbands are already dead; and why should I live? But if it please not thee that I should die, command some regard to be had of me, and pity taken of me, that I hear no more reproach.

[16] So the prayers of them both were heard before the majesty of the great God.

[17] And Raphael was sent to heal them both, that is, to scale away the whiteness of Tobit's eyes, and to give Sara the daughter of Raguel for a wife to Tobias the son of Tobit; and to bind Asmodeus the evil spirit; because she belonged to Tobias by right of inheritance. The selfsame time came Tobit home, and entered into his house, and Sara the daughter of Raguel came down from her upper chamber.

Tobit 4

[1] Then I being grieved did weep, and in my sorrow prayed, saying,

[2] O Lord, thou art just, and all thy works and all thy ways are mercy and truth, and thou judgest truly and justly for ever.

[3] Remember me, and look on me, punish me not for my sins and ignorances, and the sins of my fathers, who have sinned before thee:

[4] For they obeyed not thy commandments: wherefore thou hast delivered us for a spoil, and unto captivity, and unto death, and for a proverb of reproach to all the nations among whom we are dispersed.

[5] And now thy judgments are many and true: deal with me according to my sins and my fathers': because we have not kept thy commandments, neither have walked in truth before thee.

[6] Now therefore deal with me as seemeth best unto thee, and command my spirit to be taken from me, that I may be dissolved, and become earth: for it is profitable for me to die rather than to live, because I have heard false reproaches, and have much sorrow: command therefore that I may now be delivered out of this distress, and go into the everlasting place: turn not thy face away from me.

[7] It came to pass the same day, that in Ecbatane a city of Media Sara the daughter of Raguel was also reproached by her father's maids;

[8] Because that she had been married to seven husbands, whom Asmodeus the evil spirit had killed, before they had lain with her. Dost thou not know, said they, that thou hast strangled thine husbands? thou hast had already seven husbands, neither wast thou named after any of them.

[9] Wherefore dost thou beat us for them? if they be dead, go thy ways after them, let us never see of thee either son or daughter.

[10] Whe she heard these things, she was very sorrowful, so that she thought to have strangled herself; and she said, I am the only daughter of my father, and if I do this, it shall be a reproach unto him, and I shall bring his old age with sorrow unto the grave.

[11] Then she prayed toward the window, and said, Blessed art thou, O Lord my God, and thine holy and glorious name is blessed and honourable for ever: let all thy works praise thee for ever.

[12] And now, O Lord, I set mine eyes and my face toward thee,

[13] And say, Take me out of the earth, that I may hear no more the reproach.

[14] Thou knowest, Lord, that I am pure from all sin with man,

[15] And that I never polluted my name, nor the name of my father, in the land of my captivity: I am the only daughter of my father, neither hath he any child to be his heir, neither any near kinsman, nor any son of his alive, to whom I may keep myself for a wife: my seven husbands are already dead; and why should I live? but if it please not thee that I should die, command some regard to be had of me, and pity taken of me, that I hear no more reproach.

[16]So the prayers of them both were heard before the majesty of the great God.

[17] And Raphael was sent to heal them both, that is, to scale away the whiteness of Tobit's eyes, and to give Sara the daughter of Raguel for a wife to Tobias the son of Tobit; and to bind Asmodeus the evil spirit; because she belonged to Tobias by right of inheritance. The selfsame time came Tobit home, and entered into his house, and Sara the daughter of Raguel came down from her upper chamber.

Tobit 5

[1] Tobias then answered and said, Father, I will do all things which thou hast commanded me:

[2] But how can I receive the money, seeing I know him not?

[3] Then he gave him the handwriting, and said unto him, Seek thee a man which may go with thee, whiles I yet live, and I will give him wages: and go and receive the money.

[4] Therefore when he went to seek a man, he found Raphael that was an angel.

[5] But he knew not; and he said unto him, Canst thou go with me to Rages? and knowest thou those places well?

[6] To whom the angel said, I will go with thee, and I know the way well: for I have lodged with our brother Gabael.

[7] Then Tobias said unto him, Tarry for me, till I tell my father.

[8] Then he said unto him, Go and tarry not. So he went in and said to his father, Behold, I have found one which will go with me. Then he said, Call him unto me, that I may know of what tribe he is, and whether he be a trusty man to go with thee.

[9] So he called him, and he came in, and they saluted one another.

[10] Then Tobit said unto him, Brother, shew me of what tribe and family thou art.

[11] To whom he said, Dost thou seek for a tribe or family, or an hired man to go with thy son? Then Tobit said unto him, I would know, brother, thy kindred and name.

[12] Then he said, I am Azarias, the son of Ananias the great, and of thy brethren.

[13] Then Tobit said, Thou art welcome, brother; be not now angry with me, because I have enquired to know thy tribe and thy family; for thou art my brother, of an honest and good stock: for I know Ananias and Jonathas, sons of that great Samaias, as we went together to Jerusalem to worship, and offered the firstborn, and the tenths of the fruits; and they were not seduced with the error of our brethren: my brother, thou art of a good stock.

[14] But tell me, what wages shall I give thee? Wilt thou a drachm a day, and things necessary, as to mine own son?

[15] Yea, moreover, if ye return safe, I will add something to thy wages.

[16] So they were well pleased. Then said he to Tobias, Prepare thyself for the journey, and God send you a good journey. And when his son had prepared all things for the journey, his father said, Go thou with this man, and God, which dwelleth in heaven, prosper your journey, and the angel of God keep you company. So they went forth both, and the young man's dog with them.

[17] But Anna his mother wept, and said to Tobit, Why hast thou sent away our son? Is he not the staff of our hand, in going in and out before us?

[18] Be not greedy to add money to money: but let it be as refuse in respect of our child.

[19] For that which the Lord hath given us to live with doth suffice us.

[20] Then said Tobit to her, Take no care, my sister; he shall return in safety, and thine eyes shall see him.

[21] For the good angel will keep him company, and his journey shall be prosperous, and he shall return safe.

[22] Then she made an end of weeping.

Tobit 6

[1] And as they went on their journey, they came in the evening to the river Tigris, and they lodged there.

[2] And when the young man went down to wash himself, a fish leaped out of the river, and would have devoured him.

[3] Then the angel said unto him, Take the fish. And the young man laid hold of the fish, and drew it to land.

[4] To whom the angel said, Open the fish, and take the heart and the liver and the gall, and put them up safely.

[5] So the young man did as the angel commanded him; and when they had roasted the fish, they did eat it: then they both went on their way, till they drew near to Ecbatane.

[6] Then the young man said to the angel, Brother Azarias, to what use is the heart and the liver and the gal of the fish?

[7] And he said unto him, Touching the heart and the liver, if a devil or an evil spirit trouble any, we must make a smoke thereof before the man or the woman, and the party shall be no more vexed.

[8] As for the gall, it is good to anoint a man that hath whiteness in his eyes, and he shall be healed.

[9] And when they were come near to Rages,

[10] The angel said to the young man, Brother, to day we shall lodge with Raguel, who is thy cousin; he also hath one only daughter, named Sara; I will speak for her, that she may be given thee for a wife.

[11] For to thee doth the right of her appertain, seeing thou only art of her kindred.

[12] And the maid is fair and wise: now therefore hear me, and I will speak to her father; and when we return from Rages we will celebrate the marriage: for I know that Raguel cannot marry her to another according to the law of Moses, but he shall be guilty of death, because the right of inheritance doth rather appertain to thee than to any other.

[13] Then the young man answered the angel, I have heard, brother Azarias that this maid hath been given to seven men, who all died in the marriage chamber.

[14] And now I am the only son of my father, and I am afraid, lest if I go in unto her, I die, as the other before: for a wicked spirit loveth her, which hurteth no body, but those which come unto her; wherefore I also fear lest I die, and bring my father's and my mother's life because of me to the grave with sorrow: for they have no other son to bury them.

[15] Then the angel said unto him, Dost thou not remember the precepts which thy father gave thee, that thou shouldest marry a wife of thine own kindred? wherefore hear me, O my brother; for she shall be given thee to wife; and make thou no reckoning of the evil spirit; for this same night shall she be given thee in marriage.

[16 And when thou shalt come into the marriage chamber, thou shalt take the ashes of perfume, and shalt lay upon them some of the heart and liver of the fish, and shalt make a smoke with it:

[17] And the devil shall smell it, and flee away, and never come again any more: but when thou shalt come to her, rise up both of you, and pray to God which is merciful, who will have pity on you, and save you: fear not, for she is appointed unto thee from the beginning; and thou shalt preserve her, and she shall go with thee. Moreover I suppose that she shall bear thee children. Now when

Tobias had heard these things, he loved her, and his heart was effectually joined to her.

Tobit 7

[1] And when they were come to Ecbatane, they came to the house of Raguel, and Sara met them: and after they had saluted one another, she brought them into the house.

[2] Then said Raguel to Edna his wife, How like is this young man to Tobit my cousin!

[3] And Raguel asked them, From whence are ye, brethren? To whom they said, We are of the sons of Nephthalim, which are captives in Nineve.

[4] Then he said to them, Do ye know Tobit our kinsman? And they said, We know him. Then said he, Is he in good health?

[5] And they said, He is both alive, and in good health: and Tobias said, He is my father.

[6] Then Raguel leaped up, and kissed him, and wept,

[7] And blessed him, and said unto him, Thou art the son of an honest and good man. But when he had heard that Tobit was blind, he was sorrowful, and wept.

[8] And likewise Edna his wife and Sara his daughter wept. Moreover they entertained them cheerfully; and after that they had killed a ram of the flock, they set store of meat on the table. Then said Tobias to Raphael, Brother Azarias, speak of those things of which thou didst talk in the way, and let this business be dispatched.

[9] So he communicated the matter with Raguel: and Raguel said to Tobias, Eat and drink, and make merry:

[10] For it is meet that thou shouldest marry my daughter: nevertheless I will declare unto thee the truth.

[11] I have given my daughter in marriage to seven men, who died that night they came in unto her: nevertheless for the present be merry. But Tobias said, I will eat nothing here, till we agree and swear one to another.

[12] Raguel said, Then take her from henceforth according to the manner, for thou art her cousin, and she is thine, and the merciful God give you good success in all things.

[13] Then he called his daughter Sara, and she came to her father, and he took her by the hand, and gave her to be wife to Tobias, saying, Behold, take her after the law of Moses, and lead her away to thy father. And he blessed them;

[14] And called Edna his wife, and took paper, and did write an instrument of covenants, and sealed it.

[15] Then they began to eat.

[16] After Raguel called his wife Edna, and said unto her, Sister, prepare another chamber, and bring her in thither.

[17] Which when she had done as he had bidden her, she brought her thither: and she wept, and she received the tears of her daughter, and said unto her,

[18] Be of good comfort, my daughter; the Lord of heaven and earth give thee joy for this thy sorrow: be of good comfort, my daughter.

Tobit 8

[1] And when they had supped, they brought Tobias in unto her.

[2] And as he went, he remembered the words of Raphael, and took the ashes of the perfumes, and put the heart and the liver of the fish thereupon, and made a smoke therewith.

[3] The which smell when the evil spirit had smelled, he fled into the utmost parts of Egypt, and the angel bound him.

[4] And after that they were both shut in together, Tobias rose out of the bed, and said, Sister, arise, and let us pray that God would have pity on us.

[5] Then began Tobias to say, Blessed art thou, O God of our fathers, and blessed is thy holy and glorious name for ever; let the heavens bless thee, and all thy creatures.

[6] Thou madest Adam, and gavest him Eve his wife for an helper and stay: of them came mankind: thou hast said, It is not good that man should be alone; let us make unto him an aid like unto himself.

[7] And now, O Lord, I take not this my sister for lust but uprightly: therefore mercifully ordain that we may become aged together.

[8] And she said with him, Amen.

[9] So they slept both that night. And Raguel arose, and went and made a grave,

[10] Saying, I fear lest he also be dead.

[11] But when Raguel was come into his house,

[12] He said unto his wife Edna. Send one of the maids, and let her see whether he be alive: if he be not, that we may bury him, and no man know it.

[13] So the maid opened the door, and went in, and found them both asleep,

[14] And came forth, and told them that he was alive.

[15] Then Raguel praised God, and said, O God, thou art worthy to be praised with all pure and holy praise; therefore let thy saints praise thee with all thy creatures; and let all thine

angels and thine elect praise thee for ever.

[16] Thou art to be praised, for thou hast made me joyful; and that is not come to me which I suspected; but thou hast dealt with us according to thy great mercy.

[17] Thou art to be praised because thou hast had mercy of two that were the only begotten children of their fathers: grant them mercy, O Lord, and finish their life in health with joy and mercy.

[18] Then Raguel bade his servants to fill the grave.

[19] And he kept the wedding feast fourteen days.

[20] For before the days of the marriage were finished, Raguel had said unto him by an oath, that he should not depart till the fourteen days of the marriage were expired;

[21] And then he should take the half of his goods, and go in safety to his father; and should have the rest when I and my wife be dead.

Tobit 9

[1] Then Tobias called Raphael, and said unto him,

[2] Brother Azarias, take with thee a servant, and two camels, and go to Rages of Media to Gabael, and bring me the money, and bring him to the wedding.

[3] For Raguel hath sworn that I shall not depart.

[4] But my father counteth the days; and if I tarry long, he will be very sorry.

[5] So Raphael went out, and lodged with Gabael, and gave him the handwriting: who brought forth bags which were sealed up, and gave them to him.

[6] And early in the morning they went forth both together, and came to the wedding: and Tobias blessed his wife.

Tobit 10

[1] Now Tobit his father counted every day: and when the days of the journey were expired, and they came not,

[2] Then Tobit said, Are they detained? or is Gabael dead, and there is no man to give him the money?

[3] Therefore he was very sorry.

[4] Then his wife said unto him, My son is dead, seeing he stayeth long; and she began to wail him, and said,

[5] Now I care for nothing, my son, since I have let thee go, the light of mine eyes.

[6] To whom Tobit said, Hold thy peace, take no care, for he is safe.

[7] But she said, Hold thy peace, and deceive me not; my son is dead. And she went out every day into the way

which they went, and did eat no meat on the daytime, and ceased not whole nights to bewail her son Tobias, until the fourteen days of the wedding were expired, which Raguel had sworn that he should spend there. Then Tobias said to Raguel, Let me go, for my father and my mother look no more to see me.

[8] But his father in law said unto him, Tarry with me, and I will send to thy father, and they shall declare unto him how things go with thee.

[9] But Tobias said, No; but let me go to my father.

[10] Then Raguel arose, and gave him Sara his wife, and half his goods, servants, and cattle, and money:

[11] And he blessed them, and sent them away, saying, The God of heaven give you a prosperous journey, my children.

[12] And he said to his daughter, Honour thy father and thy mother in law, which are now thy parents, that I may hear good report of thee. And he kissed her. Edna also said to Tobias, The Lord of heaven restore thee, my dear brother, and grant that I may see thy children of my daughter Sara before I die, that I may rejoice before the Lord: behold, I commit my daughter unto thee of special trust; where are do not entreat her evil.

Tobit 11

[1] After these things Tobias went his way, praising God that he had given him a prosperous journey, and blessed Raguel and Edna his wife, and went on his way till they drew near unto Nineve.

[2] Then Raphael said to Tobias, Thou knowest, brother, how thou didst leave thy father:

[3] Let us haste before thy wife, and prepare the house.

[4] And take in thine hand the gall of the fish. So they went their way, and the dog went after them.

[5] Now Anna sat looking about toward the way for her son.

[6] And when she espied him coming, she said to his father, Behold, thy son cometh, and the man that went with him.

[7] Then said Raphael, I know, Tobias, that thy father will open his eyes.

[8] Therefore anoint thou his eyes with the gall, and being pricked therewith, he shall rub, and the whiteness shall fall away, and he shall see thee.

[9] Then Anna ran forth, and fell upon the neck of her son, and said unto him, Seeing I have seen thee, my son, from henceforth I am content to die. And they wept both.

[10] Tobit also went forth toward the door, and stumbled: but his son ran unto him,

[11] And took hold of his father: and he strake of the gall on his fathers' eyes, saying, Be of good hope, my father.

[12] And when his eyes began to smart, he rubbed them;

[13] And the whiteness pilled away from the corners of his eyes: and when he saw his son, he fell upon his neck.

[14] And he wept, and said, Blessed art thou, O God, and blessed is thy name for ever; and blessed are all thine holy angels:

[15] For thou hast scourged, and hast taken pity on me: for, behold, I see my son Tobias. And his son went in rejoicing, and told his father the great things that had happened to him in Media.

[16] Then Tobit went out to meet his daughter in law at the gate of Nineve, rejoicing and praising God: and they which saw him go marvelled, because he had received his sight.

[17] But Tobias gave thanks before them, because God had mercy on him. And when he came near to Sara his daughter in law, he blessed her, saying, Thou art welcome, daughter: God be blessed, which hath brought thee unto us, and blessed be thy father and thy mother. And there was joy among all his brethren which were at Nineve.

[18] And Achiacharus, and Nasbas his brother's son, came:

[19] And Tobias' wedding was kept seven days with great joy.

Tobit 12

[1] Then Tobit called his son Tobias, and said unto him, My son, see that the man have his wages, which went with thee, and thou must give him more.

[2] And Tobias said unto him, O father, it is no harm to me to give him half of those things which I have brought:

[3] For he hath brought me again to thee in safety, and made whole my wife, and brought me the money, and likewise healed thee.

[4] Then the old man said, It is due unto him.

[5] So he called the angel, and he said unto him, Take half of all that ye have brought and go away in safety.

[6] Then he took them both apart, and said unto them, Bless God, praise him, and magnify him, and praise him for the things which he hath done unto you in the sight of all that live. It is good to praise God, and exalt his name, and honourably to shew forth the works of God; therefore be not slack to praise him.

[7] It is good to keep close the secret of a king, but it is honourable to reveal the works of God. Do that which is good, and no evil shall touch you.

[8] Prayer is good with fasting and alms and righteousness. A little with righteousness is better than much with unrighteousness. It is better to give alms than to lay up gold:

[9] For alms doth deliver from death, and shall purge away all sin. Those that exercise alms and righteousness shall be filled with life:

[10] But they that sin are enemies to their own life.

[11] Surely I will keep close nothing from you. For I said, It was good to keep close the secret of a king, but that it was honourable to reveal the works of God.

[12] Now therefore, when thou didst pray, and Sara thy daughter in law, I did bring the remembrance of your prayers before the Holy One: and when thou didst bury the dead, I was with thee likewise.

[13] And when thou didst not delay to rise up, and leave thy dinner, to go and cover the dead, thy good deed was not hid from me: but I was with thee.

[14] And now God hath sent me to heal thee and Sara thy daughter in law.

[15] I am Raphael, one of the seven holy angels, which present the prayers of the saints, and which go in and out before the glory of the Holy One.

[16] Then they were both troubled, and fell upon their faces: for they feared.

[17] But he said unto them, Fear not, for it shall go well with you; praise God therefore.

[18] For not of any favour of mine, but by the will of our God I came; wherefore praise him for ever.

[19] All these days I did appear unto you; but I did neither eat nor drink, but ye did see a vision.

[20] Now therefore give God thanks: for I go up to him that sent me; but write all things which are done in a book.

[21] And when they arose, they saw him no more.

[22] Then they confessed the great and wonderful works of God, and how the angel of the Lord had appeared unto them.

Tobit 13

[1] Then Tobit wrote a prayer of rejoicing, and said, Blessed be God that liveth for ever, and blessed be his kingdom.

[2] For he doth scourge, and hath mercy: he leadeth down to hell, and

bringeth up again: neither is there any that can avoid his hand.

[3] Confess him before the Gentiles, ye children of Israel: for he hath scattered us among them.

[4] There declare his greatness, and extol him before all the living: for he is our Lord, and he is the God our Father for ever.

[5] And he will scourge us for our iniquities, and will have mercy again, and will gather us out of all nations, among whom he hath scattered us.

[6] If ye turn to him with your whole heart, and with your whole mind, and deal uprightly before him, then will he turn unto you, and will not hide his face from you. Therefore see what he will do with you, and confess him with your whole mouth, and praise the Lord of might, and extol the everlasting King. In the land of my captivity do I praise him, and declare his might and majesty to a sinful nation. O ye sinners, turn and do justice before him: who can tell if he will accept you, and have mercy on you?

[7] I will extol my God, and my soul shall praise the King of heaven, and shall rejoice in his greatness.

[8] Let all men speak, and let all praise him for his righteousness.

[9] O Jerusalem, the holy city, he will scourge thee for thy children's works, and will have mercy again on the sons of the righteous.

[10] Give praise to the Lord, for he is good: and praise the everlasting King, that his tabernacle may be builded in thee again with joy, and let him make joyful there in thee those that are captives, and love in thee for ever those that are miserable.

[11] Many nations shall come from far to the name of the Lord God with gifts in their hands, even gifts to the King of heaven; all generations shall praise thee with great joy.

[12] Cursed are all they which hate thee, and blessed shall all be which love thee for ever.

[13] Rejoice and be glad for the children of the just: for they shall be gathered together, and shall bless the Lord of the just.

[14] O blessed are they which love thee, for they shall rejoice in thy peace: blessed are they which have been sorrowful for all thy scourges; for they shall rejoice for thee, when they have seen all thy glory, and shall be glad for ever.

[15] Let my soul bless God the great King.

[16] For Jerusalem shall be built up with sapphires and emeralds, and precious stone: thy walls and towers and battlements with pure gold.

[17] And the streets of Jerusalem shall be paved with beryl and carbuncle and stones of Ophir.

[18] And all her streets shall say, Alleluia; and they shall praise him, saying, Blessed be God, which hath extolled it for ever.

Tobit 14

[1] So Tobit made an end of praising God.

[2] And he was eight and fifty years old when he lost his sight, which was restored to him after eight years: and he gave alms, and he increased in the fear of the Lord God, and praised him.

[3] And when he was very aged he called his son, and the sons of his son, and said to him, My son, take thy children; for, behold, I am aged, and am ready to depart out of this life.

[4] Go into Media my son, for I surely believe those things which Jonas the prophet spake of Nineve, that it shall be overthrown; and that for a time peace shall rather be in Media; and that our brethren shall lie scattered in the earth from that good land: and Jerusalem shall be desolate, and the house of God in it shall be burned, and shall be desolate for a time;

[5] And that again God will have mercy on them, and bring them again into the land, where they shall build a temple, but not like to the first, until the time of that age be fulfilled; and afterward they shall return from all places of their captivity, and build up Jerusalem

gloriously, and the house of God shall be built in it for ever with a glorious building, as the prophets have spoken thereof.

[6] And all nations shall turn, and fear the Lord God truly, and shall bury their idols.

[7] So shall all nations praise the Lord, and his people shall confess God, and the Lord shall exalt his people; and all those which love the Lord God in truth and justice shall rejoice, shewing mercy to our brethren.

[8] And now, my son, depart out of Nineve, because that those things which the prophet Jonas spake shall surely come to pass.

[9] But keep thou the law and the commandments, and shew thyself merciful and just, that it may go well with thee.

[10] And bury me decently, and thy mother with me; but tarry no longer at Nineve. Remember, my son, how Aman handled Achiacharus that brought him up, how out of light he brought him into darkness, and how he rewarded him again: yet Achiacharus was saved, but the other had his reward: for he went down into darkness. Manasses gave alms, and escaped the snares of death which they had set for him: but Aman fell into the snare, and perished.

[11] Wherefore now, my son, consider what alms doeth, and how righteousness doth deliver. When he had said these things, he gave up the ghost in the bed, being an hundred and eight and fifty years old; and he buried him honourably.

[12] And when Anna his mother was dead, he buried her with his father. But Tobias departed with his wife and children to Ecbatane to Raguel his father in law,

[13] Where he became old with honour, and he buried his father and mother in law honourably, and he inherited their substance, and his father Tobit's.

[14] And he died at Ecbatane in Media, being an hundred and seven and twenty years old.

[15] But before he died he heard of the destruction of Nineve, which was taken by Nabuchodonosor and Assuerus: and before his death he rejoiced over Nineve.

THE BOOK OF JUDITH

Judith 1

1 In the twelfth year of the reign of Nabuchodonosor, who reigned in Nineve, the great city; in the days of Arphaxad, which reigned over the Medes in Ecbatane,

2 And built in Ecbatane walls round about of stones hewn three cubits broad and six cubits long, and made the height of the wall seventy cubits, and the breadth thereof fifty cubits:

3 And set the towers thereof upon the gates of it an hundred cubits high, and the breadth thereof in the foundation threescore cubits:

4 And he made the gates thereof, even gates that were raised to the height of seventy cubits, and the breadth of them was forty cubits, for the going forth of his mighty armies, and for the setting in array of his footmen:

5 Even in those days king Nabuchodonosor made war with king Arphaxad in the great plain, which is the plain in the borders of Ragau.

6 And there came unto him all they that dwelt in the hill country, and all that dwelt by Euphrates, and Tigris and Hydaspes, and the plain of Arioch the king of the Elymeans, and very many nations of the sons of Chelod, assembled themselves to the battle.

7 Then Nabuchodonosor king of the Assyrians sent unto all that dwelt in Persia, and to all that dwelt westward, and to those that dwelt in Cilicia, and Damascus, and Libanus, and Antilibanus, and to all that dwelt upon the sea coast,

8 And to those among the nations that were of Carmel, and Galaad, and the higher Galilee, and the great plain of Esdrelom,

9 And to all that were in Samaria and the cities thereof, and beyond Jordan unto Jerusalem, and Betane, and Chelus, and Kades, and the river of Egypt, and Taphnes, and Ramesse, and all the land of Gesem,

10 Until ye come beyond Tanis and Memphis, and to all the inhabitants of Egypt, until ye come to the borders of Ethiopia.

11 But all the inhabitants of the land made light of the commandment of Nabuchodonosor king of the Assyrians, neither went they with him to the battle; for they were not afraid of him: yea, he was before them as one man, and they sent away his ambassadors from them without effect, and with disgrace.

12 Therefore Nabuchodonosor was very angry with all this country, and sware by his throne and kingdom, that he would surely be avenged upon all those coasts of Cilicia, and

Damascus, and Syria, and that he would slay with the sword all the inhabitants of the land of Moab, and the children of Ammon, and all Judea, and all that were in Egypt, till ye come to the borders of the two seas.

13 Then he marched in battle array with his power against king Arphaxad in the seventeenth year, and he prevailed in his battle: for he overthrew all the power of Arphaxad, and all his horsemen, and all his chariots,

14 And became lord of his cities, and came unto Ecbatane, and took the towers, and spoiled the streets thereof, and turned the beauty thereof into shame.

15 He took also Arphaxad in the mountains of Ragau, and smote him through with his darts, and destroyed him utterly that day.

16 So he returned afterward to Nineve, both he and all his company of sundry nations being a very great multitude of men of war, and there he took his ease, and banqueted, both he and his army, an hundred and twenty days.

Judith 2

1 And in the eighteenth year, the two and twentieth day of the first month, there was talk in the house of Nabuchodonosor king of the Assyrians that he should, as he said, avenge himself on all the earth.

2 So he called unto him all his officers, and all his nobles, and communicated with them his secret counsel, and concluded the afflicting of the whole earth out of his own mouth.

3 Then they decreed to destroy all flesh, that did not obey the commandment of his mouth.

4 And when he had ended his counsel, Nabuchodonosor king of the Assyrians called Holofernes the chief captain of his army, which was next unto him, and said unto him.

5 Thus saith the great king, the lord of the whole earth, Behold, thou shalt go forth from my presence, and take with thee men that trust in their own strength, of footmen an hundred and twenty thousand; and the number of horses with their riders twelve thousand.

6 And thou shalt go against all the west country, because they disobeyed my commandment.

7 And thou shalt declare unto that they prepare for me earth and water: for I will go forth in my wrath against them and will cover the whole face of the earth with the feet of mine army, and I will give them for a spoil unto them:

8 So that their slain shall fill their valleys and brooks and the river shall be filled with their dead, till it overflow:

9 And I will lead them captives to the utmost parts of all the earth.

10 Thou therefore shalt go forth. and take beforehand for me all their coasts: and if they will yield themselves unto thee, thou shalt reserve them for me till the day of their punishment.

11 But concerning them that rebel, let not thine eye spare them; but put them to the slaughter, and spoil them wheresoever thou goest.

12 For as I live, and by the power of my kingdom, whatsoever I have spoken, that will I do by mine hand.

13 And take thou heed that thou transgress none of the commandments of thy lord, but accomplish them fully, as I have commanded thee, and defer not to do them.

14 Then Holofernes went forth from the presence of his lord, and called all the governors and captains, and the officers of the army of Assur;

15 And he mustered the chosen men for the battle, as his lord had commanded him, unto an hundred and twenty thousand, and twelve thousand archers on horseback;

16 And he ranged them, as a great army is ordered for the war.

17 And he took camels and asses for their carriages, a very great number; and sheep and oxen and goats without number for their provision:

18 And plenty of victual for every man of the army, and very much gold and silver out of the king's house.

19 Then he went forth and all his power to go before king Nabuchodonosor in the voyage, and to cover all the face of the earth westward with their chariots, and horsemen, and their chosen footmen.

20 A great number also sundry countries came with them like locusts, and like the sand of the earth: for the multitude was without number.

21 And they went forth of Nineve three days' journey toward the plain of Bectileth, and pitched from Bectileth near the mountain which is at the left hand of the upper Cilicia.

22 Then he took all his army, his footmen, and horsemen and chariots, and went from thence into the hill country;

23 And destroyed Phud and Lud, and spoiled all the children of Rasses, and the children of Israel, which were toward the wilderness at the south of the land of the Chellians.

24 Then he went over Euphrates, and went through Mesopotamia, and destroyed all the high cities that were upon the river Arbonai, till ye come to the sea.

25 And he took the borders of Cilicia, and killed all that resisted him, and came to the borders of Japheth, which were toward the south, over against Arabia.

26 He compassed also all the children of Madian, and burned up their tabernacles, and spoiled their sheepcotes.

27 Then he went down into the plain of Damascus in the time of wheat harvest, and burnt up all their fields, and destroyed their flocks and herds, also he spoiled their cities, and utterly wasted their countries, and smote all their young men with the edge of the sword.

28 Therefore the fear and dread of him fell upon all the inhabitants of the sea coasts, which were in Sidon and Tyrus, and them that dwelt in Sur and Ocina, and all that dwelt in Jemnaan; and they that dwelt in Azotus and Ascalon feared him greatly.

Judith 3

1 So they sent ambassadors unto him to treat of peace, saying,

2 Behold, we the servants of Nabuchodonosor the great king lie before thee; use us as shall be good in thy sight.

3 Behold, our houses, and all our places, and all our fields of wheat, and flocks, and herds, and all the lodges of our tents lie before thy face; use them as it pleaseth thee.

4 Behold, even our cities and the inhabitants thereof are thy servants; come and deal with them as seemeth good unto thee.

5 So the men came to Holofernes, and declared unto him after this manner.

6 Then came he down toward the sea coast, both he and his army, and set garrisons in the high cities, and took out of them chosen men for aid.

7 So they and all the country round about received them with garlands, with dances, and with timbrels.

8 Yet he did cast down their frontiers, and cut down their groves: for he had decreed to destroy all the gods of the land, that all nations should worship Nabuchodonosor only, and that all tongues and tribes should call upon him as god.

9 Also he came over against Esdraelon near unto Judea, over against the great strait of Judea.

10 And he pitched between Geba and Scythopolis, and there he tarried a whole month, that he might gather together all the carriages of his army.

Judith 4

1 Now the children of Israel, that dwelt in Judea, heard all that Holofernes the chief captain of Nabuchodonosor king of the Assyrians had done to the nations, and after what manner he had

spoiled all their temples, and brought them to nought.

2 Therefore they were exceedingly afraid of him, and were troubled for Jerusalem, and for the temple of the Lord their God:

3 For they were newly returned from the captivity, and all the people of Judea were lately gathered together: and the vessels, and the altar, and the house, were sanctified after the profanation.

4 Therefore they sent into all the coasts of Samaria, and the villages and to Bethoron, and Belmen, and Jericho, and to Choba, and Esora, and to the valley of Salem:

5 And possessed themselves beforehand of all the tops of the high mountains, and fortified the villages that were in them, and laid up victuals for the provision of war: for their fields were of late reaped.

6 Also Joacim the high priest, which was in those days in Jerusalem, wrote to them that dwelt in Bethulia, and Betomestham, which is over against Esdraelon toward the open country, near to Dothaim,

7 Charging them to keep the passages of the hill country: for by them there was an entrance into Judea, and it was easy to stop them that would come up, because the passage was straight, for two men at the most.

8 And the children of Israel did as Joacim the high priest had commanded them, with the ancients of all the people of Israel, which dwelt at Jerusalem.

9 Then every man of Israel cried to God with great fervency, and with great vehemency did they humble their souls:

10 Both they, and their wives and their children, and their cattle, and every stranger and hireling, and their servants bought with money, put sackcloth upon their loins.

11 Thus every man and women, and the little children, and the inhabitants of Jerusalem, fell before the temple, and cast ashes upon their heads, and spread out their sackcloth before the face of the Lord: also they put sackcloth about the altar,

12 And cried to the God of Israel all with one consent earnestly, that he would not give their children for a prey, and their wives for a spoil, and the cities of their inheritance to destruction, and the sanctuary to profanation and reproach, and for the nations to rejoice at.

13 So God heard their prayers, and looked upon their afflictions: for the people fasted many days in all Judea and Jerusalem before the sanctuary of the Lord Almighty.

14 And Joacim the high priest, and all the priests that stood before the Lord, and they which ministered unto

the Lord, had their loins girt with sackcloth, and offered the daily burnt offerings, with the vows and free gifts of the people,

15 And had ashes on their mitres, and cried unto the Lord with all their power, that he would look upon all the house of Israel graciously.

Judith 5

1 Then was it declared to Holofernes, the chief captain of the army of Assur, that the children of Israel had prepared for war, and had shut up the passages of the hill country, and had fortified all the tops of the high hills and had laid impediments in the champaign countries:

2 Wherewith he was very angry, and called all the princes of Moab, and the captains of Ammon, and all the governors of the sea coast,

3 And he said unto them, Tell me now, ye sons of Chanaan, who this people is, that dwelleth in the hill country, and what are the cities that they inhabit, and what is the multitude of their army, and wherein is their power and strength, and what king is set over them, or captain of their army;

4 And why have they determined not to come and meet me, more than all the inhabitants of the west.

5 Then said Achior, the captain of all the sons of Ammon, Let my lord now hear a word from the mouth of thy servant, and I will declare unto thee the truth concerning this people, which dwelleth near thee, and inhabiteth the hill countries: and there shall no lie come out of the mouth of thy servant.

6 This people are descended of the Chaldeans:

7 And they sojourned heretofore in Mesopotamia, because they would not follow the gods of their fathers, which were in the land of Chaldea.

8 For they left the way of their ancestors, and worshipped the God of heaven, the God whom they knew: so they cast them out from the face of their gods, and they fled into Mesopotamia, and sojourned there many days.

9 Then their God commanded them to depart from the place where they sojourned, and to go into the land of Chanaan: where they dwelt, and were increased with gold and silver, and with very much cattle.

10 But when a famine covered all the land of Chanaan, they went down into Egypt, and sojourned there, while they were nourished, and became there a great multitude, so that one could not number their nation.

11 Therefore the king of Egypt rose up against them, and dealt subtilly with them, and brought them low with labouring in brick, and made them slaves.

12 Then they cried unto their God, and he smote all the land of Egypt with incurable plagues: so the Egyptians cast them out of their sight.

13 And God dried the Red sea before them,

14 And brought them to mount Sina, and Cades-Barne, and cast forth all that dwelt in the wilderness.

15 So they dwelt in the land of the Amorites, and they destroyed by their strength all them of Esebon, and passing over Jordan they possessed all the hill country.

16 And they cast forth before them the Chanaanite, the Pherezite, the Jebusite, and the Sychemite, and all the Gergesites, and they dwelt in that country many days.

17 And whilst they sinned not before their God, they prospered, because the God that hateth iniquity was with them.

18 But when they departed from the way which he appointed them, they were destroyed in many battles very sore, and were led captives into a land that was not their's, and the temple of their God was cast to the ground, and their cities were taken by the enemies.

19 But now are they returned to their God, and are come up from the places where they were scattered, and have possessed Jerusalem, where their sanctuary is, and are seated in the hill country; for it was desolate.

20 Now therefore, my lord and governor, if there be any error against this people, and they sin against their God, let us consider that this shall be their ruin, and let us go up, and we shall overcome them.

21 But if there be no iniquity in their nation, let my lord now pass by, lest their Lord defend them, and their God be for them, and we become a reproach before all the world.

22 And when Achior had finished these sayings, all the people standing round about the tent murmured, and the chief men of Holofernes, and all that dwelt by the sea side, and in Moab, spake that he should kill him.

23 For, say they, we will not be afraid of the face of the children of Israel: for, lo, it is a people that have no strength nor power for a strong battle

24 Now therefore, lord Holofernes, we will go up, and they shall be a prey to be devoured of all thine army.

Judith 6

1 And when the tumult of men that were about the council was ceased, Holofernes the chief captain of the army of Assur said unto Achior and all the Moabites before all the company of other nations,

2 And who art thou, Achior, and the hirelings of Ephraim, that thou hast prophesied against us as to day, and hast said, that we should not make war with the people of Israel, because their God will defend them? and who is God but Nabuchodonosor?

3 He will send his power, and will destroy them from the face of the earth, and their God shall not deliver them: but we his servants will destroy them as one man; for they are not able to sustain the power of our horses.

4 For with them we will tread them under foot, and their mountains shall be drunken with their blood, and their fields shall be filled with their dead bodies, and their footsteps shall not be able to stand before us, for they shall utterly perish, saith king Nabuchodonosor, lord of all the earth: for he said, None of my words shall be in vain.

5 And thou, Achior, an hireling of Ammon, which hast spoken these words in the day of thine iniquity, shalt see my face no more from this day, until I take vengeance of this nation that came out of Egypt.

6 And then shall the sword of mine army, and the multitude of them that serve me, pass through thy sides, and thou shalt fall among their slain, when I return.

7 Now therefore my servants shall bring thee back into the hill country, and shall set thee in one of the cities of the passages:

8 And thou shalt not perish, till thou be destroyed with them.

9 And if thou persuade thyself in thy mind that they shall be taken, let not thy countenance fall: I have spoken it, and none of my words shall be in vain.

10 Then Holofernes commanded his servants, that waited in his tent, to take Achior, and bring him to Bethulia, and deliver him into the hands of the children of Israel.

11 So his servants took him, and brought him out of the camp into the plain, and they went from the midst of the plain into the hill country, and came unto the fountains that were under Bethulia.

12 And when the men of the city saw them, they took up their weapons, and went out of the city to the top of the hill: and every man that used a sling kept them from coming up by casting of stones against them.

13 Nevertheless having gotten privily under the hill, they bound Achior, and cast him down, and left him at the foot of the hill, and returned to their lord.

14 But the Israelites descended from their city, and came unto him, and loosed him, and brought him to Bethulia, and presented him to the governors of the city:

15 Which were in those days Ozias the son of Micha, of the tribe of Simeon, and Chabris the son of Gothoniel, and Charmis the son of Melchiel.

16 And they called together all the ancients of the city, and all their youth ran together, and their women, to the assembly, and they set Achior in the midst of all their people. Then Ozias asked him of that which was done.

17 And he answered and declared unto them the words of the council of Holofernes, and all the words that he had spoken in the midst of the princes of Assur, and whatsoever Holofernes had spoken proudly against the house of Israel.

18 Then the people fell down and worshipped God, and cried unto God. saying,

19 O Lord God of heaven, behold their pride, and pity the low estate of our nation, and look upon the face of those that are sanctified unto thee this day.

20 Then they comforted Achior, and praised him greatly.

21 And Ozias took him out of the assembly unto his house, and made a feast to the elders; and they called on the God of Israel all that night for help.

Judith 7

1 The next day Holofernes commanded all his army, and all his people which were come to take his part, that they should remove their camp against Bethulia, to take aforehand the ascents of the hill country, and to make war against the children of Israel.

2 Then their strong men removed their camps in that day, and the army of the men of war was an hundred and seventy thousand footmen, and twelve thousand horsemen, beside the baggage, and other men that were afoot among them, a very great multitude.

3 And they camped in the valley near unto Bethulia, by the fountain, and they spread themselves in breadth over Dothaim even to Belmaim, and in length from Bethulia unto Cynamon, which is over against Esdraelon.

4 Now the children of Israel, when they saw the multitude of them, were greatly troubled, and said every one to his neighbour, Now will these men lick up the face of the earth; for neither the high mountains, nor the valleys, nor the hills, are able to bear their weight.

5 Then every man took up his weapons of war, and when they had kindled fires upon their towers, they remained and watched all that night.

6 But in the second day Holofernes brought forth all his horsemen in the sight of the children of Israel which were in Bethulia,

7 And viewed the passages up to the city, and came to the fountains of their waters, and took them, and set garrisons of men of war over them, and he himself removed toward his people.

8 Then came unto him all the chief of the children of Esau, and all the governors of the people of Moab, and the captains of the sea coast, and said,

9 Let our lord now hear a word, that there be not an overthrow in thine army.

10 For this people of the children of Israel do not trust in their spears, but in the height of the mountains wherein they dwell, because it is not easy to come up to the tops of their mountains.

11 Now therefore, my lord, fight not against them in battle array, and there shall not so much as one man of thy people perish.

12 Remain in thy camp, and keep all the men of thine army, and let thy servants get into their hands the fountain of water, which issueth forth of the foot of the mountain:

13 For all the inhabitants of Bethulia have their water thence; so shall thirst kill them, and they shall give up their city, and we and our people shall go up to the tops of the mountains that are near, and will camp upon them, to watch that none go out of the city.

14 So they and their wives and their children shall be consumed with fire, and before the sword come against them, they shall be overthrown in the streets where they dwell.

15 Thus shalt thou render them an evil reward; because they rebelled, and met not thy person peaceably.

16 And these words pleased Holofernes and all his servants, and he appointed to do as they had spoken.

17 So the camp of the children of Ammon departed, and with them five thousand of the Assyrians, and they pitched in the valley, and took the waters, and the fountains of the waters of the children of Israel.

18 Then the children of Esau went up with the children of Ammon, and camped in the hill country over against Dothaim: and they sent some of them toward the south, and toward the east over against Ekrebel, which is near unto Chusi, that is upon the brook Mochmur; and the rest of the army of the Assyrians camped in the plain, and covered the face of the whole land; and their tents and carriages were pitched to a very great multitude.

19 Then the children of Israel cried unto the Lord their God, because

their heart failed, for all their enemies had compassed them round about, and there was no way to escape out from among them.

20 Thus all the company of Assur remained about them, both their footmen, chariots, and horsemen, four and thirty days, so that all their vessels of water failed all the inhibitants of Bethulia.

21 And the cisterns were emptied, and they had not water to drink their fill for one day; for they gave them drink by measure.

22 Therefore their young children were out of heart, and their women and young men fainted for thirst, and fell down in the streets of the city, and by the passages of the gates, and there was no longer any strength in them.

23 Then all the people assembled to Ozias, and to the chief of the city, both young men, and women, and children, and cried with a loud voice, and said before all the elders,

24 God be judge between us and you: for ye have done us great injury, in that ye have not required peace of the children of Assur.

25 For now we have no helper: but God hath sold us into their hands, that we should be thrown down before them with thirst and great destruction.

26 Now therefore call them unto you, and deliver the whole city for a spoil to the people of Holofernes, and to all his army.

27 For it is better for us to be made a spoil unto them, than to die for thirst: for we will be his servants, that our souls may live, and not see the death of our infants before our eyes, nor our wives nor our children to die.

28 We take to witness against you the heaven and the earth, and our God and Lord of our fathers, which punisheth us according to our sins and the sins of our fathers, that he do not according as we have said this day.

29 Then there was great weeping with one consent in the midst of the assembly; and they cried unto the Lord God with a loud voice.

30 Then said Ozias to them, Brethren, be of good courage, let us yet endure five days, in the which space the Lord our God may turn his mercy toward us; for he will not forsake us utterly.

31 And if these days pass, and there come no help unto us, I will do according to your word.

32 And he dispersed the people, every one to their own charge; and they went unto the walls and towers of their city, and sent the women and children into their houses: and they were very low brought in the city.

Judith 8

1 Now at that time Judith heard thereof, which was the daughter of Merari, the son of Ox, the son of Joseph, the son of Ozel, the son of Elcia, the son of Ananias, the son of Gedeon, the son of Raphaim, the son of Acitho, the son of Eliu, the son of Eliab, the son of Nathanael, the son of Samael, the son of Salasadal, the son of Israel.

2 And Manasses was her husband, of her tribe and kindred, who died in the barley harvest.

3 For as he stood overseeing them that bound sheaves in the field, the heat came upon his head, and he fell on his bed, and died in the city of Bethulia: and they buried him with his fathers in the field between Dothaim and Balamo.

4 So Judith was a widow in her house three years and four months.

5 And she made her a tent upon the top of her house, and put on sackcloth upon her loins and ware her widow's apparel.

6 And she fasted all the days of her widowhood, save the eves of the sabbaths, and the sabbaths, and the eves of the new moons, and the new moons and the feasts and solemn days of the house of Israel.

7 She was also of a goodly countenance, and very beautiful to behold: and her husband Manasses had left her gold, and silver, and menservants and maidservants, and cattle, and lands; and she remained upon them.

8 And there was none that gave her an ill word; as she feared God greatly.

9 Now when she heard the evil words of the people against the governor, that they fainted for lack of water; for Judith had heard all the words that Ozias had spoken unto them, and that he had sworn to deliver the city unto the Assyrians after five days;

10 Then she sent her waiting woman, that had the government of all things that she had, to call Ozias and Chabris and Charmis, the ancients of the city.

11 And they came unto her, and she said unto them, Hear me now, O ye governors of the inhabitants of Bethulia: for your words that ye have spoken before the people this day are not right, touching this oath which ye made and pronounced between God and you, and have promised to deliver the city to our enemies, unless within these days the Lord turn to help you.

12 And now who are ye that have tempted God this day, and stand instead of God among the children of men?

13 And now try the Lord Almighty, but ye shall never know any thing.

14 For ye cannot find the depth of the heart of man, neither can ye perceive the things that he thinketh: then how can ye search out God, that hath made all these things, and know his mind, or comprehend his purpose? Nay, my brethren, provoke not the Lord our God to anger.

15 For if he will not help us within these five days, he hath power to defend us when he will, even every day, or to destroy us before our enemies.

16 Do not bind the counsels of the Lord our God: for God is not as man, that he may be threatened; neither is he as the son of man, that he should be wavering.

17 Therefore let us wait for salvation of him, and call upon him to help us, and he will hear our voice, if it please him.

18 For there arose none in our age, neither is there any now in these days neither tribe, nor family, nor people, nor city among us, which worship gods made with hands, as hath been aforetime.

19 For the which cause our fathers were given to the sword, and for a spoil, and had a great fall before our enemies.

20 But we know none other god, therefore we trust that he will not despise us, nor any of our nation.

21 For if we be taken so, all Judea shall lie waste, and our sanctuary shall be spoiled; and he will require the profanation thereof at our mouth.

22 And the slaughter of our brethren, and the captivity of the country, and the desolation of our inheritance, will he turn upon our heads among the Gentiles, wheresoever we shall be in bondage; and we shall be an offence and a reproach to all them that possess us.

23 For our servitude shall not be directed to favour: but the Lord our God shall turn it to dishonour.

24 Now therefore, O brethren, let us shew an example to our brethren, because their hearts depend upon us, and the sanctuary, and the house, and the altar, rest upon us.

25 Moreover let us give thanks to the Lord our God, which trieth us, even as he did our fathers.

26 Remember what things he did to Abraham, and how he tried Isaac, and what happened to Jacob in Mesopotamia of Syria, when he kept the sheep of Laban his mother's brother.

27 For he hath not tried us in the fire, as he did them, for the examination of their hearts, neither hath he taken vengeance on us: but the Lord doth scourge them that come near unto him, to admonish them.

28 Then said Ozias to her, All that thou hast spoken hast thou spoken with a good heart, and there is none that may gainsay thy words.

29 For this is not the first day wherein thy wisdom is manifested; but from the beginning of thy days all the people have known thy understanding, because the disposition of thine heart is good.

30 But the people were very thirsty, and compelled us to do unto them as we have spoken, and to bring an oath upon ourselves, which we will not break.

31 Therefore now pray thou for us, because thou art a godly woman, and the Lord will send us rain to fill our cisterns, and we shall faint no more.

32 Then said Judith unto them, Hear me, and I will do a thing, which shall go throughout all generations to the children of our nation.

33 Ye shall stand this night in the gate, and I will go forth with my waitingwoman: and within the days that ye have promised to deliver the city to our enemies the Lord will visit Israel by mine hand.

34 But enquire not ye of mine act: for I will not declare it unto you, till the things be finished that I do.

35 Then said Ozias and the princes unto her, Go in peace, and the Lord God be before thee, to take vengeance on our enemies.

36 So they returned from the tent, and went to their wards.

Judith 9

1 Judith fell upon her face, and put ashes upon her head, and uncovered the sackcloth wherewith she was clothed; and about the time that the incense of that evening was offered in Jerusalem in the house of the Lord Judith cried with a loud voice, and said,

2 O Lord God of my father Simeon, to whom thou gavest a sword to take vengeance of the strangers, who loosened the girdle of a maid to defile her, and discovered the thigh to her shame, and polluted her virginity to her reproach; for thou saidst, It shall not be so; and yet they did so:

3 Wherefore thou gavest their rulers to be slain, so that they dyed their bed in blood, being deceived, and smotest the servants with their lords, and the lords upon their thrones;

4 And hast given their wives for a prey, and their daughters to be captives, and all their spoils to be divided among thy dear children; which were moved with thy zeal, and abhorred the pollution of their blood, and called upon thee for aid: O God, O my God, hear me also a widow.

5 For thou hast wrought not only those things, but also the things which fell out before, and which ensued after; thou hast thought upon the things which are now, and which are to come.

6 Yea, what things thou didst determine were ready at hand, and said, Lo, we are here: for all thy ways are prepared, and thy judgments are in thy foreknowledge.

7 For, behold, the Assyrians are multiplied in their power; they are exalted with horse and man; they glory in the strength of their footmen; they trust in shield, and spear, and bow, and sling; and know not that thou art the Lord that breakest the battles: the Lord is thy name.

8 Throw down their strength in thy power, and bring down their force in thy wrath: for they have purposed to defile thy sanctuary, and to pollute the tabernacle where thy glorious name resteth and to cast down with sword the horn of thy altar.

9 Behold their pride, and send thy wrath upon their heads: give into mine hand, which am a widow, the power that I have conceived.

10 Smite by the deceit of my lips the servant with the prince, and the prince with the servant: break down their stateliness by the hand of a woman.

11 For thy power standeth not in multitude nor thy might in strong men: for thou art a God of the afflicted, an helper of the oppressed, an upholder of the weak, a protector of the forlorn, a saviour of them that are without hope.

12 I pray thee, I pray thee, O God of my father, and God of the inheritance of Israel, Lord of the heavens and earth, Creator of the waters, king of every creature, hear thou my prayer:

13 And make my speech and deceit to be their wound and stripe, who have purposed cruel things against thy covenant, and thy hallowed house, and against the top of Sion, and against the house of the possession of thy children.

14 And make every nation and tribe to acknowledge that thou art the God of all power and might, and that there is none other that protecteth the people of Israel but thou.

Judith 10

1 Now after that she had ceased to cry unto the God of Israel, and had made an end of all these words.

2 She rose where she had fallen down, and called her maid, and went down into the house in the which she abode in the sabbath days, and in her feast days,

3 And pulled off the sackcloth which she had on, and put off the garments of her widowhood, and washed her body all over with water, and anointed herself with precious ointment, and braided the hair of her head, and put on a tire upon it, and put on her garments of gladness, wherewith she was clad during the life of Manasses her husband.

4 And she took sandals upon her feet, and put about her her bracelets, and her chains, and her rings, and her earrings, and all her ornaments, and decked herself bravely, to allure the eyes of all men that should see her.

5 Then she gave her maid a bottle of wine, and a cruse of oil, and filled a bag with parched corn, and lumps of figs, and with fine bread; so she folded all these things together, and laid them upon her.

6 Thus they went forth to the gate of the city of Bethulia, and found standing there Ozias and the ancients of the city, Chabris and Charmis.

7 And when they saw her, that her countenance was altered, and her apparel was changed, they wondered at her beauty very greatly, and said unto her.

8 The God, the God of our fathers give thee favour, and accomplish thine enterprizes to the glory of the children of Israel, and to the exaltation of Jerusalem. Then they worshipped God.

9 And she said unto them, Command the gates of the city to be opened unto me, that I may go forth to accomplish the things whereof ye have spoken with me. So they commanded the young men to open unto her, as she had spoken.

10 And when they had done so, Judith went out, she, and her maid with her; and the men of the city looked after her, until she was gone down the mountain, and till she had passed the valley, and could see her no more.

11 Thus they went straight forth in the valley: and the first watch of the Assyrians met her,

12 And took her, and asked her, Of what people art thou? and whence comest thou? and whither goest thou? And she said, I am a woman of the Hebrews, and am fled from them: for they shall be given you to be consumed:

13 And I am coming before Holofernes the chief captain of your army, to declare words of truth; and I will shew him a way, whereby he shall go, and win all the hill country, without losing the body or life of any one of his men.

14 Now when the men heard her words, and beheld her countenance, they wondered greatly at her beauty, and said unto her,

15 Thou hast saved thy life, in that thou hast hasted to come down to the presence of our lord: now therefore come to his tent, and some of us shall conduct thee, until they have delivered thee to his hands.

16 And when thou standest before him, be not afraid in thine heart, but

shew unto him according to thy word; and he will entreat thee well.

17 Then they chose out of them an hundred men to accompany her and her maid; and they brought her to the tent of Holofernes.

18 Then was there a concourse throughout all the camp: for her coming was noised among the tents, and they came about her, as she stood without the tent of Holofernes, till they told him of her.

19 And they wondered at her beauty, and admired the children of Israel because of her, and every one said to his neighbour, Who would despise this people, that have among them such women? surely it is not good that one man of them be left who being let go might deceive the whole earth.

20 And they that lay near Holofernes went out, and all his servants and they brought her into the tent.

21 Now Holofernes rested upon his bed under a canopy, which was woven with purple, and gold, and emeralds, and precious stones.

22 So they shewed him of her; and he came out before his tent with silver lamps going before him.

23 And when Judith was come before him and his servants they all marvelled at the beauty of her countenance; and she fell down upon her face, and did reverence unto him: and his servants took her up.

Judith 11

1 Then said Holofernes unto her, Woman, be of good comfort, fear not in thine heart: for I never hurt any that was willing to serve Nabuchodonosor, the king of all the earth.

2 Now therefore, if thy people that dwelleth in the mountains had not set light by me, I would not have lifted up my spear against them: but they have done these things to themselves.

3 But now tell me wherefore thou art fled from them, and art come unto us: for thou art come for safeguard; be of good comfort, thou shalt live this night, and hereafter:

4 For none shall hurt thee, but entreat thee well, as they do the servants of king Nabuchodonosor my lord.

5 Then Judith said unto him, Receive the words of thy servant, and suffer thine handmaid to speak in thy presence, and I will declare no lie to my lord this night.

6 And if thou wilt follow the words of thine handmaid, God will bring the thing perfectly to pass by thee; and my lord shall not fail of his purposes.

7 As Nabuchodonosor king of all the earth liveth, and as his power liveth, who hath sent thee for the upholding

of every living thing: for not only men shall serve him by thee, but also the beasts of the field, and the cattle, and the fowls of the air, shall live by thy power under Nabuchodonosor and all his house.

8 For we have heard of thy wisdom and thy policies, and it is reported in all the earth, that thou only art excellent in all the kingdom, and mighty in knowledge, and wonderful in feats of war.

9 Now as concerning the matter, which Achior did speak in thy council, we have heard his words; for the men of Bethulia saved him, and he declared unto them all that he had spoken unto thee.

10 Therefore, O lord and governor, respect not his word; but lay it up in thine heart, for it is true: for our nation shall not be punished, neither can sword prevail against them, except they sin against their God.

11 And now, that my lord be not defeated and frustrate of his purpose, even death is now fallen upon them, and their sin hath overtaken them, wherewith they will provoke their God to anger whensoever they shall do that which is not fit to be done:

12 For their victuals fail them, and all their water is scant, and they have determined to lay hands upon their cattle, and purposed to consume all those things, that God hath forbidden them to eat by his laws:

13 And are resolved to spend the firstfruits of the tenths of wine and oil, which they had sanctified, and reserved for the priests that serve in Jerusalem before the face of our God; the which things it is not lawful for any of the people so much as to touch with their hands.

14 For they have sent some to Jerusalem, because they also that dwell there have done the like, to bring them a licence from the senate.

15 Now when they shall bring them word, they will forthwith do it, and they shall be given to thee to be destroyed the same day.

16 Wherefore I thine handmaid, knowing all this, am fled from their presence; and God hath sent me to work things with thee, whereat all the earth shall be astonished, and whosoever shall hear it.

17 For thy servant is religious, and serveth the God of heaven day and night: now therefore, my lord, I will remain with thee, and thy servant will go out by night into the valley, and I will pray unto God, and he will tell me when they have committed their sins:

18 And I will come and shew it unto thee: then thou shalt go forth with all thine army, and there shall be none of them that shall resist thee.

19 And I will lead thee through the midst of Judea, until thou come before Jerusalem; and I will set thy

throne in the midst thereof; and thou shalt drive them as sheep that have no shepherd, and a dog shall not so much as open his mouth at thee: for these things were told me according to my foreknowledge, and they were declared unto me, and I am sent to tell thee.

20 Then her words pleased Holofernes and all his servants; and they marvelled at her wisdom, and said,

21 There is not such a woman from one end of the earth to the other, both for beauty of face, and wisdom of words.

22 Likewise Holofernes said unto her. God hath done well to send thee before the people, that strength might be in our hands and destruction upon them that lightly regard my lord.

23 And now thou art both beautiful in thy countenance, and witty in thy words: surely if thou do as thou hast spoken thy God shall be my God, and thou shalt dwell in the house of king Nabuchodonosor, and shalt be renowned through the whole earth.

Judith 12

1 Then he commanded to bring her in where his plate was set; and bade that they should prepare for her of his own meats, and that she should drink of his own wine.

2 And Judith said, I will not eat thereof, lest there be an offence: but provision shall be made for me of the things that I have brought.

3 Then Holofernes said unto her, If thy provision should fail, how should we give thee the like? for there be none with us of thy nation.

4 Then said Judith unto him As thy soul liveth, my lord, thine handmaid shall not spend those things that I have, before the Lord work by mine hand the things that he hath determined.

5 Then the servants of Holofernes brought her into the tent, and she slept till midnight, and she arose when it was toward the morning watch,

6 And sent to Holofernes, saving, Let my lord now command that thine handmaid may go forth unto prayer.

7 Then Holofernes commanded his guard that they should not stay her: thus she abode in the camp three days, and went out in the night into the valley of Bethulia, and washed herself in a fountain of water by the camp.

8 And when she came out, she besought the Lord God of Israel to direct her way to the raising up of the children of her people.

9 So she came in clean, and remained in the tent, until she did eat her meat at evening.

10 And in the fourth day Holofernes made a feast to his own servants

only, and called none of the officers to the banquet.

11 Then said he to Bagoas the eunuch, who had charge over all that he had, Go now, and persuade this Hebrew woman which is with thee, that she come unto us, and eat and drink with us.

12 For, lo, it will be a shame for our person, if we shall let such a woman go, not having had her company; for if we draw her not unto us, she will laugh us to scorn.

13 Then went Bagoas from the presence of Holofernes, and came to her, and he said, Let not this fair damsel fear to come to my lord, and to be honoured in his presence, and drink wine, and be merry with us and be made this day as one of the daughters of the Assyrians, which serve in the house of Nabuchodonosor.

14 Then said Judith unto him, Who am I now, that I should gainsay my lord? surely whatsoever pleaseth him I will do speedily, and it shall be my joy unto the day of my death.

15 So she arose, and decked herself with her apparel and all her woman's attire, and her maid went and laid soft skins on the ground for her over against Holofernes, which she had received of Bagoas for her daily use, that she might sit and eat upon them.

16 Now when Judith came in and sat down, Holofernes his heart was ravished with her, and his mind was moved, and he desired greatly her company; for he waited a time to deceive her, from the day that he had seen her.

17 Then said Holofernes unto her, Drink now, and be merry with us.

18 So Judith said, I will drink now, my lord, because my life is magnified in me this day more than all the days since I was born.

19 Then she took and ate and drank before him what her maid had prepared.

20 And Holofernes took great delight in her, and drank more wine than he had drunk at any time in one day since he was born.

Judith 13

1 Now when the evening was come, his servants made haste to depart, and Bagoas shut his tent without, and dismissed the waiters from the presence of his lord; and they went to their beds: for they were all weary, because the feast had been long.

2 And Judith was left alone in the tent, and Holofernes lying alone upon his bed: for he was filled with wine.

3 Now Judith had commanded her maid to stand without her bedchamber, and to wait for her. coming forth, as she did daily: for she said she would go forth to her

prayers, and she spake to Bagoas according to the same purpose.

4 So all went forth and none was left in the bedchamber, neither little nor great. Then Judith, standing by his bed, said in her heart, O Lord God of all power, look at this present upon the works of mine hands for the exaltation of Jerusalem.

5 For now is the time to help thine inheritance, and to execute thine enterprizes to the destruction of the enemies which are risen against us.

6 Then she came to the pillar of the bed, which was at Holofernes' head, and took down his fauchion from thence,

7 And approached to his bed, and took hold of the hair of his head, and said, Strengthen me, O Lord God of Israel, this day.

8 And she smote twice upon his neck with all her might, and she took away his head from him.

9 And tumbled his body down from the bed, and pulled down the canopy from the pillars; and anon after she went forth, and gave Holofernes his head to her maid;

10 And she put it in her bag of meat: so they twain went together according to their custom unto prayer: and when they passed the camp, they compassed the valley, and went up the mountain of Bethulia, and came to the gates thereof.

11 Then said Judith afar off, to the watchmen at the gate, Open, open now the gate: God, even our God, is with us, to shew his power yet in Jerusalem, and his forces against the enemy, as he hath even done this day.

12 Now when the men of her city heard her voice, they made haste to go down to the gate of their city, and they called the elders of the city.

13 And then they ran all together, both small and great, for it was strange unto them that she was come: so they opened the gate, and received them, and made a fire for a light, and stood round about them.

14 Then she said to them with a loud voice, Praise, praise God, praise God, I say, for he hath not taken away his mercy from the house of Israel, but hath destroyed our enemies by mine hands this night.

15 So she took the head out of the bag, and shewed it, and said unto them, behold the head of Holofernes, the chief captain of the army of Assur, and behold the canopy, wherein he did lie in his drunkenness; and the Lord hath smitten him by the hand of a woman.

16 As the Lord liveth, who hath kept me in my way that I went, my countenance hath deceived him to his destruction, and yet hath he not committed sin with me, to defile and shame me.

17 Then all the people were wonderfully astonished, and bowed themselves and worshipped God, and said with one accord, Blessed be thou, O our God, which hast this day brought to nought the enemies of thy people.

18 Then said Ozias unto her, O daughter, blessed art thou of the most high God above all the women upon the earth; and blessed be the Lord God, which hath created the heavens and the earth, which hath directed thee to the cutting off of the head of the chief of our enemies.

19 For this thy confidence shall not depart from the heart of men, which remember the power of God for ever.

20 And God turn these things to thee for a perpetual praise, to visit thee in good things because thou hast not spared thy life for the affliction of our nation, but hast revenged our ruin, walking a straight way before our God. And all the people said; So be it, so be it.

Judith 14

1 Then said Judith unto them, Hear me now, my brethren, and take this head, and hang it upon the highest place of your walls.

2 And so soon as the morning shall appear, and the sun shall come forth upon the earth, take ye every one his weapons, and go forth every valiant man out of the city, and set ye a captain over them, as though ye would go down into the field toward the watch of the Assyrians; but go not down.

3 Then they shall take their armour, and shall go into their camp, and raise up the captains of the army of Assur, and shall run to the tent of Holofernes, but shall not find him: then fear shall fall upon them, and they shall flee before your face.

4 So ye, and all that inhabit the coast of Israel, shall pursue them, and overthrow them as they go.

5 But before ye do these things, call me Achior the Ammonite, that he may see and know him that despised the house of Israel, and that sent him to us as it were to his death.

6 Then they called Achior out of the house of Ozias; and when he was come, and saw the head of Holofernes in a man's hand in the assembly of the people, he fell down on his face, and his spirit failed.

7 But when they had recovered him, he fell at Judith's feet, and reverenced her, and said, Blessed art thou in all the tabernacles of Juda, and in all nations, which hearing thy name shall be astonished.

8 Now therefore tell me all the things that thou hast done in these days. Then Judith declared unto him in the midst of the people all that she had done, from the day that she went

forth until that hour she spake unto them.

9 And when she had left off speaking, the people shouted with a loud voice, and made a joyful noise in their city.

10 And when Achior had seen all that the God of Israel had done, he believed in God greatly, and circumcised the flesh of his foreskin, and was joined unto the house of Israel unto this day.

11 And as soon as the morning arose, they hanged the head of Holofernes upon the wall, and every man took his weapons, and they went forth by bands unto the straits of the mountain.

12 But when the Assyrians saw them, they sent to their leaders, which came to their captains and tribunes, and to every one of their rulers.

13 So they came to Holofernes' tent, and said to him that had the charge of all his things, Waken now our lord: for the slaves have been bold to come down against us to battle, that they may be utterly destroyed.

14 Then went in Bagoas, and knocked at the door of the tent; for he thought that he had slept with Judith.

15 But because none answered, he opened it, and went into the bedchamber, and found him cast upon the floor dead, and his head was taken from him.

16 Therefore he cried with a loud voice, with weeping, and sighing, and a mighty cry, and rent his garments.

17 After he went into the tent where Judith lodged: and when he found her not, he leaped out to the people, and cried,

18 These slaves have dealt treacherously; one woman of the Hebrews hath brought shame upon the house of king Nabuchodonosor: for, behold, Holofernes lieth upon the ground without a head.

19 When the captains of the Assyrians' army heard these words, they rent their coats and their minds were wonderfully troubled, and there was a cry and a very great noise throughout the camp.

Judith 15

1 And when they that were in the tents heard, they were astonished at the thing that was done.

2 And fear and trembling fell upon them, so that there was no man that durst abide in the sight of his neighbour, but rushing out all together, they fled into every way of the plain, and of the hill country.

3 They also that had camped in the mountains round about Bethulia fled away. Then the children of Israel,

every one that was a warrior among them, rushed out upon them.

4 Then sent Ozias to Betomasthem, and to Bebai, and Chobai, and Cola and to all the coasts of Israel, such as should tell the things that were done, and that all should rush forth upon their enemies to destroy them.

5 Now when the children of Israel heard it, they all fell upon them with one consent, and slew them unto Chobai: likewise also they that came from Jerusalem, and from all the hill country, (for men had told them what things were done in the camp of their enemies) and they that were in Galaad, and in Galilee, chased them with a great slaughter, until they were past Damascus and the borders thereof.

6 And the residue that dwelt at Bethulia, fell upon the camp of Assur, and spoiled them, and were greatly enriched.

7 And the children of Israel that returned from the slaughter had that which remained; and the villages and the cities, that were in the mountains and in the plain, gat many spoils: for the multitude was very great.

8 Then Joacim the high priest, and the ancients of the children of Israel that dwelt in Jerusalem, came to behold the good things that God had shewed to Israel, and to see Judith, and to salute her.

9 And when they came unto her, they blessed her with one accord, and said unto her, Thou art the exaltation of Jerusalem, thou art the great glory of Israel, thou art the great rejoicing of our nation:

10 Thou hast done all these things by thine hand: thou hast done much good to Israel, and God is pleased therewith: blessed be thou of the Almighty Lord for evermore. And all the people said, So be it.

11 And the people spoiled the camp the space of thirty days: and they gave unto Judith Holofernes his tent, and all his plate, and beds, and vessels, and all his stuff: and she took it and laid it on her mule; and made ready her carts, and laid them thereon.

12 Then all the women of Israel ran together to see her, and blessed her, and made a dance among them for her: and she took branches in her hand, and gave also to the women that were with her.

13 And they put a garland of olive upon her and her maid that was with her, and she went before all the people in the dance, leading all the women: and all the men of Israel followed in their armour with garlands, and with songs in their mouths.

Judith 16

1 Then Judith began to sing this thanksgiving in all Israel, and all the

people sang after her this song of praise.

2 And Judith said, Begin unto my God with timbrels, sing unto my Lord with cymbals: tune unto him a new psalm: exalt him, and call upon his name.

3 For God breaketh the battles: for among the camps in the midst of the people he hath delivered me out of the hands of them that persecuted me.

4 Assur came out of the mountains from the north, he came with ten thousands of his army, the multitude whereof stopped the torrents, and their horsemen have covered the hills.

5 He bragged that he would burn up my borders, and kill my young men with the sword, and dash the sucking children against the ground, and make mine infants as a prey, and my virgins as a spoil.

6 But the Almighty Lord hath disappointed them by the hand of a woman.

7 For the mighty one did not fall by the young men, neither did the sons of the Titans smite him, nor high giants set upon him: but Judith the daughter of Merari weakened him with the beauty of her countenance.

8 For she put off the garment of her widowhood for the exaltation of those that were oppressed in Israel, and anointed her face with ointment,

and bound her hair in a tire, and took a linen garment to deceive him.

9 Her sandals ravished his eyes, her beauty took his mind prisoner, and the fauchion passed through his neck.

10 The Persians quaked at her boldness, and the Medes were daunted at her hardiness.

11 Then my afflicted shouted for joy, and my weak ones cried aloud; but they were astonished: these lifted up their voices, but they were overthrown.

12 The sons of the damsels have pierced them through, and wounded them as fugatives' children: they perished by the battle of the Lord.

13 I will sing unto the Lord a new song: O Lord, thou art great and glorious, wonderful in strength, and invincible.

14 Let all creatures serve thee: for thou spakest, and they were made, thou didst send forth thy spirit, and it created them, and there is none that can resist thy voice.

15 For the mountains shall be moved from their foundations with the waters, the rocks shall melt as wax at thy presence: yet thou art merciful to them that fear thee.

16 For all sacrifice is too little for a sweet savour unto thee, and all the fat is not sufficient for thy burnt

offering: but he that feareth the Lord is great at all times.

17 Woe to the nations that rise up against my kindred! the Lord Almighty will take vengeance of them in the day of judgment, in putting fire and worms in their flesh; and they shall feel them, and weep for ever.

18 Now as soon as they entered into Jerusalem, they worshipped the Lord; and as soon as the people were purified, they offered their burnt offerings, and their free offerings, and their gifts.

19 Judith also dedicated all the stuff of Holofernes, which the people had given her, and gave the canopy, which she had taken out of his bedchamber, for a gift unto the Lord.

20 So the people continued feasting in Jerusalem before the sanctuary for the space of three months and Judith remained with them.

21 After this time every one returned to his own inheritance, and Judith went to Bethulia, and remained in her own possession, and was in her time honourable in all the country.

22 And many desired her, but none knew her all the days of her life, after that Manasses her husband was dead, and was gathered to his people.

23 But she increased more and more in honour, and waxed old in her husband's house, being an hundred and five years old, and made her maid free; so she died in Bethulia: and they buried her in the cave of her husband Manasses.

24 And the house of Israel lamented her seven days: and before she died, she did distribute her goods to all them that were nearest of kindred to Manasses her husband, and to them that were the nearest of her kindred.

25 And there was none that made the children of Israel any more afraid in the days of Judith, nor a long time after her death.

ADDITIONS TO ESTHER

Esther 10

4 Then Mardocheus said, God hath done these things.

5 For I remember a dream which I saw concerning these matters, and nothing thereof hath failed.

6 A little fountain became a river, and there was light, and the sun, and much water: this river is Esther, whom the king married, and made queen:

7 And the two dragons are I and Aman.

8 And the nations were those that were assembled to destroy the name of the Jews:

9 And my nation is this Israel, which cried to God, and were saved: for the Lord hath saved his people, and the Lord hath delivered us from all those evils, and God hath wrought signs and great wonders, which have not been done among the Gentiles.

10 Therefore hath he made two lots, one for the people of God, and another for all the Gentiles.

11 And these two lots came at the hour, and time, and day of judgment, before God among all nations.

12 So God remembered his people, and justified his inheritance.

13 Therefore those days shall be unto them in the month Adar, the fourteenth and fifteenth day of the same month, with an assembly, and joy, and with gladness before God, according to the generations for ever among his people.

Esther 11

1 In the fourth year of the reign of Ptolemeus and Cleopatra, Dositheus, who said he was a priest and Levite, and Ptolemeus his son, brought this epistle of Phurim, which they said was the same, and that Lysimachus the son of Ptolemeus, that was in Jerusalem, had interpreted it.

2 In the second year of the reign of Artexerxes the great, in the first day of the month Nisan, Mardocheus the son of Jairus, the son of Semei, the son of Cisai, of the tribe of Benjamin, had a dream;

3 Who was a Jew, and dwelt in the city of Susa, a great man, being a servitor in the king's court.

4 He was also one of the captives, which Nabuchodonosor the king of Babylon carried from Jerusalem with Jechonias king of Judea; and this was his dream:

5 Behold a noise of a tumult, with thunder, and earthquakes, and uproar in the land:

6 And, behold, two great dragons came forth ready to fight, and their cry was great.

7 And at their cry all nations were prepared to battle, that they might fight against the righteous people.

8 And lo a day of darkness and obscurity, tribulation and anguish, affliction and great uproar, upon earth.

9 And the whole righteous nation was troubled, fearing their own evils, and were ready to perish.

10 Then they cried unto God, and upon their cry, as it were from a little fountain, was made a great flood, even much water.

11 The light and the sun rose up, and the lowly were exalted, and devoured the glorious.

12 Now when Mardocheus, who had seen this dream, and what God had determined to do, was awake, he bare this dream in mind, and until night by all means was desirous to know it.

Esther 12

1 And Mardocheus took his rest in the court with Gabatha and Tharra, the two eunuchs of the king, and keepers of the palace.

2 And he heard their devices, and searched out their purposes, and learned that they were about to lay hands upon Artexerxes the king; and so he certified the king of them.

3 Then the king examined the two eunuchs, and after that they had confessed it, they were strangled.

4 And the king made a record of these things, and Mardocheus also wrote thereof.

5 So the king commanded, Mardocheus to serve in the court, and for this he rewarded him.

6 Howbeit Aman the son of Amadathus the Agagite, who was in great honour with the king, sought to molest Mardocheus and his people because of the two eunuchs of the king.

Esther 13

1 The copy of the letters was this: The great king Artexerxes writeth these things to the princes and governours that are under him from India unto Ethiopia in an hundred and seven and twenty provinces.

2 After that I became lord over many nations and had dominion over the whole world, not lifted up with presumption of my authority, but carrying myself always with equity and mildness, I purposed to settle my subjects continually in a quiet life, and making my kingdom peaceable, and open for passage to the utmost coasts, to renew peace, which is desired of all men.

3 Now when I asked my counsellors how this might be brought to pass, Aman, that excelled in wisdom among us, and was approved for his constant good will and steadfast fidelity, and had the honour of the second place in the kingdom,

4 Declared unto us, that in all nations throughout the world there was scattered a certain malicious people, that had laws contrary to ail nations, and continually despised the commandments of kings, so as the uniting of our kingdoms, honourably intended by us cannot go forward. 5 Seeing then we understand that this people alone is continually in opposition unto all men, differing in the strange manner of their laws, and evil affected to our state, working all the mischief they can that our kingdom may not be firmly established:

6 Therefore have we commanded, that all they that are signified in writing unto you by Aman, who is ordained over the affairs, and is next unto us, shall all, with their wives and children, be utterly destroyed by the sword of their enemies, without all mercy and pity, the fourteenth day of the twelfth month Adar of this present year:

7 That they, who of old and now also are malicious, may in one day with violence go into the grave, and so ever hereafter cause our affairs to be well settled, and without trouble.

8 Then Mardocheus thought upon all the works of the Lord, and made his prayer unto him,

9 Saying, O Lord, Lord, the King Almighty: for the whole world is in thy power, and if thou hast appointed to save Israel, there is no man that can gainsay thee:

10 For thou hast made heaven and earth, and all the wondrous things under the heaven.

11 Thou art Lord of all things, and and there is no man that can resist thee, which art the Lord.

12 Thou knowest all things, and thou knowest, Lord, that it was neither in contempt nor pride, nor for any desire of glory, that I did not bow down to proud Aman.

13 For I could have been content with good will for the salvation of Israel to kiss the soles of his feet.

14 But I did this, that I might not prefer the glory of man above the glory of God: neither will I worship any but thee, O God, neither will I do it in pride.

15 And now, O Lord God and King, spare thy people: for their eyes are upon us to bring us to nought; yea, they desire to destroy the inheritance, that hath been thine from the beginning.

16 Despise not the portion, which thou hast delivered out of Egypt for thine own self.

17 Hear my prayer, and be merciful unto thine inheritance: turn our sorrow into joy, that we may live, O Lord, and praise thy name: and destroy not the mouths of them that praise thee, O Lord.

18 All Israel in like manner cried most earnestly unto the Lord,

because their death was before their eyes.

Esther 14

1 Queen Esther also, being in fear of death, resorted unto the Lord:

2 And laid away her glorious apparel, and put on the garments of anguish and mourning: and instead of precious ointments, she covered her head with ashes and dung, and she humbled her body greatly, and all the places of her joy she filled with her torn hair.

3 And she prayed unto the Lord God of Israel, saying, O my Lord, thou only art our King: help me, desolate woman, which have no helper but thee:

4 For my danger is in mine hand.

5 From my youth up I have heard in the tribe of my family that thou, O Lord, tookest Israel from among all people, and our fathers from all their predecessors, for a perpetual inheritance, and thou hast performed whatsoever thou didst promise them.

6 And now we have sinned before thee: therefore hast thou given us into the hands of our enemies,

7 Because we worshipped their gods: O Lord, thou art righteous.

8 Nevertheless it satisfieth them not, that we are in bitter captivity: but they have stricken hands with their idols,

9 That they will abolish the thing that thou with thy mouth hast ordained, and destroy thine inheritance, and stop the mouth of them that praise thee, and quench the glory of thy house, and of thine altar,

10 And open the mouths of the heathen to set forth the praises of the idols, and to magnify a fleshly king for ever. 11 O Lord, give not thy sceptre unto them that be nothing, and let them not laugh at our fall; but turn their device upon themselves, and make him an example, that hath begun this against us.

12 Remember, O Lord, make thyself known in time of our affliction, and give me boldness, O King of the nations, and Lord of all power.

13 Give me eloquent speech in my mouth before the lion: turn his heart to hate him that fighteth against us, that there may be an end of him, and of all that are likeminded to him:

14 But deliver us with thine hand, and help me that am desolate, and which have no other help but thee.

15 Thou knowest all things, O Lord; thou knowest that I hate the glory of the unrighteous, and abhor the bed of the uncircumcised, and of all the heathen.

16 Thou knowest my necessity: for I abhor the sign of my high estate, which is upon mine head in the days wherein I shew myself, and that I abhor it as a menstruous rag, and

that I wear it not when I am private by myself.

17 And that thine handmaid hath not eaten at Aman's table, and that I have not greatly esteemed the king's feast, nor drunk the wine of the drink offerings.

18 Neither had thine handmaid any joy since the day that I was brought hither to this present, but in thee, O Lord God of Abraham.

19 O thou mighty God above all, hear the voice of the forlorn and deliver us out of the hands of the mischievous, and deliver me out of my fear.

Esther 15

1 And upon the third day, when she had ended her prayers, she laid away her mourning garments, and put on her glorious apparel.

2 And being gloriously adorned, after she had called upon God, who is the beholder and saviour of all things, she took two maids with her:

3 And upon the one she leaned, as carrying herself daintily;

4 And the other followed, bearing up her train.

5 And she was ruddy through the perfection of her beauty, and her countenance was cheerful and very amiable: but her heart was in anguish for fear.

6 Then having passed through all the doors, she stood before the king, who sat upon his royal throne, and was clothed with all his robes of majesty, all glittering with gold and precious stones; and he was very dreadful.

7 Then lifting up his countenance that shone with majesty, he looked very fiercely upon her: and the queen fell down, and was pale, and fainted, and bowed herself upon the head of the maid that went before her.

8 Then God changed the spirit of the king into mildness, who in a fear leaped from his throne, and took her in his arms, till she came to herself again, and comforted her with loving words and said unto her,

9 Esther, what is the matter? I am thy brother, be of good cheer:

10 Thou shalt not die, though our commandment be general: come near.

11 And so be held up his golden sceptre, and laid it upon her neck,

12 And embraced her, and said, Speak unto me.

13 Then said she unto him, I saw thee, my lord, as an angel of God, and my heart was troubled for fear of thy majesty. 14 For wonderful art thou, lord, and thy countenance is full of grace.

15 And as she was speaking, she fell down for faintness. 16 Then the king was troubled, and ail his servants comforted her.

Esther 16

1 The great king Artexerxes unto the princes and governors of an hundred and seven and twenty provinces from India unto Ethiopia, and unto all our faithful subjects, greeting.

2 Many, the more often they are honoured with the great bounty of their gracious princes, the more proud they are waxen,

3 And endeavour to hurt not our subjects only, but not being able to bear abundance, do take in hand to practise also against those that do them good:

4 And take not only thankfulness away from among men, but also lifted up with the glorious words of lewd persons, that were never good, they think to escape the justice of God, that seeth all things and hateth evil.

5 Oftentimes also fair speech of those, that are put in trust to manage their friends' affairs, hath caused many that are in authority to be partakers of innocent blood, and hath enwrapped them in remediless calamities:

6 Beguiling with the falsehood and deceit of their lewd disposition the innocency and goodness of princes.

7 Now ye may see this, as we have declared, not so much by ancient histories, as ye may, if ye search what hath been wickedly done of late through the pestilent behaviour of them that are unworthily placed in authority. 8 And we must take care for the time to come, that our kingdom may be quiet and peaceable for all men,

9 Both by changing our purposes, and always judging things that are evident with more equal proceeding.

10 For Aman, a Macedonian, the son of Amadatha, being indeed a stranger from the Persian blood, and far distant from our goodness, and as a stranger received of us,

11 Had so far forth obtained the favour that we shew toward every nation, as that he was called our father, and was continually honoured of all the next person unto the king.

12 But he, not bearing his great dignity, went about to deprive us of our kingdom and life:

13 Having by manifold and cunning deceits sought of us the destruction, as well of Mardocheus, who saved our life, and continually procured our good, as also of blameless Esther, partaker of our kingdom, with their whole nation.

14 For by these means he thought, finding us destitute of friends to have translated the kingdom of the Persians to the Macedonians.

15 But we find that the Jews, whom this wicked wretch hath delivered to utter destruction, are no evildoers, but live by most just laws:

16 And that they be children of the most high and most mighty, living God, who hath ordered the kingdom both unto us and to our progenitors in the most excellent manner.

17 Wherefore ye shall do well not to put in execution the letters sent unto you by Aman the son of Amadatha.

18 For he that was the worker of these things, is hanged at the gates of Susa with all his family: God, who ruleth all things, speedily rendering vengeance to him according to his deserts.

19 Therefore ye shall publish the copy of this letter in all places, that the Jews may freely live after their own laws. 20 And ye shall aid them, that even the same day, being the thirteenth day of the twelfth month Adar, they may be avenged on them, who in the time of their affliction shall set upon them.

21 For Almighty God hath turned to joy unto them the day, wherein the chosen people should have perished.

22 Ye shall therefore among your solemn feasts keep it an high day with all feasting:

23 That both now and hereafter there may be safety to us and the well affected Persians; but to those which do conspire against us a memorial of destruction.

24 Therefore every city and country whatsoever, which shall not do according to these things, shall be destroyed without mercy with fire and sword, and shall be made not only unpassable for men, but also most hateful to wild beasts and fowls for ever.

WISDOM OF SOLOMON

Solomon 1

1 Love righteousness, ye that be judges of the earth: think of the Lord with a good (heart,) and in simplicity of heart seek him.

2 For he will be found of them that tempt him not; and sheweth himself unto such as do not distrust him.

3 For froward thoughts separate from God: and his power, when it is tried, reproveth the unwise.

4 For into a malicious soul wisdom shall not enter; nor dwell in the body that is subject unto sin.

5 For the holy spirit of discipline will flee deceit, and remove from thoughts that are without understanding, and will not abide when unrighteousness cometh in.

6 For wisdom is a loving spirit; and will not acquit a blasphemer of his words: for God is witness of his reins, and a true beholder of his heart, and a hearer of his tongue.

7 For the Spirit of the Lord filleth the world: and that which containeth all things hath knowledge of the voice.

8 Therefore he that speaketh unrighteous things cannot be hid: neither shall vengeance, when it punisheth, pass by him.

9 For inquisition shall be made into the counsels of the ungodly: and the sound of his words shall come unto the Lord for the manifestation of his wicked deeds.

10 For the ear of jealousy heareth all things: and the noise of murmurings is not hid.

11 Therefore beware of murmuring, which is unprofitable; and refrain your tongue from backbiting: for there is no word so secret, that shall go for nought: and the mouth that belieth slayeth the soul.

12 Seek not death in the error of your life: and pull not upon yourselves destruction with the works of your hands.

13 For God made not death: neither hath he pleasure in the destruction of the living.

14 For he created all things, that they might have their being: and the generations of the world were healthful; and there is no poison of destruction in them, nor the kingdom of death upon the earth:

15 (For righteousness is immortal:)

16 But ungodly men with their works and words called it to them: for when they thought to have it their friend, they consumed to nought, and made a covenant with it, because they are worthy to take part with it.

Solomon 2

1 For the ungodly said, reasoning with themselves, but not aright, Our life is short and tedious, and in the death of a man there is no remedy: neither was there any man known to have returned from the grave.

2 For we are born at all adventure: and we shall be hereafter as though we had never been: for the breath in our nostrils is as smoke, and a little spark in the moving of our heart:

3 Which being extinguished, our body shall be turned into ashes, and our spirit shall vanish as the soft air,

4 And our name shall be forgotten in time, and no man shall have our works in remembrance, and our life shall pass away as the trace of a cloud, and shall be dispersed as a mist, that is driven away with the beams of the sun, and overcome with the heat thereof.

5 For our time is a very shadow that passeth away; and after our end there is no returning: for it is fast sealed, so that no man cometh again.

6 Come on therefore, let us enjoy the good things that are present: and let us speedily use the creatures like as in youth.

7 Let us fill ourselves with costly wine and ointments: and let no flower of the spring pass by us:

8 Let us crown ourselves with rosebuds, before they be withered:

9 Let none of us go without his part of our voluptuousness: let us leave tokens of our joyfulness in every place: for this is our portion, and our lot is this.

10 Let us oppress the poor righteous man, let us not spare the widow, nor reverence the ancient gray hairs of the aged.

11 Let our strength be the law of justice: for that which is feeble is found to be nothing worth.

12 Therefore let us lie in wait for the righteous; because he is not for our turn, and he is clean contrary to our doings: he upbraideth us with our offending the law, and objecteth to our infamy the transgressings of our education.

13 He professeth to have the knowledge of God: and he calleth himself the child of the Lord.

14 He was made to reprove our thoughts.

15 He is grievous unto us even to behold: for his life is not like other men's, his ways are of another fashion.

16 We are esteemed of him as counterfeits: he abstaineth from our ways as from filthiness: he pronounceth the end of the just to be blessed, and maketh his boast that God is his father.

17 Let us see if his words be true: and let us prove what shall happen in the end of him.

18 For if the just man be the son of God, he will help him, and deliver him from the hand of his enemies.

19 Let us examine him with despitefulness and torture, that we may know his meekness, and prove his patience.

20 Let us condemn him with a shameful death: for by his own saying he shall be respected.

21 Such things they did imagine, and were deceived: for their own wickedness hath blinded them.

22 As for the mysteries of God, they knew them not: neither hoped they for the wages of righteousness, nor discerned a reward for blameless souls.

23 For God created man to be immortal, and made him to be an image of his own eternity.

24 Nevertheless through envy of the devil came death into the world: and they that do hold of his side do find it.

Solomon 3

1 But the souls of the righteous are in the hand of God, and there shall no torment touch them.

2 In the sight of the unwise they seemed to die: and their departure is taken for misery,

3 And their going from us to be utter destruction: but they are in peace.

4 For though they be punished in the sight of men, yet is their hope full of immortality.

5 And having been a little chastised, they shall be greatly rewarded: for God proved them, and found them worthy for himself.

6 As gold in the furnace hath he tried them, and received them as a burnt offering.

7 And in the time of their visitation they shall shine, and run to and fro like sparks among the stubble.

8 They shall judge the nations, and have dominion over the people, and their Lord shall reign for ever.

9 They that put their trust in him shall understand the truth: and such as be faithful in love shall abide with him: for grace and mercy is to his saints, and he hath care for his elect.

10 But the ungodly shall be punished according to their own imaginations, which have neglected the righteous, and forsaken the Lord.

11 For whoso despiseth wisdom and nurture, he is miserable, and their hope is vain, their labours unfruitful, and their works unprofitable:

12 Their wives are foolish, and their children wicked:

13 Their offspring is cursed. Wherefore blessed is the barren that

is undefiled, which hath not known the sinful bed: she shall have fruit in the visitation of souls.

14 And blessed is the eunuch, which with his hands hath wrought no iniquity, nor imagined wicked things against God: for unto him shall be given the special gift of faith, and an inheritance in the temple of the Lord more acceptable to his mind.

15 For glorious is the fruit of good labours: and the root of wisdom shall never fall away.

16 As for the children of adulterers, they shall not come to their perfection, and the seed of an unrighteous bed shall be rooted out.

17 For though they live long, yet shall they be nothing regarded: and their last age shall be without honour.

18 Or, if they die quickly, they have no hope, neither comfort in the day of trial.

19 For horrible is the end of the unrighteous generation.

Solomon 4

1 Better it is to have no children, and to have virtue: for the memorial thereof is immortal: because it is known with God, and with men.

2 When it is present, men take example at it; and when it is gone, they desire it: it weareth a crown, and triumpheth for ever, having

gotten the victory, striving for undefiled rewards.

3 But the multiplying brood of the ungodly shall not thrive, nor take deep rooting from bastard slips, nor lay any fast foundation.

4 For though they flourish in branches for a time; yet standing not last, they shall be shaken with the wind, and through the force of winds they shall be rooted out.

5 The imperfect branches shall be broken off, their fruit unprofitable, not ripe to eat, yea, meet for nothing.

6 For children begotten of unlawful beds are witnesses of wickedness against their parents in their trial.

7 But though the righteous be prevented with death, yet shall he be in rest.

8 For honourable age is not that which standeth in length of time, nor that is measured by number of years.

9 But wisdom is the gray hair unto men, and an unspotted life is old age.

10 He pleased God, and was beloved of him: so that living among sinners he was translated.

11 Yea speedily was he taken away, lest that wickedness should alter his understanding, or deceit beguile his soul.

12 For the bewitching of naughtiness doth obscure things that are honest; and the wandering of concupiscence doth undermine the simple mind.

13 He, being made perfect in a short time, fulfilled a long time:

14 For his soul pleased the Lord: therefore hasted he to take him away from among the wicked.

15 This the people saw, and understood it not, neither laid they up this in their minds, That his grace and mercy is with his saints, and that he hath respect unto his chosen.

16 Thus the righteous that is dead shall condemn the ungodly which are living; and youth that is soon perfected the many years and old age of the unrighteous.

17 For they shall see the end of the wise, and shall not understand what God in his counsel hath decreed of him, and to what end the Lord hath set him in safety.

18 They shall see him, and despise him; but God shall laugh them to scorn: and they shall hereafter be a vile carcase, and a reproach among the dead for evermore.

19 For he shall rend them, and cast them down headlong, that they shall be speechless; and he shall shake them from the foundation; and they shall be utterly laid waste, and be in sorrow; and their memorial shall perish.

20 And when they cast up the accounts of their sins, they shall come with fear: and their own iniquities shall convince them to their face.

Solomon 5

1 Then shall the righteous man stand in great boldness before the face of such as have afflicted him, and made no account of his labours.

2 When they see it, they shall be troubled with terrible fear, and shall be amazed at the strangeness of his salvation, so far beyond all that they looked for.

3 And they repenting and groaning for anguish of spirit shall say within themselves, This was he, whom we had sometimes in derision, and a proverb of reproach:

4 We fools accounted his life madness, and his end to be without honour:

5 How is he numbered among the children of God, and his lot is among the saints!

6 Therefore have we erred from the way of truth, and the light of righteousness hath not shined unto us, and the sun of righteousness rose not upon us.

7 We wearied ourselves in the way of wickedness and destruction: yea, we have gone through deserts, where there lay no way: but as for

the way of the Lord, we have not known it.

8 What hath pride profited us? or what good hath riches with our vaunting brought us?

9 All those things are passed away like a shadow, and as a post that hasted by;

10 And as a ship that passeth over the waves of the water, which when it is gone by, the trace thereof cannot be found, neither the pathway of the keel in the waves;

11 Or as when a bird hath flown through the air, there is no token of her way to be found, but the light air being beaten with the stroke of her wings and parted with the violent noise and motion of them, is passed through, and therein afterwards no sign where she went is to be found;

12 Or like as when an arrow is shot at a mark, it parteth the air, which immediately cometh together again, so that a man cannot know where it went through:

13 Even so we in like manner, as soon as we were born, began to draw to our end, and had no sign of virtue to shew; but were consumed in our own wickedness.

14 For the hope of the ungodly is like dust that is blown away with the wind; like a thin froth that is driven away with the storm; like as the smoke which is dispersed here and there with a tempest, and passeth

away as the remembrance of a guest that tarrieth but a day.

15 But the righteous live for evermore; their reward also is with the Lord, and the care of them is with the most High.

16 Therefore shall they receive a glorious kingdom, and a beautiful crown from the Lord's hand: for with his right hand shall he cover them, and with his arm shall he protect them.

17 He shall take to him his jealousy for complete armour, and make the creature his weapon for the revenge of his enemies.

18 He shall put on righteousness as a breastplate, and true judgment instead of an helmet.

19 He shall take holiness for an invincible shield.

20 His severe wrath shall he sharpen for a sword, and the world shall fight with him against the unwise.

21 Then shall the right aiming thunderbolts go abroad; and from the clouds, as from a well drawn bow, shall they fly to the mark.

22 And hailstones full of wrath shall be cast as out of a stone bow, and the water of the sea shall rage against them, and the floods shall cruelly drown them.

23 Yea, a mighty wind shall stand up against them, and like a storm shall blow them away: thus iniquity shall

lay waste the whole earth, and ill dealing shall overthrow the thrones of the mighty.

Solomon 6

1 Hear therefore, O ye kings, and understand; learn, ye that be judges of the ends of the earth.

2 Give ear, ye that rule the people, and glory in the multitude of nations.

3 For power is given you of the Lord, and sovereignty from the Highest, who shall try your works, and search out your counsels.

4 Because, being ministers of his kingdom, ye have not judged aright, nor kept the law, nor walked after the counsel of God;

5 Horribly and speedily shall he come upon you: for a sharp judgment shall be to them that be in high places.

6 For mercy will soon pardon the meanest: but mighty men shall be mightily tormented.

7 For he which is Lord over all shall fear no man's person, neither shall he stand in awe of any man's greatness: for he hath made the small and great, and careth for all alike.

8 But a sore trial shall come upon the mighty.

9 Unto you therefore, O kings, do I speak, that ye may learn wisdom, and not fall away.

10 For they that keep holiness holily shall be judged holy: and they that have learned such things shall find what to answer.

11 Wherefore set your affection upon my words; desire them, and ye shall be instructed.

12 Wisdom is glorious, and never fadeth away: yea, she is easily seen of them that love her, and found of such as seek her.

13 She preventeth them that desire her, in making herself first known unto them.

14 Whoso seeketh her early shall have no great travail: for he shall find her sitting at his doors.

15 To think therefore upon her is perfection of wisdom: and whoso watcheth for her shall quickly be without care.

16 For she goeth about seeking such as are worthy of her, sheweth herself favourably unto them in the ways, and meeteth them in every thought.

17 For the very true beginning of her is the desire of discipline; and the care of discipline is love;

18 And love is the keeping of her laws; and the giving heed unto her laws is the assurance of incorruption;

19 And incorruption maketh us near unto God:

20 Therefore the desire of wisdom bringeth to a kingdom.

21 If your delight be then in thrones and sceptres, O ye kings of the people, honour wisdom, that ye may reign for evermore.

22 As for wisdom, what she is, and how she came up, I will tell you, and will not hide mysteries from you: but will seek her out from the beginning of her nativity, and bring the knowledge of her into light, and will not pass over the truth.

23 Neither will I go with consuming envy; for such a man shall have no fellowship with wisdom.

24 But the multitude of the wise is the welfare of the world: and a wise king is the upholding of the people.

25 Receive therefore instruction through my words, and it shall do you good.

Solomon 7

1 I myself also am a mortal man, like to all, and the offspring of him that was first made of the earth,

2 And in my mother's womb was fashioned to be flesh in the time of ten months, being compacted in blood, of the seed of man, and the pleasure that came with sleep.

3 And when I was born, I drew in the common air, and fell upon the earth, which is of like nature, and the first voice which I uttered was crying, as all others do.

4 I was nursed in swaddling clothes, and that with cares.

5 For there is no king that had any other beginning of birth.

6 For all men have one entrance into life, and the like going out.

7 Wherefore I prayed, and understanding was given me: I called upon God, and the spirit of wisdom came to me.

8 I preferred her before sceptres and thrones, and esteemed riches nothing in comparison of her.

9 Neither compared I unto her any precious stone, because all gold in respect of her is as a little sand, and silver shall be counted as clay before her.

10 I loved her above health and beauty, and chose to have her instead of light: for the light that cometh from her never goeth out.

11 All good things together came to me with her, and innumerable riches in her hands.

12 And I rejoiced in them all, because wisdom goeth before them: and I knew not that she was the mother of them.

13 I learned diligently, and do communicate her liberally: I do not hide her riches.

14 For she is a treasure unto men that never faileth: which they that use become the friends of God, being commended for the gifts that come from learning.

15 God hath granted me to speak as I would, and to conceive as is meet for the things that are given me: because it is he that leadeth unto wisdom, and directeth the wise.

16 For in his hand are both we and our words; all wisdom also, and knowledge of workmanship.

17 For he hath given me certain knowledge of the things that are, namely, to know how the world was made, and the operation of the elements:

18 The beginning, ending, and midst of the times: the alterations of the turning of the sun, and the change of seasons:

19 The circuits of years, and the positions of stars:

20 The natures of living creatures, and the furies of wild beasts: the violence of winds, and the reasonings of men: the diversities of plants and the virtues of roots:

21 And all such things as are either secret or manifest, them I know.

22 For wisdom, which is the worker of all things, taught me: for in her is an understanding spirit holy, one only, manifold, subtil, lively, clear, undefiled, plain, not subject to hurt, loving the thing that is good quick, which cannot be letted, ready to do good,

23 Kind to man, steadfast, sure, free from care, having all power, overseeing all things, and going through all understanding, pure, and most subtil, spirits.

24 For wisdom is more moving than any motion: she passeth and goeth through all things by reason of her pureness.

25 For she is the breath of the power of God, and a pure influence flowing from the glory of the Almighty: therefore can no defiled thing fall into her.

26 For she is the brightness of the everlasting light, the unspotted mirror of the power of God, and the image of his goodness.

27 And being but one, she can do all things: and remaining in herself, she maketh all things new: and in all ages entering into holy souls, she maketh them friends of God, and prophets.

28 For God loveth none but him that dwelleth with wisdom.

29 For she is more beautiful than the sun, and above all the order of stars: being compared with the light, she is found before it.

30 For after this cometh night: but vice shall not prevail against wisdom.

Solomon 8

1 Wisdom reacheth from one end to another mightily: and sweetly doth she order all things.

2 I loved her, and sought her out from my youth, I desired to make her my spouse, and I was a lover of her beauty.

3 In that she is conversant with God, she magnifieth her nobility: yea, the Lord of all things himself loved her.

4 For she is privy to the mysteries of the knowledge of God, and a lover of his works.

5 If riches be a possession to be desired in this life; what is richer than wisdom, that worketh all things?

6 And if prudence work; who of all that are is a more cunning workman than she?

7 And if a man love righteousness her labours are virtues: for she teacheth temperance and prudence, justice and fortitude: which are such things, as men can have nothing more profitable in their life.

8 If a man desire much experience, she knoweth things of old, and conjectureth aright what is to come: she knoweth the subtilties of speeches, and can expound dark sentences: she foreseeth signs and wonders, and the events of seasons and times.

9 Therefore I purposed to take her to me to live with me, knowing that she would be a counsellor of good things, and a comfort in cares and grief.

10 For her sake I shall have estimation among the multitude, and honour with the elders, though I be young.

11 I shall be found of a quick conceit in judgment, and shall be admired in the sight of great men.

12 When I hold my tongue, they shall bide my leisure, and when I speak, they shall give good ear unto me: if I talk much, they shall lay their hands upon their mouth.

13 Moreover by the means of her I shall obtain immortality, and leave behind me an everlasting memorial to them that come after me.

14 I shall set the people in order, and the nations shall be subject unto me.

15 Horrible tyrants shall be afraid, when they do but hear of me; I shall be found good among the multitude, and valiant in war.

16 After I am come into mine house, I will repose myself with her: for her conversation hath no bitterness; and to live with her hath no sorrow, but mirth and joy.

17 Now when I considered these things in myself, and pondered them in my heart, how that to be allied unto wisdom is immortality;

18 And great pleasure it is to have her friendship; and in the works of her hands are infinite riches; and in the exercise of conference with her, prudence; and in talking with her, a

good report; I went about seeking how to take her to me.

19 For I was a witty child, and had a good spirit.

20 Yea rather, being good, I came into a body undefiled.

21 Nevertheless, when I perceived that I could not otherwise obtain her, except God gave her me; and that was a point of wisdom also to know whose gift she was; I prayed unto the Lord, and besought him, and with my whole heart I said,

Solomon 9

1 O God of my fathers, and Lord of mercy, who hast made all things with thy word,

2 And ordained man through thy wisdom, that he should have dominion over the creatures which thou hast made,

3 And order the world according to equity and righteousness, and execute judgment with an upright heart:

4 Give me wisdom, that sitteth by thy throne; and reject me not from among thy children:

5 For I thy servant and son of thine handmaid am a feeble person, and of a short time, and too young for the understanding of judgment and laws.

6 For though a man be never so perfect among the children of men,

yet if thy wisdom be not with him, he shall be nothing regarded.

7 Thou hast chosen me to be a king of thy people, and a judge of thy sons and daughters:

8 Thou hast commanded me to build a temple upon thy holy mount, and an altar in the city wherein thou dwellest, a resemblance of the holy tabernacle, which thou hast prepared from the beginning.

9 And wisdom was with thee: which knoweth thy works, and was present when thou madest the world, and knew what was acceptable in thy sight, and right in thy commandments.

10 O send her out of thy holy heavens, and from the throne of thy glory, that being present she may labour with me, that I may know what is pleasing unto thee.

11 For she knoweth and understandeth all things, and she shall lead me soberly in my doings, and preserve me in her power.

12 So shall my works be acceptable, and then shall I judge thy people righteously, and be worthy to sit in my father's seat.

13 For what man is he that can know the counsel of God? or who can think what the will of the Lord is?

14 For the thoughts of mortal men are miserable, and our devices are but uncertain.

15 For the corruptible body presseth down the soul, and the earthy tabernacle weigheth down the mind that museth upon many things.

16 And hardly do we guess aright at things that are upon earth, and with labour do we find the things that are before us: but the things that are in heaven who hath searched out?

17 And thy counsel who hath known, except thou give wisdom, and send thy Holy Spirit from above?

18 For so the ways of them which lived on the earth were reformed, and men were taught the things that are pleasing unto thee, and were saved through wisdom.

Solomon 10

1 She preserved the first formed father of the world, that was created alone, and brought him out of his fall,

2 And gave him power to rule all things.

3 But when the unrighteous went away from her in his anger, he perished also in the fury wherewith he murdered his brother.

4 For whose cause the earth being drowned with the flood, wisdom again preserved it, and directed the course of the righteous in a piece of wood of small value.

5 Moreover, the nations in their wicked conspiracy being confounded, she found out the righteous, and preserved him blameless unto God, and kept him strong against his tender compassion toward his son.

6 When the ungodly perished, she delivered the righteous man, who fled from the fire which fell down upon the five cities.

7 Of whose wickedness even to this day the waste land that smoketh is a testimony, and plants bearing fruit that never come to ripeness: and a standing pillar of salt is a monument of an unbelieving soul.

8 For regarding not wisdom, they gat not only this hurt, that they knew not the things which were good; but also left behind them to the world a memorial of their foolishness: so that in the things wherein they offended they could not so much as be hid.

9 But wisdom delivered from pain those that attended upon her.

10 When the righteous fled from his brother's wrath she guided him in right paths, shewed him the kingdom of God, and gave him knowledge of holy things, made him rich in his travels, and multiplied the fruit of his labours.

11 In the covetousness of such as oppressed him she stood by him, and made him rich.

12 She defended him from his enemies, and kept him safe from those that lay in wait, and in a sore conflict she gave him the victory; that

he might know that goodness is stronger than all.

13 When the righteous was sold, she forsook him not, but delivered him from sin: she went down with him into the pit,

14 And left him not in bonds, till she brought him the sceptre of the kingdom, and power against those that oppressed him: as for them that had accused him, she shewed them to be liars, and gave him perpetual glory.

15 She delivered the righteous people and blameless seed from the nation that oppressed them.

16 She entered into the soul of the servant of the Lord, and withstood dreadful kings in wonders and signs;

17 Rendered to the righteous a reward of their labours, guided them in a marvellous way, and was unto them for a cover by day, and a light of stars in the night season;

18 Brought them through the Red sea, and led them through much water:

19 But she drowned their enemies, and cast them up out of the bottom of the deep.

20 Therefore the righteous spoiled the ungodly, and praised thy holy name, O Lord, and magnified with one accord thine hand, that fought for them.

21 For wisdom opened the mouth of the dumb, and made the tongues of them that cannot speak eloquent.

Solomon 11

1 She prospered their works in the hand of the holy prophet.

2 They went through the wilderness that was not inhabited, and pitched tents in places where there lay no way.

3 They stood against their enemies, and were avenged of their adversaries.

4 When they were thirsty, they called upon thee, and water was given them out of the flinty rock, and their thirst was quenched out of the hard stone.

5 For by what things their enemies were punished, by the same they in their need were benefited.

6 For instead of a perpetual running river troubled with foul blood,

7 For a manifest reproof of that commandment, whereby the infants were slain, thou gavest unto them abundance of water by a means which they hoped not for:

8 Declaring by that thirst then how thou hadst punished their adversaries.

9 For when they were tried albeit but in mercy chastised, they knew how the ungodly were judged in wrath

and tormented, thirsting in another manner than the just.

10 For these thou didst admonish and try, as a father: but the other, as a severe king, thou didst condemn and punish.

11 Whether they were absent or present, they were vexed alike.

12 For a double grief came upon them, and a groaning for the remembrance of things past.

13 For when they heard by their own punishments the other to be benefited, they had some feeling of the Lord.

14 For whom they respected with scorn, when he was long before thrown out at the casting forth of the infants, him in the end, when they saw what came to pass, they admired.

15 But for the foolish devices of their wickedness, wherewith being deceived they worshipped serpents void of reason, and vile beasts, thou didst send a multitude of unreasonable beasts upon them for vengeance;

16 That they might know, that wherewithal a man sinneth, by the same also shall he be punished.

17 For thy Almighty hand, that made the world of matter without form, wanted not means to send among them a multitude of bears or fierce lions,

18 Or unknown wild beasts, full of rage, newly created, breathing out either a fiery vapour, or filthy scents of scattered smoke, or shooting horrible sparkles out of their eyes:

19 Whereof not only the harm might dispatch them at once, but also the terrible sight utterly destroy them.

20 Yea, and without these might they have fallen down with one blast, being persecuted of vengeance, and scattered abroad through the breath of thy power: but thou hast ordered all things in measure and number and weight.

21 For thou canst shew thy great strength at all times when thou wilt; and who may withstand the power of thine arm?

22 For the whole world before thee is as a little grain of the balance, yea, as a drop of the morning dew that falleth down upon the earth.

23 But thou hast mercy upon all; for thou canst do all things, and winkest at the sins of men, because they should amend.

24 For thou lovest all the things that are, and abhorrest nothing which thou hast made: for never wouldest thou have made any thing, if thou hadst hated it.

25 And how could any thing have endured, if it had not been thy will? or been preserved, if not called by thee?

26 But thou sparest all: for they are thine, O Lord, thou lover of souls.

Solomon 12

1 For thine incorruptible Spirit is in all things.

2 Therefore chastenest thou them by little and little that offend, and warnest them by putting them in remembrance wherein they have offended, that leaving their wickedness they may believe on thee, O Lord.

3 For it was thy will to destroy by the hands of our fathers both those old inhabitants of thy holy land,

4 Whom thou hatedst for doing most odious works of witchcrafts, and wicked sacrifices;

5 And also those merciless murderers of children, and devourers of man's flesh, and the feasts of blood,

6 With their priests out of the midst of their idolatrous crew, and the parents, that killed with their own hands souls destitute of help:

7 That the land, which thou esteemedst above all other, might receive a worthy colony of God's children.

8 Nevertheless even those thou sparedst as men, and didst send wasps, forerunners of thine host, to destroy them by little and little.

9 Not that thou wast unable to bring the ungodly under the hand of the righteous in battle, or to destroy them at once with cruel beasts, or with one rough word:

10 But executing thy judgments upon them by little and little, thou gavest them place of repentance, not being ignorant that they were a naughty generation, and that their malice was bred in them, and that their cogitation would never be changed.

11 For it was a cursed seed from the beginning; neither didst thou for fear of any man give them pardon for those things wherein they sinned.

12 For who shall say, What hast thou done? or who shall withstand thy judgment? or who shall accuse thee for the nations that perish, whom thou made? or who shall come to stand against thee, to be revenged for the unrighteous men?

13 For neither is there any God but thou that careth for all, to whom thou mightest shew that thy judgment is not unright.

14 Neither shall king or tyrant be able to set his face against thee for any whom thou hast punished.

15 Forsomuch then as thou art righteous thyself, thou orderest all things righteously: thinking it not agreeable with thy power to condemn him that hath not deserved to be punished.

16 For thy power is the beginning of righteousness, and because thou art the Lord of all, it maketh thee to be gracious unto all.

17 For when men will not believe that thou art of a full power, thou shewest thy strength, and among them that know it thou makest their boldness manifest.

18 But thou, mastering thy power, judgest with equity, and orderest us with great favour: for thou mayest use power when thou wilt.

19 But by such works hast thou taught thy people that the just man should be merciful, and hast made thy children to be of a good hope that thou givest repentance for sins.

20 For if thou didst punish the enemies of thy children, and the condemned to death, with such deliberation, giving them time and place, whereby they might be delivered from their malice:

21 With how great circumspection didst thou judge thine own sons, unto whose fathers thou hast sworn, and made covenants of good promises?

22 Therefore, whereas thou dost chasten us, thou scourgest our enemies a thousand times more, to the intent that, when we judge, we should carefully think of thy goodness, and when we ourselves are judged, we should look for mercy.

23 Wherefore, whereas men have lived dissolutely and unrighteously, thou hast tormented them with their own abominations.

24 For they went astray very far in the ways of error, and held them for gods, which even among the beasts of their enemies were despised, being deceived, as children of no understanding.

25 Therefore unto them, as to children without the use of reason, thou didst send a judgment to mock them.

26 But they that would not be reformed by that correction, wherein he dallied with them, shall feel a judgment worthy of God.

27 For, look, for what things they grudged, when they were punished, that is, for them whom they thought to be gods; now being punished in them, when they saw it, they acknowledged him to be the true God, whom before they denied to know: and therefore came extreme damnation upon them.

Solomon 13

1 Surely vain are all men by nature, who are ignorant of God, and could not out of the good things that are seen know him that is: neither by considering the works did they acknowledge the workmaster;

2 But deemed either fire, or wind, or the swift air, or the circle of the stars, or the violent water, or the lights of

heaven, to be the gods which govern the world.

3 With whose beauty if they being delighted took them to be gods; let them know how much better the Lord of them is: for the first author of beauty hath created them.

4 But if they were astonished at their power and virtue, let them understand by them, how much mightier he is that made them.

5 For by the greatness and beauty of the creatures proportionably the maker of them is seen.

6 But yet for this they are the less to be blamed: for they peradventure err, seeking God, and desirous to find him.

7 For being conversant in his works they search him diligently, and believe their sight: because the things are beautiful that are seen.

8 Howbeit neither are they to be pardoned.

9 For if they were able to know so much, that they could aim at the world; how did they not sooner find out the Lord thereof?

10 But miserable are they, and in dead things is their hope, who call them gods, which are the works of men's hands, gold and silver, to shew art in, and resemblances of beasts, or a stone good for nothing, the work of an ancient hand.

11 Now a carpenter that felleth timber, after he hath sawn down a tree meet for the purpose, and taken off all the bark skilfully round about, and hath wrought it handsomely, and made a vessel thereof fit for the service of man's life;

12 And after spending the refuse of his work to dress his meat, hath filled himself;

13 And taking the very refuse among those which served to no use, being a crooked piece of wood, and full of knots, hath carved it diligently, when he had nothing else to do, and formed it by the skill of his understanding, and fashioned it to the image of a man;

14 Or made it like some vile beast, laying it over with vermilion, and with paint colouring it red, and covering every spot therein;

15 And when he had made a convenient room for it, set it in a wall, and made it fast with iron:

16 For he provided for it that it might not fall, knowing that it was unable to help itself; for it is an image, and hath need of help:

17 Then maketh he prayer for his goods, for his wife and children, and is not ashamed to speak to that which hath no life.

18 For health he calleth upon that which is weak: for life prayeth to that which is dead; for aid humbly beseecheth that which hath least

means to help: and for a good journey he asketh of that which cannot set a foot forward:

19 And for gaining and getting, and for good success of his hands, asketh ability to do of him, that is most unable to do any thing.

Solomon 14

1 Again, one preparing himself to sail, and about to pass through the raging waves, calleth upon a piece of wood more rotten than the vessel that carrieth him.

2 For verily desire of gain devised that, and the workman built it by his skill.

3 But thy providence, O Father, governeth it: for thou hast made a way in the sea, and a safe path in the waves;

4 Shewing that thou canst save from all danger: yea, though a man went to sea without art.

5 Nevertheless thou wouldest not that the works of thy wisdom should be idle, and therefore do men commit their lives to a small piece of wood, and passing the rough sea in a weak vessel are saved.

6 For in the old time also, when the proud giants perished, the hope of the world governed by thy hand escaped in a weak vessel, and left to all ages a seed of generation.

7 For blessed is the wood whereby righteousness cometh.

8 But that which is made with hands is cursed, as well it, as he that made it: he, because he made it; and it, because, being corruptible, it was called god.

9 For the ungodly and his ungodliness are both alike hateful unto God.

10 For that which is made shall be punished together with him that made it.

11 Therefore even upon the idols of the Gentiles shall there be a visitation: because in the creature of God they are become an abomination, and stumblingblocks to the souls of men, and a snare to the feet of the unwise.

12 For the devising of idols was the beginning of spiritual fornication, and the invention of them the corruption of life.

13 For neither were they from the beginning, neither shall they be for ever.

14 For by the vain glory of men they entered into the world, and therefore shall they come shortly to an end.

15 For a father afflicted with untimely mourning, when he hath made an image of his child soon taken away, now honoured him as a god, which was then a dead man, and delivered to those that were under him ceremonies and sacrifices.

16 Thus in process of time an ungodly custom grown strong was kept as a law, and graven images were worshipped by the commandments of kings.

17 Whom men could not honour in presence, because they dwelt far off, they took the counterfeit of his visage from far, and made an express image of a king whom they honoured, to the end that by this their forwardness they might flatter him that was absent, as if he were present.

18 Also the singular diligence of the artificer did help to set forward the ignorant to more superstition.

19 For he, peradventure willing to please one in authority, forced all his skill to make the resemblance of the best fashion.

20 And so the multitude, allured by the grace of the work, took him now for a god, which a little before was but honoured.

21 And this was an occasion to deceive the world: for men, serving either calamity or tyranny, did ascribe unto stones and stocks the incommunicable name.

22 Moreover this was not enough for them, that they erred in the knowledge of God; but whereas they lived in the great war of ignorance, those so great plagues called they peace.

23 For whilst they slew their children in sacrifices, or used secret ceremonies, or made revellings of strange rites;

24 They kept neither lives nor marriages any longer undefiled: but either one slew another traiterously, or grieved him by adultery.

25 So that there reigned in all men without exception blood, manslaughter, theft, and dissimulation, corruption, unfaithfulness, tumults, perjury,

26 Disquieting of good men, forgetfulness of good turns, defiling of souls, changing of kind, disorder in marriages, adultery, and shameless uncleanness.

27 For the worshipping of idols not to be named is the beginning, the cause, and the end, of all evil.

28 For either they are mad when they be merry, or prophesy lies, or live unjustly, or else lightly forswear themselves.

29 For insomuch as their trust is in idols, which have no life; though they swear falsely, yet they look not to be hurt.

30 Howbeit for both causes shall they be justly punished: both because they thought not well of God, giving heed unto idols, and also unjustly swore in deceit, despising holiness.

31 For it is not the power of them by whom they swear: but it is the just vengeance of sinners, that punisheth always the offence of the ungodly.

Solomon 15

1 But thou, O God, art gracious and true, longsuffering, and in mercy ordering all things,

2 For if we sin, we are thine, knowing thy power: but we will not sin, knowing that we are counted thine.

3 For to know thee is perfect righteousness: yea, to know thy power is the root of immortality.

4 For neither did the mischievous invention of men deceive us, nor an image spotted with divers colours, the painter's fruitless labour;

5 The sight whereof enticeth fools to lust after it, and so they desire the form of a dead image, that hath no breath.

6 Both they that make them, they that desire them, and they that worship them, are lovers of evil things, and are worthy to have such things to trust upon.

7 For the potter, tempering soft earth, fashioneth every vessel with much labour for our service: yea, of the same clay he maketh both the vessels that serve for clean uses, and likewise also all such as serve to the contrary: but what is the use of either sort, the potter himself is the judge.

8 And employing his labours lewdly, he maketh a vain god of the same clay, even he which a little before was made of earth himself, and within a little while after returneth to the same, out when his life which was lent him shall be demanded.

9 Notwithstanding his care is, not that he shall have much labour, nor that his life is short: but striveth to excel goldsmiths and silversmiths, and endeavoureth to do like the workers in brass, and counteth it his glory to make counterfeit things.

10 His heart is ashes, his hope is more vile than earth, and his life of less value than clay:

11 Forasmuch as he knew not his Maker, and him that inspired into him an active soul, and breathed in a living spirit.

12 But they counted our life a pastime, and our time here a market for gain: for, say they, we must be getting every way, though it be by evil means.

13 For this man, that of earthly matter maketh brittle vessels and graven images, knoweth himself to offend above all others.

14 And all the enemies of thy people, that hold them in subjection, are most foolish, and are more miserable than very babes.

15 For they counted all the idols of the heathen to be gods: which neither have the use of eyes to see,

nor noses to draw breath, nor ears to hear, nor fingers of hands to handle; and as for their feet, they are slow to go.

16 For man made them, and he that borrowed his own spirit fashioned them: but no man can make a god like unto himself.

17 For being mortal, he worketh a dead thing with wicked hands: for he himself is better than the things which he worshippeth: whereas he lived once, but they never.

18 Yea, they worshipped those beasts also that are most hateful: for being compared together, some are worse than others.

19 Neither are they beautiful, so much as to be desired in respect of beasts: but they went without the praise of God and his blessing.

Solomon 16

1 Therefore by the like were they punished worthily, and by the multitude of beasts tormented.

2 Instead of which punishment, dealing graciously with thine own people, thou preparedst for them meat of a strange taste, even quails to stir up their appetite:

3 To the end that they, desiring food, might for the ugly sight of the beasts sent among them lothe even that, which they must needs desire; but these, suffering penury for a short space, might be made partakers of a strange taste.

4 For it was requisite, that upon them exercising tyranny should come penury, which they could not avoid: but to these it should only be shewed how their enemies were tormented.

5 For when the horrible fierceness of beasts came upon these, and they perished with the stings of crooked serpents, thy wrath endured not for ever:

6 But they were troubled for a small season, that they might be admonished, having a sign of salvation, to put them in remembrance of the commandment of thy law.

7 For he that turned himself toward it was not saved by the thing that he saw, but by thee, that art the Saviour of all.

8 And in this thou madest thine enemies confess, that it is thou who deliverest from all evil:

9 For them the bitings of grasshoppers and flies killed, neither was there found any remedy for their life: for they were worthy to be punished by such.

10 But thy sons not the very teeth of venomous dragons overcame: for thy mercy was ever by them, and healed them.

11 For they were pricked, that they should remember thy words; and

were quickly saved, that not falling into deep forgetfulness, they might be continually mindful of thy goodness.

12 For it was neither herb, nor mollifying plaister, that restored them to health: but thy word, O Lord, which healeth all things.

13 For thou hast power of life and death: thou leadest to the gates of hell, and bringest up again.

14 A man indeed killeth through his malice: and the spirit, when it is gone forth, returneth not; neither the soul received up cometh again.

15 But it is not possible to escape thine hand.

16 For the ungodly, that denied to know thee, were scourged by the strength of thine arm: with strange rains, hails, and showers, were they persecuted, that they could not avoid, and through fire were they consumed.

17 For, which is most to be wondered at, the fire had more force in the water, that quencheth all things: for the world fighteth for the righteous.

18 For sometime the flame was mitigated, that it might not burn up the beasts that were sent against the ungodly; but themselves might see and perceive that they were persecuted with the judgment of God.

19 And at another time it burneth even in the midst of water above the power of fire, that it might destroy the fruits of an unjust land.

20 Instead whereof thou feddest thine own people with angels' food, and didst send them from heaven bread prepared without their labour, able to content every man's delight, and agreeing to every taste.

21 For thy sustenance declared thy sweetness unto thy children, and serving to the appetite of the eater, tempered itself to every man's liking.

22 But snow and ice endured the fire, and melted not, that they might know that fire burning in the hail, and sparkling in the rain, did destroy the fruits of the enemies.

23 But this again did even forget his own strength, that the righteous might be nourished.

24 For the creature that serveth thee, who art the Maker increaseth his strength against the unrighteous for their punishment, and abateth his strength for the benefit of such as put their trust in thee.

25 Therefore even then was it altered into all fashions, and was obedient to thy grace, that nourisheth all things, according to the desire of them that had need:

26 That thy children, O Lord, whom thou lovest, might know, that it is not the growing of fruits that nourisheth man: but that it is thy word, which

preserveth them that put their trust in thee.

27 For that which was not destroyed of the fire, being warmed with a little sunbeam, soon melted away:

28 That it might be known, that we must prevent the sun to give thee thanks, and at the dayspring pray unto thee.

29 For the hope of the unthankful shall melt away as the winter's hoar frost, and shall run away as unprofitable water.

Solomon 17

1 For great are thy judgments, and cannot be expressed: therefore unnurtured souls have erred.

2 For when unrighteous men thought to oppress the holy nation; they being shut up in their houses, the prisoners of darkness, and fettered with the bonds of a long night, lay there exiled from the eternal providence.

3 For while they supposed to lie hid in their secret sins, they were scattered under a dark veil of forgetfulness, being horribly astonished, and troubled with strange apparitions.

4 For neither might the corner that held them keep them from fear: but noises as of waters falling down sounded about them, and sad visions appeared unto them with heavy countenances.

5 No power of the fire might give them light: neither could the bright flames of the stars endure to lighten that horrible night.

6 Only there appeared unto them a fire kindled of itself, very dreadful: for being much terrified, they thought the things which they saw to be worse than the sight they saw not.

7 As for the illusions of art magick, they were put down, and their vaunting in wisdom was reproved with disgrace.

8 For they, that promised to drive away terrors and troubles from a sick soul, were sick themselves of fear, worthy to be laughed at.

9 For though no terrible thing did fear them; yet being scared with beasts that passed by, and hissing of serpents,

10 They died for fear, denying that they saw the air, which could of no side be avoided.

11 For wickedness, condemned by her own witness, is very timorous, and being pressed with conscience, always forecasteth grievous things.

12 For fear is nothing else but a betraying of the succours which reason offereth.

13 And the expectation from within, being less, counteth the ignorance more than the cause which bringeth the torment.

14 But they sleeping the same sleep that night, which was indeed intolerable, and which came upon them out of the bottoms of inevitable hell,

15 Were partly vexed with monstrous apparitions, and partly fainted, their heart failing them: for a sudden fear, and not looked for, came upon them.

16 So then whosoever there fell down was straitly kept, shut up in a prison without iron bars,

17 For whether he were husbandman, or shepherd, or a labourer in the field, he was overtaken, and endured that necessity, which could not be avoided: for they were all bound with one chain of darkness.

18 Whether it were a whistling wind, or a melodious noise of birds among the spreading branches, or a pleasing fall of water running violently,

19 Or a terrible sound of stones cast down, or a running that could not be seen of skipping beasts, or a roaring voice of most savage wild beasts, or a rebounding echo from the hollow mountains; these things made them to swoon for fear.

20 For the whole world shined with clear light, and none were hindered in their labour:

21 Over them only was spread an heavy night, an image of that darkness which should afterward receive them: but yet were they unto themselves more grievous than the darkness.

Solomon 18

1 Nevertheless thy saints had a very great light, whose voice they hearing, and not seeing their shape, because they also had not suffered the same things, they counted them happy.

2 But for that they did not hurt them now, of whom they had been wronged before, they thanked them, and besought them pardon for that they had been enemies.

3 Instead whereof thou gavest them a burning pillar of fire, both to be a guide of the unknown journey, and an harmless sun to entertain them honourably.

4 For they were worthy to be deprived of light and imprisoned in darkness, who had kept thy sons shut up, by whom the uncorrupt light of the law was to be given unto the world.

5 And when they had determined to slay the babes of the saints, one child being cast forth, and saved, to reprove them, thou tookest away the multitude of their children, and destroyedst them altogether in a mighty water.

6 Of that night were our fathers certified afore, that assuredly knowing unto what oaths they had

given credence, they might afterwards be of good cheer.

7 So of thy people was accepted both the salvation of the righteous, and destruction of the enemies.

8 For wherewith thou didst punish our adversaries, by the same thou didst glorify us, whom thou hadst called.

9 For the righteous children of good men did sacrifice secretly, and with one consent made a holy law, that the saints should be like partakers of the same good and evil, the fathers now singing out the songs of praise.

10 But on the other side there sounded an ill according cry of the enemies, and a lamentable noise was carried abroad for children that were bewailed.

11 The master and the servant were punished after one manner; and like as the king, so suffered the common person.

12 So they all together had innumerable dead with one kind of death; neither were the living sufficient to bury them: for in one moment the noblest offspring of them was destroyed.

13 For whereas they would not believe any thing by reason of the enchantments; upon the destruction of the firstborn, they acknowledged this people to be the sons of God.

14 For while all things were in quiet silence, and that night was in the midst of her swift course,

15 Thine Almighty word leaped down from heaven out of thy royal throne, as a fierce man of war into the midst of a land of destruction,

16 And brought thine unfeigned commandment as a sharp sword, and standing up filled all things with death; and it touched the heaven, but it stood upon the earth.

17 Then suddenly visions of horrible dreams troubled them sore, and terrors came upon them unlooked for.

18 And one thrown here, and another there, half dead, shewed the cause of his death.

19 For the dreams that troubled them did foreshew this, lest they should perish, and not know why they were afflicted.

20 Yea, the tasting of death touched the righteous also, and there was a destruction of the multitude in the wilderness: but the wrath endured not long.

21 For then the blameless man made haste, and stood forth to defend them; and bringing the shield of his proper ministry, even prayer, and the propitiation of incense, set himself against the wrath, and so brought the calamity to an end, declaring that he was thy servant.

22 So he overcame the destroyer, not with strength of body, nor force of arms, but with a word subdued him that punished, alleging the oaths and covenants made with the fathers.

23 For when the dead were now fallen down by heaps one upon another, standing between, he stayed the wrath, and parted the way to the living.

24 For in the long garment was the whole world, and in the four rows of the stones was the glory of the fathers graven, and thy Majesty upon the diadem of his head.

25 Unto these the destroyer gave place, and was afraid of them: for it was enough that they only tasted of the wrath.

Solomon 19

1 As for the ungodly, wrath came upon them without mercy unto the end: for he knew before what they would do;

2 How that having given them leave to depart, and sent them hastily away, they would repent and pursue them.

3 For whilst they were yet mourning and making lamentation at the graves of the dead, they added another foolish device, and pursued them as fugitives, whom they had intreated to be gone.

4 For the destiny, whereof they were worthy, drew them unto this end, and made them forget the things that had already happened, that they might fulfil the punishment which was wanting to their torments:

5 And that thy people might pass a wonderful way: but they might find a strange death.

6 For the whole creature in his proper kind was fashioned again anew, serving the peculiar commandments that were given unto them, that thy children might be kept without hurt:

7 As namely, a cloud shadowing the camp; and where water stood before, dry land appeared; and out of the Red sea a way without impediment; and out of the violent stream a green field:

8 Wherethrough all the people went that were defended with thy hand, seeing thy marvellous strange wonders.

9 For they went at large like horses, and leaped like lambs, praising thee, O Lord, who hadst delivered them.

10 For they were yet mindful of the things that were done while they sojourned in the strange land, how the ground brought forth flies instead of cattle, and how the river cast up a multitude of frogs instead of fishes.

11 But afterwards they saw a new generation of fowls, when, being led

with their appetite, they asked delicate meats.

12 For quails came up unto them from the sea for their contentment.

13 And punishments came upon the sinners not without former signs by the force of thunders: for they suffered justly according to their own wickedness, insomuch as they used a more hard and hateful behaviour toward strangers.

14 For the Sodomites did not receive those, whom they knew not when they came: but these brought friends into bondage, that had well deserved of them.

15 And not only so, but peradventure some respect shall be had of those, because they used strangers not friendly:

16 But these very grievously afflicted them, whom they had received with feastings, and were already made partakers of the same laws with them.

17 Therefore even with blindness were these stricken, as those were at the doors of the righteous man: when, being compassed about with horrible great darkness, every one sought the passage of his own doors.

18 For the elements were changed in themselves by a kind of harmony, like as in a psaltery notes change the name of the tune, and yet are always sounds; which may well be perceived by the sight of the things that have been done.

19 For earthly things were turned into watery, and the things, that before swam in the water, now went upon the ground.

20 The fire had power in the water, forgetting his own virtue: and the water forgat his own quenching nature.

21 On the other side, the flames wasted not the flesh of the corruptible living things, though they walked therein; neither melted they the icy kind of heavenly meat that was of nature apt to melt.

22 For in all things, O Lord, thou didst magnify thy people, and glorify them, neither didst thou lightly regard them: but didst assist them in every time and place.

ECCLESIASTICUS OR THE WISDOM OF JESUS BEN SIRACH

Ecclesiasticus 1

1 All wisdom cometh from the Lord, and is with him for ever.

2 Who can number the sand of the sea, and the drops of rain, and the days of eternity?

3 Who can find out the height of heaven, and the breadth of the earth, and the deep, and wisdom?

4 Wisdom hath been created before all things, and the understanding of prudence from everlasting.

5 The word of God most high is the fountain of wisdom; and her ways are everlasting commandments.

6 To whom hath the root of wisdom been revealed? or who hath known her wise counsels?

7 Unto whom hath the knowledge of wisdom been made manifest? and who hath understood her great experience?

8 There is one wise and greatly to be feared, the Lord sitting upon his throne.

9 He created her, and saw her, and numbered her, and poured her out upon all his works.

10 She is with all flesh according to his gift, and he hath given her to them that love him.

11 The fear of the Lord is honour, and glory, and gladness, and a crown of rejoicing.

12 The fear of the Lord maketh a merry heart, and giveth joy, and gladness, and a long life.

13 Whoso feareth the Lord, it shall go well with him at the last, and he shall find favour in the day of his death.

14 To fear the Lord is the beginning of wisdom: and it was created with the faithful in the womb.

15 She hath built an everlasting foundation with men, and she shall continue with their seed.

16 To fear the Lord is fulness of wisdom, and filleth men with her fruits.

17 She filleth all their house with things desirable, and the garners with her increase.

18 The fear of the Lord is a crown of wisdom, making peace and perfect health to flourish; both which are the gifts of God: and it enlargeth their rejoicing that love him.

19 Wisdom raineth down skill and knowledge of understanding standing, and exalteth them to honour that hold her fast.

20 The root of wisdom is to fear the Lord, and the branches thereof are long life.

21 The fear of the Lord driveth away sins: and where it is present, it turneth away wrath.

22 A furious man cannot be justified; for the sway of his fury shall be his destruction.

23 A patient man will tear for a time, and afterward joy shall spring up unto him.

24 He will hide his words for a time, and the lips of many shall declare his wisdom.

25 The parables of knowledge are in the treasures of wisdom: but godliness is an abomination to a sinner.

26 If thou desire wisdom, keep the commandments, and the Lord shall give her unto thee.

27 For the fear of the Lord is wisdom and instruction: and faith and meekness are his delight.

28 Distrust not the fear of the Lord when thou art poor: and come not unto him with a double heart.

29 Be not an hypocrite in the sight of men, and take good heed what thou speakest.

30 Exalt not thyself, lest thou fall, and bring dishonour upon thy soul, and so God discover thy secrets, and cast thee down in the midst of the congregation, because thou camest not in truth to the fear of the Lord, but thy heart is full of deceit.

Ecclesiasticus 2

1 My son, if thou come to serve the Lord, prepare thy soul for temptation.

2 Set thy heart aright, and constantly endure, and make not haste in time of trouble.

3 Cleave unto him, and depart not away, that thou mayest be increased at thy last end.

4 Whatsoever is brought upon thee take cheerfully, and be patient when thou art changed to a low estate.

5 For gold is tried in the fire, and acceptable men in the furnace of adversity.

6 Believe in him, and he will help thee; order thy way aright, and trust in him.

7 Ye that fear the Lord, wait for his mercy; and go not aside, lest ye fall.

8 Ye that fear the Lord, believe him; and your reward shall not fail.

9 Ye that fear the Lord, hope for good, and for everlasting joy and mercy.

10 Look at the generations of old, and see; did ever any trust in the Lord, and was confounded? or did any abide in his fear, and was forsaken? or whom did he ever despise, that called upon him?

11 For the Lord is full of compassion and mercy, longsuffering, and very pitiful, and forgiveth sins, and saveth in time of affliction.

12 Woe be to fearful hearts, and faint hands, and the sinner that goeth two ways!

13 Woe unto him that is fainthearted! for he believeth not; therefore shall he not be defended.

14 Woe unto you that have lost patience! and what will ye do when the Lord shall visit you?

15 They that fear the Lord will not disobey his Word; and they that love him will keep his ways.

16 They that fear the Lord will seek that which is well, pleasing unto him; and they that love him shall be filled with the law.

17 They that fear the Lord will prepare their hearts, and humble their souls in his sight,

18 Saying, We will fall into the hands of the Lord, and not into the hands of men: for as his majesty is, so is his mercy.

Ecclesiasticus 3

1 Hear me your father, O children, and do thereafter, that ye may be safe.

2 For the Lord hath given the father honour over the children, and hath confirmed the authority of the mother over the sons.

3 Whoso honoureth his father maketh an atonement for his sins:

4 And he that honoureth his mother is as one that layeth up treasure.

5 Whoso honoureth his father shall have joy of his own children; and when he maketh his prayer, he shall be heard.

6 He that honoureth his father shall have a long life; and he that is obedient unto the Lord shall be a comfort to his mother.

7 He that feareth the Lord will honour his father, and will do service unto his parents, as to his masters.

8 Honour thy father and mother both in word and deed, that a blessing may come upon thee from them.

9 For the blessing of the father establisheth the houses of children; but the curse of the mother rooteth out foundations.

10 Glory not in the dishonour of thy father; for thy father's dishonour is no glory unto thee.

11 For the glory of a man is from the honour of his father; and a mother in dishonour is a reproach to the children.

12 My son, help thy father in his age, and grieve him not as long as he liveth.

13 And if his understanding fail, have patience with him; and despise him not when thou art in thy full strength.

14 For the relieving of thy father shall not be forgotten: and instead of sins it shall be added to build thee up.

15 In the day of thine affliction it shall be remembered; thy sins also shall melt away, as the ice in the fair warm weather.

16 He that forsaketh his father is as a blasphemer; and he that angereth his mother is cursed: of God.

17 My son, go on with thy business in meekness; so shalt thou be beloved of him that is approved.

18 The greater thou art, the more humble thyself, and thou shalt find favour before the Lord.

19 Many are in high place, and of renown: but mysteries are revealed unto the meek.

20 For the power of the Lord is great, and he is honoured of the lowly.

21 Seek not out things that are too hard for thee, neither search the things that are above thy strength.

22 But what is commanded thee, think thereupon with reverence, for it is not needful for thee to see with thine eyes the things that are in secret.

23 Be not curious in unnecessary matters: for more things are shewed unto thee than men understand.

24 For many are deceived by their own vain opinion; and an evil suspicion hath overthrown their judgment.

25 Without eyes thou shalt want light: profess not the knowledge therefore that thou hast not.

26 A stubborn heart shall fare evil at the last; and he that loveth danger shall perish therein.

27 An obstinate heart shall be laden with sorrows; and the wicked man shall heap sin upon sin.

28 In the punishment of the proud there is no remedy; for the plant of wickedness hath taken root in him.

29 The heart of the prudent will understand a parable; and an attentive ear is the desire of a wise man.

30 Water will quench a flaming fire; and alms maketh an atonement for sins.

31 And he that requiteth good turns is mindful of that which may come hereafter; and when he falleth, he shall find a stay.

Ecclesiasticus 4

1 My son, defraud not the poor of his living, and make not the needy eyes to wait long.

2 Make not an hungry soul sorrowful; neither provoke a man in his distress.

3 Add not more trouble to an heart that is vexed; and defer not to give to him that is in need.

4 Reject not the supplication of the afflicted; neither turn away thy face from a poor man.

5 Turn not away thine eye from the needy, and give him none occasion to curse thee:

6 For if he curse thee in the bitterness of his soul, his prayer shall be heard of him that made him.

7 Get thyself the love of the congregation, and bow thy head to a great man.

8 Let it not grieve thee to bow down thine ear to the poor, and give him a friendly answer with meekness.

9 Deliver him that suffereth wrong from the hand of the oppressor; and be not fainthearted when thou sittest in judgment.

10 Be as a father unto the fatherless, and instead of an husband unto their mother: so shalt thou be as the son of the most High, and he shall love thee more than thy mother doth.

11 Wisdom exalteth her children, and layeth hold of them that seek her.

12 He that loveth her loveth life; and they that seek to her early shall be filled with joy.

13 He that holdeth her fast shall inherit glory; and wheresoever she entereth, the Lord will bless.

14 They that serve her shall minister to the Holy One: and them that love her the Lord doth love.

15 Whoso giveth ear unto her shall judge the nations: and he that attendeth unto her shall dwell securely.

16 If a man commit himself unto her, he shall inherit her; and his generation shall hold her in possession.

17 For at the first she will walk with him by crooked ways, and bring fear and dread upon him, and torment him with her discipline, until she may trust his soul, and try him by her laws.

18 Then will she return the straight way unto him, and comfort him, and shew him her secrets.

19 But if he go wrong, she will forsake him, and give him over to his own ruin.

20 Observe the opportunity, and beware of evil; and be not ashamed when it concerneth thy soul.

21 For there is a shame that bringeth sin; and there is a shame which is glory and grace.

22 Accept no person against thy soul, and let not the reverence of any man cause thee to fall.

23 And refrain not to speak, when there is occasion to do good, and hide not thy wisdom in her beauty.

24 For by speech wisdom shall be known: and learning by the word of the tongue.

25 In no wise speak against the truth; but be abashed of the error of thine ignorance.

26 Be not ashamed to confess thy sins; and force not the course of the river.

27 Make not thyself an underling to a foolish man; neither accept the person of the mighty.

28 Strive for the truth unto death, and the Lord shall fight for thee.

29 Be not hasty in thy tongue, and in thy deeds slack and remiss.

30 Be not as a lion in thy house, nor frantick among thy servants.

31 Let not thine hand be stretched out to receive, and shut when thou shouldest repay.

Ecclesiasticus 5

1 Set thy heart upon thy goods; and say not, I have enough for my life.

2 Follow not thine own mind and thy strength, to walk in the ways of thy heart:

3 And say not, Who shall controul me for my works? for the Lord will surely revenge thy pride.

4 Say not, I have sinned, and what harm hath happened unto me? for the Lord is longsuffering, he will in no wise let thee go.

5 Concerning propitiation, be not without fear to add sin unto sin:

6 And say not His mercy is great; he will be pacified for the multitude of my sins: for mercy and wrath come from him, and his indignation resteth upon sinners.

7 Make no tarrying to turn to the Lord, and put not off from day to day: for suddenly shall the wrath of the Lord come forth, and in thy security thou shalt be destroyed, and perish in the day of vengeance.

8 Set not thine heart upon goods unjustly gotten, for they shall not profit thee in the day of calamity.

9 Winnow not with every wind, and go not into every way: for so doth the sinner that hath a double tongue.

10 Be stedfast in thy understanding; and let thy word be the same.

11 Be swift to hear; and let thy life be sincere; and with patience give answer.

12 If thou hast understanding, answer thy neighbour; if not, lay thy hand upon thy mouth.

13 Honour and shame is in talk: and the tongue of man is his fall.

14 Be not called a whisperer, and lie not in wait with thy tongue: for a foul shame is upon the thief, and an evil condemnation upon the double tongue.

15 Be not ignorant of any thing in a great matter or a small.

Ecclesiasticus 6

1 Instead of a friend become not an enemy; for thereby thou shalt inherit an ill name, shame, and reproach: even so shall a sinner that hath a double tongue.

2 Extol not thyself in the counsel of thine own heart; that thy soul be not torn in pieces as a bull straying alone.

3 Thou shalt eat up thy leaves, and lose thy fruit, and leave thyself as a dry tree.

4 A wicked soul shall destroy him that hath it, and shall make him to be laughed to scorn of his enemies.

5 Sweet language will multiply friends: and a fairspeaking tongue will increase kind greetings.

6 Be in peace with many: nevertheless have but one counsellor of a thousand.

7 If thou wouldest get a friend, prove him first and be not hasty to credit him.

8 For some man is a friend for his own occasion, and will not abide in the day of thy trouble.

9 And there is a friend, who being turned to enmity, and strife will discover thy reproach.

10 Again, some friend is a companion at the table, and will not continue in the day of thy affliction.

11 But in thy prosperity he will be as thyself, and will be bold over thy servants.

12 If thou be brought low, he will be against thee, and will hide himself from thy face.

13 Separate thyself from thine enemies, and take heed of thy friends.

14 A faithfull friend is a strong defence: and he that hath found such an one hath found a treasure.

15 Nothing doth countervail a faithful friend, and his excellency is invaluable.

16 A faithful friend is the medicine of life; and they that fear the Lord shall find him.

17 Whoso feareth the Lord shall direct his friendship aright: for as he is, so shall his neighbour be also.

18 My son, gather instruction from thy youth up: so shalt thou find wisdom till thine old age.

19 Come unto her as one that ploweth and soweth, and wait for her good fruits: for thou shalt not toil much in labouring about her, but thou shalt eat of her fruits right soon.

20 She is very unpleasant to the unlearned: he that is without

understanding will not remain with her.

21 She will lie upon him as a mighty stone of trial; and he will cast her from him ere it be long.

22 For wisdom is according to her name, and she is not manifest unto many.

23 Give ear, my son, receive my advice, and refuse not my counsel,

24 And put thy feet into her fetters, and thy neck into her chain.

25 Bow down thy shoulder, and bear her, and be not grieved with her bonds.

26 Come unto her with thy whole heart, and keep her ways with all thy power.

27 Search, and seek, and she shall be made known unto thee: and when thou hast got hold of her, let her not go.

28 For at the last thou shalt find her rest, and that shall be turned to thy joy.

29 Then shall her fetters be a strong defence for thee, and her chains a robe of glory.

30 For there is a golden ornament upon her, and her bands are purple lace.

31 Thou shalt put her on as a robe of honour, and shalt put her about thee as a crown of joy.

32 My son, if thou wilt, thou shalt be taught: and if thou wilt apply thy mind, thou shalt be prudent.

33 If thou love to hear, thou shalt receive understanding: and if thou bow thine ear, thou shalt be wise,

34 Stand in the multitude of the elders; and cleave unto him that is wise.

35 Be willing to hear every godly discourse; and let not the parables of understanding escape thee.

36 And if thou seest a man of understanding, get thee betimes unto him, and let thy foot wear the steps of his door.

37 Let thy mind be upon the ordinances of the Lord and meditate continually in his commandments: he shall establish thine heart, and give thee wisdom at thine owns desire.

Ecclesiasticus 7

1 Do no evil, so shall no harm come unto thee.

2 Depart from the unjust, and iniquity shall turn away from thee.

3 My son, sow not upon the furrows of unrighteousness, and thou shalt not reap them sevenfold.

4 Seek not of the Lord preeminence, neither of the king the seat of honour.

5 Justify not thyself before the Lord; and boast not of thy wisdom before the king.

6 Seek not to be judge, being not able to take away iniquity; lest at any time thou fear the person of the mighty, an stumblingblock in the way of thy uprightness.

7 Offend not against the multitude of a city, and then thou shalt not cast thyself down among the people.

8 Bind not one sin upon another; for in one thou shalt not be unpunished.

9 Say not, God will look upon the multitude of my oblations, and when I offer to the most high God, he will accept it.

10 Be not fainthearted when thou makest thy prayer, and neglect not to give alms.

11 Laugh no man to scorn in the bitterness of his soul: for there is one which humbleth and exalteth.

12 Devise not a lie against thy brother; neither do the like to thy friend.

13 Use not to make any manner of lie: for the custom thereof is not good.

14 Use not many words in a multitude of elders, and make not much babbling when thou prayest.

15 Hate not laborious work, neither husbandry, which the most High hath ordained.

16 Number not thyself among the multitude of sinners, but remember that wrath will not tarry long.

17 Humble thyself greatly: for the vengeance of the ungodly is fire and worms.

18 Change not a friend for any good by no means; neither a faithful brother for the gold of Ophir.

19 Forego not a wise and good woman: for her grace is above gold.

20 Whereas thy servant worketh truly, entreat him not evil, nor the hireling that bestoweth himself wholly for thee.

21 Let thy soul love a good servant, and defraud him not of liberty.

22 Hast thou cattle? have an eye to them: and if they be for thy profit, keep them with thee.

23 Hast thou children? instruct them, and bow down their neck from their youth.

24 Hast thou daughters? have a care of their body, and shew not thyself cheerful toward them.

25 Marry thy daughter, and so shalt thou have performed a weighty matter: but give her to a man of understanding.

26 Hast thou a wife after thy mind? forsake her not: but give not thyself over to a light woman.

27 Honour thy father with thy whole heart, and forget not the sorrows of thy mother.

28 Remember that thou wast begotten of them; and how canst

thou recompense them the things that they have done for thee?

29 Fear the Lord with all thy soul, and reverence his priests.

30 Love him that made thee with all thy strength, and forsake not his ministers.

31 Fear the Lord, and honor the priest; and give him his portion, as it is commanded thee; the firstfruits, and the trespass offering, and the gift of the shoulders, and the sacrifice of sanctification, and the firstfruits of the holy things.

32 And stretch thine hand unto the poor, that thy blessing may be perfected.

33 A gift hath grace in the sight of every man living; and for the dead detain it not.

34 Fail not to be with them that weep, and mourn with them that mourn.

35 Be not slow to visit the sick: for that shall make thee to be beloved.

36 Whatsoever thou takest in hand, remember the end, and thou shalt never do amiss.

Ecclesiasticus 8

1 Strive not with a mighty man' lest thou fall into his hands.

2 Be not at variance with a rich man, lest he overweigh thee: for gold hath destroyed many, and perverted the hearts of kings.

3 Strive not with a man that is full of tongue, and heap not wood upon his fire.

4 Jest not with a rude man, lest thy ancestors be disgraced.

5 Reproach not a man that turneth from sin, but remember that we are all worthy of punishment.

6 Dishonour not a man in his old age: for even some of us wax old.

7 Rejoice not over thy greatest enemy being dead, but remember that we die all.

8 Despise not the discourse of the wise, but acquaint thyself with their proverbs: for of them thou shalt learn instruction, and how to serve great men with ease.

9 Miss not the discourse of the elders: for they also learned of their fathers, and of them thou shalt learn understanding, and to give answer as need requireth.

10 Kindle not the coals of a sinner, lest thou be burnt with the flame of his fire.

11 Rise not up in anger at the presence of an injurious person, lest he lie in wait to entrap thee in thy words

12 Lend not unto him that is mightier than thyself; for if thou lendest him, count it but lost.

13 Be not surety above thy power: for if thou be surety, take care to pay it.

14 Go not to law with a judge; for they will judge for him according to his honour.

15 Travel not by the way with a bold fellow, lest he become grievous unto thee: for he will do according to his own will, and thou shalt perish with him through his folly.

16 Strive not with an angry man, and go not with him into a solitary place: for blood is as nothing in his sight, and where there is no help, he will overthrow thee.

17 Consult not with a fool; for he cannot keep counsel.

18 Do no secret thing before a stranger; for thou knowest not what he will bring forth.

19 Open not thine heart to every man, lest he requite thee with a shrewd turn.

Ecclesiasticus 9

1 Be not jealous over the wife of thy bosom, and teach her not an evil lesson against thyself.

2 Give not thy soul unto a woman to set her foot upon thy substance.

3 Meet not with an harlot, lest thou fall into her snares.

4 Use not much the company of a woman that is a singer, lest thou be taken with her attempts.

5 Gaze not on a maid, that thou fall not by those things that are precious in her.

6 Give not thy soul unto harlots, that thou lose not thine inheritance.

7 Look not round about thee in the streets of the city, neither wander thou in the solitary place thereof.

8 Turn away thine eye from a beautiful woman, and look not upon another's beauty; for many have been deceived by the beauty of a woman; for herewith love is kindled as a fire.

9 Sit not at all with another man's wife, nor sit down with her in thine arms, and spend not thy money with her at the wine; lest thine heart incline unto her, and so through thy desire thou fall into destruction.

10 Forsake not an old friend; for the new is not comparable to him: a new friend is as new wine; when it is old, thou shalt drink it with pleasure.

11 Envy not the glory of a sinner: for thou knowest not what shall be his end.

12 Delight not in the thing that the ungodly have pleasure in; but remember they shall not go unpunished unto their grave.

13 Keep thee far from the man that hath power to kill; so shalt thou not doubt the fear of death: and if thou come unto him, make no fault, lest he take away thy life presently:

remember that thou goest in the midst of snares, and that thou walkest upon the battlements of the city.

14 As near as thou canst, guess at thy neighbour, and consult with the wise.

15 Let thy talk be with the wise, and all thy communication in the law of the most High.

16 And let just men eat and drink with thee; and let thy glorying be in the fear of the Lord.

17 For the hand of the artificer the work shall be commended: and the wise ruler of the people for his speech.

18 A man of an ill tongue is dangerous in his city; and he that is rash in his talk shall be hated.

Ecclesiasticus 10

1 A wise judge will instruct his people; and the government of a prudent man is well ordered.

2 As the judge of the people is himself, so are his officers; and what manner of man the ruler of the city is, such are all they that dwell therein.

3 An unwise king destroyeth his people; but through the prudence of them which are in authority the city shall be inhabited.

4 The power of the earth is in the hand of the Lord, and in due time he will set over it one that is profitable.

5 In the hand of God is the prosperity of man: and upon the person of the scribe shall he lay his honour.

6 Bear not hatred to thy neighbour for every wrong; and do nothing at all by injurious practices.

7 Pride is hateful before God and man: and by both doth one commit iniquity.

8 Because of unrighteous dealings, injuries, and riches got by deceit, the kingdom is translated from one people to another.

9 Why is earth and ashes proud? There is not a more wicked thing than a covetous man: for such an one setteth his own soul to sale; because while he liveth he casteth away his bowels.

10 The physician cutteth off a long disease; and he that is to day a king to morrow shall die.

11 For when a man is dead, he shall inherit creeping things, beasts, and worms.

12 The beginning of pride is when one departeth from God, and his heart is turned away from his Maker.

13 For pride is the beginning of sin, and he that hath it shall pour out abomination: and therefore the Lord brought upon them strange

calamities, and overthrew them utterly.

14 The Lord hath cast down the thrones of proud princes, and set up the meek in their stead.

15 The Lord hath plucked up the roots of the proud nations, and planted the lowly in their place.

16 The Lord overthrew countries of the heathen, and destroyed them to the foundations of the earth.

17 He took some of them away, and destroyed them, and hath made their memorial to cease from the earth.

18 Pride was not made for men, nor furious anger for them that are born of a woman.

19 They that fear the Lord are a sure seed, and they that love him an honourable plant: they that regard not the law are a dishonourable seed; they that transgress the commandments are a deceivable seed.

20 Among brethren he that is chief is honorable; so are they that fear the Lord in his eyes.

21 The fear of the Lord goeth before the obtaining of authority: but roughness and pride is the losing thereof.

22 Whether he be rich, noble, or poor, their glory is the fear of the Lord.

23 It is not meet to despise the poor man that hath understanding; neither is it convenient to magnify a sinful man.

24 Great men, and judges, and potentates, shall be honoured; yet is there none of them greater than he that feareth the Lord.

25 Unto the servant that is wise shall they that are free do service: and he that hath knowledge will not grudge when he is reformed.

26 Be not overwise in doing thy business; and boast not thyself in the time of thy distress.

27 Better is he that laboureth, and aboundeth in all things, than he that boasteth himself, and wanteth bread.

28 My son, glorify thy soul in meekness, and give it honour according to the dignity thereof.

29 Who will justify him that sinneth against his own soul? and who will honour him that dishonoureth his own life?

30 The poor man is honoured for his skill, and the rich man is honoured for his riches.

31 He that is honoured in poverty, how much more in riches? and he that is dishonourable in riches, how much more in poverty?

Ecclesiasticus 11

1 Wisdom lifteth up the head of him that is of low degree, and maketh him to sit among great men.

2 Commend not a man for his beauty; neither abhor a man for his outward appearance.

3 The bee is little among such as fly; but her fruit is the chief of sweet things.

4 Boast not of thy clothing and raiment, and exalt not thyself in the day of honour: for the works of the Lord are wonderful, and his works among men are hidden.

5 Many kings have sat down upon the ground; and one that was never thought of hath worn the crown.

6 Many mighty men have been greatly disgraced; and the honourable delivered into other men's hands.

7 Blame not before thou hast examined the truth: understand first, and then rebuke.

8 Answer not before thou hast heard the cause: neither interrupt men in the midst of their talk.

9 Strive not in a matter that concerneth thee not; and sit not in judgment with sinners.

10 My son, meddle not with many matters: for if thou meddle much, thou shalt not be innocent; and if thou follow after, thou shalt not obtain, neither shalt thou escape by fleeing.

11 There is one that laboureth, and taketh pains, and maketh haste, and is so much the more behind.

12 Again, there is another that is slow, and hath need of help, wanting ability, and full of poverty; yet the eye of the Lord looked upon him for good, and set him up from his low estate,

13 And lifted up his head from misery; so that many that saw it marvelled at him.

14 Prosperity and adversity, life and death, poverty and riches, come of the Lord.

15 Wisdom, knowledge, and understanding of the law, are of the Lord: love, and the way of good works, are from him.

16 Error and darkness had their beginning together with sinners: and evil shall wax old with them that glory therein.

17 The gift of the Lord remaineth with the godly, and his favour bringeth prosperity for ever.

18 There is that waxeth rich by his wariness and pinching, and this his the portion of his reward:

19 Whereas he saith, I have found rest, and now will eat continually of my goods; and yet he knoweth not what time shall come upon him, and

that he must leave those things to others, and die.

20 Be stedfast in thy covenant, and be conversant therein, and wax old in thy work.

21 Marvel not at the works of sinners; but trust in the Lord, and abide in thy labour: for it is an easy thing in the sight of the Lord on the sudden to make a poor man rich.

22 The blessing of the Lord is in the reward of the godly, and suddenly he maketh his blessing flourish.

23 Say not, What profit is there of my service? and what good things shall I have hereafter?

24 Again, say not, I have enough, and possess many things, and what evil shall I have hereafter?

25 In the day of prosperity there is a forgetfulness of affliction: and in the day of affliction there is no more remembrance of prosperity.

26 For it is an easy thing unto the Lord in the day of death to reward a man according to his ways.

27 The affliction of an hour maketh a man forget pleasure: and in his end his deeds shall be discovered.

28 Judge none blessed before his death: for a man shall be known in his children.

29 Bring not every man into thine house: for the deceitful man hath many trains.

30 Like as a partridge taken and kept in a cage, so is the heart of the proud; and like as a spy, watcheth he for thy fall:

31 For he lieth in wait, and turneth good into evil, and in things worthy praise will lay blame upon thee.

32 Of a spark of fire a heap of coals is kindled: and a sinful man layeth wait for blood.

33 Take heed of a mischievous man, for he worketh wickedness; lest he bring upon thee a perpetual blot.

34 Receive a stranger into thine house, and he will disturb thee, and turn thee out of thine own.

Ecclesiasticus 12

1 When thou wilt do good know to whom thou doest it; so shalt thou be thanked for thy benefits.

2 Do good to the godly man, and thou shalt find a recompence; and if not from him, yet from the most High.

3 There can no good come to him that is always occupied in evil, nor to him that giveth no alms.

4 Give to the godly man, and help not a sinner.

5 Do well unto him that is lowly, but give not to the ungodly: hold back thy bread, and give it not unto him, lest he overmaster thee thereby: for else thou shalt receive twice as much evil for all the good thou shalt have done unto him.

6 For the most High hateth sinners, and will repay vengeance unto the ungodly, and keepeth them against the mighty day of their punishment.

7 Give unto the good, and help not the sinner.

8 A friend cannot be known in prosperity: and an enemy cannot be hidden in adversity.

9 In the prosperity of a man enemies will be grieved: but in his adversity even a friend will depart.

10 Never trust thine enemy: for like as iron rusteth, so is his wickedness.

11 Though he humble himself, and go crouching, yet take good heed and beware of him, and thou shalt be unto him as if thou hadst wiped a lookingglass, and thou shalt know that his rust hath not been altogether wiped away.

12 Set him not by thee, lest, when he hath overthrown thee, he stand up in thy place; neither let him sit at thy right hand, lest he seek to take thy seat, and thou at the last remember my words, and be pricked therewith.

13 Who will pity a charmer that is bitten with a serpent, or any such as come nigh wild beasts?

14 So one that goeth to a sinner, and is defiled with him in his sins, who will pity?

15 For a while he will abide with thee, but if thou begin to fall, he will not tarry.

16 An enemy speaketh sweetly with his lips, but in his heart he imagineth how to throw thee into a pit: he will weep with his eyes, but if he find opportunity, he will not be satisfied with blood.

17 If adversity come upon thee, thou shalt find him there first; and though he pretend to help thee, yet shall he undermine thee.

18 He will shake his head, and clap his hands, and whisper much, and change his countenance.

Ecclesiasticus 13

1 He that toucheth pitch shall be defiled therewith; and he that hath fellowship with a proud man shall be like unto him.

2 Burden not thyself above thy power while thou livest; and have no fellowship with one that is mightier and richer than thyself: for how agree the kettle and the earthen pot together? for if the one be smitten against the other, it shall be broken.

3 The rich man hath done wrong, and yet he threateneth withal: the poor is wronged, and he must intreat also.

4 If thou be for his profit, he will use thee: but if thou have nothing, he will forsake thee.

5 If thou have any thing, he will live with thee: yea, he will make thee bare, and will not be sorry for it.

6 If he have need of thee, he will deceive thee, and smile upon thee, and put thee in hope; he will speak thee fair, and say, What wantest thou?

7 And he will shame thee by his meats, until he have drawn thee dry twice or thrice, and at the last he will laugh thee to scorn afterward, when he seeth thee, he will forsake thee, and shake his head at thee.

8 Beware that thou be not deceived and brought down in thy jollity.

9 If thou be invited of a mighty man, withdraw thyself, and so much the more will he invite thee.

10 Press thou not upon him, lest thou be put back; stand not far off, lest thou be forgotten.

11 Affect not to be made equal unto him in talk, and believe not his many words: for with much communication will he tempt thee, and smiling upon thee will get out thy secrets:

12 But cruelly he will lay up thy words, and will not spare to do thee hurt, and to put thee in prison.

13 Observe, and take good heed, for thou walkest in peril of thy overthrowing: when thou hearest these things, awake in thy sleep.

14 Love the Lord all thy life, and call upon him for thy salvation.

15 Every beast loveth his like, and every man loveth his neighbor.

16 All flesh consorteth according to kind, and a man will cleave to his like.

17 What fellowship hath the wolf with the lamb? so the sinner with the godly.

18 What agreement is there between the hyena and a dog? and what peace between the rich and the poor?

19 As the wild ass is the lion's prey in the wilderness: so the rich eat up the poor.

20 As the proud hate humility: so doth the rich abhor the poor.

21 A rich man beginning to fall is held up of his friends: but a poor man being down is thrust away by his friends.

22 When a rich man is fallen, he hath many helpers: he speaketh things not to be spoken, and yet men justify him: the poor man slipped, and yet they rebuked him too; he spake wisely, and could have no place.

23 When a rich man speaketh, every man holdeth his tongue, and, look, what he saith, they extol it to the clouds: but if the poor man speak, they say, What fellow is this? and if he stumble, they will help to overthrow him.

24 Riches are good unto him that hath no sin, and poverty is evil in the mouth of the ungodly.

25 The heart of a man changeth his countenance, whether it be for good or evil: and a merry heart maketh a cheerful countenance.

26 A cheerful countenance is a token of a heart that is in prosperity; and the finding out of parables is a wearisome labour of the mind.

Ecclesiasticus 14

1 Blessed is the man that hath not slipped with his mouth, and is not pricked with the multitude of sins.

2 Blessed is he whose conscience hath not condemned him, and who is not fallen from his hope in the Lord.

3 Riches are not comely for a niggard: and what should an envious man do with money?

4 He that gathereth by defrauding his own soul gathereth for others, that shall spend his goods riotously.

5 He that is evil to himself, to whom will he be good? he shall not take pleasure in his goods.

6 There is none worse than he that envieth himself; and this is a recompence of his wickedness.

7 And if he doeth good, he doeth it unwillingly; and at the last he will declare his wickedness.

8 The envious man hath a wicked eye; he turneth away his face, and despiseth men.

9 A covetous man's eye is not satisfied with his portion; and the iniquity of the wicked drieth up his soul.

10 A wicked eye envieth his bread, and he is a niggard at his table.

11 My son, according to thy ability do good to thyself, and give the Lord his due offering.

12 Remember that death will not be long in coming, and that the covenant of the grave is not shewed unto thee.

13 Do good unto thy friend before thou die, and according to thy ability stretch out thy hand and give to him.

14 Defraud not thyself of the good day, and let not the part of a good desire overpass thee.

15 Shalt thou not leave thy travails unto another? and thy labours to be divided by lot?

16 Give, and take, and sanctify thy soul; for there is no seeking of dainties in the grave.

17 All flesh waxeth old as a garment: for the covenant from the beginning is, Thou shalt die the death.

18 As of the green leaves on a thick tree, some fall, and some grow; so is the generation of flesh and blood, one cometh to an end, and another is born.

19 Every work rotteth and consumeth away, and the worker thereof shall go withal.

20 Blessed is the man that doth meditate good things in wisdom, and that reasoneth of holy things by his understanding.

21 He that considereth her ways in his heart shall also have understanding in her secrets.

22 Go after her as one that traceth, and lie in wait in her ways.

23 He that prieth in at her windows shall also hearken at her doors.

24 He that doth lodge near her house shall also fasten a pin in her walls.

25 He shall pitch his tent nigh unto her, and shall lodge in a lodging where good things are.

26 He shall set his children under her shelter, and shall lodge under her branches.

27 By her he shall be covered from heat, and in her glory shall he dwell.

Ecclesiasticus 15

1 He that feareth the Lord will do good, and he that hath the knowledge of the law shall obtain her.

2 And as a mother shall she meet him, and receive him as a wife married of a virgin.

3 With the bread of understanding shall she feed him, and give him the water of wisdom to drink.

4 He shall be stayed upon her, and shall not be moved; and shall rely upon her, and shall not be confounded.

5 She shall exalt him above his neighbours, and in the midst of the congregation shall she open his mouth.

6 He shall find joy and a crown of gladness, and she shall cause him to inherit an everlasting name.

7 But foolish men shall not attain unto her, and sinners shall not see her.

8 For she is far from pride, and men that are liars cannot remember her.

9 Praise is not seemly in the mouth of a sinner, for it was not sent him of the Lord.

10 For praise shall be uttered in wisdom, and the Lord will prosper it.

11 Say not thou, It is through the Lord that I fell away: for thou oughtest not to do the things that he hateth.

12 Say not thou, He hath caused me to err: for he hath no need of the sinful man.

13 The Lord hateth all abomination; and they that fear God love it not.

14 He himself made man from the beginning, and left him in the hand of his counsel;

15 If thou wilt, to keep the commandments, and to perform acceptable faithfulness.

16 He hath set fire and water before thee: stretch forth thy hand unto whether thou wilt.

17 Before man is life and death; and whether him liketh shall be given him.

18 For the wisdom of the Lord is great, and he is mighty in power, and beholdeth all things:

19 And his eyes are upon them that fear him, and he knoweth every work of man.

20 He hath commanded no man to do wickedly, neither hath he given any man licence to sin.

Ecclesiasticus 16

1 Desire not a multitude of unprofitable children, neither delight in ungodly sons.

2 Though they multiply, rejoice not in them, except the fear of the Lord be with them.

3 Trust not thou in their life, neither respect their multitude: for one that is just is better than a thousand; and better it is to die without children, than to have them that are ungodly.

4 For by one that hath understanding shall the city be replenished: but the kindred of the wicked shall speedily become desolate.

5 Many such things have I seen with mine eyes, and mine ear hath heard greater things than these.

6 In the congregation of the ungodly shall a fire be kindled; and in a rebellious nation wrath is set on fire.

7 He was not pacified toward the old giants, who fell away in the strength of their foolishness.

8 Neither spared he the place where Lot sojourned, but abhorred them for their pride.

9 He pitied not the people of perdition, who were taken away in their sins:

10 Nor the six hundred thousand footmen, who were gathered together in the hardness of their hearts.

11 And if there be one stiffnecked among the people, it is marvel if he escape unpunished: for mercy and wrath are with him; he is mighty to forgive, and to pour out displeasure.

12 As his mercy is great, so is his correction also: he judgeth a man according to his works

13 The sinner shall not escape with his spoils: and the patience of the godly shall not be frustrate.

14 Make way for every work of mercy: for every man shall find according to his works.

15 The Lord hardened Pharaoh, that he should not know him, that his

powerful works might be known to the world.

16 His mercy is manifest to every creature; and he hath separated his light from the darkness with an adamant.

17 Say not thou, I will hide myself from the Lord: shall any remember me from above? I shall not be remembered among so many people: for what is my soul among such an infinite number of creatures?

18 Behold, the heaven, and the heaven of heavens, the deep, and the earth, and all that therein is, shall be moved when he shall visit.

19 The mountains also and foundations of the earth be shaken with trembling, when the Lord looketh upon them.

20 No heart can think upon these things worthily: and who is able to conceive his ways?

21 It is a tempest which no man can see: for the most part of his works are hid.

22 Who can declare the works of his justice? or who can endure them? for his covenant is afar off, and the trial of all things is in the end.

23 He that wanteth understanding will think upon vain things: and a foolish man erring imagineth follies.

24 my son, hearken unto me, and learn knowledge, and mark my words with thy heart.

25 I will shew forth doctrine in weight, and declare his knowledge exactly.

26 The works of the Lord are done in judgment from the beginning: and from the time he made them he disposed the parts thereof.

27 He garnished his works for ever, and in his hand are the chief of them unto all generations: they neither labour, nor are weary, nor cease from their works.

28 None of them hindereth another, and they shall never disobey his word.

29 After this the Lord looked upon the earth, and filled it with his blessings.

30 With all manner of living things hath he covered the face thereof; and they shall return into it again.

Ecclesiasticus 17

1 The Lord created man of the earth, and turned him into it again.

2 He gave them few days, and a short time, and power also over the things therein.

3 He endued them with strength by themselves, and made them according to his image,

4 And put the fear of man upon all flesh, and gave him dominion over beasts and fowls.

5 They received the use of the five operations of the Lord, and in the

sixth place he imparted them understanding, and in the seventh speech, an interpreter of the cogitations thereof.

6 Counsel, and a tongue, and eyes, ears, and a heart, gave he them to understand.

7 Withal he filled them with the knowledge of understanding, and shewed them good and evil.

8 He set his eye upon their hearts, that he might shew them the greatness of his works.

9 He gave them to glory in his marvellous acts for ever, that they might declare his works with understanding.

10 And the elect shall praise his holy name.

11 Beside this he gave them knowledge, and the law of life for an heritage.

12 He made an everlasting covenant with them, and shewed them his judgments.

13 Their eyes saw the majesty of his glory, and their ears heard his glorious voice.

14 And he said unto them, Beware of all unrighteousness; and he gave every man commandment concerning his neighbour.

15 Their ways are ever before him, and shall not be hid from his eyes.

16 Every man from his youth is given to evil; neither could they make to themselves fleshy hearts for stony.

17 For in the division of the nations of the whole earth he set a ruler over every people; but Israel is the Lord's portion:

18 Whom, being his firstborn, he nourisheth with discipline, and giving him the light of his love doth not forsake him.

19 Therefore all their works are as the sun before him, and his eyes are continually upon their ways.

20 None of their unrighteous deeds are hid from him, but all their sins are before the Lord

21 But the Lord being gracious and knowing his workmanship, neither left nor forsook them, but spared them.

22 The alms of a man is as a signet with him, and he will keep the good deeds of man as the apple of the eye, and give repentance to his sons and daughters.

23 Afterwards he will rise up and reward them, and render their recompence upon their heads.

24 But unto them that repent, he granted them return, and comforted those that failed in patience.

25 Return unto the Lord, and forsake thy sins, make thy prayer before his face, and offend less.

26 Turn again to the most High, and turn away from iniquity: for he will lead thee out of darkness into the light of health, and hate thou abomination vehemently.

27 Who shall praise the most High in the grave, instead of them which live and give thanks?

28 Thanksgiving perisheth from the dead, as from one that is not: the living and sound in heart shall praise the Lord.

29 How great is the lovingkindness of the Lord our God, and his compassion unto such as turn unto him in holiness!

30 For all things cannot be in men, because the son of man is not immortal.

31 What is brighter than the sun? yet the light thereof faileth; and flesh and blood will imagine evil.

32 He vieweth the power of the height of heaven; and all men are but earth and ashes.

Ecclesiasticus 18

1 He that liveth for ever Hath created all things in general.

2 The Lord only is righteous, and there is none other but he,

3 Who governeth the world with the palm of his hand, and all things obey his will: for he is the King of all, by his power dividing holy things among them from profane.

4 To whom hath he given power to declare his works? and who shall find out his noble acts?

5 Who shall number the strength of his majesty? and who shall also tell out his mercies?

6 As for the wondrous works of the Lord, there may nothing be taken from them, neither may any thing be put unto them, neither can the ground of them be found out.

7 When a man hath done, then he beginneth; and when he leaveth off, then he shall be doubtful.

8 What is man, and whereto serveth he? what is his good, and what is his evil?

9 The number of a man's days at the most are an hundred years.

10 As a drop of water unto the sea, and a gravelstone in comparison of the sand; so are a thousand years to the days of eternity.

11 Therefore is God patient with them, and poureth forth his mercy upon them.

12 He saw and perceived their end to be evil; therefore he multiplied his compassion.

13 The mercy of man is toward his neighbour; but the mercy of the Lord is upon all flesh: he reproveth, and nurtureth, and teacheth and bringeth again, as a shepherd his flock.

14 He hath mercy on them that receive discipline, and that diligently seek after his judgments.

15 My son, blemish not thy good deeds, neither use uncomfortable words when thou givest any thing.

16 Shall not the dew asswage the heat? so is a word better than a gift.

17 Lo, is not a word better than a gift? but both are with a gracious man.

18 A fool will upbraid churlishly, and a gift of the envious consumeth the eyes.

19 Learn before thou speak, and use physick or ever thou be sick.

20 Before judgment examine thyself, and in the day of visitation thou shalt find mercy.

21 Humble thyself before thou be sick, and in the time of sins shew repentance.

22 Let nothing hinder thee to pay thy vow in due time, and defer not until death to be justified.

23 Before thou prayest, prepare thyself; and be not as one that tempteth the Lord.

24 Think upon the wrath that shall be at the end, and the time of vengeance, when he shall turn away his face.

25 When thou hast enough, remember the time of hunger: and when thou art rich, think upon poverty and need.

26 From the morning until the evening the time is changed, and all things are soon done before the Lord.

27 A wise man will fear in every thing, and in the day of sinning he will beware of offence: but a fool will not observe time.

28 Every man of understanding knoweth wisdom, and will give praise unto him that found her.

29 They that were of understanding in sayings became also wise themselves, and poured forth exquisite parables.

30 Go not after thy lusts, but refrain thyself from thine appetites.

31 If thou givest thy soul the desires that please her, she will make thee a laughingstock to thine enemies that malign thee.

32 Take not pleasure in much good cheer, neither be tied to the expence thereof.

33 Be not made a beggar by banqueting upon borrowing, when thou hast nothing in thy purse: for thou shalt lie in wait for thine own life, and be talked on.

Ecclesiasticus 19

1 A labouring man that A is given to drunkenness shall not be rich: and

he that contemneth small things shall fall by little and little.

2 Wine and women will make men of understanding to fall away: and he that cleaveth to harlots will become impudent.

3 Moths and worms shall have him to heritage, and a bold man shall be taken away.

4 He that is hasty to give credit is lightminded; and he that sinneth shall offend against his own soul.

5 Whoso taketh pleasure in wickedness shall be condemned: but he that resisteth pleasures crowneth his life.

6 He that can rule his tongue shall live without strife; and he that hateth babbling shall have less evil.

7 Rehearse not unto another that which is told unto thee, and thou shalt fare never the worse.

8 Whether it be to friend or foe, talk not of other men's lives; and if thou canst without offence, reveal them not.

9 For he heard and observed thee, and when time cometh he will hate thee.

10 If thou hast heard a word, let it die with thee; and be bold, it will not burst thee.

11 A fool travaileth with a word, as a woman in labour of a child.

12 As an arrow that sticketh in a man's thigh, so is a word within a fool's belly.

13 Admonish a friend, it may be he hath not done it: and if he have done it, that he do it no more.

14 Admonish thy friend, it may be he hath not said it: and if he have, that he speak it not again.

15 Admonish a friend: for many times it is a slander, and believe not every tale.

16 There is one that slippeth in his speech, but not from his heart; and who is he that hath not offended with his tongue?

17 Admonish thy neighbour before thou threaten him; and not being angry, give place to the law of the most High.

18 The fear of the Lord is the first step to be accepted of him, and wisdom obtaineth his love.

19 The knowledge of the commandments of the Lord is the doctrine of life: and they that do things that please him shall receive the fruit of the tree of immortality.

20 The fear of the Lord is all wisdom; and in all wisdom is the performance of the law, and the knowledge of his omnipotency.

21 If a servant say to his master, I will not do as it pleaseth thee; though afterward he do it, he angereth him that nourisheth him.

22 The knowledge of wickedness is not wisdom, neither at any time the counsel of sinners prudence.

23 There is a wickedness, and the same an abomination; and there is a fool wanting in wisdom.

24 He that hath small understanding, and feareth God, is better than one that hath much wisdom, and transgresseth the law of the most High.

25 There is an exquisite subtilty, and the same is unjust; and there is one that turneth aside to make judgment appear; and there is a wise man that justifieth in judgment.

26 There is a wicked man that hangeth down his head sadly; but inwardly he is full of deceit,

27 Casting down his countenance, and making as if he heard not: where he is not known, he will do thee a mischief before thou be aware.

28 And if for want of power he be hindered from sinning, yet when he findeth opportunity he will do evil.

29 A man may be known by his look, and one that hath understanding by his countenance, when thou meetest him.

30 A man's attire, and excessive laughter, and gait, shew what he is.

Ecclesiasticus 20

1 There is a reproof that is not comely: again, some man holdeth his tongue, and he is wise.

2 It is much better to reprove, than to be angry secretly: and he that confesseth his fault shall be preserved from hurt.

3 How good is it, when thou art reproved, to shew repentance! for so shalt thou escape wilful sin.

4 As is the lust of an eunuch to deflower a virgin; so is he that executeth judgment with violence.

5 There is one that keepeth silence, and is found wise: and another by much babbling becometh hateful.

6 Some man holdeth his tongue, because he hath not to answer: and some keepeth silence, knowing his time.

7 A wise man will hold his tongue till he see opportunity: but a babbler and a fool will regard no time.

8 He that useth many words shall be abhorred; and he that taketh to himself authority therein shall be hated.

9 There is a sinner that hath good success in evil things; and there is a gain that turneth to loss.

10 There is a gift that shall not profit thee; and there is a gift whose recompence is double.

11 There is an abasement because of glory; and there is that lifteth up his head from a low estate.

12 There is that buyeth much for a little, and repayeth it sevenfold.

13 A wise man by his words maketh him beloved: but the graces of fools shall be poured out.

14 The gift of a fool shall do thee no good when thou hast it; neither yet of the envious for his necessity: for he looketh to receive many things for one.

15 He giveth little, and upbraideth much; he openeth his mouth like a crier; to day he lendeth, and to morrow will he ask it again: such an one is to be hated of God and man.

16 The fool saith, I have no friends, I have no thank for all my good deeds, and they that eat my bread speak evil of me.

17 How oft, and of how many shall he be laughed to scorn! for he knoweth not aright what it is to have; and it is all one unto him as if he had it not.

18 To slip upon a pavement is better than to slip with the tongue: so the fall of the wicked shall come speedily.

19 An unseasonable tale will always be in the mouth of the unwise.

20 A wise sentence shall be rejected when it cometh out of a fool's mouth; for he will not speak it in due season.

21 There is that is hindered from sinning through want: and when he taketh rest, he shall not be troubled.

22 There is that destroyeth his own soul through bashfulness, and by accepting of persons overthroweth himself.

23 There is that for bashfulness promiseth to his friend, and maketh him his enemy for nothing.

24 A lie is a foul blot in a man, yet it is continually in the mouth of the untaught.

25 A thief is better than a man that is accustomed to lie: but they both shall have destruction to heritage.

26 The disposition of a liar is dishonourable, and his shame is ever with him.

27 A wise man shall promote himself to honour with his words: and he that hath understanding will please great men.

28 He that tilleth his land shall increase his heap: and he that pleaseth great men shall get pardon for iniquity.

29 Presents and gifts blind the eyes of the wise, and stop up his mouth that he cannot reprove.

30 Wisdom that is hid, and treasure that is hoarded up, what profit is in them both?

31 Better is he that hideth his folly than a man that hideth his wisdom.

32 Necessary patience in seeking the Lord is better than he that leadeth his life without a guide.

THE BOOK OF BARUCH

Baruch 1

1 And these are the words of the book, which Baruch the son of Nerias, the son of Maasias, the son of Sedecias, the son of Asadias, the son of Chelcias, wrote in Babylon,

2 In the fifth year, and in the seventh day of the month, what time as the Chaldeans took Jerusalem, and burnt it with fire.

3 And Baruch did read the words of this book in the hearing of Jechonias the son of Joachim king of Juda, and in the ears of all the people that came to hear the book,

4 And in the hearing of the nobles, and of the king's sons, and in the hearing of the elders, and of all the people, from the lowest unto the highest, even of all them that dwelt at Babylon by the river Sud.

5 Whereupon they wept, fasted, and prayed before the Lord.

6 They made also a collection of money according to every man's power:

7 And they sent it to Jerusalem unto Joachim the high priest, the son of Chelcias, son of Salom, and to the priests, and to all the people which were found with him at Jerusalem,

8 At the same time when he received the vessels of the house of the Lord, that were carried out of the temple, to return them into the land of Juda, the tenth day of the month Sivan, namely, silver vessels, which Sedecias the son of Josias king of Jada had made,

9 After that Nabuchodonosor king of Babylon had carried away Jechonias, and the princes, and the captives, and the mighty men, and the people of the land, from Jerusalem, and brought them unto Babylon.

10 And they said, Behold, we have sent you money to buy you burnt offerings, and sin offerings, and incense, and prepare ye manna, and offer upon the altar of the Lord our God;

11 And pray for the life of Nabuchodonosor king of Babylon, and for the life of Balthasar his son, that their days may be upon earth as the days of heaven:

12 And the Lord will give us strength, and lighten our eyes, and we shall live under the shadow of Nabuchodonosor king of Babylon, and under the shadow of Balthasar his son, and we shall serve them many days, and find favour in their sight.

13 Pray for us also unto the Lord our God, for we have sinned against the Lord our God; and unto this day the

fury of the Lord and his wrath is not turned from us.

14 And ye shall read this book which we have sent unto you, to make confession in the house of the Lord, upon the feasts and solemn days.

15 And ye shall say, To the Lord our God belongeth righteousness, but unto us the confusion of faces, as it is come to pass this day, unto them of Juda, and to the inhabitants of Jerusalem,

16 And to our kings, and to our princes, and to our priests, and to our prophets, and to our fathers:

17 For we have sinned before the Lord,

18 And disobeyed him, and have not hearkened unto the voice of the Lord our God, to walk in the commandments that he gave us openly:

19 Since the day that the Lord brought our forefathers out of the land of Egypt, unto this present day, we have been disobedient unto the Lord our God, and we have been negligent in not hearing his voice.

20 Wherefore the evils cleaved unto us, and the curse, which the Lord appointed by Moses his servant at the time that he brought our fathers out of the land of Egypt, to give us a land that floweth with milk and honey, like as it is to see this day.

21 Nevertheless we have not hearkened unto the voice of the Lord our God, according unto all the words of the prophets, whom he sent unto us:

22 But every man followed the imagination of his own wicked heart, to serve strange gods, and to do evil in the sight of the Lord our God.

Baruch 2

1 Therefore the Lord hath made good his word, which he pronounced against us, and against our judges that judged Israel, and against our kings, and against our princes, and against the men of Israel and Juda,

2 To bring upon us great plagues, such as never happened under the whole heaven, as it came to pass in Jerusalem, according to the things that were written in the law of Moses;

3 That a man should eat the flesh of his own son, and the flesh of his own daughter.

4 Moreover he hath delivered them to be in subjection to all the kingdoms that are round about us, to be as a reproach and desolation among all the people round about, where the Lord hath scattered them.

5 Thus we were cast down, and not exalted, because we have sinned against the Lord our God, and have not been obedient unto his voice.

6 To the Lord our God appertaineth righteousness: but unto us and to

our fathers open shame, as appeareth this day.

7 For all these plagues are come upon us, which the Lord hath pronounced against us

8 Yet have we not prayed before the Lord, that we might turn every one from the imaginations of his wicked heart.

9 Wherefore the Lord watched over us for evil, and the Lord hath brought it upon us: for the Lord is righteous in all his works which he hath commanded us.

10 Yet we have not hearkened unto his voice, to walk in the commandments of the Lord, that he hath set before us.

11 And now, O Lord God of Israel, that hast brought thy people out of the land of Egypt with a mighty hand, and high arm, and with signs, and with wonders, and with great power, and hast gotten thyself a name, as appeareth this day:

12 O Lord our God, we have sinned, we have done ungodly, we have dealt unrighteously in all thine ordinances.

13 Let thy wrath turn from us: for we are but a few left among the heathen, where thou hast scattered us.

14 Hear our prayers, O Lord, and our petitions, and deliver us for thine own sake, and give us favour in the sight of them which have led us away:

15 That all the earth may know that thou art the Lord our God, because Israel and his posterity is called by thy name.

16 O Lord, look down from thine holy house, and consider us: bow down thine ear, O Lord, to hear us.

17 Open thine eyes, and behold; for the dead that are in the graves, whose souls are taken from their bodies, will give unto the Lord neither praise nor righteousness:

18 But the soul that is greatly vexed, which goeth stooping and feeble, and the eyes that fail, and the hungry soul, will give thee praise and righteousness, O Lord.

19 Therefore we do not make our humble supplication before thee, O Lord our God, for the righteousness of our fathers, and of our kings.

20 For thou hast sent out thy wrath and indignation upon us, as thou hast spoken by thy servants the prophets, saying,

21 Thus saith the Lord, Bow down your shoulders to serve the king of Babylon: so shall ye remain in the land that I gave unto your fathers.

22 But if ye will not hear the voice of the Lord, to serve the king of Babylon,

23 I will cause to cease out of the cites of Judah, and from without

Jerusalem, the voice of mirth, and the voice of joy, the voice of the bridegroom, and the voice of the bride: and the whole land shall be desolate of inhabitants.

24 But we would not hearken unto thy voice, to serve the king of Babylon: therefore hast thou made good the words that thou spakest by thy servants the prophets, namely, that the bones of our kings, and the bones of our fathers, should be taken out of their place.

25 And, lo, they are cast out to the heat of the day, and to the frost of the night, and they died in great miseries by famine, by sword, and by pestilence.

26 And the house which is called by thy name hast thou laid waste, as it is to be seen this day, for the wickedness of the house of Israel and the house of Juda.

27 O Lord our God, thou hast dealt with us after all thy goodness, and according to all that great mercy of thine,

28 As thou spakest by thy servant Moses in the day when thou didst command him to write the law before the children of Israel, saying,

29 If ye will not hear my voice, surely this very great multitude shall be turned into a small number among the nations, where I will scatter them.

30 For I knew that they would not hear me, because it is a stiffnecked people: but in the land of their captivities they shall remember themselves.

31 And shall know that I am the Lord their God: for I will give them an heart, and ears to hear:

32 And they shall praise me in the land of their captivity, and think upon my name,

33 And return from their stiff neck, and from their wicked deeds: for they shall remember the way of their fathers, which sinned before the Lord.

34 And I will bring them again into the land which I promised with an oath unto their fathers, Abraham, Isaac, and Jacob, and they shall be lords of it: and I will increase them, and they shall not be diminished.

35 And I will make an everlasting covenant with them to be their God, and they shall be my people: and I will no more drive my people of Israel out of the land that I have given them.

Baruch 3

1 O Lord Almighty, God of Israel, the soul in anguish the troubled spirit, crieth unto thee.

2 Hear, O Lord, and have mercy; for thou art merciful: and have pity upon us, because we have sinned before thee.

3 For thou endurest for ever, and we perish utterly.

4 O Lord Almighty, thou God of Israel, hear now the prayers of the dead Israelites, and of their children, which have sinned before thee, and not hearkened unto the voice of thee their God: for the which cause these plagues cleave unto us.

5 Remember not the iniquities of our forefathers: but think upon thy power and thy name now at this time.

6 For thou art the Lord our God, and thee, O Lord, will we praise.

7 And for this cause thou hast put thy fear in our hearts, to the intent that we should call upon thy name, and praise thee in our captivity: for we have called to mind all the iniquity of our forefathers, that sinned before thee.

8 Behold, we are yet this day in our captivity, where thou hast scattered us, for a reproach and a curse, and to be subject to payments, according to all the iniquities of our fathers, which departed from the Lord our God.

9 Hear, Israel, the commandments of life: give ear to understand wisdom.

10 How happeneth it Israel, that thou art in thine enemies' land, that thou art waxen old in a strange country, that thou art defiled with the dead,

11 That thou art counted with them that go down into the grave?

12 Thou hast forsaken the fountain of wisdom.

13 For if thou hadst walked in the way of God, thou shouldest have dwelled in peace for ever.

14 Learn where is wisdom, where is strength, where is understanding; that thou mayest know also where is length of days, and life, where is the light of the eyes, and peace.

15 Who hath found out her place? or who hath come into her treasures?

16 Where are the princes of the heathen become, and such as ruled the beasts upon the earth;

17 They that had their pastime with the fowls of the air, and they that hoarded up silver and gold, wherein men trust, and made no end of their getting?

18 For they that wrought in silver, and were so careful, and whose works are unsearchable,

19 They are vanished and gone down to the grave, and others are come up in their steads.

20 Young men have seen light, and dwelt upon the earth: but the way of knowledge have they not known,

21 Nor understood the paths thereof, nor laid hold of it: their children were far off from that way.

22 It hath not been heard of in Chanaan, neither hath it been seen in Theman.

23 The Agarenes that seek wisdom upon earth, the merchants of Meran

and of Theman, the authors of fables, and searchers out of understanding; none of these have known the way of wisdom, or remember her paths.

24 O Israel, how great is the house of God! and how large is the place of his possession!

25 Great, and hath none end; high, and unmeasurable.

26 There were the giants famous from the beginning, that were of so great stature, and so expert in war.

27 Those did not the Lord choose, neither gave he the way of knowledge unto them:

28 But they were destroyed, because they had no wisdom, and perished through their own foolishness.

29 Who hath gone up into heaven, and taken her, and brought her down from the clouds?

30 Who hath gone over the sea, and found her, and will bring her for pure gold?

31 No man knoweth her way, nor thinketh of her path.

32 But he that knoweth all things knoweth her, and hath found her out with his understanding: he that prepared the earth for evermore hath filled it with fourfooted beasts:

33 He that sendeth forth light, and it goeth, calleth it again, and it obeyeth him with fear.

34 The stars shined in their watches, and rejoiced: when he calleth them, they say, Here we be; and so with cheerfulness they shewed light unto him that made them.

35 This is our God, and there shall none other be accounted of in comparison of him

36 He hath found out all the way of knowledge, and hath given it unto Jacob his servant, and to Israel his beloved.

37 Afterward did he shew himself upon earth, and conversed with men.

Baruch 4

1 This is the book of the commandments of God, and the law that endureth for ever: all they that keep it shall come to life; but such as leave it shall die.

2 Turn thee, O Jacob, and take hold of it: walk in the presence of the light thereof, that thou mayest be illuminated.

3 Give not thine honour to another, nor the things that are profitable unto thee to a strange nation.

4 O Israel, happy are we: for things that are pleasing to God are made known unto us.

5 Be of good cheer, my people, the memorial of Israel.

6 Ye were sold to the nations, not for your destruction: but because ye moved God to wrath, ye were delivered unto the enemies.

7 For ye provoked him that made you by sacrificing unto devils, and not to God.

8 Ye have forgotten the everlasting God, that brought you up; and ye have grieved Jerusalem, that nursed you.

9 For when she saw the wrath of God coming upon you, she said, Hearken, O ye that dwell about Sion: God hath brought upon me great mourning;

10 For I saw the captivity of my sons and daughters, which the Everlasting brought upon them.

11 With joy did I nourish them; but sent them away with weeping and mourning.

12 Let no man rejoice over me, a widow, and forsaken of many, who for the sins of my children am left desolate; because they departed from the law of God.

13 They knew not his statutes, nor walked in the ways of his commandments, nor trod in the paths of discipline in his righteousness.

14 Let them that dwell about Sion come, and remember ye the captivity of my sons and daughters, which the Everlasting hath brought upon them.

15 For he hath brought a nation upon them from far, a shameless nation, and of a strange language, who neither reverenced old man, nor pitied child.

16 These have carried away the dear beloved children of the widow, and left her that was alone desolate without daughters.

17 But what can I help you?

18 For he that brought these plagues upon you will deliver you from the hands of your enemies.

19 Go your way, O my children, go your way: for I am left desolate.

20 I have put off the clothing of peace, and put upon me the sackcloth of my prayer: I will cry unto the Everlasting in my days.

21 Be of good cheer, O my children, cry unto the Lord, and he will deliver you from the power and hand of the enemies.

22 For my hope is in the Everlasting, that he will save you; and joy is come unto me from the Holy One, because of the mercy which shall soon come unto you from the Everlasting our Saviour.

23 For I sent you out with mourning and weeping: but God will give you to me again with joy and gladness for ever.

24 Like as now the neighbours of Sion have seen your captivity: so shall they see shortly your salvation

from our God which shall come upon you with great glory, and brightness of the Everlasting.

25 My children, suffer patiently the wrath that is come upon you from God: for thine enemy hath persecuted thee; but shortly thou shalt see his destruction, and shalt tread upon his neck.

26 My delicate ones have gone rough ways, and were taken away as a flock caught of the enemies.

27 Be of good comfort, O my children, and cry unto God: for ye shall be remembered of him that brought these things upon you.

28 For as it was your mind to go astray from God: so, being returned, seek him ten times more.

29 For he that hath brought these plagues upon you shall bring you everlasting joy with your salvation.

30 Take a good heart, O Jerusalem: for he that gave thee that name will comfort thee.

31 Miserable are they that afflicted thee, and rejoiced at thy fall.

32 Miserable are the cities which thy children served: miserable is she that received thy sons.

33 For as she rejoiced at thy ruin, and was glad of thy fall: so shall she be grieved for her own desolation.

34 For I will take away the rejoicing of her great multitude, and her pride shall be turned into mourning.

35 For fire shall come upon her from the Everlasting, long to endure; and she shall be inhabited of devils for a great time.

36 O Jerusalem, look about thee toward the east, and behold the joy that cometh unto thee from God.

37 Lo, thy sons come, whom thou sentest away, they come gathered together from the east to the west by the word of the Holy One, rejoicing in the glory of God.

Baruch 5

1 Put off, O Jerusalem, the garment of mourning and affliction, and put on the comeliness of the glory that cometh from God for ever.

2 Cast about thee a double garment of the righteousness which cometh from God; and set a diadem on thine head of the glory of the Everlasting.

3 For God will shew thy brightness unto every country under heaven.

4 For thy name shall be called of God for ever The peace of righteousness, and The glory of God's worship.

5 Arise, O Jerusalem, and stand on high, and look about toward the east, and behold thy children gathered from the west unto the east by the word of the Holy One, rejoicing in the remembrance of God.

6 For they departed from thee on foot, and were led away of their enemies: but God bringeth them unto thee exalted with glory, as children of the kingdom.

7 For God hath appointed that every high hill, and banks of long continuance, should be cast down, and valleys filled up, to make even the ground, that Israel may go safely in the glory of God,

8 Moreover even the woods and every sweetsmelling tree shall overshadow Israel by the commandment of God.

9 For God shall lead Israel with joy in the light of his glory with the mercy and righteousness that cometh from him.

LETTER OF JEREMIAH

1 A copy of an epistle, which Jeremy sent unto them which were to be led captives into Babylon by the king of the Babylonians, to certify them, as it was commanded him of God.

2 Because of the sins which ye have committed before God, ye shall be led away captives into Babylon by Nabuchodonosor king of the Babylonians.

3 So when ye be come unto Babylon, ye shall remain there many years, and for a long season, namely, seven generations: and after that I will bring you away peaceably from thence.

4 Now shall ye see in Babylon gods of silver, and of gold, and of wood, borne upon shoulders, which cause the nations to fear.

5 Beware therefore that ye in no wise be like to strangers, neither be ye and of them, when ye see the multitude before them and behind them, worshipping them.

6 But say ye in your hearts, O Lord, we must worship thee.

7 For mine angel is with you, and I myself caring for your souls.

8 As for their tongue, it is polished by the workman, and they themselves are gilded and laid over with silver; yet are they but false, and cannot speak.

9 And taking gold, as it were for a virgin that loveth to go gay, they make crowns for the heads of their gods.

10 Sometimes also the priests convey from their gods gold and silver, and bestow it upon themselves.

11 Yea, they will give thereof to the common harlots, and deck them as men with garments, being gods of silver, and gods of gold, and wood.

12 Yet cannot these gods save themselves from rust and moth, though they be covered with purple raiment.

13 They wipe their faces because of the dust of the temple, when there is much upon them.

14 And he that cannot put to death one that offendeth him holdeth a sceptre, as though he were a judge of the country.

15 He hath also in his right hand a dagger and an ax: but cannot deliver himself from war and thieves.

16 Whereby they are known not to be gods: therefore fear them not.

17 For like as a vessel that a man useth is nothing worth when it is broken; even so it is with their gods: when they be set up in the temple, their eyes be full of dust through the feet of them that come in.

18 And as the doors are made sure on every side upon him that offendeth the king, as being committed to suffer death: even so the priests make fast their temples with doors, with locks, and bars, lest their gods be spoiled with robbers.

19 They light them candles, yea, more than for themselves, whereof they cannot see one.

20 They are as one of the beams of the temple, yet they say their hearts are gnawed upon by things creeping out of the earth; and when they eat them and their clothes, they feel it not.

21 Their faces are blacked through the smoke that cometh out of the temple.

22 Upon their bodies and heads sit bats, swallows, and birds, and the cats also.

23 By this ye may know that they are no gods: therefore fear them not.

24 Notwithstanding the gold that is about them to make them beautiful, except they wipe off the rust, they will not shine: for neither when they were molten did they feel it.

25 The things wherein there is no breath are bought for a most high price.

26 They are borne upon shoulders, having no feet whereby they declare unto men that they be nothing worth.

27 They also that serve them are ashamed: for if they fall to the ground at any time, they cannot rise up again of themselves: neither, if one set them upright, can they move of themselves: neither, if they be bowed down, can they make themselves straight: but they set gifts before them as unto dead men.

28 As for the things that are sacrificed unto them, their priests sell and abuse; in like manner their wives lay up part thereof in salt; but unto the poor and impotent they give nothing of it.

29 Menstruous women and women in childbed eat their sacrifices: by these things ye may know that they are no gods: fear them not.

30 For how can they be called gods? because women set meat before the gods of silver, gold, and wood.

31 And the priests sit in their temples, having their clothes rent, and their heads and beards shaven, and nothing upon their heads.

32 They roar and cry before their gods, as men do at the feast when one is dead.

33 The priests also take off their garments, and clothe their wives and children.

34 Whether it be evil that one doeth unto them, or good, they are not able to recompense it: they can neither set up a king, nor put him down.

35 In like manner, they can neither give riches nor money: though a man make a vow unto them, and keep it not, they will not require it.

36 They can save no man from death, neither deliver the weak from the mighty.

37 They cannot restore a blind man to his sight, nor help any man in his distress.

38 They can shew no mercy to the widow, nor do good to the fatherless.

39 Their gods of wood, and which are overlaid with gold and silver, are like the stones that be hewn out of the mountain: they that worship them shall be confounded.

40 How should a man then think and say that they are gods, when even the Chaldeans themselves dishonour them?

41 Who if they shall see one dumb that cannot speak, they bring him, and intreat Bel that he may speak, as though he were able to understand.

42 Yet they cannot understand this themselves, and leave them: for they have no knowledge.

43 The women also with cords about them, sitting in the ways, burn bran for perfume: but if any of them, drawn by some that passeth by, lie with him, she reproacheth her fellow, that she was not thought as worthy as herself, nor her cord broken.

44 Whatsoever is done among them is false: how may it then be thought or said that they are gods?

45 They are made of carpenters and goldsmiths: they can be nothing else than the workmen will have them to be.

46 And they themselves that made them can never continue long; how should then the things that are made of them be gods?

47 For they left lies and reproaches to them that come after.

48 For when there cometh any war or plague upon them, the priests consult with themselves, where they may be hidden with them.

49 How then cannot men perceive that they be no gods, which can neither save themselves from war, nor from plague?

50 For seeing they be but of wood, and overlaid with silver and gold, it shall be known hereafter that they are false:

51 And it shall manifestly appear to all nations and kings that they are no gods, but the works of men's hands, and that there is no work of God in them.

52 Who then may not know that they are no gods?

53 For neither can they set up a king in the land, nor give rain unto men.

54 Neither can they judge their own cause, nor redress a wrong, being unable: for they are as crows between heaven and earth.

55 Whereupon when fire falleth upon the house of gods of wood, or laid over with gold or silver, their priests will flee away, and escape; but they themselves shall be burned asunder like beams.

56 Moreover they cannot withstand any king or enemies: how can it then be thought or said that they be gods?

57 Neither are those gods of wood, and laid over with silver or gold, able to escape either from thieves or robbers.

58 Whose gold, and silver, and garments wherewith they are clothed, they that are strong take, and go away withal: neither are they able to help themselves.

59 Therefore it is better to be a king that sheweth his power, or else a profitable vessel in an house, which the owner shall have use of, than such false gods; or to be a door in an house, to keep such things therein, than such false gods. or a pillar of wood in a a palace, than such false gods.

60 For sun, moon, and stars, being bright and sent to do their offices, are obedient.

61 In like manner the lightning when it breaketh forth is easy to be seen;

and after the same manner the wind bloweth in every country.

62 And when God commandeth the clouds to go over the whole world, they do as they are bidden.

63 And the fire sent from above to consume hills and woods doeth as it is commanded: but these are like unto them neither in shew nor power.

64 Wherefore it is neither to be supposed nor said that they are gods, seeing, they are able neither to judge causes, nor to do good unto men.

65 Knowing therefore that they are no gods, fear them not,

66 For they can neither curse nor bless kings:

67 Neither can they shew signs in the heavens among the heathen, nor shine as the sun, nor give light as the moon.

68 The beasts are better than they: for they can get under a cover and help themselves.

69 It is then by no means manifest unto us that they are gods: therefore fear them not.

70 For as a scarecrow in a garden of cucumbers keepeth nothing: so are their gods of wood, and laid over with silver and gold.

71 And likewise their gods of wood, and laid over with silver and gold, are like to a white thorn in an

orchard, that every bird sitteth upon; as also to a dead body, that is east into the dark.

72 And ye shall know them to be no gods by the bright purple that rotteth upon them: and they themselves afterward shall be eaten, and shall be a reproach in the country.

73 Better therefore is the just man that hath none idols: for he shall be far from reproach.

PRAYER OF AZARIAH

1 And they walked in the midst of the fire, praising God, and blessing the Lord.

2 Then Azarias stood up, and prayed on this manner; and opening his mouth in the midst of the fire said,

3 Blessed art thou, O Lord God of our fathers: thy name is worthy to be praised and glorified for evermore:

4 For thou art righteous in all the things that thou hast done to us: yea, true are all thy works, thy ways are right, and all thy judgments truth.

5 In all the things that thou hast brought upon us, and upon the holy city of our fathers, even Jerusalem, thou hast executed true judgment: for according to truth and judgment didst thou bring all these things upon us because of our sins.

6 For we have sinned and committed iniquity, departing from thee.

7 In all things have we trespassed, and not obeyed thy commandments, nor kept them, neither done as thou hast commanded us, that it might go well with us.

8 Wherefore all that thou hast brought upon us, and every thing that thou hast done to us, thou hast done in true judgment.

9 And thou didst deliver us into the hands of lawless enemies, most hateful forsakers of God, and to an unjust king, and the most wicked in all the world.

10 And now we cannot open our mouths, we are become a shame and reproach to thy servants; and to them that worship thee.

11 Yet deliver us not up wholly, for thy name's sake, neither disannul thou thy covenant:

12 And cause not thy mercy to depart from us, for thy beloved Abraham's sake, for thy servant Issac's sake, and for thy holy Israel's sake;

13 To whom thou hast spoken and promised, that thou wouldest multiply their seed as the stars of heaven, and as the sand that lieth upon the seashore.

14 For we, O Lord, are become less than any nation, and be kept under this day in all the world because of our sins.

15 Neither is there at this time prince, or prophet, or leader, or burnt offering, or sacrifice, or oblation, or incense, or place to sacrifice before thee, and to find mercy.

16 Nevertheless in a contrite heart and an humble spirit let us be accepted.

17 Like as in the burnt offerings of rams and bullocks, and like as in ten

thousands of fat lambs: so let our sacrifice be in thy sight this day, and grant that we may wholly go after thee: for they shall not be confounded that put their trust in thee.

18 And now we follow thee with all our heart, we fear thee, and seek thy face.

19 Put us not to shame: but deal with us after thy lovingkindness, and according to the multitude of thy mercies.

20 Deliver us also according to thy marvellous works, and give glory to thy name, O Lord: and let all them that do thy servants hurt be ashamed;

21 And let them be confounded in all their power and might, and let their strength be broken;

22 And let them know that thou art God, the only God, and glorious over the whole world.

23 And the king's servants, that put them in, ceased not to make the oven hot with rosin, pitch, tow, and small wood;

24 So that the flame streamed forth above the furnace forty and nine cubits.

25 And it passed through, and burned those Chaldeans it found about the furnace.

26 But the angel of the Lord came down into the oven together with Azarias and his fellows, and smote the flame of the fire out of the oven;

27 And made the midst of the furnace as it had been a moist whistling wind, so that the fire touched them not at all, neither hurt nor troubled them.

28 Then the three, as out of one mouth, praised, glorified, and blessed, God in the furnace, saying,

29 Blessed art thou, O Lord God of our fathers: and to be praised and exalted above all for ever.

30 And blessed is thy glorious and holy name: and to be praised and exalted above all for ever.

31 Blessed art thou in the temple of thine holy glory: and to be praised and glorified above all for ever.

32 Blessed art thou that beholdest the depths, and sittest upon the cherubims: and to be praised and exalted above all for ever.

33 Blessed art thou on the glorious throne of thy kingdom: and to be praised and glorified above all for ever.

34 Blessed art thou in the firmament of heaven: and above all to be praised and glorified for ever.

35 O all ye works of the Lord, bless ye the Lord: praise and exalt him above all for ever,

36 O ye heavens, bless ye the Lord: praise and exalt him above all for ever.

37 O ye angels of the Lord, bless ye the Lord: praise and exalt him above all for ever.

38 O all ye waters that be above the heaven, bless ye the Lord: praise and exalt him above all for ever.

39 O all ye powers of the Lord, bless ye the Lord: praise and exalt him above all for ever.

40 O ye sun and moon, bless ye the Lord: praise and exalt him above all for ever.

41 O ye stars of heaven, bless ye the Lord: praise and exalt him above all for ever.

42 O every shower and dew, bless ye the Lord: praise and exalt him above all for ever.

43 O all ye winds, bless ye the Lord: praise and exalt him above all for ever,

44 O ye fire and heat, bless ye the Lord: praise and exalt him above all for ever.

45 O ye winter and summer, bless ye the Lord: praise and exalt him above all for ever.

46 O ye dews and storms of snow, bless ye the Lord: praise and exalt him above all for ever.

47 O ye nights and days, bless ye the Lord: bless and exalt him above all for ever.

48 O ye light and darkness, bless ye the Lord: praise and exalt him above all for ever.

49 O ye ice and cold, bless ye the Lord: praise and exalt him above all for ever.

50 O ye frost and snow, bless ye the Lord: praise and exalt him above all for ever.

51 O ye lightnings and clouds, bless ye the Lord: praise and exalt him above all for ever.

52 O let the earth bless the Lord: praise and exalt him above all for ever.

53 O ye mountains and little hills, bless ye the Lord: praise and exalt him above all for ever.

54 O all ye things that grow in the earth, bless ye the Lord: praise and exalt him above all for ever.

55 O ye mountains, bless ye the Lord: Praise and exalt him above all for ever.

56 O ye seas and rivers, bless ye the Lord: praise and exalt him above all for ever.

57 O ye whales, and all that move in the waters, bless ye the Lord: praise and exalt him above all for ever.

58 O all ye fowls of the air, bless ye the Lord: praise and exalt him above all for ever.

59 O all ye beasts and cattle, bless ye the Lord: praise and exalt him above all for ever.

60 O ye children of men, bless ye the Lord: praise and exalt him above all for ever.

61 O Israel, bless ye the Lord: praise and exalt him above all for ever.

62 O ye priests of the Lord, bless ye the Lord: praise and exalt him above all for ever.

63 O ye servants of the Lord, bless ye the Lord: praise and exalt him above all for ever.

64 O ye spirits and souls of the righteous, bless ye the Lord: praise and exalt him above all for ever.

65 O ye holy and humble men of heart, bless ye the Lord: praise and exalt him above all for ever.

66 O Ananias, Azarias, and Misael, bless ye the Lord: praise and exalt him above all for ever: for he hath delivered us from hell, and saved us from the hand of death, and delivered us out of the midst of the furnace and burning flame: even out of the midst of the fire hath he delivered us.

67 O give thanks unto the Lord, because he is gracious: for his mercy endureth for ever.

68 O all ye that worship the Lord, bless the God of gods, praise him, and give him thanks: for his mercy endureth for ever.

BOOK OF SUSANNA

1 There dwelt a man in Babylon, called Joacim:

2 And he took a wife, whose name was Susanna, the daughter of Chelcias, a very fair woman, and one that feared the Lord.

3 Her parents also were righteous, and taught their daughter according to the law of Moses.

4 Now Joacim was a great rich man, and had a fair garden joining unto his house: and to him resorted the Jews; because he was more honourable than all others.

5 The same year were appointed two of the ancients of the people to be judges, such as the Lord spake of, that wickedness came from Babylon from ancient judges, who seemed to govern the people.

6 These kept much at Joacim's house: and all that had any suits in law came unto them.

7 Now when the people departed away at noon, Susanna went into her husband's garden to walk.

8 And the two elders saw her going in every day, and walking; so that their lust was inflamed toward her.

9 And they perverted their own mind, and turned away their eyes, that they might not look unto heaven, nor remember just judgments.

10 And albeit they both were wounded with her love, yet durst not one shew another his grief.

11 For they were ashamed to declare their lust, that they desired to have to do with her.

12 Yet they watched diligently from day to day to see her.

13 And the one said to the other, Let us now go home: for it is dinner time.

14 So when they were gone out, they parted the one from the other, and turning back again they came to the same place; and after that they had asked one another the cause, they acknowledged their lust: then appointed they a time both together, when they might find her alone.

15 And it fell out, as they watched a fit time, she went in as before with two maids only, and she was desirous to wash herself in the garden: for it was hot.

16 And there was no body there save the two elders, that had hid themselves, and watched her.

17 Then she said to her maids, Bring me oil and washing balls, and shut the garden doors, that I may wash me.

18 And they did as she bade them, and shut the garden doors, and went out themselves at privy doors to fetch the things that she had

commanded them: but they saw not the elders, because they were hid.

19 Now when the maids were gone forth, the two elders rose up, and ran unto her, saying,

20 Behold, the garden doors are shut, that no man can see us, and we are in love with thee; therefore consent unto us, and lie with us.

21 If thou wilt not, we will bear witness against thee, that a young man was with thee: and therefore thou didst send away thy maids from thee.

22 Then Susanna sighed, and said, I am straitened on every side: for if I do this thing, it is death unto me: and if I do it not I cannot escape your hands.

23 It is better for me to fall into your hands, and not do it, than to sin in the sight of the Lord.

24 With that Susanna cried with a loud voice: and the two elders cried out against her.

25 Then ran the one, and opened the garden door.

26 So when the servants of the house heard the cry in the garden, they rushed in at the privy door, to see what was done unto her.

27 But when the elders had declared their matter, the servants were greatly ashamed: for there was never such a report made of Susanna.

28 And it came to pass the next day, when the people were assembled to her husband Joacim, the two elders came also full of mischievous imagination against Susanna to put her to death;

29 And said before the people, Send for Susanna, the daughter of Chelcias, Joacim's wife. And so they sent.

30 So she came with her father and mother, her children, and all her kindred.

31 Now Susanna was a very delicate woman, and beauteous to behold.

32 And these wicked men commanded to uncover her face, (for she was covered) that they might be filled with her beauty.

33 Therefore her friends and all that saw her wept.

34 Then the two elders stood up in the midst of the people, and laid their hands upon her head.

35 And she weeping looked up toward heaven: for her heart trusted in the Lord.

36 And the elders said, As we walked in the garden alone, this woman came in with two maids, and shut the garden doors, and sent the maids away.

37 Then a young man, who there was hid, came unto her, and lay with her.

38 Then we that stood in a corner of the garden, seeing this wickedness, ran unto them.

39 And when we saw them together, the man we could not hold: for he was stronger than we, and opened the door, and leaped out.

40 But having taken this woman, we asked who the young man was, but she would not tell us: these things do we testify.

41 Then the assembly believed them as those that were the elders and judges of the people: so they condemned her to death.

42 Then Susanna cried out with a loud voice, and said, O everlasting God, that knowest the secrets, and knowest all things before they be:

43 Thou knowest that they have borne false witness against me, and, behold, I must die; whereas I never did such things as these men have maliciously invented against me.

44 And the Lord heard her voice.

45 Therefore when she was led to be put to death, the Lord raised up the holy spirit of a young youth whose name was Daniel:

46 Who cried with a loud voice, I am clear from the blood of this woman.

47 Then all the people turned them toward him, and said, What mean these words that thou hast spoken?

48 So he standing in the midst of them said, Are ye such fools, ye sons of Israel, that without examination or knowledge of the truth ye have condemned a daughter of Israel?

49 Return again to the place of judgment: for they have borne false witness against her.

50 Wherefore all the people turned again in haste, and the elders said unto him, Come, sit down among us, and shew it us, seeing God hath given thee the honour of an elder.

51 Then said Daniel unto them, Put these two aside one far from another, and I will examine them.

52 So when they were put asunder one from another, he called one of them, and said unto him, O thou that art waxen old in wickedness, now thy sins which thou hast committed aforetime are come to light.

53 For thou hast pronounced false judgment and hast condemned the innocent and hast let the guilty go free; albeit the Lord saith, The innocent and righteous shalt thou not slay.

54 Now then, if thou hast seen her, tell me, Under what tree sawest thou them companying together? Who answered, Under a mastick tree.

55 And Daniel said, Very well; thou hast lied against thine own head; for even now the angel of God hath

received the sentence of God to cut thee in two.

56 So he put him aside, and commanded to bring the other, and said unto him, O thou seed of Chanaan, and not of Juda, beauty hath deceived thee, and lust hath perverted thine heart.

57 Thus have ye dealt with the daughters of Israel, and they for fear companied with you: but the daughter of Juda would not abide your wickedness.

58 Now therefore tell me, Under what tree didst thou take them companying together? Who answered, Under an holm tree.

59 Then said Daniel unto him, Well; thou hast also lied against thine own head: for the angel of God waiteth with the sword to cut thee in two, that he may destroy you.

60 With that all the assembly cried out with a loud voice, and praised God, who saveth them that trust in him.

61 And they arose against the two elders, for Daniel had convicted them of false witness by their own mouth:

62 And according to the law of Moses they did unto them in such sort as they maliciously intended to do to their neighbour: and they put them to death. Thus the innocent blood was saved the same day.

63 Therefore Chelcias and his wife praised God for their daughter Susanna, with Joacim her husband, and all the kindred, because there was no dishonesty found in her.

64 From that day forth was Daniel had in great reputation in the sight of the people.

BEL AND THE DRAGON

1 And king Astyages was gathered to his fathers, and Cyrus of Persia received his kingdom.

2 And Daniel conversed with the king, and was honoured above all his friends.

3 Now the Babylons had an idol, called Bel, and there were spent upon him every day twelve great measures of fine flour, and forty sheep, and six vessels of wine.

4 And the king worshipped it and went daily to adore it: but Daniel worshipped his own God. And the king said unto him, Why dost not thou worship Bel?

5 Who answered and said, Because I may not worship idols made with hands, but the living God, who hath created the heaven and the earth, and hath sovereignty over all flesh.

6 Then said the king unto him, Thinkest thou not that Bel is a living God? seest thou not how much he eateth and drinketh every day?

7 Then Daniel smiled, and said, O king, be not deceived: for this is but clay within, and brass without, and did never eat or drink any thing.

8 So the king was wroth, and called for his priests, and said unto them, If ye tell me not who this is that devoureth these expences, ye shall die.

9 But if ye can certify me that Bel devoureth them, then Daniel shall die: for he hath spoken blasphemy against Bel. And Daniel said unto the king, Let it be according to thy word.

10 Now the priests of Bel were threescore and ten, beside their wives and children. And the king went with Daniel into the temple of Bel.

11 So Bel's priests said, Lo, we go out: but thou, O king, set on the meat, and make ready the wine, and shut the door fast and seal it with thine own signet;

12 And to morrow when thou comest in, if thou findest not that Bel hath eaten up all, we will suffer death: or else Daniel, that speaketh falsely against us.

13 And they little regarded it: for under the table they had made a privy entrance, whereby they entered in continually, and consumed those things.

14 So when they were gone forth, the king set meats before Bel. Now Daniel had commanded his servants to bring ashes, and those they strewed throughout all the temple in the presence of the king alone: then went they out, and shut the door, and sealed it with the king's signet, and so departed.

15 Now in the night came the priests with their wives and children, as they were wont to do, and did eat and drink up all.

16 In the morning betime the king arose, and Daniel with him.

17 And the king said, Daniel, are the seals whole? And he said, Yea, O king, they be whole.

18 And as soon as he had opened the dour, the king looked upon the table, and cried with a loud voice, Great art thou, O Bel, and with thee is no deceit at all.

19 Then laughed Daniel, and held the king that he should not go in, and said, Behold now the pavement, and mark well whose footsteps are these.

20 And the king said, I see the footsteps of men, women, and children. And then the king was angry,

21 And took the priests with their wives and children, who shewed him the privy doors, where they came in, and consumed such things as were upon the table.

22 Therefore the king slew them, and delivered Bel into Daniel's power, who destroyed him and his temple.

23 And in that same place there was a great dragon, which they of Babylon worshipped.

24 And the king said unto Daniel, Wilt thou also say that this is of brass? lo, he liveth, he eateth and drinketh; thou canst not say that he is no living god: therefore worship him.

25 Then said Daniel unto the king, I will worship the Lord my God: for he is the living God.

26 But give me leave, O king, and I shall slay this dragon without sword or staff. The king said, I give thee leave.

27 Then Daniel took pitch, and fat, and hair, and did seethe them together, and made lumps thereof: this he put in the dragon's mouth, and so the dragon burst in sunder: and Daniel said, Lo, these are the gods ye worship.

28 When they of Babylon heard that, they took great indignation, and conspired against the king, saying, The king is become a Jew, and he hath destroyed Bel, he hath slain the dragon, and put the priests to death.

29 So they came to the king, and said, Deliver us Daniel, or else we will destroy thee and thine house.

30 Now when the king saw that they pressed him sore, being constrained, he delivered Daniel unto them:

31 Who cast him into the lions' den: where he was six days.

32 And in the den there were seven lions, and they had given them every day two carcases, and two sheep: which then were not given to them,

to the intent they might devour Daniel.

33 Now there was in Jewry a prophet, called Habbacuc, who had made pottage, and had broken bread in a bowl, and was going into the field, for to bring it to the reapers.

34 But the angel of the Lord said unto Habbacuc, Go, carry the dinner that thou hast into Babylon unto Daniel, who is in the lions' den.

35 And Habbacuc said, Lord, I never saw Babylon; neither do I know where the den is.

36 Then the angel of the Lord took him by the crown, and bare him by the hair of his head, and through the vehemency of his spirit set him in Babylon over the den.

37 And Habbacuc cried, saying, O Daniel, Daniel, take the dinner which God hath sent thee.

38 And Daniel said, Thou hast remembered me, O God: neither hast thou forsaken them that seek thee and love thee.

39 So Daniel arose, and did eat: and the angel of the Lord set Habbacuc in his own place again immediately.

40 Upon the seventh day the king went to bewail Daniel: and when he came to the den, he looked in, and behold, Daniel was sitting.

41 Then cried the king with a loud voice, saying, Great art Lord God of Daniel, and there is none other beside thee.

42 And he drew him out, and cast those that were the cause of his destruction into the den: and they were devoured in a moment before his face.

PRAYER OF MANASSEH

1 O Lord, Almighty God of our fathers, Abraham, Isaac, and Jacob, and of their righteous seed; who hast made heaven and earth, with all the ornament thereof; who hast bound the sea by the word of thy commandment; who hast shut up the deep, and sealed it by thy terrible and glorious name; whom all men fear, and tremble before thy power; for the majesty of thy glory cannot be borne, and thine angry threatening toward sinners is importable: but thy merciful promise is unmeasurable and unsearchable; for thou art the most high Lord, of great compassion, longsuffering, very merciful, and repentest of the evils of men. Thou, O Lord, according to thy great goodness hast promised repentance and forgiveness to them that have sinned against thee: and of thine infinite mercies hast appointed repentance unto sinners, that they may be saved. Thou therefore, O Lord, that art the God of the just, hast not appointed repentance to the just, as to Abraham, and Isaac, and Jacob, which have not sinned against thee; but thou hast appointed repentance unto me that am a sinner: for I have sinned above the number of the sands of the sea. My transgressions, O Lord, are multiplied: my transgressions are multiplied, and I am not worthy to behold and see the height of heaven for the multitude of mine iniquities. I am bowed down with many iron bands, that I cannot lift up mine head, neither have any release: for I have provoked thy wrath, and done evil before thee: I did not thy will, neither kept I thy commandments: I have set up abominations, and have multiplied offences. Now therefore I bow the knee of mine heart, beseeching thee of grace. I have sinned, O Lord, I have sinned, and I acknowledge mine iniquities: wherefore, I humbly beseech thee, forgive me, O Lord, forgive me, and destroy me not with mine iniquites. Be not angry with me for ever, by reserving evil for me; neither condemn me to the lower parts of the earth. For thou art the God, even the God of them that repent; and in me thou wilt shew all thy goodness: for thou wilt save me, that am unworthy, according to thy great mercy. Therefore I will praise thee for ever all the days of my life: for all the powers of the heavens do praise thee, and thine is the glory for ever and ever. Amen.

1 MACCABEES

1 Maccabees 1

1 And it happened, after that Alexander son of Philip, the Macedonian, who came out of the land of Chettiim, had smitten Darius king of the Persians and Medes, that he reigned in his stead, the first over Greece,

2 And made many wars, and won many strong holds, and slew the kings of the earth,

3 And went through to the ends of the earth, and took spoils of many nations, insomuch that the earth was quiet before him; whereupon he was exalted and his heart was lifted up.

4 And he gathered a mighty strong host and ruled over countries, and nations, and kings, who became tributaries unto him.

5 And after these things he fell sick, and perceived that he should die.

6 Wherefore he called his servants, such as were honourable, and had been brought up with him from his youth, and parted his kingdom among them, while he was yet alive.

7 So Alexander reigned twelves years, and then died.

8 And his servants bare rule every one in his place.

9 And after his death they all put crowns upon themselves; so did their sons after them many years: and evils were multiplied in the earth.

10 And there came out of them a wicked root Antiochus surnamed Epiphanes, son of Antiochus the king, who had been an hostage at Rome, and he reigned in the hundred and thirty and seventh year of the kingdom of the Greeks.

11 In those days went there out of Israel wicked men, who persuaded many, saying, Let us go and make a covenant with the heathen that are round about us: for since we departed from them we have had much sorrow.

12 So this device pleased them well.

13 Then certain of the people were so forward herein, that they went to the king, who gave them licence to do after the ordinances of the heathen:

14 Whereupon they built a place of exercise at Jerusalem according to the customs of the heathen:

15 And made themselves uncircumcised, and forsook the holy covenant, and joined themselves to the heathen, and were sold to do mischief.

16 Now when the kingdom was established before Antiochus, he thought to reign over Egypt that he might have the dominion of two realms.

17 Wherefore he entered into Egypt with a great multitude, with chariots, and elephants, and horsemen, and a great navy,

18 And made war against Ptolemee king of Egypt: but Ptolemee was afraid of him, and fled; and many were wounded to death.

19 Thus they got the strong cities in the land of Egypt and he took the spoils thereof.

20 And after that Antiochus had smitten Egypt, he returned again in the hundred forty and third year, and went up against Israel and Jerusalem with a great multitude,

21 And entered proudly into the sanctuary, and took away the golden altar, and the candlestick of light, and all the vessels thereof,

22 And the table of the shewbread, and the pouring vessels, and the vials. and the censers of gold, and the veil, and the crown, and the golden ornaments that were before the temple, all which he pulled off.

23 He took also the silver and the gold, and the precious vessels: also he took the hidden treasures which he found.

24 And when he had taken all away, he went into his own land, having made a great massacre, and spoken very proudly.

25 Therefore there was a great mourning in Israel, in every place where they were;

26 So that the princes and elders mourned, the virgins and young men were made feeble, and the beauty of women was changed.

27 Every bridegroom took up lamentation, and she that sat in the marriage chamber was in heaviness,

28 The land also was moved for the inhabitants thereof, and all the house of Jacob was covered with confusion.

29 And after two years fully expired the king sent his chief collector of tribute unto the cities of Juda, who came unto Jerusalem with a great multitude,

30 And spake peaceable words unto them, but all was deceit: for when they had given him credence, he fell suddenly upon the city, and smote it very sore, and destroyed much people of Israel.

31 And when he had taken the spoils of the city, he set it on fire, and pulled down the houses and walls thereof on every side.

32 But the women and children took they captive, and possessed the cattle.

33 Then builded they the city of David with a great and strong wall, and with mighty towers, and made it a strong hold for them.

34 And they put therein a sinful nation, wicked men, and fortified themselves therein.

35 They stored it also with armour and victuals, and when they had gathered together the spoils of Jerusalem, they laid them up there, and so they became a sore snare:

36 For it was a place to lie in wait against the sanctuary, and an evil adversary to Israel.

37 Thus they shed innocent blood on every side of the sanctuary, and defiled it:

38 Insomuch that the inhabitants of Jerusalem fled because of them: whereupon the city was made an habitation of strangers, and became strange to those that were born in her; and her own children left her.

39 Her sanctuary was laid waste like a wilderness, her feasts were turned into mourning, her sabbaths into reproach her honour into contempt.

40 As had been her glory, so was her dishonour increased, and her excellency was turned into mourning.

41 Moreover king Antiochus wrote to his whole kingdom, that all should be one people,

42 And every one should leave his laws: so all the heathen agreed according to the commandment of the king.

43 Yea, many also of the Israelites consented to his religion, and sacrificed unto idols, and profaned the sabbath.

44 For the king had sent letters by messengers unto Jerusalem and the cities of Juda that they should follow the strange laws of the land,

45 And forbid burnt offerings, and sacrifice, and drink offerings, in the temple; and that they should profane the sabbaths and festival days:

46 And pollute the sanctuary and holy people:

47 Set up altars, and groves, and chapels of idols, and sacrifice swine's flesh, and unclean beasts:

48 That they should also leave their children uncircumcised, and make their souls abominable with all manner of uncleanness and profanation:

49 To the end they might forget the law, and change all the ordinances.

50 And whosoever would not do according to the commandment of the king, he said, he should die.

51 In the selfsame manner wrote he to his whole kingdom, and appointed overseers over all the people, commanding the cities of Juda to sacrifice, city by city.

52 Then many of the people were gathered unto them, to wit every one that forsook the law; and so they committed evils in the land;

53 And drove the Israelites into secret places, even wheresoever they could flee for succour.

54 Now the fifteenth day of the month Casleu, in the hundred forty and fifth year, they set up the abomination of desolation upon the altar, and builded idol altars throughout the cities of Juda on every side;

55 And burnt incense at the doors of their houses, and in the streets.

56 And when they had rent in pieces the books of the law which they found, they burnt them with fire.

57 And whosoever was found with any the book of the testament, or if any committed to the law, the king's commandment was, that they should put him to death.

58 Thus did they by their authority unto the Israelites every month, to as many as were found in the cities.

59 Now the five and twentieth day of the month they did sacrifice upon the idol altar, which was upon the altar of God.

60 At which time according to the commandment they put to death certain women, that had caused their children to be circumcised.

61 And they hanged the infants about their necks, and rifled their houses, and slew them that had circumcised them.

62 Howbeit many in Israel were fully resolved and confirmed in themselves not to eat any unclean thing.

63 Wherefore the rather to die, that they might not be defiled with meats, and that they might not profane the holy covenant: so then they died.

64 And there was very great wrath upon Israel.

1 Maccabees 2

1 In those days arose Mattathias the son of John, the son of Simeon, a priest of the sons of Joarib, from Jerusalem, and dwelt in Modin.

2 And he had five sons, Joannan, called Caddis:

3 Simon; called Thassi:

4 Judas, who was called Maccabeus:

5 Eleazar, called Avaran: and Jonathan, whose surname was Apphus.

6 And when he saw the blasphemies that were committed in Juda and Jerusalem,

7 He said, Woe is me! wherefore was I born to see this misery of my people, and of the holy city, and to dwell there, when it was delivered into the hand of the enemy, and the sanctuary into the hand of strangers?

8 Her temple is become as a man without glory.

9 Her glorious vessels are carried away into captivity, her infants are slain in the streets, her young men with the sword of the enemy.

10 What nation hath not had a part in her kingdom and gotten of her spoils?

11 All her ornaments are taken away; of a free woman she is become a bondslave.

12 And, behold, our sanctuary, even our beauty and our glory, is laid waste, and the Gentiles have profaned it.

13 To what end therefore shall we live any longer?

14 Then Mattathias and his sons rent their clothes, and put on sackcloth, and mourned very sore.

15 In the mean while the king's officers, such as compelled the people to revolt, came into the city Modin, to make them sacrifice.

16 And when many of Israel came unto them, Mattathias also and his sons came together.

17 Then answered the king's officers, and said to Mattathias on this wise, Thou art a ruler, and an honourable and great man in this city, and strengthened with sons and brethren:

18 Now therefore come thou first, and fulfil the king's commandment, like as all the heathen have done, yea, and the men of Juda also, and such as remain at Jerusalem: so shalt thou and thy house be in the number of the king's friends, and thou and thy children shall be honoured with silver and gold, and many rewards.

19 Then Mattathias answered and spake with a loud voice, Though all the nations that are under the king's dominion obey him, and fall away every one from the religion of their fathers, and give consent to his commandments:

20 Yet will I and my sons and my brethren walk in the covenant of our fathers.

21 God forbid that we should forsake the law and the ordinances.

22 We will not hearken to the king's words, to go from our religion, either on the right hand, or the left.

23 Now when he had left speaking these words, there came one of the Jews in the sight of all to sacrifice on the altar which was at Modin, according to the king's commandment.

24 Which thing when Mattathias saw, he was inflamed with zeal, and his reins trembled, neither could he forbear to shew his anger according to judgment: wherefore he ran, and slew him upon the altar.

25 Also the king's commissioner, who compelled men to sacrifice, he killed at that time, and the altar he pulled down.

26 Thus dealt he zealously for the law of God like as Phinees did unto Zambri the son of Salom.

27 And Mattathias cried throughout the city with a loud voice, saying, Whosoever is zealous of the law, and maintaineth the covenant, let him follow me.

28 So he and his sons fled into the mountains, and left all that ever they had in the city.

29 Then many that sought after justice and judgment went down into the wilderness, to dwell there:

30 Both they, and their children, and their wives; and their cattle; because afflictions increased sore upon them.

31 Now when it was told the king's servants, and the host that was at Jerusalem, in the city of David, that certain men, who had broken the king's commandment, were gone down into the secret places in the wilderness,

32 They pursued after them a great number, and having overtaken them, they camped against them, and made war against them on the sabbath day.

33 And they said unto them, Let that which ye have done hitherto suffice; come forth, and do according to the commandment of the king, and ye shall live.

34 But they said, We will not come forth, neither will we do the king's commandment, to profane the sabbath day.

35 So then they gave them the battle with all speed.

36 Howbeit they answered them not, neither cast they a stone at them, nor stopped the places where they lay hid;

37 But said, Let us die all in our innocency: heaven and earth will testify for us, that ye put us to death wrongfully.

38 So they rose up against them in battle on the sabbath, and they slew them, with their wives and children and their cattle, to the number of a thousand people.

39 Now when Mattathias and his friends understood hereof, they mourned for them right sore.

40 And one of them said to another, If we all do as our brethren have done, and fight not for our lives and laws against the heathen, they will now quickly root us out of the earth.

41 At that time therefore they decreed, saying, Whosoever shall come to make battle with us on the sabbath day, we will fight against him; neither will we die all, as our brethren that were murdered in the secret places.

42 Then came there unto him a company of Assideans who were mighty men of Israel, even all such

as were voluntarily devoted unto the law.

43 Also all they that fled for persecution joined themselves unto them, and were a stay unto them.

44 So they joined their forces, and smote sinful men in their anger, and wicked men in their wrath: but the rest fled to the heathen for succour.

45 Then Mattathias and his friends went round about, and pulled down the altars:

46 And what children soever they found within the coast of Israel uncircumcised, those they circumcised valiantly.

47 They pursued also after the proud men, and the work prospered in their hand.

48 So they recovered the law out of the hand of the Gentiles, and out of the hand of kings, neither suffered they the sinner to triumph.

49 Now when the time drew near that Mattathias should die, he said unto his sons, Now hath pride and rebuke gotten strength, and the time of destruction, and the wrath of indignation:

50 Now therefore, my sons, be ye zealous for the law, and give your lives for the covenant of your fathers.

51 Call to remembrance what acts our fathers did in their time; so shall ye receive great honour and an everlasting name.

52 Was not Abraham found faithful in temptation, and it was imputed unto him for righteousness?

53 Joseph in the time of his distress kept the commandment and was made lord of Egypt.

54 Phinees our father in being zealous and fervent obtained the covenant of an everlasting priesthood.

55 Jesus for fulfilling the word was made a judge in Israel.

56 Caleb for bearing witness before the congregation received the heritage of the land.

57 David for being merciful possessed the throne of an everlasting kingdom.

58 Elias for being zealous and fervent for the law was taken up into heaven.

59 Ananias, Azarias, and Misael, by believing were saved out of the flame.

60 Daniel for his innocency was delivered from the mouth of lions.

61 And thus consider ye throughout all ages, that none that put their trust in him shall be overcome.

62 Fear not then the words of a sinful man: for his glory shall be dung and worms.

63 To day he shall be lifted up and to morrow he shall not be found,

because he is returned into his dust, and his thought is come to nothing.

64 Wherefore, ye my sons, be valiant and shew yourselves men in the behalf of the law; for by it shall ye obtain glory.

65 And behold, I know that your brother Simon is a man of counsel, give ear unto him alway: he shall be a father unto you.

66 As for Judas Maccabeus, he hath been mighty and strong, even from his youth up: let him be your captain, and fight the battle of the people.

67 Take also unto you all those that observe the law, and avenge ye the wrong of your people.

68 Recompense fully the heathen, and take heed to the commandments of the law.

69 So he blessed them, and was gathered to his fathers.

70 And he died in the hundred forty and sixth year, and his sons buried him in the sepulchres of his fathers at Modin, and all Israel made great lamentation for him.

1 Maccabees 3

1 Then his son Judas, called Maccabeus, rose up in his stead.

2 And all his brethren helped him, and so did all they that held with his father, and they fought with cheerfulness the battle of Israel.

3 So he gat his people great honour, and put on a breastplate as a giant, and girt his warlike harness about him, and he made battles, protecting the host with his sword.

4 In his acts he was like a lion, and like a lion's whelp roaring for his prey.

5 For He pursued the wicked, and sought them out, and burnt up those that vexed his people.

6 Wherefore the wicked shrunk for fear of him, and all the workers of iniquity were troubled, because salvation prospered in his hand.

7 He grieved also many kings, and made Jacob glad with his acts, and his memorial is blessed for ever.

8 Moreover he went through the cities of Juda, destroying the ungodly out of them, and turning away wrath from Israel:

9 So that he was renowned unto the utmost part of the earth, and he received unto him such as were ready to perish.

10 Then Apollonius gathered the Gentiles together, and a great host out of Samaria, to fight against Israel.

11 Which thing when Judas perceived, he went forth to meet him, and so he smote him, and slew him: many also fell down slain, but the rest fled.

12 Wherefore Judas took their spoils, and Apollonius' sword also, and therewith he fought all his life long.

13 Now when Seron, a prince of the army of Syria, heard say that Judas had gathered unto him a multitude and company of the faithful to go out with him to war;

14 He said, I will get me a name and honour in the kingdom; for I will go fight with Judas and them that are with him, who despise the king's commandment.

15 So he made him ready to go up, and there went with him a mighty host of the ungodly to help him, and to be avenged of the children of Israel.

16 And when he came near to the going up of Bethhoron, Judas went forth to meet him with a small company:

17 Who, when they saw the host coming to meet them, said unto Judas, How shall we be able, being so few, to fight against so great a multitude and so strong, seeing we are ready to faint with fasting all this day?

18 Unto whom Judas answered, It is no hard matter for many to be shut up in the hands of a few; and with the God of heaven it is all one, to deliver with a great multitude, or a small company:

19 For the victory of battle standeth not in the multitude of an host; but strength cometh from heaven.

20 They come against us in much pride and iniquity to destroy us, and our wives and children, and to spoil us:

21 But we fight for our lives and our laws.

22 Wherefore the Lord himself will overthrow them before our face: and as for you, be ye not afraid of them.

23 Now as soon as he had left off speaking, he leapt suddenly upon them, and so Seron and his host was overthrown before him.

24 And they pursued them from the going down of Bethhoron unto the plain, where were slain about eight hundred men of them; and the residue fled into the land of the Philistines.

25 Then began the fear of Judas and his brethren, and an exceeding great dread, to fall upon the nations round about them:

26 Insomuch as his fame came unto the king, and all nations talked of the battles of Judas.

27 Now when king Antiochus heard these things, he was full of indignation: wherefore he sent and gathered together all the forces of his realm, even a very strong army.

28 He opened also his treasure, and gave his soldiers pay for a year,

commanding them to be ready whensoever he should need them.

29 Nevertheless, when he saw that the money of his treasures failed and that the tributes in the country were small, because of the dissension and plague, which he had brought upon the land in taking away the laws which had been of old time;

30 He feared that he should not be able to bear the charges any longer, nor to have such gifts to give so liberally as he did before: for he had abounded above the kings that were before him.

31 Wherefore, being greatly perplexed in his mind, he determined to go into Persia, there to take the tributes of the countries, and to gather much money.

32 So he left Lysias, a nobleman, and one of the blood royal, to oversee the affairs of the king from the river Euphrates unto the borders of Egypt:

33 And to bring up his son Antiochus, until he came again.

34 Moreover he delivered unto him the half of his forces, and the elephants, and gave him charge of all things that he would have done, as also concerning them that dwelt in Juda and Jerusalem:

35 To wit, that he should send an army against them, to destroy and root out the strength of Israel, and the remnant of Jerusalem, and to take away their memorial from that place;

36 And that he should place strangers in all their quarters, and divide their land by lot.

37 So the king took the half of the forces that remained, and departed from Antioch, his royal city, the hundred forty and seventh year; and having passed the river Euphrates, he went through the high countries.

38 Then Lysias chose Ptolemee the son of Dorymenes, Nicanor, and Gorgias, mighty men of the king's friends:

39 And with them he sent forty thousand footmen, and seven thousand horsemen, to go into the land of Juda, and to destroy it, as the king commanded.

40 So they went forth with all their power, and came and pitched by Emmaus in the plain country.

41 And the merchants of the country, hearing the fame of them, took silver and gold very much, with servants, and came into the camp to buy the children of Israel for slaves: a power also of Syria and of the land of the Philistines joined themselves unto them.

42 Now when Judas and his brethren saw that miseries were multiplied, and that the forces did encamp themselves in their borders: for they knew how the king had given

commandment to destroy the people, and utterly abolish them;

43 They said one to another, Let us restore the decayed fortune of our people, and let us fight for our people and the sanctuary.

44 Then was the congregation gathered together, that they might be ready for battle, and that they might pray, and ask mercy and compassion.

45 Now Jerusalem lay void as a wilderness, there was none of her children that went in or out: the sanctuary also was trodden down, and aliens kept the strong hold; the heathen had their habitation in that place; and joy was taken from Jacob, and the pipe with the harp ceased.

46 Wherefore the Israelites assembled themselves together, and came to Maspha, over against Jerusalem; for in Maspha was the place where they prayed aforetime in Israel.

47 Then they fasted that day, and put on sackcloth, and cast ashes upon their heads, and rent their clothes,

48 And laid open the book of the law, wherein the heathen had sought to paint the likeness of their images.

49 They brought also the priests' garments, and the firstfruits, and the tithes: and the Nazarites they stirred up, who had accomplished their days.

50 Then cried they with a loud voice toward heaven, saying, What shall we do with these, and whither shall we carry them away?

51 For thy sanctuary is trodden down and profaned, and thy priests are in heaviness, and brought low.

52 And lo, the heathen are assembled together against us to destroy us: what things they imagine against us, thou knowest.

53 How shall we be able to stand against them, except thou, O God, be our help?

54 Then sounded they with trumpets, and cried with a loud voice.

55 And after this Judas ordained captains over the people, even captains over thousands, and over hundreds, and over fifties, and over tens.

56 But as for such as were building houses, or had betrothed wives, or were planting vineyards, or were fearful, those he commanded that they should return, every man to his own house, according to the law.

57 So the camp removed, and pitched upon the south side of Emmaus.

58 And Judas said, arm yourselves, and be valiant men, and see that ye be in readiness against the morning, that ye may fight with these nations, that are assembled together against us to destroy us and our sanctuary:

59 For it is better for us to die in battle, than to behold the calamities of our people and our sanctuary.

60 Nevertheless, as the will of God is in heaven, so let him do.

1 Maccabees 4

1 Then took Gorgias five thousand footmen, and a thousand of the best horsemen, and removed out of the camp by night;

2 To the end he might rush in upon the camp of the Jews, and smite them suddenly. And the men of the fortress were his guides.

3 Now when Judas heard thereof he himself removed, and the valiant men with him, that he might smite the king's army which was at Emmaus,

4 While as yet the forces were dispersed from the camp.

5 In the mean season came Gorgias by night into the camp of Judas: and when he found no man there, he sought them in the mountains: for said he, These fellows flee from us

6 But as soon as it was day, Judas shewed himself in the plain with three thousand men, who nevertheless had neither armour nor swords to their minds.

7 And they saw the camp of the heathen, that it was strong and well harnessed, and compassed round about with horsemen; and these were expert of war.

8 Then said Judas to the men that were with him, Fear ye not their multitude, neither be ye afraid of their assault.

9 Remember how our fathers were delivered in the Red sea, when Pharaoh pursued them with an army.

10 Now therefore let us cry unto heaven, if peradventure the Lord will have mercy upon us, and remember the covenant of our fathers, and destroy this host before our face this day:

11 That so all the heathen may know that there is one who delivereth and saveth Israel.

12 Then the strangers lifted up their eyes, and saw them coming over against them.

13 Wherefore they went out of the camp to battle; but they that were with Judas sounded their trumpets.

14 So they joined battle, and the heathen being discomfited fled into the plain.

15 Howbeit all the hindmost of them were slain with the sword: for they pursued them unto Gazera, and unto the plains of Idumea, and Azotus, and Jamnia, so that there were slain of them upon a three thousand men.

16 This done, Judas returned again with his host from pursuing them,

17 And said to the people, Be not greedy of the spoil inasmuch as there is a battle before us,

18 And Gorgias and his host are here by us in the mountain: but stand ye now against our enemies, and overcome them, and after this ye may boldly take the spoils.

19 As Judas was yet speaking these words, there appeared a part of them looking out of the mountain:

20 Who when they perceived that the Jews had put their host to flight and were burning the tents; for the smoke that was seen declared what was done:

21 When therefore they perceived these things, they were sore afraid, and seeing also the host of Judas in the plain ready to fight,

22 They fled every one into the land of strangers.

23 Then Judas returned to spoil the tents, where they got much gold, and silver, and blue silk, and purple of the sea, and great riches.

24 After this they went home, and sung a song of thanksgiving, and praised the Lord in heaven: because it is good, because his mercy endureth forever.

25 Thus Israel had a great deliverance that day.

26 Now all the strangers that had escaped came and told Lysias what had happened:

27 Who, when he heard thereof, was confounded and discouraged, because neither such things as he would were done unto Israel, nor such things as the king commanded him were come to pass.

28 The next year therefore following Lysias gathered together threescore thousand choice men of foot, and five thousand horsemen, that he might subdue them.

29 So they came into Idumea, and pitched their tents at Bethsura, and Judas met them with ten thousand men.

30 And when he saw that mighty army, he prayed and said, Blessed art thou, O Saviour of Israel, who didst quell the violence of the mighty man by the hand of thy servant David, and gavest the host of strangers into the hands of Jonathan the son of Saul, and his armourbearer;

31 Shut up this army in the hand of thy people Israel, and let them be confounded in their power and horsemen:

32 Make them to be of no courage, and cause the boldness of their strength to fall away, and let them quake at their destruction:

33 Cast them down with the sword of them that love thee, and let all those that know thy name praise thee with thanksgiving.

34 So they joined battle; and there were slain of the host of Lysias about five thousand men, even before them were they slain.

35 Now when Lysias saw his army put to flight, and the manliness of Judas' soldiers, and how they were ready either to live or die valiantly, he went into Antiochia, and gathered together a company of strangers, and having made his army greater than it was, he purposed to come again into Judea.

36 Then said Judas and his brethren, Behold, our enemies are discomfited: let us go up to cleanse and dedicate the sanctuary.

37 Upon this all the host assembled themselves together, and went up into mount Sion.

38 And when they saw the sanctuary desolate, and the altar profaned, and the gates burned up, and shrubs growing in the courts as in a forest, or in one of the mountains, yea, and the priests' chambers pulled down;

39 They rent their clothes, and made great lamentation, and cast ashes upon their heads,

40 And fell down flat to the ground upon their faces, and blew an alarm with the trumpets, and cried toward heaven.

41 Then Judas appointed certain men to fight against those that were in the fortress, until he had cleansed the sanctuary.

42 So he chose priests of blameless conversation, such as had pleasure in the law:

43 Who cleansed the sanctuary, and bare out the defiled stones into an unclean place.

44 And when as they consulted what to do with the altar of burnt offerings, which was profaned;

45 They thought it best to pull it down, lest it should be a reproach to them, because the heathen had defiled it: wherefore they pulled it down,

46 And laid up the stones in the mountain of the temple in a convenient place, until there should come a prophet to shew what should be done with them.

47 Then they took whole stones according to the law, and built a new altar according to the former;

48 And made up the sanctuary, and the things that were within the temple, and hallowed the courts.

49 They made also new holy vessels, and into the temple they brought the candlestick, and the altar of burnt offerings, and of incense, and the table.

50 And upon the altar they burned incense, and the lamps that were upon the candlestick they lighted, that they might give light in the temple.

51 Furthermore they set the loaves upon the table, and spread out the veils, and finished all the works which they had begun to make.

52 Now on the five and twentieth day of the ninth month, which is called the month Casleu, in the hundred forty and eighth year, they rose up betimes in the morning,

53 And offered sacrifice according to the law upon the new altar of burnt offerings, which they had made.

54 Look, at what time and what day the heathen had profaned it, even in that was it dedicated with songs, and citherns, and harps, and cymbals.

55 Then all the people fell upon their faces, worshipping and praising the God of heaven, who had given them good success.

56 And so they kept the dedication of the altar eight days and offered burnt offerings with gladness, and sacrificed the sacrifice of deliverance and praise.

57 They decked also the forefront of the temple with crowns of gold, and with shields; and the gates and the chambers they renewed, and hanged doors upon them.

58 Thus was there very great gladness among the people, for that the reproach of the heathen was put away.

59 Moreover Judas and his brethren with the whole congregation of Israel ordained, that the days of the dedication of the altar should be kept in their season from year to year by the space of eight days, from the five and twentieth day of the month Casleu, with mirth and gladness.

60 At that time also they builded up the mount Sion with high walls and strong towers round about, lest the Gentiles should come and tread it down as they had done before.

61 And they set there a garrison to keep it, and fortified Bethsura to preserve it; that the people might have a defence against Idumea.

1 Maccabees 5

1 Now when the nations round about heard that the altar was built and the sanctuary renewed as before, it displeased them very much.

2 Wherefore they thought to destroy the generation of Jacob that was among them, and thereupon they began to slay and destroy the people.

3 Then Judas fought against the children of Esau in Idumea at Arabattine, because they besieged Gael: and he gave them a great overthrow, and abated their courage, and took their spoils.

4 Also he remembered the injury of the children of Bean, who had been a snare and an offence unto the people, in that they lay in wait for them in the ways.

5 He shut them up therefore in the towers, and encamped against them, and destroyed them utterly, and

burned the towers of that place with fire, and all that were therein.

6 Afterward he passed over to the children of Ammon, where he found a mighty power, and much people, with Timotheus their captain.

7 So he fought many battles with them, till at length they were discomfited before him; and he smote them.

8 And when he had taken Jazar, with the towns belonging thereto, he returned into Judea.

9 Then the heathen that were at Galaad assembled themselves together against the Israelites that were in their quarters, to destroy them; but they fled to the fortress of Dathema.

10 And sent letters unto Judas and his brethren, The heathen that are round about us are assembled together against us to destroy us:

11 And they are preparing to come and take the fortress whereunto we are fled, Timotheus being captain of their host.

12 Come now therefore, and deliver us from their hands, for many of us are slain:

13 Yea, all our brethren that were in the places of Tobie are put to death: their wives and their children also they have carried away captives, and borne away their stuff; and they have destroyed there about a thousand men.

14 While these letters were yet reading, behold, there came other messengers from Galilee with their clothes rent, who reported on this wise,

15 And said, They of Ptolemais, and of Tyrus, and Sidon, and all Galilee of the Gentiles, are assembled together against us to consume us.

16 Now when Judas and the people heard these words, there assembled a great congregation together, to consult what they should do for their brethren, that were in trouble, and assaulted of them.

17 Then said Judas unto Simon his brother, Choose thee out men, and go and deliver thy brethren that are in Galilee, for I and Jonathan my brother will go into the country of Galaad.

18 So he left Joseph the son of Zacharias, and Azarias, captains of the people, with the remnant of the host in Judea to keep it.

19 Unto whom he gave commandment, saying, Take ye the charge of this people, and see that ye make not war against the heathen until the time that we come again.

20 Now unto Simon were given three thousand men to go into Galilee, and unto Judas eight thousand men for the country of Galaad.

21 Then went Simon into Galilee, where he fought many battles with the heathen, so that the heathen were discomfited by him.

22 And he pursued them unto the gate of Ptolemais; and there were slain of the heathen about three thousand men, whose spoils he took.

23 And those that were in Galilee, and in Arbattis, with their wives and their children, and all that they had, took he away with him, and brought them into Judea with great joy.

24 Judas Maccabeus also and his brother Jonathan went over Jordan, and travelled three days' journey in the wilderness,

25 Where they met with the Nabathites, who came unto them in a peaceable manner, and told them every thing that had happened to their brethren in the land of Galaad:

26 And how that many of them were shut up in Bosora, and Bosor, and Alema, Casphor, Maked, and Carnaim; all these cities are strong and great:

27 And that they were shut up in the rest of the cities of the country of Galaad, and that against to morrow they had appointed to bring their host against the forts, and to take them, and to destroy them all in one day.

28 Hereupon Judas and his host turned suddenly by the way of the wilderness unto Bosora; and when he had won the city, he slew all the males with the edge of the sword, and took all their spoils, and burned the city with fire,

29 From whence he removed by night, and went till he came to the fortress.

30 And betimes in the morning they looked up, and, behold, there was an innumerable people bearing ladders and other engines of war, to take the fortress: for they assaulted them.

31 When Judas therefore saw that the battle was begun, and that the cry of the city went up to heaven, with trumpets, and a great sound,

32 He said unto his host, Fight this day for your brethren.

33 So he went forth behind them in three companies, who sounded their trumpets, and cried with prayer.

34 Then the host of Timotheus, knowing that it was Maccabeus, fled from him: wherefore he smote them with a great slaughter; so that there were killed of them that day about eight thousand men.

35 This done, Judas turned aside to Maspha; and after he had assaulted it he took and slew all the males therein, and received the spoils thereof and and burnt it with fire.

36 From thence went he, and took Casphon, Maged, Bosor, and the other cities of the country of Galaad.

37 After these things gathered Timotheus another host and encamped against Raphon beyond the brook.

38 So Judas sent men to espy the host, who brought him word, saying, All the heathen that be round about us are assembled unto them, even a very great host.

39 He hath also hired the Arabians to help them and they have pitched their tents beyond the brook, ready to come and fight against thee. Upon this Judas went to meet them.

40 Then Timotheus said unto the captains of his host, When Judas and his host come near the brook, if he pass over first unto us, we shall not be able to withstand him; for he will mightily prevail against us:

41 But if he be afraid, and camp beyond the river, we shall go over unto him, and prevail against him.

42 Now when Judas came near the brook, he caused the scribes of the people to remain by the brook: unto whom he gave commandment, saying, Suffer no man to remain in the camp, but let all come to the battle.

43 So he went first over unto them, and all the people after him: then all the heathen, being discomfited before him, cast away their weapons, and fled unto the temple that was at Carnaim.

44 But they took the city, and burned the temple with all that were therein. Thus was Carnaim subdued, neither could they stand any longer before Judas.

45 Then Judas gathered together all the Israelites that were in the country of Galaad, from the least unto the greatest, even their wives, and their children, and their stuff, a very great host, to the end they might come into the land of Judea.

46 Now when they came unto Ephron, (this was a great city in the way as they should go, very well fortified) they could not turn from it, either on the right hand or the left, but must needs pass through the midst of it.

47 Then they of the city shut them out, and stopped up the gates with stones.

48 Whereupon Judas sent unto them in peaceable manner, saying, Let us pass through your land to go into our own country, and none shall do you any hurt; we will only pass through on foot: howbeit they would not open unto him.

49 Wherefore Judas commanded a proclamation to be made throughout the host, that every man should pitch his tent in the place where he was.

50 So the soldiers pitched, and assaulted the city all that day and all that night, till at the length the city was delivered into his hands:

51 Who then slew all the males with the edge of the sword, and rased the city, and took the spoils thereof, and passed through the city over them that were slain.

52 After this went they over Jordan into the great plain before Bethsan.

53 And Judas gathered together those that came behind, and exhorted the people all the way through, till they came into the land of Judea.

54 So they went up to mount Sion with joy and gladness, where they offered burnt offerings, because not one of them were slain until they had returned in peace.

55 Now what time as Judas and Jonathan were in the land of Galaad, and Simon his brother in Galilee before Ptolemais,

56 Joseph the son of Zacharias, and Azarias, captains of the garrisons, heard of the valiant acts and warlike deeds which they had done.

57 Wherefore they said, Let us also get us a name, and go fight against the heathen that are round about us.

58 So when they had given charge unto the garrison that was with them, they went toward Jamnia.

59 Then came Gorgias and his men out of the city to fight against them.

60 And so it was, that Joseph and Azaras were put to flight, and pursued unto the borders of Judea:

and there were slain that day of the people of Israel about two thousand men.

61 Thus was there a great overthrow among the children of Israel, because they were not obedient unto Judas and his brethren, but thought to do some valiant act.

62 Moreover these men came not of the seed of those, by whose hand deliverance was given unto Israel.

63 Howbeit the man Judas and his brethren were greatly renowned in the sight of all Israel, and of all the heathen, wheresoever their name was heard of;

64 Insomuch as the people assembled unto them with joyful acclamations.

65 Afterward went Judas forth with his brethren, and fought against the children of Esau in the land toward the south, where he smote Hebron, and the towns thereof, and pulled down the fortress of it, and burned the towers thereof round about.

66 From thence he removed to go into the land of the Philistines, and passed through Samaria.

67 At that time certain priests, desirous to shew their valour, were slain in battle, for that they went out to fight unadvisedly.

68 So Judas turned to Azotus in the land of the Philistines, and when he had pulled down their altars, and

burned their carved images with fire, and spoiled their cities, he returned into the land of Judea.

1 Maccabees 6

1 About that time king Antiochus travelling through the high countries heard say, that Elymais in the country of Persia was a city greatly renowned for riches, silver, and gold;

2 And that there was in it a very rich temple, wherein were coverings of gold, and breastplates, and shields, which Alexander, son of Philip, the Macedonian king, who reigned first among the Grecians, had left there.

3 Wherefore he came and sought to take the city, and to spoil it; but he was not able, because they of the city, having had warning thereof,

4 Rose up against him in battle: so he fled, and departed thence with great heaviness, and returned to Babylon.

5 Moreover there came one who brought him tidings into Persia, that the armies, which went against the land of Judea, were put to flight:

6 And that Lysias, who went forth first with a great power was driven away of the Jews; and that they were made strong by the armour, and power, and store of spoils, which they had gotten of the armies, whom they had destroyed:

7 Also that they had pulled down the abomination, which he had set up upon the altar in Jerusalem, and that they had compassed about the sanctuary with high walls, as before, and his city Bethsura.

8 Now when the king heard these words, he was astonished and sore moved: whereupon he laid him down upon his bed, and fell sick for grief, because it had not befallen him as he looked for.

9 And there he continued many days: for his grief was ever more and more, and he made account that he should die.

10 Wherefore he called for all his friends, and said unto them, The sleep is gone from mine eyes, and my heart faileth for very care.

11 And I thought with myself, Into what tribulation am I come, and how great a flood of misery is it, wherein now I am! for I was bountiful and beloved in my power.

12 But now I remember the evils that I did at Jerusalem, and that I took all the vessels of gold and silver that were therein, and sent to destroy the inhabitants of Judea without a cause.

13 I perceive therefore that for this cause these troubles are come upon me, and, behold, I perish through great grief in a strange land.

14 Then called he for Philip, one of his friends, who he made ruler over all his realm,

15 And gave him the crown, and his robe, and his signet, to the end he should bring up his son Antiochus, and nourish him up for the kingdom.

16 So king Antiochus died there in the hundred forty and ninth year.

17 Now when Lysias knew that the king was dead, he set up Antiochus his son, whom he had brought up being young, to reign in his stead, and his name he called Eupator.

18 About this time they that were in the tower shut up the Israelites round about the sanctuary, and sought always their hurt, and the strengthening of the heathen.

19 Wherefore Judas, purposing to destroy them, called all the people together to besiege them.

20 So they came together, and besieged them in the hundred and fiftieth year, and he made mounts for shot against them, and other engines.

21 Howbeit certain of them that were besieged got forth, unto whom some ungodly men of Israel joined themselves:

22 And they went unto the king, and said, How long will it be ere thou execute judgment, and avenge our brethren?

23 We have been willing to serve thy father, and to do as he would have us, and to obey his commandments;

24 For which cause they of our nation besiege the tower, and are alienated from us: moreover as many of us as they could light on they slew, and spoiled our inheritance.

25 Neither have they stretched out their hand against us only, but also against their borders.

26 And, behold, this day are they besieging the tower at Jerusalem, to take it: the sanctuary also and Bethsura have they fortified.

27 Wherefore if thou dost not prevent them quickly, they will do the greater things than these, neither shalt thou be able to rule them.

28 Now when the king heard this, he was angry, and gathered together all his friends, and the captains of his army, and those that had charge of the horse.

29 There came also unto him from other kingdoms, and from isles of the sea, bands of hired soldiers.

30 So that the number of his army was an hundred thousand footmen, and twenty thousand horsemen, and two and thirty elephants exercised in battle.

31 These went through Idumea, and pitched against Bethsura, which they assaulted many days, making engines of war; but they of Bethsura came out, and burned them with fire, and fought valiantly.

32 Upon this Judas removed from the tower, and pitched in Bathzacharias, over against the king's camp.

33 Then the king rising very early marched fiercely with his host toward Bathzacharias, where his armies made them ready to battle, and sounded the trumpets.

34 And to the end they might provoke the elephants to fight, they shewed them the blood of grapes and mulberries.

35 Moreover they divided the beasts among the armies, and for every elephant they appointed a thousand men, armed with coats of mail, and with helmets of brass on their heads; and beside this, for every beast were ordained five hundred horsemen of the best.

36 These were ready at every occasion: wheresoever the beast was, and whithersoever the beast went, they went also, neither departed they from him.

37 And upon the beasts were there strong towers of wood, which covered every one of them, and were girt fast unto them with devices: there were also upon every one two and thirty strong men, that fought upon them, beside the Indian that ruled him.

38 As for the remnant of the horsemen, they set them on this side and that side at the two parts of the host giving them signs what to do, and being harnessed all over amidst the ranks.

39 Now when the sun shone upon the shields of gold and brass, the mountains glistered therewith, and shined like lamps of fire.

40 So part of the king's army being spread upon the high mountains, and part on the valleys below, they marched on safely and in order.

41 Wherefore all that heard the noise of their multitude, and the marching of the company, and the rattling of the harness, were moved: for the army was very great and mighty.

42 Then Judas and his host drew near, and entered into battle, and there were slain of the king's army six hundred men.

43 Eleazar also, surnamed Savaran, perceiving that one of the beasts, armed with royal harness, was higher than all the rest, and supposing that the king was upon him,

44 Put himself in jeopardy, to the end he might deliver his people, and get him a perpetual name:

45 Wherefore he ran upon him courageously through the midst of the battle, slaying on the right hand and on the left, so that they were divided from him on both sides.

46 Which done, he crept under the elephant, and thrust him under, and

slew him: whereupon the elephant fell down upon him, and there he died.

47 Howbeit the rest of the Jews seeing the strength of the king, and the violence of his forces, turned away from them.

48 Then the king's army went up to Jerusalem to meet them, and the king pitched his tents against Judea, and against mount Sion.

49 But with them that were in Bethsura he made peace: for they came out of the city, because they had no victuals there to endure the siege, it being a year of rest to the land.

50 So the king took Bethsura, and set a garrison there to keep it.

51 As for the sanctuary, he besieged it many days: and set there artillery with engines and instruments to cast fire and stones, and pieces to cast darts and slings.

52 Whereupon they also made engines against their engines, and held them battle a long season.

53 Yet at the last, their vessels being without victuals, (for that it was the seventh year, and they in Judea that were delivered from the Gentiles, had eaten up the residue of the store;)

54 There were but a few left in the sanctuary, because the famine did so prevail against them, that they were fain to disperse themselves, every man to his own place.

55 At that time Lysias heard say, that Philip, whom Antiochus the king, whiles he lived, had appointed to bring up his son Antiochus, that he might be king,

56 Was returned out of Persia and Media, and the king's host also that went with him, and that he sought to take unto him the ruling of the affairs.

57 Wherefore he went in all haste, and said to the king and the captains of the host and the company, We decay daily, and our victuals are but small, and the place we lay siege unto is strong, and the affairs of the kingdom lie upon us:

58 Now therefore let us be friends with these men, and make peace with them, and with all their nation;

59 And covenant with them, that they shall live after their laws, as they did before: for they are therefore displeased, and have done all these things, because we abolished their laws.

60 So the king and the princes were content: wherefore he sent unto them to make peace; and they accepted thereof.

61 Also the king and the princes made an oath unto them: whereupon they went out of the strong hold.

62 Then the king entered into mount Sion; but when he saw the strength

of the place, he broke his oath that he had made, and gave commandment to pull down the wall round about.

63 Afterward departed he in all haste, and returned unto Antiochia, where he found Philip to be master of the city: so he fought against him, and took the city by force.

1 Maccabees 7

1 In the hundred and one and fiftieth year Demetrius the son of Seleucus departed from Rome, and came up with a few men unto a city of the sea coast, and reigned there.

2 And as he entered into the palace of his ancestors, so it was, that his forces had taken Antiochus and Lysias, to bring them unto him.

3 Wherefore, when he knew it, he said, Let me not see their faces.

4 So his host slew them. Now when Demetrius was set upon the throne of his kingdom,

5 There came unto him all the wicked and ungodly men of Israel, having Alcimus, who was desirous to be high priest, for their captain:

6 And they accused the people to the king, saying, Judas and his brethren have slain all thy friends, and driven us out of our own land.

7 Now therefore send some man whom thou trustest, and let him go and see what havock he hath made among us, and in the king's land,

and let him punish them with all them that aid them.

8 Then the king chose Bacchides, a friend of the king, who ruled beyond the flood, and was a great man in the kingdom, and faithful to the king,

9 And him he sent with that wicked Alcimus, whom he made high priest, and commanded that he should take vengeance of the children of Israel.

10 So they departed, and came with a great power into the land of Judea, where they sent messengers to Judas and his brethren with peaceable words deceitfully.

11 But they gave no heed to their words; for they saw that they were come with a great power.

12 Then did there assemble unto Alcimus and Bacchides a company of scribes, to require justice.

13 Now the Assideans were the first among the children of Israel that sought peace of them:

14 For said they, One that is a priest of the seed of Aaron is come with this army, and he will do us no wrong.

15 So he spake unto them, peaceably, and sware unto them, saying, we will procure the harm neither of you nor your friends.

16 Whereupon they believed him: howbeit he took of them threescore men, and slew them in one day,

according to the words which he wrote,

17 The flesh of thy saints have they cast out, and their blood have they shed round about Jerusalem, and there was none to bury them.

18 Wherefore the fear and dread of them fell upon all the people, who said, There is neither truth nor righteousness in them; for they have broken the covenant and oath that they made.

19 After this, removed Bacchides from Jerusalem, and pitched his tents in Bezeth, where he sent and took many of the men that had forsaken him, and certain of the people also, and when he had slain them, he cast them into the great pit.

20 Then committed he the country to Alcimus, and left with him a power to aid him: so Bacchides went to the king.

21 But Alcimus contended for the high priesthood.

22 And unto him resorted all such as troubled the people, who, after they had gotten the land of Juda into their power, did much hurt in Israel.

23 Now when Judas saw all the mischief that Alcimus and his company had done among the Israelites, even above the heathen,

24 He went out into all the coasts of Judea round about, and took vengeance of them that had revolted from him, so that they durst no more go forth into the country.

25 On the other side, when Alcimus saw that Judas and his company had gotten the upper hand, and knew that he was not able to abide their force, he went again to the king, and said all the worst of them that he could.

26 Then the king sent Nicanor, one of his honourable princes, a man that bare deadly hate unto Israel, with commandment to destroy the people.

27 So Nicanor came to Jerusalem with a great force; and sent unto Judas and his brethren deceitfully with friendly words, saying,

28 Let there be no battle between me and you; I will come with a few men, that I may see you in peace.

29 He came therefore to Judas, and they saluted one another peaceably. Howbeit the enemies were prepared to take away Judas by violence.

30 Which thing after it was known to Judas, to wit, that he came unto him with deceit, he was sore afraid of him, and would see his face no more.

31 Nicanor also, when he saw that his counsel was discovered, went out to fight against Judas beside Capharsalama:

32 Where there were slain of Nicanor's side about five thousand

men, and the rest fled into the city of David.

33 After this went Nicanor up to mount Sion, and there came out of the sanctuary certain of the priests and certain of the elders of the people, to salute him peaceably, and to shew him the burnt sacrifice that was offered for the king.

34 But he mocked them, and laughed at them, and abused them shamefully, and spake proudly,

35 And sware in his wrath, saying, Unless Judas and his host be now delivered into my hands, if ever I come again in safety, I will burn up this house: and with that he went out in a great rage.

36 Then the priests entered in, and stood before the altar and the temple, weeping, and saying,

37 Thou, O Lord, didst choose this house to be called by thy name, and to be a house of prayer and petition for thy people:

38 Be avenged of this man and his host, and let them fall by the sword: remember their blasphemies, and suffer them not to continue any longer.

39 So Nicanor went out of Jerusalem, and pitched his tents in Bethhoron, where an host out of Syria met him.

40 But Judas pitched in Adasa with three thousand men, and there he prayed, saying,

41 O Lord, when they that were sent from the king of the Assyrians blasphemed, thine angel went out, and smote an hundred fourscore and five thousand of them.

42 Even so destroy thou this host before us this day, that the rest may know that he hath spoken blasphemously against thy sanctuary, and judge thou him according to his wickedness.

43 So the thirteenth day of the month Adar the hosts joined battle: but Nicanor's host was discomfited, and he himself was first slain in the battle.

44 Now when Nicanor's host saw that he was slain, they cast away their weapons, and fled.

45 Then they pursued after them a day's journey, from Adasa unto Gazera, sounding an alarm after them with their trumpets.

46 Whereupon they came forth out of all the towns of Judea round about, and closed them in; so that they, turning back upon them that pursued them, were all slain with the sword, and not one of them was left.

47 Afterwards they took the spoils, and the prey, and smote off Nicanors head, and his right hand, which he stretched out so proudly, and

brought them away, and hanged them up toward Jerusalem.

48 For this cause the people rejoiced greatly, and they kept that day a day of great gladness.

49 Moreover they ordained to keep yearly this day, being the thirteenth of Adar.

50 Thus the land of Juda was in rest a little while.

1 Maccabees 8

1 Now Judas had heard of the Romans, that they were mighty and valiant men, and such as would lovingly accept all that joined themselves unto them, and make a league of amity with all that came unto them;

2 And that they were men of great valour. It was told him also of their wars and noble acts which they had done among the Galatians, and how they had conquered them, and brought them under tribute;

3 And what they had done in the country of Spain, for the winning of the mines of the silver and gold which is there;

4 And that by their policy and patience they had conquered all the place, though it were very far from them; and the kings also that came against them from the uttermost part of the earth, till they had discomfited them, and given them a great

overthrow, so that the rest did give them tribute every year:

5 Beside this, how they had discomfited in battle Philip, and Perseus, king of the Citims, with others that lifted up themselves against them, and had overcome them:

6 How also Antiochus the great king of Asia, that came against them in battle, having an hundred and twenty elephants, with horsemen, and chariots, and a very great army, was discomfited by them;

7 And how they took him alive, and covenanted that he and such as reigned after him should pay a great tribute, and give hostages, and that which was agreed upon,

8 And the country of India, and Media and Lydia and of the goodliest countries, which they took of him, and gave to king Eumenes:

9 Moreover how the Grecians had determined to come and destroy them;

10 And that they, having knowledge thereof sent against them a certain captain, and fighting with them slew many of them, and carried away captives their wives and their children, and spoiled them, and took possession of their lands, and pulled down their strong holds, and brought them to be their servants unto this day:

11 It was told him besides, how they destroyed and brought under their dominion all other kingdoms and isles that at any time resisted them;

12 But with their friends and such as relied upon them they kept amity: and that they had conquered kingdoms both far and nigh, insomuch as all that heard of their name were afraid of them:

13 Also that, whom they would help to a kingdom, those reign; and whom again they would, they displace: finally, that they were greatly exalted:

14 Yet for all this none of them wore a crown or was clothed in purple, to be magnified thereby:

15 Moreover how they had made for themselves a senate house, wherein three hundred and twenty men sat in council daily, consulting alway for the people, to the end they might be well ordered:

16 And that they committed their government to one man every year, who ruled over all their country, and that all were obedient to that one, and that there was neither envy nor emmulation among them.

17 In consideration of these things, Judas chose Eupolemus the son of John, the son of Accos, and Jason the son of Eleazar, and sent them to Rome, to make a league of amity and confederacy with them,

18 And to intreat them that they would take the yoke from them; for they saw that the kingdom of the Grecians did oppress Israel with servitude.

19 They went therefore to Rome, which was a very great journey, and came into the senate, where they spake and said.

20 Judas Maccabeus with his brethren, and the people of the Jews, have sent us unto you, to make a confederacy and peace with you, and that we might be registered your confederates and friends.

21 So that matter pleased the Romans well.

22 And this is the copy of the epistle which the senate wrote back again in tables of brass, and sent to Jerusalem, that there they might have by them a memorial of peace and confederacy:

23 Good success be to the Romans, and to the people of the Jews, by sea and by land for ever: the sword also and enemy be far from them,

24 If there come first any war upon the Romans or any of their confederates throughout all their dominion,

25 The people of the Jews shall help them, as the time shall be appointed, with all their heart:

26 Neither shall they give any thing unto them that make war upon them, or aid them with victuals, weapons, money, or ships, as it hath seemed

good unto the Romans; but they shall keep their covenants without taking any thing therefore.

27 In the same manner also, if war come first upon the nation of the Jews, the Romans shall help them with all their heart, according as the time shall be appointed them:

28 Neither shall victuals be given to them that take part against them, or weapons, or money, or ships, as it hath seemed good to the Romans; but they shall keep their covenants, and that without deceit.

29 According to these articles did the Romans make a covenant with the people of the Jews.

30 Howbeit if hereafter the one party or the other shall think to meet to add or diminish any thing, they may do it at their pleasures, and whatsoever they shall add or take away shall be ratified.

31 And as touching the evils that Demetrius doeth to the Jews, we have written unto him, saying, Wherefore thou made thy yoke heavy upon our friends and confederates the Jews?

32 If therefore they complain any more against thee, we will do them justice, and fight with thee by sea and by land.

1 Maccabees 9

1 Furthermore, when Demetrius heard the Nicanor and his host were slain in battle, he sent Bacchides and Alcimus into the land of Judea the second time, and with them the chief strength of his host:

2 Who went forth by the way that leadeth to Galgala, and pitched their tents before Masaloth, which is in Arbela, and after they had won it, they slew much people.

3 Also the first month of the hundred fifty and second year they encamped before Jerusalem:

4 From whence they removed, and went to Berea, with twenty thousand footmen and two thousand horsemen.

5 Now Judas had pitched his tents at Eleasa, and three thousand chosen men with him:

6 Who seeing the multitude of the other army to he so great were sore afraid; whereupon many conveyed themselves out of the host, insomuch as abode of them no more but eight hundred men.

7 When Judas therefore saw that his host slipt away, and that the battle pressed upon him, he was sore troubled in mind, and much distressed, for that he had no time to gather them together.

8 Nevertheless unto them that remained he said, Let us arise and go up against our enemies, if peradventure we may be able to fight with them.

9 But they dehorted him, saying, We shall never be able: let us now rather save our lives, and hereafter we will return with our brethren, and fight against them: for we are but few.

10 Then Judas said, God forbid that I should do this thing, and flee away from them: if our time be come, let us die manfully for our brethren, and let us not stain our honour.

11 With that the host of Bacchides removed out of their tents, and stood over against them, their horsemen being divided into two troops, and their slingers and archers going before the host and they that marched in the foreward were all mighty men.

12 As for Bacchides, he was in the right wing: so the host drew near on the two parts, and sounded their trumpets.

13 They also of Judas' side, even they sounded their trumpets also, so that the earth shook at the noise of the armies, and the battle continued from morning till night.

14 Now when Judas perceived that Bacchides and the strength of his army were on the right side, he took with him all the hardy men,

15 Who discomfited the right wing, and pursued them unto the mount Azotus.

16 But when they of the left wing saw that they of the right wing were discomfited, they followed upon Judas and those that were with him hard at the heels from behind:

17 Whereupon there was a sore battle, insomuch as many were slain on both parts.

18 Judas also was killed, and the remnant fled.

19 Then Jonathan and Simon took Judas their brother, and buried him in the sepulchre of his fathers in Modin.

20 Moreover they bewailed him, and all Israel made great lamentation for him, and mourned many days, saying,

21 How is the valiant man fallen, that delivered Israel!

22 As for the other things concerning Judas and his wars, and the noble acts which he did, and his greatness, they are not written: for they were very many.

23 Now after the death of Judas the wicked began to put forth their heads in all the coasts of Israel, and there arose up all such as wrought iniquity.

24 In those days also was there a very great famine, by reason whereof the country revolted, and went with them.

25 Then Bacchides chose the wicked men, and made them lords of the country.

26 And they made enquiry and search for Judas' friends, and

brought them unto Bacchides, who took vengeance of them, and used them despitefully.

27 So was there a great affliction in Israel, the like whereof was not since the time that a prophet was not seen among them.

28 For this cause all Judas' friends came together, and said unto Jonathan,

29 Since thy brother Judas died, we have no man like him to go forth against our enemies, and Bacchides, and against them of our nation that are adversaries to us.

30 Now therefore we have chosen thee this day to be our prince and captain in his stead, that thou mayest fight our battles.

31 Upon this Jonathan took the governance upon him at that time, and rose up instead of his brother Judas.

32 But when Bacchides gat knowledge thereof, he sought for to slay him

33 Then Jonathan, and Simon his brother, and all that were with him, perceiving that, fled into the wilderness of Thecoe, and pitched their tents by the water of the pool Asphar.

34 Which when Bacchides understood, he came near to Jordan with all his host upon the sabbath day.

35 Now Jonathan had sent his brother John, a captain of the people, to pray his friends the Nabathites, that they might leave with them their carriage, which was much.

36 But the children of Jambri came out of Medaba, and took John, and all that he had, and went their way with it.

37 After this came word to Jonathan and Simon his brother, that the children of Jambri made a great marriage, and were bringing the bride from Nadabatha with a great train, as being the daughter of one of the great princes of Chanaan.

38 Therefore they remembered John their brother, and went up, and hid themselves under the covert of the mountain:

39 Where they lifted up their eyes, and looked, and, behold, there was much ado and great carriage: and the bridegroom came forth, and his friends and brethren, to meet them with drums, and instruments of musick, and many weapons.

40 Then Jonathan and they that were with him rose up against them from the place where they lay in ambush, and made a slaughter of them in such sort, as many fell down dead, and the remnant fled into the mountain, and they took all their spoils.

41 Thus was the marriage turned into mourning, and the noise of their melody into lamentation.

42 So when they had avenged fully the blood of their brother, they turned again to the marsh of Jordan.

43 Now when Bacchides heard hereof, he came on the sabbath day unto the banks of Jordan with a great power.

44 Then Jonathan said to his company, Let us go up now and fight for our lives, for it standeth not with us to day, as in time past:

45 For, behold, the battle is before us and behind us, and the water of Jordan on this side and that side, the marsh likewise and wood, neither is there place for us to turn aside.

46 Wherefore cry ye now unto heaven, that ye may be delivered from the hand of your enemies.

47 With that they joined battle, and Jonathan stretched forth his hand to smite Bacchides, but he turned back from him.

48 Then Jonathan and they that were with him leapt into Jordan, and swam over unto the other bank: howbeit the other passed not over Jordan unto them.

49 So there were slain of Bacchides' side that day about a thousand men.

50 Afterward returned Bacchides to Jerusalem and repaired the strong cites in Judea; the fort in Jericho,

and Emmaus, and Bethhoron, and Bethel, and Thamnatha, Pharathoni, and Taphon, these did he strengthen with high walls, with gates and with bars.

51 And in them he set a garrison, that they might work malice upon Israel.

52 He fortified also the city Bethsura, and Gazera, and the tower, and put forces in them, and provision of victuals.

53 Besides, he took the chief men's sons in the country for hostages, and put them into the tower at Jerusalem to be kept.

54 Moreover in the hundred fifty and third year, in the second month, Alcimus commanded that the wall of the inner court of the sanctuary should be pulled down; he pulled down also the works of the prophets

55 And as he began to pull down, even at that time was Alcimus plagued, and his enterprizes hindered: for his mouth was stopped, and he was taken with a palsy, so that he could no more speak any thing, nor give order concerning his house.

56 So Alcimus died at that time with great torment.

57 Now when Bacchides saw that Alcimus was dead, he returned to the king: whereupon the land of Judea was in rest two years.

58 Then all the ungodly men held a council, saying, Behold, Jonathan and his company are at ease, and dwell without care: now therefore we will bring Bacchides hither, who shall take them all in one night.

59 So they went and consulted with him.

60 Then removed he, and came with a great host, and sent letters privily to his adherents in Judea, that they should take Jonathan and those that were with him: howbeit they could not, because their counsel was known unto them.

61 Wherefore they took of the men of the country, that were authors of that mischief, about fifty persons, and slew them.

62 Afterward Jonathan, and Simon, and they that were with him, got them away to Bethbasi, which is in the wilderness, and they repaired the decays thereof, and made it strong.

63 Which thing when Bacchides knew, he gathered together all his host, and sent word to them that were of Judea.

64 Then went he and laid siege against Bethbasi; and they fought against it a long season and made engines of war.

65 But Jonathan left his brother Simon in the city, and went forth himself into the country, and with a certain number went he forth.

66 And he smote Odonarkes and his brethren, and the children of Phasiron in their tent.

67 And when he began to smite them, and came up with his forces, Simon and his company went out of the city, and burned up the engines of war,

68 And fought against Bacchides, who was discomfited by them, and they afflicted him sore: for his counsel and travail was in vain.

69 Wherefore he was very wroth at the wicked men that gave him counsel to come into the country, inasmuch as he slew many of them, and purposed to return into his own country.

70 Whereof when Jonathan had knowledge, he sent ambassadors unto him, to the end he should make peace with him, and deliver them the prisoners.

71 Which thing he accepted, and did according to his demands, and sware unto him that he would never do him harm all the days of his life.

72 When therefore he had restored unto him the prisoners that he had taken aforetime out of the land of Judea, he returned and went his way into his own land, neither came he any more into their borders.

73 Thus the sword ceased from Israel: but Jonathan dwelt at Machmas, and began to govern the

people; and he destroyed the ungodly men out of Israel.

1 Maccabees 10

1 In the hundred and sixtieth year Alexander, the son of Antiochus surnamed Epiphanes, went up and took Ptolemais: for the people had received him, by means whereof he reigned there,

2 Now when king Demetrius heard thereof, he gathered together an exceeding great host, and went forth against him to fight.

3 Moreover Demetrius sent letters unto Jonathan with loving words, so as he magnified him.

4 For said he, Let us first make peace with him, before he join with Alexander against us:

5 Else he will remember all the evils that we have done against him, and against his brethren and his people.

6 Wherefore he gave him authority to gather together an host, and to provide weapons, that he might aid him in battle: he commanded also that the hostages that were in the tower should be delivered him.

7 Then came Jonathan to Jerusalem, and read the letters in the audience of all the people, and of them that were in the tower:

8 Who were sore afraid, when they heard that the king had given him authority to gather together an host.

9 Whereupon they of the tower delivered their hostages unto Jonathan, and he delivered them unto their parents.

10 This done, Jonathan settled himself in Jerusalem, and began to build and repair the city.

11 And he commanded the workmen to build the walls and the mount Sion and about with square stones for fortification; and they did so.

12 Then the strangers, that were in the fortresses which Bacchides had built, fled away;

13 Insomuch as every man left his place, and went into his own country.

14 Only at Bethsura certain of those that had forsaken the law and the commandments remained still: for it was their place of refuge.

15 Now when king Alexander had heard what promises Demetrius had sent unto Jonathan: when also it was told him of the battles and noble acts which he and his brethren had done, and of the pains that they had endured,

16 He said, Shall we find such another man? now therefore we will make him our friend and confederate.

17 Upon this he wrote a letter, and sent it unto him, according to these words, saying,

18 King Alexander to his brother Jonathan sendeth greeting:

19 We have heard of thee, that thou art a man of great power, and meet to be our friend.

20 Wherefore now this day we ordain thee to be the high priest of thy nation, and to be called the king's friend; (and therewithal he sent him a purple robe and a crown of gold:) and require thee to take our part, and keep friendship with us.

21 So in the seventh month of the hundred and sixtieth year, at the feast of the tabernacles, Jonathan put on the holy robe, and gathered together forces, and provided much armour.

22 Whereof when Demetrius heard, he was very sorry, and said,

23 What have we done, that Alexander hath prevented us in making amity with the Jews to strengthen himself?

24 I also will write unto them words of encouragement, and promise them dignities and gifts, that I may have their aid.

25 He sent unto them therefore to this effect: King Demetrius unto the people of the Jews sendeth greeting:

26 Whereas ye have kept covenants with us, and continued in our friendship, not joining yourselves with our enemies, we have heard hereof, and are glad.

27 Wherefore now continue ye still to be faithful unto us, and we will well recompense you for the things ye do in our behalf,

28 And will grant you many immunities, and give you rewards.

29 And now do I free you, and for your sake I release all the Jews, from tributes, and from the customs of salt, and from crown taxes,

30 And from that which appertaineth unto me to receive for the third part or the seed, and the half of the fruit of the trees, I release it from this day forth, so that they shall not be taken of the land of Judea, nor of the three governments which are added thereunto out of the country of Samaria and Galilee, from this day forth for evermore.

31 Let Jerusalem also be holy and free, with the borders thereof, both from tenths and tributes.

32 And as for the tower which is at Jerusalem, I yield up authority over it, and give the high priest, that he may set in it such men as he shall choose to keep it.

33 Moreover I freely set at liberty every one of the Jews, that were carried captives out of the land of Judea into any part of my kingdom, and I will that all my officers remit the tributes even of their cattle.

34 Furthermore I will that all the feasts, and sabbaths, and new moons, and solemn days, and the three days before the feast, and the three days after the feast shall be all

of immunity and freedom for all the Jews in my realm.

35 Also no man shall have authority to meddle with or to molest any of them in any matter.

36 I will further, that there be enrolled among the king's forces about thirty thousand men of the Jews, unto whom pay shall be given, as belongeth to all king's forces.

37 And of them some shall be placed in the king's strong holds, of whom also some shall be set over the affairs of the kingdom, which are of trust: and I will that their overseers and governors be of themselves, and that they live after their own laws, even as the king hath commanded in the land of Judea.

38 And concerning the three governments that are added to Judea from the country of Samaria, let them be joined with Judea, that they may be reckoned to be under one, nor bound to obey other authority than the high priest's.

39 As for Ptolemais, and the land pertaining thereto, I give it as a free gift to the sanctuary at Jerusalem for the necessary expences of the sanctuary.

40 Moreover I give every year fifteen thousand shekels of silver out of the king's accounts from the places appertaining.

41 And all the overplus, which the officers payed not in as in former time, from henceforth shall be given toward the works of the temple.

42 And beside this, the five thousand shekels of silver, which they took from the uses of the temple out of the accounts year by year, even those things shall be released, because they appertain to the priests that minister.

43 And whosoever they be that flee unto the temple at Jerusalem, or be within the liberties hereof, being indebted unto the king, or for any other matter, let them be at liberty, and all that they have in my realm.

44 For the building also and repairing of the works of the sanctuary expences shall be given of the king's accounts.

45 Yea, and for the building of the walls of Jerusalem, and the fortifying thereof round about, expences shall be given out of the king's accounts, as also for the building of the walls in Judea.

46 Now when Jonathan and the people heard these words, they gave no credit unto them, nor received them, because they remembered the great evil that he had done in Israel; for he had afflicted them very sore.

47 But with Alexander they were well pleased, because he was the first that entreated of true peace with them, and they were confederate with him always.

48 Then gathered king Alexander great forces, and camped over against Demetrius.

49 And after the two kings had joined battle, Demetrius' host fled: but Alexander followed after him, and prevailed against them.

50 And he continued the battle very sore until the sun went down: and that day was Demetrius slain.

51 Afterward Alexander sent ambassadors to Ptolemee king of Egypt with a message to this effect:

52 Forasmuch as I am come again to my realm, and am set in the throne of my progenitors, and have gotten the dominion, and overthrown Demetrius, and recovered our country;

53 For after I had joined battle with him, both he and his host was discomfited by us, so that we sit in the throne of his kingdom:

54 Now therefore let us make a league of amity together, and give me now thy daughter to wife: and I will be thy son in law, and will give both thee and her as according to thy dignity.

55 Then Ptolemee the king gave answer, saying, Happy be the day wherein thou didst return into the land of thy fathers, and satest in the throne of their kingdom.

56 And now will I do to thee, as thou hast written: meet me therefore at Ptolemais, that we may see one another; for I will marry my daughter to thee according to thy desire.

57 So Ptolemee went out of Egypt with his daughter Cleopatra, and they came unto Ptolemais in the hundred threescore and second year:

58 Where king Alexander meeting him, he gave unto him his daughter Cleopatra, and celebrated her marriage at Ptolemais with great glory, as the manner of kings is.

59 Now king Alexander had written unto Jonathan, that he should come and meet him.

60 Who thereupon went honourably to Ptolemais, where he met the two kings, and gave them and their friends silver and gold, and many presents, and found favour in their sight.

61 At that time certain pestilent fellows of Israel, men of a wicked life, assembled themselves against him, to accuse him: but the king would not hear them.

62 Yea more than that, the king commanded to take off his garments, and clothe him in purple: and they did so.

63 And he made him sit by himself, and said into his princes, Go with him into the midst of the city, and make proclamation, that no man complain against him of any matter,

and that no man trouble him for any manner of cause.

64 Now when his accusers saw that he was honored according to the proclamation, and clothed in purple, they fled all away.

65 So the king honoured him, and wrote him among his chief friends, and made him a duke, and partaker of his dominion.

66 Afterward Jonathan returned to Jerusalem with peace and gladness.

67 Furthermore in the; hundred threescore and fifth year came Demetrius son of Demetrius out of Crete into the land of his fathers:

68 Whereof when king Alexander heard tell, he was right sorry, and returned into Antioch.

69 Then Demetrius made Apollonius the governor of Celosyria his general, who gathered together a great host, and camped in Jamnia, and sent unto Jonathan the high priest, saying,

70 Thou alone liftest up thyself against us, and I am laughed to scorn for thy sake, and reproached: and why dost thou vaunt thy power against us in the mountains?

71 Now therefore, if thou trustest in thine own strength, come down to us into the plain field, and there let us try the matter together: for with me is the power of the cities.

72 Ask and learn who I am, and the rest that take our part, and they shall tell thee that thy foot is not able to to flight in their own land.

73 Wherefore now thou shalt not be able to abide the horsemen and so great a power in the plain, where is neither stone nor flint, nor place to flee unto.

74 So when Jonathan heard these words of Apollonius, he was moved in his mind, and choosing ten thousand men he went out of Jerusalem, where Simon his brother met him for to help him.

75 And he pitched his tents against Joppa: but; they of Joppa shut him out of the city, because Apollonius had a garrison there.

76 Then Jonathan laid siege unto it: whereupon they of the city let him in for fear: and so Jonathan won Joppa.

77 Whereof when Apollonius heard, he took three thousand horsemen, with a great host of footmen, and went to Azotus as one that journeyed, and therewithal drew him forth into the plain. because he had a great number of horsemen, in whom he put his trust.

78 Then Jonathan followed after him to Azotus, where the armies joined battle.

79 Now Apollonius had left a thousand horsemen in ambush.

80 And Jonathan knew that there was an ambushment behind him; for they had compassed in his host, and cast darts at the people, from morning till evening.

81 But the people stood still, as Jonathan had commanded them: and so the enemies' horses were tired.

82 Then brought Simon forth his host, and set them against the footmen, (for the horsemen were spent) who were discomfited by him, and fled.

83 The horsemen also, being scattered in the field, fled to Azotus, and went into Bethdagon, their idol's temple, for safety.

84 But Jonathan set fire on Azotus, and the cities round about it, and took their spoils; and the temple of Dagon, with them that were fled into it, he burned with fire.

85 Thus there were burned and slain with the sword well nigh eight thousand men.

86 And from thence Jonathan removed his host, and camped against Ascalon, where the men of the city came forth, and met him with great pomp.

87 After this returned Jonathan and his host unto Jerusalem, having any spoils.

88 Now when king Alexander heard these things, he honoured Jonathan yet more.

89 And sent him a buckle of gold, as the use is to be given to such as are of the king's blood: he gave him also Accaron with the borders thereof in possession.

1 Maccabees 11

1 And the king of Egypt gathered together a great host, like the sand that lieth upon the sea shore, and many ships, and went about through deceit to get Alexander's kingdom, and join it to his own.

2 Whereupon he took his journey into Spain in peaceable manner, so as they of the cities opened unto him, and met him: for king Alexander had commanded them so to do, because he was his brother in law.

3 Now as Ptolemee entered into the cities, he set in every one of them a garrison of soldiers to keep it.

4 And when he came near to Azotus, they shewed him the temple of Dagon that was burnt, and Azotus and the suburbs thereof that were destroyed, and the bodies that were cast abroad and them that he had burnt in the battle; for they had made heaps of them by the way where he should pass.

5 Also they told the king whatsoever Jonathan had done, to the intent he might blame him: but the king held his peace.

6 Then Jonathan met the king with great pomp at Joppa, where they saluted one another, and lodged.

7 Afterward Jonathan, when he had gone with the king to the river called Eleutherus, returned again to Jerusalem.

8 King Ptolemee therefore, having gotten the dominion of the cities by the sea unto Seleucia upon the sea coast, imagined wicked counsels against Alexander.

9 Whereupon he sent ambasadors unto king Demetrius, saying, Come, let us make a league betwixt us, and I will give thee my daughter whom Alexander hath, and thou shalt reign in thy father's kingdom:

10 For I repent that I gave my daughter unto him, for he sought to slay me.

11 Thus did he slander him, because he was desirous of his kingdom.

12 Wherefore he took his daughter from him, and gave her to Demetrius, and forsook Alexander, so that their hatred was openly known.

13 Then Ptolemee entered into Antioch, where he set two crowns upon his head, the crown of Asia, and of Egypt.

14 In the mean season was king Alexander in Cilicia, because those that dwelt in those parts had revolted from him.

15 But when Alexander heard of this, he came to war against him: whereupon king Ptolemee brought forth his host, and met him with a mighty power, and put him to flight.

16 So Alexander fled into Arabia there to be defended; but king Ptolemee was exalted:

17 For Zabdiel the Arabian took off Alexander's head, and sent it unto Ptolemee.

18 King Ptolemee also died the third day after, and they that were in the strong holds were slain one of another.

19 By this means Demetrius reigned in the hundred threescore and seventh year.

20 At the same time Jonathan gathered together them that were in Judea to take the tower that was in Jerusalem: and he made many engines of war against it.

21 Then came ungodly persons, who hated their own people, went unto the king, and told him that Jonathan besieged the tower,

22 Whereof when he heard, he was angry, and immediately removing, he came to Ptolemais, and wrote unto Jonathan, that he should not lay siege to the tower, but come and speak with him at Ptolemais in great haste.

23 Nevertheless Jonathan, when he heard this, commanded to besiege it

still: and he chose certain of the elders of Israel and the priests, and put himself in peril;

24 And took silver and gold, and raiment, and divers presents besides, and went to Ptolemais unto the king, where he found favour in his sight.

25 And though certain ungodly men of the people had made complaints against him,

26 Yet the king entreated him as his predecessors had done before, and promoted him in the sight of all his friends,

27 And confirmed him in the high priesthood, and in all the honours that he had before, and gave him preeminence among his chief friends.

28 Then Jonathan desired the king, that he would make Judea free from tribute, as also the three governments, with the country of Samaria; and he promised him three hundred talents.

29 So the king consented, and wrote letters unto Jonathan of all these things after this manner:

30 King Demetrius unto his brother Jonathan, and unto the nation of the Jews, sendeth greeting:

31 We send you here a copy of the letter which we did write unto our cousin Lasthenes concerning you, that ye might see it.

32 King Demetrius unto his father Lasthenes sendeth greeting:

33 We are determined to do good to the people of the Jews, who are our friends, and keep covenants with us, because of their good will toward us.

34 Wherefore we have ratified unto them the borders of Judea, with the three governments of Apherema and Lydda and Ramathem, that are added unto Judea from the country of Samaria, and all things appertaining unto them, for all such as do sacrifice in Jerusalem, instead of the payments which the king received of them yearly aforetime out of the fruits of the earth and of trees.

35 And as for other things that belong unto us, of the tithes and customs pertaining unto us, as also the saltpits, and the crown taxes, which are due unto us, we discharge them of them all for their relief.

36 And nothing hereof shall be revoked from this time forth for ever.

37 Now therefore see that thou make a copy of these things, and let it be delivered unto Jonathan, and set upon the holy mount in a conspicuous place.

38 After this, when king Demetrius saw that the land was quiet before him, and that no resistance was made against him, he sent away all his forces, every one to his own place, except certain bands of strangers, whom he had gathered

from the isles of the heathen: wherefore all the forces of his fathers hated him.

39 Moreover there was one Tryphon, that had been of Alexander's part afore, who, seeing that all the host murmured against Demetrius, went to Simalcue the Arabian that brought up Antiochus the young son of Alexander,

40 And lay sore upon him to deliver him this young Antiochus, that he might reign in his father's stead: he told him therefore all that Demetrius had done, and how his men of war were at enmity with him, and there he remained a long season.

41 In the mean time Jonathan sent unto king Demetrius, that he would cast those of the tower out of Jerusalem, and those also in the fortresses: for they fought against Israel.

42 So Demetrius sent unto Jonathan, saying, I will not only do this for thee and thy people, but I will greatly honour thee and thy nation, if opportunity serve.

43 Now therefore thou shalt do well, if thou send me men to help me; for all my forces are gone from me.

44 Upon this Jonathan sent him three thousand strong men unto Antioch: and when they came to the king, the king was very glad of their coming.

45 Howbeit they that were of the city gathered themselves together into the midst of the city, to the number of an hundred and twenty thousand men, and would have slain the king.

46 Wherefore the king fled into the court, but they of the city kept the passages of the city, and began to fight.

47 Then the king called to the Jews for help, who came unto him all at once, and dispersing themselves through the city slew that day in the city to the number of an hundred thousand.

48 Also they set fire on the city, and gat many spoils that day, and delivered the king.

49 So when they of the city saw that the Jews had got the city as they would, their courage was abated: wherefore they made supplication to the king, and cried, saying,

50 Grant us peace, and let the Jews cease from assaulting us and the city.

51 With that they cast away their weapons, and made peace; and the Jews were honoured in the sight of the king, and in the sight of all that were in his realm; and they returned to Jerusalem, having great spoils.

52 So king Demetrius sat on the throne of his kingdom, and the land was quiet before him.

53 Nevertheless he dissembled in all that ever he spake, and estranged himself from Jonathan, neither rewarded he him according to the benefits which he had received of him, but troubled him very sore.

54 After this returned Tryphon, and with him the young child Antiochus, who reigned, and was crowned.

55 Then there gathered unto him all the men of war, whom Demetrius had put away, and they fought against Demetrius, who turned his back and fled.

56 Moreover Tryphon took the elephants, and won Antioch.

57 At that time young Antiochus wrote unto Jonathan, saying, I confirm thee in the high priesthood, and appoint thee ruler over the four governments, and to be one of the king's friends.

58 Upon this he sent him golden vessels to be served in, and gave him leave to drink in gold, and to be clothed in purple, and to wear a golden buckle.

59 His brother Simon also he made captain from the place called The ladder of Tyrus unto the borders of Egypt.

60 Then Jonathan went forth, and passed through the cities beyond the water, and all the forces of Syria gathered themselves unto him for to help him: and when he came to Ascalon, they of the city met him honourably.

61 From whence he went to Gaza, but they of Gaza shut him out; wherefore he laid siege unto it, and burned the suburbs thereof with fire, and spoiled them.

62 Afterward, when they of Gaza made supplication unto Jonathan, he made peace with them, and took the sons of their chief men for hostages, and sent them to Jerusalem, and passed through the country unto Damascus.

63 Now when Jonathan heard that Demetrius' princes were come to Cades, which is in Galilee, with a great power, purposing to remove him out of the country,

64 He went to meet them, and left Simon his brother in the country.

65 Then Simon encamped against Bethsura and fought against it a long season, and shut it up:

66 But they desired to have peace with him, which he granted them, and then put them out from thence, and took the city, and set a garrison in it.

67 As for Jonathan and his host, they pitched at the water of Gennesar, from whence betimes in the morning they gat them to the plain of Nasor.

68 And, behold, the host of strangers met them in the plain, who, having

laid men in ambush for him in the mountains, came themselves over against him.

69 So when they that lay in ambush rose out of their places and joined battle, all that were of Jonathan's side fled;

70 Insomuch as there was not one of them left, except Mattathias the son of Absalom, and Judas the son of Calphi, the captains of the host.

71 Then Jonathan rent his clothes, and cast earth upon his head, and prayed.

72 Afterwards turning again to battle, he put them to flight, and so they ran away.

73 Now when his own men that were fled saw this, they turned again unto him, and with him pursued them to Cades, even unto their own tents, and there they camped.

74 So there were slain of the heathen that day about three thousand men: but Jonathan returned to Jerusalem.

1 Maccabees 12

1 Now when Jonathan saw that time served him, he chose certain men, and sent them to Rome, for to confirm and renew the friendship that they had with them.

2 He sent letters also to the Lacedemonians, and to other places, for the same purpose.

3 So they went unto Rome, and entered into the senate, and said, Jonathan the high priest, and the people of the Jews, sent us unto you, to the end ye should renew the friendship, which ye had with them, and league, as in former time.

4 Upon this the Romans gave them letters unto the governors of every place that they should bring them into the land of Judea peaceably.

5 And this is the copy of the letters which Jonathan wrote to the Lacedemonians:

6 Jonathan the high priest, and the elders of the nation, and the priests, and the other of the Jews, unto the Lacedemonians their brethren send greeting:

7 There were letters sent in times past unto Onias the high priest from Darius, who reigned then among you, to signify that ye are our brethren, as the copy here underwritten doth specify.

8 At which time Onias entreated the ambassador that was sent honourably, and received the letters, wherein declaration was made of the league and friendship.

9 Therefore we also, albeit we need none of these things, that we have the holy books of scripture in our hands to comfort us,

10 Have nevertheless attempted to send unto you for the renewing of brotherhood and friendship, lest we

should become strangers unto you altogether: for there is a long time passed since ye sent unto us.

11 We therefore at all times without ceasing, both in our feasts, and other convenient days, do remember you in the sacrifices which we offer, and in our prayers, as reason is, and as it becometh us to think upon our brethren:

12 And we are right glad of your honour.

13 As for ourselves, we have had great troubles and wars on every side, forsomuch as the kings that are round about us have fought against us.

14 Howbeit we would not be troublesome unto you, nor to others of our confederates and friends, in these wars:

15 For we have help from heaven that succoureth us, so as we are delivered from our enemies, and our enemies are brought under foot.

16 For this cause we chose Numenius the son of Antiochus, and Antipater the son of Jason, and sent them unto the Romans, to renew the amity that we had with them, and the former league.

17 We commanded them also to go unto you, and to salute and to deliver you our letters concerning the renewing of our brotherhood.

18 Wherefore now ye shall do well to give us an answer thereto.

19 And this is the copy of the letters which Oniares sent.

20 Areus king of the Lacedemonians to Onias the high priest, greeting:

21 It is found in writing, that the Lacedemonians and Jews are brethren, and that they are of the stock of Abraham:

22 Now therefore, since this is come to our knowledge, ye shall do well to write unto us of your prosperity.

23 We do write back again to you, that your cattle and goods are our's, and our's are your's We do command therefore our ambassadors to make report unto you on this wise.

24 Now when Jonathan heard that Demebius' princes were come to fight against him with a greater host than afore,

25 He removed from Jerusalem, and met them in the land of Amathis: for he gave them no respite to enter his country.

26 He sent spies also unto their tents, who came again, and told him that they were appointed to come upon them in the night season.

27 Wherefore so soon as the sun was down, Jonathan commanded his men to watch, and to be in arms, that all the night long they might be ready

to fight: also he sent forth centinels round about the host.

28 But when the adversaries heard that Jonathan and his men were ready for battle, they feared, and trembled in their hearts, and they kindled fires in their camp.

29 Howbeit Jonathan and his company knew it not till the morning: for they saw the lights burning.

30 Then Jonathan pursued after them, but overtook them not: for they were gone over the river Eleutherus.

31 Wherefore Jonathan turned to the Arabians, who were called Zabadeans, and smote them, and took their spoils.

32 And removing thence, he came to Damascus, and so passed through all the country,

33 Simon also went forth, and passed through the country unto Ascalon, and the holds there adjoining, from whence he turned aside to Joppa, and won it.

34 For he had heard that they would deliver the hold unto them that took Demetrius' part; wherefore he set a garrison there to keep it.

35 After this came Jonathan home again, and calling the elders of the people together, he consulted with them about building strong holds in Judea,

36 And making the walls of Jerusalem higher, and raising a great mount between the tower and the city, for to separate it from the city, that so it might be alone, that men might neither sell nor buy in it.

37 Upon this they came together to build up the city, forasmuch as part of the wall toward the brook on the east side was fallen down, and they repaired that which was called Caphenatha.

38 Simon also set up Adida in Sephela, and made it strong with gates and bars.

39 Now Tryphon went about to get the kingdom of Asia, and to kill Antiochus the king, that he might set the crown upon his own head.

40 Howbeit he was afraid that Jonathan would not suffer him, and that he would fight against him; wherefore he sought a way how to take Jonathan, that he might kill him. So he removed, and came to Bethsan.

41 Then Jonathan went out to meet him with forty thousand men chosen for the battle, and came to Bethsan.

42 Now when Tryphon saw Jonathan came with so great a force, he durst not stretch his hand against him;

43 But received him honourably, and commended him unto all his friends, and gave him gifts, and commanded his men of war to be as obedient unto him, as to himself.

44 Unto Jonathan also he said, Why hast thou brought all this people to so great trouble, seeing there is no war betwixt us?

45 Therefore send them now home again, and choose a few men to wait on thee, and come thou with me to Ptolemais, for I will give it thee, and the rest of the strong holds and forces, and all that have any charge: as for me, I will return and depart: for this is the cause of my coming.

46 So Jonathan believing him did as he bade him, and sent away his host, who went into the land of Judea.

47 And with himself he retained but three thousand men, of whom he sent two thousand into Galilee, and one thousand went with him.

48 Now as soon as Jonathan entered into Ptolemais, they of Ptolemais shut the gates and took him, and all them that came with him they slew with the sword.

49 Then sent Tryphon an host of footmen and horsemen into Galilee, and into the great plain, to destroy all Jonathan's company.

50 But when they knew that Jonathan and they that were with him were taken and slain, they encouraged one another; and went close together, prepared to fight.

51 They therefore that followed upon them, perceiving that they were ready to fight for their lives, turned back again.

52 Whereupon they all came into the land of Judea peaceably, and there they bewailed Jonathan, and them that were with him, and they were sore afraid; wherefore all Israel made great lamentation.

53 Then all the heathen that were round about then sought to destroy them: for said they, They have no captain, nor any to help them: now therefore let us make war upon them, and take away their memorial from among men.

1 Maccabees 13

1 Now when Simon heard that Tryphon had gathered together a great host to invade the land of Judea, and destroy it,

2 And saw that the people was in great trembling and fear, he went up to Jerusalem, and gathered the people together,

3 And gave them exhortation, saying, Ye yourselves know what great things I, and my brethren, and my father's house, have done for the laws and the sanctuary, the battles also and troubles which we have seen.

4 By reason whereof all my brethren are slain for Israel's sake, and I am left alone.

5 Now therefore be it far from me, that I should spare mine own life in

any time of trouble: for I am no better than my brethren.

6 Doubtless I will avenge my nation, and the sanctuary, and our wives, and our children: for all the heathen are gathered to destroy us of very malice.

7 Now as soon as the people heard these words, their spirit revived.

8 And they answered with a loud voice, saying, Thou shalt be our leader instead of Judas and Jonathan thy brother.

9 Fight thou our battles, and whatsoever, thou commandest us, that will we do.

10 So then he gathered together all the men of war, and made haste to finish the walls of Jerusalem, and he fortified it round about.

11 Also he sent Jonathan the son of Absolom, and with him a great power, to Joppa: who casting out them that were therein remained there in it.

12 So Tryphon removed from Ptolemaus with a great power to invade the land of Judea, and Jonathan was with him in ward.

13 But Simon pitched his tents at Adida, over against the plain.

14 Now when Tryphon knew that Simon was risen up instead of his brother Jonathan, and meant to join battle with him, he sent messengers unto him, saying,

15 Whereas we have Jonathan thy brother in hold, it is for money that he is owing unto the king's treasure, concerning the business that was committed unto him.

16 Wherefore now send an hundred talents of silver, and two of his sons for hostages, that when he is at liberty he may not revolt from us, and we will let him go.

17 Hereupon Simon, albeit he perceived that they spake deceitfully unto him yet sent he the money and the children, lest peradventure he should procure to himself great hatred of the people:

18 Who might have said, Because I sent him not the money and the children, therefore is Jonathan dead.

19 So he sent them the children and the hundred talents: howbeit Tryphon dissembled neither would he let Jonathan go.

20 And after this came Tryphon to invade the land, and destroy it, going round about by the way that leadeth unto Adora: but Simon and his host marched against him in every place, wheresoever he went.

21 Now they that were in the tower sent messengers unto Tryphon, to the end that he should hasten his coming unto them by the wilderness, and send them victuals.

22 Wherefore Tryphon made ready all his horsemen to come that night: but there fell a very great snow, by

reason whereof he came not. So he departed, and came into the country of Galaad.

23 And when he came near to Bascama he slew Jonathan, who was buried there.

24 Afterward Tryphon returned and went into his own land.

25 Then sent Simon, and took the bones of Jonathan his brother, and buried them in Modin, the city of his fathers.

26 And all Israel made great lamentation for him, and bewailed him many days.

27 Simon also built a monument upon the sepulchre of his father and his brethren, and raised it aloft to the sight, with hewn stone behind and before.

28 Moreover he set up seven pyramids, one against another, for his father, and his mother, and his four brethren.

29 And in these he made cunning devices, about the which he set great pillars, and upon the pillars he made all their armour for a perpetual memory, and by the armour ships carved, that they might be seen of all that sail on the sea.

30 This is the sepulchre which he made at Modin, and it standeth yet unto this day.

31 Now Tryphon dealt deceitfully with the young king Antiochus, and slew him.

32 And he reigned in his stead, and crowned himself king of Asia, and brought a great calamity upon the land.

33 Then Simon built up the strong holds in Judea, and fenced them about with high towers, and great walls, and gates, and bars, and laid up victuals therein.

34 Moreover Simon chose men, and sent to king Demetrius, to the end he should give the land an immunity, because all that Tryphon did was to spoil.

35 Unto whom king Demetrius answered and wrote after this manner:

36 King Demetrius unto Simon the high priest, and friend of kings, as also unto the elders and nation of the Jews, sendeth greeting:

37 The golden crown, and the scarlet robe, which ye sent unto us, we have received: and we are ready to make a stedfast peace with you, yea, and to write unto our officers, to confirm the immunities which we have granted.

38 And whatsoever covenants we have made with you shall stand; and the strong holds, which ye have builded, shall be your own.

39 As for any oversight or fault committed unto this day, we forgive it, and the crown tax also, which ye owe us: and if there were any other tribute paid in Jerusalem, it shall no more be paid.

40 And look who are meet among you to be in our court, let then be enrolled, and let there be peace betwixt us.

41 Thus the yoke of the heathen was taken away from Israel in the hundred and seventieth year.

42 Then the people of Israel began to write in their instruments and contracts, In the first year of Simon the high priest, the governor and leader of the Jews.

43 In those days Simon camped against Gaza and besieged it round about; he made also an engine of war, and set it by the city, and battered a certain tower, and took it.

44 And they that were in the engine leaped into the city; whereupon there was a great uproar in the city:

45 Insomuch as the people of the city rent their clothes, and climbed upon the walls with their wives and children, and cried with a loud voice, beseeching Simon to grant them peace.

46 And they said, Deal not with us according to our wickedness, but according to thy mercy.

47 So Simon was appeased toward them, and fought no more against them, but put them out of the city, and cleansed the houses wherein the idols were, and so entered into it with songs and thanksgiving.

48 Yea, he put all uncleanness out of it, and placed such men there as would keep the law, and made it stronger than it was before, and built therein a dwellingplace for himself.

49 They also of the tower in Jerusalem were kept so strait, that they could neither come forth, nor go into the country, nor buy, nor sell: wherefore they were in great distress for want of victuals, and a great number of them perished through famine.

50 Then cried they to Simon, beseeching him to be at one with them: which thing he granted them; and when he had put them out from thence, he cleansed the tower from pollutions:

51 And entered into it the three and twentieth day of the second month in the hundred seventy and first year, with thanksgiving, and branches of palm trees, and with harps, and cymbals, and with viols, and hymns, and songs: because there was destroyed a great enemy out of Israel.

52 He ordained also that that day should be kept every year with gladness. Moreover the hill of the temple that was by the tower he

made stronger than it was, and there he dwelt himself with his company.

53 And when Simon saw that John his son was a valiant man, he made him captain of all the hosts; and he dwelt in Gazera.

1 Maccabees 14

1 Now in the hundred threescore and twelfth year king Demetrius gathered his forces together, and went into Media to get him help to fight against Tryphone.

2 But when Arsaces, the king of Persia and Media, heard that Demetrius was entered within his borders, he sent one of his princes to take him alive:

3 Who went and smote the host of Demetrius, and took him, and brought him to Arsaces, by whom he was put in ward.

4 As for the land of Judea, that was quiet all the days of Simon; for he sought the good of his nation in such wise, as that evermore his authority and honour pleased them well.

5 And as he was honourable in all his acts, so in this, that he took Joppa for an haven, and made an entrance to the isles of the sea,

6 And enlarged the bounds of his nation, and recovered the country,

7 And gathered together a great number of captives, and had the dominion of Gazera, and Bethsura, and the tower, out of the which he took all uncleanness, neither was there any that resisted him.

8 Then did they till their ground in peace, and the earth gave her increase, and the trees of the field their fruit.

9 The ancient men sat all in the streets, communing together of good things, and the young men put on glorious and warlike apparel.

10 He provided victuals for the cities, and set in them all manner of munition, so that his honourable name was renowned unto the end of the world.

11 He made peace in the land, and Israel rejoiced with great joy:

12 For every man sat under his vine and his fig tree, and there was none to fray them:

13 Neither was there any left in the land to fight against them: yea, the kings themselves were overthrown in those days.

14 Moreover he strengthened all those of his people that were brought low: the law he searched out; and every contemner of the law and wicked person he took away.

15 He beautified the sanctuary, and multiplied vessels of the temple.

16 Now when it was heard at Rome, and as far as Sparta, that Jonathan was dead, they were very sorry.

17 But as soon as they heard that his brother Simon was made high priest in his stead, and ruled the country, and the cities therein:

18 They wrote unto him in tables of brass, to renew the friendship and league which they had made with Judas and Jonathan his brethren:

19 Which writings were read before the congregation at Jerusalem.

20 And this is the copy of the letters that the Lacedemonians sent; The rulers of the Lacedemonians, with the city, unto Simon the high priest, and the elders, and priests, and residue of the people of the Jews, our brethren, send greeting:

21 The ambassadors that were sent unto our people certified us of your glory and honour: wherefore we were glad of their coming,

22 And did register the things that they spake in the council of the people in this manner; Numenius son of Antiochus, and Antipater son of Jason, the Jews' ambassadors, came unto us to renew the friendship they had with us.

23 And it pleased the people to entertain the men honourably, and to put the copy of their ambassage in publick records, to the end the people of the Lacedemonians might have a memorial thereof: furthermore we have written a copy thereof unto Simon the high priest.

24 After this Simon sent Numenius to Rome with a great shield of gold of a thousand pound weight to confirm the league with them.

25 Whereof when the people heard, they said, What thanks shall we give to Simon and his sons?

26 For he and his brethren and the house of his father have established Israel, and chased away in fight their enemies from them, and confirmed their liberty.

27 So then they wrote it in tables of brass, which they set upon pillars in mount Sion: and this is the copy of the writing; The eighteenth day of the month Elul, in the hundred threescore and twelfth year, being the third year of Simon the high priest,

28 At Saramel in the great congregation of the priests, and people, and rulers of the nation, and elders of the country, were these things notified unto us.

29 Forasmuch as oftentimes there have been wars in the country, wherein for the maintenance of their sanctuary, and the law, Simon the son of Mattathias, of the posterity of Jarib, together with his brethren, put themselves in jeopardy, and resisting the enemies of their nation did their nation great honour:

30 (For after that Jonathan, having gathered his nation together, and

been their high priest, was added to his people,

31 Their enemies prepared to invade their country, that they might destroy it, and lay hands on the sanctuary:

32 At which time Simon rose up, and fought for his nation, and spent much of his own substance, and armed the valiant men of his nation and gave them wages,

33 And fortified the cities of Judea, together with Bethsura, that lieth upon the borders of Judea, where the armour of the enemies had been before; but he set a garrison of Jews there:

34 Moreover he fortified Joppa, which lieth upon the sea, and Gazera, that bordereth upon Azotus, where the enemies had dwelt before: but he placed Jews there, and furnished them with all things convenient for the reparation thereof.)

35 The people therefore sang the acts of Simon, and unto what glory he thought to bring his nation, made him their governor and chief priest, because he had done all these things, and for the justice and faith which he kept to his nation, and for that he sought by all means to exalt his people.

36 For in his time things prospered in his hands, so that the heathen were taken out of their country, and they also that were in the city of David in Jerusalem, who had made themselves a tower, out of which they issued, and polluted all about the sanctuary, and did much hurt in the holy place:

37 But he placed Jews therein. and fortified it for the safety of the country and the city, and raised up the walls of Jerusalem.

38 King Demetrius also confirmed him in the high priesthood according to those things,

39 And made him one of his friends, and honoured him with great honour.

40 For he had heard say, that the Romans had called the Jews their friends and confederates and brethren; and that they had entertained the ambassadors of Simon honourably;

41 Also that the Jews and priests were well pleased that Simon should be their governor and high priest for ever, until there should arise a faithful prophet;

42 Moreover that he should be their captain, and should take charge of the sanctuary, to set them over their works, and over the country, and over the armour, and over the fortresses, that, I say, he should take charge of the sanctuary;

43 Beside this, that he should be obeyed of every man, and that all the writings in the country should be made in his name, and that he

should be clothed in purple, and wear gold:

44 Also that it should be lawful for none of the people or priests to break any of these things, or to gainsay his words, or to gather an assembly in the country without him, or to be clothed in purple, or wear a buckle of gold;

45 And whosoever should do otherwise, or break any of these things, he should be punished.

46 Thus it liked all the people to deal with Simon, and to do as hath been said.

47 Then Simon accepted hereof, and was well pleased to be high priest, and captain and governor of the Jews and priests, and to defend them all.

48 So they commanded that this writing should be put in tables of brass, and that they should be set up within the compass of the sanctuary in a conspicuous place;

49 Also that the copies thereof should be laid up in the treasury, to the end that Simon and his sons might have them.

1 Maccabees 15

1 Moreover Antiochus son of Demetrius the king sent letters from the isles of the sea unto Simon the priest and prince of the Jews, and to all the people;

2 The contents whereof were these: King Antiochus to Simon the high priest and prince of his nation, and to the people of the Jews, greeting:

3 Forasmuch as certain pestilent men have usurped the kingdom of our fathers, and my purpose is to challenge it again, that I may restore it to the old estate, and to that end have gathered a multitude of foreign soldiers together, and prepared ships of war;

4 My meaning also being to go through the country, that I may be avenged of them that have destroyed it, and made many cities in the kingdom desolate:

5 Now therefore I confirm unto thee all the oblations which the kings before me granted thee, and whatsoever gifts besides they granted.

6 I give thee leave also to coin money for thy country with thine own stamp.

7 And as concerning Jerusalem and the sanctuary, let them be free; and all the armour that thou hast made, and fortresses that thou hast built, and keepest in thine hands, let them remain unto thee.

8 And if anything be, or shall be, owing to the king, let it be forgiven thee from this time forth for evermore.

9 Furthermore, when we have obtained our kingdom, we will

honour thee, and thy nation, and thy temple, with great honour, so that your honour shall be known throughout the world.

10 In the hundred threescore and fourteenth year went Antiochus into the land of his fathers: at which time all the forces came together unto him, so that few were left with Tryphon.

11 Wherefore being pursued by king Antiochus, he fled unto Dora, which lieth by the sea side:

12 For he saw that troubles came upon him all at once, and that his forces had forsaken him.

13 Then camped Antiochus against Dora, having with him an hundred and twenty thousand men of war, and eight thousand horsemen.

14 And when he had compassed the city round about, and joined ships close to the town on the sea side, he vexed the city by land and by sea, neither suffered he any to go out or in.

15 In the mean season came Numenius and his company from Rome, having letters to the kings and countries; wherein were written these things:

16 Lucius, consul of the Romans unto king Ptolemee, greeting:

17 The Jews' ambassadors, our friends and confederates, came unto us to renew the old friendship and league, being sent from Simon the high priest, and from the people of the Jews:

18 And they brought a shield of gold of a thousand pound.

19 We thought it good therefore to write unto the kings and countries, that they should do them no harm, nor fight against them, their cities, or countries, nor yet aid their enemies against them.

20 It seemed also good to us to receive the shield of them.

21 If therefore there be any pestilent fellows, that have fled from their country unto you, deliver them unto Simon the high priest, that he may punish them according to their own law.

22 The same things wrote he likewise unto Demetrius the king, and Attalus, to Ariarathes, and Arsaces,

23 And to all the countries and to Sampsames, and the Lacedemonians, and to Delus, and Myndus, and Sicyon, and Caria, and Samos, and Pamphylia, and Lycia, and Halicarnassus, and Rhodus, and Aradus, and Cos, and Side, and Aradus, and Gortyna, and Cnidus, and Cyprus, and Cyrene.

24 And the copy hereof they wrote to Simon the high priest.

25 So Antiochus the king camped against Dora the second day,

assaulting it continually, and making engines, by which means he shut up Tryphon, that he could neither go out nor in.

26 At that time Simon sent him two thousand chosen men to aid him; silver also, and gold, and much armour.

27 Nevertheless he would not receive them, but brake all the covenants which he had made with him afore, and became strange unto him.

28 Furthermore he sent unto him Athenobius, one of his friends, to commune with him, and say, Ye withhold Joppa and Gazera; with the tower that is in Jerusalem, which are cities of my realm.

29 The borders thereof ye have wasted, and done great hurt in the land, and got the dominion of many places within my kingdom.

30 Now therefore deliver the cities which ye have taken, and the tributes of the places, whereof ye have gotten dominion without the borders of Judea:

31 Or else give me for them five hundred talents of silver; and for the harm that ye have done, and the tributes of the cities, other five hundred talents: if not, we will come and fight against you

32 So Athenobius the king's friend came to Jerusalem: and when he saw the glory of Simon, and the cupboard of gold and silver plate, and his great attendance, he was astonished, and told him the king's message.

33 Then answered Simon, and said unto him, We have neither taken other men's land, nor holden that which appertaineth to others, but the inheritance of our fathers, which our enemies had wrongfully in possession a certain time.

34 Wherefore we, having opportunity, hold the inheritance of our fathers.

35 And whereas thou demandest Joppa and Gazera, albeit they did great harm unto the people in our country, yet will we give thee an hundred talents for them. Hereunto Athenobius answered him not a word;

36 But returned in a rage to the king, and made report unto him of these speeches, and of the glory of Simon, and of all that he had seen: whereupon the king was exceeding wroth.

37 In the mean time fled Tryphon by ship unto Orthosias.

38 Then the king made Cendebeus captain of the sea coast, and gave him an host of footmen and horsemen,

39 And commanded him to remove his host toward Judea; also he commanded him to build up Cedron, and to fortify the gates, and to war

against the people; but as for the king himself, he pursued Tryphon.

40 So Cendebeus came to Jamnia and began to provoke the people and to invade Judea, and to take the people prisoners, and slay them.

41 And when he had built up Cedrou, he set horsemen there, and an host of footmen, to the end that issuing out they might make outroads upon the ways of Judea, as the king had commanded him.

1 Maccabees 16

1 Then came up John from Gazera, and told Simon his father what Cendebeus had done.

2 Wherefore Simon called his two eldest sons, Judas and John, and said unto them, I, and my brethren, and my father's house, have ever from my youth unto this day fought against the enemies of Israel; and things have prospered so well in our hands, that we have delivered Israel oftentimes.

3 But now I am old, and ye, by God's mercy, are of a sufficient age: be ye instead of me and my brother, and go and fight for our nation, and the help from heaven be with you.

4 So he chose out of the country twenty thousand men of war with horsemen, who went out against Cendebeus, and rested that night at Modin.

5 And when as they rose in the morning, and went into the plain, behold, a mighty great host both of footmen and horsemen came against them: howbeit there was a water brook betwixt them.

6 So he and his people pitched over against them: and when he saw that the people were afraid to go over the water brook, he went first over himself, and then the men seeing him passed through after him.

7 That done, he divided his men, and set the horsemen in the midst of the footmen: for the enemies' horsemen were very many.

8 Then sounded they with the holy trumpets: whereupon Cendebeus and his host were put to flight, so that many of them were slain, and the remnant gat them to the strong hold.

9 At that time was Judas John's brother wounded; but John still followed after them, until he came to Cedron, which Cendebeus had built.

10 So they fled even unto the towers in the fields of Azotus; wherefore he burned it with fire: so that there were slain of them about two thousand men. Afterward he returned into the land of Judea in peace.

11 Moreover in the plain of Jericho was Ptolemeus the son of Abubus made captain, and he had abundance of silver and gold:

12 For he was the high priest's son in law.

13 Wherefore his heart being lifted up, he thought to get the country to himself, and thereupon consulted deceitfully against Simon and his sons to destroy them.

14 Now Simon was visiting the cities that were in the country, and taking care for the good ordering of them; at which time he came down himself to Jericho with his sons, Mattathias and Judas, in the hundred threescore and seventeenth year, in the eleventh month, called Sabat:

15 Where the son of Abubus receiving them deceitfully into a little hold, called Docus, which he had built, made them a great banquet: howbeit he had hid men there.

16 So when Simon and his sons had drunk largely, Ptolemee and his men rose up, and took their weapons, and came upon Simon into the banqueting place, and slew him, and his two sons, and certain of his servants.

17 In which doing he committed a great treachery, and recompensed evil for good.

18 Then Ptolemee wrote these things, and sent to the king, that he should send him an host to aid him, and he would deliver him the country and cities.

19 He sent others also to Gazera to kill John: and unto the tribunes he sent letters to come unto him, that he might give them silver, and gold, and rewards.

20 And others he sent to take Jerusalem, and the mountain of the temple.

21 Now one had run afore to Gazera and told John that his father and brethren were slain, and, quoth he, Ptolemee hath sent to slay thee also.

22 Hereof when he heard, he was sore astonished: so he laid hands on them that were come to destroy him, and slew them; for he knew that they sought to make him away.

23 As concerning the rest of the acts of John, and his wars, and worthy deeds which he did, and the building of the walls which he made, and his doings,

24 Behold, these are written in the chronicles of his priesthood, from the time he was made high priest after his father.

2 MACCABEES

2 Maccabees 1

1 The brethren, the Jews that be at Jerusalem and in the land of Judea, wish unto the brethren, the Jews that are throughout Egypt health and peace:

2 God be gracious unto you, and remember his covenant that he made with Abraham, Isaac, and Jacob, his faithful servants;

3 And give you all an heart to serve him, and to do his will, with a good courage and a willing mind;

4 And open your hearts in his law and commandments, and send you peace,

5 And hear your prayers, and be at one with you, and never forsake you in time of trouble.

6 And now we be here praying for you.

7 What time as Demetrius reigned, in the hundred threescore and ninth year, we the Jews wrote unto you in the extremity of trouble that came upon us in those years, from the time that Jason and his company revolted from the holy land and kingdom,

8 And burned the porch, and shed innocent blood: then we prayed unto the Lord, and were heard; we offered also sacrifices and fine flour, and lighted the lamps, and set forth the loaves.

9 And now see that ye keep the feast of tabernacles in the month Casleu.

10 In the hundred fourscore and eighth year, the people that were at Jerusalem and in Judea, and the council, and Judas, sent greeting and health unto Aristobulus, king Ptolemeus' master, who was of the stock of the anointed priests, and to the Jews that were in Egypt:

11 Insomuch as God hath delivered us from great perils, we thank him highly, as having been in battle against a king.

12 For he cast them out that fought within the holy city.

13 For when the leader was come into Persia, and the army with him that seemed invincible, they were slain in the temple of Nanea by the deceit of Nanea's priests.

14 For Antiochus, as though he would marry her, came into the place, and his friends that were with him, to receive money in name of a dowry.

15 Which when the priests of Nanea had set forth, and he was entered with a small company into the compass of the temple, they shut the temple as soon as Antiochus was come in:

16 And opening a privy door of the roof, they threw stones like thunderbolts, and struck down the captain, hewed them in pieces,

smote off their heads and cast them to those that were without.

17 Blessed be our God in all things, who hath delivered up the ungodly.

18 Therefore whereas we are now purposed to keep the purification of the temple upon the five and twentieth day of the month Casleu, we thought it necessary to certify you thereof, that ye also might keep it, as the feast of the tabernacles, and of the fire, which was given us when Neemias offered sacrifice, after that he had builded the temple and the altar.

19 For when our fathers were led into Persia, the priests that were then devout took the fire of the altar privily, and hid it in an hollow place of a pit without water, where they kept it sure, so that the place was unknown to all men.

20 Now after many years, when it pleased God, Neemias, being sent from the king of Persia, did send of the posterity of those priests that had hid it to the fire: but when they told us they found no fire, but thick water;

21 Then commanded he them to draw it up, and to bring it; and when the sacrifices were laid on, Neemias commanded the priests to sprinkle the wood and the things laid thereupon with the water.

22 When this was done, and the time came that the sun shone, which afore was hid in the cloud, there was a great fire kindled, so that every man marvelled.

23 And the priests made a prayer whilst the sacrifice was consuming, I say, both the priests, and all the rest, Jonathan beginning, and the rest answering thereunto, as Neemias did.

24 And the prayer was after this manner; O Lord, Lord God, Creator of all things, who art fearful and strong, and righteous, and merciful, and the only and gracious King,

25 The only giver of all things, the only just, almighty, and everlasting, thou that deliverest Israel from all trouble, and didst choose the fathers, and sanctify them:

26 Receive the sacrifice for thy whole people Israel, and preserve thine own portion, and sanctify it.

27 Gather those together that are scattered from us, deliver them that serve among the heathen, look upon them that are despised and abhorred, and let the heathen know that thou art our God.

28 Punish them that oppress us, and with pride do us wrong.

29 Plant thy people again in thy holy place, as Moses hath spoken.

30 And the priests sung psalms of thanksgiving.

31 Now when the sacrifice was consumed, Neemias commanded

the water that was left to be poured on the great stones.

32 When this was done, there was kindled a flame: but it was consumed by the light that shined from the altar.

33 So when this matter was known, it was told the king of Persia, that in the place, where the priests that were led away had hid the fire, there appeared water, and that Neemias had purified the sacrifices therewith.

34 Then the king, inclosing the place, made it holy, after he had tried the matter.

35 And the king took many gifts, and bestowed thereof on those whom he would gratify.

36 And Neemias called this thing Naphthar, which is as much as to say, a cleansing: but many men call it Nephi.

2 Maccabees 2

1 It is also found in the records, that Jeremy the prophet commanded them that were carried away to take of the fire, as it hath been signified:

2 And how that the prophet, having given them the law, charged them not to forget the commandments of the Lord, and that they should not err in their minds, when they see images of silver and gold, with their ornaments.

3 And with other such speeches exhorted he them, that the law should not depart from their hearts.

4 It was also contained in the same writing, that the prophet, being warned of God, commanded the tabernacle and the ark to go with him, as he went forth into the mountain, where Moses climbed up, and saw the heritage of God.

5 And when Jeremy came thither, he found an hollow cave, wherein he laid the tabernacle, and the ark, and the altar of incense, and so stopped the door.

6 And some of those that followed him came to mark the way, but they could not find it.

7 Which when Jeremy perceived, he blamed them, saying, As for that place, it shall be unknown until the time that God gather his people again together, and receive them unto mercy.

8 Then shall the Lord shew them these things, and the glory of the Lord shall appear, and the cloud also, as it was shewed under Moses, and as when Solomon desired that the place might be honourably sanctified.

9 It was also declared, that he being wise offered the sacrifice of dedication, and of the finishing of the temple.

10 And as when Moses prayed unto the Lord, the fire came down from heaven, and consumed the sacrifices: even so prayed Solomon also, and the fire came down from

heaven, and consumed the burnt offerings.

11 And Moses said, Because the sin offering was not to be eaten, it was consumed.

12 So Solomon kept those eight days.

13 The same things also were reported in the writings and commentaries of Neemias; and how he founding a library gathered together the acts of the kings, and the prophets, and of David, and the epistles of the kings concerning the holy gifts.

14 In like manner also Judas gathered together all those things that were lost by reason of the war we had, and they remain with us,

15 Wherefore if ye have need thereof, send some to fetch them unto you.

16 Whereas we then are about to celebrate the purification, we have written unto you, and ye shall do well, if ye keep the same days.

17 We hope also, that the God, that delivered all his people, and gave them all an heritage, and the kingdom, and the priesthood, and the sanctuary,

18 As he promised in the law, will shortly have mercy upon us, and gather us together out of every land under heaven into the holy place: for

he hath delivered us out of great troubles, and hath purified the place.

19 Now as concerning Judas Maccabeus, and his brethren, and the purification of the great temple, and the dedication of the altar,

20 And the wars against Antiochus Epiphanes, and Eupator his son,

21 And the manifest signs that came from heaven unto those that behaved themselves manfully to their honour for Judaism: so that, being but a few, they overcame the whole country, and chased barbarous multitudes,

22 And recovered again the temple renowned all the world over, and freed the city, and upheld the laws which were going down, the Lord being gracious unto them with all favour:

23 All these things, I say, being declared by Jason of Cyrene in five books, we will assay to abridge in one volume.

24 For considering the infinite number, and the difficulty which they find that desire to look into the narrations of the story, for the variety of the matter,

25 We have been careful, that they that will read may have delight, and that they that are desirous to commit to memory might have ease, and that all into whose hands it comes might have profit.

26 Therefore to us, that have taken upon us this painful labour of abridging, it was not easy, but a matter of sweat and watching;

27 Even as it is no ease unto him that prepareth a banquet, and seeketh the benefit of others: yet for the pleasuring of many we will undertake gladly this great pains;

28 Leaving to the author the exact handling of every particular, and labouring to follow the rules of an abridgement.

29 For as the master builder of a new house must care for the whole building; but he that undertaketh to set it out, and paint it, must seek out fit things for the adorning thereof: even so I think it is with us.

30 To stand upon every point, and go over things at large, and to be curious in particulars, belongeth to the first author of the story:

31 But to use brevity, and avoid much labouring of the work, is to be granted to him that will make an abridgment.

32 Here then will we begin the story: only adding thus much to that which hath been said, that it is a foolish thing to make a long prologue, and to be short in the story itself.

2 Maccabees 3

1 Now when the holy city was inhabited with all peace, and the laws were kept very well, because of the godliness of Onias the high priest, and his hatred of wickedness,

2 It came to pass that even the kings themselves did honour the place, and magnify the temple with their best gifts;

3 Insomuch that Seleucus of Asia of his own revenues bare all the costs belonging to the service of the sacrifices.

4 But one Simon of the tribe of Benjamin, who was made governor of the temple, fell out with the high priest about disorder in the city.

5 And when he could not overcome Onias, he gat him to Apollonius the son of Thraseas, who then was governor of Celosyria and Phenice,

6 And told him that the treasury in Jerusalem was full of infinite sums of money, so that the multitude of their riches, which did not pertain to the account of the sacrifices, was innumerable, and that it was possible to bring all into the king's hand.

7 Now when Apollonius came to the king, and had shewed him of the money whereof he was told, the king chose out Heliodorus his treasurer, and sent him with a commandment to bring him the foresaid money.

8 So forthwith Heliodorus took his journey; under a colour of visiting the cities of Celosyria and Phenice, but indeed to fulfil the king's purpose.

9 And when he was come to Jerusalem, and had been courteously received of the high priest of the city, he told him what intelligence was given of the money, and declared wherefore he came, and asked if these things were so indeed.

10 Then the high priest told him that there was such money laid up for the relief of widows and fatherless children:

11 And that some of it belonged to Hircanus son of Tobias, a man of great dignity, and not as that wicked Simon had misinformed: the sum whereof in all was four hundred talents of silver, and two hundred of gold:

12 And that it was altogether impossible that such wrongs should be done unto them, that had committed it to the holiness of the place, and to the majesty and inviolable sanctity of the temple, honoured over all the world.

13 But Heliodorus, because of the king's commandment given him, said, That in any wise it must be brought into the king's treasury.

14 So at the day which he appointed he entered in to order this matter: wherefore there was no small agony throughout the whole city.

15 But the priests, prostrating themselves before the altar in their priests' vestments, called unto heaven upon him that made a law concerning things given to he kept, that they should safely be preserved for such as had committed them to be kept.

16 Then whoso had looked the high priest in the face, it would have wounded his heart: for his countenance and the changing of his colour declared the inward agony of his mind.

17 For the man was so compassed with fear and horror of the body, that it was manifest to them that looked upon him, what sorrow he had now in his heart.

18 Others ran flocking out of their houses to the general supplication, because the place was like to come into contempt.

19 And the women, girt with sackcloth under their breasts, abounded in the streets, and the virgins that were kept in ran, some to the gates, and some to the walls, and others looked out of the windows.

20 And all, holding their hands toward heaven, made supplication.

21 Then it would have pitied a man to see the falling down of the multitude of all sorts, and the fear of the high priest being in such an agony.

22 They then called upon the Almighty Lord to keep the things

committed of trust safe and sure for those that had committed them.

23 Nevertheless Heliodorus executed that which was decreed.

24 Now as he was there present himself with his guard about the treasury, the Lord of spirits, and the Prince of all power, caused a great apparition, so that all that presumed to come in with him were astonished at the power of God, and fainted, and were sore afraid.

25 For there appeared unto them an horse with a terrible rider upon him, and adorned with a very fair covering, and he ran fiercely, and smote at Heliodorus with his forefeet, and it seemed that he that sat upon the horse had complete harness of gold.

26 Moreover two other young men appeared before him, notable in strength, excellent in beauty, and comely in apparel, who stood by him on either side; and scourged him continually, and gave him many sore stripes.

27 And Heliodorus fell suddenly unto the ground, and was compassed with great darkness: but they that were with him took him up, and put him into a litter.

28 Thus him, that lately came with a great train and with all his guard into the said treasury, they carried out, being unable to help himself with his weapons: and manifestly they acknowledged the power of God.

29 For he by the hand of God was cast down, and lay speechless without all hope of life.

30 But they praised the Lord, that had miraculously honoured his own place: for the temple; which a little afore was full of fear and trouble, when the Almighty Lord appeared, was filled with joy and gladness.

31 Then straightways certain of Heliodorus' friends prayed Onias, that he would call upon the most High to grant him his life, who lay ready to give up the ghost.

32 So the high priest, suspecting lest the king should misconceive that some treachery had been done to Heliodorus by the Jews, offered a sacrifice for the health of the man.

33 Now as the high priest was making an atonement, the same young men in the same clothing appeared and stood beside Heliodorus, saying, Give Onias the high priest great thanks, insomuch as for his sake the Lord hath granted thee life:

34 And seeing that thou hast been scourged from heaven, declare unto all men the mighty power of God. And when they had spoken these words, they appeared no more.

35 So Heliodorus, after he had offered sacrifice unto the Lord, and made great vows unto him that had

saved his life, and saluted Onias, returned with his host to the king.

36 Then testified he to all men the works of the great God, which he had seen with his eyes.

37 And when the king Heliodorus, who might be a fit man to be sent yet once again to Jerusalem, he said,

38 If thou hast any enemy or traitor, send him thither, and thou shalt receive him well scourged, if he escape with his life: for in that place, no doubt; there is an especial power of God.

39 For he that dwelleth in heaven hath his eye on that place, and defendeth it; and he beateth and destroyeth them that come to hurt it.

40 And the things concerning Heliodorus, and the keeping of the treasury, fell out on this sort.

2 Maccabees 4

1 This Simon now, of whom we spake afore, having been a betrayer of the money, and of his country, slandered Onias, as if he had terrified Heliodorus, and been the worker of these evils.

2 Thus was he bold to call him a traitor, that had deserved well of the city, and tendered his own nation, and was so zealous of the laws.

3 But when their hatred went so far, that by one of Simon's faction murders were committed,

4 Onias seeing the danger of this contention, and that Apollonius, as being the governor of Celosyria and Phenice, did rage, and increase Simon's malice,

5 He went to the king, not to be an accuser of his countrymen, but seeking the good of all, both publick and private:

6 For he saw that it was impossible that the state should continue quiet, and Simon leave his folly, unless the king did look thereunto.

7 But after the death of Seleucus, when Antiochus, called Epiphanes, took the kingdom, Jason the brother of Onias laboured underhand to be high priest,

8 Promising unto the king by intercession three hundred and threescore talents of silver, and of another revenue eighty talents:

9 Beside this, he promised to assign an hundred and fifty more, if he might have licence to set him up a place for exercise, and for the training up of youth in the fashions of the heathen, and to write them of Jerusalem by the name of Antiochians.

10 Which when the king had granted, and he had gotten into his hand the rule he forthwith brought his own nation to Greekish fashion.

11 And the royal privileges granted of special favour to the Jews by the means of John the father of

Eupolemus, who went ambassador to Rome for amity and aid, he took away; and putting down the governments which were according to the law, he brought up new customs against the law:

12 For he built gladly a place of exercise under the tower itself, and brought the chief young men under his subjection, and made them wear a hat.

13 Now such was the height of Greek fashions, and increase of heathenish manners, through the exceeding profaneness of Jason, that ungodly wretch, and no high priest;

14 That the priests had no courage to serve any more at the altar, but despising the temple, and neglecting the sacrifices, hastened to be partakers of the unlawful allowance in the place of exercise, after the game of Discus called them forth;

15 Not setting by the honours of their fathers, but liking the glory of the Grecians best of all.

16 By reason whereof sore calamity came upon them: for they had them to be their enemies and avengers, whose custom they followed so earnestly, and unto whom they desired to be like in all things.

17 For it is not a light thing to do wickedly against the laws of God: but the time following shall declare these things.

18 Now when the game that was used every faith year was kept at Tyrus, the king being present,

19 This ungracious Jason sent special messengers from Jerusalem, who were Antiochians, to carry three hundred drachms of silver to the sacrifice of Hercules, which even the bearers thereof thought fit not to bestow upon the sacrifice, because it was not convenient, but to be reserved for other charges.

20 This money then, in regard of the sender, was appointed to Hercules' sacrifice; but because of the bearers thereof, it was employed to the making of gallies.

21 Now when Apollonius the son of Menestheus was sent into Egypt for the coronation of king Ptolemeus Philometor, Antiochus, understanding him not to be well affected to his affairs, provided for his own safety: whereupon he came to Joppa, and from thence to Jerusalem:

22 Where he was honourably received of Jason, and of the city, and was brought in with torch alight, and with great shoutings: and so afterward went with his host unto Phenice.

23 Three years afterward Jason sent Menelaus, the aforesaid Simon's brother, to bear the money unto the king, and to put him in mind of certain necessary matters.

24 But he being brought to the presence of the king, when he had magnified him for the glorious appearance of his power, got the priesthood to himself, offering more than Jason by three hundred talents of silver.

25 So he came with the king's mandate, bringing nothing worthy the high priesthood, but having the fury of a cruel tyrant, and the rage of a savage beast.

26 Then Jason, who had undermined his own brother, being undermined by another, was compelled to flee into the country of the Ammonites.

27 So Menelaus got the principality: but as for the money that he had promised unto the king, he took no good order for it, albeit Sostratis the ruler of the castle required it:

28 For unto him appertained the gathering of the customs. Wherefore they were both called before the king.

29 Now Menelaus left his brother Lysimachus in his stead in the priesthood; and Sostratus left Crates, who was governor of the Cyprians.

30 While those things were in doing, they of Tarsus and Mallos made insurrection, because they were given to the king's concubine, called Antiochus.

31 Then came the king in all haste to appease matters, leaving Andronicus, a man in authority, for his deputy.

32 Now Menelaus, supposing that he had gotten a convenient time, stole certain vessels of gold out of the temple, and gave some of them to Andronicus, and some he sold into Tyrus and the cities round about.

33 Which when Onias knew of a surety, he reproved him, and withdrew himself into a sanctuary at Daphne, that lieth by Antiochia.

34 Wherefore Menelaus, taking Andronicus apart, prayed, him to get Onias into his hands; who being persuaded thereunto, and coming to Onias in deceit, gave him his right hand with oaths; and though he were suspected by him, yet persuaded he him to come forth of the sanctuary: whom forthwith he shut up without regard of justice.

35 For the which cause not only the Jews, but many also of other nations, took great indignation, and were much grieved for the unjust murder of the man.

36 And when the king was come again from the places about Cilicia, the Jews that were in the city, and certain of the Greeks that abhorred the fact also, complained because Onias was slain without cause.

37 Therefore Antiochus was heartily sorry, and moved to pity, and wept,

because of the sober and modest behaviour of him that was dead.

38 And being kindled with anger, forthwith he took away Andronicus his purple, and rent off his clothes, and leading him through the whole city unto that very place, where he had committed impiety against Onias, there slew he the cursed murderer. Thus the Lord rewarded him his punishment, as he had deserved.

39 Now when many sacrileges had been committed in the city by Lysimachus with the consent of Menelaus, and the fruit thereof was spread abroad, the multitude gathered themselves together against Lysimachus, many vessels of gold being already carried away.

40 Whereupon the common people rising, and being filled with rage, Lysimachus armed about three thousand men, and began first to offer violence; one Auranus being the leader, a man far gone in years, and no less in folly.

41 They then seeing the attempt of Lysimachus, some of them caught stones, some clubs, others taking handfuls of dust, that was next at hand, cast them all together upon Lysimachus, and those that set upon them.

42 Thus many of them they wounded, and some they struck to the ground, and all of them they forced to flee: but as for the churchrobber himself, him they killed beside the treasury.

43 Of these matters therefore there was an accusation laid against Menelaus.

44 Now when the king came to Tyrus, three men that were sent from the senate pleaded the cause before him:

45 But Menelaus, being now convicted, promised Ptolemee the son of Dorymenes to give him much money, if he would pacify the king toward him.

46 Whereupon Ptolemee taking the king aside into a certain gallery, as it were to take the air, brought him to be of another mind:

47 Insomuch that he discharged Menelaus from the accusations, who notwithstanding was cause of all the mischief: and those poor men, who, if they had told their cause, yea, before the Scythians, should have been judged innocent, them he condemned to death.

48 Thus they that followed the matter for the city, and for the people, and for the holy vessels, did soon suffer unjust punishment.

49 Wherefore even they of Tyrus, moved with hatred of that wicked deed, caused them to be honourably buried.

50 And so through the covetousness of them that were of power Menelaus

remained still in authority, increasing in malice, and being a great traitor to the citizens.

2 Maccabees 5

1 About the same time Antiochus prepared his second voyage into Egypt:

2 And then it happened, that through all the city, for the space almost of forty days, there were seen horsemen running in the air, in cloth of gold, and armed with lances, like a band of soldiers,

3 And troops of horsemen in array, encountering and running one against another, with shaking of shields, and multitude of pikes, and drawing of swords, and casting of darts, and glittering of golden ornaments, and harness of all sorts.

4 Wherefore every man prayed that that apparition might turn to good.

5 Now when there was gone forth a false rumour, as though Antiochus had been dead, Jason took at the least a thousand men, and suddenly made an assault upon the city; and they that were upon the walls being put back, and the city at length taken, Menelaus fled into the castle:

6 But Jason slew his own citizens without mercy, not considering that to get the day of them of his own nation would be a most unhappy day for him; but thinking they had been his enemies, and not his countrymen, whom he conquered.

7 Howbeit for all this he obtained not the principality, but at the last received shame for the reward of his treason, and fled again into the country of the Ammonites.

8 In the end therefore he had an unhappy return, being accused before Aretas the king of the Arabians, fleeing from city to city, pursued of all men, hated as a forsaker of the laws, and being had in abomination as an open enemy of his country and countrymen, he was cast out into Egypt.

9 Thus he that had driven many out of their country perished in a strange land, retiring to the Lacedemonians, and thinking there to find succour by reason of his kindred:

10 And he that had cast out many unburied had none to mourn for him, nor any solemn funerals at all, nor sepulchre with his fathers.

11 Now when this that was done came to the king's car, he thought that Judea had revolted: whereupon removing out of Egypt in a furious mind, he took the city by force of arms,

12 And commanded his men of war not to spare such as they met, and to slay such as went up upon the houses.

13 Thus there was killing of young and old, making away of men, women, and children, slaying of virgins and infants.

14 And there were destroyed within the space of three whole days fourscore thousand, whereof forty thousand were slain in the conflict; and no fewer sold than slain.

15 Yet was he not content with this, but presumed to go into the most holy temple of all the world; Menelaus, that traitor to the laws, and to his own country, being his guide:

16 And taking the holy vessels with polluted hands, and with profane hands pulling down the things that were dedicated by other kings to the augmentation and glory and honour of the place, he gave them away.

17 And so haughty was Antiochus in mind, that he considered not that the Lord was angry for a while for the sins of them that dwelt in the city, and therefore his eye was not upon the place.

18 For had they not been formerly wrapped in many sins, this man, as soon as he had come, had forthwith been scourged, and put back from his presumption, as Heliodorus was, whom Seleucus the king sent to view the treasury.

19 Nevertheless God did not choose the people for the place's sake, but the place far the people's sake.

20 And therefore the place itself, that was partaker with them of the adversity that happened to the nation, did afterward communicate in the benefits sent from the Lord: and as it was forsaken in the wrath of the Almighty, so again, the great Lord being reconciled, it was set up with all glory.

21 So when Antiochus had carried out of the temple a thousand and eight hundred talents, he departed in all haste unto Antiochia, weening in his pride to make the land navigable, and the sea passable by foot: such was the haughtiness of his mind.

22 And he left governors to vex the nation: at Jerusalem, Philip, for his country a Phrygian, and for manners more barbarous than he that set him there;

23 And at Garizim, Andronicus; and besides, Menelaus, who worse than all the rest bare an heavy hand over the citizens, having a malicious mind against his countrymen the Jews.

24 He sent also that detestable ringleader Apollonius with an army of two and twenty thousand, commanding him to slay all those that were in their best age, and to sell the women and the younger sort:

25 Who coming to Jerusalem, and pretending peace, did forbear till the holy day of the sabbath, when taking the Jews keeping holy day, he commanded his men to arm themselves.

26 And so he slew all them that were gone to the celebrating of the sabbath, and running through the

city with weapons slew great multitudes.

27 But Judas Maccabeus with nine others, or thereabout, withdrew himself into the wilderness, and lived in the mountains after the manner of beasts, with his company, who fed on herbs continually, lest they should be partakers of the pollution.

2 Maccabees 6

1 Not long after this the king sent an old man of Athens to compel the Jews to depart from the laws of their fathers, and not to live after the laws of God:

2 And to pollute also the temple in Jerusalem, and to call it the temple of Jupiter Olympius; and that in Garizim, of Jupiter the Defender of strangers, as they did desire that dwelt in the place.

3 The coming in of this mischief was sore and grievous to the people:

4 For the temple was filled with riot and revelling by the Gentiles, who dallied with harlots, and had to do with women within the circuit of the holy places, and besides that brought in things that were not lawful.

5 The altar also was filled with profane things, which the law forbiddeth.

6 Neither was it lawful for a man to keep sabbath days or ancient fasts, or to profess himself at all to be a Jew.

7 And in the day of the king's birth every month they were brought by bitter constraint to eat of the sacrifices; and when the fast of Bacchus was kept, the Jews were compelled to go in procession to Bacchus, carrying ivy.

8 Moreover there went out a decree to the neighbour cities of the heathen, by the suggestion of Ptolemee, against the Jews, that they should observe the same fashions, and be partakers of their sacrifices:

9 And whoso would not conform themselves to the manners of the Gentiles should be put to death. Then might a man have seen the present misery.

10 For there were two women brought, who had circumcised their children; whom when they had openly led round about the city, the babes handing at their breasts, they cast them down headlong from the wall.

11 And others, that had run together into caves near by, to keep the sabbath day secretly, being discovered by Philip, were all burnt together, because they made a conscience to help themselves for the honour of the most sacred day.

12 Now I beseech those that read this book, that they be not

discouraged for these calamities, but that they judge those punishments not to be for destruction, but for a chastening of our nation.

13 For it is a token of his great goodness, when wicked doers are not suffered any long time, but forthwith punished.

14 For not as with other nations, whom the Lord patiently forbeareth to punish, till they be come to the fulness of their sins, so dealeth he with us,

15 Lest that, being come to the height of sin, afterwards he should take vengeance of us.

16 And therefore he never withdraweth his mercy from us: and though he punish with adversity, yet doth he never forsake his people.

17 But let this that we at spoken be for a warning unto us. And now will we come to the declaring of the matter in a few words.

18 Eleazar, one of the principal scribes, an aged man, and of a well favoured countenance, was constrained to open his mouth, and to eat swine's flesh.

19 But he, choosing rather to die gloriously, than to live stained with such an abomination, spit it forth, and came of his own accord to the torment,

20 As it behoved them to come, that are resolute to stand out against such things, as are not lawful for love of life to be tasted.

21 But they that had the charge of that wicked feast, for the old acquaintance they had with the man, taking him aside, besought him to bring flesh of his own provision, such as was lawful for him to use, and make as if he did eat of the flesh taken from the sacrifice commanded by the king;

22 That in so doing he might be delivered from death, and for the old friendship with them find favour.

23 But he began to consider discreetly, and as became his age, and the excellency of his ancient years, and the honour of his gray head, whereon was come, and his most honest education from a child, or rather the holy law made and given by God: therefore he answered accordingly, and willed them straightways to send him to the grave.

24 For it becometh not our age, said he, in any wise to dissemble, whereby many young persons might think that Eleazar, being fourscore years old and ten, were now gone to a strange religion;

25 And so they through mine hypocrisy, and desire to live a little time and a moment longer, should be deceived by me, and I get a stain to mine old age, and make it abominable.

26 For though for the present time I should be delivered from the punishment of men: yet should I not escape the hand of the Almighty, neither alive, nor dead.

27 Wherefore now, manfully changing this life, I will shew myself such an one as mine age requireth,

28 And leave a notable example to such as be young to die willingly and courageously for the honourable and holy laws. And when he had said these words, immediately he went to the torment:

29 They that led him changing the good will they bare him a little before into hatred, because the foresaid speeches proceeded, as they thought, from a desperate mind.

30 But when he was ready to die with stripes, he groaned, and said, It is manifest unto the Lord, that hath the holy knowledge, that whereas I might have been delivered from death, I now endure sore pains in body by being beaten: but in soul am well content to suffer these things, because I fear him.

31 And thus this man died, leaving his death for an example of a noble courage, and a memorial of virtue, not only unto young men, but unto all his nation.

2 Maccabees 7

1 It came to pass also, that seven brethren with their mother were taken, and compelled by the king against the law to taste swine's flesh, and were tormented with scourges and whips.

2 But one of them that spake first said thus, What wouldest thou ask or learn of us? we are ready to die, rather than to transgress the laws of our fathers.

3 Then the king, being in a rage, commanded pans and caldrons to be made hot:

4 Which forthwith being heated, he commanded to cut out the tongue of him that spake first, and to cut off the utmost parts of his body, the rest of his brethren and his mother looking on.

5 Now when he was thus maimed in all his members, he commanded him being yet alive to be brought to the fire, and to be fried in the pan: and as the vapour of the pan was for a good space dispersed, they exhorted one another with the mother to die manfully, saying thus,

6 The Lord God looketh upon us, and in truth hath comfort in us, as Moses in his song, which witnessed to their faces, declared, saying, And he shall be comforted in his servants.

7 So when the first was dead after this number, they brought the second to make him a mocking stock: and when they had pulled off the skin of his head with the hair, they asked him, Wilt thou eat, before

thou be punished throughout every member of thy body?

8 But he answered in his own language, and said, No. Wherefore he also received the next torment in order, as the former did.

9 And when he was at the last gasp, he said, Thou like a fury takest us out of this present life, but the King of the world shall raise us up, who have died for his laws, unto everlasting life.

10 After him was the third made a mocking stock: and when he was required, he put out his tongue, and that right soon, holding forth his hands manfully.

11 And said courageously, These I had from heaven; and for his laws I despise them; and from him I hope to receive them again.

12 Insomuch that the king, and they that were with him, marvelled at the young man's courage, for that he nothing regarded the pains.

13 Now when this man was dead also, they tormented and mangled the fourth in like manner.

14 So when he was ready to die he said thus, It is good, being put to death by men, to look for hope from God to be raised up again by him: as for thee, thou shalt have no resurrection to life.

15 Afterward they brought the fifth also, and mangled him.

16 Then looked he unto the king, and said, Thou hast power over men, thou art corruptible, thou doest what thou wilt; yet think not that our nation is forsaken of God;

17 But abide a while, and behold his great power, how he will torment thee and thy seed.

18 After him also they brought the sixth, who being ready to die said, Be not deceived without cause: for we suffer these things for ourselves, having sinned against our God: therefore marvellous things are done unto us.

19 But think not thou, that takest in hand to strive against God, that thou shalt escape unpunished.

20 But the mother was marvellous above all, and worthy of honourable memory: for when she saw her seven sons slain within the space of one day, she bare it with a good courage, because of the hope that she had in the Lord.

21 Yea, she exhorted every one of them in her own language, filled with courageous spirits; and stirring up her womanish thoughts with a manly stomach, she said unto them,

22 I cannot tell how ye came into my womb: for I neither gave you breath nor life, neither was it I that formed the members of every one of you;

23 But doubtless the Creator of the world, who formed the generation of man, and found out the beginning of

all things, will also of his own mercy give you breath and life again, as ye now regard not your own selves for his laws' sake.

24 Now Antiochus, thinking himself despised, and suspecting it to be a reproachful speech, whilst the youngest was yet alive, did not only exhort him by words, but also assured him with oaths, that he would make him both a rich and a happy man, if he would turn from the laws of his fathers; and that also he would take him for his friend, and trust him with affairs.

25 But when the young man would in no case hearken unto him, the king called his mother, and exhorted her that she would counsel the young man to save his life.

26 And when he had exhorted her with many words, she promised him that she would counsel her son.

27 But she bowing herself toward him, laughing the cruel tyrant to scorn, spake in her country language on this manner; O my son, have pity upon me that bare thee nine months in my womb, and gave thee such three years, and nourished thee, and brought thee up unto this age, and endured the troubles of education.

28 I beseech thee, my son, look upon the heaven and the earth, and all that is therein, and consider that God made them of things that were not; and so was mankind made likewise.

29 Fear not this tormentor, but, being worthy of thy brethren, take thy death that I may receive thee again in mercy with thy brethren.

30 Whiles she was yet speaking these words, the young man said, Whom wait ye for? I will not obey the king's commandment: but I will obey the commandment of the law that was given unto our fathers by Moses.

31 And thou, that hast been the author of all mischief against the Hebrews, shalt not escape the hands of God.

32 For we suffer because of our sins.

33 And though the living Lord be angry with us a little while for our chastening and correction, yet shall he be at one again with his servants.

34 But thou, O godless man, and of all other most wicked, be not lifted up without a cause, nor puffed up with uncertain hopes, lifting up thy hand against the servants of God:

35 For thou hast not yet escaped the judgment of Almighty God, who seeth all things.

36 For our brethren, who now have suffered a short pain, are dead under God's covenant of everlasting life: but thou, through the judgment of God, shalt receive just punishment for thy pride.

37 But I, as my brethren, offer up my body and life for the laws of our

fathers, beseeching God that he would speedily be merciful unto our nation; and that thou by torments and plagues mayest confess, that he alone is God;

38 And that in me and my brethren the wrath of the Almighty, which is justly brought upon our nation, may cease.

39 Than the king' being in a rage, handed him worse than all the rest, and took it grievously that he was mocked.

40 So this man died undefiled, and put his whole trust in the Lord.

41 Last of all after the sons the mother died.

42 Let this be enough now to have spoken concerning the idolatrous feasts, and the extreme tortures.

2 Maccabees 8

1 Then Judas Maccabeus, and they that were with him, went privily into the towns, and called their kinsfolks together, and took unto them all such as continued in the Jews' religion, and assembled about six thousand men.

2 And they called upon the Lord, that he would look upon the people that was trodden down of all; and also pity the temple profaned of ungodly men;

3 And that he would have compassion upon the city, sore defaced, and ready to be made even with the ground; and hear the blood that cried unto him,

4 And remember the wicked slaughter of harmless infants, and the blasphemies committed against his name; and that he would shew his hatred against the wicked.

5 Now when Maccabeus had his company about him, he could not be withstood by the heathen: for the wrath of the Lord was turned into mercy.

6 Therefore he came at unawares, and burnt up towns and cities, and got into his hands the most commodious places, and overcame and put to flight no small number of his enemies.

7 But specially took he advantage of the night for such privy attempts, insomuch that the fruit of his holiness was spread every where.

8 So when Philip saw that this man increased by little and little, and that things prospered with him still more and more, he wrote unto Ptolemeus, the governor of Celosyria and Phenice, to yield more aid to the king's affairs.

9 Then forthwith choosing Nicanor the son of Patroclus, one of his special friends, he sent him with no fewer than twenty thousand of all nations under him, to root out the whole generation of the Jews; and with him he joined also Gorgias a

captain, who in matters of war had great experience.

10 So Nicanor undertook to make so much money of the captive Jews, as should defray the tribute of two thousand talents, which the king was to pay to the Romans.

11 Wherefore immediately he sent to the cities upon the sea coast, proclaiming a sale of the captive Jews, and promising that they should have fourscore and ten bodies for one talent, not expecting the vengeance that was to follow upon him from the Almighty God.

12 Now when word was brought unto Judas of Nicanor's coming, and he had imparted unto those that were with him that the army was at hand,

13 They that were fearful, and distrusted the justice of God, fled, and conveyed themselves away.

14 Others sold all that they had left, and withal besought the Lord to deliver them, sold by the wicked Nicanor before they met together:

15 And if not for their own sakes, yet for the covenants he had made with their fathers, and for his holy and glorious name's sake, by which they were called.

16 So Maccabeus called his men together unto the number of six thousand, and exhorted them not to be stricken with terror of the enemy, nor to fear the great multitude of the heathen, who came wrongly against them; but to fight manfully,

17 And to set before their eyes the injury that they had unjustly done to the holy place, and the cruel handling of the city, whereof they made a mockery, and also the taking away of the government of their forefathers:

18 For they, said he, trust in their weapons and boldness; but our confidence is in the Almighty who at a beck can cast down both them that come against us, and also all the world.

19 Moreover, he recounted unto them what helps their forefathers had found, and how they were delivered, when under Sennacherib an hundred fourscore and five thousand perished.

20 And he told them of the battle that they had in Babylon with the Galatians, how they came but eight thousand in all to the business, with four thousand Macedonians, and that the Macedonians being perplexed, the eight thousand destroyed an hundred and twenty thousand because of the help that they had from heaven, and so received a great booty.

21 Thus when he had made them bold with these words, and ready to die for the law and the country, he divided his army into four parts;

22 And joined with himself his own brethren, leaders of each band, to wit Simon, and Joseph, and Jonathan, giving each one fifteen hundred men.

23 Also he appointed Eleazar to read the holy book: and when he had given them this watchword, The help of God; himself leading the first band,

24 And by the help of the Almighty they slew above nine thousand of their enemies, and wounded and maimed the most part of Nicanor's host, and so put all to flight;

25 And took their money that came to buy them, and pursued them far: but lacking time they returned:

26 For it was the day before the sabbath, and therefore they would no longer pursue them.

27 So when they had gathered their armour together, and spoiled their enemies, they occupied themselves about the sabbath, yielding exceeding praise and thanks to the Lord, who had preserved them unto that day, which was the beginning of mercy distilling upon them.

28 And after the sabbath, when they had given part of the spoils to the maimed, and the widows, and orphans, the residue they divided among themselves and their servants.

29 When this was done, and they had made a common supplication, they besought the merciful Lord to be reconciled with his servants for ever.

30 Moreover of those that were with Timotheus and Bacchides, who fought against them, they slew above twenty thousand, and very easily got high and strong holds, and divided among themselves many spoils more, and made the maimed, orphans, widows, yea, and the aged also, equal in spoils with themselves.

31 And when they had gathered their armour together, they laid them up all carefully in convenient places, and the remnant of the spoils they brought to Jerusalem.

32 They slew also Philarches, that wicked person, who was with Timotheus, and had annoyed the Jews many ways.

33 Furthermore at such time as they kept the feast for the victory in their country they burnt Callisthenes, that had set fire upon the holy gates, who had fled into a little house; and so he received a reward meet for his wickedness.

34 As for that most ungracious Nicanor, who had brought a thousand merchants to buy the Jews,

35 He was through the help of the Lord brought down by them, of whom he made least account; and putting off his glorious apparel, and discharging his company, he came

like a fugitive servant through the midland unto Antioch having very great dishonour, for that his host was destroyed.

36 Thus he, that took upon him to make good to the Romans their tribute by means of captives in Jerusalem, told abroad, that the Jews had God to fight for them, and therefore they could not be hurt, because they followed the laws that he gave them.

2 Maccabees 9

1 About that time came Antiochus with dishonour out of the country of Persia

2 For he had entered the city called Persepolis, and went about to rob the temple, and to hold the city; whereupon the multitude running to defend themselves with their weapons put them to flight; and so it happened, that Antiochus being put to flight of the inhabitants returned with shame.

3 Now when he came to Ecbatane, news was brought him what had happened unto Nicanor and Timotheus.

4 Then swelling with anger. he thought to avenge upon the Jews the disgrace done unto him by those that made him flee. Therefore commanded he his chariotman to drive without ceasing, and to dispatch the journey, the judgment of God now following him. For he had

spoken proudly in this sort, That he would come to Jerusalem and make it a common burying place of the Jews.

5 But the Lord Almighty, the God of Isreal, smote him with an incurable and invisible plague: or as soon as he had spoken these words, a pain of the bowels that was remediless came upon him, and sore torments of the inner parts;

6 And that most justly: for he had tormented other men's bowels with many and strange torments.

7 Howbeit he nothing at all ceased from his bragging, but still was filled with pride, breathing out fire in his rage against the Jews, and commanding to haste the journey: but it came to pass that he fell down from his chariot, carried violently; so that having a sore fall, all the members of his body were much pained.

8 And thus he that a little afore thought he might command the waves of the sea, (so proud was he beyond the condition of man) and weigh the high mountains in a balance, was now cast on the ground, and carried in an horselitter, shewing forth unto all the manifest power of God.

9 So that the worms rose up out of the body of this wicked man, and whiles he lived in sorrow and pain, his flesh fell away, and the filthiness

of his smell was noisome to all his army.

10 And the man, that thought a little afore he could reach to the stars of heaven, no man could endure to carry for his intolerable stink.

11 Here therefore, being plagued, he began to leave off his great pride, and to come to the knowledge of himself by the scourge of God, his pain increasing every moment.

12 And when he himself could not abide his own smell, he said these words, It is meet to be subject unto God, and that a man that is mortal should not proudly think of himself if he were God.

13 This wicked person vowed also unto the Lord, who now no more would have mercy upon him, saying thus,

14 That the holy city (to the which he was going in haste to lay it even with the ground, and to make it a common buryingplace,) he would set at liberty:

15 And as touching the Jews, whom he had judged not worthy so much as to be buried, but to be cast out with their children to be devoured of the fowls and wild beasts, he would make them all equals to the citizens of Athens:

16 And the holy temple, which before he had spoiled, he would garnish with goodly gifts, and restore all the holy vessels with many more, and out of his own revenue defray the charges belonging to the sacrifices:

17 Yea, and that also he would become a Jew himself, and go through all the world that was inhabited, and declare the power of God.

18 But for all this his pains would not cease: for the just judgment of God was come upon him: therefore despairing of his health, he wrote unto the Jews the letter underwritten, containing the form of a supplication, after this manner:

19 Antiochus, king and governor, to the good Jews his citizens wisheth much joy, health, and prosperity:

20 If ye and your children fare well, and your affairs be to your contentment, I give very great thanks to God, having my hope in heaven.

21 As for me, I was weak, or else I would have remembered kindly your honour and good will returning out of Persia, and being taken with a grievous disease, I thought it necessary to care for the common safety of all:

22 Not distrusting mine health, but having great hope to escape this sickness.

23 But considering that even my father, at what time he led an army into the high countries. appointed a successor,

24 To the end that, if any thing fell out contrary to expectation, or if any tidings were brought that were grievous, they of the land, knowing to whom the state was left, might not be troubled:

25 Again, considering how that the princes that are borderers and neighbours unto my kingdom wait for opportunities, and expect what shall be the event. I have appointed my son Antiochus king, whom I often committed and commended unto many of you, when I went up into the high provinces; to whom I have written as followeth:

26 Therefore I pray and request you to remember the benefits that I have done unto you generally, and in special, and that every man will be still faithful to me and my son.

27 For I am persuaded that he understanding my mind will favourably and graciously yield to your desires.

28 Thus the murderer and blasphemer having suffered most grievously, as he entreated other men, so died he a miserable death in a strange country in the mountains.

29 And Philip, that was brought up with him, carried away his body, who also fearing the son of Antiochus went into Egypt to Ptolemeus Philometor.

2 Maccabees 10

1 Now Maccabeus and his company, the Lord guiding them, recovered the temple and the city:

2 But the altars which the heathen had built in the open street, and also the chapels, they pulled down.

3 And having cleansed the temple they made another altar, and striking stones they took fire out of them, and offered a sacrifice after two years, and set forth incense, and lights, and shewbread.

4 When that was done, they fell flat down, and besought the Lord that they might come no more into such troubles; but if they sinned any more against him, that he himself would chasten them with mercy, and that they might not be delivered unto the blasphemous and barbarous nations.

5 Now upon the same day that the strangers profaned the temple, on the very same day it was cleansed again, even the five and twentieth day of the same month, which is Casleu.

6 And they kept the eight days with gladness, as in the feast of the tabernacles, remembering that not long afore they had held the feast of the tabernacles, when as they wandered in the mountains and dens like beasts.

7 Therefore they bare branches, and fair boughs, and palms also, and sang psalms unto him that had given

them good success in cleansing his place.

8 They ordained also by a common statute and decree, That every year those days should be kept of the whole nation of the Jews.

9 And this was the end of Antiochus, called Epiphanes.

10 Now will we declare the acts of Antiochus Eupator, who was the son of this wicked man, gathering briefly the calamities of the wars.

11 So when he was come to the crown, he set one Lysias over the affairs of his realm, and appointed him his chief governor of Celosyria and Phenice.

12 For Ptolemeus, that was called Macron, choosing rather to do justice unto the Jews for the wrong that had been done unto them, endeavoured to continue peace with them.

13 Whereupon being accused of the king's friends before Eupator, and called traitor at every word because he had left Cyprus, that Philometor had committed unto him, and departed to Antiochus Epiphanes, and seeing that he was in no honourable place, he was so discouraged, that he poisoned himself and died.

14 But when Gorgias was governor of the holds, he hired soldiers, and nourished war continually with the Jews:

15 And therewithall the Idumeans, having gotten into their hands the most commodious holds, kept the Jews occupied, and receiving those that were banished from Jerusalem, they went about to nourish war.

16 Then they that were with Maccabeus made supplication, and besought God that he would be their helper; and so they ran with violence upon the strong holds of the Idumeans,

17 And assaulting them strongly, they won the holds, and kept off all that fought upon the wall, and slew all that fell into their hands, and killed no fewer than twenty thousand.

18 And because certain, who were no less than nine thousand, were fled together into two very strong castles, having all manner of things convenient to sustain the siege,

19 Maccabeus left Simon and Joseph, and Zaccheus also, and them that were with him, who were enough to besiege them, and departed himself unto those places which more needed his help.

20 Now they that were with Simon, being led with covetousness, were persuaded for money through certain of those that were in the castle, and took seventy thousand drachms, and let some of them escape.

21 But when it was told Maccabeus what was done, he called the governors of the people together,

and accused those men, that they had sold their brethren for money, and set their enemies free to fight against them.

22 So he slew those that were found traitors, and immediately took the two castles.

23 And having good success with his weapons in all things he took in hand, he slew in the two holds more than twenty thousand.

24 Now Timotheus, whom the Jews had overcome before, when he had gathered a great multitude of foreign forces, and horses out of Asia not a few, came as though he would take Jewry by force of arms.

25 But when he drew near, they that were with Maccabeus turned themselves to pray unto God, and sprinkled earth upon their heads, and girded their loins with sackcloth,

26 And fell down at the foot of the altar, and besought him to be merciful to them, and to be an enemy to their enemies, and an adversary to their adversaries, as the law declareth.

27 So after the prayer they took their weapons, and went on further from the city: and when they drew near to their enemies, they kept by themselves.

28 Now the sun being newly risen, they joined both together; the one part having together with their virtue their refuge also unto the Lord for a pledge of their success and victory: the other side making their rage leader of their battle

29 But when the battle waxed strong, there appeared unto the enemies from heaven five comely men upon horses, with bridles of gold, and two of them led the Jews,

30 And took Maccabeus betwixt them, and covered him on every side weapons, and kept him safe, but shot arrows and lightnings against the enemies: so that being confounded with blindness, and full of trouble, they were killed.

31 And there were slain of footmen twenty thousand and five hundred, and six hundred horsemen.

32 As for Timotheus himself, he fled into a very strong hold, called Gawra, where Chereas was governor.

33 But they that were with Maccabeus laid siege against the fortress courageously four days.

34 And they that were within, trusting to the strength of the place, blasphemed exceedingly, and uttered wicked words.

35 Nevertheless upon the fifth day early twenty young men of Maccabeus' company, inflamed with anger because of the blasphemies, assaulted the wall manly, and with a fierce courage killed all that they met withal.

36 Others likewise ascending after them, whiles they were busied with them that were within, burnt the towers, and kindling fires burnt the blasphemers alive; and others broke open the gates, and, having received in the rest of the army, took the city,

37 And killed Timotheus, that was hid in a certain pit, and Chereas his brother, with Apollophanes.

38 When this was done, they praised the Lord with psalms and thanksgiving, who had done so great things for Israel, and given them the victory.

2 Maccabees 11

1 Not long after the, Lysias the king's protector and cousin, who also managed the affairs, took sore displeasure for the things that were done.

2 And when he had gathered about fourscore thousand with all the horsemen, he came against the Jews, thinking to make the city an habitation of the Gentiles,

3 And to make a gain of the temple, as of the other chapels of the heathen, and to set the high priesthood to sale every year:

4 Not at all considering the power of God but puffed up with his ten thousands of footmen, and his thousands of horsemen, and his fourscore elephants.

5 So he came to Judea, and drew near to Bethsura, which was a strong town, but distant from Jerusalem about five furlongs, and he laid sore siege unto it.

6 Now when they that were with Maccabeus heard that he besieged the holds, they and all the people with lamentation and tears besought the Lord that he would send a good angel to deliver Israel.

7 Then Maccabeus himself first of all took weapons, exhorting the other that they would jeopard themselves together with him to help their brethren: so they went forth together with a willing mind.

8 And as they were at Jerusalem, there appeared before them on horseback one in white clothing, shaking his armour of gold.

9 Then they praised the merciful God all together, and took heart, insomuch that they were ready not only to fight with men, but with most cruel beasts, and to pierce through walls of iron.

10 Thus they marched forward in their armour, having an helper from heaven: for the Lord was merciful unto them

11 And giving a charge upon their enemies like lions, they slew eleven thousand footmen, and sixteen hundred horsemen, and put all the other to flight.

12 Many of them also being wounded escaped naked; and Lysias himself fled away shamefully, and so escaped.

13 Who, as he was a man of understanding, casting with himself what loss he had had, and considering that the Hebrews could not be overcome, because the Almighty God helped them, he sent unto them,

14 And persuaded them to agree to all reasonable conditions, and promised that he would persuade the king that he must needs be a friend unto them.

15 Then Maccabeus consented to all that Lysias desired, being careful of the common good; and whatsoever Maccabeus wrote unto Lysias concerning the Jews, the king granted it.

16 For there were letters written unto the Jews from Lysias to this effect: Lysias unto the people of the Jews sendeth greeting:

17 John and Absolom, who were sent from you, delivered me the petition subscribed, and made request for the performance of the contents thereof.

18 Therefore what things soever were meet to be reported to the king, I have declared them, and he hath granted as much as might be.

19 And if then ye will keep yourselves loyal to the state, hereafter also will I endeavour to be a means of your good.

20 But of the particulars I have given order both to these and the other that came from me, to commune with you.

21 Fare ye well. The hundred and eight and fortieth year, the four and twentieth day of the month Dioscorinthius.

22 Now the king's letter contained these words: King Antiochus unto his brother Lysias sendeth greeting:

23 Since our father is translated unto the gods, our will is, that they that are in our realm live quietly, that every one may attend upon his own affairs.

24 We understand also that the Jews would not consent to our father, for to be brought unto the custom of the Gentiles, but had rather keep their own manner of living: for the which cause they require of us, that we should suffer them to live after their own laws.

25 Wherefore our mind is, that this nation shall be in rest, and we have determined to restore them their temple, that they may live according to the customs of their forefathers.

26 Thou shalt do well therefore to send unto them, and grant them peace, that when they are certified of our mind, they may be of good comfort, and ever go cheerfully about their own affairs.

27 And the letter of the king unto the nation of the Jews was after this manner: King Antiochus sendeth greeting unto the council, and the rest of the Jews:

28 If ye fare well, we have our desire; we are also in good health.

29 Menelaus declared unto us, that your desire was to return home, and to follow your own business:

30 Wherefore they that will depart shall have safe conduct till the thirtieth day of Xanthicus with security.

31 And the Jews shall use their own kind of meats and laws, as before; and none of them any manner of ways shall be molested for things ignorantly done.

32 I have sent also Menelaus, that he may comfort you.

33 Fare ye well. In the hundred forty and eighth year, and the fifteenth day of the month Xanthicus.

34 The Romans also sent unto them a letter containing these words: Quintus Memmius and Titus Manlius, ambassadors of the Romans, send greeting unto the people of the Jews.

35 Whatsoever Lysias the king's cousin hath granted, therewith we also are well pleased.

36 But touching such things as he judged to be referred to the king, after ye have advised thereof, send one forthwith, that we may declare as it is convenient for you: for we are now going to Antioch.

37 Therefore send some with speed, that we may know what is your mind.

38 Farewell. This hundred and eight and fortieth year, the fifteenth day of the month Xanthicus.

2 Maccabees 12

1 When these covenants were made, Lysias went unto the king, and the Jews were about their husbandry.

2 But of the governours of several places, Timotheus, and Apollonius the son of Genneus, also Hieronymus, and Demophon, and beside them Nicanor the governor of Cyprus, would not suffer them to be quiet and live in peace.

3 The men of Joppa also did such an ungodly deed: they prayed the Jews that dwelt among them to go with their wives and children into the boats which they had prepared, as though they had meant them no hurt.

4 Who accepted of it according to the common decree of the city, as being desirous to live in peace, and suspecting nothing: but when they were gone forth into the deep, they drowned no less than two hundred of them.

5 When Judas heard of this cruelty done unto his countrymen, he commanded those that were with him to make them ready.

6 And calling upon God the righteous Judge, he came against those murderers of his brethren, and burnt the haven by night, and set the boats on fire, and those that fled thither he slew.

7 And when the town was shut up, he went backward, as if he would return to root out all them of the city of Joppa.

8 But when he heard that the Jamnites were minded to do in like manner unto the Jews that dwelt among them,

9 He came upon the Jamnites also by night, and set fire on the haven and the navy, so that the light of the fire was seen at Jerusalem two hundred and forty furlongs off.

10 Now when they were gone from thence nine furlongs in their journey toward Timotheus, no fewer than five thousand men on foot and five hundred horsemen of the Arabians set upon him.

11 Whereupon there was a very sore battle; but Judas' side by the help of God got the victory; so that the Nomades of Arabia, being overcome, besought Judas for peace, promising both to give him cattle, and to pleasure him otherwise.

12 Then Judas, thinking indeed that they would be profitable in many things, granted them peace:

whereupon they shook hands, and so they departed to their tents.

13 He went also about to make a bridge to a certain strong city, which was fenced about with walls, and inhabited by people of divers countries; and the name of it was Caspis.

14 But they that were within it put such trust in the strength of the walls and provision of victuals, that they behaved themselves rudely toward them that were with Judas, railing and blaspheming, and uttering such words as were not to be spoken.

15 Wherefore Judas with his company, calling upon the great Lord of the world, who without rams or engines of war did cast down Jericho in the time of Joshua, gave a fierce assault against the walls,

16 And took the city by the will of God, and made unspeakable slaughters, insomuch that a lake two furlongs broad near adjoining thereunto, being filled full, was seen running with blood.

17 Then departed they from thence seven hundred and fifty furlongs, and came to Characa unto the Jews that are called Tubieni.

18 But as for Timotheus, they found him not in the places: for before he had dispatched any thing, he departed from thence, having left a very strong garrison in a certain hold.

19 Howbeit Dositheus and Sosipater, who were of Maccabeus' captains, went forth, and slew those that Timotheus had left in the fortress, above ten thousand men.

20 And Maccabeus ranged his army by bands, and set them over the bands, and went against Timotheus, who had about him an hundred and twenty thousand men of foot, and two thousand and five hundred horsemen.

21 Now when Timotheus had knowledge of Judas' coming, he sent the women and children and the other baggage unto a fortress called Carnion: for the town was hard to besiege, and uneasy to come unto, by reason of the straitness of all the places.

22 But when Judas his first band came in sight, the enemies, being smitten with fear and terror through the appearing of him who seeth all things, fled amain, one running into this way, another that way, so as that they were often hurt of their own men, and wounded with the points of their own swords.

23 Judas also was very earnest in pursuing them, killing those wicked wretches, of whom he slew about thirty thousand men.

24 Moreover Timotheus himself fell into the hands of Dositheus and Sosipater, whom he besought with much craft to let him go with his life, because he had many of the Jews'

parents, and the brethren of some of them, who, if they put him to death, should not be regarded.

25 So when he had assured them with many words that he would restore them without hurt, according to the agreement, they let him go for the saving of their brethren.

26 Then Maccabeus marched forth to Carnion, and to the temple of Atargatis, and there he slew five and twenty thousand persons.

27 And after he had put to flight and destroyed them, Judas removed the host toward Ephron, a strong city, wherein Lysias abode, and a great multitude of divers nations, and the strong young men kept the walls, and defended them mightily: wherein also was great provision of engines and darts.

28 But when Judas and his company had called upon Almighty God, who with his power breaketh the strength of his enemies, they won the city, and slew twenty and five thousand of them that were within,

29 From thence they departed to Scythopolis, which lieth six hundred furlongs from Jerusalem,

30 But when the Jews that dwelt there had testified that the Scythopolitans dealt lovingly with them, and entreated them kindly in the time of their adversity;

31 They gave them thanks, desiring them to be friendly still unto them:

and so they came to Jerusalem, the feast of the weeks approaching.

32 And after the feast, called Pentecost, they went forth against Gorgias the governor of Idumea,

33 Who came out with three thousand men of foot and four hundred horsemen.

34 And it happened that in their fighting together a few of the Jews were slain.

35 At which time Dositheus, one of Bacenor's company, who was on horseback, and a strong man, was still upon Gorgias, and taking hold of his coat drew him by force; and when he would have taken that cursed man alive, a horseman of Thracia coming upon him smote off his shoulder, so that Gorgias fled unto Marisa.

36 Now when they that were with Gorgias had fought long, and were weary, Judas called upon the Lord, that he would shew himself to be their helper and leader of the battle.

37 And with that he began in his own language, and sung psalms with a loud voice, and rushing unawares upon Gorgias' men, he put them to flight.

38 So Judas gathered his host, and came into the city of Odollam, And when the seventh day came, they purified themselves, as the custom was, and kept the sabbath in the same place.

39 And upon the day following, as the use had been, Judas and his company came to take up the bodies of them that were slain, and to bury them with their kinsmen in their fathers' graves.

40 Now under the coats of every one that was slain they found things consecrated to the idols of the Jamnites, which is forbidden the Jews by the law. Then every man saw that this was the cause wherefore they were slain.

41 All men therefore praising the Lord, the righteous Judge, who had opened the things that were hid,

42 Betook themselves unto prayer, and besought him that the sin committed might wholly be put out of remembrance. Besides, that noble Judas exhorted the people to keep themselves from sin, forsomuch as they saw before their eyes the things that came to pass for the sins of those that were slain.

43 And when he had made a gathering throughout the company to the sum of two thousand drachms of silver, he sent it to Jerusalem to offer a sin offering, doing therein very well and honestly, in that he was mindful of the resurrection:

44 For if he had not hoped that they that were slain should have risen again, it had been superfluous and vain to pray for the dead.

45 And also in that he perceived that there was great favour laid up for those that died godly, it was an holy and good thought. Whereupon he made a reconciliation for the dead, that they might be delivered from sin.

2 Maccabees 13

1 In the hundred forty and ninth year it was told Judas, that Antiochus Eupator was coming with a great power into Judea,

2 And with him Lysias his protector, and ruler of his affairs, having either of them a Grecian power of footmen, an hundred and ten thousand, and horsemen five thousand and three hundred, and elephants two and twenty, and three hundred chariots armed with hooks.

3 Menelaus also joined himself with them, and with great dissimulation encouraged Antiochus, not for the safeguard of the country, but because he thought to have been made governor.

4 But the King of kings moved Antiochus' mind against this wicked wretch, and Lysias informed the king that this man was the cause of all mischief, so that the king commanded to bring him unto Berea, and to put him to death, as the manner is in that place.

5 Now there was in that place a tower of fifty cubits high, full of ashes, and it had a round instrument which on every side hanged down into the ashes.

6 And whosoever was condemned of sacrilege, or had committed any other grievous crime, there did all men thrust him unto death.

7 Such a death it happened that wicked man to die, not having so much as burial in the earth; and that most justly:

8 For inasmuch as he had committed many sins about the altar, whose fire and ashes were holy, he received his death in ashes.

9 Now the king came with a barbarous and haughty mind to do far worse to the Jews, than had been done in his father's time.

10 Which things when Judas perceived, he commanded the multitude to call upon the Lord night and day, that if ever at any other time, he would now also help them, being at the point to be put from their law, from their country, and from the holy temple:

11 And that he would not suffer the people, that had even now been but a little refreshed, to be in subjection to the blasphemous nations.

12 So when they had all done this together, and besought the merciful Lord with weeping and fasting, and lying flat upon the ground three days long, Judas, having exhorted them, commanded they should be in a readiness.

13 And Judas, being apart with the elders, determined, before the king's host should enter into Judea, and get the city, to go forth and try the matter in fight by the help of the Lord.

14 So when he had committed all to the Creator of the world, and exhorted his soldiers to fight manfully, even unto death, for the laws, the temple, the city, the country, and the commonwealth, he camped by Modin:

15 And having given the watchword to them that were about him, Victory is of God; with the most valiant and choice young men he went in into the king's tent by night, and slew in the camp about four thousand men, and the chiefest of the elephants, with all that were upon him.

16 And at last they filled the camp with fear and tumult, and departed with good success.

17 This was done in the break of the day, because the protection of the Lord did help him.

18 Now when the king had taken a taste of the manliness of the Jews, he went about to take the holds by policy,

19 And marched toward Bethsura, which was a strong hold of the Jews: but he was put to flight, failed, and lost of his men:

20 For Judas had conveyed unto them that were in it such things as were necessary.

21 But Rhodocus, who was in the Jews' host, disclosed the secrets to the enemies; therefore he was sought out, and when they had gotten him, they put him in prison.

22 The king treated with them in Bethsum the second time, gave his hand, took their's, departed, fought with Judas, was overcome;

23 Heard that Philip, who was left over the affairs in Antioch, was desperately bent, confounded, intreated the Jews, submitted himself, and sware to all equal conditions, agreed with them, and offered sacrifice, honoured the temple, and dealt kindly with the place,

24 And accepted well of Maccabeus, made him principal governor from Ptolemais unto the Gerrhenians;

25 Came to Ptolemais: the people there were grieved for the covenants; for they stormed, because they would make their covenants void:

26 Lysias went up to the judgment seat, said as much as could be in defence of the cause, persuaded, pacified, made them well affected, returned to Antioch. Thus it went touching the king's coming and departing.

2 Maccabees 14

1 After three years was Judas informed, that Demetrius the son of Seleucus, having entered by the

haven of Tripolis with a great power and navy,

2 Had taken the country, and killed Antiochus, and Lysias his protector.

3 Now one Alcimus, who had been high priest, and had defiled himself wilfully in the times of their mingling with the Gentiles, seeing that by no means he could save himself, nor have any more access to the holy altar,

4 Came to king Demetrius in the hundred and one and fiftieth year, presenting unto him a crown of gold, and a palm, and also of the boughs which were used solemnly in the temple: and so that day he held his peace.

5 Howbeit having gotten opportunity to further his foolish enterprize, and being called into counsel by Demetrius, and asked how the Jews stood affected, and what they intended, he answered thereunto:

6 Those of the Jews that he called Assideans, whose captain is Judas Maccabeus, nourish war and are seditious, and will not let the rest be in peace.

7 Therefore I, being deprived of mine ancestors' honour, I mean the high priesthood, am now come hither:

8 First, verily for the unfeigned care I have of things pertaining to the king; and secondly, even for that I intend the good of mine own countrymen: for all our nation is in no small misery through the unadvised dealing of them aforersaid.

9 Wherefore, O king, seeing knowest all these things, be careful for the country, and our nation, which is pressed on every side, according to the clemency that thou readily shewest unto all.

10 For as long as Judas liveth, it is not possible that the state should be quiet.

11 This was no sooner spoken of him, but others of the king's friends, being maliciously set against Judas, did more incense Demetrius.

12 And forthwith calling Nicanor, who had been master of the elephants, and making him governor over Judea, he sent him forth,

13 Commanding him to slay Judas, and to scatter them that were with him, and to make Alcimus high priest of the great temple.

14 Then the heathen, that had fled out of Judea from Judas, came to Nicanor by flocks, thinking the harm and calamities of the Jews to be their welfare.

15 Now when the Jews heard of Nicanor's coming, and that the heathen were up against them, they cast earth upon their heads, and made supplication to him that had established his people for ever, and who always helpeth his portion with manifestation of his presence.

16 So at the commandment of the captain they removed straightways from thence, and came near unto them at the town of Dessau.

17 Now Simon, Judas' brother, had joined battle with Nicanor, but was somewhat discomfited through the sudden silence of his enemies.

18 Nevertheless Nicanor, hearing of the manliness of them that were with Judas, and the courageousness that they had to fight for their country, durst not try the matter by the sword.

19 Wherefore he sent Posidonius, and Theodotus, and Mattathias, to make peace.

20 So when they had taken long advisement thereupon, and the captain had made the multitude acquainted therewith, and it appeared that they were all of one mind, they consented to the covenants,

21 And appointed a day to meet in together by themselves: and when the day came, and stools were set for either of them,

22 Ludas placed armed men ready in convenient places, lest some treachery should be suddenly practised by the enemies: so they made a peaceable conference.

23 Now Nicanor abode in Jerusalem, and did no hurt, but sent away the people that came flocking unto him.

24 And he would not willingly have Judas out of his sight: for he love the man from his heart

25 He prayed him also to take a wife, and to beget children: so he married, was quiet, and took part of this life.

26 But Alcimus, perceiving the love that was betwixt them, and considering the covenants that were made, came to Demetrius, and told him that Nicanor was not well affected toward the state; for that he had ordained Judas, a traitor to his realm, to be the king's successor.

27 Then the king being in a rage, and provoked with the accusations of the most wicked man, wrote to Nicanor, signifying that he was much displeased with the covenants, and commanding him that he should send Maccabeus prisoner in all haste unto Antioch.

28 When this came to Nicanor's hearing, he was much confounded in himself, and took it grievously that he should make void the articles which were agreed upon, the man being in no fault.

29 But because there was no dealing against the king, he watched his time to accomplish this thing by policy.

30 Notwithstanding, when Maccabeus saw that Nicanor began to be churlish unto him, and that he entreated him more roughly than he was wont, perceiving that such sour behaviour came not of good, he

gathered together not a few of his men, and withdrew himself from Nicanor.

31 But the other, knowing that he was notably prevented by Judas' policy, came into the great and holy temple, and commanded the priests, that were offering their usual sacrifices, to deliver him the man.

32 And when they sware that they could not tell where the man was whom he sought,

33 He stretched out his right hand toward the temple, and made an oath in this manner: If ye will not deliver me Judas as a prisoner, I will lay this temple of God even with the ground, and I will break down the altar, and erect a notable temple unto Bacchus.

34 After these words he departed. Then the priests lifted up their hands toward heaven, and besought him that was ever a defender of their nation, saying in this manner;

35 Thou, O Lord of all things, who hast need of nothing, wast pleased that the temple of thine habitation should be among us:

36 Therefore now, O holy Lord of all holiness, keep this house ever undefiled, which lately was cleansed, and stop every unrighteous mouth.

37 Now was there accused unto Nicanor one Razis, one of the elders of Jerusalem, a lover of his countrymen, and a man of very good

report, who for his kindness was called a father of the Jews.

38 For in the former times, when they mingled not themselves with the Gentiles, he had been accused of Judaism, and did boldly jeopard his body and life with all vehemency for the religion of the Jews.

39 So Nicanor, willing to declare the hate that he bare unto the Jews, sent above five hundred men of war to take him:

40 For he thought by taking him to do the Jews much hurt.

41 Now when the multitude would have taken the tower, and violently broken into the outer door, and bade that fire should be brought to burn it, he being ready to be taken on every side fell upon his sword;

42 Choosing rather to die manfully, than to come into the hands of the wicked, to be abused otherwise than beseemed his noble birth:

43 But missing his stroke through haste, the multitude also rushing within the doors, he ran boldly up to the wall, and cast himself down manfully among the thickest of them.

44 But they quickly giving back, and a space being made, he fell down into the midst of the void place.

45 Nevertheless, while there was yet breath within him, being inflamed with anger, he rose up; and though his blood gushed out like spouts of

water, and his wounds were grievous, yet he ran through the midst of the throng; and standing upon a steep rock,

46 When as his blood was now quite gone, he plucked out his bowels, and taking them in both his hands, he cast them upon the throng, and calling upon the Lord of life and spirit to restore him those again, he thus died.

2 Maccabees 15

1 But Nicanor, hearing that Judas and his company were in the strong places about Samaria, resolved without any danger to set upon them on the sabbath day.

2 Nevertheless the Jews that were compelled to go with him said, O destroy not so cruelly and barbarously, but give honour to that day, which he, that seeth all things, hath honoured with holiness above all other days.

3 Then the most ungracious wretch demanded, if there were a Mighty one in heaven, that had commanded the sabbath day to be kept.

4 And when they said, There is in heaven a living Lord, and mighty, who commanded the seventh day to be kept:

5 Then said the other, And I also am mighty upon earth, and I command to take arms, and to do the king's business. Yet he obtained not to have his wicked will done.

6 So Nicanor in exceeding pride and haughtiness determined to set up a publick monument of his victory over Judas and them that were with him.

7 But Maccabeus had ever sure confidence that the Lord would help him:

8 Wherefore he exhorted his people not to fear the coming of the heathen against them, but to remember the help which in former times they had received from heaven, and now to expect the victory and aid, which should come unto them from the Almighty.

9 And so comforting them out of the law and the prophets, and withal putting them in mind of the battles that they won afore, he made them more cheerful.

10 And when he had stirred up their minds, he gave them their charge, shewing them therewithall the falsehood of the heathen, and the breach of oaths.

11 Thus he armed every one of them, not so much with defence of shields and spears, as with comfortable and good words: and beside that, he told them a dream worthy to be believed, as if it had been so indeed, which did not a little rejoice them.

12 And this was his vision: That Onias, who had been high priest, a virtuous and a good man, reverend in conversation, gentle in condition,

well spoken also, and exercised from a child in all points of virtue, holding up his hands prayed for the whole body of the Jews.

13 This done, in like manner there appeared a man with gray hairs, and exceeding glorious, who was of a wonderful and excellent majesty.

14 Then Onias answered, saying, This is a lover of the brethren, who prayeth much for the people, and for the holy city, to wit, Jeremias the prophet of God.

15 Whereupon Jeremias holding forth his right hand gave to Judas a sword of gold, and in giving it spake thus,

16 Take this holy sword, a gift from God, with the which thou shalt wound the adversaries.

17 Thus being well comforted by the words of Judas, which were very good, and able to stir them up to valour, and to encourage the hearts of the young men, they determined not to pitch camp, but courageously to set upon them, and manfully to try the matter by conflict, because the city and the sanctuary and the temple were in danger.

18 For the care that they took for their wives, and their children, their brethren, and folks, was in least account with them: but the greatest and principal fear was for the holy temple.

19 Also they that were in the city took not the least care, being troubled for the conflict abroad.

20 And now, when as all looked what should be the trial, and the enemies were already come near, and the army was set in array, and the beasts conveniently placed, and the horsemen set in wings,

21 Maccabeus seeing the coming of the multitude, and the divers preparations of armour, and the fierceness of the beasts, stretched out his hands toward heaven, and called upon the Lord that worketh wonders, knowing that victory cometh not by arms, but even as it seemeth good to him, he giveth it to such as are worthy:

22 Therefore in his prayer he said after this manner; O Lord, thou didst send thine angel in the time of Ezekias king of Judea, and didst slay in the host of Sennacherib an hundred fourscore and five thousand:

23 Wherefore now also, O Lord of heaven, send a good angel before us for a fear and dread unto them;

24 And through the might of thine arm let those be stricken with terror, that come against thy holy people to blaspheme. And he ended thus.

25 Then Nicanor and they that were with him came forward with trumpets and songs.

26 But Judas and his company encountered the enemies with invocation and prayer.

27 So that fighting with their hands, and praying unto God with their hearts, they slew no less than thirty and five thousand men: for through the appearance of God they were greatly cheered.

28 Now when the battle was done, returning again with joy, they knew that Nicanor lay dead in his harness.

29 Then they made a great shout and a noise, praising the Almighty in their own language.

30 And Judas, who was ever the chief defender of the citizens both in body and mind, and who continued his love toward his countrymen all his life, commanded to strike off Nicanor's head, and his hand with his shoulder, and bring them to Jerusalem.

31 So when he was there, and called them of his nation together, and set the priests before the altar, he sent for them that were of the tower,

32 And shewed them vile Nicanor's head, and the hand of that blasphemer, which with proud brags he had stretched out against the holy temple of the Almighty.

33 And when he had cut out the tongue of that ungodly Nicanor, he commanded that they should give it by pieces unto the fowls, and hang up the reward of his madness before the temple.

34 So every man praised toward the heaven the glorious Lord, saying, Blessed be he that hath kept his own place undefiled.

35 He hanged also Nicanor's head upon the tower, an evident and manifest sign unto all of the help of the Lord.

36 And they ordained all with a common decree in no case to let that day pass without solemnity, but to celebrate the thirtieth day of the twelfth month, which in the Syrian tongue is called Adar, the day before Mardocheus' day.

37 Thus went it with Nicanor: and from that time forth the Hebrews had the city in their power. And here will I make an end.

38 And if I have done well, and as is fitting the story, it is that which I desired: but if slenderly and meanly, it is that which I could attain unto.

39 For as it is hurtful to drink wine or water alone; and as wine mingled with water is pleasant, and delighteth the taste: even so speech finely framed delighteth the ears of them that read the story. And here shall be an   end.

THE BOOK OF ENOCH

Enoch I

1 The word of the blessing of Enoch, how he blessed the elect and the righteous, who were to exist in the time of trouble; rejecting all the wicked and ungodly. Enoch, a righteous man, who was (1) with God, answered and spoke, while his eyes were open, and while he saw a holy vision in the heavens. This the angels showed me.

2 From them I heard all things, and understood what I saw; that which will not take place in this generation, but in a generation which is to succeed at a distant period, on account of the elect.

3 Upon their account I spoke and conversed with him, who will go forth from his habitation, the Holy and Mighty One, the God of the world:

4 Who will hereafter tread upon Mount Sinai; appear with his hosts; and be manifested in the strength of his power from heaven.

5 All shall be afraid, and the Watchers be terrified.

6 Great fear and trembling shall seize them, even to the ends of the earth. The lofty mountains shall be troubled, and the exalted hills depressed, melting like a honeycomb in the flame. The earth shall be immerged, and all things which are in it perish; while judgment shall come upon all, even upon all the righteous:

7 But to them shall he give peace: he shall preserve the elect, and towards them exercise clemency.

8 Then shall all belong to God; be happy and blessed; and the splendour of the Godhead shall illuminate them.

Enoch 2

Behold, he comes with ten thousands of his saints, to execute judgment upon them, and destroy the wicked, and reprove all the carnal for everything which the sinful and ungodly have done, and committed against him. (Quoted by Jude, vss. 14, 15.)

Enoch 3

1 All who are in the heavens know what is transacted there.

2 They know that the heavenly luminaries change not their paths; that each rises and sets regularly, every one at its proper period, without transgressing the commands which they have received. They behold the earth, and understand what is there transacted, from the beginning to the end of it.

3 They see that every work of God is invariable in the period of its appearance. They behold summer and winter: perceiving that the whole earth is full of water; and that the cloud, the dew, and the rain refresh it.

Enoch 4

They consider and behold every tree, how it appears to wither, and every leaf to fall off, except of fourteen trees, which are not deciduous; which wait from the old, to the appearance of the new leaf, for two or three winters.

Enoch 5

Again they consider the days of summer, that the sun is upon it at its very beginning; while you seek for a covered and shady spot on account of the burning sun; while the earth is scorched up with fervid heat, and you become incapable of walking either upon the ground or upon the rocks in consequence of that heat.

Enoch 6

1 They consider how the trees, when they put forth their green leaves, become covered, and produce fruit; understanding everything, and knowing that He who lives for ever does all these things for you:

2 That the works at the beginning of every existing year, that all his works, are subservient to him, and invariable; yet as God has appointed, so are all things brought to pass.

3 They see, too, how the seas and the rivers together complete their respective operations:

4 But you endure not patiently, nor fulfil the commandments of the Lord; but you transgress and calumniate his greatness; and malignant are the words in your polluted mouths against his Majesty.

5. Ye withered in heart, no peace shall be to you!

6 Therefore your days shall you curse, and the years of your lives shall perish; perpetual execration shall be multiplied, and you shall not obtain mercy.

7 In those days shall you resign your peace with the eternal maledictions of all the righteous, and sinners shall perpetually execrate you;

8 Shall execrate you with the ungodly.

9 The elect shall possess light, joy, and peace; and they shall inherit the earth.

10 But you, ye unholy, shall be accursed.

11 Then shall wisdom be given to the elect, all of whom shall live, and not again transgress by impiety or pride; but shall humble themselves, possessing prudence, and shall not repeat transgression.

12 They shall not be condemned the whole period of their lives, nor die in torment and indignation; but the sum of their days 1 shall be completed, and they shall grow old in peace; while the years of their happiness shall be multiplied with joy, and with peace, for ever, the whole duration of their existence.

Enoch 7 [SECT. II.]

1 It happened after the sons of men had multiplied in those days, that daughters were born to them, elegant and beautiful.

2 And when the angels, the sons of heaven, beheld them, they became enamoured of them, saying to each other, Come, let us select for ourselves wives from the progeny of men, and let us beget children.

3 Then their leader Samyaza said to them; I fear that you may perhaps be indisposed to the performance of this enterprise;

4 And that I alone shall suffer for so grievous a crime.

5 But they answered him and said; We all swear;

6 And bind ourselves by mutual execrations, that we will not change our intention, but execute our projected undertaking.

7 Then they swore all together, and all bound themselves by mutual execrations. Their whole number was two hundred, who descended upon Ardis, which is the top of mount Armon.

8 That mountain therefore was called Armon, because they had sworn upon it, and bound themselves by mutual execrations.

9 These are the names of their chiefs: Samyaza, who was their leader, Urakabarameel, Akibeel, Tamiel, Ramuel, Danel, Azkeel, Saraknyal, Asael, Armers, Batraal, Anane, Zavebe, Samsaveel, Ertael, Turel, Yomyael, Arazyal. These were the prefects of the two hundred angels, and the remainder were all with them.

10 Then they took wives, each choosing for himself; whom they began to approach, and with whom they cohabited; teaching them sorcery, incantations, and the dividing of roots and trees.

11 And the women conceiving brought forth giants,

12 Whose stature was each three hundred cubits. These devoured all which the labour of men produced; until it became impossible to feed them;

13 When they turned themselves against men, in order to devour them;

14 And began to injure birds, beasts, reptiles, and fishes, to eat their flesh one after another, and to drink their blood.

15 Then the earth reproved the unrighteous.

Enoch 8

1 Moreover Azazyel taught men to make swords, knives, shields, breastplates, the fabrication of mirrors, and the workmanship of bracelets and ornaments, the use of paint, the beautifying of the eyebrows, the use of stones of every valuable and select kind, and of all sorts of dyes, so that the world became altered.

2 Impiety increased; fornication multiplied; and they transgressed and corrupted all their ways.

3 Amazarak taught all the sorcerers, and dividers of roots:

4 Armers taught the solution of sorcery;

5 Barkayal taught the observers of the stars;

6 Akibeel taught signs;

7 Tamiel taught astronomy;

8 And Asaradel taught the motion of the moon.

9 And men, being destroyed, cried out; and their voice reached to heaven.

Enoch 9

1 Then Michael and Gabriel, Raphael, Suryal, and Uriel, looked down from heaven, and saw the quantity of blood which was shed on earth, and all the iniquity which was done upon it, and said one to another, It is the voice of their cries;

2 The earth deprived of her children has cried even to the gate of heaven.

3 And now to you, O ye holy ones of heaven, the souls of men complain, saying, Obtain Justice for us with 1 the Most High. Then they said to their Lord, the King, Thou art Lord of lords, God of gods, King of kings. The throne of thy glory is for ever and ever, and for ever and ever is thy name sanctified and glorified. Thou art blessed and glorified.

4 Thou hast made all things; thou possessest power over all things; and all things are open and manifest before thee. Thou beholdest all things, and nothing, can be concealed from thee.

5 Thou hast seen what Azazyel has done, how he as taught every species of iniquity upon earth, and has disclosed to the world all the secret things which are done in the heavens.

6 Samyaza also has taught sorcery, to whom thou hast given authority over those who are associated with him. They have gone together to the daughters of men; have lain with them; have become polluted;

7 And have discovered crimes to them.

8 The women likewise have brought forth giants.

9 Thus has the whole earth been filled with blood and with iniquity.

10 And now behold the souls of those who are dead, cry out.

11 And complain even to the gate of heaven.

12 Their groaning ascends; nor can they escape from the unrighteousness which is committed on earth. Thou knowest all things, before they exist.

13 Thou knowest these things, and what has been done by them; yet thou dost not speak to us.

14 What on account of these things ought we to do to them?

Enoch 10

1 Then the Most High, the Great and Holy One spoke,

2 And sent Arsayalalyur to the son of Lamech,

3 Saying, Say to him in my name, Conceal thyself.

4 Then explain to him the consummation which is about to take place; for all the earth shall perish; the waters of a deluge shall come over the whole earth, and all things which are in it shall be destroyed.

5 And now teach him how he may escape, and how his seed may remain in all the earth.

6 Again the Lord said to Raphael, Bind Azazyel hand and foot; cast him into darkness; and opening the desert which is in Dudael, cast him in there.

7 Throw upon him hurled and pointed stones, covering him with darkness;

8 There shall he remain for ever; cover his face, that he may not see the light.

9 And in the great day of judgment let him be cast into the fire.

10 Restore the earth, which the angels have corrupted; and announce life to it, that I may revive it.

11 All the sons of men shall not perish in consequence of every secret, by which the Watchers have destroyed, and which they have taught, their offspring.

12 All the earth has been corrupted by the effects of the teaching of Azazyel. To him therefore ascribe the whole crime.

13 To Gabriel also the Lord said, Go to the biters, to the reprobates, to the children of fornication; and destroy the children of fornication, the offspring of the Watchers, from among men; bring them forth, and excite them one against another. Let them perish by mutual slaughter; for length of days shall not be theirs.

14 They shall all entreat thee, but their fathers shall not obtain their wishes respecting them; for they shall hope for eternal life, and that they may live, each of them, five hundred years.

15 To Michael likewise the Lord said, Go and announce his crime to Samyaza, and to the others

who are with him, who have been associated with women, that they might be polluted with all their impurity. And when all their sons shall be slain, when they shall see the perdition of their beloved, bind them for seventy generations underneath the earth, even to the day of judgment, and of consummation, until the judgment, the effect of which will last for ever, be completed.

16 Then shall they be taken away into the lowest depths of the fire in torments; and in confinement shall they be shut up for ever.

17 Immediately after this shall he, together with them, burn and perish; they shall be bound until the consummation of many generations.

18 Destroy all the souls addicted to dalliance, and the offspring of the Watchers, for they have tyrannized over mankind.

19 Let every oppressor perish from the face of the earth;

20 Let every evil work be destroyed;

21 The plant of righteousness and of rectitude appear, and its produce 2 become a blessing.

22 Righteousness and rectitude shall be for ever planted with delight.

23. And then shall all the saints give thanks, and live until they have begotten a thousand children,

while the whole period of their youth, and their sabbaths shall be completed in peace. In those days all the earth shall be cultivated in righteousness; it shall be wholly planted with trees, and filled with benediction; every tree of delight shall be planted in it.

24 In it shall vines be planted; and the vine which shall be planted in it shall yield fruit to satiety; every seed, which shall be sown in it, shall produce for one measure a thousand; and one measure of olives shall produce ten presses of oil.

25 Purify the earth from all oppression, from all injustice, from all crime, from all impiety, and from all the pollution which is committed upon it. Exterminate them from the earth.

26 Then shall all the children of men be righteous, and all nations shall pay me divine honours, and bless me; and all shall adore me.

27 The earth shall be cleansed from all corruption, from every crime, from all punishment, and from all

suffering; neither will I again send a deluge upon it from generation to generation for ever.

28 In those days I will open the treasures of blessing which are in heaven, that I may cause them to descend upon earth, and upon all the works and labour of man.

29 Peace and equity shall associate with the sons of men all the days of the world, in every generation of it.

Enoch 11

1. And in those days I will open the store chambers of blessing which are in the heaven, so as to send them down [upon the earth] over the work and labour of the children of men. 2. And truth and peace shall be associated together throughout all the days of the world and throughout all the generations of men.

Enoch 12 [SECT. III.]

1 Before all these things Enoch was concealed; nor did any one of the sons of men know where he was concealed, where he had been, and what had happened.

2 He was wholly engaged with the holy ones, and with the Watchers in his days.

3 I, Enoch, was blessing the great Lord and King of peace.

4 And behold the Watchers called me Enoch the scribe.

5 Then the Lord said to me: Enoch, scribe of righteousness, go tell the Watchers of heaven, who have deserted the lofty sky, and their holy everlasting station, who have been polluted with women.

6 And have done as the sons of men do, by taking to themselves wives, and who have been greatly corrupted on the earth;

7 That on the earth they shall never obtain peace and remission of sin. For they shall not rejoice in their offspring; they shall behold the slaughter of their beloved; shall lament for the destruction of their sons; and shall petition for ever; but shall not obtain mercy and peace.

Enoch 13

1 Then Enoch, passing on, said to Azazyel: Thou shalt not obtain peace. A great sentence is gone forth against thee. He shall bind thee;

2 Neither shall relief, mercy, and supplication be thine, on account of the oppression which thou hast taught;

3 And on account of every act of blasphemy, tyranny, and sin, which thou hast discovered to the children of men.

4 Then departing from him I spoke to them all together;

5 And they all became terrified, and trembled;

6 Beseeching me to write for them a memorial of supplication, that they might obtain forgiveness; and that I might make the memorial of their prayer ascend up before the God of heaven; because they could not themselves thenceforwards address him, nor raise up their eyes to heaven on account of the disgraceful offence for which they were judged.

7 Then I wrote a memorial of their prayer and supplication, for their spirits, for everything which they had done, and for the subject of their entreaty, that they might obtain remission and rest.

8 Proceeding on, I continued over the waters of Danbadan, which is on the right to the west of Armon, reading the memorial of their prayer, until I fell asleep.

9 And behold a dream came to me, and visions appeared above me. I fell down and saw a vision of punishment, that I might relate it to the sons of heaven, and reprove them. When I awoke I went to them. All being collected together stood weeping in Oubelseyael, which is situated between Libanos and Seneser, with their faces veiled.

10 I related in their presence all the visions which I had seen, and my dream;

11 And began to utter these words of righteousness, reproving the Watchers of heaven.

Enoch 14

1 This is the book of the words of righteousness, and of the reproof of the Watchers, who belong to the world, according to that which He, who is holy and great, commanded in the vision. I perceived in my dream, that I was now speaking with a tongue of flesh, and with my breath, which the Mighty One has put into the mouth of men, that they might converse with it.

2 And understand with the heart. As he has created and given to men the power of comprehending the word of understanding, so has he created and given to me the power of reproving the Watchers, the offspring of heaven. I have written your petition; and in my vision it has been shown me, that what you request will not be granted you as long as the world endures.

3 Judgment has been passed upon you: your request will not be granted you.

4 From this time forward, never shall you ascend into heaven; He has said, that on the earth He will bind you, as long as the world endures.

5 But before these things you shall behold the destruction of your beloved sons; you shall not possess them, but they shall fall before you by the sword.

6 Neither shall you entreat for them, nor for yourselves;

7 But you shall weep and supplicate in silence. The words of the book which I wrote.

8 A vision thus appeared to me.

9 Behold, in that vision clouds and a mist invited me; agitated stars and flashes of lightning impelled and pressed me forwards, while winds in the vision assisted my flight, accelerating my progress.

10 They elevated me aloft to heaven. I proceeded, until I arrived at a wall built with stones of crystal. A vibrating flame surrounded it, which began to strike me with terror.

11 Into this vibrating flame I entered;

12 And drew nigh to a spacious habitation built also with stones of crystal. Its walls too, as well as pavement, were formed with stones of crystal, and crystal likewise was the ground. Its roof had the appearance of agitated stars and flashes of lightning; and among them were cherubim of fire in a stormy sky. A flame burned around its walls; and its portal blazed with fire. When I entered into this dwelling, it was hot as fire and cold as ice. No trace of delight or of life was there. Terror overwhelmed me, and a fearful shaking seized me.

13 Violently agitated and trembling, I fell upon my face. In the vision I looked,

14 And behold there was another habitation more spacious than the former, every entrance to which was open before me, erected in the midst of a vibrating flame.

15 So greatly did it excel in all points, in glory, in magnificence, and in magnitude, that it is impossible to describe to you either the splendour or the extent of it.

16 Its floor was on fire; above were lightnings and agitated stars, while its roof exhibited a blazing fire.

17 Attentively I surveyed it, and saw that it contained an exalted throne;

18 The appearance of which was like that of frost; while its circumference resembled the orb of the brilliant sun; and there was the voice of the cherubim.

19 From underneath this mighty throne rivers of flaming fire issued.

20 To look upon it was impossible.

21 One great in glory sat upon it:

22 Whose robe was brighter than the sun, and whiter than snow.

23 No angel was capable of penetrating to view the face of Him, the Glorious and the Effulgent; nor could any mortal behold Him. A fire was flaming around Him.

24 A fire also of great extent continued to rise up before Him; so that not one of those who surrounded Him was capable of

approaching Him, among the myriads of 'myriads who were before Him. To Him holy consultation was needless. Yet did not the sanctified, who were near Him, depart far from Him either by night or by day; nor were they removed from Him. I also was so far advanced, with a veil on my face, and trembling. Then the Lord with his own mouth called me, saying, Approach hither, Enoch, at my holy word.

25 And He raised me up, making me draw near even to the entrance. My eye was directed to the ground.

Enoch 15

1 Then addressing me, He spoke and said, Hear, neither be afraid, O righteous Enoch, thou scribe of righteousness: approach hither, and hear my voice. Go, say to the Watchers of heaven, who have sent thee to pray for them, You ought to pray for men, and not men for you.

2 Wherefore have you forsaken the lofty and holy heaven, which endures for ever, and have lain with women; have defiled yourselves with the daughters of men; have taken to yourselves wives; have acted like the sons of the earth, and have begotten an impious offspring?

3 You being spiritual, holy, and possessing a life which is eternal, have polluted yourselves with women; have begotten in carnal blood; have lusted in the blood of men; and have done as those who are flesh and blood do.

4 These however die and perish.

5 Therefore have I given to them wives, that they might cohabit with them; that sons might be born of them; and that this might be transacted upon earth.

6 But you from the beginning were made spiritual, possessing a life which is eternal, and not subject to death for ever.

7 Therefore I made not wives for you, because, being spiritual, your dwelling is in heaven.

8 Now the giants, who lave been born of spirit and of flesh, shall be called upon earth evil spirits, and on earth shall be their habitation. Evil spirits shall proceed from their flesh, because they were created from above; from the holy Watchers was their beginning and primary foundation. Evil spirits shall they be upon earth, and the spirits of the wicked shall they be called. The habitation of the spirits of heaven shall be in heaven; but upon earth shall be the habitation of terrestrial spirits, who are born on earth.

9 The spirits of the giants shall be like clouds, which shall oppress, corrupt, fall, contend, and bruise upon earth.

10 They shall cause lamentation. No food shall they eat; and they shall be

thirsty; they shall be concealed, and shall not 1 rise up against the sons of men, and against women; for they come forth during the days of slaughter and destruction.

Enoch 16

1 And as to the death of the giants, wheresoever their spirits depart from their bodies, let their flesh, that which is perishable, be without judgment. Thus shall they perish, until the day of the great consummation of the great world. A destruction shall take place of the Watchers and the impious.

2 And now to the Watchers, who have sent thee to pray for them, who in the beginning were in heaven,

3 Say, In heaven have you been; secret things, however, have not been manifested to you; yet have you known a reprobated mystery.

4 And this you have related to women in the hardness of your heart, and by that mystery have women and mankind multiplied evils upon the earth.

5 Say to them, Never therefore shall you obtain peace.

Enoch 17 [SECT. IV.]

1 They raised me up into a certain place, where there was the appearance of a burning fire; and when they pleased they assumed the likeness of men.

2 They carried me to a lofty spot, to a mountain, the top of which reached to heaven.

3 And I beheld the receptacles of light and of thunder at the extremities of the place, where it was deepest. There was a bow of fire, and arrows in their quiver, a sword of fire, and every species of lightning.

4 Then they elevated me to a babbling stream, and to a fire in the west, which received all the setting of the sun. I came to a river of fire, which flowed like water, and emptied itself into the great sea westwards.

5 I saw every large river, until I arrived at the great darkness. I went to where all of flesh migrate; and I beheld the mountains of the gloom which constitutes winter, and the place from which issues the water in every abyss.

6 I saw also the mouths of all the rivers in the world, and the mouths of the deep.

Enoch 18

1 I then surveyed the receptacles of all the winds, perceiving that they contributed to adorn the whole creation, and to preserve the foundation of the earth.

2. I surveyed the stone which supports the corners of the earth.

3. I also beheld the four winds, which bear up the earth, and the firmament of heaven.

4. And I beheld the winds occupying the exalted sky.

5. Arising in the midst of heaven and of earth, and constituting the pillars of heaven.

6. I saw the winds which turn the sky, which cause the orb of the sun and of all the stars to set; and over the earth I saw the winds which support the clouds.

7. I saw the path of the angels.

8 I perceived at the extremity of the earth the firmament of heaven above it. Then I passed on towards the south;

9 Where burnt, both by day and night, six mountains formed of glorious stones; three towards the east, and three towards the south.

10 Those which were towards the east were of a variegated stone; one of which was of margarite, and another of antimony. Those towards the south were of a red stone. The middle one reached to heaven like the throne of God; a throne composed of alabaster, the top of which was of sapphire. I saw, too, a blazing fire hanging over 1 all the mountains.

11 And there I saw a place on the other side of an extended territory, where waters were collected.

12. I likewise beheld terrestrial fountains, deep in the fiery columns of heaven.

13. And in the columns of heaven I beheld fires, which descended without number, but neither on high, nor into the deep. Over these fountains also I perceived a place which had neither the firmament of heaven above it, nor the solid ground underneath it; neither was there water above it, nor anything on wing; but the spot was desolate.

14. And there I beheld seven stars, like great blazing mountains, and like spirits entreating me.

15. Then the angel said, This place, until the consummation of heaven and earth, will be the prison of the stars, and the host of heaven.

16. The stars which roll over fire are those which transgressed the commandment of God before their time arrived; for they came not in their proper season. Therefore was He offended with them, and bound them, until the period of the consummation of their crimes in the secret year.

Enoch 19

1. Then Uriel said, Here the angels, who cohabited with women, appointed their leaders;

2. And being numerous in appearance made men profane, and caused them to err; so that they sacrificed to devils as to gods. For in the great day there shall be a judgment, with which they shall be judged, until they are consumed; and

their wives also shall be judged, who led astray the angels of heaven that they might salute them.

3. And I, Enoch, I alone saw the likeness of the end of all things. Nor did any human being see it, as I saw it.

Enoch 20

1. These are the names of the angels who watch.

2. Uriel, one of the holy angels, who presides over clamour and terror.

3. Raphael, one of the holy angels, who presides over the spirits of men.

4. Raguel, one of the holy angels, who inflicts punishment on the world and the luminaries.

5. Michael, one of the holy angels, who, presiding over human virtue, commands the nations.

6. Sarakiel, one of the holy angels, who presides over the spirits of the children of men that transgress.

7. Gabriel, one of the holy angels, who presides over Ikisat, over paradise, and over the cherubim.

Enoch 21

1. Then I made a circuit to a place in which nothing was completed.

2. And there I beheld neither the tremendous workmanship of an exalted heaven, nor of an established earth, but a desolate spot, prepared, and terrific.

3. There, too, I beheld seven stars of heaven bound in it together, like great mountains, and like a blazing fire. I exclaimed, For what species of crime have they been bound, and why have they been removed to this place? Then Uriel, one of the holy angels who was with me, and who conducted me, answered: Enoch, wherefore dost thou ask; wherefore reason with thyself, and anxiously inquire? These are those of the stars which have transgressed the commandment of the most high God; and are here bound, until the infinite number of the days of their crimes be completed.

4. From thence I afterwards passed on to another terrific place;

5. Where I beheld the operation of a great fire blazing and glittering, in the midst of which there was a division. Columns of fire struggled together to the end of the abyss, and deep was their descent. But neither its measurement nor magnitude was I able to discover; neither could I perceive its origin. Then I exclaimed, How terrible is this place, and how difficult to explore!

6. Uriel, one of the holy angels who was with me, answered and said: Enoch, why art thou alarmed and amazed at this terrific place, at the sight of this place of suffering? This, he said, is the prison of the angels; and here they are kept for ever.

Enoch 22 [SECT. V.]

1. From thence I proceeded to another spot, where I saw on the west a great and lofty mountain, a strong rock, and four delightful places.

2. Internally it was deep, capacious, and very smooth; as smooth as if it had been rolled over: it was both deep and dark to behold.

3. Then Raphael, one of the holy angels who were with me, answered and said, These are the delightful places where the spirits, the souls of the dead, will be collected; for them were they formed; and here will be collected all the souls of the sons of men.

4. These places, in which they dwell, shall they occupy until the day of judgment, and until their appointed period.

5. Their appointed period will be long, even until the great judgment. And I saw the spirits of the sons of men who were dead; and their voices reached to heaven, while they were accusing.

6. Then I inquired of Raphael, an angel who was with me, and said, Whose spirit is that, the voice of which reaches to heaven, and accuses?

7. He answered, saying, This is the spirit of Abel, who was slain by Cain his brother; and who will accuse that brother, until his seed be destroyed from the face of the earth;

8. Until his seed perish from the seed of the human race.

9. At that time therefore I inquired respecting him, and respecting the general judgment, saying, Why is one separated from another? He answered, Three separations have been made between the spirits of the dead, and thus have the spirits of the righteous been separated.

10. Namely, by a chasm, by water, and by light above it.

11. And in the same way likewise are sinners separated when they die, and are buried in the earth; judgment not overtaking them in their lifetime.

12. Here their souls are separated. Moreover, abundant is their suffering until the time of the great judgment, the castigation, and the torment of those who eternally execrate, whose souls are punished and bound there for ever.

13. And thus has it been from the beginning of the world. Thus has there existed a separation between the souls of those who utter complaints, and of those who watch for their destruction, to slaughter them in the day of sinners.

14. A receptacle of this sort has been formed for the souls of unrighteous men, and of sinners; of those who have completed crime,

and associated with the impious, whom they resemble. Their souls shall not be annihilated in the day of judgment, neither shall they arise from this place. Then I blessed God,

15. And said, Blessed be my Lord, the Lord of glory and of righteousness, who reigns over all for ever and for ever.

Enoch 23

1. From thence I went to another place, towards the west, unto the extremities of the earth.

2. Where I beheld a fire blazing and running along without cessation, which intermitted its course neither by day nor by night; but continued always the same.

3. I inquired, saying, What is this, which never ceases?

4. Then Raguel, one of the holy angels who were with me, answered,

5. And said, This blazing fire, which thou beholdest running towards the west, is that of all the luminaries of heaven.

Enoch 24

1. I went from thence to another place, and saw a mountain of fire flashing both by day and night. I proceeded towards it; and perceived seven splendid mountains, which were all different from each other.

2. Their stones were brilliant and beautiful; all were brilliant and splendid to behold; and beautiful was their surface. Three mountains were towards the east, and strengthened by being placed one upon another; and three were towards the south, strengthened in a similar manner. There were likewise deep valleys, which did not approach each other. And the seventh mountain was in the midst of them. In length they all resembled the seat of a throne, and odoriferous trees surrounded them.

3. Among these there was a tree of an unceasing smell; nor of those which were in Eden was there one of all the fragrant trees which smelt like this. Its leaf, its flower, and its bark never withered, and its fruit was beautiful.

4. Its fruit resembled the cluster of the palm. I exclaimed, Behold! this tree is goodly in aspect, pleasing in its leaf, and the sight of its fruit is delightful to the eye. Then Michael, one of the holy and glorious angels who were with me, and one who presided over them, answered,

5. And said: Enoch, why dost thou inquire respecting the odour of this tree?

6. Why art thou inquisitive to know it?

7. Then I, Enoch, replied to him, and said, Concerning everything I am desirous of instruction, but particularly concerning this tree.

8. He answered me, saying, That mountain which thou beholdest, the extent of whose head resembles the seat of the Lord, will be the seat on which shall sit the holy and great Lord of glory, the everlasting King, when he shall come and descend to visit the earth with goodness.

9. And that tree of an agreeable smell, not one of carnal odour, 1 there shall be no power to touch, until the period of the great judgment. When all shall be punished and consumed for ever, this shall be bestowed on the righteous and humble. The fruit of this tree shall be given to the elect. For towards the north life shall be planted in the holy place, towards the habitation of the everlasting King.

10. Then shall they greatly rejoice and exult in the Holy One. The sweet odour shall enter into their bones; and they shall live a long life on the earth, as thy forefathers have lived; neither in their days shall sorrow, distress, trouble, and punishment afflict them.

11. And I blessed the Lord of glory, the everlasting King, because He has prepared this tree for the saints, formed it, and declared that He would give it to them.

Enoch 25

1. From thence I proceeded to the middle of the earth, and beheld a happy and fertile spot, which contained branches continually sprouting from the trees which were planted in it. There I saw a holy mountain, and underneath it water on the eastern side, which flowed towards the south. I saw also on the east another mountain as high as that; and between them there were deep, but not wide valleys.

2. Water ran towards the mountain to the west of this; and underneath there was likewise another mountain.

3. There was a valley, but not a wide one, below it; and in the midst of them were other deep and dry valleys towards the extremity of the three. All these valleys, which were deep, but not wide, consisted of a strong rock, with a tree which was planted in them. And I wondered at the rock and at the valleys, being extremely surprised.

Enoch 26

1. Then I said, What means this blessed land, all these lofty trees, and the accursed valley between them?

2. Then Uriel, one of the holy angels who were with me, replied, This valley is the accursed of the accursed for ever. Here shall be collected all who utter with their mouths unbecoming language against God, and speak harsh things of His glory. Here shall they be collected. Here shall be their territory.

3. In the latter days an example of judgment shall be made of them in righteousness before the saints: while those who have received mercy shall for ever, all their days, bless God, the everlasting King.

4. And at the period of judgment shall they bless Him for his mercy, as He has distributed it to them. Then I blessed God, addressing myself to Him, and making mention, as was meet, of His greatness.

Enoch 27

1. From thence I proceeded towards the east, to the middle of the mountain in the desert, the level surface only of which I perceived.

2. It was full of trees of the seed alluded to; and water leaped down upon it.

3. There appeared a cataract composed as of many cataracts both towards the west and towards the east. Upon one side were trees; upon the other water and dew.

Enoch 28

1. Then I went to another place from the desert, towards the east of that mountain which I had approached.

2. There I beheld choice trees, particularly those which produce the sweet-smelling drugs, frankincense and myrrh; and trees unlike to each other.

3. And over it, above them, was the elevation of the eastern mountain at no great distance.

Enoch 29

1. I likewise saw another place with valleys of water which never wasted,

2. Where I perceived a goodly tree, which in smell resembled Zasakinon.

3. And towards the sides of these valleys I perceived cinnamon of a sweet odour. Over them I advanced towards the east.

Enoch 30

1. Then I beheld another mountain containing trees, from which water flowed like Neketro. Its name was Sarira, and Kalboneba. And upon this mountain I beheld another mountain, upon which were trees of Alva.

2. These trees were full, like almond trees, and strong; and when they produced fruit, it was superior to all perfume.

Enoch 31

1. After these things, surveying the entrances of the north, above the mountains, I perceived seven mountains replete with pure nard, odoriferous trees, cinnamon and papyrus.

2. From thence I passed on above the summits of those mountains to some distance eastwards, and went over the Erythræan sea. And when I

was advanced far beyond it, I passed along above the angel Zateel, and arrived at the garden of righteousness. In this garden I beheld, among other trees, some which were numerous and large, and which flourished there.

3. Their fragrance was agreeable and powerful, and their appearance both varied and elegant. The tree of knowledge also was there, of which if any one eats, he becomes endowed with great wisdom.

4. It was like a species of the tamarind tree, bearing fruit which resembled grapes extremely fine; and its fragrance extended to a considerable distance. I exclaimed, How beautiful is this tree, and how delightful is its appearance!

5. Then holy Raphael, an angel who was with me, answered and said, This is the tree of knowledge, of which thy ancient father and thy aged mother ate, who were before thee; and who, obtaining knowledge, their eyes being opened, and knowing themselves to be naked, were expelled from the garden.

Enoch 32

1. From thence I went on towards the extremities of the earth; where I saw large beasts different from each other, and birds various in their countenances and forms, as well as with notes of different sounds.

2. To the east of these beasts I perceived the extremities of the earth, where heaven ceased. The gates of heaven stood open, and I beheld the celestial stars come forth. I numbered them as they proceeded out of the gate, and wrote them all down, as they came out one by one according to their number. I wrote down their names altogether, their times and their seasons, as the angel Uriel, who was with me, pointed them out to me.

3. He showed them all to me, and wrote down an account of them.

4. He also wrote down for me their names, their regulations, and their operations.

Enoch 33

1. From thence I advanced on towards the north, to the extremities of the earth.

2. And there I saw a great and glorious wonder at the extremities of the whole earth.

3. I saw there heavenly gates opening into heaven; three of them distinctly separated. The northern winds proceeded from them, blowing cold, hail, frost, snow, dew, and rain.

4. From one of the gates they blew mildly; but when they blew from the two other gates, it was with violence and force. They blew over the earth strongly.

Enoch 34

1. From thence I went to the extremities of the world westwards;

2. Where I perceived three gates open, as I had seen in the north; the gates and passages through them being of equal magnitude.

Enoch 35

1. Then I proceeded to the extremities of the earth southwards; where I saw three gates open to the south, from which issued dew, rain, and wind.

2. From thence I went to the extremities of heaven eastwards; where I saw three heavenly gates open to the east, which had smaller gates within them. Through each of these small gates the stars of heaven passed on, and proceeded towards the west by a path which was seen by them, and that at every period of their appearance.

3. When I beheld them, I blessed; every time in which they appeared, I blessed the Lord of glory, who had made those great and splendid signs, that they might display the magnificence of his works to angels and to the souls of men; and that these might glorify all his works and operations; might see the effect of his power; might glorify the great labour of his hands; and bless him for ever.

Enoch 36

1. And from thence I went to the south to the ends of the earth, and saw there three open portals of the heaven: and thence there come dew, rain, †and wind†.

2. And from thence I went to the east to the ends of the heaven, and saw here the three eastern portals of heaven open and small portals above them.

3. Through each of these small portals pass the stars of heaven and run their course to the west on the path which is shown to them.

4. And as often as I saw I blessed always the Lord of Glory, and I continued to bless the Lord of Glory who has wrought great and glorious wonders, to show the greatness of His work to the angels and to spirits and to men, that they might praise His work and all His creation: that they might see the work of His might and praise the great work of His hands and bless Him for ever.

Enoch 37 [SECT. VI.]

1. The vision which he saw, the second vision of wisdom, which Enoch saw, the son of Jared, the son of Malaleel, the son of Canan, the son of Enos, the son of Seth, the son of Adam. This is the commencement of the word of wisdom, which I received to declare and tell to those who dwell upon earth. Hear from the beginning, and understand to the

end, the holy things which I utter in the presence of the Lord of spirits. Those who were before us thought it good to speak;

2. And let not us, who come after, obstruct the beginning of wisdom. Until the present period never has there been given before the Lord of spirits that which I have received, wisdom according to the capacity of my intellect, and according to the pleasure of the Lord of spirits; that which I have received from him, 4 a portion of life eternal.

3. And I obtained three parables, which I declared to the inhabitants of the world.

Enoch 38

1. Parable the first. When the congregation of the righteous shall be manifested; and sinners be judged for their crimes, and be troubled in the sight of the world;

2. When righteousness shall be manifested in the presence of the righteous themselves, who will be elected for their good works duly weighed by the Lord of spirits; and when the light of the righteous and the elect, who dwell on earth, shall be manifested; where will the habitation of sinners be? and where the place of rest for those who have rejected the Lord of spirits? It would have been better for them, had they never been born.

3. When, too, the secrets of the righteous shall be revealed, then shall sinners be judged; and impious men shall be afflicted in the presence of the righteous and the elect.

4. From that period those who possess the earth shall cease to be powerful and exalted. Neither shall they be capable of beholding the countenances of the holy; for the light of the countenances of the holy, the righteous, and the elect, has been seen by the Lord of spirits.

5. Yet shall not the mighty kings of that period be destroyed; but be delivered into the hands of the righteous and the holy.

6. Nor thenceforwards shall any obtain commiseration from the Lord of spirits, because their lives in this world will have been completed.

Enoch 39

1. In those days shall the elect and holy race descend from the upper heavens, and their seed shall then be with the sons of men. Enoch received books of indignation and wrath, and books of hurry and agitation.

2. Never shall they obtain mercy, saith the Lord of spirits.

3. A cloud then snatched me up, and the wind raised me above the surface of the earth, placing me at the extremity of the heavens.

4. There I saw another vision; I saw the habitations and couches of the saints. There my eyes beheld their habitations with the angels, and their couches with the holy ones. They were entreating, supplicating, and praying for the sons of men; while righteousness like water flowed before them, and mercy like dew was scattered over the earth. And thus shall it be with them for ever and for ever.

5. At that time my eyes beheld the dwelling of the elect, of truth, faith, and righteousness.

6. Countless shall be the number of the holy and the elect, in the presence of God for ever and for ever.

7. Their residence I beheld under the wings of the Lord of spirits. All the holy and the elect sung before him, in appearance like a blaze of fire; their mouths being full of blessings, and their lips glorifying the name of the Lord of spirits. And righteousness incessantly dwelt before him,

8. There was I desirous of remaining, and my soul longed for that habitation. There was my antecedent inheritance; for thus had I prevailed before the Lord of spirits.

9. At that time I glorified and extolled the name of the Lord of spirits with blessing and with praise; for he has established it with blessing and with praise, according to his own good pleasure.

10. That place long did my eyes contemplate. I blessed and said, Blessed be he, blessed from the beginning for ever. In the beginning, before the world was created, and without end is his knowledge.

11. What is this world? Of every existing generation those shall bless thee who do not sleep in the dust, but stand before thy glory, blessing, glorifying, exalting thee, and saying, The holy, holy, Lord of spirits, fills the whole world of spirits.

12. There my eyes beheld all who, without sleeping, stand before him and bless him, saying, Blessed be thou, and blessed be the name of God for ever and for ever. Then my countenance became changed, until I was incapable of seeing.

Enoch 40

1. After this I beheld thousands of thousands, and myriads of myriads, and an infinite number of people, standing before the Lord of spirits.

2. On the four wings likewise of the Lord of spirits, on the four sides, I perceived others, besides those who were standing before him. Their names, too, I know; because the angel, who proceeded with me, declared them to me, discovering to me every secret thing.

3. Then I heard the voices of those upon the four sides magnifying the Lord of glory.

4. The first voice blessed the Lord of spirits for ever and for ever.

5. The second voice I heard blessing the elect One, and the elect who suffer on account of the Lords of spirits.

6. The third voice I heard petitioning and praying for those who dwell upon earth, and supplicate the name of the Lord of spirits.

7. The fourth voice I heard expelling the impious angels, and prohibiting them from entering into presence of the Lord of spirits, to prefer accusations against the inhabitants of the earth.

8. After this I besought the angel of peace, who proceeded with me, to explain all that was concealed. I said to him, Who are those whom I have seen on the four sides, and whose words I have heard and written down? He replied, The first is the merciful, the patient, the holy Michael.

9. The second is he who presides over every suffering and every affliction of the sons of men, the holy Raphael. The third, who presides over all that is powerful, is Gabriel. And the fourth, who presides over repentance, and the hope of those who will inherit eternal life, is Phanuel. These are the four angels of the most high God, and their four voices, which at that time I heard.

Enoch 41

1. After this I beheld the secrets of the heavens and of paradise, according to its divisions; and of human action, as they weigh it there in balances. I saw the habitations of the elect, and the habitations of the holy. And there my eyes beheld all the sinners, who denied the Lord of glory, and whom they were expelling from thence, and dragging away, as they stood there; no punishment proceeding against them from the Lord of spirits.

2. There, too, my eyes beheld the secrets of the lightning and the thunder; and the secrets of the winds, how they are distributed as they blow over the earth: the secrets of the winds, of the dew, and of the clouds. There I perceived the place from which they issued forth, and became saturated with the dust of the earth.

3. There I saw the wooden 1 receptacles out of which the winds became separated, the receptacle of hail, the receptacle of snow, the receptacle of the clouds, and the cloud itself, which continued over the earth before the creation of the world.

4. I beheld also the receptacles of the moon, whence the moons came, whither they proceeded, their

337

glorious return, and how one became more splendid than another. I marked their rich progress, their unchangeable progress, their disunited and undiminished progress; their observance of a mutual fidelity by a stable oath; their proceeding forth before the sun, and their adherence to the path allotted them, in obedience to the command of the Lord of spirits. Potent is his name for ever and for ever.

5. After this I perceived, that the path both concealed and manifest of the moon, as well as the progress of its path, was there completed by day and by night; while each, one with another, looked towards the Lord of spirits, magnifying and praising without cessation, since praise to them is rest; for in the splendid sun there is a frequent conversion to blessing and to malediction.

6. The course of the moon's path to the righteous is light, but to sinners it is darkness; in the name of the Lord of spirits, who created a division between light and darkness, and, separating the spirits of men, strengthened the spirits of the righteous in the name of his own righteousness.

7. Nor does the angel prevent this, neither is he endowed with the power of preventing it; for the Judge beholds them all, and judges them all in his own presence.

Enoch 42

1. Wisdom found not a place on earth where she could inhabit; her dwelling therefore is in heaven.

2. Wisdom went forth to dwell among the sons of men, but she obtained not an habitation. Wisdom returned to her place, and seated herself in the midst of the angels. But iniquity went forth after her return, who unwillingly found an habitation, and resided among them, as rain in the desert, and as a dew in a thirsty land.

Enoch 43

1. I beheld another splendour, and the stars of heaven. I observed that he called them all by their respective names, and that they heard. In a righteous balance I saw that he weighed out with their light the amplitude of their places, and the day of their appearance, and their conversion. Splendour produced splendour; and their conversion was into the number of the angels, and of the faithful.

2. Then I inquired of the angel, who proceeded with me, and explained to me secret things, What their names were. He answered, A similitude of those has the Lord of spirits shown thee. They are names of the righteous who dwell upon earth, and who believe in the name of the Lord of spirits for ever and for ever.

Enoch 44

Another thing also I saw respecting splendour; that it rises out of the stars, and becomes splendour; being incapable of forsaking them.

Enoch 45 [SECT. VII.]

1. Parable the second, respecting these who deny the name of the habitation of the holy ones, and of the Lord of spirits.

2. Heaven they shall not ascend, nor shall they come on the earth. This shall be the portion of sinners, who deny the name of the Lord of spirits, and who are thus reserved for the day of punishment and of affliction.

3. In that day shall the Elect One sit upon a throne of glory; and shall choose their conditions and countless habitations (while their spirits within them shall be strengthened, when they behold my Elect One), shall choose them for those who have fled for protection to my holy and glorious name.

4. In that day I will cause my Elect One to dwell in the midst of them; will change the face of heaven; will bless it, and illuminate it for ever.

5. I will also change the face of the earth; will bless it; and cause those whom I have elected to dwell upon it. But those who have committed sin and iniquity shall not inhabit it, for I have marked their proceedings. My righteous ones will I satisfy with peace, placing them before me; but the condemnation of sinners shall draw near, that I may destroy them from the face of the earth.

Enoch 46

1. There I beheld the Ancient of days, whose head was like white wool, and with him another, whose countenance resembled that of man. His countenance was full of grace, like that of one of the holy angels. Then I inquired of one of the angels, who went with me, and who showed me every secret thing, concerning this Son of man; who he was; whence he was; and why he accompanied the Ancient of days.

2. He answered and said to me, This is the Son of man, to whom righteousness belongs; with whom righteousness has dwelt; and who will reveal all the treasures of that which is concealed: for the Lord of spirits has chosen him; and his portion has surpassed all before the Lord of spirits in everlasting uprightness.

3. This Son of man, whom thou beholdest, shall raise up kings and the mighty from their couches, and the powerful from their thrones; shall loosen the bridles of the powerful, and break in pieces the teeth of sinners.

4. He shall hurl kings from their thrones and their dominions; because they will not exalt and

praise him, nor humble themselves before him, by whom their kingdoms were granted to them. The countenance likewise of the mighty shall He cast down, filling them with confusion. Darkness shall be their habitation, and worms shall be their bed; nor from that their bed shall they hope to be again raised, because they exalted not the name of the Lord of spirits.

5. They shall condemn the stars of heaven, shall lift up their hands against the Most High, shall tread upon and inhabit the earth, exhibiting all their works of iniquity, even their works of iniquity. Their strength shall be in their riches, and their faith in the gods whom they have formed with their own hands. They shall deny the name of the Lord of spirits, and shall expel him from the temples, in which they assemble;

6. And with him the faithful, who suffer in the name of the Lord of spirits.

Enoch 47

1. In that day the prayer of the holy and the righteous, and the blood of the righteous, shall ascend from the earth into the presence of the Lord of spirits.

2. In that day shall the holy ones assemble, who dwell above the heavens, and with united voice petition, supplicate, praise, laud, and bless the name of the Lord of spirits,

on account of the blood of the righteous which has been shed; that the prayer of the righteous may not be intermitted before the Lord of spirits; that for them he would execute judgment; and that his patience may not endure for ever.

3. At that time I beheld the Ancient of days, while he sat upon the throne of his glory, while the book of the living was opened in his presence, and while all the powers which were above the heavens stood around and before him.

4. Then were the hearts of the saints full of joy, because the consummation of righteousness was arrived, the supplication of the saints heard, and the blood of the righteous appreciated by the Lord of spirits.

Enoch 48 [1]

1. In that place I beheld a fountain of righteousness, which never failed, encircled by many springs of wisdom. Of these all the thirsty drank, and were filled with wisdom, having their habitation with the righteous, the elect, and the holy.

2. In that hour was this Son of man invoked before the Lord of spirits, and his name in the presence of the Ancient of days.

3. Before the sun and the signs were created, before the stars of heaven were formed, his name was invoked in the presence of the Lord of spirits. A support shall he be for the

righteous and the holy to lean upon, without falling; and he shall be the light of nations.

4. He shall be the hope of those whose hearts are troubled. All, who dwell on earth, shall fall down and worship before him; shall bless and glorify him, and sing praises to the name of the Lord of spirits.

5. Therefore the Elect and the Concealed One existed in his presence, before the world was created, and for ever.

6. In his presence he existed, and has revealed to the saints and to the righteous the wisdom of the Lord of spirits; for he has preserved the lot of the righteous, because they have hated and rejected this world of iniquity, and have detested all its works and ways, in the name of the Lord of spirits.

7. For in his name shall they be preserved; and his will shall be their life. In those days shall the kings of the earth and the mighty men, who have gained the world by their achievements, 1 become humble in countenance.

8. For in the day of their anxiety and trouble their souls shall not be saved; and they shall be in subjection to those whom I have chosen.

9. I will cast them like hay into the fire, and like lead into the water. Thus shall they burn in the presence

of the righteous, and sink in the presence of the holy; nor shall a tenth part of them be found.

10. But in the day of their trouble, the world shall obtain tranquillity.

11. In his presence shall they fall, and not be raised up again; nor shall there be any one to take them out of his hands, and to lift them up: for they have denied the Lord of spirits, and his Messiah. The name of the Lord of spirits shall be blessed.

Enoch 48 [II]

1. Wisdom is poured forth like water, and glory fails not before him for ever and ever; for potent is he in all the secrets of righteousness.

2. But iniquity passes away like a shadow, and possesses not a fixed station: for the Elect One stands before the Lord of spirits; and his glory is for ever and ever; and his power from generation to generation.

3. With him dwells the spirit of intellectual wisdom, the spirit of instruction and of power, and the spirit of those who sleep in righteousness; he shall judge secret things.

4. Nor shall any be able to utter a single word before him; for the Elect One is in the presence of the Lord of spirits, according to his own pleasure.

341

Enoch 49

1. In those days the saints and the chosen shall undergo a change. The light of day shall rest upon them; and the splendour and glory of the saints shall be changed.

2. In the day of trouble evil shall be heaped up upon sinners; but the righteous shall triumph in the name of the Lord of spirits.

3. Others shall be made to see, that they must repent, and forsake the works of their hands; and that glory awaits them not in the presence of the Lord of spirits; yet that by his name they may be saved. The Lord of spirits will have compassion on them: for great is his mercy; and righteousness is in his judgment, and in the presence of his glory; nor in his judgment shall iniquity stand. He who repents not before him shall perish.

4. Henceforward I will not have mercy on them, saith the Lord of spirits.

Enoch 50

1. In those days shall the earth deliver up from her womb, and hell deliver up from hers, that which it has received; and destruction shall restore that which it owes.

2. He shall select the righteous and holy from among them; for the day of their salvation has approached.

3. And in those days shall the Elect One sit upon his throne, while every secret of intellectual wisdom shall proceed from his mouth; for the Lord of spirits has gifted and glorified him.

4. In those days the mountains shall skip like rams, and the hills shall leap like young sheep satiated with milk; and all the righteous shall become angels in heaven.

5. Their countenance shall be bright with joy; for in those days shall the Elect One be exalted. The earth shall rejoice; the righteous shall inhabit it, and the elect possess it.

Enoch 51

1. After that period, in the place where I had seen every secret sight, I was snatched up in a whirlwind, and carried off westwards.

2. There my eyes beheld the secrets of heaven, and all which existed on earth; a mountain of iron, a mountain of copper, a mountain of silver, a mountain of gold, a mountain of fluid metal, and a mountain of lead.

3. And I inquired of the angel who went with me, saying, What are these things, which in secret I behold?

4. He said, All these things which thou beholdest shall be for the dominion of the Messiah, that he may command, and be powerful upon earth.

5. And that angel of peace answered me, saying, Wait but a short time, and thou shalt understand, and every secret thing shall be revealed to thee, which the Lord of spirits has decreed. Those mountains which thou hast seen, the mountain of iron, the mountain of copper, the mountain of silver, the mountain of gold, the mountain of fluid metal, and the mountain of lead, all these in the presence of the Elect One shall be like a honeycomb before the fire, and like water descending from above upon these mountains; and shall become debilitated before his feet.

6. In those days men shall not be saved by gold and by silver.

7. Nor shall they have it in their power to secure themselves, and to fly.

8. There shall be neither iron for war, nor a coat of mail for the breast.

9. Copper shall be useless; useless also that which neither rusts nor consumes away; and lead shall not be coveted.

10. All these things shall be rejected, and perish from off the earth, when the Elect One shall appear in the presence of the Lord of spirits

Enoch 52

1. There my eyes beheld a deep valley; and wide was its entrance.

2. All who dwell on land, on the sea, and in islands, shall bring to it gifts, presents, and offerings; yet that deep valley shall not be full. Their hands shall commit iniquity. Whatsoever they produce by labour, the sinners shall devour with crime. But they shall perish front the face of the Lord of spirits, and from the face of his earth. They shall stand up, and shall not fail for ever and ever.

3. I beheld the angels of punishment, who were dwelling there, and preparing every instrument of Satan.

4. Then I inquired of the angel of peace, who proceeded with me, for whom those instruments were preparing.

5. He said, These they are preparing for the kings and powerful ones of the earth, that thus they may perish.

6. After which the righteous and chosen house of his congregation shall appear, thenceforward unchangeable, in the name of the Lord of spirits.

7. Nor shall those mountains exist in his presence, as the earth and the hills, as the fountains of water exist. And the righteous shall be relieved from the vexation of sinners.

Enoch 53

1. Then I looked and turned myself to another part of the earth, where I beheld a deep valley burning with fire.

2. To this valley they brought monarchs and the mighty.

3. And there my eyes beheld the instruments which they were making, fetters of iron without weight.

4. Then I inquired of the angel of peace, who proceeded with me, saying, For whom are these fetters and instruments prepared?

5. He replied, These are prepared for the host of Azazeel, that they may be delivered over and adjudged to the lowest condemnation; and that their angels may be overwhelmed with hurled stones, as the Lord of' spirits has commanded.

6. Michael and Gabriel, Raphael and Phanuel shall be strengthened in that day, and shall then cast them into a furnace of blazing fire, that the Lord of spirits may be avenged of them for their crimes; because they became ministers of Satan, and seduced those who dwell upon earth.

7. In those days shall punishment go forth from the Lord of spirits; and the receptacles of water which are above the heavens shall be opened, and the fountains likewise, which are under the heavens and under the earth.

8. All the waters, which are in the heavens and above them, shall be mixed together.

9. The water which is above heaven shall be the agent;

10. And the water which is under the earth shall be the recipient: and all shall be destroyed who dwell upon earth, and who dwell under the extremities of heaven.

11. By these means shall they understand the iniquity which they have committed on earth: and by these means shall they perish.

Enoch 54

1. Afterwards the Ancient of days repented, and said, In vain have I destroyed all the inhabitants of the earth.

2. And he sware by his great name, saying, Henceforwards I will not act thus towards all those who dwell upon earth.

3. But I will place a sign in the heavens; and it shall be a faithful witness between me and them for ever, as long as the days of heaven and earth last upon the earth.

4. Afterwards, according to this my decree, when I shall be disposed to seize them beforehand, by the instrumentality of angels, in the day of affliction and trouble, my wrath and my punishment shall remain upon them, my punishment and my wrath, saith God the Lord of spirits.

5. O ye kings, O ye mighty, who inhabit the world, you shall behold my Elect One, sitting upon the throne of my glory. And he shall judge Azazeel, all his associates, and all

his hosts, in the name of the Lord of spirits.

6. There likewise I beheld hosts of angels who were moving in punishment, confined in a net-work of iron and brass. Then I inquired of the angel of peace, who proceeded with me, To whom those under confinement were going.

7. He said, To each of their elect and their beloved, that they may be cast into the fountains and deep recesses of the valley.

8. And that valley shall be filled with their elect and beloved; the days of whose life shall be consumed, but the days of their error shall be innumerable.

9. Then shall princes combine together, and conspire. The chiefs of the east, among the Parthians and Medes, shall remove kings, in whom a spirit of perturbation shall enter. They shall hurl them from their thrones, springing as lions from their dens, and like famished wolves into the midst of the flock.

10. They shall go up, and tread upon the land of their elect. The land of their elect shall be before them. The threshing-floor, the path, and the city of my righteous people shall impede the progress of their horses. They shall rise up to destroy each other; their right hand shall be strengthened; nor shall a man

acknowledge his friend or his brother;

11. Nor the son his father and his mother; until the number of the dead bodies shall be completed, by their death and punishment. Neither shall this take place without cause.

12. In those days shall the mouth of hell be opened, into which they shall be immerged; hell shall destroy and swallow up sinners from the face of the elect.

Enoch 55

1. After this I beheld another army of chariots, with men riding in them.

2. And they came upon the wind from the east, from the west, and from the south.

3. The sound of the noise of their chariots was heard.

4. And when that agitation took place, the saints out of heaven perceived it; the pillar of the earth shook from its foundation; and the sound was heard from the extremities of the earth unto the extremities of heaven at the same time.

5. Then they all fell down, and worshipped the Lord of spirits.

6. This is the end of the second parable.

Enoch 56 [SECT. IX.]

1. I now began to utter the third parable, concerning the saints and the elect.

2. Blessed are ye, O saints and elect, for glorious is your lot.

3. The saints shall exist in the light of the sun, and the elect in the light of everlasting life, the days of whose life shall never terminate; nor shall the days of the saints be numbered, who seek for light, and obtain righteousness with the Lord of spirits.

4. Peace be to the saints with the Lord of the world.

5. Henceforward shall the saints be told to seek in heaven the secrets of righteousness, the portion of faith; for like the sun has it arisen upon the earth, while darkness has passed away. There shall be light interminable: nor shall they enter upon the enumeration of time; for darkness shall be previously destroyed, and light shall increase before the Lord of spirits; before the Lord of spirits shall the light of uprightness increase for ever.

Enoch 57

1. In those days my eyes beheld the secrets of the lightnings and the splendours, and the judgment belonging to them.

2. They lighten for a blessing and for a curse, according to the will of the Lord of spirits.

3. And there I saw the secrets of the thunder, when it rattles above in heaven, and its sound is heard.

4. The habitations also of the earth were shown to me. The sound of the thunder is for peace and for blessing, as well as for a curse, according to the word of the Lord of spirits.

5. Afterwards every secret of the splendours and of the lightnings was seen by me. For blessing and for fertility they lighten.

Enoch 58 [SECT. X.]

1. In the five hundredth year, and in the seventh month, on the fourteenth day of the month, of the lifetime of Enoch, in that parable, I saw that the heaven of heavens shook; that it shook violently; and that the powers of the Most High, and the angels, thousands of thousands, and myriads of myriads, were agitated with great agitation. And when I looked, the Ancient of days was sitting on the throne of his glory, while the angels and saints were standing around him. A great trembling came upon me, and terror seized me. My loins were bowed down and loosened; my reins were dissolved; and I fell upon my face. The holy Michael, another holy angel, one of the holy ones, was sent, who raised me up.

2. And when he raised me, my spirit returned; for I was incapable of enduring this vision of violence, its agitation, and the concussion of heaven.

3. Then holy Michael said to me, Wherefore art thou disturbed at this vision?

4. Hitherto has existed the day of mercy; and he has been merciful and longsuffering towards all who dwell upon the earth.

5. But when the time shall come, then shall the power, the punishment, and the judgment take place, which the Lord of spirits has prepared for those who prostrate themselves to the judgment of righteousness, for those who abjure that judgment, and for those who take his name in vain.

6. That day has been prepared for the elect as a day of covenant; and for sinners as a day of inquisition.

7. In that day shall be distributed for food two monsters; a female monster, whose name is Leviathan, dwelling in the depths of the sea, above the springs of waters;

S. And a male monster, whose name is Behemoth; which possesses, moving on his breast, the invisible wilderness.

9. His name was Dendayen in the east of the garden, where the elect and the righteous will dwell; where

he received it from my ancestor, who was man, from Adam the first of men, whom the Lord of spirits made.

10. Then I asked of another angel to show me the power of those monsters, how they became separated on the same day, one being in the depths of the sea, and one in the dry desert.

11. And he said, Thou, son of man, art here desirous of understanding secret things.

12. And the angel of peace, who was with me, said, These two monsters are by the power of God prepared to become food, that the punishment of God may not be in vain.

13. Then shall children be slain with their mothers, and sons with their fathers.

14. And when the punishment of the Lord of spirits shall continue, upon them shall it continue, that the punishment of the Lord of spirits may not take place in vain. After that, judgment shall exist with mercy and longsuffering.

Enoch 59

1. Then another angel, who proceeded with me, spoke to me;

2. And showed me the first and last secrets in heaven above, and in the depths of the earth:

3. In the extremities of heaven, and in the foundations of it, and in the receptacle of the winds.

4. He showed me how their spirits were divided; how they were balanced; and how both the springs and the winds were numbered according to the force of their spirit.

5. He showed me the power of the moon's light, that its power is a just one; as well as the divisions of the stars, according to their respective names;

6. That every division is divided; that the lightning flashes;

7. That its troops immediately obey; and that a cessation takes place during thunder in continuance of its sound. Nor are the thunder and the lightning separated; neither do both of them move with one spirit; yet are they not separated.

8. For when the lightning lightens, the thunder sounds, and the spirit at a proper period pauses, making an equal division between them; for the receptacle, upon which their periods depend, is loose as sand. Each of them at a proper season is restrained with a bridle; and turned by the power of the spirit, which thus propels them according to the spacious extent of the earth.

9. The spirit likewise of the sea is potent and strong; and as a strong power causes it to ebb, so is it driven forwards, and scattered against the mountains of the earth. The spirit of the frost has its angel; in the spirit of hail there is a good angel; the spirit of snow ceases in its strength, and a solitary spirit is in it, which ascends from it like vapour, and is called refrigeration.

10. The spirit also of mist dwells with them in their receptacle; but it has a receptacle to itself; for its progress is in splendour,

11. In light, and in darkness, in winter and in summer. It receptacle is bright, and an angel is in it.

12. The spirit of dew has its abode in the extremities of heaven, in connection with the receptacle of rain; and its progress is in winter and in summer. The cloud produced by it, and the cloud of the mist, become united; one gives to the other; and when the spirit of rain is in motion from its receptacle, angels come, and opening its receptacle, bring it forth.

13. When likewise it is sprinkled over all the earth, it forms an union with every kind of water on the ground; for the waters remain on the ground, because they afford nourishment to the earth from the Most High, who is in heaven.

14. Upon this account therefore there is a regulation in the quantity of rain, which the angels receive.

15. These things I saw; all of them, even paradise.

Enoch 60

1. In those days I beheld long ropes given to those angels; who took to their wings, and fled, advancing towards the north.

2. And I inquired of the angel, saying, Wherefore have they taken those long ropes, and gone forth? He said, They are gone forth to measure.

3. The angel, who proceeded with me, said, These are the measures of the righteous; and cords shall the righteous bring, that they may trust in the name of the Lord of spirits for ever and ever.

4. The elect shall begin to dwell with the elect.

5. And these are the measures which shall be given to faith, and which shall strengthen the words of righteousness.

6. These measures shall reveal all the secrets in the depth of the earth.

7. And it shall be, that those who have been destroyed in the desert, and who have been devoured by the fish of the sea, and by wild beasts, shall return, and trust in the day of the Elect One; for none shall perish in the presence of the Lord of spirits, nor shall any be capable of perishing.

8. Then they received the commandment, all who were in the heavens above; to whom a combined power, voice, and splendour, like fire, were given.

9. And first, with their voice, they blessed him, they exalted him, they glorified him with wisdom, and ascribed to him wisdom with the word, and with the breath of life.

10. Then the Lord of spirits seated upon the throne of his glory the Elect One;

11. Who shall judge all the works of the holy, in heaven above, and in a balance shall he weigh their actions. And when he shall lift up his countenance to judge their secret ways in the word of the name of the Lord of spirits, and their progress in the path of the righteous judgment of God most high;

12. They shall all speak with united voice; and bless, glorify, exalt, and praise, in the name of the Lord of spirits.

13. He shall call to every power of the heavens, to all the holy above, and to the power of God. The Cherubim, the Seraphim, and the Ophanin, all the angels of power, and all the angels of the Lords, namely, of the Elect One, and of the other Power, who was upon earth over the water on that day,

14. Shall raise their united voice; shall bless, glorify, praise, and exalt with the spirit of faith, with the spirit of wisdom and patience, with the spirit of mercy, with the spirit of

judgment and peace, and with the spirit of benevolence; all shall say with united voice: Blessed is He; and the name of the Lord of spirits shall be blessed for ever and for ever; all, who sleep not, shall bless it in heaven above.

15. All the holy in heaven shall bless it; all the elect who dwell in the garden of life; and every spirit of light, who is capable of blessing, glorifying, exalting, and praising thy holy name; and every mortal man, more than the powers of heaven, shall glorify and bless thy name for ever and ever.

16. For great is the mercy of the Lord of spirits; long-suffering is he; and all his works, all his power, great as are the things which he has done, has he revealed to the saints and to the elect, in the name of the Lord of spirits.

Enoch 61

1. Thus the Lord commanded the kings, the princes, the exalted, and those who dwell on earth, saying, Open your eyes, and lift up your horns, if you are capable of comprehending the Elect One.

2. The Lord of spirits sat upon the throne of his glory.

3. And the spirit of righteousness was poured out over him.

4. The word of his mouth shall destroy all the sinners and all the ungodly, who shall perish at his presence.

5. In that day shall all the kings, the princes, the exalted, and those who possess the earth, stand up, behold, and perceive, that he is sitting on the throne of his glory; that before him the saints shall be judged in righteousness;

6. And that nothing, which shall be spoken before him, shall be spoken in vain.

7. Trouble shall come upon them, as upon a woman in travail, whose labour is severe, when her child comes to the mouth of the womb, and she finds it difficult to bring forth.

8. One portion of them shall look upon another. They shall be astonished, and shall humble their countenance;

9. And trouble shall seize them, when they shall behold this Son of woman sitting upon the throne of his glory.

10. Then shall the kings, the princes, and all who possess the earth, glorify him who has dominion over all things, him who was concealed; for from the beginning the Son of man existed in secret, whom the Most High preserved in the presence of his power, and revealed to the elect.

11. He shall sow the congregation of the saints, and of the elect; and all

the elect shall stand before him in that day.

12. All the kings, the princes, the exalted, and those who rule over the earth, shall fall down on their faces before him, and shall worship him.

13. They shall fix their hopes on this Son of man, shall pray to him, and petition him for mercy.

14. Then shall the Lord of spirits hasten to expel them from his presence. Their faces shall be full of confusion, and their faces shall darkness cover. The angels shall take them to punishment, that vengeance may be inflicted on those who have oppressed his children and his elect. And they shall become an example to the saints and to his elect. Through them shall these be made joyful; for the anger of the Lord of spirits shall rest upon them.

15. Then the sword of the Lord of spirits shall be drunk with their blood; but the saints and elect shall be safe in that day; nor the face of the sinners and the ungodly shall they thenceforwards behold.

16. The Lord of spirits shall remain over them:

17. And with this Son of man shall they dwell, eat, lie down, and rise up, for ever and ever.

18. The saints and the elect have arisen from the earth, have left off to depress their countenances, and

have been clothed with the garment of life. That garment of life is with the Lord of spirits, in whose presence your garment shall not wax old, nor shall your glory diminish.

Enoch 62

1. In those days the kings who possess the earth shall be punished by the angels of his wrath, wheresoever they shall be delivered up, that he may give rest for a short period; and that they may fall down and worship before the Lord of spirits, confessing their sins before him.

2. They shall bless and glorify the Lord of spirits, saying, Blessed is the Lord of spirits, the Lord of kings, the Lord of princes, the Lord of the rich, the Lord of glory, and the Lord of wisdom.

3. He shall enlighten every secret thing.

4. Thy power is from generation to generation; and thy glory for ever and ever.

5. Deep are all thy secrets, and numberless; and thy righteousness cannot be computed.

6. Now we know, that we should glorify and bless the Lord of kings, him who is King over all things.

7. They shall also say, Who has granted us rest to glorify, laud, bless, and confess in the presence of his glory?

8. And now small is the rest we desire; but we do not find it; we reject, and do not possess it. Light has passed away from before us; and darkness has covered our thrones for ever.

9. For we have not confessed before him; we have not glorified the name of the Lord of kings; we have not glorified the Lord in all his works; but we have trusted in the sceptre of our dominion and of our glory.

10. In the day of our suffering and of our trouble he will not save us, neither shall we find rest. We confess that our Lord is faithful in all his works, in all his judgments, and in his righteousness.

11. In his judgments he pays no respect to persons; and we must depart from his presence, on account of our evil deeds.

12. All our sins are truly without number.

13. Then shall they say to themselves, Our souls are satiated with the instruments of crime;

14. But that prevents us not from descending to the flaming womb of hell.

15. Afterwards, their countenances shall be filled with darkness and confusion before the Son of man; from whose presence they shall be expelled, and before whom the sword shall remain to expel them.

16. Thus saith the Lord of spirits, This is the decree and the judgment against the princes, the kings, the exalted, and those who possess the earth, in the presence of the Lord of spirits.

Enoch 63

1. I saw also other countenances in that secret place. I heard the voice of an angel, saying, These are the angels who have descended from heaven to earth, and have revealed secrets to the sons of men, and have seduced the sons of men to the commission of sin.

Enoch 64 [SECT. XI.]

1. In those days Noah saw that the earth became inclined, and that destruction approached.

2. Then he lifted up his feet, and went to the ends of the earth, to the dwelling of his great-grandfather Enoch.

3. And Noah cried with a bitter voice, Hear me; hear me; hear me: three times. And he said, Tell me what is transacting upon earth; for the earth labours, and is violently shaken. Surely I shall perish with it.

4. After this there was a great perturbation on earth, and a voice was heard from heaven. I fell down on my face, when my great-grandfather Enoch came and stood by me.

5. He said to me, Why hast thou cried out to me with a bitter cry and lamentation?

6. A commandment has gone forth from the Lord against those who dwell on the earth, that they may be destroyed; for they know every secret of the angels, every oppressive and secret power of the devils, and every power of those who commit sorcery, as well as of those who make molten images in the whole earth.

7. They know how silver is produced from the dust of the earth, and how on the earth the metallic drop exists; for lead and tin are not produced from earth, as the primary fountain of their production.

8. There is an angel standing upon it, and that angel struggles to prevail.

9. Afterwards my great-grandfather Enoch seized me with his hand, raising me up, and saying to me, Go, for I have asked the Lord of spirits respecting this perturbation of the earth; who replied, On account of their impiety have their innumerable judgments been consummated before me. Respecting the moons have they inquired, and they have known that the earth will perish with those who dwell upon it, and that to these there will be no place of refuge for ever.

10. They have discovered secrets, and they are those who have been judged; but not thou, my son. The Lord of spirits knows that thou art pure and good, free from the reproach of discovering secrets.

11. He, the holy One, will establish thy name in the midst of the saints, and will preserve thee from those who dwell upon the earth. He will establish thy seed in righteousness, with dominion and great glory; 1 and from thy seed shall spring forth righteous and holy men without number for ever.

Enoch 65

1. After this he showed me the angels of punishment, who were prepared to come, and to open all the mighty waters under the earth:

2. That they may be for judgment, and for the destruction of all those who remain and dwell upon the earth.

3. And the Lord of spirits commanded the angels who went forth, not to take up the men and preserve them.

4. For those angels presided over all the mighty waters. Then I went out from the presence of Enoch.

Enoch 66

1. In those days the word of God came to me, and said, Noah, behold, thy lot has ascended up to me, a lot void of crime, a lot beloved and upright.

2. Now then shall the angels labour at the trees; but when they proceed to this, I will put my hand upon it, and preserve it.

3. The seed of life shall arise from it, and a change shall take place, that the dry land may not be left empty. I will establish thy seed before me for ever and ever, and the seed of those who dwell with thee on the surface of the earth. It shall be blessed and multiplied in the presence of the earth, in the name of the Lord.

4. And they shall confine those angels who disclosed impiety. In that burning valley it is, that they shall be confined, which at first my great-grandfather Enoch showed me in the west, where there were mountains of gold and silver, of iron, of fluid metal, and of tin.

5. I beheld that valley in which there was great perturbation, and where the waters were troubled.

6. And when all this was effected, from the fluid mass of fire, and the perturbation which prevailed in that place, there arose a strong smell of sulphur, which became mixed with the waters; and the valley of the angels, who had been guilty of seduction, burned underneath its soil.

7. Through that valley also rivers of fire were flowing, to which those angels shall be condemned, who seduced the inhabitants of the earth.

8. And in those days shall these waters be to kings, to princes, to the exalted, and to the inhabitants of the earth, for the healing of the soul and body, and for the judgment of the spirit.

9. Their spirits shall be full of revelry, that they may be judged in their bodies; because they have denied the Lord of spirits, and although they perceive their condemnation day by day, they believe not in his name.

10. And as the inflammation of their bodies shall be great, so shall their spirits undergo a change for ever.

11. For no word which is uttered before the Lord of spirits shall be in vain.

12. Judgment has come upon them, because they trusted in their carnal revelry, and denied the Lord of spirits.

13. In those days shall the waters of that valley be changed; for when the angels shall be judged, then shall the heat of those springs of water experience an alteration.

14. And when the angels shall ascend, the water of the springs shall again undergo a change, and be frozen. Then I heard holy Michael answering and saying, This judgment, with which the angels shall be judged, shall bear testimony against the kings, the princes, and those who possess the earth.

15. For these waters of judgment shall be for their healing, and for the death of their bodies. But they shall not perceive and believe that the waters will be changed, and become a fire, which shall blaze for ever.

Enoch 67

1. After this he gave me the characteristical marks of all the secret things in the book of my great-grandfather Enoch, and in the parables which had been given to him; inserting them for me among the words of the book of parables.

2. At that time holy Michael answered and said to Raphael, The power of the spirit hurries me away, and impels me on. The severity of the judgment, of the secret judgment of the angels, who is capable of beholding—the endurance of that severe judgment which has taken place and been made permanent—without being melted at the sight of it? Again holy Michael answered and said to holy Raphael, Who is there whose heart is not softened by it, and whose reins are not troubled at this thing?

3. Judgment has gone forth against them by those who have thus dragged them away; and that was, when they stood in the presence of the Lord of spirits.

4. In like manner also holy Rakael said to Raphael, They shall not be before the eye of the Lord; since the Lord of spirits has been offended with them; for like Lords have they conducted themselves. Therefore will he bring upon them a secret judgment for ever and ever.

5. For neither shall angel nor man receive a portion of it; but they alone shall receive their own judgment for ever and ever.

Enoch 68

1. After this judgment they shall be astonished and irritated; for it shall be exhibited to the inhabitants of the earth.

2. Behold the names of those angels. These are their names. The first of them is Samyaza; the second, Arstikapha: the third, Armen; the fourth, Kakabael; the fifth, Turel; the sixth, Rumyel; the seventh, Danyal; the eighth, Kael; the ninth, Barakel; the tenth, Azazel; the eleventh, Armers; the twelfth, Bataryal; the thirteenth, Basasael; the fourteenth, Ananel; the fifteenth, Turyal; the sixteenth, Simapiseel; the seventeenth, Yetarel; the eighteenth, Tumael; the nineteenth, Tarel; the twentieth, Rumel; the twenty-first, Azazyel.

3. These are the chiefs of their angels, and the names of the leaders of their hundreds, and the leaders of their fifties, and the leaders of their tens.

4. The name of the first is Yekun: he it was who seduced all the sons of

the holy angels; and causing them to descend on earth, led astray the offspring of men.

5. The name of the second is Kesabel, who pointed out evil counsel to the sons of the holy angels, and induced them to corrupt their bodies by generating mankind.

6. The name of the third is Gadrel: he discovered every stroke of death to the children of men.

7. He seduced Eve; and discovered to the children of men the instruments of death, the coat of mail, the shield, and the sword for slaughter; every instrument of death to the children of men.

8. From his hand were these things derived to them who dwell upon earth, from that period for ever.

9. The name of the fourth is Penemue: he discovered to the children of men bitterness and sweetness;

10. And pointed out to them every secret of their wisdom.

11. He taught men to understand writing, and the use of f ink and paper.

12. Therefore numerous have been those who have gone astray from every period of the world, even to this day.

13. For men were not born for this, thus with pen and with ink to confirm their faith;

14. Since they were not created, except that, like the angels, they might remain righteous and pure.

15. Nor would death, which destroys everything, have affected them;

16. But by this their knowledge they perish, and by this also its power consumes them.

17. The name of the fifth is Kasyade: he discovered to the children of men every wicked stroke of spirits and of demons:

18. The stroke of the embryo in the womb, to diminish it; the stroke of the spirit by the bite of the serpent, and the stroke which is given in the mid-day by the offspring of the serpent, the name of which is Tabaet.

19. This is the number of the Kesbel; the principal part of the oath which the Most High, dwelling in glory, revealed to the holy ones.

20. Its name is Beka. He spoke to holy Michael to discover to them the sacred name, that they might understand that secret name, and thus remember the oath; and that those who pointed out every secret thing to the children of men might tremble at that name and oath.

21. This is the power of that oath; for powerful it is, and strong.

22. And he established this oath of Akae by the instrumentality of the holy Michael.

23. These are the secrets of this oath, and by it were they confirmed.

24. Heaven was suspended by it before the world was made, for ever.

25. By it has the earth been founded upon the flood; while from the concealed parts of the hills the agitated waters proceed forth from the creation to the end of the world.

26. By this oath the sea has been formed, and the foundation of it.

27. During the period of its fury he has established the sand against it, which continues unchanged for ever; and by this oath the abyss has been made strong; nor is it removable from its station for ever and ever.

28. By this oath the sun and moon complete their progress, never swerving from the command given to them for ever and ever.

29. By this oath the stars complete their progress;

30. And when their names are called, they return an answer, for ever and ever.

31. Thus in the heavens take place the blowings of the winds: all of them have breathings, and effect a complete combination of breathings.

32. There the treasures of thunder are kept, and the splendour of the lightning.

33. There are kept the treasures of hail and of frost, the treasures of snow, the treasures of rain and of dew.

34. All these confess and laud before the Lord of spirits.

35. They glorify with all their power of praise; and he sustains them in all that act of thanksgiving; while they laud, glorify, and exalt the name of the Lord of spirits for ever and ever.

36. And with them he establishes this oath, by which they and their paths are preserved; nor does their progress perish.

37. Great was their joy.

38. They blessed, glorified, and exalted, because the name of the Son of man was revealed to them.

39. He sat upon the throne of his glory; and the principal part of the judgment was assigned to him, the Son of man. Sinners shall disappear and perish from the face of the earth, while those who seduced them shall be bound with chains for ever.

40. According to their ranks of corruption shall they be imprisoned, and all their works shall disappear from the face of the earth; nor thenceforward shall there be any to corrupt; for the Son of man has been

seen, sitting on the throne of his glory.

41. Everything wicked shall disappear, and depart from before his face; and the word of the Son of man shall become powerful in the presence of the Lord of spirits.

42. This is the third parable of Enoch.

Enoch 69 [SECT. XII.]

1. After this the name of the Son of man, living with the Lord of spirits, was exalted by the inhabitants of the earth.

2. It was exalted in the chariots of the Spirit; and the name went forth in the midst of them.

3. From that time I was not drawn in the midst of them; but he seated me between two spirits, between the north and the west, where the angels received their ropes, to measure out a place for the elect and the righteous.

4. There I beheld the fathers of the first men, and the saints, who dwell in that place for ever.

Enoch 70

1. Afterwards my spirit was concealed, ascending into the heavens. I beheld the sons of the holy angels treading on flaming fire, whose garments and robes were white, and whose countenances were transparent as crystal.

2. I saw two rivers of fire glittering like the hyacinth,

3. Then I fell on my face before the Lord of spirits.

4. And Michael, one of the archangels, took me by my right hand, raised me up, and brought me out to where was every secret of mercy and secret of righteousness.

5. He showed me all the hidden things of the extremities of heaven, all the receptacles of the stars, and the splendours of all, from whence they went forth before the face of the holy.

6. And he concealed the spirit of Enoch in the heaven of heavens.

7. There I beheld, in the midst of that light, a building raised with stones of ice;

8. And in the midst of these stones vibrations of living fire. My spirit saw around the circle of this flaming habitation, on one of its extremities, that there were rivers full of living fire, which encompassed it.

9. Then the Seraphim, the Cherubim, and Ophanin surrounded it these are those who never sleep, but watch the throne of his glory.

10. And I beheld angels innumerable, thousands of thousands, and myriads of myriads, who surrounded that habitation.

11. Michael, Raphael, Gabriel, Phanuel, and the holy angels who were in the heavens above, went in and out of it. Michael, Raphael, and Gabriel went out of that habitation, and holy angels innumerable.

12. With them was the Ancient of days, whose head was white as wool, and pure, and his robe was indescribable.

13. Then I fell upon my face, while all my flesh was dissolved, and my spirit became changed.

14. I cried out with a loud voice, with a powerful spirit, blessing, glorifying, and exalting.

15. And those blessings, which proceeded from my mouth, became acceptable in the presence of the Ancient of days.

16. The Ancient of days came with Michael and Gabriel, Raphael and Phanuel, with thousands of thousands, and myriads of myriads, which could not be numbered.

17. Then that angel came to me, and with his voice saluted me, saying, Thou art the offspring of man, who art born for righteousness, and righteousness has rested on thee.

18. The righteousness of the Ancient of days shall not forsake thee.

19. He said, On thee shall he confer peace 1 in the name of the existing world; for from thence has peace gone forth since the world was created.

20. And thus shall it happen to thee for ever and ever.

21. All who shall exist, and who shall walk in thy path of righteousness, shall not forsake thee for ever.

22. With thee shall be their habitations, with thee their lot; nor from thee shall they be separated for ever and ever.

23. And thus shall length of days be with the offspring of man.

24. Peace shall be to the righteous; and the path of integrity shall the righteous pursue, in the name of the Lord of spirits, for ever and ever.

Enoch 71 [SECT. XIII.]

1. The book of the revolutions of the luminaries of heaven, according to their respective classes, their respective powers, their respective periods, their respective names, the places where they commence their progress, and their respective months, which Uriel, the holy angel who was with me, explained to me; he who conducts them. The whole account of them, according to every year of the world for ever, until a new work shall be effected, which will be eternal.

2. This is the first law of the luminaries. The sun and the light arrive at the gates of heaven, which

359

are on the east, and on the west of it at the western gates of heaven.

3. I beheld the gates whence the sun goes forth; and the gates where the sun sets;

4. In which gates also the moon rises and sets; and I beheld the conductors of the stars, among those who precede them; six gates were at the rising, and six at the setting of the sun.

5. All these respectively, one after another, are on a level; and numerous windows are on the right and on the left sides of those gates.

6. First proceeds forth that great luminary, which is called the sun; the orb of which is as the orb of heaven, the whole of it being replete with splendid and flaming fire.

7. Its chariot, where it ascends, the wind blows.

8. The sun sets in heaven, and, returning by the north, to proceed towards the east, is conducted so as to enter by that gate, and illuminate the face of heaven.

9. In the same manner it goes forth in the first month by a great gate.

10. It goes forth through the fourth of those six gates, which are at the rising of the sun.

11. And in the fourth gate, through which the sun with the moon proceeds, in the first part of it, there are twelve open windows; from which issues out a flame, when they are opened at their proper periods.

12. When the sun rises in heaven, it goes forth through this fourth gate thirty days, and by the fourth gate in the west of heaven on a level with it descends.

13. During that period the day is lengthened from the day, and the night curtailed from the night for thirty days. And then the day is longer by two parts than the night.

14. The day is precisely ten parts, and the night is eight.

15. The sun goes forth through this fourth gate, and sets in it, and turns to the fifth gate during thirty days; after which it proceeds from, and sets in, the fifth gate.

16. Then the day becomes lengthened by a second portion, so that it is eleven parts: while the night becomes shortened, and is only seven parts.

17. The sun now returns to the east, entering into the sixth gate, and rising and setting in the sixth gate thirty-one days, on account of its signs.

18. At that period the day is longer than the night, being twice as long as the night; and becomes twelve parts;

19. But the night is shortened, and becomes six parts. Then the sun

rises up, that the day may be shortened, and the night lengthened.

20. And the sun returns towards the east, entering into the sixth gate, where it rises and sets for thirty days.

21. When that period is completed, the day becomes shortened precisely one part, so that it is eleven parts, while the night is seven parts.

22. Then the sun goes from the west, from that sixth gate, and proceeds eastwards, rising in the fifth gate for thirty days, and setting again westwards in the fifth gate of the west.

23. At that period the day becomes shortened two parts; and is ten parts, while the night is eight parts.

24. Then the sun goes from the fifth gate, as it sets in the fifth gate of the west; and rises in the fourth gate for thirty-one days, on account of its signs, setting in the west.

25. At that period the day is made equal with the night; and, being equal with it, the night becomes nine parts, and the day nine parts.

26. Then the sun goes from that gate, as it sets in the west; and returning to the east proceeds by the third gate for thirty days, setting in the west at the third gate.

27. At that period the night is lengthened from the day during thirty mornings, and the day is curtailed

from the day during thirty days; the night being ten parts precisely, and the day eight parts.

28. The sun now goes from the third gate, as it sets in the third gate in the west; but returning to the east, it proceeds by the second gate of the east for thirty days.

29. In like manner also it sets in the second gate in the west of heaven.

30. At that period the night is eleven parts, and the day seven parts.

31. Then the sun goes at that time from the second gate, as it sets in the second gate in the west; but returns to the east, proceeding by the first gate, for thirty-one days.

32. And sets in the west in the first gate.

33. At that period the night is lengthened as much again as the day.

34. It is twelve parts precisely, while the day is six parts.

35. The sun has thus completed its beginnings, and a second time goes round from these beginnings.

36. Into that gate it enters for thirty days, and sets in the west, in the opposite part of heaven.

37. At that period the night is contracted in its length a fourth part, that is, one portion, and becomes eleven parts.

38. The day is seven parts.

39. Then the sun returns, and enters into the second gate of the east.

40. It returns by these beginnings thirty days, rising and setting.

41. At that period the night is contracted in its length. It becomes ten parts, and the day eight parts. Then the sun goes from that second gate, and sets in the west; but returns to the east, and rises in the east, in the third gate, thirty-one days, setting in the west of heaven.

42. At that period the night becomes shortened. It is nine parts. And the night is equal with the day. The year is precisely three hundred and sixty-four days.

43. The lengthening of the day and night, and the contraction of the day and night, are made to differ from each other by the progress of the sun.

44. By means of this progress the day is daily lengthened, and the night greatly shortened.

45. This is the law and progress of the sun, and its turning when it turns back, turning during sixty days, and going forth. This is the great everlasting luminary, that which he names the sun for ever and ever.

46. This also is that which goes forth a great luminary, and which is named after its peculiar kind, as God commanded.

47. And thus it goes in and out, neither slackening nor resting; but running on in its chariot by day and by night. It shines with a seventh portion of light from the moon; but the dimensions of both are equal.

Enoch 72 [SECT. XIV.]

1. After this law I beheld another law of an inferior luminary, the name of which is the moon, and the orb of which is as the orb of heaven.

2. Its chariot, which it secretly ascends, the wind blows; and light is given to it by measure.

3. Every month at its exit and entrance it becomes changed; and its periods are as the periods of the sun. And when in like manner its light is to exist, its light is a seventh portion from the light of the sun.

4. Thus it rises, and at its commencement towards the east goes forth for thirty days.

5. At that time it appears, and becomes to you the beginning of the month. Thirty days it is with the sun in the gate from which the sun goes forth.

6. Half of it is in extent seven portions, one half; and the whole of its orb is void of light, except a seventh portion out of the fourteen portions of its light. And in a day it receives a seventh portion, or half that portion, of its light. Its light is by

sevens, by one portion, and by the half of a portion. It sets with the sun.

7. And when the sun rises, the moon rises with it; receiving half a portion of light.

8. On that night, when it commences its period, previously to the day of the month, the moon sets with the sun.

9. And on that night it is dark in its fourteen portions, that is, in each half; but it rises on that day with one seventh portion precisely, and in its progress declines from the rising of the sun.

10. During the remainder of its period its light increases to fourteen portions.

Enoch 73

1. Then I saw another progress and regulation which He effected in the law of the moon. The progress of the moons, and everything relating to them, Uriel showed me, the holy angel who conducted them all.

2. Their stations I wrote down as he showed them to me.

3. I wrote down their months, as they occur, and the appearance of their light, until it is completed in fifteen days.

4. In each of its two seven portions it completes all its light at rising and at setting.

5. On stated months it changes its settings; and on stated months it makes its progress through each gate. In two gates the moon sets with the sun, viz. in those two gates which are in the midst, in the third and fourth gate. From the third gate it goes forth for seven days, and makes its circuit.

6. Again it returns to the gate whence the sun goes forth, and in that completes the whole of its light. Then it declines from the sun, and enters in eight days into the sixth gate, and returns in seven days to the third gate, from which the sun goes forth.

7. When the sun proceeds to the fourth gate, the moon goes forth for seven days, until it passes from the fifth gate.

8. Again it returns in seven days to the fourth gate, and completing all its light, declines, and passes on by the first gate in eight days;

9. And returns in seven days to the fourth gate, from which the sun goes forth.

10. Thus I beheld their stations, as according to the fixed order of the months the sun rises and sets.

11. At those times there is an excess of thirty days belonging to the sun in five years; all the days belonging to each year of the five years, when completed, amount to three hundred and sixty-four days; and to the sun

and stars belong six days; six days in each of the five years; thus thirty days belong to them;

12. So that the moon has thirty days less than the sun and stars.

13. The moon brings on all the years exactly, that their stations may come neither too forwards nor too backwards a single day; but that the years may be changed with correct precision in three hundred and sixty-four days. In three years the days are one thousand and ninety-two; in five years they are one thousand eight hundred and twenty; and in eight years two thousand nine hundred and twelve days.

14. To the moon alone belong in three years one thousand and sixty-two days; in five years it has fifty days less than the sun, for an addition being made to the one thousand and sixty-two days, in five years there are one thousand seven hundred and seventy days; and the days of the moon in eight years are two thousand eight hundred and thirty-two days.

15. For its days in eight years are less than those of the sun by eighty days, which eighty days are its diminution in eight years.

16. The year then becomes truly complete according to the station of the moons, and the station of the sun; which rise in the different gates; which rise and set in them for thirty days.

Enoch 74

1. These are the leaders of the chiefs of the thousands, those which preside over all creation, and over all the stars; with the four days which are added and never separated from the place allotted them, according to the complete computation of the year.

2. And these serve four days, which are not computed in the computation of the year.

3. Respecting them, men greatly err, for these luminaries truly serve, in the mansion of the world, one day in the first gate, one in the third gate, one in the fourth, and one in the sixth gate.

4. And the harmony of the world becomes complete every three hundred and sixty-fourth state of it. For the signs,

5. The seasons,

6. The years,

7. And the days, Uriel showed me; the angel whom the Lord of glory appointed over all the luminaries.

8. Of heaven in heaven, and in the world; that they might rule in the face of the sky, and appearing over the earth, become

9. Conductors of the days and nights: the sun, the moon, the stars,

and all the ministers of heaven, which make their circuit with all the chariots of heaven.

10. Thus Uriel showed me twelve gates open for the circuit of the chariots of the sun in heaven, from which the rays of the sun shoot forth.

11. From these proceed heat over the earth, when they are opened in their stated seasons. They are for the winds, and the spirit of the dew, when in their seasons they are opened; opened in heaven at its extremities.

12. Twelve gates I beheld in heaven, at the extremities of the earth, through which the sun, moon, and stars, and all the works of heaven, proceed at their rising and setting.

13. Many windows also are open on the right and on the left.

14. One window at a certain season grows extremely hot. So also are there gates from which the stars go forth as they are commanded, and in which they set according to their number.

15. I saw likewise the chariots of heaven, running in the world above to those gates in which the stars turn, which never set. One of these is greater than all, which goes round the whole world.

Enoch 75 [SECT. XV.]

1. And at the extremities of the earth I beheld twelve gates open for all the winds, from which they proceed and blow over the earth.

2. Three of them are open in the front of heaven, three in the west, three on the right side of heaven, and three on the left. The first three are those which are towards the east, three are towards the north, three behind those which are upon the left, towards the south, and three on the west.

3. From four of them proceed winds of blessing, and of health; and from eight proceed winds of punishment; when they are sent to destroy the earth, and the heaven above it, all its inhabitants, and all which are in the waters, or on dry land.

4. The first of these winds proceeds from the gate termed the eastern, through the first gate on the east, which inclines southwards. From this goes forth destruction, drought, heat, and perdition.

5. From the second gate, the middle one, proceeds equity. There issue from it rain, fruitfulness, health, and dew; and from the third gate northwards, proceed cold and drought.

6. After these proceed the south winds through three principal gates; through their first gate, which inclines eastwards, proceeds a hot wind.

7. But from the middle gate proceed grateful odour, dew, rain, health, and life.

8. From the third gate, which is westwards, proceed dew, rain, blight, and destruction.

9. After these are the winds to the north, which is called the sea. They proceed from three gates. The first gate is that which is on the east, inclining southwards; from this proceed dew, rain, blight, and destruction. From the middle direct gate proceed rain, dew, life, and health. And from the third gate, which is westwards, inclining towards the south, proceed mist, frost, snow, rain, dew, and blight.

10. After these in the fourth quarter are the winds to the west. From the first gate, inclining northwards, proceed dew, rain, frost, cold, snow, and chill; from the middle gate proceed rain, health, and blessing;

11. And from the last gate, which is southwards, proceed drought, destruction, scorching, and perdition.

12. The account of the twelve gates of the four quarters of heaven is ended.

13. All their laws, all their infliction of punishment, and the health produced by them, have I explained to thee, my son Mathusala.

Enoch 76

1. The first wind is called the eastern, because it is the first.

2. The second is called the south, because the Most High there descends, and frequently there descends he who is blessed for ever.

3. The western wind has the name of diminution, because there all the luminaries of heaven are diminished, and descend.

4. The fourth wind, which is named the north, is divided into three parts; one of which is for the habitation of man; another for seas of water, with valleys, woods, rivers, shady places, and snow; and the third part contains paradise.

5. Seven high mountains I beheld, higher than all the mountains of the earth, from which frost proceeds; while days, seasons, and years depart and pass away.

6. Seven rivers I beheld upon earth, greater than all rivers, one of which takes its course from the west; into a great sea its water flows.

7. Two come from the north to the sea, their waters flowing into the Erythræan sea, on the east. And with respect to the remaining four, they take their course in the cavity of the north, two to their sea, the Erythræan sea, and two are poured into a great sea, where also it is said there is a desert.

8. Seven great islands I saw in the sea and on the earth. Seven in the great sea.

Enoch 77

1. The names of the sun are these: one Aryares, the other Tomas.

2. The moon has four names. The first is Asonya; the second, Ebla; the third, Benase; and the fourth, Erae.

3. These are the two great luminaries, whose orbs are as the orbs of heaven; and the dimensions of both are equal.

4. In the orb of the sun there is a seventh portion of light, which is added to it from the moon. By measure it is put in, until a seventh portion of the light of the sun is departed. They set, enter into the western gate, circuit by the north, and through the eastern gate go forth over the face of heaven.

5. When the moon rises, it appears in heaven; and the half of a seventh portion of light is all which is in it.

6. In fourteen days the whole of its light is completed.

7. By three quintuples light is put into it, until in fifteen days its light is completed, according to the signs of the year; it has three quintuples.

8. The moon has the half of a seventh portion.

9. During its diminution on the first day its light decreases a fourteenth part; on the second day it decreases a thirteenth part; on the third day a twelfth part; on the fourth day an eleventh part; on the fifth day a tenth part; on the sixth day a ninth part; on the seventh day it decreases an eighth part; on the eighth day it decreases a seventh part; on the ninth day it decreases a sixth part; on the tenth day it decreases a fifth part; on the eleventh day it decreases a fourth part; on the twelfth day it decreases a third part; on the thirteenth day it decreases a second part; on the fourteenth day it decreases a half of its seventh part; and on the fifteenth day the whole remainder of its light is consumed.

10. On stated months the moon has twenty-nine days.

11. It also has a period of twenty-eight days.

12. Uriel likewise showed me another regulation, when light is poured into the moon, how it is poured into it from the sun.

13. All the time that the moon is in progress with its light, it is poured into it in the presence of the sun, until its light is in fourteen days completed in heaven.

14. And when it is wholly extinguished, its light is consumed in heaven; and on the first day it is called the new moon, for on that day light is received into it.

15. It becomes precisely completed on the day that the sun descends into the west, while the moon ascends at night from the east.

16. The moon then shines all the night, until the sun rises before it; when the moon disappears in turn before the sun.

17. Where light comes to the moon, there again it decreases, until all its light is extinguished, and the days of the moon pass away.

18. Then its orb remains solitary without light.

19. During three months it effects in thirty days each month its period; and during three more months it effects it in twenty-nine days each. These are the times in which it effects its decrease in its first period, and in the first gate, namely, in one hundred and seventy-seven days.

20. And at the time of its going forth during three months it appears thirty days each, and during three more months it appears twenty-nine days each.

21. In the night it appears for each twenty days as the face of a man, and in the day as heaven; for it is nothing else except its light.

Enoch 78

1. And now, my son Mathusala, I have shown thee everything; and the account of every ordinance of the stars of heaven is finished.

2. He showed me every ordinance respecting these, which takes place at all times and in all seasons under every influence, in all years, at the arrival and under the rule of each, during every month and every week. He showed me also the decrease of the moon, which is effected in the sixth gate; for in that sixth gate is its light consumed.

3. From this is the beginning of the month; and its decrease is effected in the sixth gate in its period, until a hundred and seventy-seven days are completed; according to the mode of computation by weeks, twenty-five weeks and two days.

4. Its period is less than that of the sun, according to the ordinance of the stars, by five days in one half year precisely.

5. When that their visible situation is completed. Such is the appearance and likeness of every luminary, which Thiel, the great angel who conducts them, showed to me.

Enoch 79

1. In those days Uriel answered and said to me, Behold, I have showed thee all things, O Enoch;

2. And all things have I revealed to thee. Thou seest the sun, the moon, and those which conduct the stars of heaven, which cause all their operations, seasons, and arrivals to return.

3. In the days of sinners the years shall be shortened.

4. Their seed shall be backward in their prolific soil; and everything

done on earth shall be subverted, and disappear in its season. The rain shall be restrained, and heaven shall stand still.

5. In those days the fruits of the earth shall be late, and not flourish in their season; and in their season the fruits of the trees shall be withholden.

6. The moon shall change its laws, and not be seen at its proper period. But in those days shall heaven be seen; and barrenness shall take place in the borders of the great chariots in the west. Heaven shall shine more than when illuminated by the orders of light; while many chiefs among the stars of authority shall err, perverting their ways and works.

7. Those shall not appear in their season, who command them, and all the classes of the stars shall be shut up against sinners.

8. The thoughts of those who dwell on earth shall transgress within them; and they shall be perverted in all their ways.

9. They shall transgress, and think themselves gods; while evil shall be multiplied among them.

10. And punishment shall come upon them, so that all of them shall be destroyed.

Enoch 80

1. He said, O Enoch, look on the book which heaven has gradually dropped down; 1 and, reading that which is written in it, understand every part of it.

2. Then I looked on all which was written, and understood all, reading the book and everything written in it, all the works of man;

3. And of all the children of flesh upon earth, during the generations of the world.

4. Immediately after I blessed the Lord, the King of glory, who has thus for ever formed the whole workmanship of the world.

5. And I glorified the Lord, on account of his long-suffering and blessing towards the children of the world.

6. At that time I said, Blessed is the man, who shall die righteous and good, against whom no catalogue of crime has been written, and with whom iniquity is not found.

7. Then those three holy ones caused me to approach, and placed me on the earth, before the door of my house.

8. And they said unto me, Explain everything to Mathusala thy son; and inform all thy children, that no flesh shall be justified before the Lord; for he is their Creator.

9. During one year we will leave thee with thy children, until thou shalt again recover thy strength, that thou mayest instruct thy family, write

these things, and explain them to all thy children. But in another year they shall take thee from the midst of them, and thy heart shall be strengthened; for the elect shall point out righteousness to the elect; the righteous with the righteous shall rejoice, congratulating each other; but sinners with sinners shall die,

10. And the perverted with the perverted shall be drowned.

11. Those likewise who act righteously shall die on account of the works of man, and shall be gathered together on account of the works of the wicked.

12. In those days they finished conversing with me.

13. And I returned to my fellow men, blessing the Lord of worlds.

Enoch 81

1. Now, my son Mathusala, all these things I speak unto thee, and write for thee. To thee I have revealed all, and have given thee books of everything.

2. Preserve, my son Mathusala, the books written by thy father; that thou mayest transmit them to future generations.

3. Wisdom have I given to thee, to thy children, and thy posterity, that they may transmit to their children, for generations for ever, this wisdom in their thoughts; and that those who comprehend it may not slumber, but

hear with their ears; that they may learn this wisdom, and be deemed worthy of eating this wholesome food.

4. Blessed are all the righteous; blessed all who walk in the paths of righteousness; in whom no crime is found, as in sinners, when all their days are numbered.

5. With respect to the progress of the sun in heaven, it enters and goes out of each gate for thirty days, with the leaders of the thousand classes of the stars; with four which are added, and appertain to the four quarters of the year, which conduct them, and accompany them at four periods.

6. Respecting these, men greatly err, and do not compute them in the computation of every age; for they greatly err respecting them; nor do men know accurately that they are in the computation of the year. But indeed these are marked down for ever; one in the first gate, one in the third, one in the fourth, and one in the sixth:

7. So that the year is completed in three hundred and sixty-four days.

8. Truly has been stated, and accurately has been computed that which is marked down; for the luminaries, the months, the fixed periods, the years, and the days, Uriel has explained to me, and communicated to me; whom the Lord of all creation, on my account,

commanded (according to the might of heaven, and the power which it possesses both by night and by day) to explain the laws of light to man, of the sun, moon, and stars, and of all the powers of heaven, which are turned with their respective orbs.

9. This is the ordinance of the stars, which set in their places, in their seasons, in their periods, in their days, and in their months.

10. These are the names of those who conduct them, who watch and enter in their seasons, according to their ordinance in their periods, in their months, in the times of their influence, and in their stations.

11. Four conductors of them first enter, who separate the four quarters of the year. After these, twelve conductors of their classes, who separate the months and the year into three hundred and sixty-four days, with the leaders of a thousand, who distinguish between the days, as well as between the four additional ones; which, as conductors, divide the four quarters of the year.

12. These leaders of a thousand are in the midst of the conductors, and the conductors are added each behind his station, and their conductors make the separation. These are the names of the conductors, who separate the four quarters of the year, who are

appointed over them: Melkel, Helammelak,

13. Meliyal, and Narel.

14. And the names of those who conduct them are Adnarel, Jyasusal, and Jyelumeal.

15. These are the three who follow after the conductors of the classes of stars; each following after the three conductors of the classes, which themselves follow after those conductors of the stations, who divide the four quarters of the year.

16. In the first part of the year rises and rules Melkyas, who is named Tamani, and Zahay.

17. All the days of his influence, during which he rules, are ninety-one days.

18. And these are the signs of the days which are seen upon earth. In the days of his influence there is perspiration, heat, and trouble. All the trees become fruitful; the leaf of every tree comes forth; the corn is reaped; the rose and every species of flowers blossoms in the field; and the trees of winter are dried up.

19. These are the names of the conductors who are under them: Barkel, Zelsabel; and another additional conductor of a thousand is named Heloyalef, the days of whose influence have been completed. The other conductor next after them is

Helemmelek, whose name they call the splendid Zahay.

20. All the days of his light are ninety-one days.

21. These are the signs of the days upon earth, heat and drought; while the trees bring forth their fruits, warmed and concocted, and give their fruits to dry.

22. The flocks follow and yean. All the fruits of the earth are collected, with everything in the fields, and the vines are trodden. This takes place during the time of his influence.

23. These are their names and orders, and the names of the conductors who are under them, of those who are chiefs of a thousand: Gedaeyal, Keel, Heel.

24. And the name of the additional leader of a thousand is Asphael.

25. The days of his influence have been completed.

Enoch 82

1. And now I have shown thee, my son Mathusala, every sight which I saw prior to thy birth. I will relate another vision, which I saw before I was married; they resemble each other.

2. The first was when I was learning a book; and the other before I was married to thy mother. I saw a potent vision;

3. And on account of these things besought the Lord.

4. I was lying down in the house of my grandfather Malalel, when I saw in a vision heaven purifying, and snatched away.

5. And falling to the earth, I saw likewise the earth absorbed by a great abyss; and mountains suspended over mountains.

6. Hills were sinking upon hills, lofty trees were gliding off from their trunks, and were in the act of being projected, and of sinking into the abyss.

7. Being alarmed at these things, my voice faltered. I cried out and said, The earth is destroyed. Then my grandfather Malalel raised me up, and said to me: Why dost thou thus cry out, my son? and wherefore dost thou thus lament?

8. I related to him the whole vision which I had seen. He said to me, Confirmed is that which thou hast seen, my son;

9. And potent the vision of thy dream respecting every secret sin of the earth. Its substance shall sink into the abyss, and a great destruction take place.

10. Now, my son, rise up; and beseech the Lord of glory (for thou art faithful), that a remnant may be left upon earth, and that he would not wholly destroy it. My son, all this

calamity upon earth comes down from heaven; upon earth shall there be a great destruction.

11. Then I arose, prayed, and entreated; and wrote down my prayer for the generations of the world, explaining everything to my son Mathusala.

12. When I went out below, and looking up to heaven, beheld the sun proceeding from the east, the moon descending to the west, a few scattered stars, and everything which God has known from the beginning, I blessed the Lord of judgment, and magnified him: because he hath sent forth the sun from the chambers of the east; that, ascending and rising in the face of heaven, it might spring up, and pursue the path which has been pointed out to it.

Enoch 83

1. I lifted up my hands in righteousness, and blessed the holy, and the Great One. I spoke with the breath of my mouth, and with a tongue of flesh, which God has formed for all the sons of mortal men, that with it they may speak; giving them breath, a mouth, and a tongue to converse with.

2. Blessed art thou, O Lord, the King, great and powerful in thy greatness, Lord of all the creatures of heaven, King of kings, God of the whole world, whose reign, whose kingdom, and whose majesty endure for ever and ever.

3. From generation to generation shall thy dominion exist. All the heavens are thy throne for ever, and all the earth thy footstool for ever and for ever.

4. For thou hast made them, and over all thou reignest. No act whatsoever exceeds thy power. With thee wisdom is unchangeable; nor from thy throne and from thy presence is it ever averted. Thou knowest all things, seest and hearest them; nor is anything concealed from thee; for thou perceivest all things.

5. The angels of thy heavens have transgressed; and on mortal flesh shall thy wrath remain, until the day of the great judgment.

6. Now then, O God, Lord and mighty King, I entreat thee, and beseech thee to grant my prayer, that a posterity may be left to me on earth, and that the whole human race may not perish;

7. That the earth may not be left destitute, and destruction take place for ever.

8. O my Lord, let the race perish from off the earth which has offended thee, but a righteous and upright race establish for a posterity for ever. Hide not thy face, O Lord, from the prayer of thy servant.

Enoch 84 [SECT. XVII.]

1. After this I saw another dream, and explained it all to thee, my son. Enoch arose and said to his son Mathusala, To thee, my son, will I speak. Hear my word; and incline thine ear to the visionary dream of thy father. Before I married thy mother Edna, I saw a vision on my bed;

2. And behold, a cow sprung forth from the earth;

3. And this cow was white.

4. Afterwards a female heifer sprung forth; and with it another heifer: one of them was black, and one was red.

5. The black heifer then struck the red one, and pursued it over the earth.

6. From that period I could see nothing more of the red heifer; but the black one increased in bulk, and a female heifer came with him.

7. After this I saw that many cows proceeded forth, resembling him, and following after him.

8. The first female young one also went out in the presence of the first cow; and sought the red heifer; but found him not.

9. And she lamented with a great lamentation, while she was seeking him.

10. Then I looked until that first cow came to her, from which time she became silent, and ceased to lament.

11. Afterwards she calved another white cow.

12. And again calved many cows and black heifers.

13. In my sleep also I perceived a white bull, which in like manner grew, and became a large white bull.

14. After him many white cows came forth, resembling him.

15. And they began to calve many other white cows, which resembled them and followed each other.

Enoch 85

1. Again I looked attentively, 1 while sleeping, and surveyed heaven above.

2. And behold a single star fell from heaven.

3. Which being raised up, ate and fed among those cows.

4. After that I perceived other large and black cows; and behold all of them changed their stalls and pastures, while their young began to lament one with another. Again I looked in my vision, and surveyed heaven; when behold I saw many stars which descended, and projected themselves from heaven to where the first star was,

5. Into the midst of those young ones; while the cows were with them, feeding in the midst of them.

6. I looked at and observed them; when behold, they all acted after the manner of horses, and began to approach the young cows, all of whom became pregnant, and brought forth elephants, camels, and asses.

7. At these all the cows were alarmed and terrified; when they began biting with their teeth, swallowing, and striking with their horns.

8. They began also to devour the cows; and behold all the children of the earth trembled, shook with terror at them, and suddenly fled away.

Enoch 86

1. Again I perceived them, when they began to strike and to swallow each other; and the earth cried out. Then I raised my eyes a second time towards heaven, and saw in a vision, that, behold, there came forth from heaven as it were the likeness of white men. One came forth from thence, and three with him.

2. Those three, who came forth last, seized me by my hand; and raising me up from the generations of the earth, elevated me to a high station.

3. Then they showed me a lofty tower on the earth, while every hill became diminished. And they said,

Remain here, until thou perceivest what shall come upon those elephants, camels, and asses, upon the stars, and upon all the cows.

Enoch 87

1. Then I looked at that one of the four white men, who came forth first.

2. He seized the first star which fell down from heaven.

3. And, binding it hand and foot, he cast it into a valley; a valley narrow, deep, stupendous, and gloomy.

4. Then one of them drew his sword, and gave it to the elephants, camels, and asses, who began to strike each other. And the whole earth shook on account of them.

5. And when I looked in the vision, behold, one of those four angels, who came forth, hurled from heaven, collected together, and took all the great stars, whose form partly resembled that of horses; and binding them all hand and foot, cast them into the cavities of the earth.

Enoch 88

1. Then one of those four went to the white cows, and taught them a mystery. While the cow was trembling, it was born, and became a man, and fabricated for himself a large ship. In this he dwelt, and three cows dwelt with him in that ship, which covered them.

2. Again I lifted up my eyes towards heaven, and saw a lofty roof. Above it were seven cataracts, which poured forth on a certain village much water.

3. Again I looked, and behold there were fountains open on the earth in that large village.

4. The water began to boil up, and rose over the earth; so that the village was not seen, while its whole soil was covered with water.

5. Much water was over it, darkness, and clouds. Then I surveyed the height of this water; and it was elevated above the village.

6. It flowed over the village, and stood higher than the earth.

7. Then all the cows which were collected there, while I looked on them, were drowned, swallowed up, and destroyed in the water.

8. But the ship floated above it. All the cows, the elephants, the camels, and the asses, were drowned on the earth, and all cattle. Nor could I perceive them. Neither were they able to get out, but perished, and sunk into the deep.

9. Again I looked in the vision until those cataracts from that lofty roof were removed, and the fountains of the earth became equalized, while other depths were opened;

10. Into which the water began to descend, until the dry ground appeared.

11. The ship remained on the earth; the darkness receded; and it became light.

12. Then the white cow, which became a man, went out of the ship, and the three cows with him.

13. One of the three cows was white, resembling that cow; one of them was red as blood; and one of them was black. And the white cow left them.

14. Then began wild beasts and birds to bring forth.

15. Of all these the different kinds assembled together, lions, tigers, wolves, dogs, wild boars, foxes, rabbits, and the hanzar,

16. The siset, the avest, kites, the phonkas, and ravens.

17. Then a white cow was born in the midst of them.

18. And they began to bite each other; when the white cow, which was born in the midst of them, brought forth a wild ass and a white cow at the same time, and after that many wild asses. Then the white cow, which was born, brought forth a black wild sow and a white sheep.

19. That wild sow also brought forth many swine;

20. And that sheep brought forth twelve sheep.

21. When those twelve sheep grew up, they delivered one of them to the asses.

22. Again those asses delivered that sheep to the wolves;

23. And he grew up in the midst of them.

24. Then the Lord brought the eleven other sheep, that they might dwell and feed with him in the midst of the wolves.

25. They multiplied, and there was abundance of pasture for them.

26. But the wolves began to frighten and oppress them, while they destroyed their young ones.

27. And they left their young in torrents of deep water.

28. Now the sheep began to cry out on account of their young, and fled for refuge to their Lord. One however, which was saved, escaped, and went away to the wild asses.

29. I beheld the sheep moaning, crying, and petitioning their Lord,

30. With all their might, until the Lord of the sheep descended at their voice from his lofty habitation; went to them; and inspected them.

31. He called to that sheep which had secretly stolen away from the wolves, and told him to make the wolves understand that they were not to touch the sheep.

32. Then that sheep went to the wolves with the word of the Lord, when another met him, and proceeded with him.

33. Both of them together entered the dwelling of the wolves; and conversing with them made them understand, that from thenceforwards they were not to touch the sheep.

34. Afterwards I perceived the wolves greatly prevailing over the sheep with their whole force. The sheep cried out; and their Lord came to them.

35. He began to strike the wolves, who commenced a grievous lamentation; but the sheep were silent, nor from that time did they cry out.

36. I then looked at them, until they departed from the wolves. The eyes of the wolves were blind, who went out and followed them with all their might. But the Lord of the sheep proceeded with them, and conducted them.

37. All his sheep followed him.

38. His countenance was terrific and splendid, and glorious was his aspect. Yet the wolves began to follow the sheep, until they overtook them in a certain lake of water.

39. Then that lake became divided; the water standing up on both sides before their face.

40. And while their Lord was conducting them, he placed himself between them and the wolves.

41. The wolves however perceived not the sheep, but went into the midst of the lake, following them, and running after them into the lake of water.

42. But when they saw the Lord of the sheep, they turned to fly from before his face.

43. Then the water of the lake returned, and that suddenly, according to its nature. It became full, and was raised up, until it covered the wolves. And I saw that all of them which had followed the sheep perished, and were drowned.

44. But the sheep passed over this water, proceeding to a wilderness, which was without both water and grass. And they began to open their eves and to see.

45. Then I beheld the Lord of the sheep inspecting them, and giving them water and grass.

46. The sheep already mentioned was proceeding with them, and conducting them.

47. And when he had ascended the top of a lofty rock, the Lord of the sheep sent him to them.

48. Afterwards I perceived their Lord standing before them, with an aspect terrific and severe.

49. And when they all beheld him, they were frightened at his countenance.

50. All of them were alarmed, and trembled. They cried out after that sheep; and to the other sheep who had been with him, and who was in the midst of them, saying, We are not able to stand before our Lord, or to look upon him.

51. Then that sheep who conducted them went away, and ascended the top of the rock;

52. When the rest of the sheep began to grow blind, and to wander from the path which he had shown them; but he knew it not.

53. Their Lord however was moved with great indignation against them; and when that sheep had learned what had happened,

54. He descended from the top of the rock, and coming to them, found that there were many,

55. Which had become blind;

56. And had wandered from his path. As soon as they beheld him, they feared, and trembled at his presence;

57. And became desirous of returning to their fold.

58. Then that sheep, taking with him other sheep, went to those which had wandered.

59. And afterwards began to kill them. They were terrified at his countenance. Then he caused those which had wandered to return; who went back to their fold.

60. I likewise saw there in the vision, that this sheep became a man, built an house for the Lord of the sheep, and made them all stand in that house.

61. I perceived also that the sheep which proceeded to meet this sheep, their conductor, died. I saw, too, that all the great sheep perished, while smaller ones rose up in their place, entered into a pasture, and approached a river of water.

62. Then that sheep, their conductor, who became a man, was separated from them, and died.

63. All the sheep sought after him, and cried for him with bitter lamentation.

64. I saw likewise that they ceased to cry after that sheep, and passed over the river of water.

65. And that there arose other sheep, all of whom conducted them, instead of those who were dead, and who had previously conducted them.

66. Then I saw that the sheep entered into a goodly place, and a territory delectable and glorious.

67. I saw also that they became satiated; that their house was in the midst of a delectable territory: and that sometimes their eyes were opened, and that sometimes they were blind; until another sheep arose and conducted them. He brought them all back; and their eyes were opened.

68. Then dogs, foxes, and wild boars began to devour them, until again another sheep 3 arose, the master of the flock, one of themselves, a ram, to conduct them. This ram began to butt on every side those dogs, foxes, and wild boars, until they all perished.

69. But the former sheep opened his eyes, and saw the ram in the midst of them, who had laid aside his glory.

70. And he began to strike the sheep, treading upon them, and behaving himself without dignity.

71. Then their Lord sent the former sheep again to a still different sheep, and raised him up to be a ram, and to conduct them instead of that sheep who had laid aside his glory.

72. Going therefore to him, and conversing with him alone, he raised up that ram, and made him a prince and leader of the flock. All the time that the dogs troubled the sheep,

73. The first ram paid respect to this latter ram.

74. Then the latter ram arose, and fled away from before his face. And I saw that those dogs caused the first ram to fall.

75. But the latter ram arose, and conducted the smaller sheep.

76. That ram likewise begat many sheep, and died.

77. Then there was a smaller sheep, a ram, instead of him, which became a prince and leader, conducting the flock.

78. And the sheep increased in size, and multiplied.

79. And all the dogs, foxes, and wild boars feared, and fled away from him.

80. That ram also struck and killed all the wild beasts, so that they could not again prevail in the midst of the sheep, nor at any time ever snatch them away.

81. And that house was made large and wide; a lofty tower being built upon it by the sheep, for the Lord of the sheep.

82. The house was low, but the tower was elevated and very high.

83. Then the Lord of the sheep stood upon that tower, and caused a full table to approach before him.

84. Again I saw that those sheep wandered, and went various ways, forsaking that their house;

85. And that their Lord called to some among them, whom he sent to them.

86. But these the sheep began to kill. And when one of them was saved from slaughter, he leaped, and cried out against those who were desirous of killing him.

87. But the Lord of the sheep delivered him from their hands, and made him ascend to him, and remain with him.

88. He sent also many others to them, to testify, and with lamentations to exclaim against them.

89. Again I saw, when some of them forsook the house of their Lord, and his tower; wandering on all sides, and growing blind,

90. I saw that the Lord of the sheep made a great slaughter among them in their pasture, until they cried out to him in consequence of that slaughter. Then he departed from the place of his habitation, and left them in the power of lions, tigers, wolves, and the zeebt, and in the power of foxes, and of every beast.

91. And the wild beasts began to tear them.

92. I saw, too, that he forsook the house of their fathers, and their tower; giving them all into the power of lions to tear and devour them; into the power of every beast.

93. Then I began to cry out with all my might, imploring the Lord of the sheep, and showing him how the sheep were devoured by all the beasts of prey.

94. But he looked on in silence, rejoicing that they were devoured, swallowed up, and carried off; and leaving them in the power of every beast for food. He called also seventy shepherds, and resigned to them the care of the sheep, that they might overlook them;

95. Saying to them and to their associates, Every one of you henceforwards overlook the sheep, and whatsoever I command you, do; and I will deliver them to you numbered.

96. I will tell you which of them shall be slain; these destroy. And he delivered the sheep to them.

97. Then he called to another, and said, Understand, and watch everything which the shepherds shall do to these sheep; for many more of them shall perish than I have commanded.

98. Of every excess and slaughter, which the shepherds shall commit, there shall be an account; as, how many may have perished by my command, and how many they may have destroyed of their own heads.

99. Of all the destruction brought about by each of the shepherds there shall be an account; and according to the number I will cause a recital to be made before me, how many they have destroyed of their own heads, and how many they have delivered up to destruction, that I may have this testimony against them; that I may know all their proceedings; and that, delivering the sheep to them, I may see what they will do; whether they will act as I have commanded them, or not.

100. Of this, however, they shall be ignorant; neither shalt thou make any explanation to them, neither shalt thou reprove them; but there shall be an account of all the destruction done by them in their respective seasons. Then they began to kill, and destroy more than it was commanded them.

101. And they left the sheep in the power of lions, so that very many of them were devoured and swallowed up by lions and tigers; and wild boars preyed upon them. That tower they burnt, and overthrew that house.

102. Then I grieved extremely on account of the tower, and because the house of the sheep was overthrown.

103. Neither was I afterwards able to perceive whether they again entered that house.

104. The shepherds likewise, and their associates, delivered them to all the wild beasts, that they might devour them. Each of them in his

season, according to his number, was delivered up; each of them, one with another, was described in a book, how many of them, one with another, were destroyed, in a book.

105. More, however, than was ordered, every shepherd killed and destroyed.

106. Then I began to weep, and was greatly indignant, on account of the sheep.

107. In like manner also I saw in the vision him who wrote, how he wrote down one, destroyed by the shepherds, every day. He ascended, remained, and exhibited each of his books to the Lord of the sheep, containing all which they had done, and all which each of them had made away with;

108. And all which they had delivered up to destruction.

109. He took the book up in his hands, read it, sealed it, and deposited it.

110. After this, I saw shepherds overlooking for twelve hours.

111. And behold three of the sheep departed, arrived, went in; and began building all which was fallen down of that house.

112. But the wild boars hindered them, although they prevailed not.

113. Again they began to build as before, and raised up that tower, which was called a lofty tower.

114. And again they began to place before the tower a table, with every impure and unclean kind of bread upon it.

115. Moreover also all the sheep were blind, and could not see; as were the shepherds likewise.

116. Thus were they delivered up to the shepherds for a great destruction, who trod them under foot, and devoured them.

117. Yet was their Lord silent, until all the sheep in the field were destroyed. The shepherds and the sheep were all mixed together; but they did not save them from the power of the beasts.

118. Then he who wrote the book ascended, exhibited it, and read it at the residence of the Lord of the sheep. He petitioned him for them, and prayed, pointing out every act of the shepherds, and testifying before him against them all. Then taking the book, he deposited it with him, and departed.

Enoch 89

1. And I observed during the time, that thus thirty-seven shepherds were overlooking, all of whom finished in their respective periods as the first. Others then received them into their hands, that they might

overlook them in their respective periods, every shepherd in his own period.

2. Afterwards I saw in the vision, that all the birds of heaven arrived; eagles, the avest, kites and ravens. The eagle instructed them all.

3. They began to devour the sheep, to peck out their eyes, and to eat up their bodies.

4. The sheep then cried out; for their bodies were devoured by the birds.

5. I also cried out, and groaned in my sleep against that shepherd which overlooked the flock.

6. And I looked, while the sheep were eaten up by the dogs, by the eagles, and by the kites. They neither left them their body, nor their skin, nor their muscles, until their bones alone remained; until their bones fell upon the ground. And the sheep became diminished.

7. I observed likewise during the time, that twenty-three shepherds were overlooking; who completed in their respective periods fifty-eight periods.

8. Then were small lambs born of those white sheep; who began to open their eyes and to see, crying out to the sheep.

9. The sheep, however, cried not out to them, neither did they hear what they uttered to them; but were deaf, blind, and obdurate in the greatest degrees.

10. I saw in the vision that ravens flew down upon those lambs;

11. That they seized one of them; and that tearing the sheep in pieces, they devoured them.

12. I saw also, that horns grew upon those lambs; and that the ravens lighted down upon their horns.

13. I saw, too, that a large horn sprouted out on an animal 1 among the sheep, and that their eyes were opened.

14. He looked at them. Their eyes were wide open; and he cried out to them.

15. Then the dabela saw him; all of whom ran to him.

16. And besides this, all the eagles, the avest, the ravens and the kites, were still carrying off the sheep, flying down upon them, and devouring them. The sheep were silent, but the dabela lamented and cried out.

17. Then the ravens contended, and struggled with them.

18. They wished among them to break his horn; but they prevailed not over him.

19. I looked on them, until the shepherds, the eagles, the avest, and the kites came.

383

20. Who cried out to the ravens to break the horn of the dabela; to contend with him; and to kill him. But he struggled with them, and cried out, that help might come to him.

21. Then I perceived that the man came who had written down the names of the shepherds, and who ascended up before the Lord of the sheep.

22. He brought assistance, and caused every one to see him descending to the help of the dabela.

23. I perceived likewise that the Lord of the sheep came to them in wrath, while all those who saw him fled away; all fell down in his tabernacle before his face; while all the eagles, the avest, ravens, and kites assembled, and brought with them all the sheep of the field.

24. All came together, and strove to break the horn of the dabela.

25. Then I saw, that the man, who wrote the book at the word of the Lord, opened the book of destruction, of that destruction which the last twelve shepherds wrought; and pointed out before the Lord of the sheep, that they destroyed more than those who preceded them.

26. I saw also that the Lord of the sheep came to them, and taking in his hand the sceptre of his wrath seized the earth, which became rent asunder; while all the beasts and birds of heaven fell from the sheep,

and sunk into the earth, which closed over them.

27. I saw, too, that a large sword was given to the sheep, who went forth against all the beasts of the field to slay them.

28. But all the beasts and birds of heaven fled away from before their face.

29. And I saw a throne erected in a delectable land;

30. Upon this sat the Lord of the sheep, who received all the sealed books;

31. Which were open before him.

32. Then the Lord called the first seven white ones, and commanded them to bring before him the first of the first stars, which preceded the stars whose form partly resembled that of horses; the first star, which fell down first; and they brought them all before him.

33. And he spoke to the man who wrote in his presence, who was one of the seven white ones, saying, Take those seventy shepherds, to whom I delivered up the sheep, and who receiving them killed more of them than I commanded. Behold, I saw them all bound, and all standing before him. First came on the trial of the stars, which, being judged, and found guilty, went to the place of punishment. They thrust them into a place, deep, and full of flaming fire,

and full of pillars of fire. Then the seventy shepherds were judged, and being found guilty, were thrust into the flaming abyss.

34. At that time likewise I perceived, that one abyss was thus opened in the midst of the earth, which was full of fire.

35. And to this were brought the blind sheep; which being judged, and found guilty, were all thrust into that abyss of fire on the earth, and burnt.

36. The abyss was on the right of that house.

37. And I saw the sheep burning, and their bones consuming.

38. I stood beholding him immerge that ancient house, while they brought out its pillars, every plant in it, and the ivory infolding it. They brought it out, and deposited it in a place on the right side of the earth.

39. I also saw, that the Lord of the sheep produced a new house, great, and loftier than the former, which he bounded by the former circular spot. All its pillars were new, and its ivory new, as well as more abundant than the former ancient ivory, which he had brought out.

40. And while all the sheep which were left were in the midst of it, all the beasts of the earth, and all the birds of heaven, fell down and worshipped them, petitioning them, and obeying them in everything.

41. Then those three, who were clothed in white, and who, holding me by my hand, had before caused me to ascend, while the hand of him who spoke held me; raised me up, and placed me in the midst of the sheep, before the judgment took place.

42. The sheep were all white, with wool long and pure. Then all who had perished, and had been destroyed, every beast of the field, and every bird of heaven, assembled in that house: while the Lord of the sheep rejoiced with great joy, because all were good, and had come back again to his dwelling.

43. And I saw that they laid down the sword which had been given to the sheep, and returned it to his house, sealing it up in the presence of the Lord.

44. All the sheep would have been inclosed in that house, had it been capable of containing them; and the eyes of all were open, gazing on the good One; nor was there one among them who did not behold him.

45. I likewise perceived that the house was large, wide, and extremely full. I saw, too, that a white cow was born, whose horns were great; and that all the beasts of the field, and all the birds of heaven, were alarmed at him, and entreated him at all times.

46. Then I saw that the nature of all of them was changed, and that they became white cows;

47. And that the first, who was in the midst of them, spoke, when that word became a large beast, upon the head of which were great and black horns;

48. While the Lord of the sheep rejoiced over them, and over all the cows.

49. I lay down in the midst of them: I awoke; and saw the whole. This is the vision which I saw, lying down and waking. Then I blessed the Lord of righteousness, and gave glory to Him.

50. Afterwards I wept abundantly, nor did my tears cease, so that I became incapable of enduring it. While I was looking on, they flowed on account of what I saw; for all was come and gone by; every individual circumstance respecting the conduct of mankind was seen by me.

51. In that night I remembered my former dream; and therefore wept and was troubled, because I had seen that vision.

Enoch 90 [SECT. XVIII.]

1. And now, my son Mathusala, call to me all thy brethren, and assemble for me all the children of thy mother; for a voice calls me, and the spirit is poured out upon me, that I may show you everything which shall happen to you for ever.

2. Then Mathusala went, called to him all his brethren, and assembled his kindred.

3. And conversing with all his children in truth,

4. Enoch said, Hear, my children, every word of your father, and listen in uprightness to the voice of my mouth; for I would gain your attention, while I address you. My beloved, be attached to integrity, and walk in it.

5. Approach not integrity with a double heart; nor be associated with double-minded men: but walk, my children, in righteousness, which will conduct you in good paths; and be truth your companion.

6. For I know, that oppression will exist and prevail on earth; that on earth great punishment shall in the end take place; and that there shall be a consummation of all iniquity, which shall be cut off from its root, and every fabric raised by it shall pass away. Iniquity, however, shall again be renewed, and consummated on earth. Every act of crime, and every act of oppression and impiety, shall be a second time embraced.

7. When therefore iniquity, sin, blasphemy, tyranny, and every evil work, shall increase, and when transgression, impiety, and

uncleanness also shall increase, then upon them all shall great punishment be inflicted from heaven.

8. The holy Lord shall go forth in wrath, and upon them all shall great punishment from heaven be inflicted.

9. The holy Lord shall go forth in wrath, and with punishment, that he may execute judgment upon earth.

10. In those days oppression shall be cut off from its roots, and iniquity with fraud shall be eradicated, perishing from under heaven.

11. Every place of strength shall be surrendered with its inhabitants; with fire shall it be burnt. They shall be brought from every part of the earth, and be cast into a judgment of fire. They shall perish in wrath, and by a judgment overpowering them for ever.

12. Righteousness shall be raised up from slumber; and wisdom shall be raised up, and conferred upon them.

13. Then shall the roots of iniquity be cut off; sinners perish by the sword; and blasphemers be annihilated everywhere.

14. Those who meditate oppression, and those who blaspheme, by the sword shall perish.

15. And now, my children, I will describe and point out to you the path of righteousness and the path of oppression.

16. I will again point them out to you, that you may know what is to come.

17. Here now, my children, and walk in the path of righteousness, but shun that of oppression; for all who walk in the path of iniquity shall perish for ever.

Enoch 91 [SECT. XIX.]

1. That which was written by Enoch. He wrote all this instruction of wisdom for every man of dignity, and every judge of the earth; for all my children who shall dwell upon earth, and for subsequent generations, conducting themselves uprightly and peaceably.

2. Let not your spirit be grieved on account of the times; for the holy, the Great One, has prescribed a period to all.

3. Let the righteous man arise from slumber; let him arise, and proceed in the path of righteousness, in all its paths; and let him advance in goodness and in eternal clemency. Mercy shall be showed to the righteous man; upon him shall be conferred integrity and power for ever. In goodness and in righteousness shall he exist, and shall walk in everlasting light; but sin shall perish in eternal darkness, nor be seen from this time forward for evermore.

Enoch 92

1. After this, Enoch began to speak from a book.

2. And Enoch said, Concerning the children of righteousness, concerning the elect of the world, and concerning the plant of righteousness and integrity.

3. Concerning these things will I speak, and these things will I explain to you, my children: I who am Enoch. In consequence of that which has been shown to me, from my heavenly vision and from the voice of the holy angels have I acquired knowledge; and from the tablet of heaven have I acquired understanding.

4. Enoch then began to speak from a book, and said, I have been born the seventh in the first week, while judgment and righteousness wait with patience.

5. But after me, in the second week, great wickedness shall arise, and fraud shall spring forth.

6. In that week the end of the first shall take place, in which mankind shall be safe.

7. But when the first is completed, iniquity shall grow up; and he shall execute the decree upon sinners.

8. Afterwards, in the third week, during its completion, a man of the plant of righteous judgment shall be selected; and after him the plant of righteousness shall come for ever.

9. Subsequently, in the fourth week, during its completion, the visions of the holy and the righteous shall be seen, the order of generation after generation shall take place, and an habitation shall be made for them. Then in the fifth week, during its completion, the house of glory and of dominion shall be erected for ever.

10. After that, in the sixth week, all those who are in it shall be darkened, the hearts of all of them shall be forgetful of wisdom, and in it shall a man ascend.

11. And during its completion he shall burn the house of dominion with fire, and all the race of the elect root shall be dispersed.

12. Afterwards, in the seventh week, a perverse generation shall arise; abundant shall be its deeds, and all its deeds perverse. During its completion, the righteous shall be selected from the everlasting plant of righteousness; and to them shall be given the sevenfold doctrine of his whole creation.

13. Afterwards there shall be another week, the eighth of righteousness, to which shall be given a sword to execute judgment and justice upon all oppressors.

14. Sinners shall be delivered up into the hands of the righteous, who during its completion shall acquire

habitations by their righteousness; and the house of the great King shall be established for celebrations for ever. After, this, in the ninth week, shall the judgment of righteousness be revealed to the whole world.

15. Every work of the ungodly shall disappear from the whole earth; the world shall be marked for destruction; and all men shall be on the look out for the path of integrity.

16. And after this, on the seventh day of the tenth week, there shall be an everlasting judgment, which shall be executed upon the Watchers; and a spacious eternal heaven shall spring forth in the midst of the angels.

17. The former heaven shall depart and pass away; a new heaven shall appear; and all the celestial powers shine with sevenfold splendour for ever. Afterwards likewise shall there be many weeks, which shall externally exist in goodness and in righteousness.

18. Neither shall sin be named there for ever and for ever.

19. Who is there of all the children of men, capable of hearing the voice of the Holy One without emotion?

20. Who is there capable of thinking his thoughts? Who capable of contemplating all the workmanship of heaven? Who of comprehending the deeds of heaven?

21. He may behold its animation, but not its spirit. He may be capable of conversing respecting it, but not of ascending to it. He may see all the boundaries of these things, and meditate upon them; but he can make nothing like them.

22. Who of all men is able to understand the breadth and length of the earth?

23. By whom have been seen the dimensions of all these things? Is it every man who is capable of comprehending the extent of heaven; what its elevation is, and by what it is supported?

24. How many are the numbers of the stars; and where all the luminaries remain at rest?

Enoch 93

1. And now let me exhort you, my children, to love righteousness, and to walk in it; for the paths of righteousness are worthy of acceptation; but the paths of iniquity shall suddenly fail, and be diminished.

2. To men of note in their generation the paths of oppression and death are revealed; but they keep far from them, and do not follow them.

3. Now, too, let me exhort you who are righteous, not to walk in the paths of evil and oppression, nor in the paths of death. Approach them

not, that you may not perish; but covet,

4. And choose for yourselves righteousness, and a good life.

5. Walk in the paths of peace, that you may live, and be found worthy. Retain my words in your inmost thoughts, and obliterate them not from your hearts; for I know that sinners counsel men to commit crime craftily. They are not found in every place, nor does every counsel possess a little of them.

6. Woe to those who build up iniquity and oppression, and who lay the foundation of fraud; for suddenly shall they be subverted, and never obtain peace.

7. Woe to those who build up their houses with crime; for from their very foundations shall their houses be demolished, and by the sword shall they themselves fall. Those, too, who acquire gold and silver, shall justly and suddenly perish. Woe to you who are rich, for in your riches have you trusted; but from your riches you shall be removed; because you have not remembered the Most High in the days of your prosperity: [you shall be removed, because you have not remembered the Most High in the days of your prosperity.

8. You have committed blasphemy and iniquity; and. are destined to the day of the effusion of blood, to the day of darkness, and to the day of the great judgment.

9. This I declare and point out to you, that he who created you will destroy you.

10. When you fall, he will not show you mercy; but your Creator will rejoice in your destruction.

11. Let those, then, who shall be righteous among you in those days, detest sinners, and the ungodly.

Enoch 94

1. O that my eyes were clouds of water, that I might weep over you, and pour forth my tears like rain, and rest from the sorrow of my heart!

2. Who has permitted you to hate and to transgress? Judgment shall overtake you, ye sinners.

3. The righteous shall not fear the wicked; because God will again bring them into your power, that you may avenge yourselves of them according to your pleasure.

4. Woe to you who shall be so bound by execrations, that you cannot be released from them; the remedy being far removed from you on account of your sins. Woe to you who recompense your neighbour with evil; for you shall be recompensed according to your works.

5. Woe to you, ye false witnesses, you who aggravate iniquity; for you shall suddenly perish.

6. Woe to you, ye sinners; for you reject the righteous; for you receive or reject at pleasure those who commit iniquity; and their yoke shall prevail over you.

Enoch 95

1. Wait in hope, ye righteous; for suddenly shall sinners perish from before you, and you shall exercise dominion over them, according to your will.

2. In the day of the sufferings of sinners your offspring shall be elevated, and lifted up like eagles. Your nest shall be more exalted than that of the avest; you shall ascend, and enter into the cavities of the earth, and into the clefts of the rocks for ever, like conies, from the sight of the ungodly;

3. Who shall groan over you, and weep like sirens.

4. You shall not fear those who trouble you; for restoration shall be yours; a splendid light shall shine around you, and the voice of tranquillity shall be heard from heaven. Woe to you, sinners; for your wealth makes you resemble saints, but your hearts reproach you, knowing that you are sinners. This word shall testify against you, for the remembrance of crime.

5. Woe to you who feed upon the glory of the corn, and drink the strength of the deepest spring, and in the pride of your power tread down the humble.

6. Woe to you who drink water at pleasure; for suddenly shall you be recompensed, consumed, and withered, because you have forsaken the fountain of life.

7. Woe to you who act iniquitously, fraudulently, and blasphemously; there shall be a remembrance against you for evil.

8. Woe to you, ye powerful, who with power strike down righteousness; for the day of your destruction shall come; while at that very time many and good days shall be the portion of the righteous, even at the period of your judgment.

Enoch 96

1. The righteous are confident that sinners will be disgraced, and perish in the day of iniquity.

2. You shall yourselves be conscious of it; for the Most High will remember your destruction, and the angels shall rejoice over it. What will you do ye sinners, and where will you fly in the day of judgment, when you shall hear the words of the prayer of the righteous?

3. You are not like them who in this respect witness against you; you are associates of sinners.

4. In those days shall the prayers of the righteous come up before the Lord. When the day of your judgment shall arrive; and every circumstance of your iniquity be related before the great and the holy One;

5. Your faces shall be covered with shame; while every deed, strengthened by crime, shall be rejected.

6. Woe unto you, sinners, who in the midst of the sea, and on dry land, are those against whom an evil record exists. Woe to you who squander silver and gold, not obtained in righteousness, and say, We are rich, possess wealth, and have acquired everything which we can desire.

7. Now then will we do whatsoever we are disposed to do; for we have amassed silver; our barns are full, and the husbandmen of our families are like overflowing water.

8. Like water shall your falsehood pass away; for your wealth will not be permanent, but shall suddenly ascend from you, because you have obtained it all iniquitously; to extreme malediction shall you be delivered up.

9. And now I swear to you, ye crafty, as well as simple ones; that you, often contemplating the earth, you who are men, clothe yourselves more elegantly than married women, and both together more so than unmarried ones, everywhere arraying yourselves in majesty, in magnificence, in authority, and in silver: but gold, purple, honour, and wealth, like water, flow away.

10. Erudition therefore and wisdom are not theirs. Thus shall they perish, together with their riches, with all their glory, and with their honours;

11. While with disgrace, with slaughter, and in extreme penury, shall their spirits be thrust into a furnace of fire.

12. I have sworn to you, ye sinners, that neither mountain nor hill has been or shall be subservient to woman.

13. Neither in this way has crime been sent down to us upon earth, but men of their own heads have invented it; and greatly shall those who give it efficiency be execrated.

14. Barrenness shall not be previously inflicted on woman; but on account of the work of her hands shall she die childless.

15. I have sworn to you, ye sinners, by the holy and the Great One, that all your evil deeds are disclosed in the heavens; and that none of your oppressive acts are concealed and secret.

16. Think not in your minds, neither say in your hearts, that every crime is not manifested and seen. In heaven it is daily written down before

the Most High. Henceforwards shall it be manifested; for every act of oppression which you commit shall be daily recorded, until the period of your condemnation.

17. Woe to you, ye simple ones, for you shall perish in your simplicity. To the wise you will not listen, and that which is good you shall not obtain.

18. Now therefore know that you are destined to the day of destruction; nor hope that sinners shall live; but in process of time you shall die; for you are not marked for redemption;

19. But are destined to the day of the great judgment, to the day of distress, and the extreme ignominy of your souls.

20. Woe to you, ye obdurate in heart, who commit crime, and feed on blood. Whence is it that you feed on good things, drink, and are satiated? Is it not because our Lord, the Most High, has abundantly supplied every good thing upon earth? To you there shall not be peace.

21. Woe to you who love the deeds of iniquity. Why do you hope for that which is good? Know that you shall be given up into the hands of the righteous; who shall cut off your necks, slay you, and show you no compassion.

22. Woe to you who rejoice in the trouble of the righteous; for a grave shall not be dug for you.

23. Woe to you who frustrate the word of the righteous; for to you there shall be no hope of life.

24. Woe to you who write down the word of falsehood, and the word of the wicked; for their falsehood they record, that they may hear and not forget folly.

25. To them there shall be no peace; but they shall surely die suddenly.

Enoch 97

1. Woe to them who act impiously, who laud and honour the word of falsehood. You have been lost in perdition; and have never led a virtuous life.

2. Woe to you who change the words of integrity. They transgress against the everlasting decree;

3. And cause the heads of those who are not sinners to be trodden down upon the earth.

4. In those days you, O ye righteous, shall have been deemed worthy of having your prayers rise up in remembrance; and shall have deposited them in testimony before the angels, that they might record the sins of sinners in the presence of the Most High.

5. In those days the nations shall he overthrown; but the families of the nations shall rise again in the day of perdition.

6. In those days they who become pregnant shall go forth, carry off their children, and forsake them. Their offspring shall slip from them, and while suckling them shall they forsake them; they shall never return to them, and never instruct their beloved.

7. Again I swear to you, ye sinners, that crime has been prepared for the day of blood, which never ceases.

8. They shall worship stones, and engrave golden, silver, and wooden images. They shall worship impure spirits, demons, and every idol, in temples; but no help shall be obtained for them. Their hearts shall become impious through their folly, and their eyes be blinded with mental superstition. In their visionary dreams shall they be impious and superstitious, lying in all their actions, and worshipping a stone. Altogether shall they perish.

9. But in those days blessed shall they be, to whom the word of wisdom is delivered; who point out and pursue the path of the Most High; who walk in the way of righteousness, and who act not impiously with the impious.

10. They shall be saved.

11. Woe to you who expand the crime of your neighbour; for in hell shall you be slain.

12. Woe to you who lay the foundation of sin and deceit, and who are bitter on earth; for on it shall you be consumed.

13. Woe to you who build your houses by the labour of others, every part of which is constructed with brick, and with the stone of crime; I tell you, that you shall not obtain peace.

14. Woe to you who despise the extent of the everlasting inheritance of your fathers, while your souls follow after idols; for to you there shall be no tranquillity.

15. Woe to them who commit iniquity, and give aid to blasphemy, who slay their neighbour until the day of the great judgment; for your glory shall fall; malevolence shall He put into your hearts, and the spirit of his wrath shall stir you up, that every one of you may perish by the sword.

16. Then shall all the righteous and the holy remember your crimes.

Enoch 98

1. In those days shall fathers be struck down with their children in the presence of each other; and brethren with their brethren shall fall dead: until a river shall flow from their blood.

2. For a man shall not restrain his hand from his children, nor from his children's children; his mercy will be to kill them.

3. Nor shall the sinner restrain his hand from his honoured brother.

From the dawn of day to the setting sun shall the slaughter continue. The horse shall wade up to his breast, and the chariot shall sink to its axle, in the blood of sinners.

Enoch 99

1. In those days the angels shall descend into places of concealment, and gather together in one spot all who have assisted in crime.

2. In that day shall the Most High rise up to execute the great judgment upon all sinners, and to commit the guardianship of all the righteous and holy to the holy angels, that they may protect them as the apple of an eye, until every evil and every crime be annihilated.

3. Whether or no the righteous sleep securely, wise men shall then truly perceive.

4. And the sons of the earth shall understand every word of that book, knowing that their riches cannot save them in the ruin of their crimes.

5. Woe to you, ye sinners, when you shall be afflicted on account of the righteous in the day of the great trouble; shall be burnt in the fire; and be recompensed according to your deeds.

6. Woe to you, ye perverted in heart, who are watchful to obtain an accurate knowledge of evil, and to discover terrors. No one shall assist you.

7. Woe to you, ye sinners; for with the words of your mouths, and with the work of your hands, have you acted impiously; in the flame of a blazing fire shall you be burnt.

8. And now know ye, that the angels shall inquire into your conduct in heaven; of the sun, the moon, and the stars, shall they inquire respecting your sins; for upon earth you exercise jurisdiction over the righteous.

9. Every cloud shall bear witness against you, the snow, the dew, and the rain: for all of them shall be withholden from you, that they may not descend upon you, nor become subservient to your crimes.

10. Now then bring gifts of salutation to the rain; that, not being withholders, it may descend upon you; and to the dew, if it has received from you gold and silver. But when the frost, snow, cold, every snowy wind, and every suffering belonging to them, fall upon you, in those days you will be utterly incapable of standing before them.

Enoch 100

1. Attentively consider heaven, all ye progeny of heaven, and all ye works of the Most High; fear him, nor conduct yourselves criminally before him.

2. If He shut up the windows of heaven, restraining the rain and dew,

that it may not descend upon earth on your account, what will you do?

3. And if He send his wrath upon you, and upon all your deeds, you are not they who can supplicate him; you who utter against his righteousness, language proud and powerful. To you there shall be no peace.

4. Do you not see the commanders of ships, how their vessels are tossed about by the waves, torn to pieces by the winds, and exposed to the greatest peril?

5. That they therefore fear, because their whole property is embarked with them on the ocean; and} that they forbode evil in their hearts, because it may swallow them up, and they may perish in it?

6. Is not the whole sea, all its waters, and all its commotion, the work of him, the Most High; of him who has sealed up all its exertions, and girded it on every side with sand?

7. Is it not at his rebuke dried up, and alarmed; while all its fish with everything contained in it die? And will not you, ye sinners, who are on earth, fear him? Is not He the maker of heaven and earth, and of all things which are in them?

8. And who has given erudition and wisdom to all that move progressive upon the earth, and over the sea?

9. Are not the commanders of ships terrified at the ocean? And shall not sinners be terrified at the Most High?

Enoch 101

1. In those days, when He shall cast the calamity of fire upon you, whither will you fly, and where will you be safe?

2. And when He sends forth his word against you, are you not spared, and terrified?

3. All the luminaries are agitated with great fear; and all the earth is spared, while it trembles, and suffers anxiety.

4. All the angels fulfil the commands received by them, and are desirous of being concealed from the presence of the great Glory; while the children of the earth are alarmed and troubled.

5. But you, ye sinners, are for ever accursed; to you there shall be no peace.

6. Fear not, ye souls of the righteous; but wait with patient hope for the day of your death in righteousness. Grieve not, because your souls descend in great trouble, with groaning, lamentation, and sorrow, to the receptacle of the dead. In your lifetime your bodies have not received a recompense in proportion to your goodness, but in the period of your existence have

sinners existed; in the period of execration and of punishment.

7. And when you die, sinners say concerning you, "As we die, the righteous die. What profit have they in their works? Behold, like us, they expire in sorrow and in darkness. What advantage have they over us? Henceforward are we equal. What will be within their grasp, and what before their eyes for ever? For behold they are dead; and never will they again 3 perceive the light." I say unto you, ye sinners, You have been satiated with meat and drink, with human plunder and rapine, with sin, with the acquisition of wealth and with the sight of good days. Have you not marked the righteous, how their end is in peace? for no oppression is found in them even to the day of their death. They perish, and are as if they were not, while their souls descend in trouble to the receptacle of the dead.

Enoch 102

1. But now I swear to you, ye righteous, by the greatness of his splendour and his glory; by his illustrious kingdom and by his majesty, to you I swear, that I comprehend this mystery; that I have read the tablet of heaven, have seen the writing of the holy Ones, and have discovered what is written and impressed on it concerning you.

2. I have seen that all goodness, joy, and glory has been prepared for you, and been written down for the spirits of them who die eminently righteous and good. To you it shall be given in return for your troubles; and your portion of happiness shall far exceed the portion of the living.

3. The spirits of you who die in righteousness shall exist and rejoice. Their spirits shall exult; and their remembrance shall be before the face of the mighty One from generation to generation. Nor shall they now fear disgrace.

4. Woe to you, sinners, when you die in your sins; and they, who are like you, say respecting you, Blessed are these sinners. They have lived out their whole period; and now they die in happiness and in wealth. Distress and slaughter they knew not while alive; in honour they die; nor ever in their lifetime did judgment overtake them.

5. But has it not been shown to them, that, when to the receptacle of the dead t heir souls shall be made to descend, their evil deeds shall become their greatest torment? Into darkness, into the snare, and into the flame, which shall burn to the great judgment, shall their spirits enter; and the great judgment shall take effect for ever and for ever.

6. Woe to you; for to you there shall be no peace. Neither can you say to the righteous, and to the good who are alive, "In the days of our trouble have we been afflicted; every

species of trouble have we seen, and many evil things have suffered.

7. Our spirits have been consumed, lessened, and diminished.

8. We have perished; nor has there been a possibility of help for us in word or in deed: we have found none, but have been tormented and destroyed.

9. We have not expected to live day after day.

10. We hoped indeed to have been the head;

11. But we have become the tail. We have been afflicted, when we have exerted ourselves; but we have been devoured by sinners and the ungodly; their yoke has been heavy upon us.

12. Those have exercised dominion over us who detest and who goad us; and to those who hate us have we humbled our neck; but they have shown no compassion towards us.

13. We have been desirous of escaping from them, that we might fly away and be at rest; but we have found no place to which we could fly, and be secure from them. We have sought an asylum with princes in our distress, and have cried out to those who were devouring us; but our cry has not been regarded, nor have they been disposed to hear our voice;

14. But rather to assist those who plunder and devour us; those who diminish us, and hide their oppression; who remove not their yoke from us, but devour, enervate, and slay us; who conceal our slaughter, nor remember that they have lifted up their hands against us."

Enoch 103

1. I swear to you, ye righteous, that in heaven the angels record your goodness before the glory of the mighty One.

2. Wait with patient hope; for formerly you have been disgraced with evil and with affliction; but now shall you shine like the luminaries of heaven. You shall be seen, and the gates of heaven shall be opened to you. Your cries have cried for judgment; and it has appeared to you: for an account of all your sufferings shall be required from the princes, and from every one who has assisted your plunderers.

3. Wait with patient hope; nor relinquish your confidence; for great joy shall be yours, like that of the angels in heaven. Conduct yourselves as you may, still you shall not be concealed in the day of the great judgment. You shall not be found like sinners; and eternal condemnation shall be far from you, so long as the world exists.

4. And now fear not, ye righteous, when you see sinners flourishing and prosperous in their ways.

5. Be not associates with them; but keep yourselves at a distance from their oppression; be you associated with the host of heaven. You, ye sinners, say, All our transgressions shall not be taken account of, and be recorded. But all your transgressions shall be recorded daily.

6. And be assured by me, 1 that light and darkness, day and night, behold all your transgressions. Be not impious in your thoughts; lie not; surrender not the word of uprightness; lie not against the word of the holy and the mighty One; glorify not your idols; for all your lying and all your impiety is not for righteousness, but for great crime.

7. Now will I point out a mystery: Many sinners shall turn and transgress against the word of uprightness.

8. They shall speak evil things; they shall utter falsehood; execute great undertakings; and compose books in their own words. But when they shall write all my words correctly in their own languages,

9. They shall neither change or diminish them; but shall write them all correctly; all which from the first I have uttered concerning them.

10. Another mystery also I point out. To the righteous and the wise shall be given books of joy, of integrity, and of great wisdom. To them shall books be given, in which they shall believe;

11. And in which they shall rejoice. And all the righteous shall be rewarded, who from these shall acquire the knowledge of every upright path.

Enoch 104

1. In those days, saith the Lord, they shall call to the children of the earth, and make them listen to their wisdom. Show them that you are their leaders;

2. And that renumeration shall take place over the whole earth; for I and my Son will for ever hold communion with them in the paths of uprightness, while they are still alive. Peace shall be yours. Rejoice, children of integrity, in the truth.

Enoch 105

1. After a time, my son Mathusala took a wife for his son Lamech.

2. She became pregnant by him, and brought forth a child, the flesh of which was as white as snow, and red as a rose; the hair of whose head was white like wool, and long; and whose eyes were beautiful. When he opened them, he illuminated all the house, like the sun; the whole house abounded with light.

3. And when he was taken from the hand of the midwife, opening also his

mouth, he spoke to the Lord of righteousness. Then Lamech his father was afraid of him; and flying away came to his own father Mathusala, and said, I have begotten a son, unlike to other children. He is not human; but, resembling the offspring of the angels of heaven, is of a different nature from ours, being altogether unlike to us.

4. His eyes are bright as the rays of the sun; his countenance glorious, and he looks not as if he belonged to me, but to the angels.

5. I am afraid, lest something miraculous should take place on earth in his days.

6. And now, my father, let me entreat and request you to go to our progenitor Enoch, and to learn from him the truth; for his residence is with the angels.

7. When Mathusala heard the words of his son, he came to me at the extremities of the earth; for he had been informed that I was there: and he cried out.

8. I heard his voice, and went to him saying, Behold, I am here, my son; since thou art come to me.

9. He answered and said, On account of a great event have I come to thee; and on account of a sight difficult to be comprehended have I approached thee.

10. And now, my father, hear me; for to my son Lamech a child has been born, who resembles not him; and whose nature is not like the nature of man. His colour is whiter than snow; he is redder than the rose; the hair of his head is whiter than white wool; his eyes are like the rays of the sun; and when he opened them he illuminated the whole house.

11. When also he was taken from the hand of the midwife, he opened his mouth, and blessed the Lord of heaven.

12. His father Lamech feared, and fled to me, believing not that the child belonged to him, but that he resembled the angels of heaven. And behold I am come to thee, that thou mightest point out to me the truth.

Then I, Enoch, answered and said, The Lord will effect a new thing upon the earth. This have

I explained, and seen in a vision. I have shown thee that in the generations of Jared my father, those who were from heaven disregarded the word of the Lord. Behold they committed crimes; laid aside their class, and intermingled with women. With them also they transgressed; married with them, and begot children.

14. A great destruction therefore shall come upon all the earth; a

deluge, a great destruction, shall take place in one year.

15. This child which is born to you shall survive on the earth, and his three sons shall be saved with him. When all mankind who are on earth shall die, he shall be safe.

16. And his posterity shall beget on the earth giants, not spiritual, but carnal. Upon the earth shall a great punishment be inflicted, and it shall be washed from all corruption. Now therefore inform thy son Lamech, that he who is born is his child in truth; and he shall call his name Noah, for he shall be to you a survivor. He and his children shall be saved from the corruption which shall take place in the world; from all the sin and from all the iniquity which shall be consummated on earth in his days. Afterwards shall greater impiety take place than that which had been before consummated on the earth; for I am acquainted with holy mysteries, which the Lord himself has discovered and explained to me; and which I have read in the tablets of heaven.

17. In them I saw it written, that generation after generation shall transgress, until a righteous race shall arise; until transgression and crime perish from off the earth; until all goodness come upon it.

18. And now, my son, go tell thy son Lamech,

19. That the child which is born is his child in truth; and that there is no deception.

20. When Mathusala heard the word of his father Enoch, who had shown hint every secret thing, he returned with understanding, and called the name of that child Noah; because he was to console the earth on account of all its destruction.

21. Another book, which Enoch wrote for his son Mathusala, and for those who should come after him, and preserve their purity of conduct in the latter days. You, who have laboured, shall wait in those days, until the evil doers be consumed, and the power of the guilty be annihilated. Wait, until sin pass away; for their names shall be blotted out of the holy books; their seed shall be destroyed, and their spirits slain. They shall cry out and lament in the invisible waste, and in the bottomless fire shall they burn. There I perceived, as it were, a cloud which could not be seen through; for from the depth of it I was unable to look upwards. I beheld also a flame of fire blazing brightly, and, as it were, glittering mountains whirled around, and agitated from side to side.

22. Then I inquired of one of the holy angels who was with me, and said, What is this splendid object? For it is not heaven, but a flame of fire alone which blazes; and in it there is the

clamour of exclamation, of woe, and of great suffering.

23. He said, There, into that place which thou beholdest, shall be thrust the spirits of sinners and blasphemers; of those who shall do evil, and who shall pervert all which God has spoken by the mouth of the prophets; all which they ought to do.

For respecting these things there shall be writings and impressions above in heaven, that the angels may read them and know what shall happen both to sinners and to the spirits of the humble; to those who have suffered in their bodies, but have been rewarded by God; who have been injuriously treated by wicked men; who have loved God; who have been attached neither to gold nor silver, nor to any good thing in the world, but have given their bodies to torment;

24. To those who from the period of their birth have not been covetous of earthly riches; but have regarded themselves as a breath passing away.

25. Such has been their conduct; and much has the Lord tried them; and their spirits have been found pure, that they might bless his name. All their blessings have I related in a book; and He has rewarded them; for they have been found to love heaven with an everlasting aspiration. God has said, While they have been trodden down by wicked men, they have heard from them revilings and blasphemies; and have been ignominiously treated, while they were blessing me. And now will I call the spirits of the good from the generation of light, and will change those who have been born in darkness; who have not in their bodies been recompensed with glory, as their faith may have merited.

26. I will bring them into the splendid light of those who love my holy name: and I will place each of them on a throne of glory, of glory peculiarly his own, and they shall be at rest during unnumbered periods. Righteous is the judgment of God;

27. For to the faithful shall he give faith in the habitations of uprightness. They shall see those, who having been born in darkness unto darkness shall be cast; while the righteous shall be at rest. Sinners shall cry out, beholding them, while they exist in splendour and proceed forwards to the days and periods prescribed to them.

Here ends the vision of Enoch the prophet. May the benediction of his prayer, and the gift of his appointed period, be with his beloved! Amen.

402

THE BOOK OF JASHER

Jasher 1

1 And God said, Let us make man in our image, after our likeness, and God created man in his own image.

2 And God formed man from the ground, and he blew into his nostrils the breath of life, and man became a living soul endowed with speech.

3 And the Lord said, It is not good for man to be alone; I will make unto him a helpmeet.

4 And the Lord caused a deep sleep to fall upon Adam, and he slept, and he took away one of his ribs, and he built flesh upon it, and formed it and brought it to Adam, and Adam awoke from his sleep, and behold a woman was standing before him.

5 And he said, This is a bone of my bones and it shall be called woman, for this has been taken from man; and Adam called her name Eve, for she was the mother of all living.

6 And God blessed them and called their names Adam and Eve in the day that he created them, and the Lord God said, Be fruitful and multiply and fill the earth.

7 And the Lord God took Adam and his wife, and he placed them in the garden of Eden to dress it and to keep it; and he commanded them

and said unto them, From every tree of the garden you may eat, but from the tree of the knowledge of good and evil you shall not eat, for in the day that you eat thereof you shall surely die.

8 And when God had blessed and commanded them, he went from them, and Adam and his wife dwelt in the garden according to the command which the Lord had commanded them.

9 And the serpent, which God had created with them in the earth, came to them to incite them to transgress the command of God which he had commanded them.

10 And the serpent enticed and persuaded the woman to eat from the tree of knowledge, and the woman hearkened to the voice of the serpent, and she transgressed the word of God, and took from the tree of the knowledge of good and evil, and she ate, and she took from it and gave also to her husband and he ate.

11 And Adam and his wife transgressed the command of God which he commanded them, and God knew it, and his anger was kindled against them and he cursed them.

12 And the Lord God drove them that day from the garden of Eden, to till the ground from which they were taken, and they went and dwelt at

the east of the garden of Eden; and Adam knew his wife Eve and she bore two sons and three daughters.

13 And she called the name of the first born Cain, saying, I have obtained a man from the Lord, and the name of the other she called Abel, for she said, In vanity we came into the earth, and in vanity we shall be taken from it.

14 And the boys grew up and their father gave them a possession in the land; and Cain was a tiller of the ground, and Abel a keeper of sheep.

15 And it was at the expiration of a few years, that they brought an approximating offering to the Lord, and Cain brought from the fruit of the ground, and Abel brought from the firstlings of his flock from the fat thereof, and God turned and inclined to Abel and his offering, and a fire came down from the Lord from heaven and consumed it.

16 And unto Cain and his offering the Lord did not turn, and he did not incline to it, for he had brought from the inferior fruit of the ground before the Lord, and Cain was jealous against his brother Abel on account of this, and he sought a pretext to slay him.

17 And in some time after, Cain and Abel his brother, went one day into the field to do their work; and they were both in the field, Cain tilling and ploughing his ground, and Abel

feeding his flock; and the flock passed that part which Cain had ploughed in the ground, and it sorely grieved Cain on this account.

18 And Cain approached his brother Abel in anger, and he said unto him, What is there between me and thee, that thou comest to dwell and bring thy flock to feed in my land?

19 And Abel answered his brother Cain and said unto him, What is there between me and thee, that thou shalt eat the flesh of my flock and clothe thyself with their wool?

20 And now therefore, put off the wool of my sheep with which thou hast clothed thyself, and recompense me for their fruit and flesh which thou hast eaten, and when thou shalt have done this, I will then go from thy land as thou hast said?

21 And Cain said to his brother Abel, Surely if I slay thee this day, who will require thy blood from me?

22 And Abel answered Cain, saying, Surely God who has made us in the earth, he will avenge my cause, and he will require my blood from thee shouldst thou slay me, for the Lord is the judge and arbiter, and it is he who will requite man according to his evil, and the wicked man according to the wickedness that he may do upon earth.

23 And now, if thou shouldst slay me here, surely God knoweth thy secret

views, and will judge thee for the evil which thou didst declare to do unto me this day.

24 And when Cain heard the words which Abel his brother had spoken, behold the anger of Cain was kindled against his brother Abel for declaring this thing.

25 And Cain hastened and rose up, and took the iron part of his ploughing instrument, with which he suddenly smote his brother and he slew him, and Cain spilt the blood of his brother Abel upon the earth, and the blood of Abel streamed upon the earth before the flock.

26 And after this Cain repented having slain his brother, and he was sadly grieved, and he wept over him and it vexed him exceedingly.

27 And Cain rose up and dug a hole in the field, wherein he put his brother's body, and he turned the dust over it.

28 And the Lord knew what Cain had done to his brother, and the Lord appeared to Cain and said unto him, Where is Abel thy brother that was with thee?

29 And Cain dissembled, and said, I do not know, am I my brother's keeper? And the Lord said unto him, What hast thou done? The voice of thy brother's blood crieth unto me from the ground where thou hast slain him.

30 For thou hast slain thy brother and hast dissembled before me, and didst imagine in thy heart that I saw thee not, nor knew all thy actions.

31 But thou didst this thing and didst slay thy brother for naught and because he spoke rightly to thee, and now, therefore, cursed be thou from the ground which opened its mouth to receive thy brother's blood from thy hand, and wherein thou didst bury him.

32 And it shall be when thou shalt till it, it shall no more give thee its strength as in the beginning, for thorns and thistles shall the ground produce, and thou shalt be moving and wandering in the earth until the day of thy death.

33 And at that time Cain went out from the presence of the Lord, from the place where he was, and he went moving and wandering in the land toward the east of Eden, he and all belonging to him.

34 And Cain knew his wife in those days, and she conceived and bare a son, and he called his name Enoch, saying, In that time the Lord began to give him rest and quiet in the earth.

35 And at that time Cain also began to build a city: and he built the city and he called the name of the city Enoch, according to the name of his son; for in those days the Lord had given him rest upon the earth, and

he did not move about and wander as in the beginning.

36 And Irad was born to Enoch, and Irad begat Mechuyael and Mechuyael begat Methusael.

Jasher 2

1 And it was in the hundred and thirtieth year of the life of Adam upon the earth, that he again knew Eve his wife, and she conceived and bare a son in his likeness and in his image, and she called his name Seth, saying, Because God has appointed me another seed in the place of Abel, for Cain has slain him.

2 And Seth lived one hundred and five years, and he begat a son; and Seth called the name of his son Enosh, saying, Because in that time the sons of men began to multiply, and to afflict their souls and hearts by transgressing and rebelling against God.

3 And it was in the days of Enosh that the sons of men continued to rebel and transgress against God, to increase the anger of the Lord against the sons of men.

4 And the sons of men went and they served other gods, and they forgot the Lord who had created them in the earth: and in those days the sons of men made images of brass and iron, wood and stone, and they bowed down and served them.

5 And every man made his god and they bowed down to them, and the sons of men forsook the Lord all the days of Enosh and his children; and the anger of the Lord was kindled on account of their works and abominations which they did in the earth.

6 And the Lord caused the waters of the river Gihon to overwhelm them, and he destroyed and consumed them, and he destroyed the third part of the earth, and notwithstanding this, the sons of men did not turn from their evil ways, and their hands were yet extended to do evil in the sight of the Lord.

7 And in those days there was neither sowing nor reaping in the earth; and there was no food for the sons of men and the famine was very great in those days.

8 And the seed which they sowed in those days in the ground became thorns, thistles and briers; for from the days of Adam was this declaration concerning the earth, of the curse of God, which he cursed the earth, on account of the sin which Adam sinned before the Lord.

9 And it was when men continued to rebel and transgress against God, and to corrupt their ways, that the earth also became corrupt.

10 And Enosh lived ninety years and he begat Cainan;

11 And Cainan grew up and he was forty years old, and he became wise and had knowledge and skill in all wisdom, and he reigned over all the sons of men, and he led the sons of men to wisdom and knowledge; for Cainan was a very wise man and had understanding in all wisdom, and with his wisdom he ruled over spirits and demons;

12 And Cainan knew by his wisdom that God would destroy the sons of men for having sinned upon earth, and that the Lord would in the latter days bring upon them the waters of the flood.

13 And in those days Cainan wrote upon tablets of stone, what was to take place in time to come, and he put them in his treasures.

14 And Cainan reigned over the whole earth, and he turned some of the sons of men to the service of God.

15 And when Cainan was seventy years old, he begat three sons and two daughters.

16 And these are the names of the children of Cainan; the name of the first born Mahlallel, the second Enan, and the third Mered, and their sisters were Adah and Zillah; these are the five children of Cainan that were born to him.

17 And Lamech, the son of Methusael, became related to Cainan by marriage, and he took his two daughters for his wives, and Adah conceived and bare a son to Lamech, and she called his name Jabal.

18 And she again conceived and bare a son, and called his name Jubal; and Zillah, her sister, was barren in those days and had no offspring.

19 For in those days the sons of men began to trespass against God, and to transgress the commandments which he had commanded to Adam, to be fruitful and multiply in the earth.

20 And some of the sons of men caused their wives to drink a draught that would render them barren, in order that they might retain their figures and whereby their beautiful appearance might not fade.

21 And when the sons of men caused some of their wives to drink, Zillah drank with them.

22 And the child-bearing women appeared abominable in the sight of their husbands as widows, whilst their husbands lived, for to the barren ones only they were attached.

23 And in the end of days and years, when Zillah became old, the Lord opened her womb.

24 And she conceived and bare a son and she called his name Tubal Cain, saying, After I had withered away have I obtained him from the Almighty God.

25 And she conceived again and bare a daughter, and she called her name Naamah, for she said, After I had withered away have I obtained pleasure and delight.

26 And Lamech was old and advanced in years, and his eyes were dim that he could not see, and Tubal Cain, his son, was leading him and it was one day that Lamech went into the field and Tubal Cain his son was with him, and whilst they were walking in the field, Cain the son of Adam advanced towards them; for Lamech was very old and could not see much, and Tubal Cain his son was very young.

27 And Tubal Cain told his father to draw his bow, and with the arrows he smote Cain, who was yet far off, and he slew him, for he appeared to them to be an animal.

28 And the arrows entered Cain's body although he was distant from them, and he fell to the ground and died.

29 And the Lord requited Cain's evil according to his wickedness, which he had done to his brother Abel, according to the word of the Lord which he had spoken.

30 And it came to pass when Cain had died, that Lamech and Tubal went to see the animal which they had slain, and they saw, and behold Cain their grandfather was fallen dead upon the earth.

31 And Lamech was very much grieved at having done this, and in clapping his hands together he struck his son and caused his death.

32 And the wives of Lamech heard what Lamech had done, and they sought to kill him.

33 And the wives of Lamech hated him from that day, because he slew Cain and Tubal Cain, and the wives of Lamech separated from him, and would not hearken to him in those days.

34 And Lamech came to his wives, and he pressed them to listen to him about this matter.

35 And he said to his wives Adah and Zillah, Hear my voice O wives of Lamech, attend to my words, for now you have imagined and said that I slew a man with my wounds, and a child with my stripes for their having done no violence, but surely know that I am old and grey-headed, and that my eyes are heavy through age, and I did this thing unknowingly.

36 And the wives of Lamech listened to him in this matter, and they returned to him with the advice of their father Adam, but they bore no children to him from that time, knowing that God's anger was increasing in those days against the sons of men, to destroy them with the waters of the flood for their evil doings.

37 And Mahlallel the son of Cainan lived sixty-five years and he begat Jared; and Jared lived sixty-two years and he begat Enoch.

Jasher 3

1 And Enoch lived sixty-five years and he begat Methuselah; and Enoch walked with God after having begot Methuselah, and he served the Lord, and despised the evil ways of men.

2 And the soul of Enoch was wrapped up in the instruction of the Lord, in knowledge and in understanding; and he wisely retired from the sons of men, and secreted himself from them for many days.

3 And it was at the expiration of many years, whilst he was serving the Lord, and praying before him in his house, that an angel of the Lord called to him from Heaven, and he said, Here am I.

4 And he said, Rise, go forth from thy house and from the place where thou dost hide thyself, and appear to the sons of men, in order that thou mayest teach them the way in which they should go and the work which they must accomplish to enter in the ways of God.

5 And Enoch rose up according to the word of the Lord, and went forth from his house, from his place and from the chamber in which he was concealed; and he went to the sons of men and taught them the ways of the Lord, and at that time assembled the sons of men and acquainted them with the instruction of the Lord.

6 And he ordered it to be proclaimed in all places where the sons of men dwelt, saying, Where is the man who wishes to know the ways of the Lord and good works? let him come to Enoch.

7 And all the sons of men then assembled to him, for all who desired this thing went to Enoch, and Enoch reigned over the sons of men according to the word of the Lord, and they came and bowed to him and they heard his word.

8 And the spirit of God was upon Enoch, and he taught all his men the wisdom of God and his ways, and the sons of men served the Lord all the days of Enoch, and they came to hear his wisdom.

9 And all the kings of the sons of men, both first and last, together with their princes and judges, came to Enoch when they heard of his wisdom, and they bowed down to him, and they also required of Enoch to reign over them, to which he consented.

10 And they assembled in all, one hundred and thirty kings and princes, and they made Enoch king over them and they were all under his power and command.

11 And Enoch taught them wisdom, knowledge, and the ways of the

Lord; and he made peace amongst them, and peace was throughout the earth during the life of Enoch.

12 And Enoch reigned over the sons of men two hundred and forty-three years, and he did justice and righteousness with all his people, and he led them in the ways of the Lord.

13 And these are the generations of Enoch, Methuselah, Elisha, and Elimelech, three sons; and their sisters were Melca and Nahmah, and Methuselah lived eighty-seven years and he begat Lamech.

14 And it was in the fifty-sixth year of the life of Lamech when Adam died; nine hundred and thirty years old was he at his death, and his two sons, with Enoch and Methuselah his son, buried him with great pomp, as at the burial of kings, in the cave which God had told him.

15 And in that place all the sons of men made a great mourning and weeping on account of Adam; it has therefore become a custom among the sons of men to this day.

16 And Adam died because he ate of the tree of knowledge; he and his children after him, as the Lord God had spoken.

17 And it was in the year of Adam's death which was the two hundred and forty-third year of the reign of Enoch, in that time Enoch resolved to separate himself from the sons of

men and to secret himself as at first in order to serve the Lord.

18 And Enoch did so, but did not entirely secret himself from them, but kept away from the sons of men three days and then went to them for one day.

19 And during the three days that he was in his chamber, he prayed to, and praised the Lord his God, and the day on which he went and appeared to his subjects he taught them the ways of the Lord, and all they asked him about the Lord he told them.

20 And he did in this manner for many years, and he afterward concealed himself for six days, and appeared to his people one day in seven; and after that once in a month, and then once in a year, until all the kings, princes and sons of men sought for him, and desired again to see the face of Enoch, and to hear his word; but they could not, as all the sons of men were greatly afraid of Enoch, and they feared to approach him on account of the Godlike awe that was seated upon his countenance; therefore no man could look at him, fearing he might be punished and die.

21 And all the kings and princes resolved to assemble the sons of men, and to come to Enoch, thinking that they might all speak to him at the time when he should come forth amongst them, and they did so.

22 And the day came when Enoch went forth and they all assembled and came to him, and Enoch spoke to them the words of the Lord and he taught them wisdom and knowledge, and they bowed down before him and they said, May the king live! May the king live!

23 And in some time after, when the kings and princes and the sons of men were speaking to Enoch, and Enoch was teaching them the ways of God, behold an angel of the Lord then called unto Enoch from heaven, and wished to bring him up to heaven to make him reign there over the sons of God, as he had reigned over the sons of men upon earth.

24 When at that time Enoch heard this he went and assembled all the inhabitants of the earth, and taught them wisdom and knowledge and gave them divine instructions, and he said to them, I have been required to ascend into heaven, I therefore do not know the day of my going.

25 And now therefore I will teach you wisdom and knowledge and will give you instruction before I leave you, how to act upon earth whereby you may live; and he did so.

26 And he taught them wisdom and knowledge, and gave them instruction, and he reproved them, and he placed before them statutes and judgments to do upon earth, and he made peace amongst them, and

he taught them everlasting life, and dwelt with them some time teaching them all these things.

27 And at that time the sons of men were with Enoch, and Enoch was speaking to them, and they lifted up their eyes and the likeness of a great horse descended from heaven, and the horse paced in the air;

28 And they told Enoch what they had seen, and Enoch said to them, On my account does this horse descend upon earth; the time is come when I must go from you and I shall no more be seen by you.

29 And the horse descended at that time and stood before Enoch, and all the sons of men that were with Enoch saw him.

30 And Enoch then again ordered a voice to be proclaimed, saying, Where is the man who delighteth to know the ways of the Lord his God, let him come this day to Enoch before he is taken from us.

31 And all the sons of men assembled and came to Enoch that day; and all the kings of the earth with their princes and counsellors remained with him that day; and Enoch then taught the sons of men wisdom and knowledge, and gave them divine instruction; and he bade them serve the Lord and walk in his ways all the days of their lives, and he continued to make peace amongst them.

32 And it was after this that he rose up and rode upon the horse; and he went forth and all the sons of men went after him, about eight hundred thousand men; and they went with him one day's journey.

33 And the second day he said to them, Return home to your tents, why will you go? perhaps you may die; and some of them went from him, and those that remained went with him six day's journey; and Enoch said to them every day, Return to your tents, lest you may die; but they were not willing to return, and they went with him.

34 And on the sixth day some of the men remained and clung to him, and they said to him, We will go with thee to the place where thou goest; as the Lord liveth, death only shall separate us.

35 And they urged so much to go with him, that he ceased speaking to them; and they went after him and would not return;

36 And when the kings returned they caused a census to be taken, in order to know the number of remaining men that went with Enoch; and it was upon the seventh day that Enoch ascended into heaven in a whirlwind, with horses and chariots of fire.

37 And on the eighth day all the kings that had been with Enoch sent to bring back the number of men that were with Enoch, in that place from which he ascended into heaven.

38 And all those kings went to the place and they found the earth there filled with snow, and upon the snow were large stones of snow, and one said to the other, Come, let us break through the snow and see, perhaps the men that remained with Enoch are dead, and are now under the stones of snow, and they searched but could not find him, for he had ascended into heaven.

Jasher 4

1 And all the days that Enoch lived upon earth, were three hundred and sixty-five years.

2 And when Enoch had ascended into heaven, all the kings of the earth rose and took Methuselah his son and anointed him, and they caused him to reign over them in the place of his father.

3 And Methuselah acted uprightly in the sight of God, as his father Enoch had taught him, and he likewise during the whole of his life taught the sons of men wisdom, knowledge and the fear of God, and he did not turn from the good way either to the right or to the left.

4 But in the latter days of Methuselah, the sons of men turned from the Lord, they corrupted the earth, they robbed and plundered each other, and they rebelled against God and they transgressed, and they

corrupted their ways, and would not hearken to the voice of Methuselah, but rebelled against him.

5 And the Lord was exceedingly wroth against them, and the Lord continued to destroy the seed in those days, so that there was neither sowing nor reaping in the earth.

6 For when they sowed the ground in order that they might obtain food for their support, behold, thorns and thistles were produced which they did not sow.

7 And still the sons of men did not turn from their evil ways, and their hands were still extended to do evil in the sight of God, and they provoked the Lord with their evil ways, and the Lord was very wroth, and repented that he had made man.

8 And he thought to destroy and annihilate them and he did so.

9 In those days when Lamech the son of Methuselah was one hundred and sixty years old, Seth the son of Adam died.

10 And all the days that Seth lived, were nine hundred and twelve years, and he died.

11 And Lamech was one hundred and eighty years old when he took Ashmua, the daughter of Elishaa the son of Enoch his uncle, and she conceived.

12 And at that time the sons of men sowed the ground, and a little food

was produced, yet the sons of men did not turn from their evil ways, and they trespassed and rebelled against God.

13 And the wife of Lamech conceived and bare him a son at that time, at the revolution of the year.

14 And Methuselah called his name Noah, saying, The earth was in his days at rest and free from corruption, and Lamech his father called his name Menachem, saying, This one shall comfort us in our works and miserable toil in the earth, which God had cursed.

15 And the child grew up and was weaned, and he went in the ways of his father Methuselah, perfect and upright with God.

16 And all the sons of men departed from the ways of the Lord in those days as they multiplied upon the face of the earth with sons and daughters, and they taught one another their evil practices and they continued sinning against the Lord.

17 And every man made unto himself a god, and they robbed and plundered every man his neighbor as well as his relative, and they corrupted the earth, and the earth was filled with violence.

18 And their judges and rulers went to the daughters of men and took their wives by force from their husbands according to their choice, and the sons of men in those days

took from the cattle of the earth, the beasts of the field and the fowls of the air, and taught the mixture of animals of one species with the other, in order therewith to provoke the Lord; and God saw the whole earth and it was corrupt, for all flesh had corrupted its ways upon earth, all men and all animals.

19 And the Lord said, I will blot out man that I created from the face of the earth, yea from man to the birds of the air, together with cattle and beasts that are in the field for I repent that I made them.

20 And all men who walked in the ways of the Lord, died in those days, before the Lord brought the evil upon man which he had declared, for this was from the Lord, that they should not see the evil which the Lord spoke of concerning the sons of men.

21 And Noah found grace in the sight of the Lord, and the Lord chose him and his children to raise up seed from them upon the face of the whole earth.

Jasher 5

1 And it was in the eighty-fourth year of the life of Noah, that Enoch the son of Seth died, he was nine hundred and five years old at his death.

2 And in the one hundred and seventy ninth year of the life of Noah, Cainan the son of Enosh died,

and all the days of Cainan were nine hundred and ten years, and he died.

3 And in the two hundred and thirty fourth year of the life of Noah, Mahlallel the son of Cainan died, and the days of Mahlallel were eight hundred and ninety-five years, and he died.

4 And Jared the son of Mahlallel died in those days, in the three hundred and thirty-sixth year of the life of Noah; and all the days of Jared were nine hundred and sixty-two years, and he died.

5 And all who followed the Lord died in those days, before they saw the evil which God declared to do upon earth.

6 And after the lapse of many years, in the four hundred and eightieth year of the life of Noah, when all those men, who followed the Lord had died away from amongst the sons of men, and only Methuselah was then left, God said unto Noah and Methuselah, saying,

7 Speak ye, and proclaim to the sons of men, saying, Thus saith the Lord, return from your evil ways and forsake your works, and the Lord will repent of the evil that he declared to do to you, so that it shall not come to pass.

8 For thus saith the Lord, Behold I give you a period of one hundred and twenty years; if you will turn to me and forsake your evil ways, then

will I also turn away from the evil which I told you, and it shall not exist, saith the Lord.

9 And Noah and Methuselah spoke all the words of the Lord to the sons of men, day after day, constantly speaking to them.

10 But the sons of men would not hearken to them, nor incline their ears to their words, and they were stiffnecked.

11 And the Lord granted them a period of one hundred and twenty years, saying, If they will return, then will God repent of the evil, so as not to destroy the earth.

12 Noah the son of Lamech refrained from taking a wife in those days, to beget children, for he said, Surely now God will destroy the earth, wherefore then shall I beget children?

13 And Noah was a just man, he was perfect in his generation, and the Lord chose him to raise up seed from his seed upon the face of the earth.

14 And the Lord said unto Noah, Take unto thee a wife, and beget children, for I have seen thee righteous before me in this generation.

15 And thou shalt raise up seed, and thy children with thee, in the midst of the earth; and Noah went and took a wife, and he chose Naamah the daughter of Enoch, and she was five hundred and eighty years old.

16 And Noah was four hundred and ninety-eight years old, when he took Naamah for a wife.

17 And Naamah conceived and bare a son, and he called his name Japheth, saying, God has enlarged me in the earth; and she conceived again and bare a son, and he called his name Shem, saying, God has made me a remnant, to raise up seed in the midst of the earth.

18 And Noah was five hundred and two years old when Naamah bare Shem, and the boys grew up and went in the ways of the Lord, in all that Methuselah and Noah their father taught them.

19 And Lamech the father of Noah, died in those days; yet verily he did not go with all his heart in the ways of his father, and he died in the hundred and ninety-fifth year of the life of Noah.

20 And all the days of Lamech were seven hundred and seventy years, and he died.

21 And all the sons of men who knew the Lord, died in that year before the Lord brought evil upon them; for the Lord willed them to die, so as not to behold the evil that God would bring upon their brothers and relatives, as he had so declared to do.

22 In that time, the Lord said to Noah and Methuselah, Stand forth and proclaim to the sons of men all the words that I spoke to you in those days, peradventure they may turn from their evil ways, and I will then repent of the evil and will not bring it.

23 And Noah and Methuselah stood forth, and said in the ears of the sons of men, all that God had spoken concerning them.

24 But the sons of men would not hearken, neither would they incline their ears to all their declarations.

25 And it was after this that the Lord said to Noah, The end of all flesh is come before me, on account of their evil deeds, and behold I will destroy the earth.

26 And do thou take unto thee gopher wood, and go to a certain place and make a large ark, and place it in that spot.

27 And thus shalt thou make it; three hundred cubits its length, fifty cubits broad and thirty cubits high.

28 And thou shalt make unto thee a door, open at its side, and to a cubit thou shalt finish above, and cover it within and without with pitch.

29 And behold I will bring the flood of waters upon the earth, and all flesh be destroyed, from under the heavens all that is upon earth shall perish.

30 And thou and thy household shall go and gather two couple of all living things, male and female, and shall bring them to the ark, to raise up seed from them upon earth.

31 And gather unto thee all food that is eaten by all the animals, that there may be food for thee and for them.

32 And thou shalt choose for thy sons three maidens, from the daughters of men, and they shall be wives to thy sons.

33 And Noah rose up, and he made the ark, in the place where God had commanded him, and Noah did as God had ordered him.

34 In his five hundred and ninety-fifth year Noah commenced to make the ark, and he made the ark in five years, as the Lord had commanded.

35 Then Noah took the three daughters of Eliakim, son of Methuselah, for wives for his sons, as the Lord had commanded Noah.

36 And it was at that time Methuselah the son of Enoch died, nine hundred and sixty years old was he, at his death.

Jasher 6

1 At that time, after the death of Methuselah, the Lord said to Noah, Go thou with thy household into the ark; behold I will gather to thee all the animals of the earth, the beasts of the field and the fowls of the air,

and they shall all come and surround the ark.

2 And thou shalt go and seat thyself by the doors of the ark, and all the beasts, the animals, and the fowls, shall assemble and place themselves before thee, and such of them as shall come and crouch before thee, shalt thou take and deliver into the hands of thy sons, who shall bring them to the ark, and all that will stand before thee thou shalt leave.

3 And the Lord brought this about on the next day, and animals, beasts and fowls came in great multitudes and surrounded the ark.

4 And Noah went and seated himself by the door of the ark, and of all flesh that crouched before him, he brought into the ark, and all that stood before him he left upon earth.

5 And a lioness came, with her two whelps, male and female, and the three crouched before Noah, and the two whelps rose up against the lioness and smote her, and made her flee from her place, and she went away, and they returned to their places, and crouched upon the earth before Noah.

6 And the lioness ran away, and stood in the place of the lions.

7 And Noah saw this, and wondered greatly, and he rose and took the two whelps, and brought them into the ark.

8 And Noah brought into the ark from all living creatures that were upon earth, so that there was none left but which Noah brought into the ark.

9 Two and two came to Noah into the ark, but from the clean animals, and clean fowls, he brought seven couples, as God had commanded him.

10 And all the animals, and beasts, and fowls, were still there, and they surrounded the ark at every place, and the rain had not descended till seven days after.

11 And on that day, the Lord caused the whole earth to shake, and the sun darkened, and the foundations of the world raged, and the whole earth was moved violently, and the lightning flashed, and the thunder roared, and all the fountains in the earth were broken up, such as was not known to the inhabitants before; and God did this mighty act, in order to terrify the sons of men, that there might be no more evil upon earth.

12 And still the sons of men would not return from their evil ways, and they increased the anger of the Lord at that time, and did not even direct their hearts to all this.

13 And at the end of seven days, in the six hundredth year of the life of Noah, the waters of the flood were upon the earth.

14 And all the fountains of the deep were broken up, and the windows of

heaven were opened, and the rain was upon the earth forty days and forty nights.

15 And Noah and his household, and all the living creatures that were with him, came into the ark on account of the waters of the flood, and the Lord shut him in.

16 And all the sons of men that were left upon the earth, became exhausted through evil on account of the rain, for the waters were coming more violently upon the earth, and the animals and beasts were still surrounding the ark.

17 And the sons of men assembled together, about seven hundred thousand men and women, and they came unto Noah to the ark.

18 And they called to Noah, saying, Open for us that we may come to thee in the ark--and wherefore shall we die?

19 And Noah, with a loud voice, answered them from the ark, saying, Have you not all rebelled against the Lord, and said that he does not exist? and therefore the Lord brought upon you this evil, to destroy and cut you off from the face of the earth.

20 Is not this the thing that I spoke to you of one hundred and twenty years back, and you would not hearken to the voice of the Lord, and now do you desire to live upon earth?

21 And they said to Noah, We are ready to return to the Lord; only open for us that we may live and not die.

22 And Noah answered them, saying, Behold now that you see the trouble of your souls, you wish to return to the Lord; why did you not return during these hundred and twenty years, which the Lord granted you as the determined period?

23 But now you come and tell me this on account of the troubles of your souls, now also the Lord will not listen to you, neither will he give ear to you on this day, so that you will not now succeed in your wishes.

24 And the sons of men approached in order to break into the ark, to come in on account of the rain, for they could not bear the rain upon them.

25 And the Lord sent all the beasts and animals that stood round the ark. And the beasts overpowered them and drove them from that place, and every man went his way and they again scattered themselves upon the face of the earth.

26 And the rain was still descending upon the earth, and it descended forty days and forty nights, and the waters prevailed greatly upon the earth; and all flesh that was upon the earth or in the waters died, whether men, animals, beasts, creeping things or birds of the air, and there

only remained Noah and those that were with him in the ark.

27 And the waters prevailed and they greatly increased upon the earth, and they lifted up the ark and it was raised from the earth.

28 And the ark floated upon the face of the waters, and it was tossed upon the waters so that all the living creatures within were turned about like pottage in a cauldron.

29 And great anxiety seized all the living creatures that were in the ark, and the ark was like to be broken.

30 And all the living creatures that were in the ark were terrified, and the lions roared, and the oxen lowed, and the wolves howled, and every living creature in the ark spoke and lamented in its own language, so that their voices reached to a great distance, and Noah and his sons cried and wept in their troubles; they were greatly afraid that they had reached the gates of death.

31 And Noah prayed unto the Lord, and cried unto him on account of this, and he said, O Lord help us, for we have no strength to bear this evil that has encompassed us, for the waves of the waters have surrounded us, mischievous torrents have terrified us, the snares of death have come before us; answer us, O Lord, answer us, light up thy countenance toward us and be gracious to us, redeem us and deliver us.

32 And the Lord hearkened to the voice of Noah, and the Lord remembered him.

33 And a wind passed over the earth, and the waters were still and the ark rested.

34 And the fountains of the deep and the windows of heaven were stopped, and the rain from heaven was restrained.

35 And the waters decreased in those days, and the ark rested upon the mountains of Ararat.

36 And Noah then opened the windows of the ark, and Noah still called out to the Lord at that time and he said, O Lord, who didst form the earth and the heavens and all that are therein, bring forth our souls from this confinement, and from the prison wherein thou hast placed us, for I am much wearied with sighing.

37 And the Lord hearkened to the voice of Noah, and said to him, When though shalt have completed a full year thou shalt then go forth.

38 And at the revolution of the year, when a full year was completed to Noah's dwelling in the ark, the waters were dried from off the earth, and Noah put off the covering of the ark.

39 At that time, on the twenty-seventh day of the second month,

the earth was dry, but Noah and his sons, and those that were with him, did not go out from the ark until the Lord told them.

40 And the day came that the Lord told them to go out, and they all went out from the ark.

41 And they went and returned every one to his way and to his place, and Noah and his sons dwelt in the land that God had told them, and they served the Lord all their days, and the Lord blessed Noah and his sons on their going out from the ark.

42 And he said to them, Be fruitful and fill all the earth; become strong and increase abundantly in the earth and multiply therein.

Jasher 7

1 And these are the names of the sons of Noah: Japheth, Ham and Shem; and children were born to them after the flood, for they had taken wives before the flood.

2 These are the sons of Japheth; Gomer, Magog, Madai, Javan, Tubal, Meshech, and Tiras, seven sons.

3 And the sons of Gomer were Askinaz, Rephath and Tegarmah.

4 And the sons of Magog were Elichanaf and Lubal.

5 And the children of Madai were Achon, Zeelo, Chazoni and Lot.

6 And the sons of Javan were Elisha, Tarshish, Chittim and Dudonim.

7 And the sons of Tubal were Ariphi, Kesed and Taari.

8 And the sons of Meshech were Dedon, Zaron and Shebashni.

9 And the sons of Tiras were Benib, Gera, Lupirion and Gilak; these are the sons of Japheth according to their families, and their numbers in those days were about four hundred and sixty men.

10 And these are the sons of Ham; Cush, Mitzraim, Phut and Canaan, four sons; and the sons of Cush were Seba, Havilah, Sabta, Raama and Satecha, and the sons of Raama were Sheba and Dedan.

11 And the sons of Mitzraim were Lud, Anom and Pathros, Chasloth and Chaphtor.

12 And the sons of Phut were Gebul, Hadan, Benah and Adan.

13 And the sons of Canaan were Zidon, Heth, Amori, Gergashi, Hivi, Arkee, Seni, Arodi, Zimodi and Chamothi.

14 These are the sons of Ham, according to their families, and their numbers in those days were about seven hundred and thirty men.

15 And these are the sons of Shem; Elam, Ashur, Arpachshad, Lud and Aram, five sons; and the sons of

Elam were Shushan, Machul and Harmon.

16 And the sons of Ashar were Mirus and Mokil, and the sons of Arpachshad were Shelach, Anar and Ashcol.

17 And the sons of Lud were Pethor and Bizayon, and the sons of Aram were Uz, Chul, Gather and Mash.

18 These are the sons of Shem, according to their families; and their numbers in those days were about three hundred men.

19 These are the generations of Shem; Shem begat Arpachshad and Arpachshad begat Shelach, and Shelach begat Eber and to Eber were born two children, the name of one was Peleg, for in his days the sons of men were divided, and in the latter days, the earth was divided.

20 And the name of the second was Yoktan, meaning that in his day the lives of the sons of men were diminished and lessened.

21 These are the sons of Yoktan; Almodad, Shelaf, Chazarmoveth, Yerach, Hadurom, Ozel, Diklah, Obal, Abimael, Sheba, Ophir, Havilah and Jobab; all these are the sons of Yoktan.

22 And Peleg his brother begat Yen, and Yen begat Serug, and Serug begat Nahor and Nahor begat Terah, and Terah was thirty-eight years old, and he begat Haran and Nahor.

23 And Cush the son of Ham, the son of Noah, took a wife in those days in his old age, and she bare a son, and they called his name Nimrod, saying, At that time the sons of men again began to rebel and transgress against God, and the child grew up, and his father loved him exceedingly, for he was the son of his old age.

24 And the garments of skin which God made for Adam and his wife, when they went out of the garden, were given to Cush.

25 For after the death of Adam and his wife, the garments were given to Enoch, the son of Jared, and when Enoch was taken up to God, he gave them to Methuselah, his son.

26 And at the death of Methuselah, Noah took them and brought them to the ark, and they were with him until he went out of the ark.

27 And in their going out, Ham stole those garments from Noah his father, and he took them and hid them from his brothers.

28 And when Ham begat his first born Cush, he gave him the garments in secret, and they were with Cush many days.

29 And Cush also concealed them from his sons and brothers, and when Cush had begotten Nimrod, he gave him those garments through his love for him, and Nimrod grew up,

and when he was twenty years old he put on those garments.

30 And Nimrod became strong when he put on the garments, and God gave him might and strength, and he was a mighty hunter in the earth, yea, he was a mighty hunter in the field, and he hunted the animals and he built altars, and he offered upon them the animals before the Lord.

31 And Nimrod strengthened himself, and he rose up from amongst his brethren, and he fought the battles of his brethren against all their enemies round about.

32 And the Lord delivered all the enemies of his brethren in his hands, and God prospered him from time to time in his battles, and he reigned upon earth.

33 Therefore it became current in those days, when a man ushered forth those that he had trained up for battle, he would say to them, Like God did to Nimrod, who was a mighty hunter in the earth, and who succeeded in the battles that prevailed against his brethren, that he delivered them from the hands of their enemies, so may God strengthen us and deliver us this day.

34 And when Nimrod was forty years old, at that time there was a war between his brethren and the children of Japheth, so that they were in the power of their enemies.

35 And Nimrod went forth at that time, and he assembled all the sons of Cush and their families, about four hundred and sixty men, and he hired also from some of his friends and acquaintances about eighty men, and be gave them their hire, and he went with them to battle, and when he was on the road, Nimrod strengthened the hearts of the people that went with him.

36 And he said to them, Do not fear, neither be alarmed, for all our enemies will be delivered into our hands, and you may do with them as you please.

37 And all the men that went were about five hundred, and they fought against their enemies, and they destroyed them, and subdued them, and Nimrod placed standing officers over them in their respective places.

38 And he took some of their children as security, and they were all servants to Nimrod and to his brethren, and Nimrod and all the people that were with him turned homeward.

39 And when Nimrod had joyfully returned from battle, after having conquered his enemies, all his brethren, together with those who knew him before, assembled to make him king over them, and they placed the regal crown upon his head.

40 And he set over his subjects and people, princes, judges, and rulers, as is the custom amongst kings.

41 And he placed Terah the son of Nahor the prince of his host, and he dignified him and elevated him above all his princes.

42 And whilst he was reigning according to his heart's desire, after having conquered all his enemies around, he advised with his counselors to build a city for his palace, and they did so.

43 And they found a large valley opposite to the east, and they built him a large and extensive city, and Nimrod called the name of the city that he built Shinar, for the Lord had vehemently shaken his enemies and destroyed them.

44 And Nimrod dwelt in Shinar, and he reigned securely, and he fought with his enemies and he subdued them, and he prospered in all his battles, and his kingdom became very great.

45 And all nations and tongues heard of his fame, and they gathered themselves to him, and they bowed down to the earth, and they brought him offerings, and he became their lord and king, and they all dwelt with him in the city at Shinar, and Nimrod reigned in the earth over all the sons of Noah, and they were all under his power and counsel.

46 And all the earth was of one tongue and words of union, but Nimrod did not go in the ways of the Lord, and he was more wicked than all the men that were before him, from the days of the flood until those days.

47 And he made gods of wood and stone, and he bowed down to them, and he rebelled against the Lord, and taught all his subjects and the people of the earth his wicked ways; and Mardon his son was more wicked than his father.

48 And every one that heard of the acts of Mardon the son of Nimrod would say, concerning him, From the wicked goeth forth wickedness; therefore it became a proverb in the whole earth, saying, From the wicked goeth forth wickedness, and it was current in the words of men from that time to this.

49 And Terah the son of Nahor, prince of Nimrod's host, was in those days very great in the sight of the king and his subjects, and the king and princes loved him, and they elevated him very high.

50 And Terah took a wife and her name was Amthelo the daughter of Cornebo; and the wife of Terah conceived and bare him a son in those days.

51 Terah was seventy years old when he begat him, and Terah called the name of his son that was born to

him Abram, because the king had raised him in those days, and dignified him above all his princes that were with him.

Jasher 8

1 And it was in the night that Abram was born, that all the servants of Terah, and all the wise men of Nimrod, and his conjurors came and ate and drank in the house of Terah, and they rejoiced with him on that night.

2 And when all the wise men and conjurors went out from the house of Terah, they lifted up their eyes toward heaven that night to look at the stars, and they saw, and behold one very large star came from the east and ran in the heavens, and he swallowed up the four stars from the four sides of the heavens.

3 And all the wise men of the king and his conjurors were astonished at the sight, and the sages understood this matter, and they knew its import.

4 And they said to each other, This only betokens the child that has been born to Terah this night, who will grow up and be fruitful, and multiply, and possess all the earth, he and his children for ever, and he and his seed will slay great kings, and inherit their lands.

5 And the wise men and conjurors went home that night, and in the morning all these wise men and conjurors rose up early, and assembled in an appointed house.

6 And they spoke and said to each other, Behold the sight that we saw last night is hidden from the king, it has not been made known to him.

7 And should this thing get known to the king in the latter days, he will say to us, Why have you concealed this matter from me, and then we shall all suffer death; therefore, now let us go and tell the king the sight which we saw, and the interpretation thereof, and we shall then remain clear.

8 And they did so, and they all went to the king and bowed down to him to the ground, and they said, May the king live, may the king live.

9 We heard that a son was born to Terah the son of Nahor, the prince of thy host, and we yesternight came to his house, and we ate and drank and rejoiced with him that night.

10 And when thy servants went out from the house of Terah, to go to our respective homes to abide there for the night, we lifted up our eyes to heaven, and we saw a great star coming from the east, and the same star ran with great speed, and swallowed up four great stars, from the four sides of the heavens.

11 And thy servants were astonished at the sight which we saw, and were greatly terrified, and we made our judgment upon the sight, and knew by our wisdom the proper

interpretation thereof, that this thing applies to the child that is born to Terah, who will grow up and multiply greatly, and become powerful, and kill all the kings of the earth, and inherit all their lands, he and his seed forever.

12 And now our lord and king, behold we have truly acquainted thee with what we have seen concerning this child.

13 If it seemeth good to the king to give his father value for this child, we will slay him before he shall grow up and increase in the land, and his evil increase against us, that we and our children perish through his evil.

14 And the king heard their words and they seemed good in his sight, and he sent and called for Terah, and Terah came before the king.

15 And the king said to Terah, I have been told that a son was yesternight born to thee, and after this manner was observed in the heavens at his birth.

16 And now therefore give me the child, that we may slay him before his evil springs up against us, and I will give thee for his value, thy house full of silver and gold.

17 And Terah answered the king and said to him: My Lord and king, I have heard thy words, and thy servant shall do all that his king desireth.

18 But my lord and king, I will tell thee what happened to me yesternight, that I may see what advice the king will give his servant, and then I will answer the king upon what he has just spoken; and the king said, Speak.

19 And Terah said to the king, Ayon, son of Mored, came to me yesternight, saying,

20 Give unto me the great and beautiful horse that the king gave thee, and I will give thee silver and gold, and straw and provender for its value; and I said to him, Wait till I see the king concerning thy words, and behold whatever the king saith, that will I do.

21 And now my lord and king, behold I have made this thing known to thee, and the advice which my king will give unto his servant, that will I follow.

22 And the king heard the words of Terah, and his anger was kindled and he considered him in the light of a fool.

23 And the king answered Terah, and he said to him, Art thou so silly, ignorant, or deficient in understanding, to do this thing, to give thy beautiful horse for silver and gold or even for straw and provender?

24 Art thou so short of silver and gold, that thou shouldst do this thing, because thou canst not obtain straw

and provender to feed thy horse? and what is silver and gold to thee, or straw and provender, that thou shouldst give away that fine horse which I gave thee, like which there is none to be had on the whole earth?

25 And the king left off speaking, and Terah answered the king, saying, Like unto this has the king spoken to his servant;

26 I beseech thee, my lord and king, what is this which thou didst say unto me, saying, Give thy son that we may slay him, and I will give thee silver and gold for his value; what shall I do with silver and gold after the death of my son? who shall inherit me? surely then at my death, the silver and gold will return to my king who gave it.

27 And when the king heard the words of Terah, and the parable which he brought concerning the king, it grieved him greatly and he was vexed at this thing, and his anger burned within him.

28 And Terah saw that the anger of the king was kindled against him, and he answered the king, saying, All that I have is in the king's power; whatever the king desireth to do to his servant, that let him do, yea, even my son, he is in the king's power, without value in exchange, he and his two brothers that are older than he.

29 And the king said to Terah, No, but I will purchase thy younger son for a price.

30 And Terah answered the king, saying, I beseech thee my lord and king to let thy servant speak a word before thee, and let the king hear the word of his servant, and Terah said, Let my king give me three days' time till I consider this matter within myself, and consult with my family concerning the words of my king; and he pressed the king greatly to agree to this.

31 And the king hearkened to Terah, and he did so and he gave him three days' time, and Terah went out from the king's presence, and he came home to his family and spoke to them all the words of the king; and the people were greatly afraid.

32 And it was in the third day that the king sent to Terah, saying, Send me thy son for a price as I spoke to thee; and shouldst thou not do this, I will send and slay all thou hast in thy house, so that thou shalt not even have a dog remaining.

33 And Terah hastened, (as the thing was urgent from the king), and he took a child from one of his servants, which his handmaid had born to him that day, and Terah brought the child to the king and received value for him.

34 And the Lord was with Terah in this matter, that Nimrod might not

cause Abram's death, and the king took the child from Terah and with all his might dashed his head to the ground, for he thought it had been Abram; and this was concealed from him from that day, and it was forgotten by the king, as it was the will of Providence not to suffer Abram's death.

35 And Terah took Abram his son secretly, together with his mother and nurse, and he concealed them in a cave, and he brought them their provisions monthly.

36 And the Lord was with Abram in the cave and he grew up, and Abram was in the cave ten years, and the king and his princes, soothsayers and sages, thought that the king had killed Abram.

Jasher 9

1 And Haran, the son of Terah, Abram's oldest brother, took a wife in those days.

2 Haran was thirty-nine years old when he took her; and the wife of Haran conceived and bare a son, and he called his name Lot.

3 And she conceived again and bare a daughter, and she called her name Milca; and she again conceived and bare a daughter, and she called her name Sarai.

4 Haran was forty-two years old when he begat Sarai, which was in the tenth year of the life of Abram;

and in those days Abram and his mother and nurse went out from the cave, as the king and his subjects had forgotten the affair of Abram.

5 And when Abram came out from the cave, he went to Noah and his son Shem, and he remained with them to learn the instruction of the Lord and his ways, and no man knew where Abram was, and Abram served Noah and Shem his son for a long time.

6 And Abram was in Noah's house thirty-nine years, and Abram knew the Lord from three years old, and he went in the ways of the Lord until the day of his death, as Noah and his son Shem had taught him; and all the sons of the earth in those days greatly transgressed against the Lord, and they rebelled against him and they served other gods, and they forgot the Lord who had created them in the earth; and the inhabitants of the earth made unto themselves, at that time, every man his god; gods of wood and stone which could neither speak, hear, nor deliver, and the sons of men served them and they became their gods.

7 And the king and all his servants, and Terah with all his household were then the first of those that served gods of wood and stone.

20

8 And Terah had twelve gods of large size, made of wood and stone,

after the twelve months of the year, and he served each one monthly, and every month Terah would bring his meat offering and drink offering to his gods; thus did Terah all the days.

9 And all that generation were wicked in the sight of the Lord, and they thus made every man his god, but they forsook the Lord who had created them.

10 And there was not a man found in those days in the whole earth, who knew the Lord (for they served each man his own God) except Noah and his household, and all those who were under his counsel knew the Lord in those days.

11 And Abram the son of Terah was waxing great in those days in the house of Noah, and no man knew it, and the Lord was with him.

12 And the Lord gave Abram an understanding heart, and he knew all the works of that generation were vain, and that all their gods were vain and were of no avail.

13 And Abram saw the sun shining upon the earth, and Abram said unto himself Surely now this sun that shines upon the earth is God, and him will I serve.

14 And Abram served the sun in that day and he prayed to him, and when evening came the sun set as usual, and Abram said within himself, Surely this cannot be God?

15 And Abram still continued to speak within himself, Who is he who made the heavens and the earth? who created upon earth? where is he?

16 And night darkened over him, and he lifted up his eyes toward the west, north, south, and east, and he saw that the sun had vanished from the earth, and the day became dark.

17 And Abram saw the stars and moon before him, and he said, Surely this is the God who created the whole earth as well as man, and behold these his servants are gods around him: and Abram served the moon and prayed to it all that night.

18 And in the morning when it was light and the sun shone upon the earth as usual, Abram saw all the things that the Lord God had made upon earth.

19 And Abram said unto himself Surely these are not gods that made the earth and all mankind, but these are the servants of God, and Abram remained in the house of Noah and there knew the Lord and his ways' and he served the Lord all the days of his life, and all that generation forgot the Lord, and served other gods of wood and stone, and rebelled all their days.

20 And king Nimrod reigned securely, and all the earth was under his control, and all the earth was of one tongue and words of union.

21 And all the princes of Nimrod and his great men took counsel together; Phut, Mitzraim, Cush and Canaan with their families, and they said to each other, Come let us build ourselves a city and in it a strong tower, and its top reaching heaven, and we will make ourselves famed, so that we may reign upon the whole world, in order that the evil of our enemies may cease from us, that we may reign mightily over them, and that we may not become scattered over the earth on account of their wars.

22 And they all went before the king, and they told the king these words, and the king agreed with them in this affair, and he did so.

23 And all the families assembled consisting of about six hundred thousand men, and they went to seek an extensive piece of ground to build the city and the tower, and they sought in the whole earth and they found none like one valley at the east of the land of Shinar, about two days' walk, and they journeyed there and they dwelt there.

24 And they began to make bricks and burn fires to build the city and the tower that they had imagined to complete.

25 And the building of the tower was unto them a transgression and a sin, and they began to build it, and whilst they were building against the Lord God of heaven, they imagined in

their hearts to war against him and to ascend into heaven.

26 And all these people and all the families divided themselves in three parts; the first said We will ascend into heaven and fight against him; the second said, We will ascend to heaven and place our own gods there and serve them; and the third part said, We will ascend to heaven and smite him with bows and spears; and God knew all their works and all their evil thoughts, and he saw the city and the tower which they were building.

27 And when they were building they built themselves a great city and a very high and strong tower; and on account of its height the mortar and bricks did not reach the builders in their ascent to it, until those who went up had completed a full year, and after that, they reached to the builders and gave them the mortar and the bricks; thus was it done daily.

28 And behold these ascended and others descended the whole day; and if a brick should fall from their hands and get broken, they would all weep over it, and if a man fell and died, none of them would look at him.

29 And the Lord knew their thoughts, and it came to pass when they were building they cast the arrows toward the heavens, and all the arrows fell upon them filled with blood, and

when they saw them they said to each other, Surely we have slain all those that are in heaven.

30 For this was from the Lord in order to cause them to err, and in order; to destroy them from off the face of the ground.

31 And they built the tower and the city, and they did this thing daily until many days and years were elapsed.

32 And God said to the seventy angels who stood foremost before him, to those who were near to him, saying, Come let us descend and confuse their tongues, that one man shall not understand the language of his neighbor, and they did so unto them.

33 And from that day following, they forgot each man his neighbor's tongue, and they could not understand to speak in one tongue, and when the builder took from the hands of his neighbor lime or stone which he did not order, the builder would cast it away and throw it upon his neighbor, that he would die.

34 And they did so many days, and they killed many of them in this manner.

35 And the Lord smote the three divisions that were there, and he punished them according to their works and designs; those who said, We will ascend to heaven and serve our gods, became like apes and elephants; and those who said, We will smite the heaven with arrows, the Lord killed them, one man through the hand of his neighbor; and the third division of those who said, We will ascend to heaven and fight against him, the Lord scattered them throughout the earth.

36 And those who were left amongst them, when they knew and understood the evil which was coming upon them, they forsook the building, and they also became scattered upon the face of the whole earth.

37 And they ceased building the city and the tower; therefore he called that place Babel, for there the Lord confounded the Language of the whole earth; behold it was at the east of the land of Shinar.

38 And as to the tower which the sons of men built, the earth opened its mouth and swallowed up one third part thereof, and a fire also descended from heaven and burned another third, and the other third is left to this day, and it is of that part which was aloft, and its circumference is three days' walk.

39 And many of the sons of men died in that tower, a people without number.

Jasher 10

1 And Peleg the son of Eber died in those days, in the forty-eighth year of the life of Abram son of Terah, and

430

all the days of Peleg were two hundred and thirty-nine years.

2 And when the Lord had scattered the sons of men on account of their sin at the tower, behold they spread forth into many divisions, and all the sons of men were dispersed into the four corners of the earth.

3 And all the families became each according to its language, its land, or its city.

4 And the sons of men built many cities according to their families, in all the places where they went, and throughout the earth where the Lord had scattered them.

5 And some of them built cities in places from which they were afterward extirpated, and they called these cities after their own names, or the names of their children, or after their particular occurrences.

6 And the sons of Japheth the son of Noah went and built themselves cities in the places where they were scattered, and they called all their cities after their names, and the sons of Japheth were divided upon the face of the earth into many divisions and languages.

7 And these are the sons of Japheth according to their families, Gomer, Magog, Medai, Javan, Tubal, Meshech and Tiras; these are the children of Japheth according to their generations.

8 And the children of Gomer, according to their cities, were the Francum, who dwell in the land of Franza, by the river Franza, by the river Senah.

9 And the children of Rephath are the Bartonim, who dwell in the land of Bartonia by the river Ledah, which empties its waters in the great sea Gihon, that is, oceanus.

10 And the children of Tugarma are ten families, and these are their names: Buzar, Parzunac, Balgar, Elicanum, Ragbib, Tarki, Bid, Zebuc, Ongal and Tilmaz; all these spread and rested in the north and built themselves cities.

11 And they called their cities after their own names, those are they who abide by the rivers Hithlah and Italac unto this day.

12 But the families of Angoli, Balgar and Parzunac, they dwell by the great river Dubnee; and the names of their cities are also according to their own names.

13 And the children of Javan are the Javanim who dwell in the land of Makdonia, and the children of Medaiare are the Orelum that dwell in the land of Curson, and the children of Tubal are those that dwell in the land of Tuskanah by the river Pashiah.

14 And the children of Meshech are the Shibashni and the children of Tiras are Rushash, Cushni, and

Ongolis; all these went and built themselves cities; those are the cities that are situate by the sea Jabus by the river Cura, which empties itself in the river Tragan.

15 And the children of Elishah are the Almanim, and they also went and built themselves cities; those are the cities situate between the mountains of Job and Shibathmo; and of them were the people of Lumbardi who dwell opposite the mountains of Job and Shibathmo, and they conquered the land of Italia and remained there unto this day.

16 And the children of Chittim are the Romim who dwell in the valley of Canopia by the river Tibreu.

17 And the children of Dudonim are those who dwell in the cities of the sea Gihon, in the land of Bordna.

18 These are the families of the children of Japheth according to their cities and languages, when they were scattered after the tower, and they called their cities after their names and occurrences; and these are the names of all their cities according to their families, which they built in those days after the tower.

19 And the children of Ham were Cush, Mitzraim, Phut and Canaan according to their generation and cities.

20 All these went and built themselves cities as they found fit places for them, and they called their cities after the names of their fathers Cush, Mitzraim, Phut and Canaan.

21 And the children of Mitzraim are the Ludim, Anamim, Lehabim, Naphtuchim, Pathrusim, Casluchim and Caphturim, seven families.

22 All these dwell by the river Sihor, that is the brook of Egypt, and they built themselves cities and called them after their own names.

23 And the children of Pathros and Casloch intermarried together, and from them went forth the Pelishtim, the Azathim, and the Gerarim, the Githim and the Ekronim, in all five families; these also built themselves cities, and they called their cities after the names of their fathers unto this day.

24 And the children of Canaan also built themselves cities, and they called their cities after their names, eleven cities and others without number.

25 And four men from the family of Ham went to the land of the plain; these are the names of the four men, Sodom, Gomorrah, Admah and Zeboyim.

26 And these men built themselves four cities in the land of the plain, and they called the names of their cities after their own names.

27 And they and their children and all belonging to them dwelt in those

cities, and they were fruitful and multiplied greatly and dwelt peaceably.

28 And Seir the son of Hur, son of Hivi, son of Canaan, went and found a valley opposite to Mount Paran, and he built a city there, and he and his seven sons and his household dwelt there, and he called the city which he built Seir, according to his name; that is the land of Seir unto this day.

29 These are the families of the children of Ham, according to their languages and cities, when they were scattered to their countries after the tower.

30 And some of the children of Shem son of Noah, father of all the children of Eber, also went and built themselves cities in the places wherein they were scattered, and they called their cities after their names.

31 And the sons of Shem were Elam, Ashur, Arpachshad, Lud and Aram, and they built themselves cities and called the names of all their cities after their names.

32 And Ashur son of Shem and his children and household went forth at that time, a very large body of them, and they went to a distant land that they found, and they met with a very extensive valley in the land that they went to, and they built themselves four cities, and they called them after their own names and occurrences.

33 And these are the names of the cities which the children of Ashur built, Ninevah, Resen, Calach and Rehobother; and the children of Ashur dwell there unto this day.

34 And the children of Aram also went and built themselves a city, and they called the name of the city Uz after their eldest brother, and they dwell therein; that is the land of Uz to this day.

35 And in the second year after the tower a man from the house of Ashur, whose name was Bela, went from the land of Ninevah to sojourn with his household wherever he could find a place; and they came until opposite the cities of the plain against Sodom, and they dwelt there.

36 And the man rose up and built there a small city, and called its name Bela, after his name; that is the land of Zoar unto this day.

37 And these are the families of the children of Shem according to their language and cities, after they were scattered upon the earth after the tower.

38 And every kingdom, city, and family of the families of the children of Noah built themselves many cities after this.

39 And they established governments in all their cities, in order to be regulated by their orders; so did all the families of the children of Noah forever.

Jasher 11

1 And Nimrod son of Cush was still in the land of Shinar, and he reigned over it and dwelt there, and he built cities in the land of Shinar.

2 And these are the names of the four cities which he built, and he called their names after the occurrences that happened to them in the building of the tower.

3 And he called the first Babel, saying, Because the Lord there confounded the language of the whole earth; and the name of the second he called Erech, because from there God dispersed them.

4 And the third he called Eched, saying there was a great battle at that place; and the fourth he called Calnah, because his princes and mighty men were consumed there, and they vexed the Lord, they rebelled and transgressed against him.

5 And when Nimrod had built these cities in the land of Shinar, he placed in them the remainder of his people, his princes and his mighty men that were left in his kingdom.

6 And Nimrod dwelt in Babel, and he there renewed his reign over the rest of his subjects, and he reigned securely, and the subjects and princes of Nimrod called his name Amraphel, saying that at the tower his princes and men fell through his means.

7 And notwithstanding this, Nimrod did not return to the Lord, and he continued in wickedness and teaching wickedness to the sons of men; and Mardon, his son, was worse than his father, and continued to add to the abominations of his father.

8 And he caused the sons of men to sin, therefore it is said, From the wicked goeth forth wickedness.

9 At that time there was war between the families of the children of Ham, as they were dwelling in the cities which they had built.

10 And Chedorlaomer, king of Elam, went away from the families of the children of Ham, and he fought with them and he subdued them, and he went to the five cities of the plain and he fought against them and he subdued them, and they were under his control.

11 And they served him twelve years, and they gave him a yearly tax.

12 At that time died Nahor, son of Serug, in the forty-ninth year of the life of Abram son of Terah.

13 And in the fiftieth year of the life of Abram son of Terah, Abram came forth from the house of Noah, and went to his father's house.

14 And Abram knew the Lord, and he went in his ways and instructions, and the Lord his God was with him.

15 And Terah his father was in those days, still captain of the host of king Nimrod, and he still followed strange gods.

16 And Abram came to his father's house and saw twelve gods standing there in their temples, and the anger of Abram was kindled when he saw these images in his father's house.

17 And Abram said, As the Lord liveth these images shall not remain in my father's house; so shall the Lord who created me do unto me if in three days' time I do not break them all.

18 And Abram went from them, and his anger burned within him. And Abram hastened and went from the chamber to his father's outer court, and he found his father sitting in the court, and all his servants with him, and Abram came and sat before him.

19 And Abram asked his father, saying, Father, tell me where is God who created heaven and earth, and all the sons of men upon earth, and who created thee and me. And Terah answered his son Abram and said, Behold those who created us are all with us in the house.

20 And Abram said to his father, My lord, shew them to me I pray thee; and Terah brought Abram into the chamber of the inner court, and Abram saw, and behold the whole room was full of gods of wood and stone, twelve great images and others less than they without number.

21 And Terah said to his son, Behold these are they which made all thou seest upon earth, and which created me and thee, and all mankind.

22 And Terah bowed down to his gods, and he then went away from them, and Abram, his son, went away with him.

23 And when Abram had gone from them he went to his mother and sat before her, and he said to his mother, Behold, my father has shown me those who made heaven and earth, and all the sons of men.

24 Now, therefore, hasten and fetch a kid from the flock, and make of it savory meat, that I may bring it to my father's gods as an offering for them to eat; perhaps I may thereby become acceptable to them.

25 And his mother did so, and she fetched a kid, and made savory meat thereof, and brought it to Abram, and Abram took the savory meat from his mother and brought it before his father's gods, and he drew nigh to them that they might eat; and Terah his father, did not know of it.

26 And Abram saw on the day when he was sitting amongst them, that they had no voice, no hearing, no motion, and not one of them could stretch forth his hand to eat.

27 And Abram mocked them, and said, Surely the savory meat that I prepared has not pleased them, or perhaps it was too little for them, and for that reason they would not eat; therefore tomorrow I will prepare fresh savory meat, better and more plentiful than this, in order that I may see the result.

28 And it was on the next day that Abram directed his mother concerning the savory meat, and his mother rose and fetched three fine kids from the flock, and she made of them some excellent savory meat, such as her son was fond of, and she gave it to her son Abram; and Terah his father did not know of it.

29 And Abram took the savory meat from his mother, and brought it before his father's gods into the chamber; and he came nigh unto them that they might eat, and he placed it before them, and Abram sat before them all day, thinking perhaps they might eat.

30 And Abram viewed them, and behold they had neither voice nor hearing, nor did one of them stretch forth his hand to the meat to eat.

31 And in the evening of that day in that house Abram was clothed with the spirit of God.

32 And he called out and said, Wo unto my father and this wicked generation, whose hearts are all inclined to vanity, who serve these idols of wood and stone which can neither eat, smell, hear nor speak, who have mouths without speech, eyes without sight, ears without hearing, hands without feeling, and legs which cannot move; like them are those that made them and that trust in them.

33 And when Abram saw all these things his anger was kindled against his father, and he hastened and took a hatchet in his hand, and came unto the chamber of the gods, and he broke all his father's gods.

34 And when he had done breaking the images, he placed the hatchet in the hand of the great god which was there before them, and he went out; and Terah his father came home, for he had heard at the door the sound of the striking of the hatchet; so Terah came into the house to know what this was about.

35 And Terah, having heard the noise of the hatchet in the room of images, ran to the room to the images, and he met Abram going out.

36 And Terah entered the room and found all the idols fallen down and

broken, and the hatchet in the hand of the largest, which was not broken, and the savory meat which Abram his son had made was still before them.

37 And when Terah saw this his anger was greatly kindled, and he hastened and went from the room to Abram.

38 And he found Abram his son still sitting in the house; and he said to him, What is this work thou hast done to my gods?

39 And Abram answered Terah his father and he said, Not so my lord, for I brought savory meat before them, and when I came nigh to them with the meat that they might eat, they all at once stretched forth their hands to eat before the great one had put forth his hand to eat.

40 And the large one saw their works that they did before him, and his anger was violently kindled against them, and he went and took the hatchet that was in the house and came to them and broke them all, and behold the hatchet is yet in his hand as thou seest.

41 And Terah's anger was kindled against his son Abram, when he spoke this; and Terah said to Abram his son in his anger, What is this tale that thou hast told? Thou speakest lies to me.

42 Is there in these gods spirit, soul or power to do all thou hast told me?

Are they not wood and stone, and have I not myself made them, and canst thou speak such lies, saying that the large god that was with them smote them? It is thou that didst place the hatchet in his hands, and then sayest he smote them all.

43 And Abram answered his father and said to him, And how canst thou then serve these idols in whom there is no power to do any thing? Can those idols in which thou trustest deliver thee? can they hear thy prayers when thou callest upon them? can they deliver thee from the hands of thy enemies, or will they fight thy battles for thee against thy enemies, that thou shouldst serve wood and stone which can neither speak nor hear?

44 And now surely it is not good for thee nor for the sons of men that are connected with thee, to do these things; are you so silly, so foolish or so short of understanding that you will serve wood and stone, and do after this manner?

45 And forget the Lord God who made heaven and earth, and who created you in the earth, and thereby bring a great evil upon your souls in this matter by serving stone and wood?

46 Did not our fathers in days of old sin in this matter, and the Lord God of the universe brought the waters of the flood upon them and destroyed the whole earth?

47 And how can you continue to do this and serve gods of wood and stone, who cannot hear, or speak, or deliver you from oppression, thereby bringing down the anger of the God of the universe upon you?

48 Now therefore my father refrain from this, and bring not evil upon thy soul and the souls of thy household.

49 And Abram hastened and sprang from before his father, and took the hatchet from his father's largest idol, with which Abram broke it and ran away.

50 And Terah, seeing all that Abram had done, hastened to go from his house, and he went to the king and he came before Nimrod and stood before him, and he bowed down to the king; and the king said, What dost thou want?

51 And he said, I beseech thee my lord, to hear me--Now fifty years back a child was born to me, and thus has he done to my gods and thus has he spoken; and now therefore, my lord and king, send for him that he may come before thee, and judge him according to the law, that we may be delivered from his evil.

52 And the king sent three men of his servants, and they went and brought Abram before the king. And Nimrod and all his princes and servants were that day sitting before him, and Terah sat also before them.

53 And the king said to Abram, What is this that thou hast done to thy father and to his gods? And Abram answered the king in the words that he spoke to his father, and he said, The large god that was with them in the house did to them what thou hast heard.

54 And the king said to Abram, Had they power to speak and eat and do as thou hast said? And Abram answered the king, saying, And if there be no power in them why dost thou serve them and cause the sons of men to err through thy follies?

55 Dost thou imagine that they can deliver thee or do anything small or great, that thou shouldst serve them? And why wilt thou not sense the God of the whole universe, who created thee and in whose power it is to kill and keep alive?

56 0 foolish, simple, and ignorant king, woe unto thee forever.

57 I thought thou wouldst teach thy servants the upright way, but thou hast not done this, but hast filled the whole earth with thy sins and the sins of thy people who have followed thy ways.

58 Dost thou not know, or hast thou not heard, that this evil which thou doest, our ancestors sinned therein in days of old, and the eternal God brought the waters of the flood upon them and destroyed them all, and also destroyed the whole earth on

their account? And wilt thou and thy people rise up now and do like unto this work, in order to bring down the anger of the Lord God of the universe, and to bring evil upon thee and the whole earth?

59 Now therefore put away this evil deed which thou doest, and serve the God of the universe, as thy soul is in his hands, and then it will be well with thee.

60 And if thy wicked heart will not hearken to my words to cause thee to forsake thy evil ways, and to serve the eternal God, then wilt thou die in shame in the latter days, thou, thy people and all who are connected with thee, hearing thy words or walking in thy evil ways.

61 And when Abram had ceased speaking before the king and princes, Abram lifted up his eyes to the heavens, and he said, The Lord seeth all the wicked, and he will judge them.

Jasher 12

1 And when the king heard the words of Abram he ordered him to be put into prison; and Abram was ten days in prison.

2 And at the end of those days the king ordered that all the kings, princes and governors of different provinces and the sages should come before him, and they sat before him, and Abram was still in the house of confinement.

3 And the king said to the princes and sages, Have you heard what Abram, the son of Terah, has done to his father? Thus has he done to him, and I ordered him to be brought before me, and thus has he spoken; his heart did not misgive him, neither did he stir in my presence, and behold now he is confined in the prison.

4 And therefore decide what judgment is due to this man who reviled the king; who spoke and did all the things that you heard.

5 And they all answered the king saying, The man who revileth the king should be hanged upon a tree; but having done all the things that he said, and having despised our gods, he must therefore be burned to death, for this is the law in this matter.

6 If it pleaseth the king to do this, let him order his servants to kindle a fire both night and day in thy brick furnace, and then we will cast this man into it. And the king did so, and he commanded his servants that they should prepare a fire for three days and three nights in the king's furnace, that is in Casdim; and the king ordered them to take Abram from prison and bring him out to be burned.

7 And all the king's servants, princes, lords, governors, and judges, and all the inhabitants of the land, about

nine hundred thousand men, stood opposite the furnace to see Abram.

8 And all the women and little ones crowded upon the roofs and towers to see what was doing with Abram, and they all stood together at a distance; and there was not a man left that did not come on that day to behold the scene.

9 And when Abram was come, the conjurors of the king and the sages saw Abram, and they cried out to the king, saying, Our sovereign lord, surely this is the man whom we know to have been the child at whose birth the great star swallowed the four stars, which we declared to the king now fifty years since.

10 And behold now his father has also transgressed thy commands, and mocked thee by bringing thee another child, which thou didst kill.

11 And when the king heard their words, he was exceedingly wroth, and he ordered Terah to be brought before him.

12 And the king said, Hast thou heard what the conjurors have spoken? Now tell me truly, how didst thou; and if thou shalt speak truth thou shalt be acquitted.

13 And seeing that the king's anger was so much kindled, Terah said to the king, My lord and king, thou hast heard the truth, and what the sages have spoken is right. And the king said, How couldst thou do this thing,

to transgress my orders and to give me a child that thou didst not beget, and to take value for him?

14 And Terah answered the king, Because my tender feelings were excited for my son, at that time, and I took a son of my handmaid, and I brought him to the king.

15 And the king said Who advised thee to this? Tell me, do not hide aught from me, and then thou shalt not die.

16 And Terah was greatly terrified in the king's presence, and he said to the king, It was Haran my eldest son who advised me to this; and Haran was in those days that Abram was born, two and thirty years old.

17 But Haran did not advise his father to anything, for Terah said this to the king in order to deliver his soul from the king, for he feared greatly; and the king said to Terah, Haran thy son who advised thee to this shall die through fire with Abram; for the sentence of death is upon him for having rebelled against the king's desire in doing this thing.

18 And Haran at that time felt inclined to follow the ways of Abram, but he kept it within himself.

19 And Haran said in his heart, Behold now the king has seized Abram on account of these things which Abram did, and it shall come to pass, that if Abram prevail over

the king I will follow him, but if the king prevail I will go after the king.

20 And when Terah had spoken this to the king concerning Haran his son, the king ordered Haran to be seized with Abram.

21 And they brought them both, Abram and Haran his brother, to cast them into the fire; and all the inhabitants of the land and the king's servants and princes and all the women and little ones were there, standing that day over them.

22 And the king's servants took Abram and his brother, and they stripped them of all their clothes excepting their lower garments which were upon them.

23 And they bound their hands and feet with linen cords, and the servants of the king lifted them up and cast them both into the furnace.

24 And the Lord loved Abram and he had compassion over him, and the Lord came down and delivered Abram from the fire and he was not burned.

25 But all the cords with which they bound him were burned, while Abram remained and walked about in the fire.

26 And Haran died when they had cast him into the fire, and he was burned to ashes, for his heart was not perfect with the Lord; and those men who cast him into the fire, the flame of the fire spread over them, and they were burned, and twelve men of them died.

27 And Abram walked in the midst of the fire three days and three nights, and all the servants of the king saw him walking in the fire, and they came and told the king, saying, Behold we have seen Abram walking about in the midst of the fire, and even the lower garments which are upon him are not burned, but the cord with which he was bound is burned.

28 And when the king heard their words his heart fainted and he would not believe them; so he sent other faithful princes to see this matter, and they went and saw it and told it to the king; and the king rose to go and see it, and he saw Abram walking to and fro in the midst of the fire, and he saw Haran's body burned, and the king wondered greatly.

29 And the king ordered Abram to be taken out from the fire; and his servants approached to take him out and they could not, for the fire was round about and the flame ascending toward them from the furnace.

30 And the king's servants fled from it, and the king rebuked them, saying, Make haste and bring Abram out of the fire that you shall not die.

31 And the servants of the king again approached to bring Abram out, and the flames came upon them and burned their faces so that eight of them died.

32 And when the king saw that his servants could not approach the fire lest they should be burned, the king called to Abram, O servant of the God who is in heaven, go forth from amidst the fire and come hither before me; and Abram hearkened to the voice of the king, and he went forth from the fire and came and stood before the king.

33 And when Abram came out the king and all his servants saw Abram coming before the king, with his lower garments upon him, for they were not burned, but the cord with which he was bound was burned.

34 And the king said to Abram, How is it that thou wast not burned in the fire?

35 And Abram said to the king, The God of heaven and earth in whom I trust and who has all in his power, he delivered me from the fire into which thou didst cast me.

36 And Haran the brother of Abram was burned to ashes, and they sought for his body, and they found it consumed.

37 And Haran was eighty-two years old when he died in the fire of Casdim. And the king, princes, and inhabitants of the land, seeing that Abram was delivered from the fire, they came and bowed down to Abram.

38 And Abram said to them, Do not bow down to me, but bow down to the God of the world who made you, and serve him, and go in his ways for it is he who delivered me from out of this fire, and it is he who created the souls and spirits of all men, and formed man in his mother's womb, and brought him forth into the world, and it is he who will deliver those who trust in him from all pain.

39 And this thing seemed very wonderful in the eyes of the king and princes, that Abram was saved from the fire and that Haran was burned; and the king gave Abram many presents and he gave him his two head servants from the king's house; the name of one was Oni and the name of the other was Eliezer.

40 And all the kings, princes and servants gave Abram many gifts of silver and gold and pearl, and the king and his princes sent him away, and he went in peace.

41 And Abram went forth from the king in peace, and many of the king's servants followed him, and about three hundred men joined him.

42 And Abram returned on that day and went to his father's house, he and the men that followed him, and Abram served the Lord his God all

the days of his life, and he walked in his ways and followed his law.

43 And from that day forward Abram inclined the hearts of the sons of men to serve the Lord.

44 And at that time Nahor and Abram took unto themselves wives, the daughters of their brother Haran; the wife of Nahor was Milca and the name of Abram's wife was Sarai. And Sarai, wife of Abram, was barren; she had no offspring in those days.

45 And at the expiration of two years from Abram's going out of the fire, that is in the fifty-second year of his life, behold king Nimrod sat in Babel upon the throne, and the king fell asleep and dreamed that he was standing with his troops and hosts in a valley opposite the king's furnace.

46 And he lifted up his eyes and saw a man in the likeness of Abram coming forth from the furnace, and that he came and stood before the king with his drawn sword, and then sprang to the king with his sword, when the king fled from the man, for he was afraid; and while he was running, the man threw an egg upon the king's head, and the egg became a great river.

47 And the king dreamed that all his troops sank in that river and died, and the king took flight with three men who were before him and he escaped.

48 And the king looked at these men and they were clothed in princely dresses as the garments of kings, and had the appearance and majesty of kings.

49 And while they were running, the river again turned to an egg before the king, and there came forth from the egg a young bird which came before the king, and flew at his head and plucked out the king's eye.

50 And the king was grieved at the sight, and he awoke out of his sleep and his spirit was agitated; and he felt a great terror.

51 And in the morning the king rose from his couch in fear, and he ordered all the wise men and magicians to come before him, when the king related his dream to them.

52 And a wise servant of the king, whose name was Anuki, answered the king, saying, This is nothing else but the evil of Abram and his seed which will spring up against my Lord and king in the latter days.

53 And behold the day will come when Abram and his seed and the children of his household will war with my king, and they will smite all the king's hosts and his troops.

54 And as to what thou hast said concerning three men which thou didst see like unto thyself, and which did escape, this means that only thou wilt escape with three kings

from the kings of the earth who will be with thee in battle.

55 And that which thou sawest of the river which turned to an egg as at first, and the young bird plucking out thine eye, this means nothing else but the seed of Abram which will slay the king in latter days.

56 This is my king's dream, and this is its interpretation, and the dream is true, and the interpretation which thy servant has given thee is right.

57 Now therefore my king, surely thou knowest that it is now fifty-two years since thy sages saw this at the birth of Abram, and if my king will suffer Abram to live in the earth it will be to the injury of my lord and king, for all the days that Abram liveth neither thou nor thy kingdom will be established, for this was known formerly at his birth; and why will not my king slay him, that his evil may be kept from thee in latter days?

58 And Nimrod hearkened to the voice of Anuki, and he sent some of his servants in secret to go and seize Abram, and bring him before the king to suffer death.

59 And Eliezer, Abram's servant whom the king had given him, was at that time in the presence of the king, and he heard what Anuki had advised the king, and what the king had said to cause Abram's death.

60 And Eliezer said to Abram, Hasten, rise up and save thy soul, that thou mayest not die through the hands of the king, for thus did he see in a dream concerning thee, and thus did Anuki interpret it, and thus also did Anuki advise the king concerning thee.

61 And Abram hearkened to the voice of Eliezer, and Abram hastened and ran for safety to the house of Noah and his son Shem, and he concealed himself there and found a place of safety; and the king's servants came to Abram's house to seek him, but they could not find him, and they searched through out the country and he was not to be found, and they went and searched in every direction and he was not to be met with.

62 And when the king's servants could not find Abram they returned to the king, but the king's anger against Abram was stilled, as they did not find him, and the king drove from his mind this matter concerning Abram.

63 And Abram was concealed in Noah's house for one month, until the king had forgotten this matter, but Abram was still afraid of the king; and Terah came to see Abram his son secretly in the house of Noah, and Terah was very great in the eyes of the king.

64 And Abram said to his father, Dost thou not know that the king thinketh to slay me, and to annihilate my name from the earth by the advice of his wicked counsellors?

65 Now whom hast thou here and what hast thou in this land? Arise, let us go together to the land of Canaan, that we may be delivered from his hand, lest thou perish also through him in the latter days.

66 Dost thou not know or hast thou not heard, that it is not through love that Nimrod giveth thee all this honor, but it is only for his benefit that he bestoweth all this good upon thee?

67 And if he do unto thee greater good than this, surely these are only vanities of the world, for wealth and riches cannot avail in the day of wrath and anger.

68 Now therefore hearken to my voice, and let us arise and go to the land of Canaan, out of the reach of injury from Nimrod; and serve thou the Lord who created thee in the earth and it will be well with thee; and cast away all the vain things which thou pursuest.

69 And Abram ceased to speak, when Noah and his son Shem answered Terah, saying, True is the word which Abram hath said unto thee.

70 And Terah hearkened to the voice of his son Abram, and Terah did all that Abram said, for this was from the Lord, that the king should not cause Abram's death.

Jasher 13

1 And Terah took his son Abram and his grandson Lot, the son of Haran, and Sarai his daughter-in-law, the wife of his son Abram, and all the souls of his household and went with them from Ur Casdim to go to the land of Canaan. And when they came as far as the land of Haran they remained there, for it was exceedingly good land for pasture, and of sufficient extent for those who accompanied them.

2 And the people of the land of Haran saw that Abram was good and upright with God and men, and that the Lord his God was with him, and some of the people of the land of Haran came and joined Abram, and he taught them the instruction of the Lord and his ways; and these men remained with Abram in his house and they adhered to him.

3 And Abram remained in the land three years, and at the expiration of three years the Lord appeared to Abram and said to him; I am the Lord who brought thee forth from Ur Casdim, and delivered thee from the hands of all thine enemies.

4 And now therefore if thou wilt hearken to my voice and keep my commandments, my statutes and my laws, then will I cause thy enemies to fall before thee, and I will multiply thy seed like the stars of heaven, and I will send my blessing upon all the

works of thy hands, and thou shalt lack nothing.

5 Arise now, take thy wife and all belonging to thee and go to the land of Canaan and remain there, and I will there be unto thee for a God, and I will bless thee. And Abram rose and took his wife and all belonging to him, and he went to the land of Canaan as the Lord had told him; and Abram was fifty years old when he went from Haran.

6 And Abram came to the land of Canaan and dwelt in the midst of the city, and he there pitched his tent amongst the children of Canaan, inhabitants of the land.

7 And the Lord appeared to Abram when he came to the land of Canaan, and said to him, This is the land which I gave unto thee and to thy seed after thee forever, and I will make thy seed like the stars of heaven, and I will give unto thy seed for an inheritance all the lands which thou seest.

8 And Abram built an altar in the place where God had spoken to him, and Abram there called upon the name of the Lord.

9 At that time, at the end of three years of Abram's dwelling in the land of Canaan, in that year Noah died, which was the fifty-eighth year of the life of Abram; and all the days that Noah lived were nine hundred and fifty years and he died.

10 And Abram dwelt in the land of Canaan, he, his wife, and all belonging to him, and all those that accompanied him, together with those that joined him from the people of the land; but Nahor, Abram's brother, and Terah his father, and Lot the son of Haran and all belonging to them dwelt in Haran.

11 In the fifth year of Abram's dwelling in the land of Canaan the people of Sodom and Gomorrah and all the cities of the plain revolted from the power of Chedorlaomer, king of Elam; for all the kings of the cities of the plain had served Chedorlaomer for twelve years, and given him a yearly tax, but in those days in the thirteenth year, they rebelled against him.

12 And in the tenth year of Abram's dwelling in the land of Canaan there was war between Nimrod king of Shinar and Chedorlaomer king of Elam, and Nimrod came to fight with Chedorlaomer and to subdue him.

13 For Chedorlaomer was at that time one of the princes of the hosts of Nimrod, and when all the people at the tower were dispersed and those that remained were also scattered upon the face of the earth, Chedorlaomer went to the land of Elam and reigned over it and rebelled against his lord.

14 And in those days when Nimrod saw that the cities of the plain had rebelled, he came with pride and

anger to war with Chedorlaomer, and Nimrod assembled all his princes and subjects, about seven hundred thousand men, and went against Chedorlaomer, and Chedorlaomer went out to meet him with five thousand men, and they prepared for battle in the valley of Babel which is between Elam and Shinar.

15 And all those kings fought there, and Nimrod and his people were smitten before the people of Chedorlaomer, and there fell from Nimrod's men about six hundred thousand, and Mardon the king's son fell amongst them.

16 And Nimrod fled and returned in shame and disgrace to his land, and he was under subjection to Chedorlaomer for a long time, and Chedorlaomer returned to his land and sent princes of his host to the kings that dwelt around him, to Arioch king of Elasar, and to Tidal king of Goyim, and made a covenant with them, and they were all obedient to his commands.

17 And it was in the fifteenth year of Abram's dwelling in the land of Canaan, which is the seventieth year of the life of Abram, and the Lord appeared to Abram in that year and he said to him, I am the Lord who brought thee out from Ur Casdim to give thee this land for an inheritance.

18 Now therefore walk before me and be perfect and keep my commands, for to thee and to thy seed I will give this land for an inheritance, from the river Mitzraim unto the great river Euphrates.

19 And thou shalt come to thy fathers in peace and in good age, and the fourth generation shall return here in this land and shall inherit it forever; and Abram built an altar, and he called upon the name of the Lord who appeared to him, and he brought up sacrifices upon the altar to the Lord.

20 At that time Abram returned and went to Haran to see his father and mother, and his father's household, and Abram and his wife and all belonging to him returned to Haran, and Abram dwelt in Haran five years.

21 And many of the people of Haran, about seventy-two men, followed Abram and Abram taught them the instruction of the Lord and his ways, and he taught them to know the Lord.

22 In those days the Lord appeared to Abram in Haran, and he said to him, Behold, I spoke unto thee these twenty years back saying,

23 Go forth from thy land, from thy birth-place and from thy father's house, to the land which I have shown thee to give it to thee and to thy children, for there in that land will I bless thee, and make thee a great nation, and make thy name great, and in thee shall the families of the earth be blessed.

24 Now therefore arise, go forth from this place, thou, thy wife, and all belonging to thee, also every one born in thy house and all the souls thou hast made in Haran, and bring them out with thee from here, and rise to return to the land of Canaan.

25 And Abram arose and took his wife Sarai and all belonging to him and all that were born to him in his house and the souls which they had made in Haran, and they came out to go to the land of Canaan.

26 And Abram went and returned to the land of Canaan, according to the word of the Lord. And Lot the son of his brother Haran went with him, and Abram was seventy-five years old when he went forth from Haran to return to the land of Canaan.

27 And he came to the land of Canaan according to the word of the Lord to Abram, and he pitched his tent and he dwelt in the plain of Mamre, and with him was Lot his brother's son, and all belonging to him.

28 And the Lord again appeared to Abram and said, To thy seed will I give this land; and he there built an altar to the Lord who appeared to him, which is still to this day in the plains of Mamre.

Jasher 14

1 In those days there was in the land of Shinar a wise man who had understanding in all wisdom, and of a beautiful appearance, but he was poor and indigent; his name was Rikayon and he was hard set to support himself.

2 And he resolved to go to Egypt, to Oswiris the son of Anom king of Egypt, to show the king his wisdom; for perhaps he might find grace in his sight, to raise him up and give him maintenance; and Rikayon did so.

3 And when Rikayon came to Egypt he asked the inhabitants of Egypt concerning the king, and the inhabitants of Egypt told him the custom of the king of Egypt, for it was then the custom of the king of Egypt that he went from his royal palace and was seen abroad only one day in the year, and after that the king would return to his palace to remain there.

4 And on the day when the king went forth he passed judgment in the land, and every one having a suit came before the king that day to obtain his request.

5 And when Rikayon heard of the custom in Egypt and that he could not come into the presence of the king, he grieved greatly and was very sorrowful.

6 And in the evening Rikayon went out and found a house in ruins, formerly a bake house in Egypt, and he abode there all night in bitterness of soul and pinched with hunger, and sleep was removed from his eyes.

7 And Rikayon considered within himself what he should do in the town until the king made his appearance, and how he might maintain himself there.

8 And he rose in the morning and walked about, and met in his way those who sold vegetables and various sorts of seed with which they supplied the inhabitants.

9 And Rikayon wished to do the same in order to get a maintenance in the city, but he was unacquainted with the custom of the people, and he was like a blind man among them.

10 And he went and obtained vegetables to sell them for his support, and the rabble assembled about him and ridiculed him, and took his vegetables from him and left him nothing.

11 And he rose up from there in bitterness of soul, and went sighing to the bake house in which he had remained all the night before, and he slept there the second night.

12 And on that night again he reasoned within himself how he could save himself from starvation, and he devised a scheme how to act.

13 And he rose up in the morning and acted ingeniously, and went and hired thirty strong men of the rabble, carrying their war instruments in their hands, and he led them to the top of the Egyptian sepulchre, and he placed them there.

14 And he commanded them, saying, Thus saith the king, Strengthen yourselves and be valiant men, and let no man be buried here until two hundred pieces of silver be given, and then he may be buried; and those men did according to the order of Rikayon to the people of Egypt the whole of that year.

15 And in eight months time Rikayon and his men gathered great riches of silver and gold, and Rikayon took a great quantity of horses and other animals, and he hired more men, and he gave them horses and they remained with him.

16 And when the year came round, at the time the king went forth into the town, all the inhabitants of Egypt assembled together to speak to him concerning the work of Rikayon and his men.

17 And the king went forth on the appointed day, and all the Egyptians came before him and cried unto him, saying,

18 May the king live forever. What is this thing thou doest in the town to thy servants, not to suffer a dead body to be buried until so much silver and gold be given? Was there ever the like unto this done in the whole earth, from the days of former kings yea even from the days of Adam, unto this day, that the dead

should not be buried only for a set price?

19 We know it to be the custom of kings to take a yearly tax from the living, but thou dost not only do this, but from the dead also thou exactest a tax day by day.

20 Now, O king, we can no more bear this, for the whole city is ruined on this account, and dost thou not know it?

21 And when the king heard all that they had spoken he was very wroth, and his anger burned within him at this affair, for he had known nothing of it.

22 And the king said, Who and where is he that dares to do this wicked thing in my land without my command? Surely you will tell me.

23 And they told him all the works of Rikayon and his men, and the king's anger was aroused, and he ordered Rikayon and his men to be brought before him.

24 And Rikayon took about a thousand children, sons and daughters, and clothed them in silk and embroidery, and he set them upon horses and sent them to the king by means of his men, and he also took a great quantity of silver and gold and precious stones, and a strong and beautiful horse, as a present for the king, with which he came before the king and bowed down to the earth before him; and

the king, his servants and all the inhabitants of Egypt wondered at the work of Rikayon, and they saw his riches and the present that he had brought to the king.

25 And it greatly pleased the king and he wondered at it; and when Rikayon sat before him the king asked him concerning all his works, and Rikayon spoke all his words wisely before the king, his servants and all the inhabitants of Egypt.

26 And when the king heard the words of Rikayon and his wisdom, Rikayon found grace in his sight, and he met with grace and kindness from all the servants of the king and from all the inhabitants of Egypt, on account of his wisdom and excellent speeches, and from that time they loved him exceedingly.

27 And the king answered and said to Rikayon, Thy name shall no more be called Rikayon but Pharaoh shall be thy name, since thou didst exact a tax from the dead; and he called his name Pharaoh.

28 And the king and his subjects loved Rikayon for his wisdom, and they consulted with all the inhabitants of Egypt to make him prefect under the king.

29 And all the inhabitants of Egypt and its wise men did so, and it was made a law in Egypt.

30 And they made Rikayon Pharaoh prefect under Oswiris king of Egypt,

and Rikayon Pharaoh governed over Egypt, daily administering justice to the whole city, but Oswiris the king would judge the people of the land one day in the year, when he went out to make his appearance.

31 And Rikayon Pharaoh cunningly usurped the government of Egypt, and he exacted a tax from all the inhabitants of Egypt.

32 And all the inhabitants of Egypt greatly loved Rikayon Pharaoh, and they made a decree to call every king that should reign over them and their seed in Egypt, Pharaoh.

33 Therefore all the kings that reigned in Egypt from that time forward were called Pharaoh unto this day.

Jasher 15

1 And in that year there was a heavy famine throughout the land of Canaan, and the inhabitants of the land could not remain on account of the famine for it was very grievous.

2 And Abram and all belonging to him rose and went down to Egypt on account of the famine, and when they were at the brook Mitzraim they remained there some time to rest from the fatigue of the road.

3 And Abram and Sarai were walking at the border of the brook Mitzraim, and Abram beheld his wife Sarai that she was very beautiful.

4 And Abram said to his wife Sarai, Since God has created thee with such a beautiful countenance, I am afraid of the Egyptians lest they should slay me and take thee away, for the fear of God is not in these places.

5 Surely then thou shalt do this, Say thou art my sister to all that may ask thee, in order that it may be well with me, and that we may live and not be put to death.

6 And Abram commanded the same to all those that came with him to Egypt on account of the famine; also his nephew Lot he commanded, saying, If the Egyptians ask thee concerning Sarai say she is the sister of Abram.

7 And yet with all these orders Abram did not put confidence in them, but he took Sarai and placed her in a chest and concealed it amongst their vessels, for Abram was greatly concerned about Sarai on account of the wickedness of the Egyptians.

8 And Abram and all belonging to him rose up from the brook Mitzraim and came to Egypt; and they had scarcely entered the gates of the city when the guards stood up to them saying, Give tithe to the king from what you have, and then you may come into the town; and Abram and those that were with him did so.

9 And Abram with the people that were with him came to Egypt, and when they came they brought the chest in which Sarai was concealed and the Egyptians saw the chest.

10 And the king's servants approached Abram, saying, What hast thou here in this chest which we have not seen? Now open thou the chest and give tithe to the king of all that it contains.

11 And Abram said, This chest I will not open, but all you demand upon it I will give. And Pharaoh's officers answered Abram, saying, It is a chest of precious stones, give us the tenth thereof.

12 Abram said, All that you desire I will give, but you must not open the chest.

13 And the king's officers pressed Abram, and they reached the chest and opened it with force, and they saw, and behold a beautiful woman was in the chest.

14 And when the officers of the king beheld Sarai they were struck with admiration at her beauty, and all the princes and servants of Pharaoh assembled to see Sarai, for she was very beautiful. And the king's officers ran and told Pharaoh all that they had seen, and they praised Sarai to the king; and Pharaoh ordered her to be brought, and the woman came before the king.

15 And Pharaoh beheld Sarai and she pleased him exceedingly, and he was struck with her beauty, and the king rejoiced greatly on her account, and made presents to those who brought him the tidings concerning her.

16 And the woman was then brought to Pharaoh's house, and Abram grieved on account of his wife, and he prayed to the Lord to deliver her from the hands of Pharaoh.

17 And Sarai also prayed at that time and said, O Lord God thou didst tell my Lord Abram to go from his land and from his father's house to the land of Canaan, and thou didst promise to do well with him if he would perform thy commands; now behold we have done that which thou didst command us, and we left our land and our families, and we went to a strange land and to a people whom we have not known before.

18 And we came to this land to avoid the famine, and this evil accident has befallen me; now therefore, O Lord God, deliver us and save us from the hand of this oppressor, and do well with me for the sake of thy mercy.

19 And the Lord hearkened to the voice of Sarai, and the Lord sent an angel to deliver Sarai from the power of Pharaoh.

20 And the king came and sat before Sarai and behold an angel of the

Lord was standing over them, and he appeared to Sarai and said to her, Do not fear, for the Lord has heard thy prayer.

21 And the king approached Sarai and said to her, What is that man to thee who brought thee hither? and she said, He is my brother.

22 And the king said, It is incumbent upon us to make him great, to elevate him and to do unto him all the good which thou shalt command us; and at that time the king sent to Abram silver and gold and precious stones in abundance, together with cattle, men servants and maid servants; and the king ordered Abram to be brought, and he sat in the court of the king's house, and the king greatly exalted Abram on that night.

23 And the king approached to speak to Sarai, and he reached out his hand to touch her, when the angel smote him heavily, and he was terrified and he refrained from reaching to her.

24 And when the king came near to Sarai, the angel smote him to the ground, and acted thus to him the whole night, and the king was terrified.

25 And the angel on that night smote heavily all the servants of the king, and his whole household, on account of Sarai, and there was a great lamentation that night amongst the people of Pharaoh's house.

26 And Pharaoh, seeing the evil that befell him, said, Surely on account of this woman has this thing happened to me, and he removed himself at some distance from her and spoke pleasing words to her.

27 And the king said to Sarai, Tell me I pray thee concerning the man with whom thou camest here; and Sarai said, This man is my husband, and I said to thee that he was my brother for I was afraid, lest thou shouldst put him to death through wickedness.

28 And the king kept away from Sarai, and the plagues of the angel of the Lord ceased from him and his household; and Pharaoh knew that he was smitten on account of Sarai, and the king was greatly astonished at this.

29 And in the morning the king called for Abram and said to him, What is this thou hast done to me? Why didst thou say, She is my sister, owing to which I took her unto me for a wife, and this heavy plague has therefore come upon me and my household.

30 Now therefore here is thy wife, take her and go from our land lest we all die on her account. And Pharaoh took more cattle, men servants and maid servants, and silver and gold, to give to Abram,

and he returned unto him Sarai his wife.

31 And the king took a maiden whom he begat by his concubines, and he gave her to Sarai for a handmaid.

32 And the king said to his daughter, It is better for thee my daughter to be a handmaid in this man's house than to be mistress in my house, after we have beheld the evil that befell us on account of this woman.

33 And Abram arose, and he and all belonging to him went away from Egypt; and Pharaoh ordered some of his men to accompany him and all that went with him.

34 And Abram returned to the land of Canaan, to the place where he had made the altar, where he at first had pitched his tent.

35 And Lot the son of Haran, Abram's brother, had a heavy stock of cattle, flocks and herds and tents, for the Lord was bountiful to them on account of Abram.

36 And when Abram was dwelling in the land the herdsmen of Lot quarrelled with the herdsmen of Abram, for their property was too great for them to remain together in the land, and the land could not bear them on account of their cattle.

37 And when Abram's herdsmen went to feed their flock they would not go into the fields of the people of the land, but the cattle of Lot's herdsmen did otherwise, for they were suffered to feed in the fields of the people of the land.

38 And the people of the land saw this occurrence daily, and they came to Abram and quarrelled with him on account of Lot's herdsmen.

39 And Abram said to Lot, What is this thou art doing to me, to make me despicable to the inhabitants of the land, that thou orderest thy herdsman to feed thy cattle in the fields of other people? Dost thou not know that I am a stranger in this land amongst the children of Canaan, and why wilt thou do this unto me?

40 And Abram quarrelled daily with Lot on account of this, but Lot would not listen to Abram, and he continued to do the same and the inhabitants of the land came and told Abram.

41 And Abram said unto Lot, How long wilt thou be to me for a stumbling block with the inhabitants of the land? Now I beseech thee let there be no more quarrelling between us, for we are kinsmen.

42 But I pray thee separate from me, go and choose a place where thou mayest dwell with thy cattle and all belonging to thee, but Keep thyself at a distance from me, thou and thy household.

43 And be not afraid in going from me, for if any one do an injury to thee, let me know and I will avenge

thy cause from him, only remove from me.

44 And when Abram had spoken all these words to Lot, then Lot arose and lifted up his eyes toward the plain of Jordan.

45 And he saw that the whole of this place was well watered, and good for man as well as affording pasture for the cattle.

46 And Lot went from Abram to that place, and he there pitched his tent and he dwelt in Sodom, and they were separated from each other.

47 And Abram dwelt in the plain of Mamre, which is in Hebron, and he pitched his tent there, and Abram remained in that place many years.

Jasher 16

1 At that time Chedorlaomer king of Elam sent to all the neighboring kings, to Nimrod, king of Shinar who was then under his power, and to Tidal, king of Goyim, and to Arioch, king of Elasar, with whom he made a covenant, saying, Come up to me and assist me, that we may smite all the towns of Sodom and its inhabitants, for they have rebelled against me these thirteen years.

2 And these four kings went up with all their camps, about eight hundred thousand men, and they went as they were, and smote every man they found in their road.

3 And the five kings of Sodom and Gomorrah, Shinab king of Admah, Shemeber king of Zeboyim, Bera king of Sodom, Bersha king of Gomorrah, and Bela king of Zoar, went out to meet them, and they all joined together in the valley of Siddim.

4 And these nine kings made war in the valley of Siddim; and the kings of Sodom and Gomorrah were smitten before the kings of Elam.

5 And the valley of Siddim was full of lime pits and the kings of Elam pursued the kings of Sodom, and the kings of Sodom with their camps fled and fell into the lime pits, and all that remained went to the mountain for safety, and the five kings of Elam came after them and pursued them to the gates of Sodom, and they took all that there was in Sodom.

6 And they plundered all the cities of Sodom and Gomorrah, and they also took Lot, Abram's brother's son, and his property, and they seized all the goods of the cities of Sodom, and they went away; and Unic, Abram's servant, who was in the battle, saw this, and told Abram all that the kings had done to the cities of Sodom, and that Lot was taken captive by them.

7 And Abram heard this, and he rose up with about three hundred and eighteen men that were with him, and he that night pursued these kings and smote them, and they all fell before Abram and his men, and

there was none remaining but the four kings who fled, and they went each his own road.

8 And Abram recovered all the property of Sodom, and he also recovered Lot and his property, his wives and little ones and all belonging to him, so that Lot lacked nothing.

9 And when he returned from smiting these kings, he and his men passed the valley of Siddim where the kings had made war together.

10 And Bera king of Sodom, and the rest of his men that were with him, went out from the lime pits into which they had fallen, to meet Abram and his men.

11 And Adonizedek king of Jerusalem, the same was Shem, went out with his men to meet Abram and his people, with bread and wine, and they remained together in the valley of Melech.

12 And Adonizedek blessed Abram, and Abram gave him a tenth from all that he had brought from the spoil of his enemies, for Adonizedek was a priest before God.

13 And all the kings of Sodom and Gomorrah who were there, with their servants, approached Abram and begged of him to return them their servants whom he had made captive, and to take unto himself all the property.

14 And Abram answered the kings of Sodom, saying, As the Lord liveth who created heaven and earth, and who redeemed my soul from all affliction, and who delivered me this day from my enemies, and gave them into my hand, I will not take anything belonging to you, that you may not boast tomorrow, saying, Abram became rich from our property that he saved.

15 For the Lord my God in whom I trust said unto me, Thou shalt lack nothing, for I will bless thee in all the works of thy hands.

16 And now therefore behold, here is all belonging to you, take it and go; as the Lord liveth I will not take from you from a living soul down to a shoetie or thread, excepting the expense of the food of those who went out with me to battle, as also the portions of the men who went with me, Anar, Ashcol, and Mamre, they and their men, as well as those also who had remained to watch the baggage, they shall take their portion of the spoil.

17 And the kings of Sodom gave Abram according to all that he had said, and they pressed him to take of whatever he chose, but he would not.

18 And he sent away the kings of Sodom and the remainder of their men, and he gave them orders about Lot, and they went to their respective places.

19 And Lot, his brother's son, he also sent away with his property, and he went with them, and Lot returned to his home, to Sodom, and Abram and his people returned to their home to the plains of Mamre, which is in Hebron.

20 At that time the Lord again appeared to Abram in Hebron, and he said to him, Do not fear, thy reward is very great before me, for I will not leave thee, until I shall have multiplied thee, and blessed thee and made thy seed like the stars in heaven, which cannot be measured nor numbered.

21 And I will give unto thy seed all these lands that thou seest with thine eyes, to them will I give them for an inheritance forever, only be strong and do not fear, walk before me and be perfect.

22 And in the seventy-eighth year of the life of Abram, in that year died Reu, the son of Peleg, and all the days of Reu were two hundred and thirty-nine years, and he died.

23 And Sarai, the daughter of Haran, Abram's wife, was still barren in those days; she did not bear to Abram either son or daughter.

24 And when she saw that she bare no children she took her handmaid Hagar, whom Pharaoh had given her, and she gave her to Abram her husband for a wife.

25 For Hagar learned all the ways of Sarai as Sarai taught her, she was not in any way deficient in following her good ways.

26 And Sarai said to Abram, Behold here is my handmaid Hagar, go to her that she may bring forth upon my knees, that I may also obtain children through her.

27 And at the end of ten years of Abram's dwelling in the land of Canaan, which is the eighty-fifth year of Abram's life, Sarai gave Hagar unto him.

28 And Abram hearkened to the voice of his wife Sarai, and he took his handmaid Hagar and Abram came to her and she conceived.

29 And when Hagar saw that she had conceived she rejoiced greatly, and her mistress was despised in her eyes, and she said within herself, This can only be that I am better before God than Sarai my mistress, for all the days that my mistress has been with my lord, she did not conceive, but me the Lord has caused in so short a time to conceive by him.

30 And when Sarai saw that Hagar had conceived by Abram, Sarai was jealous of her handmaid, and Sarai said within herself, This is surely nothing else but that she must be better than I am.

31 And Sarai said unto Abram, My wrong be upon thee, for at the time

when thou didst pray before the Lord for children why didst thou not pray on my account, that the Lord should give me seed from thee?

32 And when I speak to Hagar in thy presence, she despiseth my words, because she has conceived, and thou wilt say nothing to her; may the Lord judge between me and thee for what thou hast done to me.

33 And Abram said to Sarai, Behold thy handmaid is in thy hand, do unto her as it may seem good in thy eyes; and Sarai afflicted her, and Hagar fled from her to the wilderness.

34 And an angel of the Lord found her in the place where she had fled, by a well, and he said to her, Do not fear, for I will multiply thy seed, for thou shalt bear a son and thou shalt call his name Ishmael; now then return to Sarai thy mistress, and submit thyself under her hands.

35 And Hagar called the place of that well Beer-lahai-roi, it is between Kadesh and the wilderness of Bered.

36 And Hagar at that time returned to her master's house, and at the end of days Hagar bare a son to Abram, and Abram called his name Ishmael; and Abram was eighty-six years old when he begat him.

Jasher 17

1 And in those days, in the ninety-first year of the life of Abram, the children of Chittim made war with the children of Tubal, for when the Lord had scattered the sons of men upon the face of the earth, the children of Chittim went and embodied themselves in the plain of Canopia, and they built themselves cities there and dwelt by the river Tibreu.

2 And the children of Tubal dwelt in Tuscanah, and their boundaries reached the river Tibreu, and the children of Tubal built a city in Tuscanan, and they called the name Sabinah, after the name of Sabinah son of Tubal their father, and they dwelt there unto this day.

3 And it was at that time the children of Chittim made war with the children of Tubal, and the children of Tubal were smitten before the children of Chittim, and the children of Chittim caused three hundred and seventy men to fall from the children of Tubal.

4 And at that time the children of Tubal swore to the children of Chittim, saying, You shall not intermarry amongst us, and no man shall give his daughter to any of the sons of Chittim.

5 For all the daughters of Tubal were in those days fair, for no women were then found in the whole earth so fair as the daughters of Tubal.

6 And all who delighted in the beauty of women went to the daughters of Tubal and took wives from them, and the sons of men, kings and princes,

who greatly delighted in the beauty of women, took wives in those days from the daughters of Tubal.

7 And at the end of three years after the children of Tubal had sworn to the children of Chittim not to give them their daughters for wives, about twenty men of the children of Chittim went to take some of the daughters of Tubal, but they found none.

8 For the children of Tubal kept their oaths not to intermarry with them, and they would not break their oaths.

9 And in the days of harvest the children of Tubal went into their fields to get in their harvest, when the young men of Chittim assembled and went to the city of Sabinah, and each man took a young woman from the daughters of Tubal, and they came to their cities.

10 And the children of Tubal heard of it and they went to make war with them, and they could not prevail over them, for the mountain was exceedingly high from them, and when they saw they could not prevail over them they returned to their land.

11 And at the revolution of the year the children of Tubal went and hired about ten thousand men from those cities that were near them, and they went to war with the children of Chittim.

12 And the children of Tubal went to war with the children of Chittim, to destroy their land and to distress them, and in this engagement the children of Tubal prevailed over the children of Chittim, and the children of Chittim, seeing that they were greatly distressed, lifted up the children which they had had by the daughters of Tubal, upon the wall which had been built, to be before the eyes of the children of Tubal.

13 And the children of Chittim said to them, Have you come to make war with your own sons and daughters, and have we not been considered your flesh and bones from that time till now?

14 And when the children of Tubal heard this they ceased to make war with the children of Chittim, and they went away.

15 And they returned to their cities, and the children of Chittim at that time assembled and built two cities by the sea, and they called one Purtu and the other Ariza.

16 And Abram the son of Terah was then ninety-nine years old.

17 At that time the Lord appeared to him and he said to him, I will make my covenant between me and thee, and I will greatly multiply thy seed, and this is the covenant which I make between me and thee, that every male child be circumcised, thou and thy seed after thee.

18 At eight days old shall it be circumcised, and this covenant shall

459

be in your flesh for an everlasting covenant.

19 And now therefore thy name shall no more be called Abram but Abraham, and thy wife shall no more be called Sarai but Sarah.

20 For I will bless you both, and I will multiply your seed after you that you shall become a great nation, and kings shall come forth from you.

Jasher 18

1 And Abraham rose and did all that God had ordered him, and he took the men of his household and those bought with his money, and he circumcised them as the Lord had commanded him.

2 And there was not one left whom he did not circumcise, and Abraham and his son Ishmael were circumcised in the flesh of their foreskin; thirteen years old was Ishmael when he was circumcised in the flesh of his foreskin.

3 And in the third day Abraham went out of his tent and sat at the door to enjoy the heat of the sun, during the pain of his flesh.

4 And the Lord appeared to him in the plain of Mamre, and sent three of his ministering angels to visit him, and he was sitting at the door of the tent, and he lifted his eyes and saw, and lo three men were coming from a distance, and he rose up and ran to meet them, and he bowed down to

them and brought them into his house.

5 And he said to them, If now I have found favor in your sight, turn in and eat a morsel of bread; and he pressed them, and they turned in and he gave them water and they washed their feet, and he placed them under a tree at the door of the tent.

6 And Abraham ran and took a calf, tender and good, and he hastened to kill it, and gave it to his servant Eliezer to dress.

7 And Abraham came to Sarah into the tent, and he said to her, Make ready quickly three measures of fine meal, knead it and make cakes to cover the pot containing the meat, and she did so.

8 And Abraham hastened and brought before them butter and milk, beef and mutton, and gave it before them to eat before the flesh of the calf was sufficiently done, and they did eat.

9 And when they had done eating one of them said to him, I will return to thee according to the time of life, and Sarah thy wife shall have a son.

10 And the men afterward departed and went their ways, to the places to which they were sent.

11 In those days all the people of Sodom and Gomorrah, and of the whole five cities, were exceedingly

wicked and sinful against the Lord and they provoked the Lord with their abominations, and they strengthened in aging abominably and scornfully before the Lord, and their wickedness and crimes were in those days great before the Lord.

12 And they had in their land a very extensive valley, about half a day's walk, and in it there were fountains of water and a great deal of herbage surrounding the water.

13 And all the people of Sodom and Gomorrah went there four times in the year, with their wives and children and all belonging to them, and they rejoiced there with timbrels and dances.

14 And in the time of rejoicing they would all rise and lay hold of their neighbor's wives, and some, the virgin daughters of their neighbors, and they enjoyed them, and each man saw his wife and daughter in the hands of his neighbor and did not say a word.

15 And they did so from morning to night, and they afterward returned home each man to his house and each woman to her tent; so they always did four times in the year.

16 Also when a stranger came into their cities and brought goods which he had purchased with a view to dispose of there, the people of these cities would assemble, men, women and children, young and old, and go to the man and take his goods by force, giving a little to each man until there was an end to all the goods of the owner which he had brought into the land.

17 And if the owner of the goods quarreled with them, saying, What is this work which you have done to me, then they would approach to him one by one, and each would show him the little which he took and taunt him, saying, I only took that little which thou didst give me; and when he heard this from them all, he would arise and go from them in sorrow and bitterness of soul, when they would all arise and go after him, and drive him out of the city with great noise and tumult.

18 And there was a man from the country of Elam who was leisurely going on the road, seated upon his ass, which carried a fine mantle of divers colors, and the mantle was bound with a cord upon the ass.

19 And the man was on his journey passing through the street of Sodom when the sun set in the evening, and he remained there in order to abide during the night, but no one would let him into his house; and at that time there was in Sodom a wicked and mischievous man, one skillful to do evil, and his name was Hedad.

20 And he lifted up his eyes and saw the traveler in the street of the city, and he came to him and said,

Whence comest thou and whither dost thou go?

21 And the man said to him, I am traveling from Hebron to Elam where I belong, and as I passed the sun set and no one would suffer me to enter his house, though I had bread and water and also straw and provender for my ass, and am short of nothing.

22 And Hedad answered and said to him, All that thou shalt want shall be supplied by me, but in the street thou shalt not abide all night.

23 And Hedad brought him to his house, and he took off the mantle from the ass with the cord, and brought them to his house, and he gave the ass straw and provender whilst the traveler ate and drank in Hedad's house, and he abode there that night.

24 And in the morning the traveler rose up early to continue his journey, when Hedad said to him, Wait, comfort thy heart with a morsel of bread and then go, and the man did so; and he remained with him, and they both ate and drank together during the day, when the man rose up to go.

25 And Hedad said to him, Behold now the day is declining, thou hadst better remain all night that thy heart may be comforted; and he pressed him so that he tarried there all night, and on the second day he rose up early to go away, when Hedad pressed him, saying, Comfort thy heart with a morsel of bread and then go, and he remained and ate with him also the second day, and then the man rose up to continue his journey.

26 And Hedad said to him, Behold now the day is declining, remain with me to comfort thy heart and in the morning rise up early and go thy way.

27 And the man would not remain, but rose and saddled his ass, and whilst he was saddling his ass the wife of Hedad said to her husband, Behold this man has remained with us for two days eating and drinking and he has given us nothing, and now shall he go away from us without giving anything? and Hedad said to her, Be silent.

28 And the man saddled his ass to go, and he asked Hedad to give him the cord and mantle to tie it upon the ass.

29 And Hedad said to him, What sayest thou? And he said to him, That thou my lord shalt give me the cord and the mantle made with divers colors which thou didst conceal with thee in thy house to take care of it.

30 And Hedad answered the man, saying, This is the interpretation of thy dream, the cord which thou didst see, means that thy life will be lengthened out like a cord, and

having seen the mantle colored with all sorts of colors, means that thou shalt have a vineyard in which thou wilt plant trees of all fruits.

31 And the traveler answered, saying, Not so my lord, for I was awake when I gave thee the cord and also a mantle woven with different colors, which thou didst take off the ass to put them by for me; and Hedad answered and said, Surely I have told thee the interpretation of thy dream and it is a good dream, and this is the interpretation thereof.

32 Now the sons of men give me four pieces of silver, which is my charge for interpreting dreams, and of thee only I require three pieces of silver.

33 And the man was provoked at the words of Hedad, and he cried bitterly, and he brought Hedad to Serak judge of Sodom.

34 And the man laid his cause before Serak the judge, when Hedad replied, saying, It is not so, but thus the matter stands; and the judge said to the traveler, This man Hedad telleth thee truth, for he is famed in the cities for the accurate interpretation of dreams.

35 And the man cried at the word of the judge, and he said, Not so my Lord, for it was in the day that I gave him the cord and mantle which was upon the ass, in order to put them by

in his house; and they both disputed before the judge, the one saying, Thus the matter was, and the other declaring otherwise.

36 And Hedad said to the man, Give me four pieces of silver that I charge for my interpretations of dreams; I will not make any allowance; and give me the expense of the four meals that thou didst eat in my house.

37 And the man said to Hedad, Truly I will pay thee for what I ate in thy house, only give me the cord and mantle which thou didst conceal in thy house.

38 And Hedad replied before the judge and said to the man, Did I not tell thee the interpretation of thy dream? the cord means that thy days shall be prolonged like a cord, and the mantle, that thou wilt have a vineyard in which thou wilt plant all kinds of fruit trees.

39 This is the proper interpretation of thy dream, now give me the four pieces of silver that I require as a compensation, for I will make thee no allowance.

40 And the man cried at the words of Hedad and they both quarreled before the judge, and the judge gave orders to his servants, who drove them rashly from the house.

41 And they went away quarreling from the judge, when the people of Sodom heard them, and they

gathered about them and they exclaimed against the stranger, and they drove him rashly from the city.

42 And the man continued his journey upon his ass with bitterness of soul, lamenting and weeping.

43 And whilst he was going along he wept at what had happened to him in the corrupt city of Sodom.

Jasher 19

1 And the cities of Sodom had four judges to four cities, and these were their names, Serak in the city of Sodom, Sharkad in Gomorrah, Zabnac in Admah, and Menon in Zeboyim.

2 And Eliezer Abraham's servant applied to them different names, and he converted Serak to Shakra, Sharkad to Shakrura, Zebnac to Kezobim, and Menon to Matzlodin.

3 And by desire of their four judges the people of Sodom and Gomorrah had beds erected in the streets of the cities, and if a man came to these places they laid hold of him and brought him to one of their beds, and by force made him to lie in them.

4 And as he lay down, three men would stand at his head and three at his feet, and measure him by the length of the bed, and if the man was less than the bed these six men would stretch him at each end, and when he cried out to them they would not answer him.

5 And if he was longer than the bed they would draw together the two sides of the bed at each end, until the man had reached the gates of death.

6 And if he continued to cry out to them, they would answer him, saying, Thus shall it be done to a man that cometh into our land.

7 And when men heard all these things that the people of the cities of Sodom did, they refrained from coming there.

8 And when a poor man came to their land they would give him silver and gold, and cause a proclamation in the whole city not to give him a morsel of bread to eat, and if the stranger should remain there some days, and die from hunger, not having been able to obtain a morsel of bread, then at his death all the people of the city would come and take their silver and gold which they had given to him.

9 And those that could recognize the silver or gold which they had given him took it back, and at his death they also stripped him of his garments, and they would fight about them, and he that prevailed over his neighbor took them.

10 They would after that carry him and bury him under some of the shrubs in the deserts; so they did all the days to any one that came to them and died in their land.

11 And in the course of time Sarah sent Eliezer to Sodom, to see Lot and inquire after his welfare.

12 And Eliezer went to Sodom, and he met a man of Sodom fighting with a stranger, and the man of Sodom stripped the poor man of all his clothes and went away.

13 And this poor man cried to Eliezer and supplicated his favor on account of what the man of Sodom had done to him.

14 And he said to him, Why dost thou act thus to the poor man who came to thy land?

15 And the man of Sodom answered Eliezer, saying, Is this man thy brother, or have the people of Sodom made thee a judge this day, that thou speakest about this man?

16 And Eliezer strove with the man of Sodom on account of the poor man, and when Eliezer approached to recover the poor man's clothes from the man of Sodom, he hastened and with a stone smote Eliezer in the forehead.

17 And the blood flowed copiously from Eliezer's forehead, and when the man saw the blood he caught hold of Eliezer, saying, Give me my hire for having rid thee of this bad blood that was in thy forehead, for such is the custom and the law in our land.

18 And Eliezer said to him, Thou hast wounded me and requirest me to pay thee thy hire; and Eliezer would not hearken to the words of the man of Sodom.

19 And the man laid hold of Eliezer and brought him to Shakra the judge of Sodom for judgment.

20 And the man spoke to the judge, saying, I beseech thee my lord, thus has this man done, for I smote him with a stone that the blood flowed from his forehead, and he is unwilling to give me my hire.

21 And the judge said to Eliezer, This man speaketh truth to thee, give him his hire, for this is the custom in our land; and Eliezer heard the words of the judge, and he lifted up a stone and smote the judge, and the stone struck on his forehead, and the blood flowed copiously from the forehead of the judge, and Eliezer said, If this then is the custom in your land give thou unto this man what I should have given him, for this has been thy decision, thou didst decree it.

22 And Eliezer left the man of Sodom with the judge, and he went away.

23 And when the kings of Elam had made war with the kings of Sodom, the kings of Elam captured all the property of Sodom, and they took Lot captive, with his property, and when it was told to Abraham he went and

made war with the kings of Elam, and he recovered from their hands all the property of Lot as well as the property of Sodom.

24 At that time the wife of Lot bare him a daughter, and he called her name Paltith, saying, Because God had delivered him and his whole household from the kings of Elam; and Paltith daughter of Lot grew up, and one of the men of Sodom took her for a wife.

25 And a poor man came into the city to seek a maintenance, and he remained in the city some days, and all the people of Sodom caused a proclamation of their custom not to give this man a morsel of bread to eat, until he dropped dead upon the earth, and they did so.

26 And Paltith the daughter of Lot saw this man lying in the streets starved with hunger, and no one would give him any thing to keep him alive, and he was just upon the point of death.

27 And her soul was filled with pity on account of the man, and she fed him secretly with bread for many days, and the soul of this man was revived.

28 For when she went forth to fetch water she would put the bread in the water pitcher, and when she came to the place where the poor man was, she took the bread from the pitcher and gave it him to eat; so she did many days.

29 And all the people of Sodom and Gomorrah wondered how this man could bear starvation for so many days.

30 And they said to each other, This can only be that he eats and drinks, for no man can bear starvation for so many days or live as this man has, without even his countenance changing; and three men concealed themselves in a place where the poor man was stationed, to know who it was that brought him bread to eat.

31 And Paltith daughter of Lot went forth that day to fetch water, and she put bread into her pitcher of water, and she went to draw water by the poor man's place, and she took out the bread from the pitcher and gave it to the poor man and he ate it.

32 And the three men saw what Paltith did to the poor man, and they said to her, It is thou then who hast supported him, and therefore has he not starved, nor changed in appearance nor died like the rest.

33 And the three men went out of the place in which they were concealed, and they seized Paltith and the bread which was in the poor man's hand.

34 And they took Paltith and brought her before their judges, and they said to them, Thus did she do, and it

is she who supplied the poor man with bread, therefore did he not die all this time; now therefore declare to us the punishment due to this woman for having transgressed our law.

35 And the people of Sodom and Gomorrah assembled and kindled a fire in the street of the city, and they took the woman and cast her into the fire and she was burned to ashes.

36 And in the city of Admah there was a woman to whom they did the like.

37 For a traveler came into the city of Admah to abide there all night, with the intention of going home in the morning, and he sat opposite the door of the house of the young woman's father, to remain there, as the sun had set when be had reached that place; and the young woman saw him sitting by the door of the house.

38 And he asked her for a drink of water and she said to him, Who art thou? and he said to her, I was this day going on the road, and reached here when the sun set, so I will abide here all night, and in the morning I will arise early and continue my journey.

39 And the young woman went into the house and fetched the man bread and water to eat and drink.

40 And this affair became known to the people of Admah, and they assembled and brought the young woman before the judges, that they should judge her for this act.

41 And the judge said, The judgment of death must pass upon this woman because she transgressed our law, and this therefore is the decision concerning her.

42 And the people of those cities assembled and brought out the young woman, and anointed her with honey from head to foot, as the judge had decreed, and they placed her before a swarm of bees which were then in their hives, and the bees flew upon her and stung her that her whole body was swelled.

43 And the young woman cried out on account of the bees, but no one took notice of her or pitied her, and her cries ascended to heaven.

44 And the Lord was provoked at this and at all the works of the cities of Sodom, for they had abundance of food, and had tranquility amongst them, and still would not sustain the poor and the needy, and in those days their evil doings and sins became great before the Lord.

45 And the Lord sent for two of the angels that had come to Abraham's house, to destroy Sodom and its cities.

46 And the angels rose up from the door of Abraham's tent, after they had eaten and drunk, and they reached Sodom in the evening, and

Lot was then sitting in the gate of Sodom, and when he saw them he rose to meet them, and he bowed down to the ground.

47 And he pressed them greatly and brought them into his house, and he gave them victuals which they ate, and they abode all night in his house.

48 And the angels said to Lot, Arise, go forth from this place, thou and all belonging to thee, lest thou be consumed in the iniquity of this city, for the Lord will destroy this place.

49 And the angels laid hold upon the hand of Lot and upon the hand of his wife, and upon the hands of his children, and all belonging to him, and they brought him forth and set him without the cities.

50 And they said to Lot, Escape for thy life, and he fled and all belonging to him.

51 Then the Lord rained upon Sodom and upon Gomorrah and upon all these cities brimstone and fire from the Lord out of heaven.

52 And he overthrew these cities, all the plain and all the inhabitants of the cities, and that which grew upon the ground; and Ado the wife of Lot looked back to see the destruction of the cities, for her compassion was moved on account of her daughters who remained in Sodom, for they did not go with her.

53 And when she looked back she became a pillar of salt, and it is yet in that place unto this day.

54 And the oxen which stood in that place daily licked up the salt to the extremities of their feet, and in the morning it would spring forth afresh, and they again licked it up unto this day.

55 And Lot and two of his daughters that remained with him fled and escaped to the cave of Adullam, and they remained there for some time.

56 And Abraham rose up early in the morning to see what had been done to the cities of Sodom; and he looked and beheld the smoke of the cities going up like the smoke of a furnace.

57 And Lot and his two daughters remained in the cave, and they made their father drink wine, and they lay with him, for they said there was no man upon earth that could raise up seed from them, for they thought that the whole earth was destroyed.

58 And they both lay with their father, and they conceived and bare sons, and the first born called the name of her son Moab, saying, From my father did I conceive him; he is the father of the Moabites unto this day.

59 And the younger also called her son Benami; he is the father of the children of Ammon unto this day.

60 And after this Lot and his two daughters went away from there, and he dwelt on the other side of the Jordan with his two daughters and their sons, and the sons of Lot grew up, and they went and took themselves wives from the land of Canaan, and they begat children and they were fruitful and multiplied.

Jasher 20

1 And at that time Abraham journeyed from the plain of Mamre, and he went to the land of the Philistines, and he dwelt in Gerar; it was in the twenty-fifth year of Abraham's being in the land of Canaan, and the hundredth year of the life of Abraham, that he came to Gerar in the land of the Philistines.

2 And when they entered the land he said to Sarah his wife, Say thou art my sister, to any one that shall ask thee, in order that we may escape the evil of the inhabitants of the land.

3 And as Abraham was dwelling in the land of the Philistines, the servants of Abimelech, king of the Philistines, saw that Sarah was exceedingly beautiful, and they asked Abraham concerning her, and he said, She is my sister.

4 And the servants of Abimelech went to Abimelech, saying, A man from the land of Canaan is come to dwell in the land, and he has a sister that is exceeding fair.

5 And Abimelech heard the words of his servants who praised Sarah to him, and Abimelech sent his officers, and they brought Sarah to the king.

6 And Sarah came to the house of Abimelech, and the king saw that Sarah was beautiful, and she pleased him exceedingly.

7 And he approached her and said to her, What is that man to thee with whom thou didst come to our land? and Sarah answered and said He is my brother, and we came from the land of Canaan to dwell wherever we could find a place.

8 And Abimelech said to Sarah, Behold my land is before thee, place thy brother in any part of this land that pleases thee, and it will be our duty to exalt and elevate him above all the people of the land since he is thy brother.

9 And Abimelech sent for Abraham, and Abraham came to Abimelech.

10 And Abimelech said to Abraham, Behold I have given orders that thou shalt be honored as thou desirest on account of thy sister Sarah.

11 And Abraham went forth from the king, and the king's present followed him.

12 As at evening time, before men lie down to rest, the king was sitting upon his throne, and a deep sleep fell upon him, and he lay upon the throne and slept till morning.

13 And he dreamed that an angel of the Lord came to him with a drawn sword in his hand, and the angel stood over Abimelech, and wished to slay him with the sword, and the king was terrified in his dream, and said to the angel, In what have I sinned against thee that thou comest to slay me with thy sword?

52

14 And the angel answered and said to Abimelech, Behold thou diest on account of the woman which thou didst yesternight bring to thy house, for she is a married woman, the wife of Abraham who came to thy house; now therefore return that man his wife, for she is his wife; and shouldst thou not return her, know that thou wilt surely die, thou and all belonging to thee.

15 And on that night there was a great outcry in the land of the Philistines, and the inhabitants of the land saw the figure of a man standing with a drawn sword in his hand, and he smote the inhabitants of the land with the sword, yea he continued to smite them.

16 And the angel of the Lord smote the whole land of the Philistines on that night, and there was a great confusion on that night and on the following morning.

17 And every womb was closed, and all their issues, and the hand of the Lord was upon them on account of

Sarah, wife of Abraham, whom Abimelech had taken.

18 And in the morning Abimelech rose with terror and confusion and with a great dread, and he sent and had his servants called in, and he related his dream to them, and the people were greatly afraid.

19 And one man standing amongst the servants of the king answered the king, saying, O sovereign king, restore this woman to her husband, for he is her husband, for the like happened to the king of Egypt when this man came to Egypt.

20 And he said concerning his wife, She is my sister, for such is his manner of doing when he cometh to dwell in the land in which he is a stranger.

21 And Pharaoh sent and took this woman for a wife and the Lord brought upon him grievous plagues until he returned the woman to her husband.

22 Now therefore, O sovereign king, know what happened yesternight to the whole land, for there was a very great consternation and great pain and lamentation, and we know that it was on account of the woman which thou didst take.

23 Now, therefore, restore this woman to her husband, lest it should befall us as it did to Pharaoh king of Egypt and his subjects, and that we may not die; and Abimelech

hastened and called and had Sarah called for, and she came before him, and he had Abraham called for, and he came before him.

24 And Abimelech said to them, What is this work you have been doing in saying you are brother and sister, and I took this woman for a wife?

25 And Abraham said, Because I thought I should suffer death on account of my wife; and Abimelech took flocks and herds, and men servants and maid servants, and a thousand pieces of silver, and he gave them to Abraham, and he returned Sarah to him.

26 And Abimelech said to Abraham, Behold the whole land is before thee, dwell in it wherever thou shalt choose.

27 And Abraham and Sarah, his wife, went forth from the king's presence with honor and respect, and they dwelt in the land, even in Gerar.

28 And all the inhabitants of the land of the Philistines and the king's servants were still in pain, through the plague which the angel had inflicted upon them the whole night on account of Sarah.

29 And Abimelech sent for Abraham, saying, Pray now for thy servants to the Lord thy God, that he may put away this mortality from amongst us.

30 And Abraham prayed on account of Abimelech and his subjects, and the Lord heard the prayer of Abraham, and he healed Abimelech and all his subjects.

Jasher 21

1 And it was at that time at the end of a year and four months of Abraham's dwelling in the land of the Philistines in Gerar, that God visited Sarah, and the Lord remembered her, and she conceived and bare a son to Abraham.

2 And Abraham called the name of the son which was born to him, which Sarah bare to him, Isaac.

3 And Abraham circumcised his son Isaac at eight days old, as God had commanded Abraham to do unto his seed after him; and Abraham was one hundred, and Sarah ninety years old, when Isaac was born to them.

4 And the child grew up and he was weaned, and Abraham made a great feast upon the day that Isaac was weaned.

5 And Shem and Eber and all the great people of the land, and Abimelech king of the Philistines, and his servants, and Phicol, the captain of his host, came to eat and drink and rejoice at the feast which Abraham made upon the day of his son Isaac's being weaned.

6 Also Terah, the father of Abraham, and Nahor his brother, came from

Haran, they and all belonging to them, for they greatly rejoiced on hearing that a son had been born to Sarah.

7 And they came to Abraham, and they ate and drank at the feast which Abraham made upon the day of Isaac's being weaned.

8 And Terah and Nahor rejoiced with Abraham, and they remained with him many days in the land of the Philistines.

9 At that time Serug the son of Reu died, in the first year of the birth of Isaac son of Abraham.

10 And all the days of Serug were two hundred and thirty-nine years, and he died.

11 And Ishmael the son of Abraham was grown up in those days; he was fourteen years old when Sarah bare Isaac to Abraham.

12 And God was with Ishmael the son of Abraham, and he grew up, and he learned to use the bow and became an archer.

13 And when Isaac was five years old he was sitting with Ishmael at the door of the tent.

14 And Ishmael came to Isaac and seated himself opposite to him, and he took the bow and drew it and put the arrow in it, and intended to slay Isaac.

15 And Sarah saw the act which Ishmael desired to do to her son Isaac, and it grieved her exceedingly on account of her son, and she sent for Abraham, and said to him, Cast out this bondwoman and her son, for her son shall not be heir with my son, for thus did he seek to do unto him this day.

16 And Abraham hearkened to the voice of Sarah, and he rose up early in the morning, and he took twelve loaves and a bottle of water which he gave to Hagar, and sent her away with her son, and Hagar went with her son to the wilderness, and they dwelt in the wilderness of Paran with the inhabitants of the wilderness, and Ishmael was an archer, and he dwelt in the wilderness a long time.

17 And he and his mother afterward went to the land of Egypt, and they dwelt there, and Hagar took a wife for her son from Egypt, and her name was Meribah.

18 And the wife of Ishmael conceived and bare four sons and two daughters, and Ishmael and his mother and his wife and children afterward went and returned to the wilderness.

19 And they made themselves tents in the wilderness, in which they dwelt, and they continued to travel and then to rest monthly and yearly.

20 And God gave Ishmael flocks and herds and tents on account of

Abraham his father, and the man increased in cattle.

21 And Ishmael dwelt in deserts and in tents, traveling and resting for a long time, and he did not see the face of his father.

22 And in some time after, Abraham said to Sarah his wife, I will go and see my son Ishmael, for I have a desire to see him, for I have not seen him for a long time.

23 And Abraham rode upon one of his camels to the wilderness to seek his son Ishmael, for he heard that he was dwelling in a tent in the wilderness with all belonging to him.

24 And Abraham went to the wilderness, and he reached the tent of Ishmael about noon, and he asked after Ishmael, and he found the wife of Ishmael sitting in the tent with her children, and Ishmael her husband and his mother were not with them.

25 And Abraham asked the wife of Ishmael, saying, Where has Ishmael gone? and she said, He has gone to the field to hunt, and Abraham was still mounted upon the camel, for he would not get off to the ground as he had sworn to his wife Sarah that he would not get off from the camel.

26 And Abraham said to Ishmael's wife, My daughter, give me a little water that I may drink, for I am fatigued from the journey.

27 And Ishmael's wife answered and said to Abraham, We have neither water nor bread, and she continued sitting in the tent and did not notice Abraham, neither did she ask him who he was.

28 But she was beating her children in the tent, and she was cursing them, and she also cursed her husband Ishmael and reproached him, and Abraham heard the words of Ishmael's wife to her children, and he was very angry and displeased.

29 And Abraham called to the woman to come out to him from the tent, and the woman came and stood opposite to Abraham, for Abraham was still mounted upon the camel.

30 And Abraham said to Ishmael's wife, When thy husband Ishmael returneth home say these words to him,

31 A very old man from the land of the Philistines came hither to seek thee, and thus was his appearance and figure; I did not ask him who he was, and seeing thou wast not here he spoke unto me and said, When Ishmael thy husband returneth tell him thus did this man say, When thou comest home put away this nail of the tent which thou hast placed here, and place another nail in its stead.

32 And Abraham finished his instructions to the woman, and he

turned and went off on the camel homeward.

33 And after that Ishmael came from the chase he and his mother, and returned to the tent, and his wife spoke these words to him,

34 A very old man from the land of the Philistines came to seek thee, and thus was his appearance and figure; I did not ask him who he was, and seeing thou wast not at home he said to me, When thy husband cometh home tell him, thus saith the old man, Put away the nail of the tent which thou hast placed here and place another nail in its stead.

35 And Ishmael heard the words of his wife, and he knew that it was his father, and that his wife did not honor him.

36 And Ishmael understood his father's words that he had spoken to his wife, and Ishmael hearkened to the voice of his father, and Ishmael cast off that woman and she went away.

37 And Ishmael afterward went to the land of Canaan, and he took another wife and he brought her to his tent to the place where he then dwelt.

38 And at the end of three years Abraham said, I will go again and see Ishmael my son, for I have not seen him for a long time.

39 And he rode upon his camel and went to the wilderness, and he reached the tent of Ishmael about noon.

40 And he asked after Ishmael, and his wife came out of the tent and she said, He is not here my lord, for he has gone to hunt in the fields, and to feed the camels, and the woman said to Abraham, Turn in my lord into the tent, and eat a morsel of bread, for thy soul must be wearied on account of the journey.

41 And Abraham said to her, I will not stop for I am in haste to continue my journey, but give me a little water to drink, for I have thirst; and the woman hastened and ran into the tent and she brought out water and bread to Abraham, which she placed before him and she urged him to eat, and he ate and drank and his heart was comforted and he blessed his son Ishmael.

42 And he finished his meal and he blessed the Lord, and he said to Ishmael's wife, When Ishmael cometh home say these words to him,

43 A very old man from the land of the Philistines came hither and asked after thee, and thou wast not here; and I brought him out bread and water and he ate and drank and his heart was comforted.

44 And he spoke these words to me: When Ishmael thy husband cometh

home, say unto him, The nail of the tent which thou hast is very good, do not put it away from the tent.

45 And Abraham finished commanding the woman, and he rode off to his home to the land of the Philistines; and when Ishmael came to his tent his wife went forth to meet him with joy and a cheerful heart.

46 And she said to him, An old man came here from the land of the Philistines and thus was his appearance, and he asked after thee and thou wast not here, so I brought out bread and water, and he ate and drank and his heart was comforted.

47 And he spoke these words to me, When Ishmael thy husband cometh home say to him, The nail of the tent which thou hast is very good, do not put it away from the tent.

48 And Ishmael knew that it was his father, and that his wife had honored him, and the Lord blessed Ishmael.

Jasher 22

1 And Ishmael then rose up and took his wife and his children and his cattle and all belonging to him, and he journeyed from there and he went to his father in the land of the Philistines.

2 And Abraham related to Ishmael his son the transaction with the first wife that Ishmael took, according to what she did.

3 And Ishmael and his children dwelt with Abraham many days in that land, and Abraham dwelt in the land of the Philistines a long time.

4 And the days increased and reached twenty six years, and after that Abraham with his servants and all belonging to him went from the land of the Philistines and removed to a great distance, and they came near to Hebron, and they remained there, and the servants of Abraham dug wells of water, and Abraham and all belonging to him dwelt by the water, and the servants of Abimelech king of the Philistines heard the report that Abraham's servants had dug wells of water in the borders of the land.

5 And they came and quarreled with the servants of Abraham, and they robbed them of the great well which they had dug.

6 And Abimelech king of the Philistines heard of this affair, and he with Phicol the captain of his host and twenty of his men came to Abraham, and Abimelech spoke to Abraham concerning his servants, and Abraham rebuked Abimelech concerning the well of which his servants had robbed him.

7 And Abimelech said to Abraham, As the Lord liveth who created the whole earth, I did not hear of the act which my servants did unto thy servants until this day.

8 And Abraham took seven ewe lambs and gave them to Abimelech, saying, Take these, I pray thee, from my hands that it may be a testimony for me that I dug this well.

9 And Abimelech took the seven ewe lambs which Abraham had given to him, for he had also given him cattle and herds in abundance, and Abimelech swore to Abraham concerning the well, therefore he called that well Beersheba, for there they both swore concerning it.

10 And they both made a covenant in Beersheba, and Abimelech rose up with Phicol the captain of his host and all his men, and they returned to the land of the Philistines, and Abraham and all belonging to him dwelt in Beersheba and he was in that land a long time.

11 And Abraham planted a large grove in Beersheba, and he made to it four gates facing the four sides of the earth, and he planted a vineyard in it, so that if a traveler came to Abraham he entered any gate which was in his road, and remained there and ate and drank and satisfied himself and then departed.

12 For the house of Abraham was always open to the sons of men that passed and repassed, who came daily to eat and drink in the house of Abraham.

13 And any man who had hunger and came to Abraham's house, Abraham would give him bread that he might eat and drink and be satisfied, and any one that came naked to his house he would clothe with garments as he might choose, and give him silver and gold and make known to him the Lord who had created him in the earth; this did Abraham all his life.

14 And Abraham and his children and all belonging to him dwelt in Beersheba, and he pitched his tent as far as Hebron.

15 And Abraham's brother Nahor and his father and all belonging to them dwelt in Haran, for they did not come with Abraham to the land of Canaan.

16 And children were born to Nahor which Milca the daughter of Haran, and sister to Sarah, Abraham's wife, bare to him.

17 And these are the names of those that were born to him, Uz, Buz, Kemuel, Kesed, Chazo, Pildash, Tidlaf, and Bethuel, being eight sons, these are the children of Milca which she bare to Nahor, Abraham's brother.

18 And Nahor had a concubine and her name was Reumah, and she also bare to Nahor, Zebach, Gachash, Tachash and Maacha, being four sons.

19 And the children that were born to Nahor were twelve sons besides his

daughters, and they also had children born to them in Haran.

20 And the children of Uz the first born of Nahor were Abi, Cheref, Gadin, Melus, and Deborah their sister.

21 And the sons of Buz were Berachel, Naamath, Sheva, and Madonu.

22 And the sons of Kemuel were Aram and Rechob.

23 And the sons of Kesed were Anamlech, Meshai, Benon and Yifi; and the sons of Chazo were Pildash, Mechi and Opher.

24 And the sons of Pildash were Arud, Chamum, Mered and Moloch.

25 And the sons of Tidlaf were Mushan, Cushan and Mutzi.

26 And the children of Bethuel were Sechar, Laban and their sister Rebecca.

27 These are the families of the children of Nahor, that were born to them in Haran; and Aram the son of Kemuel and Rechob his brother went away from Haran, and they found a valley in the land by the river Euphrates.

28 And they built a city there, and they called the name of the city after the name of Pethor the son of Aram, that is Aram Naherayim unto this day.

29 And the children of Kesed also went to dwell where they could find a place, and they went and they found a valley opposite to the land of Shinar, and they dwelt there.

30 And they there built themselves a city, and they called the name at the city Kesed after the name of their father, that is the land Kasdim unto this day, and the Kasdim dwelt in that land and they were fruitful and multiplied exceedingly.

31 And Terah, father of Nahor and Abraham, went and took another wife in his old age, and her name was Pelilah, and she conceived and bare him a son and he called his name Zoba.

32 And Terah lived twenty-five years after he begat Zoba.

33 And Terah died in that year, that is in the thirty-fifth year of the birth of Isaac son of Abraham.

34 And the days of Terah were two hundred and five years, and he was buried in Haran.

35 And Zoba the son of Terah lived thirty years and he begat Aram, Achlis and Merik.

36 And Aram son of Zoba son of Terah, had three wives and he begat twelve sons and three daughters; and the Lord gave to Aram the son of Zoba, riches and possessions, and abundance of cattle, and flocks

and herds, and the man increased greatly.

37 And Aram the son of Zoba and his brother and all his household journeyed from Haran, and they went to dwell where they should find a place, for their property was too great to remain in Haran; for they could not stop in Haran together with their brethren the children of Nahor.

38 And Aram the son of Zoba went with his brethren, and they found a valley at a distance toward the eastern country and they dwelt there.

39 And they also built a city there, and they called the name thereof Aram, after the name of their eldest brother; that is Aram Zoba to this day.

40 And Isaac the son of Abraham was growing up in those days, and Abraham his father taught him the way of the Lord to know the Lord, and the Lord was with him.

41 And when Isaac was thirty-seven years old, Ishmael his brother was going about with him in the tent.

42 And Ishmael boasted of himself to Isaac, saying, I was thirteen years old when the Lord spoke to my father to circumcise us, and I did according to the word of the Lord which he spoke to my father, and I gave my soul unto the Lord, and I did not transgress his word which he commanded my father.

43 And Isaac answered Ishmael, saying, Why dost thou boast to me about this, about a little bit of thy flesh which thou didst take from thy body, concerning which the Lord commanded thee?

44 As the Lord liveth, the God of my father Abraham, if the Lord should say unto my father, Take now thy son Isaac and bring him up an offering before me, I would not refrain but I would joyfully accede to it.

45 And the Lord heard the word that Isaac spoke to Ishmael, and it seemed good in the sight of the Lord, and he thought to try Abraham in this matter.

46 And the day arrived when the sons of God came and placed themselves before the Lord, and Satan also came with the sons of God before the Lord.

47 And the Lord said unto Satan, Whence comest thou? and Satan answered the Lord and said, From going to and fro in the earth, and from walking up and down in it.

48 And the Lord said to Satan, What is thy word to me concerning all the children of the earth? and Satan answered the Lord and said, I have seen all the children of the earth who serve thee and remember thee when they require anything from thee.

49 And when thou givest them the thing which they require from thee,

they sit at their ease, and forsake thee and they remember thee no more.

50 Hast thou seen Abraham the son of Terah, who at first had no children, and he served thee and erected altars to thee wherever he came, and he brought up offerings upon them, and he proclaimed thy name continually to all the children of the earth.

51 And now that his son Isaac is born to him, he has forsaken thee, he has made a great feast for all the inhabitants of the land, and the Lord he has forgotten.

52 For amidst all that he has done he brought thee no offering; neither burnt offering nor peace offering, neither ox, lamb nor goat of all that he killed on the day that his son was weaned.

53 Even from the time of his son's birth till now, being thirty-seven years, he built no altar before thee, nor brought any offering to thee, for he saw that thou didst give what he requested before thee, and he therefore forsook thee.

54 And the Lord said to Satan, Hast thou thus considered my servant Abraham? for there is none like him upon earth, a perfect and an upright man before me, one that feareth God and avoideth evil; as I live, were I to say unto him, Bring up Isaac thy son before me, he would not withhold

him from me, much more if I told him to bring up a burnt offering before me from his flock or herds.

55 And Satan answered the Lord and said, Speak then now unto Abraham as thou hast said, and thou wilt see whether he will not this day transgress and cast aside thy words.

Jasher 23

1 At that time the word of the Lord came to Abraham, and he said unto him, Abraham, and he said, Here I am.

2 And he said to him, Take now thy son, thine only son whom thou lovest, even Isaac, and go to the land of Moriah, and offer him there for a burnt offering upon one of the mountains which shall be shown to thee, for there wilt thou see a cloud and the glory of the Lord.

3 And Abraham said within himself, How shall I separate my son Isaac from Sarah his mother, in order to bring him up for a burnt offering before the Lord?

4 And Abraham came into the tent, and he sat before Sarah his wife, and he spoke these words to her,

5 My son Isaac is grown up and he has not for some time studied the service of his God, now tomorrow I will go and bring him to Shem, and Eber his son, and there he will learn the ways of the Lord, for they will teach him to know the Lord as well

as to know that when he prayeth continually before the Lord, he will answer him, therefore there he will know the way of serving the Lord his God.

6 And Sarah said, Thou hast spoken well, go my lord and do unto him as thou hast said, but remove him not at a great distance from me, neither let him remain there too long, for my soul is bound within his soul.

7 And Abraham said unto Sarah, My daughter, let us pray to the Lord our God that he may do good with us.

8 And Sarah took her son Isaac and he abode all that night with her, and she kissed and embraced him, and gave him instructions till morning.

9 And she said to him, O my son, how can my soul separate itself from thee? And she still kissed him and embraced him, and she gave Abraham instructions concerning him.

10 And Sarah said to Abraham, O my lord, I pray thee take heed of thy son, and place thine eyes over him, for I have no other son nor daughter but him.

11 O forsake him not. If he be hungry give him bread, and if he be thirsty give him water to drink; do not let him go on foot, neither let him sit in the sun.

12 Neither let him go by himself in the road, neither force him from whatever he may desire, but do unto him as he may say to thee.

13 And Sarah wept bitterly the whole night on account of Isaac, and she gave him instructions till morning.

14 And in the morning Sarah selected a very fine and beautiful garment from those garments which she had in the house, that Abimelech had given to her.

15 And she dressed Isaac her son therewith, and she put a turban upon his head, and she enclosed a precious stone in the top of the turban, and she gave them provision for the road, and they went forth, and Isaac went with his father Abraham, and some of their servants accompanied them to see them off the road.

16 And Sarah went out with them, and she accompanied them upon the road to see them off, and they said to her, Return to the tent.

17 And when Sarah heard the words of her son Isaac she wept bitterly, and Abraham her husband wept with her, and their son wept with them a great weeping; also those who went with them wept greatly.

18 And Sarah caught hold of her son Isaac, and she held him in her arms, and she embraced him and continued to weep with him, and Sarah said, Who knoweth if after this day I shall ever see thee again?

19 And they still wept together, Abraham, Sarah and Isaac, and all those that accompanied them on the road wept with them, and Sarah afterward turned away from her son, weeping bitterly, and all her men servants and maid servants returned with her to the tent.

20 And Abraham went with Isaac his son to bring him up as an offering before the Lord, as He had commanded him.

21 And Abraham took two of his young men with him, Ishmael the son of Hagar and Eliezer his servant, and they went together with them, and whilst they were walking in the road the young men spoke these words to themselves,

22 And Ishmael said to Eliezer, Now my father Abraham is going with Isaac to bring him up for a burnt offering to the Lord, as He commanded him.

23 Now when he returneth he will give unto me all that he possesses, to inherit after him, for I am his first born.

24 And Eliezer answered Ishmael and said, Surely Abraham did cast thee away with thy mother, and swear that thou shouldst not inherit any thing of all he possesses, and to whom will he give all that he has, with all his treasures, but unto me his servant, who has been faithful in his house, who has served him night and day, and has done all that he desired me? to me will he bequeath at his death all that he possesses.

25 And whilst Abraham was proceeding with his son Isaac along the road, Satan came and appeared to Abraham in the figure of a very aged man, humble and of contrite spirit, and he approached Abraham and said to him, Art thou silly or brutish, that thou goest to do this thing this day to thine only son?

26 For God gave thee a son in thy latter days, in thy old age, and wilt thou go and slaughter him this day because he committed no violence, and wilt thou cause the soul of thine only son to perish from the earth?

27 Dost thou not know and understand that this thing cannot be from the Lord? for the Lord cannot do unto man such evil upon earth to say to him, Go slaughter thy child.

28 And Abraham heard this and knew that it was the word of Satan who endeavored to draw him aside from the way of the Lord, but Abraham would not hearken to the voice of Satan, and Abraham rebuked him so that he went away.

29 And Satan returned and came to Isaac; and he appeared unto Isaac in the figure of a young man comely and well favored.

30 And he approached Isaac and said unto him, Dost thou not know and understand that thy old silly

father bringeth thee to the slaughter this day for naught?

31 Now therefore, my son, do not listen nor attend to him, for he is a silly old man, and let not thy precious soul and beautiful figure be lost from the earth.

32 And Isaac heard this, and said unto Abraham, Hast thou heard, my father, that which this man has spoken? even thus has he spoken.

33 And Abraham answered his son Isaac and said to him, Take heed of him and do not listen to his words, nor attend to him, for he is Satan, endeavoring to draw us aside this day from the commands of God.

34 And Abraham still rebuked Satan, and Satan went from them, and seeing he could not prevail over them he hid himself from them, and he went and passed before them in the road; and he transformed himself to a large brook of water in the road, and Abraham and Isaac and his two young men reached that place, and they saw a brook large and powerful as the mighty waters.

35 And they entered the brook and passed through it, and the waters at first reached their legs.

36 And they went deeper in the brook and the waters reached up to their necks, and they were all terrified on account of the water; and whilst they were going over the brook Abraham recognized that

place, and he knew that there was no water there before.

37 And Abraham said to his son Isaac, I know this place in which there was no brook nor water, now therefore it is this Satan who does all this to us, to draw us aside this day from the commands of God.

38 And Abraham rebuked him and said unto him, The Lord rebuke thee, O Satan, begone from us for we go by the commands of God.

39 And Satan was terrified at the voice of Abraham, and he went away from them, and the place again became dry land as it was at first.

40 And Abraham went with Isaac toward the place that God had told him.

41 And on the third day Abraham lifted up his eyes and saw the place at a distance which God had told him of.

42 And a pillar of fire appeared to him that reached from the earth to heaven, and a cloud of glory upon the mountain, and the glory of the Lord was seen in the cloud.

43 And Abraham said to Isaac, My son, dost thou see in that mountain, which we perceive at a distance, that which I see upon it?

44 And Isaac answered and said unto his father, I see and lo a pillar of fire and a cloud, and the glory of the Lord is seen upon the cloud.

45 And Abraham knew that his son Isaac was accepted before the Lord for a burnt offering.

46 And Abraham said unto Eliezer and unto Ishmael his son, Do you also see that which we see upon the mountain which is at a distance?

47 And they answered and said, We see nothing more than like the other mountains of the earth. And Abraham knew that they were not accepted before the Lord to go with them, and Abraham said to them, Abide ye here with the ass whilst I and Isaac my son will go to yonder mount and worship there before the Lord and then return to you.

48 And Eliezer and Ishmael remained in that place, as Abraham had commanded.

49 And Abraham took wood for a burnt offering and placed it upon his son Isaac, and he took the fire and the knife, and they both went to that place.

50 And when they were going along Isaac said to his father, Behold, I see here the fire and wood, and where then is the lamb that is to be the burnt offering before the Lord?

51 And Abraham answered his son Isaac, saying, The Lord has made choice of thee my son, to be a perfect burnt offering instead of the lamb.

52 And Isaac said unto his father, I will do all that the Lord spoke to thee with joy and cheerfulness of heart.

53 And Abraham again said unto Isaac his son, Is there in thy heart any thought or counsel concerning this, which is not proper? tell me my son, I pray thee, O my son conceal it not from me.

54 And Isaac answered his father Abraham and said unto him, O my father, as the Lord liveth and as thy soul liveth, there is nothing in my heart to cause me to deviate either to the right or to the left from the word that he has spoken to thee.

55 Neither limb nor muscle has moved or stirred at this, nor is there in my heart any thought or evil counsel concerning this.

56 But I am of joyful and cheerful heart in this matter, and I say, Blessed is the Lord who has this day chosen me to be a burnt offering before Him.

57 And Abraham greatly rejoiced at the words of Isaac, and they went on and came together to that place that the Lord had spoken of.

58 And Abraham approached to build the altar in that place, and Abraham was weeping, and Isaac took stones and mortar until they had finished building the altar.

59 And Abraham took the wood and placed it in order upon the altar which he had built.

60 And he took his son Isaac and bound him in order to place him upon the wood which was upon the altar, to slay him for a burnt offering before the Lord.

61 And Isaac said to his father, Bind me securely and then place me upon the altar lest I should turn and move, and break loose from the force of the knife upon my flesh and thereof profane the burnt offering; and Abraham did so.

62 And Isaac still said to his father, O my father, when thou shalt have slain me and burnt me for an offering, take with thee that which shall remain of my ashes to bring to Sarah my mother, and say to her, This is the sweet smelling savor of Isaac; but do not tell her this if she should sit near a well or upon any high place, lest she should cast her soul after me and die.

63 And Abraham heard the words of Isaac, and he lifted up his voice and wept when Isaac spake these words; and Abraham's tears gushed down upon Isaac his son, and Isaac wept bitterly, and he said to his father, Hasten thou, O my father, and do with me the will of the Lord our God as He has commanded thee.

64 And the hearts of Abraham and Isaac rejoiced at this thing which the Lord had commanded them; but the eye wept bitterly whilst the heart rejoiced.

65 And Abraham bound his son Isaac, and placed him on the altar upon the wood, and Isaac stretched forth his neck upon the altar before his father, and Abraham stretched forth his hand to take the knife to slay his son as a burnt offering before the Lord.

66 At that time the angels of mercy came before the Lord and spake to him concerning Isaac, saying,

67 0 Lord, thou art a merciful and compassionate King over all that thou hast created in heaven and in earth, and thou supportest them all; give therefore ransom and redemption instead of thy servant Isaac, and pity and have compassion upon Abraham and Isaac his son, who are this day performing thy commands.

68 Hast thou seen, O Lord, how Isaac the son of Abraham thy servant is bound down to the slaughter like an animal? now therefore let thy pity be roused for them, O Lord.

69 At that time the Lord appeared unto Abraham, and called to him, from heaven, and said unto him, Lay not thine hand upon the lad, neither do thou any thing unto him, for now I know that thou fearest God in performing this act, and in not

withholding thy son, thine only son, from me.

70 And Abraham lifted up his eyes and saw, and behold, a ram was caught in a thicket by his horns; that was the ram which the Lord God had created in the earth in the day that he made earth and heaven.

71 For the Lord had prepared this ram from that day, to be a burnt offering instead of Isaac.

72 And this ram was advancing to Abraham when Satan caught hold of him and entangled his horns in the thicket, that he might not advance to Abraham, in order that Abraham might slay his son.

73 And Abraham, seeing the ram advancing to him and Satan withholding him, fetched him and brought him before the altar, and he loosened his son Isaac from his binding, and he put the ram in his stead, and Abraham killed the ram upon the altar, and brought it up as an offering in the place of his son Isaac.

74 And Abraham sprinkled some of the blood of the ram upon the altar, and he exclaimed and said, This is in the place of my son, and may this be considered this day as the blood of my son before the Lord.

75 And all that Abraham did on this occasion by the altar, he would exclaim and say, This is in the room of my son, and may it this day be considered before the Lord in the place of my son; and Abraham finished the whole of the service by the altar, and the service was accepted before the Lord, and was accounted as if it had been Isaac; and the Lord blessed Abraham and his seed on that day.

76 And Satan went to Sarah, and he appeared to her in the figure of an old man very humble and meek, and Abraham was yet engaged in the burnt offering before the Lord.

77 And he said unto her, Dost thou not know all the work that Abraham has made with thine only son this day? for he took Isaac and built an altar, and killed him, and brought him up as a sacrifice upon the altar, and Isaac cried and wept before his father, but he looked not at him, neither did he have compassion over him.

78 And Satan repeated these words, and he went away from her, and Sarah heard all the words of Satan, and she imagined him to be an old man from amongst the sons of men who had been with her son, and had come and told her these things.

79 And Sarah lifted up her voice and wept and cried out bitterly on account of her son; and she threw herself upon the ground and she cast dust upon her head, and she said, O my son, Isaac my son, O that I had this day died instead of thee. And she continued to weep and said,

It grieves me for thee, O my son, my son Isaac, O that I had died this day in thy stead.

80 And she still continued to weep, and said, It grieves me for thee after that I have reared thee and have brought thee up; now my joy is turned into mourning over thee, I that had a longing for thee, and cried and prayed to God till I bare thee at ninety years old; and now hast thou served this day for the knife and the fire, to be made an offering.

81 But I console myself with thee, my son, in its being the word of the Lord, for thou didst perform the command of thy God; for who can transgress the word of our God, in whose hands is the soul of every living creature?

82 Thou art just, O Lord our God, for all thy works are good and righteous; for I also am rejoiced with thy word which thou didst command, and whilst mine eye weepeth bitterly my heart rejoiceth.

83 And Sarah laid her head upon the bosom of one of her handmaids, and she became as still as a stone.

84 She afterward rose up and went about making inquiries till she came to Hebron, and she inquired of all those whom she met walking in the road, and no one could tell her what had happened to her son.

85 And she came with her maid servants and men servants to Kireath-arba, which is Hebron, and she asked concerning her Son, and she remained there while she sent some of her servants to seek where Abraham had gone with Isaac; they went to seek him in the house of Shem and Eber, and they could not find him, and they sought throughout the land and he was not there.

86 And behold, Satan came to Sarah in the shape of an old man, and he came and stood before her, and he said unto her, I spoke falsely unto thee, for Abraham did not kill his son and he is not dead; and when she heard the word her joy was so exceedingly violent on account of her son, that her soul went out through joy; she died and was gathered to her people.

87 And when Abraham had finished his service he returned with his son Isaac to his young men, and they rose up and went together to Beersheba, and they came home.

88 And Abraham sought for Sarah, and could not find her, and he made inquiries concerning her, and they said unto him, She went as far as Hebron to seek you both where you had gone, for thus was she informed.

89 And Abraham and Isaac went to her to Hebron, and when they found that she was dead they lifted up their voices and wept bitterly over her; and Isaac fell upon his mother's face and wept over her, and he said, O my mother, my mother, how hast

thou left me, and where hast thou gone? O how, how hast thou left me!

90 And Abraham and Isaac wept greatly and all their servants wept with them on account of Sarah, and they mourned over her a great and heavy mourning.

Jasher 24

1 And the life of Sarah was one hundred and twenty-seven years, and Sarah died; and Abraham rose up from before his dead to seek a burial place to bury his wife Sarah; and he went and spoke to the children of Heth, the inhabitants of the land, saying,

2 I am a stranger and a sojourner with you in your land; give me a possession of a burial place in your land, that I may bury my dead from before me.

3 And the children of Heth said unto Abraham, behold the land is before thee, in the choice of our sepulchers bury thy dead, for no man shall withhold thee from burying thy dead.

4 And Abraham said unto them, If you are agreeable to this go and entreat for me to Ephron, the son of Zochar, requesting that he may give me the cave of Machpelah, which is in the end of his field, and I will purchase it of him for whatever he desire for it.

5 And Ephron dwelt among the children of Heth, and they went and called for him, and he came before Abraham, and Ephron said unto Abraham, Behold all thou requirest thy servant will do; and Abraham said, No, but I will buy the cave and the field which thou hast for value, In order that it may be for a possession of a burial place for ever.

6 And Ephron answered and said, Behold the field and the cave are before thee, give whatever thou desirest; and Abraham said, Only at full value will I buy it from thy hand, and from the hands of those that go in at the gate of thy city, and from the hand of thy seed for ever.

7 And Ephron and all his brethren heard this, and Abraham weighed to Ephron four hundred shekels of silver in the hands of Ephron and in the hands of all his brethren; and Abraham wrote this transaction, and he wrote it and testified it with four witnesses.

8 And these are the names of the witnesses, Amigal son of Abishna the Hittite, Adichorom son of Ashunach the Hivite, Abdon son of Achiram the Gomerite, Bakdil the son of Abudish the Zidonite.

9 And Abraham took the book of the purchase, and placed it in his treasures, and these are the words that Abraham wrote in the book, namely:

10 That the cave and the field Abraham bought from Ephron the

Hittite, and from his seed, and from those that go out of his city, and from their seed for ever, are to be a purchase to Abraham and to his seed and to those that go forth from his loins, for a possession of a burial place for ever; and he put a signet to it and testified it with witnesses.

11 And the field and the cave that was in it and all that place were made sure unto Abraham and unto his seed after him, from the children of Heth; behold it is before Mamre in Hebron, which is in the land of Canaan.

12 And after this Abraham buried his wife Sarah there, and that place and all its boundary became to Abraham and unto his seed for a possession of a burial place.

13 And Abraham buried Sarah with pomp as observed at the interment of kings, and she was buried in very fine and beautiful garments.

14 And at her bier was Shem, his sons Eber and Abimelech, together with Anar, Ashcol and Mamre, and all the grandees of the land followed her bier.

15 And the days of Sarah were one hundred and twenty-seven years and she died, and Abraham made a great and heavy mourning, and he performed the rites of mourning for seven days.

16 And all the inhabitants of the land comforted Abraham and Isaac his son on account of Sarah.

17 And when the days of their mourning passed by Abraham sent away his son Isaac, and he went to the house of Shem and Eber, to learn the ways of the Lord and his instructions, and Abraham remained there three years.

18 At that time Abraham rose up with all his servants, and they went and returned homeward to Beersheba, and Abraham and all his servants remained in Beersheba.

19 And at the revolution of the year Abimelech king of the Philistines died in that year; he was one hundred and ninety-three years old at his death; and Abraham went with his people to the land of the Philistines, and they comforted the whole household and all his servants, and he then turned and went home.

20 And it was after the death of Abimelech that the people of Gerar took Benmalich his son, and he was only twelve years old, and they made him lying in the place of his father.

21 And they called his name Abimelech after the name of his father, for thus was it their custom to do in Gerar, and Abimelech reigned instead of Abimelech his father, and he sat upon his throne.

22 And Lot the son of Haran also died in those days, in the thirty-ninth year of the life of Isaac, and all the days that Lot lived were one hundred and forty years and he died.

23 And these are the children of Lot, that were born to him by his daughters, the name of the first born was Moab, and the name of the second was Benami.

24 And the two sons of Lot went and took themselves wives from the land of Canaan, and they bare children to them, and the children of Moab were Ed, Mayon, Tarsus, and Kanvil, four sons, these are fathers to the children of Moab unto this day.

25 And all the families of the children of Lot went to dwell wherever they should light upon, for they were fruitful and increased abundantly.

26 And they went and built themselves cities in the land where they dwelt, and they called the names of the cities which they built after their own names.

27 And Nahor the son of Terah, brother to Abraham, died in those days in the fortieth year of the life of Isaac, and all the days of Nahor were one hundred and seventy-two years and he died and was buried in Haran.

28 And when Abraham heard that his brother was dead he grieved sadly, and he mourned over his brother many days.

29 And Abraham called for Eliezer his head servant, to give him orders concerning his house, and he came and stood before him.

30 And Abraham said to him, Behold I am old, I do not know the day of my death; for I am advanced in days; now therefore rise up, go forth and do not take a wife for my son from this place and from this land, from the daughters of the Canaanites amongst whom we dwell.

31 But go to my land and to my birthplace, and take from thence a wife for my son, and the Lord God of Heaven and earth who took me from my father's house and brought me to this place, and said unto me, To thy seed will I give this land for an inheritance for ever, he will send his angel before thee and prosper thy way, that thou mayest obtain a wife for my son from my family and from my father's house.

32 And the servant answered his master Abraham and said, Behold I go to thy birthplace and to thy father's house, and take a wife for thy son from there; but if the woman be not willing to follow me to this land, shall I take thy son back to the land of thy birthplace?

33 And Abraham said unto him, Take heed that thou bring not my son hither again, for the Lord before whom I have walked he will send his angel before thee and prosper thy way.

34 And Eliezer did as Abraham ordered him, and Eliezer swore unto Abraham his master upon this matter; and Eliezer rose up and took ten camels of the camels of his master, and ten men from his master's servants with him, and they rose up and went to Haran, the city of Abraham and Nahor, in order to fetch a wife for Isaac the son of Abraham; and whilst they were gone Abraham sent to the house of Shem and Eber, and they brought from thence his son Isaac.

35 And Isaac came home to his father's house to Beersheba, whilst Eliezer and his men came to Haran; and they stopped in the city by the watering place, and he made his camels to kneel down by the water and they remained there.

36 And Eliezer, Abraham's servant, prayed and said, O God of Abraham my master; send me I pray thee good speed this day and show kindness unto my master, that thou shalt appoint this day a wife for my master's son from his family.

37 And the Lord hearkened to the voice of Eliezer, for the sake of his servant Abraham, and he happened to meet with the daughter of Bethuel, the son of Milcah, the wife of Nahor, brother to Abraham, and Eliezer came to her house.

38 And Eliezer related to them all his concerns, and that he was Abraham's servant, and they greatly rejoiced at him.

39 And they all blessed the Lord who brought this thing about, and they gave him Rebecca, the daughter of Bethuel, for a wife for Isaac.

40 And the young woman was of very comely appearance, she was a virgin, and Rebecca was ten years old in those days.

41 And Bethuel and Laban and his children made a feast on that night, and Eliezer and his men came and ate and drank and rejoiced there on that night.

42 And Eliezer rose up in the morning, he and the men that were with him, and he called to the whole household of Bethuel, saying, Send me away that I may go to my master; and they rose up and sent away Rebecca and her nurse Deborah, the daughter of Uz, and they gave her silver and gold, men servants and maid servants, and they blessed her.

43 And they sent Eliezer away with his men; and the servants took Rebecca, and he went and returned to his master to the land of Canaan.

44 And Isaac took Rebecca and she became his wife, and he brought her into the tent.

45 And Isaac was forty years old when he took Rebecca, the daughter of his uncle Bethuel, for a wife.

Jasher 25

1 And it was at that time that Abraham again took a wife in his old age, and her name was Keturah, from the land of Canaan.

2 And she bare unto him Zimran, Jokshan, Medan, Midian, Ishbak and Shuach, being six sons. And the children of Zimran were Abihen, Molich and Narim.

3 And the sons of Jokshan were Sheba and Dedan, and the sons of Medan were Amida, Joab, Gochi, Elisha and Nothach; and the sons of Midian were Ephah, Epher, Chanoch, Abida and Eldaah.

4 And the sons of Ishbak were Makiro, Beyodua and Tator.

5 And the sons of Shuach were Bildad, Mamdad, Munan and Meban; all these are the families of the children of Keturah the Canaanitish woman which she bare unto Abraham the Hebrew.

6 And Abraham sent all these away, and he gave them gifts, and they went away from his son Isaac to dwell wherever they should find a place.

7 And all these went to the mountain at the east, and they built themselves six cities in which they dwelt unto this day.

8 But the children of Sheba and Dedan, children of Jokshan, with their children, did not dwell with their brethren in their cities, and they journeyed and encamped in the countries and wildernesses unto this day.

9 And the children of Midian, son of Abraham, went to the east of the land of Cush, and they there found a large valley in the eastern country, and they remained there and built a city, and they dwelt therein, that is the land of Midian unto this day.

10 And Midian dwelt in the city which he built, he and his five sons and all belonging to him.

11 And these are the names of the sons of Midian according to their names in their cities, Ephah, Epher, Chanoch, Abida and Eldaah.

12 And the sons of Ephah were Methach, Meshar, Avi and Tzanua, and the sons of Epher were Ephron, Zur, Alirun and Medin, and the sons of Chanoch were Reuel, Rekem, Azi, Alyoshub and Alad.

13 And the sons of Abida were Chur, Melud, Kerury, Molchi; and the sons of Eldaah were Miker, and Reba, and Malchiyah and Gabol; these are the names of the Midianites according to their families; and afterward the families of Midian spread throughout the land of Midian.

14 And these are the generations of Ishmael the son Abraham, whom Hagar, Sarah's handmaid, bare unto Abraham.

15 And Ishmael took a wife from the land of Egypt, and her name was Ribah, the same is Meribah.

16 And Ribah bare unto Ishmael Nebayoth, Kedar, Adbeel, Mibsam and their sister Bosmath.

17 And Ishmael cast away his wife Ribah, and she went from him and returned to Egypt to the house of her father, and she dwelt there, for she had been very bad in the sight of Ishmael, and in the sight of his father Abraham.

18 And Ishmael afterward took a wife from the land of Canaan, and her name was Malchuth, and she bare unto him Nishma, Dumah, Masa, Chadad, Tema, Yetur, Naphish and Kedma.

19 These are the sons of Ishmael, and these are their names, being twelve princes according to their nations; and the families of Ishmael afterward spread forth, and Ishmael took his children and all the property that he had gained, together with the souls of his household and all belonging to him, and they went to dwell where they should find a place.

20 And they went and dwelt near the wilderness of Paran, and their dwelling was from Havilah unto Shur, that is before Egypt as thou comest toward Assyria.

21 And Ishmael and his sons dwelt in the land, and they had children born to them, and they were fruitful and increased abundantly.

22 And these are the names of the sons of Nebayoth the first born of Ishmael; Mend, Send, Mayon; and the sons of Kedar were Alyon, Kezem, Chamad and Eli.

23 And the sons of Adbeel were Chamad and Jabin; and the sons of Mibsam were Obadiah, Ebedmelech and Yeush; these are the families of the children of Ribah the wife of Ishmael.

24 And the sons of Mishma the son of Ishmael were Shamua, Zecaryon and Obed; and the sons of Dumah were Kezed, Eli, Machmad and Amed.

25 And the sons of Masa were Melon, Mula and Ebidadon; and the sons of Chadad were Azur, Minzar and Ebedmelech; and the sons of Tema were Seir, Sadon and Yakol.

26 And the sons of Yetur were Merith, Yaish, Alyo, and Pachoth; and the sons of Naphish were Ebed-Tamed, Abiyasaph and Mir; and the sons of Kedma were Calip, Tachti, and Omir; these were the children of Malchuth the wife of Ishmael according to their families.

27 All these are the families of Ishmael according to their generations, and they dwelt in those lands wherein they had built themselves cities unto this day.

28 And Rebecca the daughter of Bethuel, the wife of Abraham's son Isaac, was barren in those days, she had no offspring; and Isaac dwelt with his father in the land of Canaan; and the Lord was with Isaac; and Arpachshad the son of Shem the son of Noah died in those days, in the forty-eighth year of the life of Isaac, and all the days that Arpachshad lived were four hundred and thirty-eight years, and he died.

Jasher 26

1 And in the fifty-ninth year of the life of Isaac the son of Abraham, Rebecca his wife was still barren in those days.

2 And Rebecca said unto Isaac, Truly I have heard, my lord, that thy mother Sarah was barren in her days until my Lord Abraham, thy father, prayed for her and she conceived by him.

3 Now therefore stand up, pray thou also to God and he will hear thy prayer and remember us through his mercies.

4 And Isaac answered his wife Rebecca, saying, Abraham has already prayed for me to God to multiply his seed, now therefore this barrenness must proceed to us from thee.

5 And Rebecca said unto him, But arise now thou also and pray, that the Lord may hear thy prayer and grant me children, and Isaac

hearkened to the words of his wife, and Isaac and his wife rose up and went to the land of Moriah to pray there and to seek the Lord, and when they had reached that place Isaac stood up and prayed to the Lord on account of his wife because she was barren.

6 And Isaac said, O Lord God of heaven and earth, whose goodness and mercies fill the earth, thou who didst take my father from his father's house and from his birthplace, and didst bring him unto this land, and didst say unto him, To thy seed will I give the land, and thou didst promise him and didst declare unto him, I will multiply thy seed as the stars of heaven and as the sand of the sea, now may thy words be verified which thou didst speak unto my father.

7 For thou art the Lord our God, our eyes are toward thee to give us seed of men, as thou didst promise us, for thou art the Lord our God and our eyes are directed toward thee only.

8 And the Lord heard the prayer of Isaac the son of Abraham, and the Lord was entreated of him and Rebecca his wife conceived.

9 And in about seven months after the children struggled together within her, and it pained her greatly that she was wearied on account of them, and she said to all the women who were then in the land, Did such a thing happen to you as it has to me? and they said unto her, No.

10 And she said unto them, Why am I alone in this amongst all the women that were upon earth? and she went to the land of Moriah to seek the Lord on account of this; and she went to Shem and Eber his son to make inquiries of them in this matter, and that they should seek the Lord in this thing respecting her.

11 And she also asked Abraham to seek and inquire of the Lord about all that had befallen her.

12 And they all inquired of the Lord concerning this matter, and they brought her word from the Lord and told her, Two children are in thy womb, and two nations shall rise from them; and one nation shall be stronger than the other, and the greater shall serve the younger.

13 And when her days to be delivered were completed, she knelt down, and behold there were twins in her womb, as the Lord had spoken to her.

14 And the first came out red all over like a hairy garment, and all the people of the land called his name Esau, saying, That this one was made complete from the womb.

15 And after that came his brother, and his hand took hold of Esau's heel, therefore they called his name Jacob.

16 And Isaac, the son of Abraham, was sixty years old when he begat them.

17 And the boys grew up to their fifteenth year, and they came amongst the society of men. Esau was a designing and deceitful man, and an expert hunter in the field, and Jacob was a man perfect and wise, dwelling in tents, feeding flocks and learning the instructions of the Lord and the commands of his father and mother.

18 And Isaac and the children of his household dwelt with his father Abraham in the land of Canaan, as God had commanded them.

19 And Ishmael the son of Abraham went with his children and all belonging to them, and they returned there to the land of Havilah, and they dwelt there.

20 And all the children of Abraham's concubines went to dwell in the land of the east, for Abraham had sent them away from his son, and had given them presents, and they went away.

21 And Abraham gave all that he had to his son Isaac, and he also gave him all his treasures.

22 And he commanded him saying, Dost thou not know and understand the Lord is God in heaven and in earth, and there is no other beside him?

23 And it was he who took me from my father's house, and from my birth place, and gave me all the delights upon earth; who delivered me from

the counsel of the wicked, for in him did I trust.

24 And he brought me to this place, and he delivered me from Ur Casdim; and he said unto me, To thy seed will I give all these lands, and they shall inherit them when they keep my commandments, my statutes and my judgments that I have commanded thee, and which I shall command them.

25 Now therefore my son, hearken to my voice, and keep the commandments of the Lord thy God, which I commanded thee, do not turn from the right way either to the right or to the left, in order that it may be well with thee and thy children after thee forever.

26 And remember the wonderful works of the Lord, and his kindness that he has shown toward us, in having delivered us from the hands of our enemies, and the Lord our God caused them to fall into our hands; and now therefore keep all that I have commanded thee, and turn not away from the commandments of thy God, and serve none beside him, in order that it may be well with thee and thy seed after thee.

27 And teach thou thy children and thy seed the instructions of the Lord and his commandments, and teach them the upright way in which they should go, in order that it may be well with them forever.

28 And Isaac answered his father and said unto him, That which my Lord has commanded that will I do, and I will not depart from the commands of the Lord my God, I will keep all that he commanded me; and Abraham blessed his son Isaac, and also his children; and Abraham taught Jacob the instruction of the Lord and his ways.

29 And it was at that time that Abraham died, in the fifteenth year of the life of Jacob and Esau, the sons of Isaac, and all the days of Abraham were one hundred and seventy-five years, and he died and was gathered to his people in good old age, old and satisfied with days, and Isaac and Ishmael his sons buried him.

30 And when the inhabitants of Canaan heard that Abraham was dead, they all came with their kings and princes and all their men to bury Abraham.

31 And all the inhabitants of the land of Haran, and all the families of the house of Abraham, and all the princes and grandees, and the sons of Abraham by the concubines, all came when they heard of Abraham's death, and they requited Abraham's kindness, and comforted Isaac his son, and they buried Abraham in the cave which he bought from Ephron the Hittite and his children, for the possession of a burial place.

32 And all the inhabitants of Canaan, and all those who had known Abraham, wept for Abraham a whole year, and men and women mourned over him.

33 And all the little children, and all the inhabitants of the land wept on account of Abraham, for Abraham had been good to them all, and because he had been upright with God and men.

34 And there arose not a man who feared God like unto Abraham, for he had feared his God from his youth, and had served the Lord, and had gone in all his ways during his life, from his childhood to the day of his death.

35 And the Lord was with him and delivered him from the counsel of Nimrod and his people, and when he made war with the four kings of Elam he conquered them.

36 And he brought all the children of the earth to the service of God, and he taught them the ways of the Lord, and caused them to know the Lord.

37 And he formed a grove and he planted a vineyard therein, and he had always prepared in his tent meat and drink to those that passed through the land, that they might satisfy themselves in his house.

38 And the Lord God delivered the whole earth on account of Abraham.

39 And it was after the death of Abraham that God blessed his son Isaac and his children, and the Lord was with Isaac as he had been with his father Abraham, for Isaac kept all the commandments of the Lord as Abraham his father had commanded him; he did not turn to the right or to the left from the right path which his father had commanded him.

Jasher 27

1 And Esau at that time, after the death of Abraham, frequently went in the field to hunt.

2 And Nimrod king of Babel, the same was Amraphel, also frequently went with his mighty men to hunt in the field, and to walk about with his men in the cool of the day.

3 And Nimrod was observing Esau all the days, for a jealousy was formed in the heart of Nimrod against Esau all the days.

4 And on a certain day Esau went in the field to hunt, and he found Nimrod walking in the wilderness with his two men.

5 And all his mighty men and his people were with him in the wilderness, but they removed at a distance from him, and they went from him in different directions to hunt, and Esau concealed himself for Nimrod, and he lurked for him in the wilderness.

6 And Nimrod and his men that were with him did not know him, and Nimrod and his men frequently walked about in the field at the cool of the day, and to know where his men were hunting in the field.

7 And Nimrod and two of his men that were with him came to the place where they were, when Esau started suddenly from his lurking place, and drew his sword, and hastened and ran to Nimrod and cut off his head.

8 And Esau fought a desperate fight with the two men that were with Nimrod, and when they called out to him, Esau turned to them and smote them to death with his sword.

9 And all the mighty men of Nimrod, who had left him to go to the wilderness, heard the cry at a distance, and they knew the voices of those two men, and they ran to know the cause of it, when they found their king and the two men that were with him lying dead in the wilderness.

10 And when Esau saw the mighty men of Nimrod coming at a distance, he fled, and thereby escaped; and Esau took the valuable garments of Nimrod, which Nimrod's father had bequeathed to Nimrod, and with which Nimrod prevailed over the whole land, and he ran and concealed them in his house.

11 And Esau took those garments and ran into the city on account of Nimrod's men, and he came unto his father's house wearied and exhausted from fight, and he was ready to die through grief when he approached his brother Jacob and sat before him.

12 And he said unto his brother Jacob, Behold I shall die this day, and wherefore then do I want the birthright? And Jacob acted wisely with Esau in this matter, and Esau sold his birthright to Jacob, for it was so brought about by the Lord.

13 And Esau's portion in the cave of the field of Machpelah, which Abraham had bought from the children of Heth for the possession of a burial ground, Esau also sold to Jacob, and Jacob bought all this from his brother Esau for value given.

14 And Jacob wrote the whole of this in a book, and he testified the same with witnesses, and he sealed it, and the book remained in the hands of Jacob.

15 And when Nimrod the son of Cush died, his men lifted him up and brought him in consternation, and buried him in his city, and all the days that Nimrod lived were two hundred and fifteen years and he died.

16 And the days that Nimrod reigned upon the people of the land were one hundred and eighty-five years; and Nimrod died by the sword of

Esau in shame and contempt, and the seed of Abraham caused his death as he had seen in his dream.

17 And at the death of Nimrod his kingdom became divided into many divisions, and all those parts that Nimrod reigned over were restored to the respective kings of the land, who recovered them after the death of Nimrod, and all the people of the house of Nimrod were for a long time enslaved to all the other kings of the land.

Jasher 28

1 And in those days, after the death of Abraham, in that year the Lord brought a heavy famine in the land, and whilst the famine was raging in the land of Canaan, Isaac rose up to go down to Egypt on account of the famine, as his father Abraham had done.

2 And the Lord appeared that night to Isaac and he said to him, Do not go down to Egypt but rise and go to Gerar, to Abimelech king of the Philistines, and remain there till the famine shall cease.

3 And Isaac rose up and went to Gerar, as the Lord commanded him, and he remained there a full year.

4 And when Isaac came to Gerar, the people of the land saw that Rebecca his wife was of a beautiful appearance, and the people of Gerar asked Isaac concerning his wife, and he said, She is my sister, for he was afraid to say she was his wife lest the people of the land should slay him on account of her.

5 And the princes of Abimelech went and praised the woman to the king, but he answered them not, neither did he attend to their words.

6 But he heard them say that Isaac declared her to be his sister, so the king reserved this within himself.

7 And when Isaac had remained three months in the land, Abimelech looked out at the window, and he saw, and behold Isaac was sporting with Rebecca his wife, for Isaac dwelt in the outer house belonging to the king, so that the house of Isaac was opposite the house of the king.

8 And the king said unto Isaac, What is this thou hast done to us in saying of thy wife, She is my sister? how easily might one of the great men of the people have lain with her, and thou wouldst then have brought guilt upon us.

9 And Isaac said unto Abimelech, Because I was afraid lest I die on account of my wife, therefore I said, She is my sister.

10 At that time Abimelech gave orders to all his princes and great men, and they took Isaac and Rebecca his wife and brought them before the king.

11 And the king commanded that they should dress them in princely

garments, and make them ride through the streets of the city, and proclaim before them throughout the land, saying, This is the man and this is his wife; whoever toucheth this man or his wife shall surely die. And Isaac returned with his wife to the king's house, and the Lord was with Isaac and he continued to wax great and lacked nothing.

12 And the Lord caused Isaac to find favor in the sight of Abimelech, and in the sight of all his subjects, and Abimelech acted well with Isaac, for Abimelech remembered the oath and the covenant that existed between his father and Abraham.

13 And Abimelech said unto Isaac, Behold the whole earth is before thee; dwell wherever it may seem good in thy sight until thou shalt return to thy land; and Abimelech gave Isaac fields and vineyards and the best part of the land of Gerar, to sow and reap and eat the fruits of the ground until the days of the famine should have passed by.

14 And Isaac sowed in that land, and received a hundred-fold in the same year, and the Lord blessed him.

15 And the man waxed great, and he had possession of flocks and possession of herds and great store of servants.

16 And when the days of the famine had passed away the Lord appeared to Isaac and said unto him, Rise up, go forth from this place and return to thy land, to the land of Canaan; and Isaac rose up and returned to Hebron which is in the land of Canaan, he and all belonging to him as the Lord commanded him.

17 And after this Shelach the son at Arpachshad died in that year, which is the eighteenth year of the lives of Jacob and Esau; and all the days that Shelach lived were four hundred and thirty-three years and he died.

18 At that time Isaac sent his younger son Jacob to the house of Shem and Eber, and he learned the instructions of the Lord, and Jacob remained in the house of Shem and Eber for thirty-two years, and Esau his brother did not go, for he was not willing to go, and he remained in his father's house in the land of Canaan.

19 And Esau was continually hunting in the fields to bring home what he could get, so did Esau all the days.

20 And Esau was a designing and deceitful man, one who hunted after the hearts of men and inveigled them, and Esau was a valiant man in the field, and in the course of time went as usual to hunt; and he came as far as the field of Seir, the same is Edom.

21 And he remained in the land of Seir hunting in the field a year and four months.

22 And Esau there saw in the land of Seir the daughter of a man of

Canaan, and her name was Jehudith, the daughter of Beeri, son of Epher, from the families of Heth the son of Canaan.

23 And Esau took her for a wife, and he came unto her; forty years old was Esau when he took her, and he brought her to Hebron, the land of his father's dwelling place, and he dwelt there.

24 And it came to pass in those days, in the hundred and tenth year of the life of Isaac, that is in the fiftieth year of the life of Jacob, in that year died Shem the son of Noah; Shem was six hundred years old at his death.

25 And when Shem died Jacob returned to his father to Hebron which is in the land of Canaan.

26 And in the fifty-sixth year of the life of Jacob, people came from Haran, and Rebecca was told concerning her brother Laban the son of Bethuel.

27 For the wife of Laban was barren in those days, and bare no children, and also all his handmaids bare none to him.

28 And the Lord afterward remembered Adinah the wife of Laban, and she conceived and bare twin daughters, and Laban called the names of his daughters, the name of the elder Leah, and the name of the younger Rachel.

29 And those people came and told these things to Rebecca, and Rebecca rejoiced greatly that the Lord had visited her brother and that he had got children.

Jasher 29

1 And Isaac the son of Abraham became old and advanced in days, and his eyes became heavy through age; they were dim and could not see.

2 At that time Isaac called unto Esau his son, saying, Get I pray thee thy weapons, thy quiver and thy bow, rise up and go forth into the field and get me some venison, and make me savory meat and bring it to me, that I may eat in order that I may bless thee before my death, as I have now become old and gray-headed.

3 And Esau did so; and he took his weapon and went forth into the field to hunt for venison, as usual, to bring to his father as he had ordered him, so that he might bless him.

4 And Rebecca heard all the words that Isaac had spoken unto Esau, and she hastened and called her son Jacob, saying, Thus did thy father speak unto thy brother Esau, and thus did I hear, now therefore hasten thou and make that which I shall tell thee.

5 Rise up and go, I pray thee, to the flock and fetch me two fine kids of the goats, and I will get the savory meat for thy father, and thou shalt

bring the savory meat that he may eat before thy brother shall have come from the chase, in order that thy father may bless thee.

6 And Jacob hastened and did as his mother had commanded him, and he made the savory meat and brought it before his father before Esau had come from his chase.

7 And Isaac said unto Jacob, Who art thou, my son? And he said, I am thy first born Esau, I have done as thou didst order me, now therefore rise up I pray thee, and eat of my hunt, in order that thy soul may bless me as thou didst speak unto me.

8 And Isaac rose up and he ate and he drank, and his heart was comforted, and he blessed Jacob and Jacob went away from his father; and as soon as Isaac had blessed Jacob and he had gone away from him, behold Esau came from his hunt from the field, and he also made savory meat and brought it to his father to eat thereof and to bless him.

9 And Isaac said unto Esau, And who was he that has taken venison and brought it me before thou camest and whom I did bless? And Esau knew that his brother Jacob had done this, and the anger of Esau was kindled against his brother Jacob that he had acted thus toward him.

10 And Esau said, Is he not rightly called Jacob? for he has supplanted me twice, he took away my birthright and now he has taken away my blessing; and Esau wept greatly; and when Isaac heard the voice of his son Esau weeping, Isaac said unto Esau, What can I do, my son, thy brother came with subtlety and took away thy blessing; and Esau hated his brother Jacob on account of the blessing that his father had given him, and his anger was greatly roused against him.

11 And Jacob was very much afraid of his brother Esau, and he rose up and fled to the house of Eber the son of Shem, and he concealed himself there on account of his brother, and Jacob was sixty-three years old when he went forth from the land of Canaan from Hebron, and Jacob was concealed in Eber's house fourteen years on account of his brother Esau, and he there continued to learn the ways of the Lord and his commandments.

12 And when Esau saw that Jacob had fled and escaped from him, and that Jacob had cunningly obtained the blessing, then Esau grieved exceedingly, and he was also vexed at his father and mother; and he also rose up and took his wife and went away from his father and mother to the land of Seir, and he dwelt there; and Esau saw there a woman from amongst the daughters of Heth whose name was Bosmath, the

daughter of Elon the Hittite, and he took her for a wife in addition to his first wife, and Esau called her name Adah, saying the blessing had in that time passed from him.

13 And Esau dwelt in the land of Seir six months without seeing his father and mother, and afterward Esau took his wives and rose up and returned to the land of Canaan, and Esau placed his two wives in his father's house in Hebron.

14 And the wives of Esau vexed and provoked Isaac and Rebecca with their works, for they walked not in the ways of the Lord, but served their father's gods of wood and stone as their father had taught them, and they were more wicked than their father.

15 And they went according to the evil desires of their hearts, and they sacrificed and burnt incense to the Baalim, and Isaac and Rebecca became weary of them.

16 And Rebecca said, I am weary of my life because of the daughters of Heth; if Jacob take a wife of the daughters of Heth, such as these which are of the daughters of the land, what good then is life unto me?

17 And in those days Adah the wife of Esau conceived and bare him a son, and Esau called the name of the son that was born unto him Eliphaz, and Esau was sixty-five years old when she bare him.

18 And Ishmael the son of Abraham died in those days, in the sixty-forth year of the life of Jacob, and all the days that Ishmael lived were one hundred and thirty-seven years and he died.

19 And when Isaac heard that Ishmael was dead he mourned for him, and Isaac lamented over him many days.

20 And at the end of fourteen years of Jacob's residing in the house of Eber, Jacob desired to see his father and mother, and Jacob came to the house of his father and mother to Hebron, and Esau had in those days forgotten what Jacob had done to him in having taken the blessing from him in those days.

21 And when Esau saw Jacob coming to his father and mother he remembered what Jacob had done to him, and he was greatly incensed against him and he sought to slay him.

22 And Isaac the son of Abraham was old and advanced in days, and Esau said, Now my father's time is drawing nigh that he must die, and when he shall die I will slay my brother Jacob.

23 And this was told to Rebecca, and she hastened and sent and called for Jacob her son, and she said unto him, Arise, go and flee to Haran to my brother Laban, and remain there for some time, until thy

brother's anger be turned from thee and then shalt thou come back.

24 And Isaac called unto Jacob and said unto him, Take not a wife from the daughters of Canaan, for thus did our father Abraham command us according to the word of the Lord which he had commanded him, saying, Unto thy seed will I give this land; if thy children keep my covenant that I have made with thee, then will I also perform to thy children that which I have spoken unto thee and I will not forsake them.

25 Now therefore my son hearken to my voice, to all that I shall command thee, and refrain from taking a wife from amongst the daughters of Canaan; arise, go to Haran to the house of Bethuel thy mother's father, and take unto thee a wife from there from the daughters of Laban thy mother's brother.

26 Therefore take heed lest thou shouldst forget the Lord thy God and all his ways in the land to which thou goest, and shouldst get connected with the people of the land and pursue vanity and forsake the Lord thy God.

27 But when thou comest to the land serve there the Lord, do not turn to the right or to the left from the way which I commanded thee and which thou didst learn.

28 And may the Almighty God grant thee favor in the sight of the people of the earth, that thou mayest take there a wife according to thy choice; one who is good and upright in the ways of the Lord.

29 And may God give unto thee and thy seed the blessing of thy father Abraham, and make thee fruitful and multiply thee, and mayest thou become a multitude of people in the land whither thou goest, and may God cause thee to return to this land, the land of thy father's dwelling, with children and with great riches, with joy and with pleasure.

30 And Isaac finished commanding Jacob and blessing him, and he gave him many gifts, together with silver and gold, and he sent him away; and Jacob hearkened to his father and mother; he kissed them and arose and went to Padan-aram; and Jacob was seventy-seven years old when he went out from the land of Canaan from Beersheba.

31 And when Jacob went away to go to Haran Esau called unto his son Eliphaz, and secretly spoke unto him, saying, Now hasten, take thy sword in thy hand and pursue Jacob and pass before him in the road, and lurk for him, and slay him with thy sword in one of the mountains, and take all belonging to him and come back.

32 And Eliphaz the son of Esau was an active man and expert with the bow as his father had taught him,

and he was a noted hunter in the field and a valiant man.

33 And Eliphaz did as his father had commanded him, and Eliphaz was at that time thirteen years old, and Eliphaz rose up and went and took ten of his mother's brothers with him and pursued Jacob.

34 And he closely followed Jacob, and he lurked for him in the border of the land of Canaan opposite to the city of Shechem.

35 And Jacob saw Eliphaz and his men pursuing him, and Jacob stood still in the place in which he was going, in order to know what this was, for he did not know the thing; and Eliphaz drew his sword and he went on advancing, he and his men, toward Jacob; and Jacob said unto them, What is to do with you that you have come hither, and what meaneth it that you pursue with your swords.

36 And Eliphaz came near to Jacob and he answered and said unto him, Thus did my father command me, and now therefore I will not deviate from the orders which my father gave me; and when Jacob saw that Esau had spoken to Eliphaz to employ force, Jacob then approached and supplicated Eliphaz and his men, saying to him,

37 Behold all that I have and which my father and mother gave unto me, that take unto thee and go from me, and do not slay me, and may this thing be accounted unto thee a righteousness.

38 And the Lord caused Jacob to find favor in the sight of Eliphaz the son of Esau, and his men, and they hearkened to the voice of Jacob, and they did not put him to death, and Eliphaz and his men took all belonging to Jacob together with the silver and gold that he had brought with him from Beersheba; they left him nothing.

39 And Eliphaz and his men went away from him and they returned to Esau to Beersheba, and they told him all that had occurred to them with Jacob, and they gave him all that they had taken from Jacob.

40 And Esau was indignant at Eliphaz his son, and at his men that were with him, because they had not put Jacob to death.

41 And they answered and said unto Esau, Because Jacob supplicated us in this matter not to slay him, our pity was excited toward him, and we took all belonging to him and brought it unto thee; and Esau took all the silver and gold which Eliphaz had taken from Jacob and he put them by in his house.

42 At that time when Esau saw that Isaac had blessed Jacob, and had commanded him, saying, Thou shalt not take a wife from amongst the daughters of Canaan, and that the

daughters of Canaan were bad in the sight of Isaac and Rebecca,

43 Then he went to the house of Ishmael his uncle, and in addition to his older wives he took Machlath the daughter of Ishmael, the sister of Nebayoth, for a wife.

Jasher 30

1 And Jacob went forth continuing his road to Haran, and he came as far as mount Moriah, and he tarried there all night near the city of Luz; and the Lord appeared there unto Jacob on that night, and he said unto him, I am the Lord God of Abraham and the God of Isaac thy father; the land upon which thou liest I will give unto thee and thy seed.

2 And behold I am with thee and will keep thee wherever thou goest, and I will multiply thy seed as the stars of Heaven, and I will cause all thine enemies to fall before thee; and when they shall make war with thee they shall not prevail over thee, and I will bring thee again unto this land with joy, with children, and with great riches.

3 And Jacob awoke from his sleep and he rejoiced greatly at the vision which he had seen; and he called the name of that place Bethel.

4 And Jacob rose up from that place quite rejoiced, and when he walked his feet felt light to him for joy, and he went from there to the land of the children of the East, and he returned to Haran and he set by the shepherd's well.

5 And he there found some men; going from Haran to feed their flocks, and Jacob made inquiries of them, and they said, We are from Haran.

6 And he said unto them, Do you know Laban, the son of Nahor? and they said, We know him, and behold his daughter Rachel is coming along to feed her father's flock.

7 Whilst he was yet speaking with them, Rachel the daughter of Laban came to feed her father's sheep, for she was a shepherdess.

8 And when Jacob saw Rachel, the daughter of Laban, his mother's brother, he ran and kissed her, and lifted up his voice and wept.

9 And Jacob told Rachel that he was the son of Rebecca, her father's sister, and Rachel ran and told her father, and Jacob continued to cry because he had nothing with him to bring to the house of Laban.

10 And when Laban heard that his sister's son Jacob had come, he ran and kissed him and embraced him and brought him into the house and gave him bread, and he ate.

11 And Jacob related to Laban what his brother Esau had done to him, and what his son Eliphaz had done to him in the road.

12 And Jacob resided in Laban's house for one month, and Jacob ate

and drank in the house of Laban, and afterward Laban said unto Jacob, Tell me what shall be thy wages, for how canst thou serve me for nought?

13 And Laban had no sons but only daughters, and his other wives and handmaids were still barren in those days; and these are the names of Laban's daughters which his wife Adinah had borne unto him; the name of the elder was Leah and the name of the younger was Rachel; and Leah was tender-eyed, but Rachel was beautiful and well favored, and Jacob loved her.

14 And Jacob said unto Laban, I will serve thee seven years for Rachel thy younger daughter; and Laban consented to this and Jacob served Laban seven years for his daughter Rachel.

15 And in the second year of Jacob's dwelling in Haran, that is in the seventy ninth year of the life of Jacob, in that year died Eber the son of Shem, he was four hundred and sixty-four years old at his death.

16 And when Jacob heard that Eber was dead he grieved exceedingly, and he lamented and mourned over him many days.

17 And in the third year of Jacob's dwelling in Haran, Bosmath, the daughter of Ishmael, the wife of Esau, bare unto him a son, and Esau called his name Reuel.

18 And in the fourth year of Jacob's residence in the house of Laban, the Lord visited Laban and remembered him on account of Jacob, and sons were born unto him, and his first born was Beor, his second was Alib, and the third was Chorash.

19 And the Lord gave Laban riches and honor, sons and daughters, and the man increased greatly on account of Jacob.

20 And Jacob in those days served Laban in all manner of work, in the house and in the field, and the blessing of the Lord was in all that belonged to Laban in the house and in the field.

21 And in the fifth year died Jehudith, the daughter of Beeri, the wife of Esau, in the land of Canaan, and she had no sons but daughters only.

22 And these are the names of her daughters which she bare to Esau, the name of the elder was Marzith, and the name of the younger was Puith.

23 And when Jehudith died, Esau rose up and went to Seir to hunt in the field, as usual, and Esau dwelt in the land of Seir for a long time.

24 And in the sixth year Esau took for a wife, in addition to his other wives, Ahlibamah, the daughter of Zebeon the Hivite, and Esau brought her to the land of Canaan.

25 And Ahlibamah conceived and bare unto Esau three sons, Yeush, Yaalan, and Korah.

26 And in those days, in the land of Canaan, there was a quarrel between the herdsmen of Esau and the herdsmen of the inhabitants of the land of Canaan, for Esau's cattle and goods were too abundant for him to remain in the land of Canaan, in his father's house, and the land of Canaan could not bear him on account of his cattle.

27 And when Esau saw that his quarreling increased with the inhabitants of the land of Canaan, he rose up and took his wives and his sons and his daughters, and all belonging to him, and the cattle which he possessed, and all his property that he had acquired in the land of Canaan, and he went away from the inhabitants of the land to the land of Seir, and Esau and all belonging to him dwelt in the land of Seir.

28 But from time to time Esau would go and see his father and mother in the land of Canaan, and Esau intermarried with the Horites, and he gave his daughters to the sons of Seir, the Horite.

29 And he gave his elder daughter Marzith to Anah, the son of Zebeon, his wife's brother, and Puith he gave to Azar, the son of Bilhan the Horite; and Esau dwelt in the mountain, he

and his children, and they were fruitful and multiplied.

Jasher 31

1 And in the seventh year, Jacob's service which he served Laban was completed, and Jacob said unto Laban, Give me my wife, for the days of my service are fulfilled; and Laban did so, and Laban and Jacob assembled all the people of that place and they made a feast.

2 And in the evening Laban came to the house, and afterward Jacob came there with the people of the feast, and Laban extinguished all the lights that were there in the house.

3 And Jacob said unto Laban, Wherefore dost thou do this thing unto us? and Laban answered, Such is our custom to act in this land.

4 And afterward Laban took his daughter Leah, and he brought her to Jacob, and he came to her and Jacob did not know that she was Leah.

5 And Laban gave his daughter Leah his maid Zilpah for a handmaid.

6 And all the people at the feast knew what Laban had done to Jacob, but they did not tell the thing to Jacob.

7 And all the neighbors came that night to Jacob's house, and they ate and drank and rejoiced, and played before Leah upon timbrels, and with

dances, and they responded before Jacob, Heleah, Heleah.

8 And Jacob heard their words but did not understand their meaning, but he thought such might be their custom in this land.

9 And the neighbors spoke these words before Jacob during the night, and all the lights that were in the house Laban had that night extinguished.

10 And in the morning, when daylight appeared, Jacob turned to his wife and he saw, and behold it was Leah that had been lying in his bosom, and Jacob said, Behold now I know what the neighbors said last night, Heleah, they said, and I knew it not.

11 And Jacob called unto Laban, and said unto him, What is this that thou didst unto me? Surely I served thee for Rachel, and why didst thou deceive me and didst give me Leah?

12 And Laban answered Jacob, saying, Not so is it done in our place to give the younger before the elder now therefore if thou desirest to take her sister likewise, take her unto thee for the service which thou wilt serve me for another seven years.

13 And Jacob did so, and he also took Rachel for a wife, and he served Laban seven years more, and Jacob also came to Rachel, and he loved Rachel more than Leah, and Laban gave her his maid Bilhah for a handmaid.

14 And when the Lord saw that Leah was hated, the Lord opened her womb, and she conceived and bare Jacob four sons in those days.

15 And these are their names, Reuben Simeon, Levi, and Judah, and she afterward left bearing.

16 And at that time Rachel was barren, and she had no offspring, and Rachel envied her sister Leah, and when Rachel saw that she bare no children to Jacob, she took her handmaid Bilhah, and she bare Jacob two sons, Dan and Naphtali.

17 And when Leah saw that she had left bearing, she also took her handmaid Zilpah, and she gave her to Jacob for a wife, and Jacob also came to Zilpah, and she also bare Jacob two sons, Gad and Asher.

18 And Leah again conceived and bare Jacob in those days two sons and one daughter, and these are their names, Issachar, Zebulon, and their sister Dinah.

19 And Rachel was still barren in those days, and Rachel prayed unto the Lord at that time, and she said, O Lord God remember me and visit me, I beseech thee, for now my husband will cast me off, for I have borne him no children.

20 Now O Lord God, hear my supplication before thee, and see my affliction, and give me children like one of the handmaids, that I may no more bear my reproach.

21 And God heard her and opened her womb, and Rachel conceived and bare a son, and she said, The Lord has taken away my reproach, and she called his name Joseph, saying, May the Lord add to me another son; and Jacob was ninety-one years old when she bare him.

22 At that time Jacob's mother, Rebecca, sent her nurse Deborah the daughter of Uz, and two of Isaac's servants unto Jacob.

23 And they came to Jacob to Haran and they said unto him, Rebecca has sent us to thee that thou shalt return to thy father's house to the land of Canaan; and Jacob hearkened unto them in this which his mother had spoken.

24 At that time, the other seven years which Jacob served Laban for Rachel were completed, and it was at the end of fourteen years that he had dwelt in Haran that Jacob said unto Laban, give me my wives and send me away, that I may go to my land, for behold my mother did send unto me from the land at Canaan that I should return to my father's house.

25 And Laban said unto him, Not so I pray thee; if I have found favor in thy sight do not leave me; appoint me thy wages and I will give them, and remain with me.

26 And Jacob said unto him, This is what thou shalt give me for wages,

that I shall this day pass through all thy flock and take away from them every lamb that is speckled and spotted and such as are brown amongst the sheep, and amongst the goats, and if thou wilt do this thing for me I will return and feed thy flock and keep them as at first.

27 And Laban did so, and Laban removed from his flock all that Jacob had said and gave them to him.

28 And Jacob placed all that he had removed from Laban's flock in the hands of his sons, and Jacob was feeding the remainder of Laban's flock.

29 And when the servants of Isaac which he had sent unto Jacob saw that Jacob would not then return with them to the land of Canaan to his father, they then went away from him, and they returned home to the land of Canaan.

30 And Deborah remained with Jacob in Haran, and she did not return with the servants of Isaac to the land of Canaan, and Deborah resided with Jacob's wives and children in Haran.

31 And Jacob served Laban six years longer, and when the sheep brought forth, Jacob removed from them such as were speckled and spotted, as he had determined with Laban, and Jacob did so at Laban's for six years, and the man increased abundantly and he had cattle and

maid servants and men servants, camels, and asses.

32 And Jacob had two hundred drove of cattle, and his cattle were of large size and of beautiful appearance and were very productive, and all the families of the sons of men desired to get some of the cattle of Jacob, for they were exceedingly prosperous.

33 And many of the sons of men came to procure some of Jacob's flock, and Jacob gave them a sheep for a man servant or a maid servant or for an ass or a camel, or whatever Jacob desired from them they gave him.

34 And Jacob obtained riches and honor and possessions by means of these transactions with the sons of men, and the children of Laban envied him of this honor.

35 And in the course of time he heard the words of Laban's sons, saying, Jacob has taken away all that was our father's, and of that which was our father's has he acquired all this glory.

36 And Jacob beheld the countenance of Laban and of his children, and behold it was not toward him in those days as it had been before.

37 And the Lord appeared to Jacob at the expiration of the six years, and said unto him, Arise, go forth out of this land, and return to the land of thy birthplace and I will be with thee.

38 And Jacob rose up at that time and he mounted his children and wives and all belonging to him upon camels, and he went forth to go to the land of Canaan to his father Isaac.

39 And Laban did not know that Jacob had gone from him, for Laban had been that day sheep-shearing.

40 And Rachel stole her father's images, and she took them and she concealed them upon the camel upon which she sat, and she went on.

41 And this is the manner of the images; in taking a man who is the first born and slaying him and taking the hair off his head, and taking salt and salting the head and anointing it in oil, then taking a small tablet of copper or a tablet of gold and writing the name upon it, and placing the tablet under his tongue, and taking the head with the tablet under the tongue and putting it in the house, and lighting up lights before it and bowing down to it.

42 And at the time when they bow down to it, it speaketh to them in all matters that they ask of it, through the power of the name which is written in it.

43 And some make them in the figures of men, of gold and silver, and go to them in times known to

510

them, and the figures receive the influence of the stars, and tell them future things, and in this manner were the images which Rachel stole from her father.

44 And Rachel stole these images which were her father's, in order that Laban might not know through them where Jacob had gone.

45 And Laban came home and he asked concerning Jacob and his household, and he was not to be found, and Laban sought his images to know where Jacob had gone, and could not find them, and he went to some other images, and he inquired of them and they told him that Jacob had fled from him to his father's, to the land of Canaan.

46 And Laban then rose up and he took his brothers and all his servants, and he went forth and pursued Jacob, and he overtook him in mount Gilead.

47 And Laban said unto Jacob, What is this thou hast done to me to flee and deceive me, and lead my daughters and their children as captives taken by the sword?

48 And thou didst not suffer me to kiss them and send them away with joy, and thou didst steal my gods and didst go away.

49 And Jacob answered Laban, saying, Because I was afraid lest thou wouldst take thy daughters by force from me; and now with

whomsoever thou findest thy gods he shall die.

50 And Laban searched for the images and he examined in all Jacob's tents and furniture, but could not find them.

51 And Laban said unto Jacob, We will make a covenant together and it shall be a testimony between me and thee; if thou shalt afflict my daughters, or shalt take other wives besides my daughters, even God shall be a witness between me and thee in this matter.

52 And they took stones and made a heap, and Laban said, This heap is a witness between me and thee, therefore he called the name thereof Gilead.

53 And Jacob and Laban offered sacrifice upon the mount, and they ate there by the heap, and they tarried in the mount all night, and Laban rose up early in the morning, and he wept with his daughters and he kissed them, and he returned unto his place.

54 And he hastened and sent off his son Beor, who was seventeen years old, with Abichorof the son of Uz, the son of Nahor, and with them were ten men.

55 And they hastened and went and passed on the road before Jacob, and they came by another road to the land of Seir.

56 And they came unto Esau and said unto him, Thus saith thy brother and relative, thy mother's brother Laban, the son of Bethuel, saying,

57 Hast thou heard what Jacob thy brother has done unto me, who first came to me naked and bare, and I went to meet him, and brought him to my house with honor, and I made him great, and I gave him my two daughters for wives and also two of my maids.

58 And God blessed him on my account, and he increased abundantly, and had sons, daughters and maid servants.

59 He has also an immense stock of flocks and herds, camels and asses, also silver and gold in abundance; and when he saw that his wealth increased, he left me whilst I went to shear my sheep, and he rose up and fled in secrecy.

60 And he lifted his wives and children upon camels, and he led away all his cattle and property which he acquired in my land, and he lifted up his countenance to go to his father Isaac, to the land of Canaan.

61 And he did not suffer me to kiss my daughters and their children, and he led my daughters as captives taken by the sword, and he also stole my gods and he fled.

62 And now I have left him in the mountain of the brook of Jabuk, him and all belonging to him; he lacketh nothing.

63 If it be thy wish to go to him, go then and there wilt thou find him, and thou canst do unto him as thy soul desireth; and Laban's messengers came and told Esau all these things.

64 And Esau heard all the words of Laban's messengers, and his anger was greatly kindled against Jacob, and he remembered his hatred, and his anger burned within him.

65 And Esau hastened and took his children and servants and the souls of his household, being sixty men, and he went and assembled all the children of Seir the Horite and their people, being three hundred and forty men, and took all this number of four hundred men with drawn swords, and he went unto Jacob to smite him.

66 And Esau divided this number into several parts, and he took the sixty men of his children and servants and the souls of his household as one head, and gave them in care of Eliphaz his eldest son.

67 And the remaining heads he gave to the care of the six sons of Seir the Horite, and he placed every man over his generations and children.

68 And the whole of this camp went as it was, and Esau went amongst them toward Jacob, and he conducted them with speed.

69 And Laban's messengers departed from Esau and went to the land of Canaan, and they came to the house of Rebecca the mother of Jacob and Esau.

70 And they told her saying, Behold thy son Esau has gone against his brother Jacob with four hundred men, for he heard that he was coming, and he is gone to make war with him, and to smite him and to take all that he has.

71 And Rebecca hastened and sent seventy two men from the servants of Isaac to meet Jacob on the road; for she said, Peradventure, Esau may make war in the road when he meets him.

72 And these messengers went on the road to meet Jacob, and they met him in the road of the brook on the opposite side of the brook Jabuk, and Jacob said when he saw them, This camp is destined to me from God, and Jacob called the name of that place Machnayim.

73 And Jacob knew all his father's people, and he kissed them and embraced them and came with them, and Jacob asked them concerning his father and mother, and they said, They were well.

74 And these messengers said unto Jacob, Rebecca thy mother has sent us to thee, saying, I have heard, my son, that thy brother Esau has gone forth against thee on the road with men from the children of Seir the Horite.

75 And therefore, my son, hearken to my voice and see with thy counsel what thou wilt do, and when he cometh up to thee, supplicate him, and do not speak rashly to him, and give him a present from what thou possessest, and from what God has favored thee with.

76 And when he asketh thee concerning thy affairs, conceal nothing from him, perhaps he may turn from his anger against thee and thou wilt thereby save thy soul, thou and all belonging to thee, for it is thy duty to honor him, for he is thy elder brother.

77 And when Jacob heard the words of his mother which the messengers had spoken to him, Jacob lifted up his voice and wept bitterly, and did as his mother then commanded him.

Jasher 32

1 And at that time Jacob sent messengers to his brother Esau toward the land of Seir, and he spoke to him words of supplication.

2 And he commanded them, saying, Thus shall ye say to my lord, to Esau, Thus saith thy servant Jacob, Let not my lord imagine that my father's blessing with which he did bless me has proved beneficial to me.

3 For I have been these twenty years with Laban, and he deceived me and changed my wages ten times, as it has all been already told unto my lord.

4 And I served him in his house very laboriously, and God afterward saw my affliction, my labor and the work of my hands, and he caused me to find grace and favor in his sight.

5 And I afterward through God's great mercy and kindness acquired oxen and asses and cattle, and men servants and maid servants.

6 And now I am coming to my land and my home to my father and mother, who are in the land of Canaan; and I have sent to let my lord know all this in order to find favor in the sight of my lord, so that he may not imagine that I have of myself obtained wealth, or that the blessing with which my father blessed me has benefited me.

7 And those messengers went to Esau, and found him on the borders of the land of Edom going toward Jacob, and four hundred men of the children of Seir the Horite were standing with drawn swords.

8 And the messengers of Jacob told Esau all the words that Jacob had spoken to them concerning Esau.

9 And Esau answered them with pride and contempt, and said unto them, Surely I have heard and truly it has been told unto me what Jacob has done to Laban, who exalted him in his house and gave him his daughters for wives, and he begat sons and daughters, and abundantly increased in wealth and riches in Laban's house through his means.

10 And when he saw that his wealth was abundant and his riches great he fled with all belonging to him, from Laban's house, and he led Laban's daughters away from the face of their father, as captives taken by the sword without telling him of it.

11 And not only to Laban has Jacob done thus but also unto me has he done so and has twice supplanted me, and shall I be silent?

12 Now therefore I have this day come with my camps to meet him, and I will do unto him according to the desire of my heart.

13 And the messengers returned and came to Jacob and said unto him, We came to thy brother, to Esau, and we told him all thy words, and thus has he answered us, and behold he cometh to meet thee with four hundred men.

14 Now then know and see what thou shalt do, and pray before God to deliver thee from him.

15 And when he heard the words of his brother which he had spoken to the messengers of Jacob, Jacob was greatly afraid and he was distressed.

16 And Jacob prayed to the Lord his God, and he said, O Lord God of my fathers, Abraham and Isaac, thou didst say unto me when I went away from my father's house, saying,

17 I am the Lord God of thy father Abraham and the God of Isaac, unto thee do I give this land and thy seed after thee, and I will make thy seed as the stars of heaven, and thou shalt spread forth to the four sides of heaven, and in thee and in thy seed shall all the families of the earth be blessed.

18 And thou didst establish thy words, and didst give unto me riches and children and cattle, as the utmost wishes of my heart didst thou give unto thy servant; thou didst give unto me all that I asked from thee, so that I lacked nothing.

19 And thou didst afterward say unto me, Return to thy parents and to thy birth place and I will still do well with thee.

20 And now that I have come, and thou didst deliver me from Laban, I shall fall in the hands of Esau who will slay me, yea, together with the mothers of my children.

21 Now therefore, O Lord God, deliver me, I pray thee, also from the hands of my brother Esau, for I am greatly afraid of him.

22 And if there is no righteousness in me, do it for the sake of Abraham and my father Isaac.

23 For I know that through kindness and mercy have I acquired this wealth; now therefore I beseech thee to deliver me this day with thy kindness and to answer me.

24 And Jacob ceased praying to the Lord, and he divided the people that were with him with the flocks and cattle into two camps, and he gave the half to the care of Damesek, the son of Eliezer, Abraham's servant, for a camp, with his children, and the other half he gave to the care of his brother Elianus the son of Eliezer, to be for a camp with his children.

25 And he commanded them, saying, Keep yourselves at a distance with your camps, and do not come too near each other, and if Esau come to one camp and slay it, the other camp at a distance from it will escape him.

26 And Jacob tarried there that night, and during the whole night he gave his servants instructions concerning the forces and his children.

27 And the Lord heard the prayer of Jacob on that day, and the Lord then delivered Jacob from the hands of his brother Esau.

28 And the Lord sent three angels of the angels of heaven, and they went before Esau and came to him.

29 And these angels appeared unto Esau and his people as two thousand men, riding upon horses furnished with all sorts of war

instruments, and they appeared in the sight of Esau and all his men to be divided into four camps, with four chiefs to them.

30 And one camp went on and they found Esau coming with four hundred men toward his brother Jacob, and this camp ran toward Esau and his people and terrified them, and Esau fell off the horse in alarm, and all his men separated from him in that place, for they were greatly afraid.

31 And the whole of the camp shouted after them when they fled from Esau, and all the warlike men answered, saying,

32 Surely we are the servants of Jacob, who is the servant of God, and who then can stand against us? And Esau said unto them, O then, my lord and brother Jacob is your lord, whom I have not seen for these twenty years, and now that I have this day come to see him, do you treat me in this manner?

33 And the angels answered him saying, As the Lord liveth, were not Jacob of whom thou speaketh thy brother, we had not let one remaining from thee and thy people, but only on account of Jacob we will do nothing to them.

34 And this camp passed from Esau and his men and it went away, and Esau and his men had gone from them about a league when the second camp came toward him with all sorts of weapons, and they also did unto Esau and his men as the first camp had done to them.

35 And when they had left it to go on, behold the third camp came toward him and they were all terrified, and Esau fell off the horse, and the whole camp cried out, and said, Surely we are the servants of Jacob, who is the servant of God, and who can stand against us?

36 And Esau again answered them saying, O then, Jacob my lord and your lord is my brother, and for twenty years I have not seen his countenance and hearing this day that he was coming, I went this day to meet him, and do you treat me in this manner?

37 And they answered him, and said unto him, As the Lord liveth, were not Jacob thy brother as thou didst say, we had not left a remnant from thee and thy men, but on account of Jacob of whom thou speakest being thy brother, we will not meddle with thee or thy men.

38 And the third camp also passed from them, and he still continued his road with his men toward Jacob, when the fourth camp came toward him, and they also did unto him and his men as the others had done.

39 And when Esau beheld the evil which the four angels had done to him and to his men, he became

greatly afraid of his brother Jacob, and he went to meet him in peace.

40 And Esau concealed his hatred against Jacob, because he was afraid of his life on account of his brother Jacob, and because he imagined that the four camps that he had lighted upon were Jacob's servants.

41 And Jacob tarried that night with his servants in their camps, and he resolved with his servants to give unto Esau a present from all that he had with him, and from all his property; and Jacob rose up in the morning, he and his men, and they chose from amongst the cattle a present for Esau.

42 And this is the amount of the present which Jacob chose from his flock to give unto his brother Esau: and he selected two hundred and forty head from the flocks, and he selected from the camels and asses thirty each, and of the herds he chose fifty kine.

43 And he put them all in ten droves, and he placed each sort by itself, and he delivered them into the hands of ten of his servants, each drove by itself.

44 And he commanded them, and said unto them, Keep yourselves at a distance from each other, and put a space between the droves, and when Esau and those who are with him shall meet you and ask you,

saying, Whose are you, and whither do you go, and to whom belongeth all this before you, you shall say unto them, We are the servants of Jacob, and we come to meet Esau in peace, and behold Jacob cometh behind us.

45 And that which is before us is a present sent from Jacob to his brother Esau.

46 And if they shall say unto you, Why doth he delay behind you, from coming to meet his brother and to see his face, then you shall say unto them, Surely he cometh joyfully behind us to meet his brother, for he said, I will appease him with the present that goeth to him, and after this I will see his face, peradventure he will accept of me.

47 So the whole present passed on in the hands of his servants, and went before him on that day, and he lodged that night with his camps by the border of the brook of Jabuk, and he rose up in the midst of the night, and he took his wives and his maid servants, and all belonging to him, and he that night passed them over the ford Jabuk.

48 And when he passed all belonging to him over the brook, Jacob was left by himself, and a man met him, and he wrestled with him that night until the breaking of the day, and the hollow of Jacob's thigh was out of joint through wrestling with him.

49 And at the break of day the man left Jacob there, and he blessed him and went away, and Jacob passed the brook at the break of day, and he halted upon his thigh.

50 And the sun rose upon him when he had passed the brook, and he came up to the place of his cattle and children.

51 And they went on till midday, and whilst they were going the present was passing on before them.

52 And Jacob lifted up his eyes and looked, and behold Esau was at a distance, coming along with many men, about four hundred, and Jacob was greatly afraid of his brother.

53 And Jacob hastened and divided his children unto his wives and his handmaids, and his daughter Dinah he put in a chest, and delivered her into the hands of his servants.

54 And he passed before his children and wives to meet his brother, and he bowed down to the ground, yea he bowed down seven times until he approached his brother, and God caused Jacob to find grace and favor in the sight of Esau and his men, for God had heard the prayer of Jacob.

55 And the fear of Jacob and his terror fell upon his brother Esau, for Esau was greatly afraid of Jacob for what the angels of God had done to Esau, and Esau's anger against Jacob was turned into kindness.

56 And when Esau saw Jacob running toward him, he also ran toward him and he embraced him, and he fell upon his neck, and they kissed and they wept.

57 And God put fear and kindness toward Jacob in the hearts of the men that came with Esau, and they also kissed Jacob and embraced him.

58 And also Eliphaz, the son of Esau, with his four brothers, sons of Esau, wept with Jacob, and they kissed him and embraced him, for the fear of Jacob had fallen upon them all.

59 And Esau lifted up his eyes and saw the women with their offspring, the children of Jacob, walking behind Jacob and bowing along the road to Esau.

60 And Esau said unto Jacob, Who are these with thee, my brother? are they thy children or thy servants? and Jacob answered Esau and said, They are my children which God hath graciously given to thy servant.

61 And whilst Jacob was speaking to Esau and his men, Esau beheld the whole camp, and he said unto Jacob, Whence didst thou get the whole of the camp that I met yesternight? and Jacob said, To find favor in the sight of my lord, it is that which God graciously gave to thy servant.

62 And the present came before Esau, and Jacob pressed Esau, saying, Take I pray thee the present that I have brought to my lord, and Esau said, Wherefore is this my purpose? keep that which thou hast unto thyself.

63 And Jacob said, It is incumbent upon me to give all this, since I have seen thy face, that thou still livest in peace.

64 And Esau refused to take the present, and Jacob said unto him, I beseech thee my lord, if now I have found favor in thy sight, then receive my present at my hand, for I have therefore seen thy face, as though I had seen a god-like face, because thou wast pleased with me.

65 And Esau took the present, and Jacob also gave unto Esau silver and gold and bdellium, for he pressed him so much that he took them.

66 And Esau divided the cattle that were in the camp, and he gave the half to the men who had come with him, for they had come on hire, and the other half he delivered unto the hands of his children.

67 And the silver and gold and bdellium he gave in the hands of Eliphaz his eldest son, and Esau said unto Jacob, Let us remain with thee, and we will go slowly along with thee until thou comest to my place with me, that we may dwell there together.

68 And Jacob answered his brother and said, I would do as my lord speaketh unto me, but my lord knoweth that the children are tender, and the flocks and herds with their young who are with me, go but slowly, for if they went swiftly they would all die, for thou knowest their burdens and their fatigue.

69 Therefore let my lord pass on before his servant, and I will go on slowly for the sake of the children and the flock, until I come to my lord's place to Seir.

70 And Esau said unto Jacob, I will place with thee some of the people that are with me to take care of thee in the road, and to bear thy fatigue and burden, and he said, What needeth it my lord, if I may find grace in thy sight?

71 Behold I will come unto thee to Seir to dwell there together as thou hast spoken, go thou then with thy people for I will follow thee.

72 And Jacob said this to Esau in order to remove Esau and his men from him, so that Jacob might afterward go to his father's house to the land of Canaan.

73 And Esau hearkened to the voice of Jacob, and Esau returned with the four hundred men that were with him on their road to Seir, and Jacob and all belonging to him went that day as

far as the extremity of the land of Canaan in its borders, and he remained there some time.

Jasher 33

1 And in some time after Jacob went away from the borders of the land, and he came to the land of Shalem, that is the city of Shechem, which is in the land of Canaan, and he rested in front of the city.

2 And he bought a parcel of the field which was there, from the children of Hamor the people of the land, for five shekels.

3 And Jacob there built himself a house, and he pitched his tent there, and he made booths for his cattle, therefore he called the name of that place Succoth.

4 And Jacob remained in Succoth a year and six months.

5 At that time some of the women of the inhabitants of the land went to the city of Shechem to dance and rejoice with the daughters of the people of the city, and when they went forth then Rachel and Leah the wives of Jacob with their families also went to behold the rejoicing of the daughters of the city.

6 And Dinah the daughter of Jacob also went along with them and saw the daughters of the city, and they remained there before these daughters whilst all the people of the city were standing by them to behold

their rejoicings, and all the great people of the city were there.

7 And Shechem the son of Hamor, the prince of the land was also standing there to see them.

8 And Shechem beheld Dinah the daughter of Jacob sitting with her mother before the daughters of the city, and the damsel pleased him greatly, and he there asked his friends and his people, saying, Whose daughter is that sitting amongst the women, whom I do not know in this city?

9 And they said unto him, Surely this is the daughter of Jacob the son of Isaac the Hebrew, who has dwelt in this city for some time, and when it was reported that the daughters of the land were going forth to rejoice she went with her mother and maid servants to sit amongst them as thou seest.

10 And Shechem beheld Dinah the daughter of Jacob, and when he looked at her his soul became fixed upon Dinah.

11 And he sent and had her taken by force, and Dinah came to the house of Shechem and he seized her forcibly and lay with her and humbled her, and he loved her exceedingly and placed her in his house.

12 And they came and told the thing unto Jacob, and when Jacob heard that Shechem had defiled his

daughter Dinah, Jacob sent twelve of his servants to fetch Dinah from the house of Shechem, and they went and came to the house of Shechem to take away Dinah from there.

13 And when they came Shechem went out to them with his men and drove them from his house, and he would not suffer them to come before Dinah, but Shechem was sitting with Dinah kissing and embracing her before their eyes.

14 And the servants of Jacob came back and told him, saying, When we came, he and his men drove us away, and thus did Shechem do unto Dinah before our eyes.

15 And Jacob knew moreover that Shechem had defiled his daughter, but he said nothing, and his sons were feeding his cattle in the field, and Jacob remained silent till their return.

16 And before his sons came home Jacob sent two maidens from his servants' daughters to take care of Dinah in the house of Shechem, and to remain with her, and Shechem sent three of his friends to his father Hamor the son of Chiddekem, the son of Pered, saying, Get me this damsel for a wife.

17 And Hamor the son of Chiddekem the Hivite came to the house of Shechem his son, and he sat before him, and Hamor said unto his son, Shechem, Is there then no woman amongst the daughters of thy people that thou wilt take an Hebrew woman who is not of thy people?

18 And Shechem said to him, Her only must thou get for me, for she is delightful in my sight; and Hamor did according to the word of his son, for he was greatly beloved by him.

19 And Hamor went forth to Jacob to commune with him concerning this matter, and when he had gone from the house of his son Shechem, before he came to Jacob to speak unto him, behold the sons of Jacob had come from the field, as soon as they heard the thing that Shechem the son of Hamor had done.

20 And the men were very much grieved concerning their sister, and they all came home fired with anger, before the time of gathering in their cattle.

21 And they came and sat before their father and they spoke unto him kindled with wrath, saying, Surely death is due to this man and to his household, because the Lord God of the whole earth commanded Noah and his children that man shall never rob, nor commit adultery; now behold Shechem has both ravaged and committed fornication with our sister, and not one of all the people of the city spoke a word to him.

22 Surely thou knowest and understandest that the judgment of death is due to Shechem, and to his

father, and to the whole city on account of the thing which he has done.

23 And whilst they were speaking before their father in this matter, behold Hamor the father of Shechem came to speak to Jacob the words of his son concerning Dinah, and he sat before Jacob and before his sons.

24 And Hamor spoke unto them, saying, The soul of my son Shechem longeth for your daughter; I pray you give her unto him for a wife and intermarry with us; give us your daughters and we will give you our daughters, and you shall dwell with us in our land and we will be as one people in the land.

25 For our land is very extensive, so dwell ye and trade therein and get possessions in it, and do therein as you desire, and no one shall prevent you by saying a word to you.

26 And Hamor ceased speaking unto Jacob and his sons, and behold Shechem his son had come after him, and he sat before them.

27 And Shechem spoke before Jacob and his sons, saying, May I find favor in your sight that you will give me your daughter, and whatever you say unto me that will I do for her.

28 Ask me for abundance of dowry and gift, and I will give it, and whatever you shall say unto me that will I do, and whoever he be that will

rebel against your orders, he shall die; only give me the damsel for a wife.

29 And Simeon and Levi answered Hamor and Shechem his son deceitfully, saying, All you have spoken unto us we will do for you.

30 And behold our sister is in your house, but keep away from her until we send to our father Isaac concerning this matter, for we can do nothing without his consent.

31 For he knoweth the ways of our father Abraham, and whatever he sayeth unto us we will tell you, we will conceal nothing from you.

32 And Simeon and Levi spoke this unto Shechem and his father in order to find a pretext, and to seek counsel what was to be done to Shechem and to his city in this matter.

33 And when Shechem and his father heard the words of Simeon and Levi, it seemed good in their sight, and Shechem and his father came forth to go home.

34 And when they had gone, the sons of Jacob said unto their father, saying, Behold, we know that death is due to these wicked ones and to their city, because they transgressed that which God had commanded unto Noah and his children and his seed after them.

35 And also because Shechem did this thing to our sister Dinah in

defiling her, for such vileness shall never be done amongst us.

36 Now therefore know and see what you will do, and seek counsel and pretext what is to be done to them, in order to kill all the inhabitants of this city.

37 And Simeon said to them, Here is a proper advice for you: tell them to circumcise every male amongst them as we are circumcised, and if they do not wish to do this, we shall take our daughter from them and go away.

38 And if they consent to do this and will do it, then when they are sunk down with pain, we will attack them with our swords, as upon one who is quiet and peaceable, and we will slay every male person amongst them.

39 And Simeon's advice pleased them, and Simeon and Levi resolved to do unto them as it was proposed.

40 And on the next morning Shechem and Hamor his father came again unto Jacob and his sons, to speak concerning Dinah, and to hear what answer the sons of Jacob would give to their words.

41 And the sons of Jacob spoke deceitfully to them, saying, We told our father Isaac all your words, and your words pleased him.

42 But he spoke unto us, saying, Thus did Abraham his father command him from God the Lord of the whole earth, that any man who is not of his descendants that should wish to take one of his daughters, shall cause every male belonging to him to be circumcised, as we are circumcised, and then we may give him our daughter for a wife.

43 Now we have made known to you all our ways that our father spoke unto us, for we cannot do this of which you spoke unto us, to give our daughter to an uncircumcised man, for it is a disgrace to us.

44 But herein will we consent to you, to give you our daughter, and we will also take unto ourselves your daughters, and will dwell amongst you and be one people as you have spoken, if you will hearken to us, and consent to be like us, to circumcise every male belonging to you, as we are circumcised.

45 And if you will not hearken unto us, to have every male circumcised as we are circumcised, as we have commanded, then we will come to you, and take our daughter from you and go away.

46 And Shechem and his father Hamor heard the words of the sons of Jacob, and the thing pleased them exceedingly, and Shechem and his father Hamor hastened to do the wishes of the sons of Jacob, for Shechem was very fond of Dinah, and his soul was riveted to her.

47 And Shechem and his father Hamor hastened to the gate of the city, and they assembled all the men of their city and spoke unto them the words of the sons of Jacob, saying,

48 We came to these men, the sons of Jacob, and we spoke unto them concerning their daughter, and these men will consent to do according to our wishes, and behold our land is of great extent for them, and they will dwell in it, and trade in it, and we shall be one people; we will take their daughters, and our daughters we will give unto them for wives.

49 But only on this condition will these men consent to do this thing, that every male amongst us be circumcised as they are circumcised, as their God commanded them, and when we shall have done according to their instructions to be circumcised, then will they dwell amongst us, together with their cattle and possessions, and we shall be as one people with them.

50 And when all the men of the city heard the words of Shechem and his father Hamor, then all the men of their city were agreeable to this proposal, and they obeyed to be circumcised, for Shechem and his father Hamor were greatly esteemed by them, being the princes of the land.

51 And on the next day, Shechem and Hamor his father rose up early in the morning, and they assembled all the men of their city into the middle of the city, and they called for the sons of Jacob, who circumcised every male belonging to them on that day and the next.

52 And they circumcised Shechem and Hamor his father, and the five brothers of Shechem, and then every one rose up and went home, for this thing was from the Lord against the city of Shechem, and from the Lord was Simeon's counsel in this matter, in order that the Lord might deliver the city of Shechem into the hands of Jacob's two sons.

Jasher 34

1 And the number of all the males that were circumcised, were six hundred and forty-five men, and two hundred and forty-six children.

2 But Chiddekem, son of Pered, the father of Hamor, and his six brothers, would not listen unto Shechem and his father Hamor, and they would not be circumcised, for the proposal of the sons of Jacob was loathsome in their sight, and their anger was greatly roused at this, that the people of the city had not hearkened to them.

3 And in the evening of the second day, they found eight small children who had not been circumcised, for their mothers had concealed them from Shechem and his father Hamor, and from the men of the city.

4 And Shechem and his father Hamor sent to have them brought before them to be circumcised, when Chiddekem and his six brothers sprang at them with their swords, and sought to slay them.

5 And they sought to slay also Shechem and his father Hamor and they sought to slay Dinah with them on account of this matter.

6 And they said unto them, What is this thing that you have done? are there no women amongst the daughters of your brethren the Canaanites, that you wish to take unto yourselves daughters of the Hebrews, whom ye knew not before, and will do this act which your fathers never commanded you?

7 Do you imagine that you will succeed through this act which you have done? and what will you answer in this affair to your brethren the Canaanites, who will come tomorrow and ask you concerning this thing?

8 And if your act shall not appear just and good in their sight, what will you do for your lives, and me for our lives, in your not having hearkened to our voices?

9 And if the inhabitants of the land and all your brethren the children of Ham, shall hear of your act, saying,

10 On account of a Hebrew woman did Shechem and Hamor his father, and all the inhabitants of their city,

do that with which they had been unacquainted and which their ancestors never commanded them, where then will you fly or where conceal your shame, all your days before your brethren, the inhabitants of the land of Canaan?

11 Now therefore we cannot bear up against this thing which you have done, neither can we be burdened with this yoke upon us, which our ancestors did not command us.

12 Behold tomorrow we will go and assemble all our brethren, the Canaanitish brethren who dwell in the land, and we will all come and smite you and all those who trust in you, that there shall not be a remnant left from you or them.

13 And when Hamor and his son Shechem and all the people of the city heard the words of Chiddekem and his brothers, they were terribly afraid of their lives at their words, and they repented of what they had done.

14 And Shechem and his father Hamor answered their father Chiddekem and his brethren, and they said unto them, All the words which you spoke unto us are true.

15 Now do not say, nor imagine in your hearts that on account of the love of the Hebrews we did this thing that our ancestors did not command us.

16 But because we saw that it was not their intention and desire to accede to our wishes concerning their daughter as to our taking her, except on this condition, so we hearkened to their voices and did this act which you saw, in order to obtain our desire from them.

17 And when we shall have obtained our request from them, we will then return to them and do unto them that which you say unto us.

18 We beseech you then to wait and tarry until our flesh shall be healed and we again become strong, and we will then go together against them, and do unto them that which is in your hearts and in ours.

19 And Dinah the daughter of Jacob heard all these words which Chiddekem and his brothers had spoken, and what Hamor and his son Shechem and the people of their city had answered them.

20 And she hastened and sent one of her maidens, that her father had sent to take care of her in the house of Shechem, to Jacob her father and to her brethren, saying:

21 Thus did Chiddekem and his brothers advise concerning you, and thus did Hamor and Shechem and the people of the city answer them.

22 And when Jacob heard these words he was filled with wrath, and he was indignant at them, and his anger was kindled against them.

23 And Simeon and Levi swore and said, As the Lord liveth, the God of the whole earth, by this time tomorrow, there shall not be a remnant left in the whole city.

24 And twenty young men had concealed themselves who were not circumcised, and these young men fought against Simeon and Levi, and Simeon and Levi killed eighteen of them, and two fled from them and escaped to some lime pits that were in the city, and Simeon and Levi sought for them, but could not find them.

25 And Simeon and Levi continued to go about in the city, and they killed all the people of the city at the edge of the sword, and they left none remaining.

26 And there was a great consternation in the midst of the city, and the cry of the people of the city ascended to heaven, and all the women and children cried aloud.

27 And Simeon and Levi slew all the city; they left not a male remaining in the whole city.

28 And they slew Hamor and Shechem his son at the edge of the sword, and they brought away Dinah from the house of Shechem and they went from there.

29 And the sons of Jacob went and returned, and came upon the slain, and spoiled all their property which was in the city and the field.

30 And whilst they were taking the spoil, three hundred men stood up and threw dust at them and struck them with stones, when Simeon turned to them and he slew them all with the edge of the sword, and Simeon turned before Levi, and came into the city.

31 And they took away their sheep and their oxen and their cattle, and also the remainder of the women and little ones, and they led all these away, and they opened a gate and went out and came unto their father Jacob with vigor.

32 And when Jacob saw all that they had done to the city, and saw the spoil that they took from them, Jacob was very angry at them, and Jacob said unto them, What is this that you have done to me? behold I obtained rest amongst the Canaanitish inhabitants of the land, and none of them meddled with me.

33 And now you have done to make me obnoxious to the inhabitants of the land, amongst the Canaanites and the Perizzites, and I am but of a small number, and they will all assemble against me and slay me when they hear of your work with their brethren, and I and my household will be destroyed.

34 And Simeon and Levi and all their brothers with them answered their father Jacob and said unto him, Behold we live in the land, and shall Shechem do this to our sister? why

art thou silent at all that Shechem has done? and shall he deal with our sister as with a harlot in the streets?

35 And the number of women whom Simeon and Levi took captives from the city of Shechem, whom they did not slay, was eighty-five who had not known man.

36 And amongst them was a young damsel of beautiful appearance and well favored, whose name was Bunah, and Simeon took her for a wife, and the number of the males which they took captives and did not slay, was forty-seven men, and the rest they slew.

37 And all the young men and women that Simeon and Levi had taken captives from the city of Shechem, were servants to the sons of Jacob and to their children after them, until the day of the sons of Jacob going forth from the land of Egypt.

38 And when Simeon and Levi had gone forth from the city, the two young men that were left, who had concealed themselves in the city, and did not die amongst the people of the city, rose up, and these young men went into the city and walked about in it, and found the city desolate without man, and only women weeping, and these young men cried out and said, Behold, this is the evil which the sons of Jacob the Hebrew did to this city in their having this day destroyed one of the

Canaanitish cities, and were not afraid of their lives of all the land of Canaan.

39 And these men left the city and went to the city of Tapnach, and they came there and told the inhabitants of Tapnach all that had befallen them, and all that the sons of Jacob had done to the city of Shechem.

40 And the information reached Jashub king of Tapnach, and he sent men to the city of Shechem to see those young men, for the king did not believe them in this account, saying, How could two men lay waste such a large town as Shechem?

41 And the messengers of Jashub came back and told him, saying, We came unto the city, and it is destroyed, there is not a man there; only weeping women; neither is any flock or cattle there, for all that was in the city the sons of Jacob took away.

42 And Jashub wondered at this, saying, How could two men do this thing, to destroy so large a city, and not one man able to stand against them?

43 For the like has not been from the days of Nimrod, and not even from the remotest time, has the like taken place; and Jashub, king of Tapnach, said to his people, Be courageous and we will go and fight against these Hebrews, and do unto them as they did unto the city, and we will

avenge the cause of the people of the city.

44 And Jashub, king of Tapnach, consulted with his counsellors about this matter, and his advisers said unto him, Alone thou wilt not prevail over the Hebrews, for they must be powerful to do this work to the whole city.

45 If two of them laid waste the whole city, and no one stood against them, surely if thou wilt go against them, they will all rise against us and destroy us likewise.

46 But if thou wilt send to all the kings that surround us, and let them come together, then we will go with them and fight against the sons of Jacob; then wilt thou prevail against them.

47 And Jashub heard the words of his counsellors, and their words pleased him and his people, and he did so; and Jashub king of Tapnach sent to all the kings of the Amorites that surrounded Shechem and Tapnach, saying,

48 Go up with me and assist me, and we will smite Jacob the Hebrew and all his sons, and destroy them from the earth, for thus did he do to the city of Shechem, and do you not know of it?

49 And all the kings of the Amorites heard the evil that the sons of Jacob had done to the city of Shechem,

and they were greatly astonished at them.

50 And the seven kings of the Amorites assembled with all their armies, about ten thousand men with drawn swords, and they came to fight against the sons of Jacob; and Jacob heard that the kings of the Amorites had assembled to fight against his sons, and Jacob was greatly afraid, and it distressed him.

51 And Jacob exclaimed against Simeon and Levi, saying, What is this act that you did? why have you injured me, to bring against me all the children of Canaan to destroy me and my household? for I was at rest, even I and my household, and you have done this thing to me, and provoked the inhabitants of the land against me by your proceedings.

52 And Judah answered his father, saying, Was it for naught my brothers Simeon and Levi killed all the inhabitants of Shechem? Surely it was because Shechem had humbled our sister, and transgressed the command of our God to Noah and his children, for Shechem took our sister away by force, and committed adultery with her.

53 And Shechem did all this evil and not one of the inhabitants of his city interfered with him, to say, Why wilt thou do this? surely for this my brothers went and smote the city, and the Lord delivered it into their

hands, because its inhabitants had transgressed the commands of our God. Is it then for naught that they have done all this?

54 And now why art thou afraid or distressed, and why art thou displeased at my brothers, and why is thine anger kindled against them?

55 Surely our God who delivered into their hand the city of Shechem and its people, he will also deliver into our hands all the Canaanitish kings who are coming against us, and we will do unto them as my brothers did unto Shechem.

56 Now be tranquil about them and cast away thy fears, but trust in the Lord our God, and pray unto him to assist us and deliver us, and deliver our enemies into our hands.

57 And Judah called to one of his father's servants, Go now and see where those kings, who are coming against us, are situated with their armies.

58 And the servant went and looked far off, and went up opposite Mount Sihon, and saw all the camps of the kings standing in the fields, and he returned to Judah and said, Behold the kings are situated in the field with all their camps, a people exceedingly numerous, like unto the sand upon the sea shore.

59 And Judah said unto Simeon and Levi, and unto all his brothers, Strengthen yourselves and be sons

of valor, for the Lord our God is with us, do not fear them.

60 Stand forth each man, girt with his weapons of war, his bow and his sword, and we will go and fight against these uncircumcised men; the Lord is our God, He will save us.

61 And they rose up, and each girt on his weapons of war, great and small, eleven sons of Jacob, and all the servants of Jacob with them.

62 And all the servants of Isaac who were with Isaac in Hebron, all came to them equipped in all sorts of war instruments, and the sons of Jacob and their servants, being one hundred and twelve men, went towards these kings, and Jacob also went with them.

63 And the sons of Jacob sent unto their father Isaac the son of Abraham to Hebron, the same is Kireath-arba, saying,

64 Pray we beseech thee for us unto the Lord our God, to protect us from the hands of the Canaanites who are coming against us, and to deliver them into our hands.

65 And Isaac the son of Abraham prayed unto the Lord for his sons, and he said, O Lord God, thou didst promise my father, saying, I will multiply thy seed as the stars of heaven, and thou didst also promise me, and establish thou thy word, now that the kings of Canaan are coming together, to make war with

my children because they committed no violence.

66 Now therefore, O Lord God, God of the whole earth, pervert, I pray thee, the counsel of these kings that they may not fight against my sons.

67 And impress the hearts of these kings and their people with the terror of my sons and bring down their pride, and that they may turn away from my sons.

68 And with thy strong hand and outstretched arm deliver my sons and their servants from them, for power and might are in thy hands to do all this.

69 And the sons of Jacob and their servants went toward these kings, and they trusted in the Lord their God, and whilst they were going, Jacob their father also prayed unto the Lord and said, O Lord God, powerful and exalted God, who has reigned from days of old, from thence till now and forever;

70 Thou art He who stirreth up wars and causeth them to cease, in thy hand are power and might to exalt and to bring down; O may my prayer be acceptable before thee that thou mayest turn to me with thy mercies, to impress the hearts of these kings and their people with the terror of my sons, and terrify them and their camps, and with thy great kindness deliver all those that trust in thee, for it is thou who canst bring people

under us and reduce nations under our power.

Jasher 35

1 And all the kings of the Amorites came and took their stand in the field to consult with their counsellors what was to be done with the sons of Jacob, for they were still afraid of them, saying, Behold, two of them slew the whole of the city of Shechem.

2 And the Lord heard the prayers of Isaac and Jacob, and he filled the hearts of all these kings' advisers with great fear and terror that they unanimously exclaimed,

3 Are you silly this day, or is there no understanding in you, that you will fight with the Hebrews, and why will you take a delight in your own destruction this day?

4 Behold two of them came to the city of Shechem without fear or terror, and they killed all the inhabitants of the city, that no man stood up against them, and how will you be able to fight with them all?

5 Surely you know that their God is exceedingly fond of them, and has done mighty things for them, such as have not been done from days of old, and amongst all the gods of nations, there is none can do like unto his mighty deeds.

6 Surely he delivered their father Abraham, the Hebrew, from the hand of Nimrod, and from the hand of all his people who had many times sought to slay him.

7 He delivered him also from the fire in which king Nimrod had cast him, and his God delivered him from it.

8 And who else can do the like? surely it was Abraham who slew the five kings of Elam, when they had touched his brother's son who in those days dwelt in Sodom.

9 And took his servant that was faithful in his house and a few of his men, and they pursued the kings of Elam in one night and killed them, and restored to his brother's son all his property which they had taken from him.

10 And surely you know the God of these Hebrews is much delighted with them, and they are also delighted with him, for they know that he delivered them from all their enemies.

11 And behold through his love toward his God, Abraham took his only and precious son and intended to bring him up as a burnt offering to his God, and had it not been for God who prevented him from doing this, he would then have done it through his love to his God.

12 And God saw all his works, and swore unto him, and promised him that he would deliver his sons and all his seed from every trouble that would befall them, because he had

done this thing, and through his love to his God stifled his compassion for his child.

13 And have you not heard what their God did to Pharaoh king of Egypt, and to Abimelech king of Gerar, through taking Abraham's wife, who said of her, She is my sister, lest they might slay him on account of her, and think of taking her for a wife? and God did unto them and their people all that you heard of.

14 And behold, we ourselves saw with our eyes that Esau, the brother of Jacob, came to him with four hundred men, with the intention of slaying him, for he called to mind that he had taken away from him his father's blessing.

15 And he went to meet him when he came from Syria, to smite the mother with the children, and who delivered him from his hands but his God in whom he trusted? he delivered him from the hand of his brother and also from the hands of his enemies, and surely he again will protect them.

16 Who does not know that it was their God who inspired them with strength to do to the town of Shechem the evil which you heard of?

17 Could it then be with their own strength that two men could destroy such a large city as Shechem had it

not been for their God in whom they trusted? he said and did unto them all this to slay the inhabitants of the city in their city.

18 And can you then prevail over them who have come forth together from your city to fight with the whole of them, even if a thousand times as many more should come to your assistance?

19 Surely you know and understand that you do not come to fight with them, but you come to war with their God who made choice of them, and you have therefore all come this day to be destroyed.

20 Now therefore refrain from this evil which you are endeavoring to bring upon yourselves, and it will be better for you not to go to battle with them, although they are but few in numbers, because their God is with them.

21 And when the kings of the Amorites heard all the words of their advisers, their hearts were filled with terror, and they were afraid of the sons of Jacob and would not fight against them.

22 And they inclined their ears to the words of their advisers, and they listened to all their words, and the words of the counsellors greatly pleased the kings, and they did so.

23 And the kings turned and refrained from the sons of Jacob, for they durst not approach them to

make war with them, for they were greatly afraid of them, and their hearts melted within them from their fear of them.

24 For this proceeded from the Lord to them, for he heard the prayers of his servants Isaac and Jacob, for they trusted in him; and all these kings returned with their camps on that day, each to his own city, and they did not at that time fight with the sons of Jacob.

25 And the sons of Jacob kept their station that day till evening opposite mount Sihon, and seeing that these kings did not come to fight against them, the sons of Jacob returned home.

Jasher 36

1 At that time the Lord appeared unto Jacob saying, Arise, go to Bethel and remain there, and make there an altar to the Lord who appeareth unto thee, who delivered thee and thy sons from affliction.

2 And Jacob rose up with his sons and all belonging to him, and they went and came to Bethel according to the word of the Lord.

3 And Jacob was ninety-nine years old when he went up to Bethel, and Jacob and his sons and all the people that were with him, remained in Bethel in Luz, and he there built an altar to the Lord who appeared unto him, and Jacob and his sons remained in Bethel six months.

4 At that time died Deborah the daughter of Uz, the nurse of Rebecca, who had been with Jacob; and Jacob buried her beneath Bethel under an oak that was there.

5 And Rebecca the daughter of Bethuel, the mother of Jacob, also died at that time in Hebron, the same is Kireath-arba, and she was buried in the cave of Machpelah which Abraham had bought from the children of Heth.

6 And the life of Rebecca was one hundred and thirty-three years, and she died and when Jacob heard that his mother Rebecca was dead he wept bitterly for his mother, and made a great mourning for her, and for Deborah her nurse beneath the oak, and he called the name of that place Allon-bachuth.

7 And Laban the Syrian died in those days, for God smote him because he transgressed the covenant that existed between him and Jacob.

8 And Jacob was a hundred years old when the Lord appeared unto him, and blessed him and called his name Israel, and Rachel the wife of Jacob conceived in those days.

9 And at that time Jacob and all belonging to him journeyed from Bethel to go to his father's house, to Hebron.

10 And whilst they were going on the road, and there was yet but a little way to come to Ephrath, Rachel bare

a son and she had hard labor and she died.

11 And Jacob buried her in the way to Ephrath, which is Bethlehem, and he set a pillar upon her grave, which is there unto this day; and the days of Rachel were forty-five years and she died.

12 And Jacob called the name of his son that was born to him, which Rachel bare unto him, Benjamin, for he was born to him in the land on the right hand.

13 And it was after the death of Rachel, that Jacob pitched his tent in the tent of her handmaid Bilhah.

14 And Reuben was jealous for his mother Leah on account of this, and he was filled with anger, and he rose up in his anger and went and entered the tent of Bilhah and he thence removed his father's bed.

15 At that time the portion of birthright, together with the kingly and priestly offices, was removed from the sons of Reuben, for he had profaned his father's bed, and the birthright was given unto Joseph, the kingly office to Judah, and the priesthood unto Levi, because Reuben had defiled his father's bed.

16 And these are the generations of Jacob who were born to him in Padan-aram, and the sons of Jacob were twelve.

17 The sons of Leah were Reuben the first born, and Simeon, Levi, Judah, Issachar, Zebulun, and their sister Dinah; and the sons of Rachel were Joseph and Benjamin.

18 The sons of Zilpah, Leah's handmaid, were Gad and Asher, and the sons of Bilhah, Rachel's handmaid, were Dan and Naphtali; these are the sons of Jacob which were born to him in Padan-aram.

19 And Jacob and his sons and all belonging to him journeyed and came to Mamre, which is Kireath-arba, that is in Hebron, where Abraham and Isaac sojourned, and Jacob with his sons and all belonging to him, dwelt with his father in Hebron.

20 And his brother Esau and his sons, and all belonging to him went to the land of Seir and dwelt there, and had possessions in the land of Seir, and the children of Esau were fruitful and multiplied exceedingly in the land of Seir.

21 And these are the generations of Esau that were born to him in the land of Canaan, and the sons of Esau were five.

22 And Adah bare to Esau his first born Eliphaz, and she also bare to him Reuel, and Ahlibamah bare to him Jeush, Yaalam and Korah.

23 These are the children of Esau who were born to him in the land of Canaan; and the sons of Eliphaz the

son of Esau were Teman, Omar, Zepho, Gatam, Kenaz and Amalex, and the sons of Reuel were Nachath, Zerach, Shamah and Mizzah.

24 And the sons of Jeush were Timnah, Alvah, Jetheth; and the sons of Yaalam were Alah, Phinor and Kenaz.

25 And the sons of Korah were Teman, Mibzar, Magdiel and Eram; these are the families of the sons of Esau according to their dukedoms in the land of Seir.

26 And these are the names of the sons of Seir the Horite, inhabitants of the land of Seir, Lotan, Shobal, Zibeon, Anah, Dishan, Ezer and Dishon, being seven sons.

27 And the children of Lotan were Hori, Heman and their sister Timna, that is Timna who came to Jacob and his sons, and they would not give ear to her, and she went and became a concubine to Eliphaz the son of Esau, and she bare to him Amalek.

28 And the sons of Shobal were Alvan, Manahath, Ebal, Shepho, and Onam, and the sons of Zibeon were Ajah, and Anah, this was that Anah who found the Yemim in the wilderness when he fed the asses of Zibeon his father.

29 And whilst he was feeding his father's asses he led them to the wilderness at different times to feed them.

30 And there was a day that he brought them to one of the deserts on the sea shore, opposite the wilderness of the people, and whilst he was feeding them, behold a very heavy storm came from the other side of the sea and rested upon the asses that were feeding there, and they all stood still.

31 And afterward about one hundred and twenty great and terrible animals came out from the wilderness at the other side of the sea, and they all came to the place where the asses were, and they placed themselves there.

32 And those animals, from their middle downward, were in the shape of the children of men, and from their middle upward, some had the likeness of bears, and some the likeness of the keephas, with tails behind them from between their shoulders reaching down to the earth, like the tails of the ducheephath, and these animals came and mounted and rode upon these asses, and led them away, and they went away unto this day.

33 And one of these animals approached Anah and smote him with his tail, and then fled from that place.

34 And when he saw this work he was exceedingly afraid of his life, and he fled and escaped to the city.

35 And he related to his sons and brothers all that had happened to him, and many men went to seek the asses but could not find them, and Anah and his brothers went no more to that place from that day following, for they were greatly afraid of their lives.

36 And the children of Anah the son of Seir, were Dishon and his sister Ahlibamah, and the children of Dishon were Hemdan, Eshban, Ithran and Cheran, and the children of Ezer were Bilhan, Zaavan and Akan, and the children of Dishon were Uz and Aran.

37 These are the families of the children of Seir the Horite, according to their dukedoms in the land of Seir.

38 And Esau and his children dwelt in the land of Seir the Horite, the inhabitant of the land, and they had possessions in it and were fruitful and multiplied exceedingly, and Jacob and his children and all belonging to them, dwelt with their father Isaac in the land of Canaan, as the Lord had commanded Abraham their father.

Jasher 37

1 And in the one hundred and fifth year of the life of Jacob, that is the ninth year of Jacob's dwelling with his children in the land of Canaan, he came from Padan-aram.

2 And in those days Jacob journeyed with his children from Hebron, and they went and returned to the city of Shechem, they and all belonging to them, and they dwelt there, for the children of Jacob obtained good and fat pasture land for their cattle in the city of Shechem, the city of Shechem having then been rebuilt, and there were in it about three hundred men and women.

3 And Jacob and his children and all belonging to him dwelt in the part of the field which Jacob had bought from Hamor the father of Shechem, when he came from Padan-aram before Simeon and Levi had smitten the city.

4 And all those kings of the Canaanites and Amorites that surrounded the city of Shechem, heard that the sons of Jacob had again come to Shechem and dwelt there.

5 And they said, Shall the sons of Jacob the Hebrew again come to the city and dwell therein, after that they have smitten its inhabitants and driven them out? shall they now return and also drive out those who are dwelling in the city or slay them?

6 And all the kings of Canaan again assembled, and they came together to make war with Jacob and his sons.

7 And Jashub king of Tapnach sent also to all his neighboring kings, to Elan king of Gaash, and to Ihuri king of Shiloh, and to Parathon king of

536

Chazar, and to Susi king of Sarton, and to Laban king of Bethchoran, and to Shabir king of Othnay-mah, saying,

8 Come up to me and assist me, and let us smite Jacob the Hebrew and his sons, and all belonging to him, for they are again come to Shechem to possess it and to slay its inhabitants as before.

9 And all these kings assembled together and came with all their camps, a people exceedingly plentiful like the sand upon the sea shore, and they were all opposite to Tapnach.

10 And Jashub king of Tapnach went forth to them with all his army, and he encamped with them opposite to Tapnach without the city, and all these kings they divided into seven divisions, being seven camps against the sons of Jacob.

11 And they sent a declaration to Jacob and his son, saying, Come you all forth to us that we may have an interview together in the plain, and revenge the cause of the men of Shechem whom you slew in their city, and you will now again return to the city of Shechem and dwell therein, and slay its inhabitants as before.

12 And the sons of Jacob heard this and their anger was kindled exceedingly at the words of the kings of Canaan, and ten of the sons of

Jacob hastened and rose up, and each of them girt on his weapons of war; and there were one hundred and two of their servants with them equipped in battle array.

13 And all these men, the sons of Jacob with their servants, went toward these kings, and Jacob their father was with them, and they all stood upon the heap of Shechem.

14 And Jacob prayed to the Lord for his sons, and he spread forth his hands to the Lord, and he said, O God, thou art an Almighty God, thou art our father, thou didst form us and we are the works of thine hands; I pray thee deliver my sons through thy mercy from the hand of their enemies, who are this day coming to fight with them and save them from their hand, for in thy hand is power and might, to save the few from the many.

15 And give unto my sons, thy servants, strength of heart and might to fight with their enemies, to subdue them, and make their enemies fall before them, and let not my sons and their servants die through the hands of the children of Canaan.

16 But if it seemeth good in thine eyes to take away the lives of my sons and their servants, take them in thy great mercy through the hands of thy ministers, that they may not perish this day by the hands of the kings of the Amorites.

17 And when Jacob ceased praying to the Lord the earth shook from its place, and the sun darkened, and all these kings were terrified and a great consternation seized them.

18 And the Lord hearkened to the prayer of Jacob, and the Lord impressed the hearts of all the kings and their hosts with the terror and awe of the sons of Jacob.

19 For the Lord caused them to hear the voice of chariots, and the voice of mighty horses from the sons of Jacob, and the voice of a great army accompanying them.

20 And these kings were seized with great terror at the sons of Jacob, and whilst they were standing in their quarters, behold the sons of Jacob advanced upon them, with one hundred and twelve men, with a great and tremendous shouting.

21 And when the kings saw the sons of Jacob advancing toward them, they were still more panic struck, and they were inclined to retreat from before the sons of Jacob as at first, and not to fight with them.

22 But they did not retreat, saying, It would be a disgrace to us thus twice to retreat from before the Hebrews.

23 And the sons of Jacob came near and advanced against all these kings and their armies, and they saw, and behold it was a very mighty people, numerous as the sand of the sea.

24 And the sons of Jacob called unto the Lord and said, Help us O Lord, help us and answer us, for we trust in thee, and let us not die by the hands of these uncircumcised men, who this day have come against us.

25 And the sons of Jacob girt on their weapons of war, and they took in their hands each man his shield and his javelin, and they approached to battle.

26 And Judah, the son of Jacob, ran first before his brethren, and ten of his servants with him, and he went toward these kings.

27 And Jashub, king of Tapnach, also came forth first with his army before Judah, and Judah saw Jashub and his army coming toward him, and Judah's wrath was kindled, and his anger burned within him, and he approached to battle in which Judah ventured his life.

28 And Jashub and all his army were advancing toward Judah, and he was riding upon a very strong and powerful horse, and Jashub was a very valiant man, and covered with iron and brass from head to foot.

29 And whilst he was upon the horse, he shot arrows with both hands from before and behind, as was his manner in all his battles, and he never missed the place to which he aimed his arrows.

30 And when Jashub came to fight with Judah, and was darting many

arrows against Judah, the Lord bound the hand of Jashub, and all the arrows that he shot rebounded upon his own men.

31 And notwithstanding this, Jashub kept advancing toward Judah, to challenge him with the arrows, but the distance between them was about thirty cubits, and when Judah saw Jashub darting forth his arrows against him, he ran to him with his wrath-excited might.

32 And Judah took up a large stone from the ground, and its weight was sixty shekels, and Judah ran toward Jashub, and with the stone struck him on his shield, that Jashub was stunned with the blow, and fell off from his horse to the ground.

33 And the shield burst asunder out of the hand of Jashub, and through the force of the blow sprang to the distance of about fifteen cubits, and the shield fell before the second camp.

34 And the kings that came with Jashub saw at a distance the strength of Judah, the son of Jacob, and what he had done to Jashub, and they were terribly afraid of Judah.

35 And they assembled near Jashub's camp, seeing his confusion, and Judah drew his sword and smote forty-two men of the camp of Jashub, and the whole of Jashub's camp fled before Judah,

and no man stood against him, and they left Jashub and fled from him, and Jashub was still prostrate upon the ground.

36 And Jashub seeing that all the men of his camp had fled from him, hastened and rose up with terror against Judah, and stood upon his legs opposite Judah.

37 And Jashub had a single combat with Judah, placing shield toward shield, and Jashub's men all fled, for they were greatly afraid of Judah.

38 And Jashub took his spear in his hand to strike Judah upon his head, but Judah had quickly placed his shield to his head against Jashub's spear, so that the shield of Judah received the blow from Jashub's spear, and the shield was split in too.

39 And when Judah saw that his shield was split, he hastily drew his sword and smote Jashub at his ankles, and cut off his feet that Jashub fell upon the ground, and the spear fell from his hand.

40 And Judah hastily picked up Jashub's spear, with which he severed his head and cast it next to his feet.

41 And when the sons of Jacob saw what Judah had done to Jashub, they all ran into the ranks of the other kings, and the sons of Jacob fought with the army of Jashub, and the armies of all the kings that were there.

42 And the sons of Jacob caused fifteen thousand of their men to fall, and they smote them as if smiting at gourds, and the rest fled for their lives.

43 And Judah was still standing by the body of Jashub, and stripped Jashub of his coat of mail.

44 And Judah also took off the iron and brass that was about Jashub, and behold nine men of the captains of Jashub came along to fight against Judah.

45 And Judah hastened and took up a stone from the ground, and with it smote one of them upon the head, and his skull was fractured, and the body also fell from the horse to the ground.

46 And the eight captains that remained, seeing the strength of Judah, were greatly afraid and they fled, and Judah with his ten men pursued them, and they overtook them and slew them.

47 And the sons of Jacob were still smiting the armies of the kings, and they slew many of them, but those kings daringly kept their stand with their captains, and did not retreat from their places, and they exclaimed against those of their armies that fled from before the sons of Jacob, but none would listen to them, for they were afraid of their lives lest they should die.

48 And all the sons of Jacob, after having smitten the armies of the kings, returned and came before Judah, and Judah was still slaying the eight captains of Jashub, and stripping off their garments.

49 And Levi saw Elon, king of Gaash, advancing toward him, with his fourteen captains to smite him, but Levi did not know it for certain.

50 And Elon with his captains approached nearer, and Levi looked back and saw that battle was given him in the rear, and Levi ran with twelve of his servants, and they went and slew Elon and his captains with the edge of the sword.

Jasher 38

1 And Ihuri king of Shiloh came up to assist Elon, and he approached Jacob, when Jacob drew his bow that was in his hand and with an arrow struck Ihuri which caused his death.

2 And when Ihuri king of Shiloh was dead, the four remaining kings fled from their station with the rest of the captains, and they endeavored to retreat, saying, We have no more strength with the Hebrews after their having killed the three kings and their captains who were more powerful than we are.

3 And when the sons of Jacob saw that the remaining kings had removed from their station, they pursued them, and Jacob also came

from the heap of Shechem from the place where he was standing, and they went after the kings and they approached them with their servants.

4 And the kings and the captains with the rest of their armies, seeing that the sons of Jacob approached them, were afraid of their lives and fled till they reached the city of Chazar.

5 And the sons of Jacob pursued them to the gate of the city of Chazar, and they smote a great smiting amongst the kings and their armies, about four thousand men, and whilst they were smiting the army of the kings, Jacob was occupied with his bow confining himself to smiting the kings, and he slew them all.

6 And he slew Parathon king of Chazar at the gate of the city of Chazar, and he afterward smote Susi king of Sarton, and Laban king of Bethchorin, and Shabir king of Machnaymah, and he slew them all with arrows, an arrow to each of them, and they died.

7 And the sons of Jacob seeing that all the kings were dead and that they were broken up and retreating, continued to carry on the battle with the armies of the kings opposite the gate of Chazar, and they still smote about four hundred of their men.

8 And three men of the servants of Jacob fell in that battle, and when Judah saw that three of his servants had died, it grieved him greatly, and his anger burned within him against the Amorites.

9 And all the men that remained of the armies of the kings were greatly afraid of their lives, and they ran and broke the gate of the walls of the city of Chazar, and they all entered the city for safety.

10 And they concealed themselves in the midst of the city of Chazar, for the city of Chazar was very large and extensive, and when all these armies had entered the city, the sons of Jacob ran after them to the city.

11 And four mighty men, experienced in battle, went forth from the city and stood against the entrance of the city, with drawn swords and spears in their hands, and they placed themselves opposite the sons of Jacob, and would not suffer them to enter the city.

12 And Naphtali ran and came between them and with his sword smote two of them, and cut off their heads at one stroke.

13 And he turned to the other two, and behold they had fled, and he pursued them, overtook them, smote them and slew them.

14 And the sons of Jacob came to the city and saw, and behold there was another wall to the city, and they sought for the gate of the wall and could not find it, and Judah sprang

upon the top of the wall, and Simeon and Levi followed him, and they all three descended from the wall into the city.

15 And Simeon and Levi slew all the men who ran for safety into the city, and also the inhabitants of the city with their wives and little ones, they slew with the edge of the sword, and the cries of the city ascended up to heaven.

16 And Dan and Naphtali sprang upon the wall to see what caused the noise of lamentation, for the sons of Jacob felt anxious about their brothers, and they heard the inhabitants of the city speaking with weeping and supplications, saying, Take all that we possess in the city and go away, only do not put us to death.

17 And when Judah, Simeon, and Levi had ceased smiting the inhabitants of the city, they ascended the wall and called to Dan and Naphtali, who were upon the wall, and to the rest of their brothers, and Simeon and Levi informed them of the entrance into the city, and all the sons of Jacob came to fetch the spoil.

18 And the sons of Jacob took the spoil of the city of Chazar, the flocks and herds, and the property, and they took all that could be captured, and went away that day from the city.

19 And on the next day the sons of Jacob went to Sarton, for they heard that the men of Sarton who had remained in the city were assembling to fight with them for having slain their king, and Sarton was a very high and fortified city, and it had a deep rampart surrounding the city.

20 And the pillar of the rampart was about fifty cubits and its breadth forty cubits, and there was no place for a man to enter the city on account of the rampart, and the sons of Jacob saw the rampart of the city, and they sought an entrance in it but could not find it.

21 For the entrance to the city was at the rear, and every man that wished to come into the city came by that road and went around the whole city, and he afterwards entered the city.

22 And the sons of Jacob seeing they could not find the way into the city, their anger was kindled greatly, and the inhabitants of the city seeing that the sons of Jacob were coming to them were greatly afraid of them, for they had heard of their strength and what they had done to Chazar.

23 And the inhabitants of the city of Sarton could not go out toward the sons of Jacob after having assembled in the city to fight against them, lest they might thereby get into the city, but when they saw that they were coming toward them, they were greatly afraid of them, for they had

heard of their strength and what they had done to Chazar.

24 So the inhabitants of Sarton speedily took away the bridge of the road of the city, from its place, before the sons of Jacob came, and they brought it into the city.

25 And the sons of Jacob came and sought the way into the city, and could not find it and the inhabitants of the city went up to the top of the wall, and saw, and behold the sons of Jacob were seeking an entrance into the city.

26 And the inhabitants of the city reproached the sons of Jacob from the top of the wall, and they cursed them, and the sons of Jacob heard the reproaches, and they were greatly incensed, and their anger burned within them.

27 And the sons of Jacob were provoked at them, and they all rose and sprang over the rampart with the force of their strength, and through their might passed the forty cubits' breadth of the rampart.

28 And when they had passed the rampart they stood under the wall of the city, and they found all the gates of the city enclosed with iron doors.

29 And the sons of Jacob came near to break open the doors of the gates of the city, and the inhabitants did not let them, for from the top of the wall they were casting stones and arrows upon them.

30 And the number of the people that were upon the wall was about four hundred men, and when the sons of Jacob saw that the men of the city would not let them open the gates of the city, they sprang and ascended the top of the wall, and Judah went up first to the east part of the city.

31 And Gad and Asher went up after him to the west corner of the city, and Simeon and Levi to the north, and Dan and Reuben to the south.

32 And the men who were on the top of the wall, the inhabitants of the city, seeing that the sons of Jacob were coming up to them, they all fled from the wall, descended into the city, and concealed themselves in the midst of the city.

33 And Issachar and Naphtali that remained under the wall approached and broke the gates of the city, and kindled a fire at the gates of the city, that the iron melted, and all the sons of Jacob came into the city, they and all their men, and they fought with the inhabitants of the city of Sarton, and smote them with the edge of the sword, and no man stood up before them.

34 And about two hundred men fled from the city, and they all went and hid themselves in a certain tower in the city, and Judah pursued them to the tower and he broke down the tower, which fell upon the men, and they all died.

35 And the sons of Jacob went up the road of the roof of that tower, and they saw, and behold there was another strong and high tower at a distance in the city, and the top of it reached to heaven, and the sons of Jacob hastened and descended, and went with all their men to that tower, and found it filled with about three hundred men, women and little ones.

36 And the sons of Jacob smote a great smiting amongst those men in the tower and they ran away and fled from them.

37 And Simeon and Levi pursued them, when twelve mighty and valiant men came out to them from the place where they had concealed themselves.

38 And those twelve men maintained a strong battle against Simeon and Levi, and Simeon and Levi could not prevail over them, and those valiant men broke the shields of Simeon and Levi, and one of them struck at Levi's head with his sword, when Levi hastily placed his hand to his head, for he was afraid of the sword, and the sword struck Levi's hand, and it wanted but little to the hand of Levi being cut off.

39 And Levi seized the sword of the valiant man in his hand, and took it forcibly from the man, and with it he struck at the head of the powerful man, and he severed his head.

40 And eleven men approached to fight with Levi, for they saw that one of them was killed, and the sons of Jacob fought, but the sons of Jacob could not prevail over them, for those men were very powerful.

41 And the sons of Jacob seeing that they could not prevail over them, Simeon gave a loud and tremendous shriek, and the eleven powerful men were stunned at the voice of Simeon's shrieking.

42 And Judah at a distance knew the voice of Simeon's shouting, and Naphtali and Judah ran with their shields to Simeon and Levi, and found them fighting with those powerful men, unable to prevail over them as their shields were broken.

43 And Naphtali saw that the shields of Simeon and Levi were broken, and he took two shields from his servants and brought them to Simeon and Levi.

44 And Simeon, Levi and Judah on that day fought all three against the eleven mighty men until the time of sunset, but they could not prevail over them.

45 And this was told unto Jacob, and he was sorely grieved, and he prayed unto the Lord, and he and Naphtali his son went against these mighty men.

46 And Jacob approached and drew his bow, and came nigh unto the mighty men, and slew three of their

men with the bow, and the remaining eight turned back, and behold, the war waged against them in the front and rear, and they were greatly afraid of their lives, and could not stand before the sons of Jacob, and they fled from before them.

47 And in their flight they met Dan and Asher coming toward them, and they suddenly fell upon them, and fought with them, and slew two of them, and Judah and his brothers pursued them, and smote the remainder of them, and slew them.

48 And all the sons of Jacob returned and walked about the city, searching if they could find any men, and they found about twenty young men in a cave in the city, and Gad and Asher smote them all, and Dan and Naphtali lighted upon the rest of the men who had fled and escaped from the second tower, and they smote them all.

49 And the sons of Jacob smote all the inhabitants of the city of Sarton, but the women and little ones they left in the city and did not slay them.

50 And all the inhabitants of the city of Sarton were powerful men, one of them would pursue a thousand, and two of them would not flee from ten thousand of the rest of men.

51 And the sons of Jacob slew all the inhabitants of the city of Sarton with the edge of the sword, that no man stood up against them, and they left the women in the city.

52 And the sons of Jacob took all the spoil of the city, and captured what they desired, and they took flocks and herds and property from the city, and the sons of Jacob did unto Sarton and its inhabitants as they had done to Chazar and its inhabitants, and they turned and went away.

Jasher 39

1 And when the sons of Jacob went from the city of Sarton, they had gone about two hundred cubits when they met the inhabitants of Tapnach coming toward them, for they went out to fight with them, because they had smitten the king of Tapnach and all his men.

2 So all that remained in the city of Tapnach came out to fight with the sons of Jacob, and they thought to retake from them the booty and the spoil which they had captured from Chazar and Sarton.

3 And the rest of the men of Tapnach fought with the sons of Jacob in that place, and the sons of Jacob smote them, and they fled before them, and they pursued them to the city of Arbelan, and they all fell before the sons of Jacob.

4 And the sons of Jacob returned and came to Tapnach, to take away the spoil of Tapnach, and when they came to Tapnach they heard that the

people of Arbelan had gone out to meet them to save the spoil of their brethren, and the sons of Jacob left ten of their men in Tapnach to plunder the city, and they went out toward the people of Arbelan.

5 And the men of Arbelan went out with their wives to fight with the sons of Jacob, for their wives were experienced in battle, and they went out, about four hundred men and women.

6 And all the sons of Jacob shouted with a loud voice, and they all ran toward the inhabitants of Arbelan, and with a great and tremendous voice.

7 And the inhabitants of Arbelan heard the noise of the shouting of the sons of Jacob, and their roaring like the noise of lions and like the roaring of the sea and its waves.

8 And fear and terror possessed their hearts on account of the sons of Jacob, and they were terribly afraid of them, and they retreated and fled before them into the city, and the sons of Jacob pursued them to the gate of the city, and they came upon them in the city.

9 And the sons of Jacob fought with them in the city, and all their women were engaged in slinging against the sons of Jacob, and the combat was very severe amongst them the whole of that day till evening.

10 And the sons of Jacob could not prevail over them, and the sons of Jacob had almost perished in that battle, and the sons of Jacob cried unto the Lord and greatly gained strength toward evening, and the sons of Jacob smote all the inhabitants of Arbelan by the edge of the sword, men, women and little ones.

11 And also the remainder of the people who had fled from Sarton, the sons of Jacob smote them in Arbelan, and the sons of Jacob did unto Arbelan and Tapnach as they had done to Chazar and Sarton, and when the women saw that all the men were dead, they went upon the roofs of the city and smote the sons of Jacob by showering down stones like rain.

12 And the sons of Jacob hastened and came into the city and seized all the women and smote them with the edge of the sword, and the sons of Jacob captured all the spoil and booty, flocks and herds and cattle.

13 And the sons of Jacob did unto Machnaymah as they had done to Tapnach, to Chazar and to Shiloh, and they turned from there and went away.

14 And on the fifth day the sons of Jacob heard that the people of Gaash had gathered against them to battle, because they had slain their king and their captains, for there had been fourteen captains in the city of

Gaash, and the sons of Jacob had slain them all in the first battle.

15 And the sons of Jacob that day girt on their weapons of war, and they marched to battle against the inhabitants of Gaash, and in Gaash there was a strong and mighty people of the people of the Amorites, and Gaash was the strongest and best fortified city of all the cities of the Amorites, and it had three walls.

16 And the sons of Jacob came to Gaash and they found the gates of the city locked, and about five hundred men standing at the top of the outer-most wall, and a people numerous as the sand upon the sea shore were in ambush for the sons of Jacob from without the city at the rear thereof.

17 And the sons of Jacob approached to open the gates of the city, and whilst they were drawing nigh, behold those who were in ambush at the rear of the city came forth from their places and surrounded the sons of Jacob.

18 And the sons of Jacob were enclosed between the people of Gaash, and the battle was both to their front and rear, and all the men that were upon the wall, were casting from the wall upon them, arrows and stones.

19 And Judah, seeing that the men of Gaash were getting too heavy for them, gave a most piercing and tremendous shriek and all the men of Gaash were terrified at the voice of Judah's cry, and men fell from the wall at his powerful shriek, and all those that were from without and within the city were greatly afraid of their lives.

20 And the sons of Jacob still came nigh to break the doors of the city, when the men of Gaash threw stones and arrows upon them from the top of the wall, and made them flee from the gate.

21 And the sons of Jacob returned against the men of Gaash who were with them from without the city, and they smote them terribly, as striking against gourds, and they could not stand against the sons of Jacob, for fright and terror had seized them at the shriek of Judah.

22 And the sons of Jacob slew all those men who were without the city, and the sons of Jacob still drew nigh to effect an entrance into the city, and to fight under the city walls, but they could not for all the inhabitants of Gaash who remained in the city had surrounded the walls of Gaash in every direction, so that the sons of Jacob were unable to approach the city to fight with them.

23 And the sons of Jacob came nigh to one corner to fight under the wall, the inhabitants of Gaash threw arrows and stones upon them like showers of rain, and they fled from under the wall.

24 And the people of Gaash who were upon the wall, seeing that the sons of Jacob could not prevail over them from under the wall, reproached the sons of Jacob in these words, saying,

25 What is the matter with you in the battle that you cannot prevail? can you then do unto the mighty city of Gaash and its inhabitants as you did to the cities of the Amorites that were not so powerful? Surely to those weak ones amongst us you did those things, and slew them in the entrance of the city, for they had no strength when they were terrified at the sound of your shouting.

26 And will you now then be able to fight in this place? Surely here you will all die, and we will avenge the cause of those cities that you have laid waste.

27 And the inhabitants of Gaash greatly reproached the sons of Jacob and reviled them with their gods, and continued to cast arrows and stones upon them from the wall.

28 And Judah and his brothers heard the words of the inhabitants of Gaash and their anger was greatly roused, and Judah was jealous of his God in this matter, and he called out and said, O Lord, help, send help to us and our brothers.

29 And he ran at a distance with all his might, with his drawn sword in his hand, and he sprang from the earth and by dint of his strength, mounted the wall, and his sword fell from his hand.

30 And Judah shouted upon the wall, and all the men that were upon the wall were terrified, and some of them fell from the wall into the city and died, and those who were yet upon the wall, when they saw Judah's strength, they were greatly afraid and fled for their lives into the city for safety.

31 And some were emboldened to fight with Judah upon the wall, and they came nigh to slay him when they saw there was no sword in Judah's hand, and they thought of casting him from the wall to his brothers, and twenty men of the city came up to assist them, and they surrounded Judah and they all shouted over him, and approached him with drawn swords, and they terrified Judah, and Judah cried out to his brothers from the wall.

32 And Jacob and his sons drew the bow from under the wall, and smote three of the men that were upon the top of the wall, and Judah continued to cry and he exclaimed, O Lord help us, O Lord deliver us, and he cried out with a loud voice upon the wall, and the cry was heard at a great distance.

33 And after this cry he again repeated to shout, and all the men who surrounded Judah on the top of the wall were terrified, and they each

threw his sword from his hand at the sound of Judah's shouting and his tremor, and fled.

34 And Judah took the swords which had fallen from their hands, and Judah fought with them and slew twenty of their men upon the wall.

35 And about eighty men and women still ascended the wall from the city and they all surrounded Judah, and the Lord impressed the fear of Judah in their hearts, that they were unable to approach him.

36 And Jacob and all who were with him drew the bow from under the wall, and they slew ten men upon the wall, and they fell below the wall, before Jacob and his sons.

37 And the people upon the wall seeing that twenty of their men had fallen, they still ran toward Judah with drawn swords, but they could not approach him for they were greatly terrified at Judah's strength.

38 And one of their mighty men whose name was Arud approached to strike Judah upon the head with his sword, when Judah hastily put his shield to his head, and the sword hit the shield, and it was split in two.

39 And this mighty man after he had struck Judah ran for his life, at the fear of Judah, and his feet slipped upon the wall and he fell amongst the sons of Jacob who were below the wall, and the sons of Jacob smote him and slew him.

40 And Judah's head pained him from the blow of the powerful man, and Judah had nearly died from it.

41 And Judah cried out upon the wall owing to the pain produced by the blow, when Dan heard him, and his anger burned within him, and he also rose up and went at a distance and ran and sprang from the earth and mounted the wall with his wrath-excited strength.

42 And when Dan came upon the wall near unto Judah all the men upon the wall fled, who had stood against Judah, and they went up to the second wall, and they threw arrows and stones upon Dan and Judah from the second wall, and endeavored to drive them from the wall.

43 And the arrows and stones struck Dan and Judah, and they had nearly been killed upon the wall, and wherever Dan and Judah fled from the wall, they were attacked with arrows and stones from the second wall.

44 And Jacob and his sons were still at the entrance of the city below the first wall, and they were not able to draw their bow against the inhabitants of the city, as they could not be seen by them, being upon the second wall.

45 And Dan and Judah when they could no longer bear the stones and arrows that fell upon them from the

second wall, they both sprang upon the second wall near the people of the city, and when the people of the city who were upon the second wall saw that Dan and Judah had come to them upon the second wall, they all cried out and descended below between the walls.

46 And Jacob and his sons heard the noise of the shouting from the people of the city, and they were still at the entrance of the city, and they were anxious about Dan and Judah who were not seen by them, they being upon the second wall.

47 And Naphtali went up with his wrath-excited might and sprang upon the first wall to see what caused the noise of shouting which they had heard in the city, and Issachar and Zebulun drew nigh to break the doors of the city, and they opened the gates of the city and came into the city.

48 And Naphtali leaped from the first wall to the second, and came to assist his brothers, and the inhabitants of Gaash who were upon the wall, seeing that Naphtali was the third who had come up to assist his brothers, they all fled and descended into the city, and Jacob and all his sons and all their young men came into the city to them.

49 And Judah and Dan and Naphtali descended from the wall into the city and pursued the inhabitants of the city, and Simeon and Levi were from without the city and knew not that the gate was opened, and they went up from there to the wall and came down to their brothers into the city.

50 And the inhabitants of the city had all descended into the city, and the sons of Jacob came to them in different directions, and the battle waged against them from the front and the rear, and the sons of Jacob smote them terribly, and slew about twenty thousand of them men and women, not one of them could stand up against the sons of Jacob.

51 And the blood flowed plentifully in the city, and it was like a brook of water, and the blood flowed like a brook to the outer part of the city, and reached the desert of Bethchorin.

52 And the people of Bethchorin saw at a distance the blood flowing from the city of Gaash, and about seventy men from amongst them ran to see the blood, and they came to the place where the blood was.

53 And they followed the track of the blood and came to the wall of the city of Gaash, and they saw the blood issue from the city, and they heard the voice of crying from the inhabitants of Gaash, for it ascended unto heaven, and the blood was continuing to flow abundantly like a brook of water.

54 And all the sons of Jacob were still smiting the inhabitants of Gaash,

and were engaged in slaying them till evening, about twenty thousand men and women, and the people of Chorin said, Surely this is the work of the Hebrews, for they are still carrying on war in all the cities of the Amorites.

55 And those people hastened and ran to Bethchorin, and each took his weapons of war, and they cried out to all the inhabitants of Bethchorin, who also girt on their weapons of war to go and fight with the sons of Jacob.

56 And when the sons of Jacob had done smiting the inhabitants of Gaash, they walked about the city to strip all the slain, and coming in the innermost part of the city and farther on they met three very powerful men, and there was no sword in their hand.

57 And the sons of Jacob came up to the place where they were, and the powerful men ran away, and one of them had taken Zebulun, who he saw was a young lad and of short stature, and with his might dashed him to the ground.

58 And Jacob ran to him with his sword and Jacob smote him below his loins with the sword, and cut him in two, and the body fell upon Zebulun.

59 And the second one approached and seized Jacob to fell him to the ground, and Jacob turned to him and shouted to him, whilst Simeon and Levi ran and smote him on the hips with the sword and felled him to the ground.

60 And the powerful man rose up from the ground with wrath-excited might, and Judah came to him before he had gained his footing, and struck him upon the head with the sword, and his head was split and he died.

61 And the third powerful man, seeing that his companions were killed, ran from before the sons of Jacob, and the sons of Jacob pursued him in the city; and whilst the powerful man was fleeing he found one of the swords of the inhabitants of the city, and he picked it up and turned to the sons of Jacob and fought them with that sword.

62 And the powerful man ran to Judah to strike him upon the head with the sword, and there was no shield in the hand of Judah; and whilst he was aiming to strike him, Naphtali hastily took his shield and put it to Judah's head, and the sword of the powerful man hit the shield of Naphtali and Judah escaped the sword.

63 And Simeon and Levi ran upon the powerful man with their swords and struck at him forcibly with their swords, and the two swords entered the body of the powerful man and divided it in two, length-wise.

64 And the sons of Jacob smote the three mighty men at that time, together with all the inhabitants of Gaash, and the day was about to decline.

65 And the sons of Jacob walked about Gaash and took all the spoil of the city, even the little ones and women they did not suffer to live, and the sons of Jacob did unto Gaash as they had done to Sarton and Shiloh.

Jasher 40

1 And the sons of Jacob led away all the spoil of Gaash, and went out of the city by night.

2 They were going out marching toward the castle of Bethchorin, and the inhabitants of Bethchorin were going to the castle to meet them, and on that night the sons of Jacob fought with the inhabitants of Bethchorin, in the castle of Bethchorin.

3 And all the inhabitants of Bethchorin were mighty men, one of them would not flee from before a thousand men, and they fought on that night upon the castle, and their shouts were heard on that night from afar, and the earth quaked at their shouting.

4 And all the sons of Jacob were afraid of those men, as they were not accustomed to fight in the dark, and they were greatly confounded, and the sons of Jacob cried unto the Lord, saying, Give help to us O Lord, deliver us that we may not die by the hands of these uncircumcised men.

5 And the Lord hearkened to the voice of the sons of Jacob, and the Lord caused great terror and confusion to seize the people of Bethchorin, and they fought amongst themselves the one with the other in the darkness of night, and smote each other in great numbers.

6 And the sons of Jacob, knowing that the Lord had brought a spirit of perverseness amongst those men, and that they fought each man with his neighbor, went forth from among the bands of the people of Bethchorin and went as far as the descent of the castle of Bethchorin, and farther, and they tarried there securely with their young men on that night.

7 And the people of Bethchorin fought the whole night, one man with his brother, and the other with his neighbor, and they cried out in every direction upon the castle, and their cry was heard at a distance, and the whole earth shook at their voice, for they were powerful above all the people of the earth.

8 And all the inhabitants of the cities of the Canaanites, the Hittites, the Amorites, the Hivites and all the kings of Canaan, and also those who were on the other side of the Jordan, heard the noise of the shouting on that night.

9 And they said, Surely these are the battles of the Hebrews who are fighting against the seven cities, who came nigh unto them; and who can stand against those Hebrews?

10 And all the inhabitants of the cities of the Canaanites, and all those who were on the other side of the Jordan, were greatly afraid of the sons of Jacob, for they said, Behold the same will be done to us as was done to those cities, for who can stand against their mighty strength?

11 And the cries of the Chorinites were very great on that night, and continued to increase; and they smote each other till morning, and numbers of them were killed.

12 And the morning appeared, and all the sons of Jacob rose up at daybreak and went up to the castle, and they smote those who remained of the Chorinites in a terrible manner, and they were all killed in the castle.

13 And the sixth day appeared, and all the inhabitants of Canaan saw at a distance all the people of Bethchorin lying dead in the castle of Bethchorin, and strewed about as the carcasses of lambs and goats.

14 And the sons of Jacob led all the spoil which they had captured from Gaash and went to Bethchorin, and they found the city full of people like the sand of the sea, and they fought with them, and the sons of Jacob smote them there till evening time.

15 And the sons of Jacob did unto Bethchorin as they had done to Gaash and Tapnach, and as they had done to Chazar, to Sarton and to Shiloh.

16 And the sons of Jacob took with them the spoil of Bethchorin and all the spoil of the cities, and on that day they went home to Shechem.

17 And the sons of Jacob came home to the city of Shechem, and they remained without the city, and they then rested there from the war, and tarried there all night.

18 And all their servants together with all the spoil that they had taken from the cities, they left without the city, and they did not enter the city, for they said, Peradventure there may be yet more fighting against us, and they may come to besiege us in Shechem.

19 And Jacob and his sons and their servants remained on that night and the next day in the portion of the field which Jacob had purchased from Hamor for five shekels, and all that they had captured was with them.

20 And all the booty which the sons of Jacob had captured, was in the portion of the field, immense as the sand upon the sea shore.

21 And the inhabitants of the land observed them from afar, and all the inhabitants of the land were afraid of the sons of Jacob who had done this

thing, for no king from the days of old had ever done the like.

22 And the seven kings of the Canaanites resolved to make peace with the sons of Jacob, for they were greatly afraid of their lives, on account of the sons of Jacob.

23 And on that day, being the seventh day, Japhia king of Hebron sent secretly to the king of Ai, and to the king of Gibeon, and to the king of Shalem, and to the king of Adulam, and to the king of Lachish, and to the king of Chazar, and to all the Canaanitish kings who were under their subjection, saying,

24 Go up with me, and come to me that we may go to the sons of Jacob, and I will make peace with them, and form a treaty with them, lest all your lands be destroyed by the swords of the sons of Jacob, as they did to Shechem and the cities around it, as you have heard and seen.

25 And when you come to me, do not come with many men, but let every king bring his three head captains, and every captain bring three of his officers.

26 And come all of you to Hebron, and we will go together to the sons of Jacob, and supplicate them that they shall form a treaty of peace with us.

27 And all those kings did as the king of Hebron had sent to them, for they were all under his counsel and command, and all the kings of Canaan assembled to go to the sons of Jacob, to make peace with them; and the sons of Jacob returned and went to the portion of the field that was in Shechem, for they did not put confidence in the kings of the land.

28 And the sons of Jacob returned and remained in the portion of the field ten days, and no one came to make war with them.

29 And when the sons of Jacob saw that there was no appearance of war, they all assembled and went to the city of Shechem, and the sons of Jacob remained in Shechem.

30 And at the expiration of forty days, all the kings of the Amorites assembled from all their places and came to Hebron, to Japhia, king of Hebron.

31 And the number of kings that came to Hebron, to make peace with the sons of Jacob, was twenty-one kings, and the number of captains that came with them was sixty-nine, and their men were one hundred and eighty-nine, and all these kings and their men rested by Mount Hebron.

32 And the king of Hebron went out with his three captains and nine men, and these kings resolved to go to the sons of Jacob to make peace.

33 And they said unto the king of Hebron, Go thou before us with thy men, and speak for us unto the sons of Jacob, and we will come after thee

and confirm thy words, and the king of Hebron did so.

34 And the sons of Jacob heard that all the kings of Canaan had gathered together and rested in Hebron, and the sons of Jacob sent four of their servants as spies, saying, Go and spy these kings, and search and examine their men whether they are few or many, and if they are but few in number, number them all and come back.

35 And the servants of Jacob went secretly to these kings, and did as the sons of Jacob had commanded them, and on that day they came back to the sons of Jacob, and said unto them, We came unto those kings, and they are but few in number, and we numbered them all, and behold, they were two hundred and eighty-eight, kings and men.

36 And the sons of Jacob said, They are but few in number, therefore we will not all go out to them; and in the morning the sons of Jacob rose up and chose sixty two of their men, and ten of the sons of Jacob went with them; and they girt on their weapons of war, for they said, They are coming to make war with us, for they knew not that they were coming to make peace with them.

37 And the sons of Jacob went with their servants to the gate of Shechem, toward those kings, and their father Jacob was with them.

38 And when they had come forth, behold, the king of Hebron and his three captains and nine men with him were coming along the road against the sons of Jacob, and the sons of Jacob lifted up their eyes, and saw at a distance Japhia, king of Hebron, with his captains, coming toward them, and the sons of Jacob took their stand at the place of the gate of Shechem, and did not proceed.

39 And the king of Hebron continued to advance, he and his captains, until he came nigh to the sons of Jacob, and he and his captains bowed down to them to the ground, and the king of Hebron sat with his captains before Jacob and his sons.

40 And the sons of Jacob said unto him, What has befallen thee, O king of Hebron? why hast thou come to us this day? what dost thou require from us? and the king of Hebron said unto Jacob, I beseech thee my lord, all the kings of the Canaanites have this day come to make peace with you.

41 And the sons of Jacob heard the words of the king of Hebron, and they would not consent to his proposals, for the sons of Jacob had no faith in him, for they imagined that the king of Hebron had spoken deceitfully to them.

42 And the king of Hebron knew from the words of the sons of Jacob, that they did not believe his words,

and the king of Hebron approached nearer to Jacob, and said unto him, I beseech thee, my lord, to be assured that all these kings have come to you on peaceable terms, for they have not come with all their men, neither did they bring their weapons of war with them, for they have come to seek peace from my lord and his sons.

43 And the sons of Jacob answered the king of Hebron, saying, Send thou to all these kings, and if thou speakest truth unto us, let them each come singly before us, and if they come unto us unarmed, we shall then know that they seek peace from us.

44 And Japhia, king of Hebron, sent one of his men to the kings, and they all came before the sons of Jacob, and bowed down to them to the ground, and these kings sat before Jacob and his sons, and they spoke unto them, saying,

45 We have heard all that you did unto the kings of the Amorites with your sword and exceedingly mighty arm, so that no man could stand up before you, and we were afraid of you for the sake of our lives, lest it should befall us as it did to them.

46 So we have come unto you to form a treaty of peace between us, and now therefore contract with us a covenant of peace and truth, that you will not meddle with us, inasmuch as we have not meddled with you.

47 And the sons of Jacob knew that they had really come to seek peace from them, and the sons of Jacob listened to them, and formed a covenant with them.

48 And the sons of Jacob swore unto them that they would not meddle with them, and all the kings of the Canaanites swore also to them, and the sons of Jacob made them tributary from that day forward.

49 And after this all the captains of these kings came with their men before Jacob, with presents in their hands for Jacob and his sons, and they bowed down to him to the ground.

50 And these kings then urged the sons of Jacob and begged of them to return all the spoil they had captured from the seven cities of the Amorites, and the sons of Jacob did so, and they returned all that they had captured, the women, the little ones, the cattle and all the spoil which they had taken, and they sent them off, and they went away each to his city.

51 And all these kings again bowed down to the sons of Jacob, and they sent or brought them many gifts in those days, and the sons of Jacob sent off these kings and their men, and they went peaceably away from them to their cities, and the sons of

Jacob also returned to their home, to Shechem.

52 And there was peace from that day forward between the sons of Jacob and the kings of the Canaanites, until the children of Israel came to inherit the land of Canaan.

Jasher 41

1 And at the revolution of the year the sons of Jacob journeyed from Shechem, and they came to Hebron, to their father Isaac, and they dwelt there, but their flocks and herds they fed daily in Shechem, for there was there in those days good and fat pasture, and Jacob and his sons and all their household dwelt in the valley of Hebron.

2 And it was in those days, in that year, being the hundred and sixth year of the life of Jacob, in the tenth year of Jacob's coming from Padan-aram, that Leah the wife of Jacob died; she was fifty-one years old when she died in Hebron.

3 And Jacob and his sons buried her in the cave of the field of Machpelah, which is in Hebron, which Abraham had bought from the children of Heth, for the possession of a burial place.

4 And the sons of Jacob dwelt with their father in the valley of Hebron, and all the inhabitants of the land knew their strength and their fame went throughout the land.

5 And Joseph the son of Jacob, and his brother Benjamin, the sons of Rachel, the wife of Jacob, were yet young in those days, and did not go out with their brethren during their battles in all the cities of the Amorites.

6 And when Joseph saw the strength of his brethren, and their greatness, he praised them and extolled them, but he ranked himself greater than them, and extolled himself above them; and Jacob, his father, also loved him more than any of his sons, for he was a son of his old age, and through his love toward him, he made him a coat of many colors.

7 And when Joseph saw that his father loved him more than his brethren, he continued to exalt himself above his brethren, and he brought unto his father evil reports concerning them.

8 And the sons of Jacob seeing the whole of Joseph's conduct toward them, and that their father loved him more than any of them, they hated him and could not speak peaceably to him all the days.

9 And Joseph was seventeen years old, and he was still magnifying himself above his brethren, and thought of raising himself above them.

10 At that time he dreamed a dream, and he came unto his brothers and told them his dream, and he said

unto them, I dreamed a dream, and behold we were all binding sheaves in the field, and my sheaf rose and placed itself upon the ground and your sheaves surrounded it and bowed down to it.

11 And his brethren answered him and said unto him, What meaneth this dream that thou didst dream? dost thou imagine in thy heart to reign or rule over us?

12 And he still came, and told the thing to his father Jacob, and Jacob kissed Joseph when he heard these words from his mouth, and Jacob blessed Joseph.

13 And when the sons of Jacob saw that their father had blessed Joseph and had kissed him, and that he loved him exceedingly, they became jealous of him and hated him the more.

14 And after this Joseph dreamed another dream and related the dream to his father in the presence of his brethren, and Joseph said unto his father and brethren, Behold I have again dreamed a dream, and behold the sun and the moon and the eleven stars bowed down to me.

15 And his father heard the words of Joseph and his dream, and seeing that his brethren hated Joseph on account of this matter, Jacob therefore rebuked Joseph before his brethren on account of this thing, saying, What meaneth this dream which thou hast dreamed, and this magnifying thyself before thy brethren who are older than thou art?

16 Dost thou imagine in thy heart that I and thy mother and thy eleven brethren will come and bow down to thee, that thou speakest these things?

17 And his brethren were jealous of him on account of his words and dreams, and they continued to hate him, and Jacob reserved the dreams in his heart.

18 And the sons of Jacob went one day to feed their father's flock in Shechem, for they were still herdsmen in those days; and whilst the sons of Jacob were that day feeding in Shechem they delayed, and the time of gathering in the cattle was passed, and they had not arrived.

19 And Jacob saw that his sons were delayed in Shechem, and Jacob said within himself, Peradventure the people of Shechem have risen up to fight against them, therefore they have delayed coming this day.

20 And Jacob called Joseph his son and commanded him, saying, Behold thy brethren are feeding in Shechem this day, and behold they have not yet come back; go now therefore and see where they are, and bring me word back concerning the welfare of

thy brethren and the welfare of the flock.

21 And Jacob sent his son Joseph to the valley of Hebron, and Joseph came for his brothers to Shechem, and could not find them, and Joseph went about the field which was near Shechem, to see where his brothers had turned, and he missed his road in the wilderness, and knew not which way he should go.

22 And an angel of the Lord found him wandering in the road toward the field, and Joseph said unto the angel of the Lord, I seek my brethren; hast thou not heard where they are feeding? and the angel of the Lord said unto Joseph, I saw thy brethren feeding here, and I heard them say they would go to feed in Dothan.

23 And Joseph hearkened to the voice of the angel of the Lord, and he went to his brethren in Dothan and he found them in Dothan feeding the flock.

24 And Joseph advanced to his brethren, and before he had come nigh unto them, they had resolved to slay him.

25 And Simeon said to his brethren, Behold the man of dreams is coming unto us this day, and now therefore come and let us kill him and cast him in one of the pits that are in the wilderness, and when his father shall seek him from us, we will say an evil beast has devoured him.

26 And Reuben heard the words of his brethren concerning Joseph, and he said unto them, You should not do this thing, for how can we look up to our father Jacob? Cast him into this pit to die there, but stretch not forth a hand upon him to spill his blood; and Reuben said this in order to deliver him from their hand, to bring him back to his father.

27 And when Joseph came to his brethren he sat before them, and they rose upon him and seized him and smote him to the earth, and stripped the coat of many colors which he had on.

28 And they took him and cast him into a pit, and in the pit there was no water, but serpents and scorpions. And Joseph was afraid of the serpents and scorpions that were in the pit. And Joseph cried out with a loud voice, and the Lord hid the serpents and scorpions in the sides of the pit, and they did no harm unto Joseph.

29 And Joseph called out from the pit to his brethren, and said unto them, What have I done unto you, and in what have I sinned? why do you not fear the Lord concerning me? am I not of your bones and flesh, and is not Jacob your father, my father? why do you do this thing unto me this day, and how will you be able to look up to our father Jacob?

30 And he continued to cry out and call unto his brethren from the pit, and he said, O Judah, Simeon, and Levi, my brethren, lift me up from the place of darkness in which you have placed me, and come this day to have compassion on me, ye children of the Lord, and sons of Jacob my father. And if I have sinned unto you, are you not the sons of Abraham, Isaac, and Jacob? if they saw an orphan they had compassion over him, or one that was hungry, they gave him bread to eat, or one that was thirsty, they gave him water to drink, or one that was naked, they covered him with garments!

31 And how then will you withhold your pity from your brother, for I am of your flesh and bones, and if I have sinned unto you, surely you will do this on account of my father!

32 And Joseph spoke these words from the pit, and his brethren could not listen to him, nor incline their ears to the words of Joseph, and Joseph was crying and weeping in the pit.

33 And Joseph said, O that my father knew, this day, the act which my brothers have done unto me, and the words which they have this day spoken unto me.

34 And all his brethren heard his cries and weeping in the pit, and his brethren went and removed themselves from the pit, so that they might not hear the cries of Joseph and his weeping in the pit.

Jasher 42

1 And they went and sat on the opposite side, about the distance of a bow-shot, and they sat there to eat bread, and whilst they were eating, they held counsel together what was to be done with him, whether to slay him or to bring him back to his father.

2 They were holding the counsel, when they lifted up their eyes, and saw, and behold there was a company of Ishmaelites coming at a distance by the road of Gilead, going down to Egypt.

3 And Judah said unto them, What gain will it be to us if we slay our brother? peradventure God will require him from us; this then is the counsel proposed concerning him, which you shall do unto him: Behold this company of Ishmaelites going down to Egypt,

4 Now therefore, come let us dispose of him to them, and let not our hand be upon him, and they will lead him along with them, and he will be lost amongst the people of the land, and we will not put him to death with our own hands. And the proposal pleased his brethren and they did according to the word of Judah.

5 And whilst they were discoursing about this matter, and before the company of Ishmaelites had come

up to them, seven trading men of Midian passed by them, and as they passed they were thirsty, and they lifted up their eyes and saw the pit in which Joseph was immured, and they looked, and behold every species of bird was upon him.

6 And these Midianites ran to the pit to drink water, for they thought that it contained water, and on coming before the pit they heard the voice of Joseph crying and weeping in the pit, and they looked down into the pit, and they saw and behold there was a youth of comely appearance and well favored.

7 And they called unto him and said, Who art thou and who brought thee hither, and who placed thee in this pit, in the wilderness? and they all assisted to raise up Joseph and they drew him out, and brought him up from the pit, and took him and went away on their journey and passed by his brethren.

8 And these said unto them, Why do you do this, to take our servant from us and to go away? surely we placed this youth in the pit because he rebelled against us, and you come and bring him up and lead him away; now then give us back our servant.

9 And the Midianites answered and said unto the sons of Jacob, Is this your servant, or does this man attend you? peradventure you are all his servants, for he is more comely and well favored than any of you,

and why do you all speak falsely unto us?

10 Now therefore we will not listen to your words, nor attend to you, for we found the youth in the pit in the wilderness, and we took him; we will therefore go on.

11 And all the sons of Jacob approached them and rose up to them and said unto them, Give us back our servant, and why will you all die by the edge of the sword? And the Midianites cried out against them, and they drew their swords, and approached to fight with the sons of Jacob.

12 And behold Simeon rose up from his seat against them, and sprang upon the ground and drew his sword and approached the Midianites and he gave a terrible shout before them, so that his shouting was heard at a distance, and the earth shook at Simeon's shouting.

13 And the Midianites were terrified on account of Simeon and the noise of his shouting, and they fell upon their faces, and were excessively alarmed.

14 And Simeon said unto them, Verily I am Simeon, the son of Jacob the Hebrew, who have, only with my brother, destroyed the city of Shechem and the cities of the Amorites; so shall God moreover do unto me, that if all your brethren the people of Midian, and also the kings

of Canaan, were to come with you, they could not fight against me.

15 Now therefore give us back the youth whom you have taken, lest I give your flesh to the birds of the skies and the beasts of the earth.

16 And the Midianites were more afraid of Simeon, and they approached the sons of Jacob with terror and fright, and with pathetic words, saying,

17 Surely you have said that the young man is your servant, and that he rebelled against you, and therefore you placed him in the pit; what then will you do with a servant who rebels against his master? Now therefore sell him unto us, and we will give you all that you require for him; and the Lord was pleased to do this in order that the sons of Jacob should not slay their brother.

18 And the Midianites saw that Joseph was of a comely appearance and well-favored; they desired him in their hearts and were urgent to purchase him from his brethren.

19 And the sons of Jacob hearkened to the Midianites and they sold their brother Joseph to them for twenty pieces of silver, and Reuben their brother was not with them, and the Midianites took Joseph and continued their journey to Gilead.

20 They were going along the road, and the Midianites repented of what they had done, in having purchased the young man, and one said to the other, What is this thing that we have done, in taking this youth from the Hebrews, who is of comely appearance and well favored.

21 Perhaps this youth is stolen from the land of the Hebrews, and why then have we done this thing? and if he should be sought for and found in our hands we shall die through him.

22 Now surely hardy and powerful men have sold him to us, the strength of one of whom you saw this day; perhaps they stole him from his land with their might and with their powerful arm, and have therefore sold him to us for the small value which we gave unto them.

23 And whilst they were thus discoursing together, they looked, and behold the company of Ishmaelites which was coming at first, and which the sons of Jacob saw, was advancing toward the Midianites, and the Midianites said to each other, Come let us sell this youth to the company of Ishmaelites who are coming toward us, and we will take for him the little that we gave for him, and we will be delivered from his evil.

24 And they did so, and they reached the Ishmaelites, and the Midianites sold Joseph to the Ishmaelites for twenty pieces of silver which they had given for him to his brethren.

25 And the Midianites went on their road to Gilead, and the Ishmaelites took Joseph and they let him ride upon one of the camels, and they were leading him to Egypt.

26 And Joseph heard that the Ishmaelites were proceeding to Egypt, and Joseph lamented and wept at this thing that he was to be so far removed from the land of Canaan, from his father, and he wept bitterly whilst he was riding upon the camel, and one of their men observed him, and made him go down from the camel and walk on foot, and notwithstanding this Joseph continued to cry and weep, and he said, O my father, my father.

27 And one of the Ishmaelites rose up and smote Joseph upon the cheek, and still he continued to weep; and Joseph was fatigued in the road, and was unable to proceed on account of the bitterness of his soul, and they all smote him and afflicted him in the road, and they terrified him in order that he might cease from weeping.

28 And the Lord saw the ambition of Joseph and his trouble, and the Lord brought down upon those men darkness and confusion, and the hand of every one that smote him became withered.

29 And they said to each other, What is this thing that God has done to us in the road? and they knew not that this befell them on account of

Joseph. And the men proceeded on the road, and they passed along the road of Ephrath where Rachel was buried.

30 And Joseph reached his mother's grave, and Joseph hastened and ran to his mother's grave, and fell upon the grave and wept.

31 And Joseph cried aloud upon his mother's grave, and he said, O my mother, my mother, O thou who didst give me birth, awake now, and rise and see thy son, how he has been sold for a slave, and no one to pity him.

32 O rise and see thy son, weep with me on account of my troubles, and see the heart of my brethren.

33 Arouse my mother, arouse, awake from thy sleep for me, and direct thy battles against my brethren. O how have they stripped me of my coat, and sold me already twice for a slave, and separated me from my father, and there is no one to pity me.

34 Arouse and lay thy cause against them before God, and see whom God will justify in the judgment, and whom he will condemn.

35 Rise, O my mother, rise, awake from thy sleep and see my father how his soul is with me this day, and comfort him and ease his heart.

36 And Joseph continued to speak these words, and Joseph cried aloud

and wept bitterly upon his mother's grave; and he ceased speaking, and from bitterness of heart he became still as a stone upon the grave.

37 And Joseph heard a voice speaking to him from beneath the ground, which answered him with bitterness of heart, and with a voice of weeping and praying in these words:

38 My son, my son Joseph, I have heard the voice of thy weeping and the voice of thy lamentation; I have seen thy tears; I know thy troubles, my son, and it grieves me for thy sake, and abundant grief is added to my grief.

39 Now therefore my son, Joseph my son, hope to the Lord, and wait for him and do not fear, for the Lord is with thee, he will deliver thee from all trouble.

40 Rise my son, go down unto Egypt with thy masters, and do not fear, for the Lord is with thee, my son. And she continued to speak like unto these words unto Joseph, and she was still.

41 And Joseph heard this, and he wondered greatly at this, and he continued to weep; and after this one of the Ishmaelites observed him crying and weeping upon the grave, and his anger was kindled against him, and he drove him from there, and he smote him and cursed him.

42 And Joseph said unto the men, May I find grace in your sight to take me back to my father's house, and he will give you abundance of riches.

43 And they answered him, saying, Art thou not a slave, and where is thy father? and if thou hadst a father thou wouldst not already twice have been sold for a slave for so little value; and their anger was still roused against him, and they continued to smite him and to chastise him, and Joseph wept bitterly.

44 And the Lord saw Joseph's affliction, and Lord again smote these men, and chastised them, and the Lord caused darkness to envelope them upon the earth, and the lightning flashed and the thunder roared, and the earth shook at the voice of the thunder and of the mighty wind, and the men were terrified and knew not where they should go.

45 And the beasts and camels stood still, and they led them, but they would not go, they smote them, and they crouched upon the ground; and the men said to each other, What is this that God has done to us? what are our transgressions, and what are our sins that this thing has thus befallen us?

46 And one of them answered and said unto them, Perhaps on account of the sin of afflicting this slave has this thing happened this day to us;

now therefore implore him strongly to forgive us, and then we shall know on whose account this evil befalleth us, and if God shall have compassion over us, then we shall know that all this cometh to us on account of the sin of afflicting this slave.

47 And the men did so, and they supplicated Joseph and pressed him to forgive them; and they said, We have sinned to the Lord and to thee, now therefore vouchsafe to request of thy God that he shall put away this death from amongst us, for we have sinned to him.

48 And Joseph did according to their words, and the Lord hearkened to Joseph, and the Lord put away the plague which he had inflicted upon those men on account of Joseph, and the beasts rose up from the ground and they conducted them, and they went on, and the raging storm abated and the earth became tranquilized, and the men proceeded on their journey to go down to Egypt, and the men knew that this evil had befallen them on account of Joseph.

49 And they said to each other, Behold we know that it was on account of his affliction that this evil befell us; now therefore why shall we bring this death upon our souls? Let us hold counsel what to do to this slave.

50 And one answered and said, Surely he told us to bring him back to his father; now therefore come, let us take him back and we will go to the place that he will tell us, and take from his family the price that we gave for him and we will then go away.

51 And one answered again and said, Behold this counsel is very good, but we cannot do so for the way is very far from us, and we cannot go out of our road.

52 And one more answered and said unto them, This is the counsel to be adopted, we will not swerve from it; behold we are this day going to Egypt, and when we shall have come to Egypt, we will sell him there at a high price, and we will be delivered from his evil.

53 And this thing pleased the men and they did so, and they continued their journey to Egypt with Joseph.

Jasher 43

1 And when the sons of Jacob had sold their brother Joseph to the Midianites, their hearts were smitten on account of him, and they repented of their acts, and they sought for him to bring him back, but could not find him.

2 And Reuben returned to the pit in which Joseph had been put, in order to lift him out, and restore him to his father, and Reuben stood by the pit, and he heard not a word, and he called out Joseph! Joseph! and no one answered or uttered a word.

3 And Reuben said, Joseph has died through fright, or some serpent has caused his death; and Reuben descended into the pit, and he searched for Joseph and could not find him in the pit, and he came out again.

4 And Reuben tore his garments and he said, The child is not there, and how shall I reconcile my father about him if he be dead? and he went to his brethren and found them grieving on account of Joseph, and counseling together how to reconcile their father about him, and Reuben said unto his brethren, I came to the pit and behold Joseph was not there, what then shall we say unto our father, for my father will only seek the lad from me.

5 And his brethren answered him saying, Thus and thus we did, and our hearts afterward smote us on account of this act, and we now sit to seek a pretext how we shall reconcile our father to it.

6 And Reuben said unto them, What is this you have done to bring down the grey hairs of our father in sorrow to the grave? the thing is not good, that you have done.

7 And Reuben sat with them, and they all rose up and swore to each other not to tell this thing unto Jacob, and they all said, The man who will tell this to our father or his household, or who will report this to any of the children of the land, we will all rise up against him and slay him with the sword.

8 And the sons of Jacob feared each other in this matter, from the youngest to the oldest, and no one spoke a word, and they concealed the thing in their hearts.

9 And they afterward sat down to determine and invent something to say unto their father Jacob concerning all these things.

10 And Issachar said unto them, Here is an advice for you if it seem good in your eyes to do this thing, take the coat which belongeth to Joseph and tear it, and kill a kid of the goats and dip it in its blood.

11 And send it to our father and when he seeth it he will say an evil beast has devoured him, therefore tear ye his coat and behold his blood will be upon his coat, and by your doing this we shall be free of our father's murmurings.

12 And Issachar's advice pleased them, and they hearkened unto him and they did according to the word of Issachar which he had counselled them.

13 And they hastened and took Joseph's coat and tore it, and they killed a kid of the goats and dipped the coat in the blood of the kid, and then trampled it in the dust, and they sent the coat to their father Jacob by the hand of Naphtali, and they commanded him to say these words:

14 We had gathered in the cattle and had come as far as the road to Shechem and farther, when we found this coat upon the road in the wilderness dipped in blood and in dust; now therefore know whether it be thy son's coat or not.

15 And Naphtali went and he came unto his father and he gave him the coat, and he spoke unto him all the words which his brethren had commanded him.

16 And Jacob saw Joseph's coat and he knew it and he fell upon his face to the ground, and became as still as a stone, and he afterward rose up and cried out with a loud and weeping voice and he said, It is the coat of my son Joseph!

17 And Jacob hastened and sent one of his servants to his sons, who went to them and found them coming along the road with the flock.

18 And the sons of Jacob came to their father about evening, and behold their garments were torn and dust was upon their heads, and they found their father crying out and weeping with a loud voice.

19 And Jacob said unto his sons, Tell me truly what evil have you this day suddenly brought upon me? and they answered their father Jacob, saying, We were coming along this day after the flock had been gathered in, and we came as far as the city of Shechem by the road in the wilderness, and we found this coat filled with blood upon the ground, and we knew it and we sent unto thee if thou couldst know it.

20 And Jacob heard the words of his sons and he cried out with a loud voice, and he said, It is the coat of my son, an evil beast has devoured him; Joseph is rent in pieces, for I sent him this day to see whether it was well with you and well with the flocks and to bring me word again from you, and he went as I commanded him, and this has happened to him this day whilst I thought my son was with you.

21 And the sons of Jacob answered and said, He did not come to us, neither have we seen him from the time of our going out from thee until now.

22 And when Jacob heard their words he again cried out aloud, and he rose up and tore his garments, and he put sackcloth upon his loins, and he wept bitterly and he mourned and lifted up his voice in weeping and exclaimed and said these words,

23 Joseph my son, O my son Joseph, I sent thee this day after the welfare of thy brethren, and behold thou hast been torn in pieces; through my hand has this happened to my son.

24 It grieves me for thee Joseph my son, it grieves me for thee; how sweet wast thou to me during life,

and now how exceedingly bitter is thy death to me.

25 0 that I had died in thy stead Joseph my son, for it grieves me sadly for thee my son, O my son, my son. Joseph my son, where art thou, and where hast thou been drawn? arouse, arouse from thy place, and come and see my grief for thee, O my son Joseph.

26 Come now and number the tears gushing from my eyes down my cheeks, and bring them up before the Lord, that his anger may turn from me.

27 0 Joseph my son, how didst thou fall, by the hand of one by whom no one had fallen from the beginning of the world unto this day; for thou hast been put to death by the smiting of an enemy, inflicted with cruelty, but surely I know that this has happened to thee, on account of the multitude of my sins.

28 Arouse now and see how bitter is my trouble for thee my son, although I did not rear thee, nor fashion thee, nor give thee breath and soul, but it was God who formed thee and built thy bones and covered them with flesh, and breathed in thy nostrils the breath of life, and then he gave thee unto me.

29 Now truly God who gave thee unto me, he has taken thee from me, and such then has befallen thee

30 And Jacob continued to speak like unto these words concerning Joseph, and he wept bitterly; he fell to the ground and became still.

31 And all the sons of Jacob seeing their father's trouble, they repented of what they had done, and they also wept bitterly.

32 And Judah rose up and lifted his father's head from the ground, and placed it upon his lap, and he wiped his father's tears from his cheeks, and Judah wept an exceeding great weeping, whilst his father's head was reclining upon his lap, still as a stone.

33 And the sons of Jacob saw their father's trouble, and they lifted up their voices and continued to weep, and Jacob was yet lying upon the ground still as a stone.

34 And all his sons and his servants and his servant's children rose up and stood round him to comfort him, and he refused to be comforted.

35 And the whole household of Jacob rose up and mourned a great mourning on account of Joseph and their father's trouble, and the intelligence reached Isaac, the son of Abraham, the father of Jacob, and he wept bitterly on account of Joseph, he and all his household, and he went from the place where he dwelt in Hebron, and his men with him, and he comforted Jacob his son, and he refused to be comforted.

36 And after this, Jacob rose up from the ground, and his tears were running down his cheeks, and he said unto his sons, Rise up and take your swords and your bows, and go forth into the field, and seek whether you can find my son's body and bring it unto me that I may bury it.

37 Seek also, I pray you, among the beasts and hunt them, and that which shall come the first before you seize and bring it unto me, perhaps the Lord will this day pity my affliction, and prepare before you that which did tear my son in pieces, and bring it unto me, and I will avenge the cause of my son.

38 And his sons did as their father had commanded them, and they rose up early in the morning, and each took his sword and his bow in his hand, and they went forth into the field to hunt the beasts.

39 And Jacob was still crying aloud and weeping and walking to and fro in the house, and smiting his hands together, saying, Joseph my son, Joseph my son.

40 And the sons of Jacob went into the wilderness to seize the beasts, and behold a wolf came toward them, and they seized him, and brought him unto their father, and they said unto him, This is the first we have found, and we have brought him unto thee as thou didst command us, and thy son's body we could not find.

41 And Jacob took the beast from the hands of his sons, and he cried out with a loud and weeping voice, holding the beast in his hand, and he spoke with a bitter heart unto the beast, Why didst thou devour my son Joseph, and how didst thou have no fear of the God of the earth, or of my trouble for my son Joseph?

42 And thou didst devour my son for naught, because he committed no violence, and didst thereby render me culpable on his account, therefore God will require him that is persecuted.

43 And the Lord opened the mouth of the beast in order to comfort Jacob with its words, and it answered Jacob and spoke these words unto him,

44 As God liveth who created us in the earth, and as thy soul liveth, my lord, I did not see thy son, neither did I tear him to pieces, but from a distant land I also came to seek my son who went from me this day, and I know not whether he be living or dead.

45 And I came this day into the field to seek my son, and your sons found me, and seized me and increased my grief, and have this day brought me before thee, and I have now spoken all my words to thee.

46 And now therefore, O son of man, I am in thy hands, and do unto me this day as it may seem good in thy

sight, but by the life of God who created me, I did not see thy son, nor did I tear him to pieces, neither has the flesh of man entered my mouth all the days of my life.

47 And when Jacob heard the words of the beast he was greatly astonished, and sent forth the beast from his hand, and she went her way.

48 And Jacob was still crying aloud and weeping for Joseph day after day, and he mourned for his son many days.

Jasher 44

1 And the sons of Ishmael who had bought Joseph from the Midianites, who had bought him from his brethren, went to Egypt with Joseph, and they came upon the borders of Egypt, and when they came near unto Egypt, they met four men of the sons of Medan the son of Abraham, who had gone forth from the land of Egypt on their journey.

2 And the Ishmaelites said unto them, Do you desire to purchase this slave from us? and they said, Deliver him over to us, and they delivered Joseph over to them, and they beheld him, that he was a very comely youth and they purchased him for twenty shekels.

3 And the Ishmaelites continued their journey to Egypt and the Medanim also returned that day to Egypt, and the Medanim said to each other,

Behold we have heard that Potiphar, an officer of Pharaoh, captain of the guard, seeketh a good servant who shall stand before him to attend him, and to make him overseer over his house and all belonging to him.

4 Now therefore come let us sell him to him for what we may desire, if he be able to give unto us that which we shall require for him.

5 And these Medanim went and came to the house of Potiphar, and said unto him, We have heard that thou seekest a good servant to attend thee, behold we have a servant that will please thee, if thou canst give unto us that which we may desire, and we will sell him unto thee.

6 And Potiphar said, Bring him before me, and I will see him, and if he please me I will give unto you that which you may require for him.

7 And the Medanim went and brought Joseph and placed him before Potiphar, and he saw him, and he pleased him exceedingly, and Potiphar said unto them, Tell me what you require for this youth?

8 And they said, Four hundred pieces of silver we desire for him, and Potiphar said, I will give it you if you bring me the record of his sale to you, and will tell me his history, for perhaps he may be stolen, for this youth is neither a slave, nor the son of a slave, but I observe in him the

appearance of a goodly and handsome person.

9 And the Medanim went and brought unto him the Ishmaelites who had sold him to them, and they told him, saying, He is a slave and we sold him to them.

10 And Potiphar heard the words of the Ishmaelites in his giving the silver unto the Medanim, and the Medanim took the silver and went on their journey, and the Ishmaelites also returned home.

11 And Potiphar took Joseph and brought him to his house that he might serve him, and Joseph found favor in the sight of Potiphar, and he placed confidence in him, and made him overseer over his house, and all that belonged to him he delivered over into his hand.

12 And the Lord was with Joseph and he became a prosperous man, and the Lord blessed the house of Potiphar for the sake of Joseph.

13 And Potiphar left all that he had in the hand of Joseph, and Joseph was one that caused things to come in and go out, and everything was regulated by his wish in the house of Potiphar.

14 And Joseph was eighteen years old, a youth with beautiful eyes and of comely appearance, and like unto him was not in the whole land of Egypt.

15 At that time whilst he was in his master's house, going in and out of the house and attending his master, Zelicah, his master's wife, lifted up her eyes toward Joseph and she looked at him, and behold he was a youth comely and well favored.

16 And she coveted his beauty in her heart, and her soul was fixed upon Joseph, and she enticed him day after day, and Zelicah persuaded Joseph daily, but Joseph did not lift up his eyes to behold his master's wife.

17 And Zelicah said unto him, How goodly are thy appearance and form, truly I have looked at all the slaves, and have not seen so beautiful a slave as thou art; and Joseph said unto her, Surely he who created me in my mother's womb created all mankind.

18 And she said unto him, How beautiful are thine eyes, with which thou hast dazzled all the inhabitants of Egypt, men and women; and he said unto her, How beautiful they are whilst we are alive, but shouldst thou behold them in the grave, surely thou wouldst move away from them.

19 And she said unto him, How beautiful and pleasing are all thy words; take now, I pray thee, the harp which is in the house, and play with thy hands and let us hear thy words.

20 And he said unto her, How beautiful and pleasing are my words when I speak the praise of my God and his glory; and she said unto him, How very beautiful is the hair of thy head, behold the golden comb which is in the house, take it I pray thee, and curl the hair of thy head.

21 And he said unto her, How long wilt thou speak these words? cease to utter these words to me, and rise and attend to thy domestic affairs.

22 And she said unto him, There is no one in my house, and there is nothing to attend to but to thy words and to thy wish; yet notwithstanding all this, she could not bring Joseph unto her, neither did he place his eye upon her, but directed his eyes below to the ground.

23 And Zelicah desired Joseph in her heart, that he should lie with her, and at the time that Joseph was sitting in the house doing his work, Zelicah came and sat before him, and she enticed him daily with her discourse to lie with her, or ever to look at her, but Joseph would not hearken to her.

24 And she said unto him, If thou wilt not do according to my words, I will chastise thee with the punishment of death, and put an iron yoke upon thee.

25 And Joseph said unto her, Surely God who created man looseth the fetters of prisoners, and it is he who will deliver me from thy prison and from thy judgment.

26 And when she could not prevail over him, to persuade him, and her soul being still fixed upon him, her desire threw her into a grievous sickness.

27 And all the women of Egypt came to visit her, and they said unto her, Why art thou in this declining state? thou that lackest nothing; surely thy husband is a great and esteemed prince in the sight of the king, shouldst thou lack anything of what thy heart desireth?

28 And Zelicah answered them, saying, This day it shall be made known to you, whence this disorder springs in which you see me, and she commanded her maid servants to prepare food for all the women, and she made a banquet for them, and all the women ate in the house of Zelicah.

29 And she gave them knives to peel the citrons to eat them, and she commanded that they should dress Joseph in costly garments, and that he should appear before them, and Joseph came before their eyes and all the women looked on Joseph, and could not take their eyes from off him, and they all cut their hands with the knives that they had in their hands, and all the citrons that were in their hands were filled with blood.

30 And they knew not what they had done but they continued to look at the beauty of Joseph, and did not turn their eyelids from him.

31 And Zelicah saw what they had done, and she said unto them, What is this work that you have done? behold I gave you citrons to eat and you have all cut your hands.

32 And all the women saw their hands, and behold they were full of blood, and their blood flowed down upon their garments, and they said unto her, this slave in your house has overcome us, and we could not turn our eyelids from him on account of his beauty.

33 And she said unto them, Surely this happened to you in the moment that you looked at him, and you could not contain yourselves from him; how then can I refrain when he is constantly in my house, and I see him day after day going in and out of my house? how then can I keep from declining or even from perishing on account of this?

34 And they said unto her, the words are true, for who can see this beautiful form in the house and refrain from him, and is he not thy slave and attendant in thy house, and why dost thou not tell him that which is in thy heart, and sufferest thy soul to perish through this matter?

35 And she said unto them, I am daily endeavoring to persuade him, and he will not consent to my wishes, and I promised him everything that is good, and yet I could meet with no return from him; I am therefore in a declining state as you see.

36 And Zelicah became very ill on account of her desire toward Joseph, and she was desperately lovesick on account of him, and all the people of the house of Zelicah and her husband knew nothing of this matter, that Zelicah was ill on account of her love to Joseph.

37 And all the people of her house asked her, saying, Why art thou ill and declining, and lackest nothing? and she said unto them, I know not this thing which is daily increasing upon me.

38 And all the women and her friends came daily to see her, and they spoke with her, and she said unto them, This can only be through the love of Joseph; and they said unto her, Entice him and seize him secretly, perhaps he may hearken to thee, and put off this death from thee.

39 And Zelicah became worse from her love to Joseph, and she continued to decline, till she had scarce strength to stand.

40 And on a certain day Joseph was doing his master's work in the house,

and Zelicah came secretly and fell suddenly upon him, and Joseph rose up against her, and he was more powerful than she, and he brought her down to the ground.

41 And Zelicah wept on account of the desire of her heart toward him, and she supplicated him with weeping, and her tears flowed down her cheeks, and she spoke unto him in a voice of supplication and in bitterness of soul, saying,

42 Hast thou ever heard, seen or known of so beautiful a woman as I am, or better than myself, who speak daily unto thee, fall into a decline through love for thee, confer all this honor upon thee, and still thou wilt not hearken to my voice?

43 And if it be through fear of thy master lest he punish thee, as the king liveth no harm shall come to thee from thy master through this thing; now, therefore pray listen to me, and consent for the sake of the honor which I have conferred upon thee, and put off this death from me, and why should I die for thy sake? and she ceased to speak.

44 And Joseph answered her, saying, Refrain from me, and leave this matter to my master; behold my master knoweth not what there is with me in the house, for all that belongeth to him he has delivered into my hand, and how shall I do these things in my master's house?

45 For he hath also greatly honored me in his house, and he hath also made me overseer over his house, and he hath exalted me, and there is no one greater in this house than I am, and my master hath refrained nothing from me, excepting thee who art his wife, how then canst thou speak these words unto me, and how can I do this great evil and sin to God and to thy husband?

46 Now therefore refrain from me, and speak no more such words as these, for I will not hearken to thy words. But Zelicah would not hearken to Joseph when he spoke these words unto her, but she daily enticed him to listen to her.

47 And it was after this that the brook of Egypt was filled above all its sides, and all the inhabitants of Egypt went forth, and also the king and princes went forth with timbrels and dances, for it was a great rejoicing in Egypt, and a holiday at the time of the inundation of the sea Sihor, and they went there to rejoice all the day.

48 And when the Egyptians went out to the river to rejoice, as was their custom, all the people of the house of Potiphar went with them, but Zelicah would not go with them, for she said, I am indisposed, and she remained alone in the house, and no other person was with her in the house.

49 And she rose up and ascended to her temple in the house, and dressed herself in princely garments, and she placed upon her head precious stones of onyx stones, inlaid with silver and gold, and she beautified her face and skin with all sorts of women's purifying liquids, and she perfumed the temple and the house with cassia and frankincense, and she spread myrrh and aloes, and she afterward sat in the entrance of the temple, in the passage of the house, through which Joseph passed to do his work, and behold Joseph came from the field, and entered the house to do his master's work.

50 And he came to the place through which he had to pass, and he saw all the work of Zelicah, and he turned back.

51 And Zelicah saw Joseph turning back from her, and she called out to him, saying What aileth thee Joseph? come to thy work, and behold I will make room for thee until thou shalt have passed to thy seat.

52 And Joseph returned and came to the house, and passed from thence to the place of his seat, and he sat down to do his master's work as usual and behold Zelicah came to him and stood before him in princely garments, and the scent from her clothes was spread to a distance.

53 And she hastened and caught hold of Joseph and his garments, and she said unto him, As the king liveth if thou wilt not perform my request thou shalt die this day, and she hastened and stretched forth her other hand and drew a sword from beneath her garments, and she placed it upon Joseph's neck, and she said, Rise and perform my request, and if not thou diest this day.

54 And Joseph was afraid of her at her doing this thing, and he rose up to flee from her, and she seized the front of his garments, and in the terror of his flight the garment which Zelicah seized was torn, and Joseph left the garment in the hand of Zelicah, and he fled and got out, for he was in fear.

55 And when Zelicah saw that Joseph's garment was torn, and that he had left it in her hand, and had fled, she was afraid of her life, lest the report should spread concerning her, and she rose up and acted with cunning, and put off the garments in which she was dressed, and she put on her other garments.

56 And she took Joseph's garment, and she laid it beside her, and she went and seated herself in the place where she had sat in her illness, before the people of her house had gone out to the river, and she called a young lad who was then in the house, and she ordered him to call the people of the house to her.

57 And when she saw them she said unto them with a loud voice and lamentation, See what a Hebrew your master has brought to me in the house, for he came this day to lie with me.

58 For when you had gone out he came to the house, and seeing that there was no person in the house, he came unto me, and caught hold of me, with intent to lie with me.

59 And I seized his garments and tore them and called out against him with a loud voice, and when I had lifted up my voice he was afraid of his life and left his garment before me, and fled.

60 And the people of her house spoke nothing, but their wrath was very much kindled against Joseph, and they went to his master and told him the words of his wile.

61 And Potiphar came home enraged, and his wife cried out to him, saying, What is this thing that thou hast done unto me in bringing a He. brew servant into my house, for he came unto me this day to sport with me; thus did he do unto me this day.

62 And Potiphar heard the words of his wife, and he ordered Joseph to be punished with severe stripes, and they did so to him.

63 And whilst they were smiting him, Joseph called out with a loud voice, and he lifted up his eyes to heaven, and he said, O Lord God, thou knowest that I am innocent of all these things, and why shall I die this day through falsehood, by the hand of these uncircumcised wicked men, whom thou knowest?

64 And whilst Potiphar's men were beating Joseph, he continued to cry out and weep, and there was a child there eleven months old, and the Lord opened the mouth of the child, and he spake these words before Potiphar's men, who were smiting Joseph, saying,

65 What do you want of this man, and why do you do this evil unto him? my mother speaketh falsely and uttereth lies; thus was the transaction.

66 And the child told them accurately all that happened, and all the words of Zelicah to Joseph day after day did he declare unto them.

67 And all the men heard the words of the child and they wondered greatly at the child's words, and the child ceased to speak and became still.

68 And Potiphar was very much ashamed at the words of his son, and he commanded his men not to beat Joseph any more, and the men ceased beating Joseph.

69 And Potiphar took Joseph and ordered him to be brought to justice before the priests, who were judges

belonging to the king, in order to judge him concerning this affair.

70 And Potiphar and Joseph came before the priests who were the king's judges, and he said unto them, Decide I pray you, what judgment is due to a servant, for thus has he done.

71 And the priests said unto Joseph, Why didst thou do this thing to thy master? and Joseph answered them, saying, Not so my lords, thus was the matter; and Potiphar said unto Joseph, Surely I entrusted in thy hands all that belonged to me, and I withheld nothing from thee but my wife, and how couldst thou do this evil?

72 And Joseph answered saying, Not so my lord, as the Lord liveth, and as thy soul liveth, my lord, the word which thou didst hear from thy wife is untrue, for thus was the affair this day.

73 A year has elapsed to me since I have been in thy house; hast thou seen any iniquity in me, or any thing which might cause thee to demand my life?

74 And the priests said unto Potiphar, Send, we pray thee, and let them bring before us Joseph's torn garment, and let us see the tear in it, and if it shall be that the tear is in front of the garment, then his face must have been opposite to her and she must have caught hold of him, to

come to her, and with deceit did thy wife do all that she has spoken.

75 And they brought Joseph's garment before the priests who were judges, and they saw and behold the tear was in front of Joseph, and all the judging priests knew that she had pressed him, and they said, The judgment of death is not due to this slave for he has done nothing, but his judgment is, that he be placed in the prison house on account of the report, which through him has gone forth against thy wife.

76 And Potiphar heard their words, and he placed him in the prison house, the place where the king's prisoners are confined, and Joseph was in the house of confinement twelve years.

77 And notwithstanding this, his master's wife did not turn from him, and she did not cease from speaking to him day after day to hearken to her, and at the end of three months Zelicah continued going to Joseph to the house of confinement day by day, and she enticed him to hearken to her, and Zelicah said unto Joseph, How long wilt thou remain in this house? but hearken now to my voice, and I will bring thee out of this house.

78 And Joseph answered her, saying, It is better for me to remain in this house than to hearken to thy words, to sin against God; and she said unto him, If thou wilt not perform

my wish, I will pluck out thine eyes, add fetters to thy feet, and will deliver thee into the hands of them whom thou didst not know before.

79 And Joseph answered her and said, Behold the God of the whole earth is able to deliver me from all that thou canst do unto me, for he openeth the eyes of the blind, and looseth those that are bound, and preserveth all strangers who are unacquainted with the land.

80 And when Zelicah was unable to persuade Joseph to hearken to her, she left off going to entice him; and Joseph was still confined in the house of confinement. And Jacob the father of Joseph, and all his brethren who were in the land of Canaan still mourned and wept in those days on account of Joseph, for Jacob refused to be comforted for his son Joseph, and Jacob cried aloud, and wept and mourned all those days.

Jasher 45

1 And it was at that time in that year, which is the year of Joseph's going down to Egypt after his brothers had sold him, that Reuben the son of Jacob went to Timnah and took unto him for a wife Eliuram, the daughter of Avi the Canaanite, and he came to her.

2 And Eliuram the wife of Reuben conceived and bare him Hanoch, Palu, Chetzron and Carmi, four sons;

and Simeon his brother took his sister Dinah for a wife, and she bare unto him Memuel, Yamin, Ohad, Jachin and Zochar, five sons.

3 And he afterward came to Bunah the Canaanitish woman, the same is Bunah whom Simeon took captive from the city of Shechem, and Bunah was before Dinah and attended upon her, and Simeon came to her, and she bare unto him Saul.

4 And Judah went at that time to Adulam, and he came to a man of Adulam, and his name was Hirah, and Judah saw there the daughter of a man from Canaan, and her name was Aliyath, the daughter of Shua, and he took her, and came to her, and Aliyath bare unto Judah, Er, Onan and Shiloh; three sons.

5 And Levi and Issachar went to the land of the east, and they took unto themselves for wives the daughters of Jobab the son of Yoktan, the son of Eber; and Jobab the son of Yoktan had two daughters; the name of the elder was Adinah, and the name of the younger was Aridah.

6 And Levi took Adinah, and Issachar took Aridah, and they came to the land of Canaan, to their father's house, and Adinah bare unto Levi, Gershon, Kehath and Merari; three sons.

7 And Aridah bare unto Issachar Tola, Puvah, Job and Shomron, four sons; and Dan went to the land of

Moab and took for a wife Aphlaleth, the daughter of Chamudan the Moabite, and he brought her to the land of Canaan.

8 And Aphlaleth was barren, she had no offspring, and God afterward remembered Aphlaleth the wife of Dan, and she conceived and bare a son, and she called his name Chushim.

9 And Gad and Naphtali went to Haran and took from thence the daughters of Amuram the son of Uz, the son of Nahor, for wives.

10 And these are the names of the daughters of Amuram; the name of the elder was Merimah, and the name of the younger Uzith; and Naphtali took Merimah, and Gad took Uzith; and brought them to the land of Canaan, to their father's house.

11 And Merimah bare unto Naphtali Yachzeel, Guni, Jazer and Shalem, four sons; and Uzith bare unto Gad Zephion, Chagi, Shuni, Ezbon, Eri, Arodi and Arali, seven sons.

12 And Asher went forth and took Adon the daughter of Aphlal, the son of Hadad, the son of Ishmael, for a wife, and he brought her to the land of Canaan.

13 And Adon the wife of Asher died in those days: she had no offspring; and it was after the death of Adon that Asher went to the other side of the river and took for a wife Hadurah the daughter of Abimael, the son of Eber, the son of Shem.

14 And the young woman was of a comely appearance, and a woman of sense, and she had been the wife of Malkiel the son of Elam, the son of Shem.

15 And Hadurah bare a daughter unto Malkiel, and he called her name Serach, and Malkiel died after this, and Hadurah went and remained in her father's house.

16 And after the death of the wife at Asher he went and took Hadurah for a wife, and brought her to the land of Canaan, and Serach her daughter he also brought with them, and she was three years old, and the damsel was brought up in Jacob's house.

17 And the damsel was of a comely appearance, and she went in the sanctified ways of the children of Jacob; she lacked nothing, and the Lord gave her wisdom and understanding.

18 And Hadurah the wife of Asher conceived and bare unto him Yimnah, Yishvah, Yishvi and Beriah; four sons.

19 And Zebulun went to Midian, and took for a wife Merishah the daughter of Molad, the son of Abida, the son of Midian, and brought her to the land of Canaan.

20 And Merushah bare unto Zebulun Sered, Elon and Yachleel; three sons.

21 And Jacob sent to Aram, the son of Zoba, the son of Terah, and he took for his son Benjamin Mechalia the daughter of Aram, and she came to the land of Canaan to the house of Jacob; and Benjamin was ten years old when he took Mechalia the daughter of Aram for a wife.

22 And Mechalia conceived and bare unto Benjamin Bela, Becher, Ashbel, Gera and Naaman, five sons; and Benjamin went afterward and took for a wife Aribath, the daughter of Shomron, the son of Abraham, in addition to his first wife, and he was eighteen years old; and Aribath bare unto Benjamin Achi, Vosh, Mupim, Chupim, and Ord; five sons.

23 And in those days Judah went to the house of Shem and took Tamar the daughter of Elam, the son of Shem, for a wife for his first born Er.

24 And Er came to his wife Tamar, and she became his wife, and when he came to her he outwardly destroyed his seed, and his work was evil in the sight of the Lord, and the Lord slew him.

25 And it was after the death of Er, Judah's first born, that Judah said unto Onan, go to thy brother's wife and marry her as the next of kin, and raise up seed to thy brother.

26 And Onan took Tamar for a wife and he came to her, and Onan also did like unto the work of his brother, and his work was evil in the sight of the Lord, and he slew him also.

27 And when Onan died, Judah said unto Tamar, Remain in thy father's house until my son Shiloh shall have grown up, and Judah did no more delight in Tamar, to give her unto Shiloh, for he said, Peradventure he will also die like his brothers.

28 And Tamar rose up and went and remained in her father's house, and Tamar was in her father's house for some time.

29 And at the revolution of the year, Aliyath the wife of Judah died; and Judah was comforted for his wife, and after the death of Aliyath, Judah went up with his friend Hirah to Timnah to shear their sheep.

30 And Tamar heard that Judah had gone up to Timnah to shear the sheep, and that Shiloh was grown up, and Judah did not delight in her.

31 And Tamar rose up and put off the garments of her widowhood, and she put a vail upon her, and she entirely covered herself, and she went and sat in the public thoroughfare, which is upon the road to Timnah.

32 And Judah passed and saw her and took her and he came to her, and she conceived by him, and at the time of being delivered, behold,

there were twins in her womb, and he called the name of the first Perez, and the name of the second Zarah.

Jasher 46

1 In those days Joseph was still confined in the prison house in the land of Egypt.

2 At that time the attendants of Pharaoh were standing before him, the chief of the butlers and the chief of the bakers which belonged to the king of Egypt.

3 And the butler took wine and placed it before the king to drink, and the baker placed bread before the king to eat, and the king drank of the wine and ate of the bread, he and his servants and ministers that ate at the king's table.

4 And whilst they were eating and drinking, the butler and the baker remained there, and Pharaoh's ministers found many flies in the wine, which the butler had brought, and stones of nitre were found in the baker's bread.

5 And the captain of the guard placed Joseph as an attendant on Pharaoh's officers, and Pharaoh's officers were in confinement one year.

6 And at the end of the year, they both dreamed dreams in one night, in the place of confinement where they were, and in the morning Joseph came to them to attend upon them as usual, and he saw them, and behold their countenances were dejected and sad.

7 And Joseph asked them, Why are your countenances sad and dejected this day? and they said unto him, We dreamed a dream, and there is no one to interpret it; and Joseph said unto them, Relate, I pray you, your dream unto me, and God shall give you an answer of peace as you desire.

8 And the butler related his dream unto Joseph, and he said, I saw in my dream, and behold a large vine was before me, and upon that vine I saw three branches, and the vine speedily blossomed and reached a great height, and its clusters were ripened and became grapes.

9 And I took the grapes and pressed them in a cup, and placed it in Pharaoh's hand and he drank; and Joseph said unto him, The three branches that were upon the vine are three days.

10 Yet within three days, the king will order thee to be brought out and he will restore thee to thy office, and thou shalt give the king his wine to drink as at first when thou wast his butler; but let me find favor in thy sight, that thou shalt remember me to Pharaoh when it will be well with thee, and do kindness unto me, and get me brought forth from this prison, for I was stolen away from the land

of Canaan and was sold for a slave in this place.

11 And also that which was told thee concerning my master's wife is false, for they placed me in this dungeon for naught; and the butler answered Joseph, saying, If the king deal well with me as at first, as thou last interpreted to me, I will do all that thou desirest, and get thee brought out of this dungeon.

12 And the baker, seeing that Joseph had accurately interpreted the butler's dream, also approached, and related the whole of his dream to Joseph.

13 And he said unto him, In my dream I saw and behold three white baskets upon my head, and I looked, and behold there were in the upper-most basket all manner of baked meats for Pharaoh, and behold the birds were eating them from off my head.

14 And Joseph said unto him, The three baskets which thou didst see are three days, yet within three days Pharaoh will take off thy head, and hang thee upon a tree, and the birds will eat thy flesh from off thee, as thou sawest in thy dream.

15 In those days the queen was about to be delivered, and upon that day she bare a son unto the king of Egypt, and they proclaimed that the king had gotten his first born son and all the people of Egypt together with

the officers and servants of Pharaoh rejoiced greatly.

16 And upon the third day of his birth Pharaoh made a feast for his officers and servants, for the hosts of the land of Zoar and of the land of Egypt.

17 And all the people of Egypt and the servants of Pharaoh came to eat and drink with the king at the feast of his son, and to rejoice at the king's rejoicing.

18 And all the officers of the king and his servants were rejoicing at that time for eight days at the feast, and they made merry with all sorts of musical instruments, with timbrels and with dances in the king's house for eight days.

19 And the butler, to whom Joseph had interpreted his dream, forgot Joseph, and he did not mention him to the king as he had promised, for this thing was from the Lord in order to punish Joseph because he had trusted in man.

20 And Joseph remained after this in the prison house two years, until he had completed twelve years.

Jasher 47

1 And Isaac the son of Abraham was still living in those days in the land of Canaan; he was very aged, one hundred and eighty years old, and Esau his son, the brother of Jacob, was in the land of Edom, and he and

his sons had possessions in it amongst the children of Seir.

2 And Esau heard that his father's time was drawing nigh to die, and he and his sons and household came unto the land of Canaan, unto his father's house, and Jacob and his sons went forth from the place where they dwelt in Hebron, and they all came to their father Isaac, and they found Esau and his sons in the tent.

3 And Jacob and his sons sat before his father Isaac, and Jacob was still mourning for his son Joseph.

4 And Isaac said unto Jacob, Bring me hither thy sons and I will bless them; and Jacob brought his eleven children before his father Isaac.

5 And Isaac placed his hands upon all the sons of Jacob, and he took hold of them and embraced them, and kissed them one by one, and Isaac blessed them on that day, and he said unto them, May the God of your fathers bless you and increase your seed like the stars of heaven for number.

6 And Isaac also blessed the sons of Esau, saying, May God cause you to be a dread and a terror to all that will behold you, and to all your enemies.

7 And Isaac called Jacob and his sons, and they all came and sat before Isaac, and Isaac said unto Jacob, The Lord God of the whole earth said unto me, Unto thy seed will I give this land for an inheritance if thy children keep my statutes and my ways, and I will perform unto them the oath which I swore unto thy father Abraham.

8 Now therefore my son, teach thy children and thy children's children to fear the Lord, and to go in the good way which will please the Lord thy God, for if you keep the ways of the Lord and his statutes the Lord will also keep unto you his covenant with Abraham, and will do well with you and your seed all the days.

9 And when Isaac had finished commanding Jacob and his children, he gave up the ghost and died, and was gathered unto his people.

10 And Jacob and Esau fell upon the face of their father Isaac, and they wept, and Isaac was one hundred and eighty years old when he died in the land of Canaan, in Hebron, and his sons carried him to the cave of Machpelah, which Abraham had bought from the children of Heth for a possession of a burial place.

11 And all the kings of the land of Canaan went with Jacob and Esau to bury Isaac, and all the kings of Canaan showed Isaac great honor at his death.

12 And the sons of Jacob and the sons of Esau went barefooted round about, walking and lamenting until they reached Kireath-arba.

13 And Jacob and Esau buried their father Isaac in the cave of

Machpelah, which is in Kireath-arba in Hebron, and they buried him with very great honor, as at the funeral of kings.

14 And Jacob and his sons, and Esau and his sons, and all the kings of Canaan made a great and heavy mourning, and they buried him and mourned for him many days.

15 And at the death of Isaac, he left his cattle and his possessions and all belonging to him to his sons; and Esau said unto Jacob, Behold I pray thee, all that our father has left we will divide it in two parts, and I will have the choice, and Jacob said, We will do so.

16 And Jacob took all that Isaac had left in the land of Canaan, the cattle and the property, and he placed them in two parts before Esau and his sons, and he said unto Esau, Behold all this is before thee, choose thou unto thyself the half which thou wilt take.

17 And Jacob said unto Esau, Hear thou I pray thee what I will speak unto thee, saying, The Lord God of heaven and earth spoke unto our fathers Abraham and Isaac, saying, Unto thy seed will I give this land for an inheritance forever.

18 Now therefore all that our father has left is before thee, and behold all the land is before thee; choose thou from them what thou desirest.

19 If thou desirest the whole land take it for thee and thy children forever, and I will take this riches, and it thou desirest the riches take it unto thee, and I will take this land for me and for my children to inherit it forever.

20 And Nebayoth, the son of Ishmael, was then in the land with his children, and Esau went on that day and consulted with him, saying.

21 Thus has Jacob spoken unto me, and thus has he answered me, now give thy advice and we will hear.

22 And Nebayoth said, What is this that Jacob hath spoken unto thee? behold all the children of Canaan are dwelling securely in their land, and Jacob sayeth he will inherit it with his seed all the days.

23 Go now therefore and take all thy father's riches and leave Jacob thy brother in the land, as he has spoken.

24 And Esau rose up and returned to Jacob, and did all that Nebayoth the son of Ishmael had advised; and Esau took all the riches that Isaac had left, the souls, the beasts, the cattle and the property, and all the riches; he gave nothing to his brother Jacob; and Jacob took all the land of Canaan, from the brook of Egypt unto the river Euphrates, and he took it for an everlasting possession, and for his children and for his seed after him forever.

25 Jacob also took from his brother Esau the cave of Machpelah, which is in Hebron, which Abraham had bought from Ephron for a possession of a burial place for him and his seed forever.

26 And Jacob wrote all these things in the book of purchase, and he signed it, and he testified all this with four faithful witnesses.

27 And these are the words which Jacob wrote in the book, saying: The land of Canaan and all the cities of the Hittites, the Hivites, the Jebusites, the Amorites, the Perizzites, and the Gergashites, all the seven nations from the river of Egypt unto the river Euphrates.

28 And the city of Hebron Kireath-arba, and the cave which is in it, the whole did Jacob buy from his brother Esau for value, for a possession and for an inheritance for his seed after him forever.

29 And Jacob took the book of purchase and the signature, the command and the statutes and the revealed book, and he placed them in an earthen vessel in order that they should remain for a long time, and he delivered them into the hands of his children.

30 Esau took all that his father had left him after his death from his brother Jacob, and he took all the property, from man and beast, camel and ass, ox and lamb, silver and gold, stones and bdellium, and all the riches which had belonged to Isaac the son of Abraham; there was nothing left which Esau did not take unto himself, from all that Isaac had left after his death.

31 And Esau took all this, and he and his children went home to the land of Seir the Horite, away from his brother Jacob and his children.

32 And Esau had possessions amongst the children of Seir, and Esau returned not to the land of Canaan from that day forward.

33 And the whole land of Canaan became an inheritance to the children of Israel for an everlasting inheritance, and Esau with all his children inherited the mountain of Seir.

Jasher 48

1 In those days, after the death of Isaac, the Lord commanded and caused a famine upon the whole earth.

2 At that time Pharaoh king of Egypt was sitting upon his throne in the land of Egypt, and lay in his bed and dreamed dreams, and Pharaoh saw in his dream that he was standing by the side of the river of Egypt.

3 And whilst he was standing he saw and behold seven fat fleshed and well favored kine came up out of the river.

4 And seven other kine, lean fleshed and ill favored, came up after them, and the seven ill favored ones swallowed up the well favored ones, and still their appearance was ill as at first.

5 And he awoke, and he slept again and he dreamed a second time, and he saw and behold seven ears of corn came up upon one stalk, rank and good, and seven thin ears blasted with the east wind sprang, up after them, and the thin ears swallowed up the full ones, and Pharaoh awoke out of his dream.

6 And in the morning the king remembered his dreams, and his spirit was sadly troubled on account of his dreams, and the king hastened and sent and called for all the magicians of Egypt, and the wise men, and they came and stood before Pharaoh.

7 And the king said unto them, I have dreamed dreams, and there is none to interpret them; and they said unto the king, relate thy dreams to thy servants and let us hear them.

8 And the king related his dreams to them, and they all answered and said with one voice to the king, may the king live forever; and this is the interpretation of thy dreams.

9 The seven good kine which thou didst see denote seven daughters that will be born unto thee in the latter days, and the seven kine which

thou sawest come up after them, and swallowed them up, are for a sign that the daughters which will be born unto thee will all die in the life-time of the king.

10 And that which thou didst see in the second dream of seven full good ears of corn coming up upon one stalk, this is their interpretation, that thou wilt build unto thyself in the latter days seven cities throughout the land of Egypt; and that which thou sawest of the seven blasted ears of corn springing up after them and swallowing them up whilst thou didst behold them with thine eyes, is for a sign that the cities which thou wilt build will all be destroyed in the latter days, in the life-time of the king.

11 And when they spoke these words the king did not incline his ear to their words, neither did he fix his heart upon them, for the king knew in his wisdom that they did not give a proper interpretation of the dreams; and when they had finished speaking before the king, the king answered them, saying, What is this thing that you have spoken unto me? surely you have uttered falsehood and spoken lies; therefore now give the proper interpretation of my dreams, that you may not die.

12 And the king commanded after this, and he sent and called again for other wise men, and they came and stood before the king, and the king

related his dreams to them, and they all answered him according to the first interpretation, and the king's anger was kindled and he was very wroth, and the king said unto them, Surely you speak lies and utter falsehood in what you have said.

13 And the king commanded that a proclamation should be issued throughout the land of Egypt, saying, It is resolved by the king and his great men, that any wise man who knoweth and understandeth the interpretation of dreams, and will not come this day before the king, shall die.

14 And the man that will declare unto the king the proper interpretation of his dreams, there shall be given unto him all that he will require from the king. And all the wise men of the land of Egypt came before the king, together with all the magicians and sorcerers that were in Egypt and in Goshen, in Rameses, in Tachpanches, in Zoar, and in all the places on the borders of Egypt, and they all stood before the king.

15 And all the nobles and the princes, and the attendants belonging to the king, came together from all the cities of Egypt, and they all sat before the king, and the king related his dreams before the wise men, and the princes, and all that sat before the king were astonished at the vision.

16 And all the wise men who were before the king were greatly divided in their interpretation of his dreams; some of them interpreted them to the king, saying, The seven good kine are seven kings, who from the king's issue will be raised over Egypt.

17 And the seven bad kine are seven princes, who will stand up against them in the latter days and destroy them; and the seven ears of corn are the seven great princes belonging to Egypt, who will fall in the hands of the seven less powerful princes of their enemies, in the wars of our lord the king.

18 And some of them interpreted to the king in this manner, saying, The seven good kine are the strong cities of Egypt, and the seven bad kine are the seven nations of the land of Canaan, who will come against the seven cities of Egypt in the latter days and destroy them.

19 And that which thou sawest in the second dream, of seven good and bad ears of corn, is a sign that the government of Egypt will again return to thy seed as at first.

20 And in his reign the people of the cities of Egypt will turn against the seven cities of Canaan who are stronger than they are, and will destroy them, and the government of Egypt will return to thy seed.

21 And some of them said unto the king, This is the interpretation of thy

dreams; the seven good kine are seven queens, whom thou wilt take for wives in the latter days, and the seven bad kine denote that those women will all die in the lifetime of the king.

22 And the seven good and bad ears of corn which thou didst see in the second dream are fourteen children, and it will be in the latter days that they will stand up and fight amongst themselves, and seven of them will smite the seven that are more powerful.

23 And some of them said these words unto the king, saying, The seven good kine denote that seven children will be born to thee, and they will slay seven of thy children's children in the latter days; and the seven good ears of corn which thou didst see in the second dream, are those princes against whom seven other less powerful princes will fight and destroy them in the latter days, and avenge thy children's cause, and the government will again return to thy seed.

24 And the king heard all the words of the wise men of Egypt and their interpretation of his dreams, and none of them pleased the king.

25 And the king knew in his wisdom that they did not altogether speak correctly in all these words, for this was from the Lord to frustrate the words of the wise men of Egypt, in order that Joseph might go forth from

the house of confinement, and in order that he should become great in Egypt.

26 And the king saw that none amongst all the wise men and magicians of Egypt spoke correctly to him, and the king's wrath was kindled, and his anger burned within him.

27 And the king commanded that all the wise men and magicians should go out from before him, and they all went out from before the king with shame and disgrace.

28 And the king commanded that a proclamation be sent throughout Egypt to slay all the magicians that were in Egypt, and not one of them should be suffered to live.

29 And the captains of the guards belonging to the king rose up, and each man drew his sword, and they began to smite the magicians of Egypt, and the wise men.

30 And after this Merod, chief butler to the king, came and bowed down before the king and sat before him.

31 And the butler said unto the king, May the king live forever, and his government be exalted in the land.

32 Thou wast angry with thy servant in those days, now two years past, and didst place me in the ward, and I was for some time in the ward, I and the chief of the bakers.

33 And there was with us a Hebrew servant belonging to the captain of the guard, his name was Joseph, for his master had been angry with him and placed him in the house of confinement, and he attended us there.

34 And in some time after when we were in the ward, we dreamed dreams in one night, I and the chief of the bakers; we dreamed, each man according to the interpretation of his dream.

35 And we came in the morning and told them to that servant, and he interpreted to us our dreams, to each man according to his dream, did he correctly interpret.

36 And it came to pass as he interpreted to us, so was the event; there fell not to the ground any of his words.

37 And now therefore my lord and king do not slay the people of Egypt for naught; behold that slave is still confined in the house by the captain of the guard his master, in the house of confinement.

38 If it pleaseth the king let him send for him that he may come before thee and he will make known to thee, the correct interpretation of the dream which thou didst dream.

39 And the king heard the words of the chief butler, and the king ordered that the wise men of Egypt should not be slain.

40 And the king ordered his servants to bring Joseph before him, and the king said unto them, Go to him and do not terrify him lest he be confused and will not know to speak properly.

41 And the servants of the king went to Joseph, and they brought him hastily out of the dungeon, and the king's servants shaved him, and he changed his prison garment and he came before the king.

42 And the king was sitting upon his royal throne in a princely dress girt around with a golden ephod, and the fine gold which was upon it sparkled, and the carbuncle and the ruby and the emerald, together with all the precious stones that were upon the king's head, dazzled the eye, and Joseph wondered greatly at the king.

43 And the throne upon which the king sat was covered with gold and silver, and with onyx stones, and it had seventy steps.

44 And it was their custom throughout the land of Egypt, that every man who came to speak to the king, if he was a prince or one that was estimable in the sight of the king, he ascended to the king's throne as far as the thirty-first step, and the king would descend to the thirty-sixth step, and speak with him.

45 If he was one of the common people, he ascended to the third step, and the king would descend to the fourth and speak to him, and

their custom was, moreover, that any man who understood to speak in all the seventy languages, he ascended the seventy steps, and went up and spoke till he reached the king.

46 And any man who could not complete the seventy, he ascended as many steps as the languages which he knew to speak in.

47 And it was customary in those days in Egypt that no one should reign over them, but who understood to speak in the seventy languages.

48 And when Joseph came before the king he bowed down to the ground before the king, and he ascended to the third step, and the king sat upon the fourth step and spoke with Joseph.

49 And the king said unto Joseph, I dreamed a dream, and there is no interpreter to interpret it properly, and I commanded this day that all the magicians of Egypt and the wise men thereof, should come before me, and I related my dreams to them, and no one has properly interpreted them to me.

50 And after this I this day heard concerning thee, that thou art a wise man, and canst correctly interpret every dream that thou hearest.

51 And Joseph answered Pharaoh, saying, Let Pharaoh relate his dreams that he dreamed; surely the interpretations belong to God; and Pharaoh related his dreams to

Joseph, the dream of the kine, and the dream of the ears of corn, and the king left off speaking.

52 And Joseph was then clothed with the spirit of God before the king, and he knew all the things that would befall the king from that day forward, and he knew the proper interpretation of the king's dream, and he spoke before the king.

53 And Joseph found favor in the sight of the king, and the king inclined his ears and his heart, and he heard all the words of Joseph. And Joseph said unto the king, Do not imagine that they are two dreams, for it is only one dream, for that which God has chosen to do throughout the land he has shown to the king in his dream, and this is the proper interpretation of thy dream:

54 The seven good kine and ears of corn are seven years, and the seven bad kine and ears of corn are also seven years; it is one dream.

55 Behold the seven years that are coming there will be a great plenty throughout the land, and after that the seven years of famine will follow them, a very grievous famine; and all the plenty will be forgotten from the land, and the famine will consume the inhabitants of the land.

56 The king dreamed one dream, and the dream was therefore repeated unto Pharaoh because the

thing is established by God, and God will shortly bring it to pass.

57 Now therefore I will give thee counsel and deliver thy soul and the souls of the inhabitants of the land from the evil of the famine, that thou seek throughout thy kingdom for a man very discreet and wise, who knoweth all the affairs of government, and appoint him to superintend over the land of Egypt.

58 And let the man whom thou placest over Egypt appoint officers under him, that they gather in all the food of the good years that are coming, and let them lay up corn and deposit it in thy appointed stores.

59 And let them keep that food for the seven years of famine, that it may be found for thee and thy people and thy whole land, and that thou and thy land be not cut off by the famine.

60 Let all the inhabitants of the land be also ordered that they gather in, every man the produce of his field, of all sorts of food, during the seven good years, and that they place it in their stores, that it may be found for them in the days of the famine and that they may live upon it.

61 This is the proper interpretation of thy dream, and this is the counsel given to save thy soul and the souls of all thy subjects.

62 And the king answered and said unto Joseph, Who sayeth and who knoweth that thy words are correct? And he said unto the king, This shall be a sign for thee respecting all my words, that they are true and that my advice is good for thee.

63 Behold thy wife sitteth this day upon the stool of delivery, and she will bear thee a son and thou wilt rejoice with him; when thy child shall have gone forth from his mother's womb, thy first born son that has been born these two years back shall die, and thou wilt be comforted in the child that will be born unto thee this day.

64 And Joseph finished speaking these words to the king, and he bowed down to the king and he went out, and when Joseph had gone out from the king's presence, those signs which Joseph had spoken unto the king came to pass on that day.

65 And the queen bare a son on that day and the king heard the glad tidings about his son, and he rejoiced, and when the reporter had gone forth from the king's presence, the king's servants found the first born son of the king fallen dead upon the ground.

66 And there was great lamentation and noise in the king's house, and the king heard it, and he said, What is the noise and lamentation that I have heard in the house? and they told the king that his first born son had died; then the king knew that all Joseph's words that he had spoken

were correct, and the king was consoled for his son by the child that was born to him on that day as Joseph had spoken.

Jasher 49

1 After these things the king sent and assembled all his officers and servants, and all the princes and nobles belonging to the king, and they all came before the king.

2 And the king said unto them, Behold you have seen and heard all the words of this Hebrew man, and all the signs which he declared would come to pass, and not any of his words have fallen to the ground.

3 You know that he has given a proper interpretation of the dream, and it will surely come to pass, now therefore take counsel, and know what you will do and how the land will be delivered from the famine.

4 Seek now and see whether the like can be found, in whose heart there is wisdom and knowledge, and I will appoint him over the land.

5 For you have heard what the Hebrew man has advised concerning this to save the land therewith from the famine, and I know that the land will not be delivered from the famine but with the advice of the Hebrew man, him that advised me.

6 And they all answered the king and said, The counsel which the Hebrew has given concerning this is good;

now therefore, our lord and king, behold the whole land is in thy hand, do that which seemeth good in thy sight.

7 Him whom thou chooses, and whom thou in thy wisdom knowest to be wise and capable of delivering the land with his wisdom, him shall the king appoint to be under him over the land.

8 And the king said to all the officers: I have thought that since God has made known to the Hebrew man all that he has spoken, there is none so discreet and wise in the whole land as he is; if it seem good in your sight I will place him over the land, for he will save the land with his wisdom.

9 And all the officers answered the king and said, But surely it is written in the laws of Egypt, and it should not be violated, that no man shall reign over Egypt, nor be the second to the king, but one who has knowledge in all the languages of the sons of men.

10 Now therefore our lord and king, behold this Hebrew man can only speak the Hebrew language, and how then can he be over us the second under government, a man who not even knoweth our language?

11 Now we pray thee send for him, and let him come before thee, and prove him in all things, and do as thou see fit.

12 And the king said, It shall be done tomorrow, and the thing that you have spoken is good; and all the officers came on that day before the king.

13 And on that night the Lord sent one of his ministering angels, and he came into the land of Egypt unto Joseph, and the angel of the Lord stood over Joseph, and behold Joseph was lying in the bed at night in his master's house in the dungeon, for his master had put him back into the dungeon on account of his wife.

14 And the angel roused him from his sleep, and Joseph rose up and stood upon his legs, and behold the angel of the Lord was standing opposite to him; and the angel of the Lord spoke with Joseph, and he taught him all the languages of man in that night, and he called his name Jehoseph.

15 And the angel of the Lord went from him, and Joseph returned and lay upon his bed, and Joseph was astonished at the vision which he saw.

16 And it came to pass in the morning that the king sent for all his officers and servants, and they all came and sat before the king, and the king ordered Joseph to be brought, and the king's servants went and brought Joseph before Pharaoh.

17 And the king came forth and ascended the steps of the throne, and Joseph spoke unto the king in all languages, and Joseph went up to him and spoke unto the king until he arrived before the king in the seventieth step, and he sat before the king.

18 And the king greatly rejoiced on account of Joseph, and all the king's officers rejoiced greatly with the king when they heard all the words of Joseph.

19 And the thing seemed good in the sight of the king and the officers, to appoint Joseph to be second to the king over the whole land of Egypt, and the king spoke to Joseph, saying,

20 Now thou didst give me counsel to appoint a wise man over the land of Egypt, in order with his wisdom to save the land from the famine; now therefore, since God has made all this known to thee, and all the words which thou hast spoken, there is not throughout the land a discreet and wise man like unto thee.

21 And thy name no more shall be called Joseph, but Zaphnath Paaneah shall be thy name; thou shalt be second to me, and according to thy word shall be all the affairs of my government, and at thy word shall my people go out and come in.

22 Also from under thy hand shall my servants and officers receive their salary which is given to them monthly, and to thee shall all the people of the land bow down; only in my throne will I be greater than thou.

23 And the king took off his ring from his hand and put it upon the hand of Joseph, and the king dressed Joseph in a princely garment, and he put a golden crown upon his head, and he put a golden chain upon his neck.

24 And the king commanded his servants, and they made him ride in the second chariot belonging to the king, that went opposite to the king's chariot, and he caused him to ride upon a great and strong horse from the king's horses, and to be conducted through the streets of the land of Egypt.

25 And the king commanded that all those that played upon timbrels, harps and other musical instruments should go forth with Joseph; one thousand timbrels, one thousand mecholoth, and one thousand nebalim went after him.

26 And five thousand men, with drawn swords glittering in their hands, and they went marching and playing before Joseph, and twenty thousand of the great men of the king girt with girdles of skin covered with gold, marched at the right hand of Joseph, and twenty thousand at his left, and all the women and damsels went upon the roofs or stood in the streets playing and rejoicing at Joseph, and gazed at the appearance of Joseph and at his beauty.

27 And the king's people went before him and behind him, perfuming the road with frankincense and with cassia, and with all sorts of fine perfume, and scattered myrrh and aloes along the road, and twenty men proclaimed these words before him throughout the land in a loud voice:

28 Do you see this man whom the king has chosen to be his second? all the affairs of government shall be regulated by him, and he that transgresses his orders, or that does not bow down before him to the ground, shall die, for he rebels against the king and his second.

29 And when the heralds had ceased proclaiming, all the people of Egypt bowed down to the ground before Joseph and said, May the king live, also may his second live; and all the inhabitants of Egypt bowed down along the road, and when the heralds approached them, they bowed down, and they rejoiced with all sorts of timbrels, mechol and nebal before Joseph.

30 And Joseph upon his horse lifted up his eyes to heaven, and called out and said, He raiseth the poor man from the dust, He lifteth up the needy from the dunghill. O Lord of

Hosts, happy is the man who trusteth in thee.

31 And Joseph passed throughout the land of Egypt with Pharaoh's servants and officers, and they showed him the whole land of Egypt and all the king's treasures.

32 And Joseph returned and came on that day before Pharaoh, and the king gave unto Joseph a possession in the land of Egypt, a possession of fields and vineyards, and the king gave unto Joseph three thousand talents of silver and one thousand talents of gold, and onyx stones and bdellium and many gifts.

33 And on the next day the king commanded all the people of Egypt to bring unto Joseph offerings and gifts, and that he that violated the command of the king should die; and they made a high place in the street of the city, and they spread out garments there, and whoever brought anything to Joseph put it into the high place.

34 And all the people of Egypt cast something into the high place, one man a golden ear-ring, and the other rings and ear-rings, and different vessels of gold and silver work, and onyx stones and bdellium did he cast upon the high place; every one gave something of what he possessed.

35 And Joseph took all these and placed them in his treasuries, and all the officers and nobles belonging to the king exalted Joseph, and they gave him many gifts, seeing that the king had chosen him to be his second.

36 And the king sent to Potiphera, the son of Ahiram priest of On, and he took his young daughter Osnath and gave her unto Joseph for a wife.

37 And the damsel was very comely, a virgin, one whom man had not known, and Joseph took her for a wife; and the king said unto Joseph, I am Pharaoh, and beside thee none shall dare to lift up his hand or his foot to regulate my people throughout the land of Egypt.

38 And Joseph was thirty years old when he stood before Pharaoh, and Joseph went out from before the king, and he became the king's second in Egypt.

39 And the king gave Joseph a hundred servants to attend him in his house, and Joseph also sent and purchased many servants and they remained in the house of Joseph.

40 Joseph then built for himself a very magnificent house like unto the houses of kings, before the court of the king's palace, and he made in the house a large temple, very elegant in appearance and convenient for his residence; three years was Joseph in erecting his house.

41 And Joseph made unto himself a very elegant throne of abundance of

gold and silver, and he covered it with onyx stones and bdellium, and he made upon it the likeness of the whole land of Egypt, and the likeness of the river of Egypt that watereth the whole land of Egypt; and Joseph sat securely upon his throne in his house and the Lord increased Joseph's wisdom.

42 And all the inhabitants of Egypt and Pharaoh's servants and his princes loved Joseph exceedingly, for this thing was from the Lord to Joseph.

43 And Joseph had an army that made war, going out in hosts and troops to the number of forty thousand six hundred men, capable of bearing arms to assist the king and Joseph against the enemy, besides the king's officers and his servants and inhabitants of Egypt without number.

44 And Joseph gave unto his mighty men, and to all his host, shields and javelins, and caps and coats of mail and stones for slinging.

Jasher 50

1 At that time the children of Tarshish came against the sons of Ishmael, and made war with them, and the children of Tarshish spoiled the Ishmaelites for a long time.

2 And the children of Ishmael were small in number in those days, and they could not prevail over the children of Tarshish, and they were sorely oppressed.

3 And the old men of the Ishmaelites sent a record to the king of Egypt, saying, Send I pray thee unto thy servants officers and hosts to help us to fight against the children of Tarshish, for we have been consuming away for a long time.

4 And Pharaoh sent Joseph with the mighty men and host which were with him, and also his mighty men from the king's house.

5 And they went to the land of Havilah to the children of Ishmael, to assist them against the children of Tarshish, and the children of Ishmael fought with the children of Tarshish, and Joseph smote the Tarshishites and he subdued all their land, and the children of Ishmael dwell therein unto this day.

6 And when the land of Tarshish was subdued, all the Tarshishites ran away, and came on the border of their brethren the children of Javan, and Joseph with all his mighty men and host returned to Egypt, not one man of them missing.

7 And at the revolution of the year, in the second year of Joseph's reigning over Egypt, the Lord gave great plenty throughout the land for seven years as Joseph had spoken, for the Lord blessed all the produce of the earth in those days for seven years,

and they ate and were greatly satisfied.

8 And Joseph at that time had officers under him, and they collected all the food of the good years, and heaped corn year by year, and they placed it in the treasuries of Joseph.

9 And at any time when they gathered the food Joseph commanded that they should bring the corn in the ears, and also bring with it some of the soil of the field, that it should not spoil.

10 And Joseph did according to this year by year, and he heaped up corn like the sand of the sea for abundance, for his stores were immense and could not be numbered for abundance.

11 And also all the inhabitants of Egypt gathered all sorts of food in their stores in great abundance during the seven good years, but they did not do unto it as Joseph did.

12 And all the food which Joseph and the Egyptians had gathered during the seven years of plenty, was secured for the land in stores for the seven years of famine, for the support of the whole land.

13 And the inhabitants of Egypt filled each man his store and his concealed place with corn, to be for support during the famine.

14 And Joseph placed all the food that he had gathered in all the cities of Egypt, and he closed all the stores and placed sentinels over them.

15 And Joseph's wife Osnath the daughter of Potiphera bare him two sons, Manasseh and Ephraim, and Joseph was thirty-four years old when he begat them.

16 And the lads grew up and they went in his ways and in his instructions, they did not deviate from the way which their father taught them, either to the right or left.

17 And the Lord was with the lads, and they grew up and had understanding and skill in all wisdom and in all the affairs of government, and all the king's officers and his great men of the inhabitants of Egypt exalted the lads, and they were brought up amongst the king's children.

18 And the seven years of plenty that were throughout the land were at an end, and the seven years of famine came after them as Joseph had spoken, and the famine was throughout the land.

19 And all the people of Egypt saw that the famine had commenced in the land of Egypt, and all the people of Egypt opened their stores of corn for the famine prevailed over them.

20 And they found all the food that was in their stores, full of vermin and not fit to eat, and the famine

prevailed throughout the land, and all the inhabitants of Egypt came and cried before Pharaoh, for the famine was heavy upon them.

21 And they said unto Pharaoh, Give food unto thy servants, and wherefore shall we die through hunger before thy eyes, even we and our little ones?

22 And Pharaoh answered them, saying, And wherefore do you cry unto me? did not Joseph command that the corn should be laid up during the seven years of plenty for the years of famine? and wherefore did you not hearken to his voice?

23 And the people of Egypt answered the king, saying, As thy soul liveth, our lord, thy servants have done all that Joseph ordered, for thy servants also gathered in all the produce of their fields during the seven years of plenty and laid it in the stores unto this day.

24 And when the famine prevailed over thy servants we opened our stores, and behold all our produce was filled with vermin and was not fit for food.

25 And when the king heard all that had befallen the inhabitants of Egypt, the king was greatly afraid on account of the famine, and he was much terrified; and the king answered the people of Egypt, saying, Since all this has happened unto you, go unto Joseph, do

whatever he shall say unto you, transgress not his commands.

26 And all the people of Egypt went forth and came unto Joseph, and said unto him, Give unto us food, and wherefore shall we die before thee through hunger? for we gathered in our produce during the seven years as thou didst command, and we put it in store, and thus has it befallen us.

27 And when Joseph heard all the words of the people of Egypt and what had befallen them, Joseph opened all his stores of the produce and he sold it unto the people of Egypt.

28 And the famine prevailed throughout the land, and the famine was in all countries, but in the land of Egypt there was produce for sale.

29 And all the inhabitants of Egypt came unto Joseph to buy corn, for the famine prevailed over them, and all their corn was spoiled, and Joseph daily sold it to all the people of Egypt.

30 And all the inhabitants of the land of Canaan and the Philistines, and those beyond the Jordan, and the children of the east and all the cities of the lands far and nigh heard that there was corn in Egypt, and they all came to Egypt to buy corn, for the famine prevailed over them.

31 And Joseph opened the stores of corn and placed officers over them,

and they daily stood and sold to all that came.

32 And Joseph knew that his brethren also would come to Egypt to buy corn, for the famine prevailed throughout the earth. And Joseph commanded all his people that they should cause it to be proclaimed throughout the land of Egypt, saying,

33 It is the pleasure of the king, of his second and of their great men, that any person who wishes to buy corn in Egypt shall not send his servants to Egypt to purchase, but his sons, and also any Egyptian or Canaanite, who shall come from any of the stores from buying corn in Egypt, and shall go and sell it throughout the land, he shall die, for no one shall buy but for the support of his household.

34 And any man leading two or three beasts shall die, for a man shall only lead his own beast.

35 And Joseph placed sentinels at the gates of Egypt, and commanded them, saying, Any person who may come to buy corn, suffer him not to enter until his name, and the name of his father, and the name of his father's father be written down, and whatever is written by day, send their names unto me in the evening that I may know their names.

36 And Joseph placed officers throughout the land of Egypt, and he commanded them to do all these things.

37 And Joseph did all these things, and made these statutes, in order that he might know when his brethren should come to Egypt to buy corn; and Joseph's people caused it daily to be proclaimed in Egypt according to these words and statutes which Joseph had commanded.

38 And all the inhabitants of the east and west country, and of all the earth, heard of the statutes and regulations which Joseph had enacted in Egypt, and the inhabitants of the extreme parts of the earth came and they bought corn in Egypt day after day, and then went away.

39 And all the officers of Egypt did as Joseph had commanded, and all that came to Egypt to buy corn, the gate keepers would write their names, and their fathers' names, and daily bring them in the evening before Joseph.

Jasher 51

1 And Jacob afterward heard that there was corn in Egypt, and he called unto his sons to go to Egypt to buy corn, for upon them also did the famine prevail, and he called unto his sons, saying,

2 Behold I hear that there is corn in Egypt, and all the people of the earth go there to purchase, now therefore why will you show yourselves

satisfied before the whole earth? go you also down to Egypt and buy us a little corn amongst those that come there, that we may not die.

3 And the sons of Jacob hearkened to the voice of their father, and they rose up to go down to Egypt in order to buy corn amongst the rest that came there.

4 And Jacob their father commanded them, saying, When you come into the city do not enter together in one gate, on account of the inhabitants of the land.

5 And the sons of Jacob went forth and they went to Egypt, and the sons of Jacob did all as their father had commanded them, and Jacob did not send Benjamin, for he said, Lest an accident might befall him on the road like his brother; and ten of Jacob's sons went forth.

6 And whilst the sons of Jacob were going on the road, they repented of what they had done to Joseph, and they spoke to each other, saying, We know that our brother Joseph went down to Egypt, and now we will seek him where we go, and if we find him we will take him from his master for a ransom, and if not, by force, and we will die for him.

7 And the sons of Jacob agreed to this thing and strengthened themselves on account of Joseph, to deliver him from the hand of his master, and the sons of Jacob went to Egypt; and when they came near to Egypt they separated from each other, and they came through ten gates of Egypt, and the gate keepers wrote their names on that day, and brought them to Joseph in the evening.

8 And Joseph read the names from the hand of the gate-keepers of the city, and he found that his brethren had entered at the ten gates of the city, and Joseph at that time commanded that it should be proclaimed throughout the land of Egypt, saying,

9 Go forth all ye store guards, close all the corn stores and let only one remain open, that those who come may purchase from it.

10 And all the officers of Joseph did so at that time, and they closed all the stores and left only one open.

11 And Joseph gave the written names of his brethren to him that was set over the open store, and he said unto him, Whosoever shall come to thee to buy corn, ask his name, and when men of these names shall come before thee, seize them and send them, and they did so.

12 And when the sons of Jacob came into the city, they joined together in the city to seek Joseph before they bought themselves corn.

13 And they went to the walls of the harlots, and they sought Joseph in

the walls of the harlots for three days, for they thought that Joseph would come in the walls of the harlots, for Joseph was very comely and well favored, and the sons of Jacob sought Joseph for three days, and they could not find him.

14 And the man who was set over the open store sought for those names which Joseph had given him, and he did not find them.

15 And he sent to Joseph, saying, These three days have passed, and those men whose names thou didst give unto me have not come; and Joseph sent servants to seek the men in all Egypt, and to bring them before Joseph.

16 And Joseph's servants went and came into Egypt and could not find them, and went to Goshen and they were not there, and then went to the city of Rameses and could not find them.

17 And Joseph continued to send sixteen servants to seek his brothers, and they went and spread themselves in the four corners of the city, and four of the servants went into the house of the harlots, and they found the ten men there seeking their brother.

18 And those four men took them and brought them before him, and they bowed down to him to the ground, and Joseph was sitting upon his throne in his temple, clothed with princely garments, and upon his head was a large crown of gold, and all the mighty men were sitting around him.

19 And the sons of Jacob saw Joseph, and his figure and comeliness and dignity of countenance seemed wonderful in their eyes, and they again bowed down to him to the ground.

20 And Joseph saw his brethren, and he knew them, but they knew him not, for Joseph was very great in their eyes, therefore they knew him not.

21 And Joseph spoke to them, saying, From whence come ye? and they all answered and said, Thy servants have come from the land of Canaan to buy corn, for the famine prevails throughout the earth, and thy servants heard that there was corn in Egypt, so they have come amongst the other comers to buy corn for their support.

22 And Joseph answered them, saying, If you have come to purchase as you say, why do you come through ten gates of the city? it can only be that you have come to spy through the land.

23 And they all together answered Joseph, and said, Not so my lord, we are right, thy servants are not spies, but we have come to buy corn, for thy servants are all brothers, the sons of one man in the land of

Canaan, and our father commanded us, saying, When you come to the city do not enter together at one gate on account of the inhabitants of the land.

24 And Joseph again answered them and said, That is the thing which I spoke unto you, you have come to spy through the land, therefore you all came through ten gates of the city; you have come to see the nakedness of the land.

25 Surely every one that cometh to buy corn goeth his way, and you are already three days in the land, and what do you do in the walls of harlots in which you have been for these three days? surely spies do like unto these things.

26 And they said unto Joseph, Far be it from our lord to speak thus, for we are twelve brothers, the sons of our father Jacob, in the land of Canaan, the son of Isaac, the son of Abraham, the Hebrew, and behold the youngest is with our father this day in the land of Canaan, and one is not, for he was lost from us, and we thought perhaps he might be in this land, so we are seeking him throughout the land, and have come even to the houses of harlots to seek him there.

27 And Joseph said unto them, And have you then sought him throughout the earth, that there only remained Egypt for you to seek him in? And what also should your brother do in the houses of harlots, although he were in Egypt? have you not said, That you are from the sons of Isaac, the son of Abraham, and what shall the sons of Jacob do then in the houses of harlots?

28 And they said unto him, Because we heard that Ishmaelites stole him from us, and it was told unto us that they sold him in Egypt, and thy servant, our brother, is very comely and well favored, so we thought he would surely be in the houses of harlots, therefore thy servants went there to seek him and give ransom for him.

29 And Joseph still answered them, saying, Surely you speak falsely and utter lies, to say of yourselves that you are the sons of Abraham; as Pharaoh liveth you are spies, therefore have you come to the houses of harlots that you should not be known.

30 And Joseph said unto them, And now if you find him, and his master requireth of you a great price, will you give it for him? and they said, It shall be given.

31 And he said unto them, And if his master will not consent to part with him for a great price, what will you do unto him on his account? and they answered him, saying, If he will not give him unto us we will slay him, and take our brother and go away.

32 And Joseph said unto them, That is the thing which I have spoken to you; you are spies, for you are come to slay the inhabitants of the land, for we heard that two of your brethren smote all the inhabitants of Shechem, in the land of Canaan, on account of your sister, and you now come to do the like in Egypt on account of your brother.

33 Only hereby shall I know that you are true men; if you will send home one from amongst you to fetch your youngest brother from your father, and to bring him here unto me, and by doing this thing I will know that you are right.

34 And Joseph called to seventy of his mighty men, and he said unto them, Take these men and bring them into the ward.

35 And the mighty men took the ten men, they laid hold of them and put them into the ward, and they were in the ward three days.

36 And on the third day Joseph had them brought out of the ward, and he said unto them, Do this for yourselves if you be true men, so that you may live, one of your brethren shall be confined in the ward whilst you go and take home the corn for your household to the land of Canaan, and fetch your youngest brother, and bring him here unto me, that I may know that you are true men when you do this thing.

37 And Joseph went out from them and came into the chamber, and wept a great weeping, for his pity was excited for them, and he washed his face, and returned to them again, and he took Simeon from them and ordered him to be bound, but Simeon was not willing to be done so, for he was a very powerful man and they could not bind him.

38 And Joseph called unto his mighty men and seventy valiant men came before him with drawn swords in their hands, and the sons of Jacob were terrified at them.

39 And Joseph said unto them, Seize this man and confine him in prison until his brethren come to him, and Joseph's valiant men hastened and they all laid hold of Simeon to bind him, and Simeon gave a loud and terrible shriek and the cry was heard at a distance.

40 And all the valiant men of Joseph were terrified at the sound of the shriek, that they fell upon their faces, and they were greatly afraid and fled.

41 And all the men that were with Joseph fled, for they were greatly afraid of their lives, and only Joseph and Manasseh his son remained there, and Manassah the son of Joseph saw the strength of Simeon, and he was exceedingly wroth.

42 And Manassah the son of Joseph rose up to Simeon, and Manassah

smote Simeon a heavy blow with his fist against the back of his neck, and Simeon was stilled of his rage.

43 And Manassah laid hold of Simeon and he seized him violently and he bound him and brought him into the house of confinement, and all the sons of Jacob were astonished at the act of the youth.

44 And Simeon said unto his brethren, None of you must say that this is the smiting of an Egyptian, but it is the smiting of the house of my father.

45 And after this Joseph ordered him to be called who was set over the storehouse, to fill their sacks with corn as much as they could carry, and to restore every man's money into his sack, and to give them provision for the road, and thus did he unto them.

46 And Joseph commanded them, saying, Take heed lest you transgress my orders to bring your brother as I have told you, and it shall be when you bring your brother hither unto me, then will I know that you are true men, and you shall traffic in the land, and I will restore unto you your brother, and you shall return in peace to your father.

47 And they all answered and said, According as our lord speaketh so will we do, and they bowed down to him to the ground.

48 And every man lifted his corn upon his ass, and they went out to go to the land of Canaan to their father; and they came to the inn and Levi spread his sack to give provender to his ass, when he saw and behold his money in full weight was still in his sack.

49 And the man was greatly afraid, and he said unto his brethren, My money is restored, and lo, it is even in my sack, and the men were greatly afraid, and they said, What is this that God hath done unto us?

50 And they all said, And where is the Lord's kindness with our fathers, with Abraham, Isaac, end Jacob, that the Lord has this day delivered us into the hands of the king of Egypt to contrive against us?

51 And Judah said unto them, Surely we are guilty sinners before the Lord our God in having sold our brother, our own flesh, and wherefore do you say, Where is the Lord's kindness with our fathers?

52 And Reuben said unto them, Said I not unto you, do not sin against the lad, and you would not listen to me? now God requireth him from us, and how dare you say, Where is the Lord's kindness with our fathers, whilst you have sinned unto the Lord?

53 And they tarried over night in that place, and they rose up early in the morning and laded their asses with

their corn, and they led them and went on and came to their father's house in the land of Canaan.

54 And Jacob and his household went out to meet his sons, and Jacob saw and behold their brother Simeon was not with them, and Jacob said unto his sons, Where is your brother Simeon, whom I do not see? and his sons told him all that had befallen them in Egypt.

Jasher 52

1 And they entered their house, and every man opened his sack and they saw and behold every man's bundle of money was there, at which they and their father were greatly terrified.

2 And Jacob said unto them, What is this that you have done to me? I sent your brother Joseph to inquire after your welfare and you said unto me, A wild beast did devour him.

3 And Simeon went with you to buy food and you say the king of Egypt hath confined him in prison, and you wish to take Benjamin to cause his death also, and bring down my grey hairs with sorrow to the grave on account of Benjamin and his brother Joseph.

4 Now therefore my son shall not go down with you, for his brother is dead and he is left alone, and mischief may befall him by the way in which you go, as it befell his brother.

5 And Reuben said unto his father, Thou shalt slay my two sons if I do not bring thy son and place him before thee; and Jacob said unto his sons, Abide ye here and do not go down to Egypt, for my son shall not go down with you to Egypt, nor die like his brother.

6 And Judah said unto them, refrain ye from him until the corn is finished, and he will then say, Take down your brother, when he will find his own life and the life of his household in danger from the famine.

7 And in those days the famine was sore throughout the land, and all the people of the earth went and came to Egypt to buy food, for the famine prevailed greatly amongst them, and the sons of Jacob remained in Canaan a year and two months until their corn was finished.

8 And it came to pass after their corn was finished, the whole household of Jacob was pinched with hunger, and all the infants of the sons of Jacob came together and they approached Jacob, and they all surrounded him, and they said unto him, Give unto us bread, and wherefore shall we all perish through hunger in thy presence?

9 Jacob heard the words of his son's children, and he wept a great weeping, and his pity was roused for them, and Jacob called unto his sons and they all came and sat before him.

10 And Jacob said unto them, And have you not seen how your children have been weeping over me this day, saying, Give unto us bread, and there is none? now therefore return and buy for us a little food.

11 And Judah answered and said unto his father, If thou wilt send our brother with us we will go down and buy corn for thee, and if thou wilt not send him then we will not go down, for surely the king of Egypt particularly enjoined us, saying, You shall not see my face unless your brother be with you, for the king of Egypt is a strong and mighty king, and behold if we shall go to him without our brother we shall all be put to death.

12 Dost thou not know and hast thou not heard that this king is very powerful and wise, and there is not like unto him in all the earth? behold we have seen all the kings of the earth and we have not seen one like that king, the king of Egypt; surely amongst all the kings of the earth there is none greater than Abimelech king of the Philistines, yet the king of Egypt is greater and mightier than he, and Abimelech can only be compared to one of his officers.

13 Father, thou hast not seen his palace and his throne, and all his servants standing before him; thou hast not seen that king upon his throne in his pomp and royal appearance, dressed in his kingly robes with a large golden crown upon his head; thou hast not seen the honor and glory which God has given unto him, for there is not like unto him in all the earth.

14 Father, thou hast not seen the wisdom, the understanding and the knowledge which God has given in his heart, nor heard his sweet voice when he spake unto us.

15 We know not, father, who made him acquainted with our names and all that befell us, yet he asked also after thee, saying, Is your father still living, and is it well with him?

16 Thou hast not seen the affairs of the government of Egypt regulated by him, without inquiring of Pharaoh his lord; thou hast not seen the awe and fear which he impressed upon all the Egyptians.

17 And also when we went from him, we threatened to do unto Egypt like unto the rest of the cities of the Amorites, and we were exceedingly wroth against all his words which he spoke concerning us as spies, and now when we shall again come before him his terror will fall upon us all, and not one of us will be able to speak to him either a little or a great thing.

18 Now therefore father, send we pray thee the lad with us, and we will go down and buy thee food for our support, and not die through hunger. And Jacob said, Why have you dealt

so ill with me to tell the king you had a brother? what is this thing that you have done unto me?

19 And Judah said unto Jacob his father, Give the lad into my care and we will rise up and go down to Egypt and buy corn, and then return, and it shall be when we return if the lad be not with us, then let me bear thy blame forever.

20 Hast thou seen all our infants weeping over thee through hunger and there is no power in thy hand to satisfy them? now let thy pity be roused for them and send our brother with us and we will go.

21 For how will the Lord's kindness to our ancestors be manifested to thee when thou sayest that the king of Egypt will take away thy son? as the Lord liveth I will not leave him until I bring him and place him before thee; but pray for us unto the Lord, that he may deal kindly with us, to cause us to be received favorably and kindly before the king of Egypt and his men, for had we not delayed surely now we had returned a second time with thy son.

22 And Jacob said unto his sons, I trust in the Lord God that he may deliver you and give you favor in the sight of the king of Egypt, and in the sight of all his men.

23 Now therefore rise up and go to the man, and take for him in your hands a present from what can be obtained in the land and bring it before him, and may the Almighty God give you mercy before him that he may send Benjamin and Simeon your brethren with you.

24 And all the men rose up, and they took their brother Benjamin, and they took in their hands a large present of the best of the land, and they also took a double portion of silver.

25 And Jacob strictly commanded his sons concerning Benjamin, Saying, Take heed of him in the way in which you are going, and do not separate yourselves from him in the road, neither in Egypt.

26 And Jacob rose up from his sons and spread forth his hands and he prayed unto the Lord on account of his sons, saying, O Lord God of heaven and earth, remember thy covenant with our father Abraham, remember it with my father Isaac and deal kindly with my sons and deliver them not into the hands of the king of Egypt; do it I pray thee O God for the sake of thy mercies and redeem all my children and rescue them from Egyptian power, and send them their two brothers.

27 And all the wives of the sons of Jacob and their children lifted up their eyes to heaven and they all wept before the Lord, and cried unto him to deliver their fathers from the hand of the king of Egypt.

28 And Jacob wrote a record to the king of Egypt and gave it into the hand of Judah and into the hands of his sons for the king of Egypt, saying,

29 From thy servant Jacob, son of Isaac, son of Abraham the Hebrew, the prince of God, to the powerful and wise king, the revealer of secrets, king of Egypt, greeting.

30 Be it known to my lord the king of Egypt, the famine was sore upon us in the land of Canaan, and I sent my sons to thee to buy us a little food from thee for our support.

31 For my sons surrounded me and I being very old cannot see with my eyes, for my eyes have become very heavy through age, as well as with daily weeping for my son, for Joseph who was lost from before me, and I commanded my sons that they should not enter the gates of the city when they came to Egypt, on account of the inhabitants of the land.

32 And I also commanded them to go about Egypt to seek for my son Joseph, perhaps they might find him there, and they did so, and thou didst consider them as spies of the land.

33 Have we not heard concerning thee that thou didst interpret Pharaoh's dream and didst speak truly unto him? how then dost thou not know in thy wisdom whether my sons are spies or not?

34 Now therefore, my lord and king, behold I have sent my son before thee, as thou didst speak unto my sons; I beseech thee to put thy eyes upon him until he is returned to me in peace with his brethren.

35 For dost thou not know, or hast thou not heard that which our God did unto Pharaoh when he took my mother Sarah, and what he did unto Abimelech king of the Philistines on account of her, and also what our father Abraham did unto the nine kings of Elam, how he smote them all with a few men that were with him?

36 And also what my two sons Simeon and Levi did unto the eight cities of the Amorites, how they destroyed them on account of their sister Dinah?

37 And also on account of their brother Benjamin they consoled themselves for the loss of his brother Joseph; what will they then do for him when they see the hand of any people prevailing over them, for his sake?

38 Dost thou not know, O king of Egypt, that the power of God is with us, and that also God ever heareth our prayers and forsaketh us not all the days?

39 And when my sons told me of thy dealings with them, I called not unto the Lord on account of thee, for then thou wouldst have perished with thy

men before my son Benjamin came before thee, but I thought that as Simeon my son was in thy house, perhaps thou mightest deal kindly with him, therefore I did not this thing unto thee.

40 Now therefore behold Benjamin my son cometh unto thee with my sons, take heed of him and put thy eyes upon him, and then will God place his eyes over thee and throughout thy kingdom.

41 Now I have told thee all that is in my heart, and behold my sons are coming to thee with their brother, examine the face of the whole earth for their sake and send them back in peace with their brethren.

42 And Jacob gave the record to his sons into the care of Judah to give it unto the king of Egypt.

Jasher 53

1 And the sons of Jacob rose up and took Benjamin and the whole of the presents, and they went and came to Egypt and they stood before Joseph.

2 And Joseph beheld his brother Benjamin with them and he saluted them, and these men came to Joseph's house.

3 And Joseph commanded the superintendent of his house to give to his brethren to eat, and he did so unto them.

4 And at noon time Joseph sent for the men to come before him with Benjamin, and the men told the superintendent of Joseph's house concerning the silver that was returned in their sacks, and he said unto them, It will be well with you, fear not, and he brought their brother Simeon unto them.

5 And Simeon said unto his brethren, The lord of the Egyptians has acted very kindly unto me, he did not keep me bound, as you saw with your eyes, for when you went out from the city he let me free and dealt kindly with me in his house.

6 And Judah took Benjamin by the hand, and they came before Joseph, and they bowed down to him to the ground.

7 And the men gave the present unto Joseph and they all sat before him, and Joseph said unto them, Is it well with you, is it well with your children, is it well with your aged father? and they said, It is well, and Judah took the record which Jacob had sent and gave it into the hand of Joseph.

8 And Joseph read the letter and knew his father's writing, and he wished to weep and he went into an inner room and he wept a great weeping; and he went out.

9 And he lifted up his eyes and beheld his brother Benjamin, and he said, Is this your brother of whom you spoke unto me? And Benjamin approached Joseph, and Joseph placed his hand upon his head and

609

he said unto him, May God be gracious unto thee my son.

10 And when Joseph saw his brother, the son of his mother, he again wished to weep, and he entered the chamber, and he wept there, and he washed his face, and went out and refrained from weeping, and he said, Prepare food.

11 And Joseph had a cup from which he drank, and it was of silver beautifully inlaid with onyx stones and bdellium, and Joseph struck the cup in the sight of his brethren whilst they were sitting to eat with him.

12 And Joseph said unto the men, I know by this cup that Reuben the first born, Simeon and Levi and Judah, Issachar and Zebulun are children from one mother, seat yourselves to eat according to your births.

13 And he also placed the others according to their births, and he said, I know that this your youngest brother has no brother, and I, like him, have no brother, he shall therefore sit down to eat with me.

14 And Benjamin went up before Joseph and sat upon the throne, and the men beheld the acts of Joseph, and they were astonished at them; and the men ate and drank at that time with Joseph, and he then gave presents unto them, and Joseph gave one gift unto Benjamin, and Manasseh and Ephraim saw the acts

of their father, and they also gave presents unto him, and Osnath gave him one present, and they were five presents in the hand of Benjamin.

15 And Joseph brought them out wine to drink, and they would not drink, and they said, From the day on which Joseph was lost we have not drunk wine, nor eaten any delicacies.

16 And Joseph swore unto them, and he pressed them hard, and they drank plentifully with him on that day, and Joseph afterward turned to his brother Benjamin to speak with him, and Benjamin was still sitting upon the throne before Joseph.

17 And Joseph said unto him, Hast thou begotten any children? and he said, Thy servant has ten sons, and these are their names, Bela, Becher, Ashbal, Gera, Naaman, Achi, Rosh, Mupim, Chupim, and Ord, and I called their names after my brother whom I have not seen.

18 And he ordered them to bring before him his map of the stars, whereby Joseph knew all the times, and Joseph said unto Benjamin, I have heard that the Hebrews are acquainted with all wisdom, dost thou know anything of this?

19 And Benjamin said, Thy servant is knowing also in all the wisdom which my father taught me, and Joseph said unto Benjamin, Look now at this instrument and

understand where thy brother Joseph is in Egypt, who you said went down to Egypt.

20 And Benjamin beheld that instrument with the map of the stars of heaven, and he was wise and looked therein to know where his brother was, and Benjamin divided the whole land of Egypt into four divisions, and he found that he who was sitting upon the throne before him was his brother Joseph, and Benjamin wondered greatly, and when Joseph saw that his brother Benjamin was so much astonished, he said unto Benjamin, What hast thou seen, and why art thou astonished?

21 And Benjamin said unto Joseph, I can see by this that Joseph my brother sitteth here with me upon the throne, and Joseph said unto him, I am Joseph thy brother, reveal not this thing unto thy brethren; behold I will send thee with them when they go away, and I will command them to be brought back again into the city, and I will take thee away from them.

22 And if they dare their lives and fight for thee, then shall I know that they have repented of what they did unto me, and I will make myself known to them, and if they forsake thee when I take thee, then shalt thou remain with me, and I will wrangle with them, and they shall go away, and I will not become known to them.

23 At that time Joseph commanded his officer to fill their sacks with food, and to put each man's money into his sack, and to put the cup in the sack of Benjamin, and to give them provision for the road, and they did so unto them.

24 And on the next day the men rose up early in the morning, and they loaded their asses with their corn, and they went forth with Benjamin, and they went to the land of Canaan with their brother Benjamin.

25 They had not gone far from Egypt when Joseph commanded him that was set over his house, saying, Rise, pursue these men before they get too far from Egypt, and say unto them, Why have you stolen my master's cup?

26 And Joseph's officer rose up and he reached them, and he spoke unto them all the words of Joseph; and when they heard this thing they became exceedingly wroth, and they said, He with whom thy master's cup shall be found shall die, and we will also become slaves.

27 And they hastened and each man brought down his sack from his ass, and they looked in their bags and the cup was found in Benjamin's bag, and they all tore their garments and they returned to the city, and they smote Benjamin in the road, continually smiting him until he came into the city, and they stood before Joseph.

28 And Judah's anger was kindled, and he said, This man has only brought me back to destroy Egypt this day.

29 And the men came to Joseph's house, and they found Joseph sitting upon his throne, and all the mighty men standing at his right and left.

30 And Joseph said unto them, What is this act that you have done, that you took away my silver cup and went away? but I know that you took my cup in order to know thereby in what part of the land your brother was.

31 And Judah said, What shall we say to our lord, what shall we speak and how shall we justify ourselves, God has this day found the iniquity of all thy servants, therefore has he done this thing to us this day.

32 And Joseph rose up and caught hold of Benjamin and took him from his brethren with violence, and he came to the house and locked the door at them, and Joseph commanded him that was set over his house that he should say unto them, Thus saith the king, Go in peace to your father, behold I have taken the man in whose hand my cup was found.

Jasher 54

1 And when Judah saw the dealings of Joseph with them, Judah approached him and broke open the door, and came with his brethren before Joseph.

2 And Judah said unto Joseph, Let it not seem grievous in the sight of my lord, may thy servant I pray thee speak a word before thee? and Joseph said unto him, Speak.

3 And Judah spoke before Joseph, and his brethren were there standing before them; and Judah said unto Joseph, Surely when we first came to our lord to buy food, thou didst consider us as spies of the land, and we brought Benjamin before thee, and thou still makest sport of us this day.

4 Now therefore let the king hear my words, and send I pray thee our brother that he may go along with us to our father, lest thy soul perish this day with all the souls of the inhabitants of Egypt.

5 Dost thou not know what two of my brethren, Simeon and Levi, did unto the city of Shechem, and unto seven cities of the Amorites, on account of our sister Dinah, and also what they would do for the sake of their brother Benjamin?

6 And I with my strength, who am greater and mightier than both of them, come this day upon thee and thy land if thou art unwilling to send our brother.

7 Hast thou not heard what our God who made choice of us did unto Pharaoh on account of Sarah our

mother, whom he took away from our father, that he smote him and his household with heavy plagues, that even unto this day the Egyptians relate this wonder to each other? so will our God do unto thee on account of Benjamin whom thou hast this day taken from his father, and on account of the evils which thou this day heapest over us in thy land; for our God will remember his covenant with our father Abraham and bring evil upon thee, because thou hast grieved the soul of our father this day.

8 Now therefore hear my words that I have this day spoken unto thee, and send our brother that he may go away lest thou and the people of thy land die by the sword, for you cannot all prevail over me.

9 And Joseph answered Judah, saying, Why hast thou opened wide thy mouth and why dost thou boast over us, saying, Strength is with thee? as Pharaoh liveth, if I command all my valiant men to fight with you, surely thou and these thy brethren would sink in the mire.

10 And Judah said unto Joseph, Surely it becometh thee and thy people to fear me; as the Lord liveth if I once draw my sword I shall not sheathe it again until I shall this day have slain all Egypt, and I will commence with thee and finish with Pharaoh thy master.

11 And Joseph answered and said unto him, Surely strength belongeth not alone to thee; I am stronger and mightier than thou, surely if thou drawest thy sword I will put it to thy neck and the necks of all thy brethren.

12 And Judah said unto him, Surely if I this day open my mouth against thee I would swallow thee up that thou be destroyed from off the earth and perish this day from thy kingdom. And Joseph said, Surely if thou openest thy mouth I have power and might to close thy mouth with a stone until thou shalt not be able to utter a word; see how many stones are before us, truly I can take a stone, and force it into thy mouth and break thy jaws.

13 And Judah said, God is witness between us, that we have not hitherto desired to battle with thee, only give us our brother and we will go from thee; and Joseph answered and said, As Pharaoh liveth, if all the kings of Canaan came together with you, you should not take him from my hand.

14 Now therefore go your way to your father, and your brother shall be unto me for a slave, for he has robbed the king's house. And Judah said, What is it to thee or to the character of the king, surely the king sendeth forth from his house, throughout the land, silver and gold either in gifts or expenses, and thou

still talkest about thy cup which thou didst place in our brother's bag and sayest that he has stolen it from thee?

15 God forbid that our brother Benjamin or any of the seed of Abraham should do this thing to steal from thee, or from any one else, whether king, prince, or any man.

16 Now therefore cease this accusation lest the whole earth hear thy words, saying, For a little silver the king of Egypt wrangled with the men, and he accused them and took their brother for a slave.

17 And Joseph answered and said, Take unto you this cup and go from me and leave your brother for a slave, for it is the judgment of a thief to be a slave.

18 And Judah said, Why art thou not ashamed of thy words, to leave our brother and to take thy cup? Surely if thou givest us thy cup, or a thousand times as much, we will not leave our brother for the silver which is found in the hand of any man, that we will not die over him.

19 And Joseph answered, And why did you forsake your brother and sell him for twenty pieces of silver unto this day, and why then will you not do the same to this your brother?

20 And Judah said, the Lord is witness between me and thee that we desire not thy battles; now therefore give us our brother and we will go from thee without quarreling.

21 And Joseph answered and said, If all the kings of the land should assemble they will not be able to take your brother from my hand; and Judah said, What shall we say unto our father, when he seeth that our brother cometh not with us, and will grieve over him?

22 And Joseph answered and said, This is the thing which you shall tell unto your father, saying, The rope has gone after the bucket.

23 And Judah said, Surely thou art a king, and why speakest thou these things, giving a false judgment? woe unto the king who is like unto thee.

24 And Joseph answered and said, There is no false judgment in the word that I spoke on account of your brother Joseph, for all of you sold him to the Midianites for twenty pieces of silver, and you all denied it to your father and said unto him, An evil beast has devoured him, Joseph has been torn to pieces.

25 And Judah said, Behold the fire of Shem burneth in my heart, now I will burn all your land with fire; and Joseph answered and said, Surely thy sister-in-law Tamar, who killed your sons, extinguished the fire of Shechem.

26 And Judah said, If I pluck out a single hair from my flesh, I will fill all Egypt with its blood.

27 And Joseph answered and said, Such is your custom to do as you did to your brother whom you sold, and you dipped his coat in blood and brought it to your father in order that he might say an evil beast devoured him and here is his blood.

28 And when Judah heard this thing he was exceedingly wroth and his anger burned within him, and there was before him in that place a stone, the weight of which was about four hundred shekels, and Judah's anger was kindled and he took the stone in one hand and cast it to the heavens and caught it with his left hand.

29 And he placed it afterward under his legs, and he sat upon it with all his strength and the stone was turned into dust from the force of Judah.

30 And Joseph saw the act of Judah and he was very much afraid, but he commanded Manassah his son and he also did with another stone like unto the act of Judah, and Judah said unto his brethren, Let not any of you say, this man is an Egyptian, but by his doing this thing he is of our father's family.

31 And Joseph said, Not to you only is strength given, for we are also powerful men, and why will you boast over us all? and Judah said unto Joseph, Send I pray thee our brother and ruin not thy country this day.

32 And Joseph answered and said unto them, Go and tell your father, an evil beast hath devoured him as you said concerning your brother Joseph.

33 And Judah spoke to his brother Naphtali, and he said unto him, Make haste, go now and number all the streets of Egypt and come and tell me; and Simeon said unto him, Let not this thing be a trouble to thee; now I will go to the mount and take up one large stone from the mount and level it at every one in Egypt, and kill all that are in it.

34 And Joseph heard all these words that his brethren spoke before him, and they did not know that Joseph understood them, for they imagined that he knew not to speak Hebrew.

35 And Joseph was greatly afraid at the words of his brethren lest they should destroy Egypt, and he commanded his son Manasseh, saying, Go now make haste and gather unto me all the inhabitants of Egypt, and all the valiant men together, and let them come to me now upon horseback and on foot and with all sorts of musical instruments, and Manasseh went and did so.

36 And Naphtali went as Judah had commanded him, for Naphtali was lightfooted as one of the swift stags, and he would go upon the ears of corn and they would not break under him.

37 And he went and numbered all the streets of Egypt, and found them to be twelve, and he came hastily and told Judah, and Judah said unto his brethren, Hasten you and put on every man his sword upon his loins and we will come over Egypt, and smite them all, and let not a remnant remain.

38 And Judah said, Behold, I will destroy three of the streets with my strength, and you shall each destroy one street; and when Judah was speaking this thing, behold the inhabitants of Egypt and all the mighty men came toward them with all sorts of musical instruments and with loud shouting.

39 And their number was five hundred cavalry and ten thousand infantry, and four hundred men who could fight without sword or spear, only with their hands and strength.

40 And all the mighty men came with great storming and shouting, and they all surrounded the sons of Jacob and terrified them, and the ground quaked at the sound of their shouting.

41 And when the sons of Jacob saw these troops they were greatly afraid of their lives, and Joseph did so in order to terrify the sons of Jacob to become tranquilized.

42 And Judah, seeing some of his brethren terrified, said unto them, Why are you afraid whilst the grace of God is with us? and when Judah saw all the people of Egypt surrounding them at the command of Joseph to terrify them, only Joseph commanded them, saying, Do not touch any of them.

43 Then Judah hastened and drew his sword, and uttered a loud and bitter scream, and he smote with his sword, and he sprang upon the ground and he still continued to shout against all the people.

44 And when he did this thing the Lord caused the terror of Judah and his brethren to fall upon the valiant men and all the people that surrounded them.

45 And they all fled at the sound of the shouting, and they were terrified and fell one upon the other, and many of them died as they fell, and they all fled from before Judah and his brethren and from before Joseph.

46 And whilst they were fleeing, Judah and his brethren pursued them unto the house of Pharaoh, and they all escaped, and Judah again sat before Joseph and roared at him like a lion, and gave a great and tremendous shriek at him.

47 And the shriek was heard at a distance, and all the inhabitants of Succoth heard it, and all Egypt quaked at the sound of the shriek, and also the walls of Egypt and of the land of Goshen fell in from the shaking of the earth, and Pharaoh

also fell from his throne upon the ground, and also all the pregnant women of Egypt and Goshen miscarried when they heard the noise of the shaking, for they were terribly afraid.

48 And Pharaoh sent word, saying, What is this thing that has this day happened in the land of Egypt? and they came and told him all the things from beginning to end, and Pharaoh was alarmed and he wondered and was greatly afraid.

49 And his fright increased when he heard all these things, and he sent unto Joseph, saying, Thou hast brought unto me the Hebrews to destroy all Egypt; what wilt thou do with that thievish slave? send him away and let him go with his brethren, and let us not perish through their evil, even we, you and all Egypt.

50 And if thou desirest not to do this thing, cast off from thee all my valuable things, and go with them to their land, if thou delightest in it, for they will this day destroy my whole country and slay all my people; even all the women of Egypt have miscarried through their screams; see what they have done merely by their shouting and speaking, moreover if they fight with the sword, they will destroy the land; now therefore choose that which thou desirest, whether me or the

Hebrews, whether Egypt or the land of the Hebrews.

51 And they came and told Joseph all the words of Pharaoh that he had said concerning him, and Joseph was greatly afraid at the words of Pharaoh and Judah and his brethren were still standing before Joseph indignant and enraged, and all the sons of Jacob roared at Joseph, like the roaring of the sea and its waves.

52 And Joseph was greatly afraid of his brethren and on account of Pharaoh, and Joseph sought a pretext to make himself known unto his brethren, lest they should destroy all Egypt.

53 And Joseph commanded his son Manasseh, and Manasseh went and approached Judah, and placed his hand upon his shoulder, and the anger of Judah was stilled.

54 And Judah said unto his brethren, Let no one of you say that this is the act of an Egyptian youth for this is the work of my father's house.

55 And Joseph seeing and knowing that Judah's anger was stilled, he approached to speak unto Judah in the language of mildness.

56 And Joseph said unto Judah, Surely you speak truth and have this day verified your assertions concerning your strength, and may your God who delighteth in you, increase your welfare; but tell me truly why from amongst all thy

brethren dost thou wrangle with me on account of the lad, as none of them have spoken one word to me concerning him.

57 And Judah answered Joseph, saying, Surely thou must know that I was security for the lad to his father, saying, If I brought him not unto him I should bear his blame forever.

58 Therefore have I approached thee from amongst all my brethren, for I saw that thou wast unwilling to suffer him to go from thee; now therefore may I find grace in thy sight that thou shalt send him to go with us, and behold I will remain as a substitute for him, to serve thee in whatever thou desirest, for wheresoever thou shalt send me I will go to serve thee with great energy.

59 Send me now to a mighty king who has rebelled against thee, and thou shalt know what I will do unto him and unto his land; although he may have cavalry and infantry or an exceeding mighty people, I will slay them all and bring the king's head before thee.

60 Dost thou not know or hast thou not heard that our father Abraham with his servant Eliezer smote all the kings of Elam with their hosts in one night, they left not one remaining? and ever since that day our father's strength was given unto us for an inheritance, for us and our seed forever.

61 And Joseph answered and said, You speak truth, and falsehood is not in your mouth, for it was also told unto us that the Hebrews have power and that the Lord their God delighteth much in them, and who then can stand before them?

62 However, on this condition will I send your brother, if you will bring before me his brother the son of his mother, of whom you said that he had gone from you down to Egypt; and it shall come to pass when you bring unto me his brother I will take him in his stead, because not one of you was security for him to your father, and when he shall come unto me, I will then send with you his brother for whom you have been security.

63 And Judah's anger was kindled against Joseph when he spoke this thing, and his eyes dropped blood with anger, and he said unto his brethren, How doth this man this day seek his own destruction and that of all Egypt!

64 And Simeon answered Joseph, saying, Did we not tell thee at first that we knew not the particular spot to which he went, and whether he be dead or alive, and wherefore speaketh my lord like unto these things?

65 And Joseph observing the countenance of Judah discerned that his anger began to kindle when he spoke unto him, saying, Bring unto

me your other brother instead of this brother.

66 And Joseph said unto his brethren, Surely you said that your brother was either dead or lost, now if I should call him this day and he should come before you, would you give him unto me instead of his brother?

67 And Joseph began to speak and call out, Joseph, Joseph, come this day before me, and appear to thy brethren and sit before them.

68 And when Joseph spoke this thing before them, they looked each a different way to see from whence Joseph would come before them.

69 And Joseph observed all their acts, and said unto them, Why do you look here and there? I am Joseph whom you sold to Egypt, now therefore let it not grieve you that you sold me, for as a support during the famine did God send me before you.

70 And his brethren were terrified at him when they heard the words of Joseph, and Judah was exceedingly terrified at him.

71 And when Benjamin heard the words of Joseph he was before them in the inner part of the house, and Benjamin ran unto Joseph his brother, and embraced him and fell upon his neck, and they wept.

72 And when Joseph's brethren saw that Benjamin had fallen upon his brother's neck and wept with him, they also fell upon Joseph and embraced him, and they wept a great weeping with Joseph.

73 And the voice was heard in the house of Joseph that they were Joseph's brethren, and it pleased Pharaoh exceedingly, for he was afraid of them lest they should destroy Egypt.

74 And Pharaoh sent his servants unto Joseph to congratulate him concerning his brethren who had come to him, and all the captains of the armies and troops that were in Egypt came to rejoice with Joseph, and all Egypt rejoiced greatly about Joseph's brethren.

75 And Pharaoh sent his servants to Joseph, saying, Tell thy brethren to fetch all belonging to them and let them come unto me, and I will place them in the best part of the land of Egypt, and they did so.

76 And Joseph commanded him that was set over his house to bring out to his brethren gifts and garments, and he brought out to them many garments being robes of royalty and many gifts, and Joseph divided them amongst his brethren.

77 And he gave unto each of his brethren a change of garments of gold and silver, and three hundred pieces of silver, and Joseph

commanded them all to be dressed in these garments, and to be brought before Pharaoh.

78 And Pharaoh seeing that all Joseph's brethren were valiant men, and of beautiful appearance, he greatly rejoiced.

79 And they afterward went out from the presence of Pharaoh to go to the land of Canaan, to their father, and their brother Benjamin was with them.

80 And Joseph rose up and gave unto them eleven chariots from Pharaoh, and Joseph gave unto them his chariot, upon which he rode on the day of his being crowned in Egypt, to fetch his father to Egypt; and Joseph sent to all his brothers' children, garments according to their numbers, and a hundred pieces of silver to each of them, and he also sent garments to the wives of his brethren from the garments of the king's wives, and he sent them.

81 And he gave unto each of his brethren ten men to go with them to the land of Canaan to serve them, to serve their children and all belonging to them in coming to Egypt.

82 And Joseph sent by the hand of his brother Benjamin ten suits of garments for his ten sons, a portion above the rest of the children of the sons of Jacob.

83 And he sent to each fifty pieces of silver, and ten chariots on the account of Pharaoh, and he sent to his father ten asses laden with all the luxuries of Egypt, and ten she asses laden with corn and bread and nourishment for his father, and to all that were with him as provisions for the road.

84 And he sent to his sister Dinah garments of silver and gold, and frankincense and myrrh, and aloes and women's ornaments in great plenty, and he sent the same from the wives of Pharaoh to the wives of Benjamin.

85 And he gave unto all his brethren, also to their wives, all sorts of onyx stones and bdellium, and from all the valuable things amongst the great people of Egypt, nothing of all the costly things was left but what Joseph sent of to his father's household.

86 And he sent his brethren away, and they went, and he sent his brother Benjamin with them.

87 And Joseph went out with them to accompany them on the road unto the borders of Egypt, and he commanded them concerning his father and his household, to come to Egypt.

88 And he said unto them, Do not quarrel on the road, for this thing was from the Lord to keep a great people from starvation, for there will be yet five years of famine in the land.

89 And he commanded them, saying, When you come unto the land of Canaan, do not come suddenly before my father in this affair, but act in your wisdom.

90 And Joseph ceased to command them, and he turned and went back to Egypt, and the sons of Jacob went to the land of Canaan with joy and cheerfulness to their father Jacob.

91 And they came unto the borders of the land, and they said to each other, What shall we do in this matter before our father, for if we come suddenly to him and tell him the matter, he will be greatly alarmed at our words and will not believe us.

92 And they went along until they came nigh unto their houses, and they found Serach, the daughter of Asher, going forth to meet them, and the damsel was very good and subtle, and knew how to play upon the harp.

93 And they called unto her and she came before them, and she kissed them, and they took her and gave unto her a harp, saying, Go now before our father, and sit before him, and strike upon the harp, and speak these words.

94 And they commanded her to go to their house, and she took the harp and hastened before them, and she came and sat near Jacob.

95 And she played well and sang, and uttered in the sweetness of her words, Joseph my uncle is living, and he ruleth throughout the land of Egypt, and is not dead.

96 And she continued to repeat and utter these words, and Jacob heard her words and they were agreeable to him.

97 He listened whilst she repeated them twice and thrice, and joy entered the heart of Jacob at the sweetness of her words, and the spirit of God was upon him, and he knew all her words to be true.

98 And Jacob blessed Serach when she spoke these words before him, and he said unto her, My daughter, may death never prevail over thee, for thou hast revived my spirit; only speak yet before me as thou hast spoken, for thou hast gladdened me with all thy words.

99 And she continued to sing these words, and Jacob listened and it pleased him, and he rejoiced, and the spirit of God was upon him.

100 Whilst he was yet speaking with her, behold his sons came to him with horses and chariots and royal garments and servants running before them.

101 And Jacob rose up to meet them, and saw his sons dressed in royal garments and he saw all the treasures that Joseph had sent to them.

102 And they said unto him, Be informed that our brother Joseph is living, and it is he who ruleth throughout the land of Egypt, and it is he who spoke unto us as we told thee.

103 And Jacob heard all the words of his sons, and his heart palpitated at their words, for he could not believe them until he saw all that Joseph had given them and what he had sent him, and all the signs which Joseph had spoken unto them.

104 And they opened out before him, and showed him all that Joseph had sent, they gave unto each what Joseph had sent him, and he knew that they had spoken the truth, and he rejoiced exceedingly an account of his son.

105 And Jacob said, It is enough for me that my son Joseph is still living, I will go and see him before I die.

106 And his sons told him all that had befallen them, and Jacob said, I will go down to Egypt to see my son and his offspring.

107 And Jacob rose up and put on the garments which Joseph had sent him, and after he had washed, and shaved his hair, he put upon his head the turban which Joseph had sent him.

108 And all the people of Jacob's house and their wives put on the garments which Joseph had sent to them, and they greatly rejoiced at Joseph that he was still living and that he was ruling in Egypt,

109 And all the inhabitants of Canaan heard of this thing, and they came and rejoiced much with Jacob that he was still living.

110 And Jacob made a feast for them for three days, and all the kings of Canaan and nobles of the land ate and drank and rejoiced in the house of Jacob.

Jasher 55

1 And it came to pass after this that Jacob said, I will go and see my son in Egypt and will then come back to the land of Canaan of which God had spoken unto Abraham, for I cannot leave the land of my birth-place.

2 Behold the word of the Lord came unto him, saying, Go down to Egypt with all thy household and remain there, fear not to go down to Egypt for I will there make thee a great nation.

3 And Jacob said within himself, I will go and see my son whether the fear of his God is yet in his heart amidst all the inhabitants of Egypt.

4 And the Lord said unto Jacob, Fear not about Joseph, for he still retaineth his integrity to serve me, as will seem good in thy sight, and Jacob rejoiced exceedingly concerning his son.

5 At that time Jacob commanded his sons and household to go to Egypt according to the word of the Lord unto him, and Jacob rose up with his sons and all his household, and he went out from the land of Canaan from Beersheba, with joy and gladness of heart, and they went to the land of Egypt.

6 And it came to pass when they came near Egypt, Jacob sent Judah before him to Joseph that he might show him a situation in Egypt, and Judah did according to the word of his father, and he hastened and ran and came to Joseph, and they assigned for them a place in the land of Goshen for all his household, and Judah returned and came along the road to his father.

7 And Joseph harnessed the chariot, and he assembled all his mighty men and his servants and all the officers of Egypt in order to go and meet his father Jacob, and Joseph's mandate was proclaimed in Egypt, saying, All that do not go to meet Jacob shall die.

8 And on the next day Joseph went forth with all Egypt a great and mighty host, all dressed in garments of fine linen and purple and with instruments of silver and gold and with their instruments of war with them.

9 And they all went to meet Jacob with all sorts of musical instruments, with drums and timbrels, strewing myrrh and aloes all along the road, and they all went after this fashion, and the earth shook at their shouting.

10 And all the women of Egypt went upon the roofs of Egypt and upon the walls to meet Jacob, and upon the head of Joseph was Pharaoh's regal crown, for Pharaoh had sent it unto him to put on at the time of his going to meet his father.

11 And when Joseph came within fifty cubits of his father, he alighted from the chariot and he walked toward his father, and when all the officers of Egypt and her nobles saw that Joseph had gone on foot toward his father, they also alighted and walked on foot toward Jacob.

12 And when Jacob approached the camp of Joseph, Jacob observed the camp that was coming toward him with Joseph, and it gratified him and Jacob was astonished at it.

13 And Jacob said unto Judah, Who is that man whom I see in the camp of Egypt dressed in kingly robes with a very red garment upon him and a royal crown upon his head, who has alighted from his chariot and is coming toward us? and Judah answered his father, saying, He is thy son Joseph the king; and Jacob rejoiced in seeing the glory of his son.

14 And Joseph came nigh unto his father and he bowed to his father,

and all the men of the camp bowed to the ground with him before Jacob.

15 And behold Jacob ran and hastened to his son Joseph and fell upon his neck and kissed him, and they wept, and Joseph also embraced his father and kissed him, and they wept and all the people of Egypt wept with them.

16 And Jacob said unto Joseph, Now I will die cheerfully after I have seen thy face, that thou art still living and with glory.

17 And the sons of Jacob and their wives and their children and their servants, and all the household of Jacob wept exceedingly with Joseph, and they kissed him and wept greatly with him.

18 And Joseph and all his people returned afterward home to Egypt, and Jacob and his sons and all the children of his household came with Joseph to Egypt, and Joseph placed them in the best part of Egypt, in the land of Goshen.

19 And Joseph said unto his father and unto his brethren, I will go up and tell Pharaoh, saying, My brethren and my father's household and all belonging to them have come unto me, and behold they are in the land of Goshen.

20 And Joseph did so and took from his brethren Reuben, Issachar Zebulun and his brother Benjamin and he placed them before Pharaoh.

21 And Joseph spoke unto Pharaoh, saying, My brethren and my father's household and all belonging to them, together with their flocks and cattle have come unto me from the land of Canaan, to sojourn in Egypt; for the famine was sore upon them.

22 And Pharaoh said unto Joseph, Place thy father and brethren in the best part of the land, withhold not from them all that is good, and cause them to eat of the fat of the land.

23 And Joseph answered, saying, Behold I have stationed them in the land of Goshen, for they are shepherds, therefore let them remain in Goshen to feed their flocks apart from the Egyptians.

24 And Pharaoh said unto Joseph, Do with thy brethren all that they shall say unto thee; and the sons of Jacob bowed down to Pharaoh, and they went forth from him in peace, and Joseph afterward brought his father before Pharaoh.

25 And Jacob came and bowed down to Pharaoh, and Jacob blessed Pharaoh, and he then went out; and Jacob and all his sons, and all his household dwelt in the land of Goshen.

26 In the second year, that is in the hundred and thirtieth year of the life of Jacob, Joseph maintained his father and his brethren, and all his father's household, with bread according to their little ones, all the

days of the famine; they lacked nothing.

27 And Joseph gave unto them the best part of the whole land; the best of Egypt had they all the days of Joseph; and Joseph also gave unto them and unto the whole of his father's household, clothes and garments year by year; and the sons of Jacob remained securely in Egypt all the days of their brother.

28 And Jacob always ate at Joseph's table, Jacob and his sons did not leave Joseph's table day or night, besides what Jacob's children consumed in their houses.

29 And all Egypt ate bread during the days of the famine from the house of Joseph, for all the Egyptians sold all belonging to them on account of the famine.

30 And Joseph purchased all the lands and fields of Egypt for bread on the account of Pharaoh, and Joseph supplied all Egypt with bread all the days of the famine, and Joseph collected all the silver and gold that came unto him for the corn which they bought throughout the land, and he accumulated much gold and silver, besides an immense quantity of onyx stones, bdellium and valuable garments which they brought unto Joseph from every part of the land when their money was spent.

31 And Joseph took all the silver and gold that came into his hand, about seventy two talents of gold and silver, and also onyx stones and bdellium in great abundance, and Joseph went and concealed them in four parts, and he concealed one part in the wilderness near the Red sea, and one part by the river Perath, and the third and fourth part he concealed in the desert opposite to the wilderness of Persia and Media.

32 And he took part of the gold and silver that was left, and gave it unto all his brothers and unto all his father's household, and unto all the women of his father's household, and the rest he brought to the house of Pharaoh, about twenty talents of gold and silver.

33 And Joseph gave all the gold and silver that was left unto Pharaoh, and Pharaoh placed it in the treasury, and the days of the famine ceased after that in the land, and they sowed and reaped in the whole land, and they obtained their usual quantity year by year; they lacked nothing.

34 And Joseph dwelt securely in Egypt, and the whole land was under his advice, and his father and all his brethren dwelt in the land of Goshen and took possession of it.

35 And Joseph was very aged, advanced in days, and his two sons, Ephraim and Manasseh, remained constantly in the house of Jacob,

together with the children of the sons of Jacob their brethren, to learn the ways of the Lord and his law.

36 And Jacob and his sons dwelt in the land of Egypt in the land of Goshen, and they took possession in it, and they were fruitful and multiplied in it.

Jasher 56

1 And Jacob lived in the land of Egypt seventeen years, and the days of Jacob, and the years of his life were a hundred and forty seven years.

2 At that time Jacob was attacked with that illness of which he died and he sent and called for his son Joseph from Egypt, and Joseph his son came from Egypt and Joseph came unto his father.

3 And Jacob said unto Joseph and unto his sons, Behold I die, and the God of your ancestors will visit you, and bring you back to the land, which the Lord sware to give unto you and unto your children after you, now therefore when I am dead, bury me in the cave which is in Machpelah in Hebron in the land of Canaan, near my ancestors.

4 And Jacob made his sons swear to bury him in Machpelah, in Hebron, and his sons swore unto him concerning this thing.

5 And he commanded them, saying, Serve the Lord your God, for he who delivered your fathers will also deliver you from all trouble.

6 And Jacob said, Call all your children unto me, and all the children of Jacob's sons came and sat before him, and Jacob blessed them, and he said unto them, The Lord God of your fathers shall grant you a thousand times as much and bless you, and may he give you the blessing of your father Abraham; and all the children of Jacob's sons went forth on that day after he had blessed them.

7 And on the next day Jacob again called for his sons, and they all assembled and came to him and sat before him, and Jacob on that day blessed his sons before his death, each man did he bless according to his blessing; behold it is written in the book of the law of the Lord appertaining to Israel.

8 And Jacob said unto Judah, I know my son that thou art a mighty man for thy brethren; reign over them, and thy sons shall reign over their sons forever.

9 Only teach thy sons the bow and all the weapons of war, in order that they may fight the battles of their brother who will rule over his enemies.

10 And Jacob again commanded his sons on that day, saying, Behold I shall be this day gathered unto my people; carry me up from Egypt, and

626

bury me in the cave of Machpelah as I have commanded you.

11 Howbeit take heed I pray you that none of your sons carry me, only yourselves, and this is the manner you shall do unto me, when you carry my body to go with it to the land of Canaan to bury me,

12 Judah, Issachar and Zebulun shall carry my bier at the eastern side; Reuben, Simeon and Gad at the south, Ephraim, Manasseh and Benjamin at the west, Dan, Asher and Naphtali at the north.

13 Let not Levi carry with you, for he and his sons will carry the ark of the covenant of the Lord with the Israelites in the camp, neither let Joseph my son carry, for as a king so let his glory be; howbeit, Ephraim and Manasseh shall be in their stead.

14 Thus shall you do unto me when you carry me away; do not neglect any thing of all that I command you; and it shall come to pass when you do this unto me, that the Lord will remember you favorably and your children after you forever.

15 And you my sons, honor each his brother and his relative, and command your children and your children's children after you to serve the Lord God of your ancestors all the days.

16 In order that you may prolong your days in the land, you and your children and your children's children for ever, when you do what is good and upright in the sight of the Lord your God, to go in all his ways.

17 And thou, Joseph my son, forgive I pray thee the prongs of thy brethren and all their misdeeds in the injury that they heaped upon thee, for God intended it for thine and thy children's benefit.

18 And O my son leave not thy brethren to the inhabitants of Egypt, neither hurt their feelings, for behold I consign them to the hand of God and in thy hand to guard them from the Egyptians; and the sons of Jacob answered their father saying, O, our father, all that thou hast commanded us, so will we do; may God only be with us.

19 And Jacob said unto his sons, So may God be with you when you keep all his ways; turn not from his ways either to the right or the left in performing what is good and upright in his sight.

20 For I know that many and grievous troubles will befall you in the latter days in the land, yea your children and children's children, only serve the Lord and he will save you from all trouble.

21 And it shall come to pass when you shall go after God to serve him and will teach your children after you, and your children's children, to know the Lord, then will the Lord

raise up unto you and your children a servant from amongst your children, and the Lord will deliver you through his hand from all affliction, and bring you out of Egypt and bring you back to the land of your fathers to inherit it securely.

22 And Jacob ceased commanding his sons, and he drew his feet into the bed, he died and was gathered to his people.

23 And Joseph fell upon his father and he cried out and wept over him and he kissed him, and he called out in a bitter voice, and he said, O my father, my father.

24 And his son's wives and all his household came and fell upon Jacob, and they wept over him, and cried in a very loud voice concerning Jacob.

25 And all the sons of Jacob rose up together, and they tore their garments, and they all put sackcloth upon their loins, and they fell upon their faces, and they cast dust upon their heads toward the heavens.

26 And the thing was told unto Osnath Joseph's wife, and she rose up and put on a sack and she with all the Egyptian women with her came and mourned and wept for Jacob.

27 And also all the people of Egypt who knew Jacob came all on that day when they heard this thing, and all Egypt wept for many days.

28 And also from the land of Canaan did the women come unto Egypt when they heard that Jacob was dead, and they wept for him in Egypt for seventy days.

29 And it came to pass after this that Joseph commanded his servants the doctors to embalm his father with myrrh and frankincense and all manner of incense and perfume, and the doctors embalmed Jacob as Joseph had commanded them.

30 And all the people of Egypt and the elders and all the inhabitants of the land of Goshen wept and mourned over Jacob, and all his sons and the children of his household lamented and mourned over their father Jacob many days.

31 And after the days of his weeping had passed away, at the end of seventy days, Joseph said unto Pharaoh, I will go up and bury my father in the land of Canaan as he made me swear, and then I will return.

32 And Pharaoh sent Joseph, saying, Go up and bury thy father as he said, and as he made thee swear; and Joseph rose up with all his brethren to go to the land of Canaan to bury their father Jacob as he had commanded them.

33 And Pharaoh commanded that it should be proclaimed throughout Egypt, saying, Whoever goeth not up with Joseph and his brethren to the

land of Canaan to bury Jacob, shall die.

34 And all Egypt heard of Pharaoh's proclamation, and they all rose up together, and all the servants of Pharaoh, and the elders of his house, and all the elders of the land of Egypt went up with Joseph, and all the officers and nobles of Pharaoh went up as the servants of Joseph, and they went to bury Jacob in the land of Canaan.

35 And the sons of Jacob carried the bier upon which he lay; according to all that their father commanded them, so did his sons unto him.

36 And the bier was of pure gold, and it was inlaid round about with onyx stones and bdellium; and the covering of the bier was gold woven work, joined with threads, and over them were hooks of onyx stones and bdellium.

37 And Joseph placed upon the head of his father Jacob a large golden crown, and he put a golden scepter in his hand, and they surrounded the bier as was the custom of kings during their lives.

38 And all the troops of Egypt went before him in this array, at first all the mighty men of Pharaoh, and the mighty men of Joseph, and after them the rest of the inhabitants of Egypt, and they were all girded with swords and equipped with coats of mail, and the trappings of war were upon them.

39 And all the weepers and mourners went at a distance opposite to the bier, going and weeping and lamenting, and the rest of the people went after the bier.

40 And Joseph and his household went together near the bier barefooted and weeping, and the rest of Joseph's servants went around him; each man had his ornaments upon him, and they were all armed with their weapons of war.

41 And fifty of Jacob's servants went in front of the bier, and they strewed along the road myrrh and aloes, and all manner of perfume, and all the sons of Jacob that carried the bier walked upon the perfumery, and the servants of Jacob went before them strewing the perfume along the road.

42 And Joseph went up with a heavy camp, and they did after this manner every day until they reached the land of Canaan, and they came to the threshing floor of Atad, which was on the other side of Jordan, and they mourned an exceeding great and heavy mourning in that place.

43 And all the kings of Canaan heard of this thing and they all went forth, each man from his house, thirty-one kings of Canaan, and they all came with their men to mourn and weep over Jacob.

44 And all these kings beheld Jacob's bier, and behold Joseph's crown was upon it, and they also put their crowns upon the bier, and encircled it with crowns.

45 And all these kings made in that place a great and heavy mourning with the sons of Jacob and Egypt over Jacob, for all the kings of Canaan knew the valor of Jacob and his sons.

46 And the report reached Esau, saying, Jacob died in Egypt, and his sons and all Egypt are conveying him to the land of Canaan to bury him.

47 And Esau heard this thing, and he was dwelling in mount Seir, and he rose up with his sons and all his people and all his household, a people exceedingly great, and they came to mourn and weep over Jacob.

48 And it came to pass, when Esau came he mourned for his brother Jacob, and all Egypt and all Canaan again rose up and mourned a great mourning with Esau over Jacob in that place

49 And Joseph and his brethren brought their father Jacob from that place, and they went to Hebron to bury Jacob in the cave by his fathers.

50 And they came unto Kireath-arba, to the cave, and as they came Esau stood with his sons against Joseph and his brethren as a hindrance in the cave, saying, Jacob shall not be buried therein, for it belongeth to us and to our father.

51 And Joseph and his brethren heard the words of Esau's sons, and they were exceedingly wroth, and Joseph approached unto Esau, saying, What is this thing which they have spoken? surely my father Jacob bought it from thee for great riches after the death of Isaac, now five and twenty years ago, and also all the land of Canaan he bought from thee and from thy sons, and thy seed after thee.

52 And Jacob bought it for his sons and his seed after him for an inheritance for ever, and why speakest thou these things this day?

53 And Esau answered, saying, Thou speakest falsely and utterest lies, for I sold not anything belonging to me in all this land, as thou sayest, neither did my brother Jacob buy aught belonging to me in this land.

54 And Esau spoke these things in order to deceive Joseph with his words, for Esau knew that Joseph was not present in those days when Esau sold all belonging to him in the land of Canaan to Jacob.

55 And Joseph said unto Esau, Surely my father inserted these things with thee in the record of purchase, and testified the record

with witnesses, and behold it is with us in Egypt.

56 And Esau answered, saying unto him, Bring the record, all that thou wilt find in the record, so will we do.

57 And Joseph called unto Naphtali his brother, and he said, Hasten quickly, stay not, and run I pray thee to Egypt and bring all the records; the record of the purchase, the sealed record and the open record, and also all the first records in which all the transactions of the birth-right are written, fetch thou.

58 And thou shalt bring them unto us hither, that we may know from them all the words of Esau and his sons which they spoke this day.

59 And Naphtali hearkened to the voice of Joseph and he hastened and ran to go down to Egypt, and Naphtali was lighter on foot than any of the stags that were upon the wilderness, for he would go upon ears of corn without crushing them.

60 And when Esau saw that Naphtali had gone to fetch the records, he and his sons increased their resistance against the cave, and Esau and all his people rose up against Joseph and his brethren to battle.

61 And all the sons of Jacob and the people of Egypt fought with Esau and his men, and the sons of Esau and his people were smitten before the sons of Jacob, and the sons of

Jacob slew of Esau's people forty men.

62 And Chushim the son of Dan, the son of Jacob, was at that time with Jacob's sons, but he was about a hundred cubits distant from the place of battle, for he remained with the children of Jacob's sons by Jacob's bier to guard it.

63 And Chushim was dumb and deaf, still he understood the voice of consternation amongst men.

64 And he asked, saying, Why do you not bury the dead, and what is this great consternation? and they answered him the words of Esau and his sons; and he ran to Esau in the midst of the battle, and he slew Esau with a sword, and he cut off his head, and it sprang to a distance, and Esau fell amongst the people of the battle.

65 And when Chushim did this thing the sons of Jacob prevailed over the sons of Esau, and the sons of Jacob buried their father Jacob by force in the cave, and the sons of Esau beheld it.

66 And Jacob was buried in Hebron, in the cave of Machpelah which Abraham had bought from the sons of Heth for the possession of a burial place, and he was buried in very costly garments.

67 And no king had such honor paid him as Joseph paid unto his father at his death, for he buried him with

great honor like unto the burial of kings.

68 And Joseph and his brethren made a mourning of seven days for their father.

Jasher 57

1 And it was after this that the sons of Esau waged war with the sons of Jacob, and the sons of Esau fought with the sons of Jacob in Hebron, and Esau was still lying dead, and not buried.

2 And the battle was heavy between them, and the sons of Esau were smitten before the sons of Jacob, and the sons of Jacob slew of the sons of Esau eighty men, and not one died of the people of the sons of Jacob; and the hand of Joseph prevailed over all the people of the sons of Esau, and he took Zepho, the son of Eliphaz, the son of Esau, and fifty of his men captive, and he bound them with chains of iron, and gave them into the hand of his servants to bring them to Egypt.

3 And it came to pass when the sons of Jacob had taken Zepho and his people captive, all those that remained were greatly afraid of their lives from the house of Esau, lest they should also be taken captive, and they all fled with Eliphaz the son of Esau and his people, with Esau's body, and they went on their road to Mount Seir.

4 And they came unto Mount Seir and they buried Esau in Seir, but they had not brought his head with them to Seir, for it was buried in that place where the battle had been in Hebron.

5 And it came to pass when the sons of Esau had fled from before the sons of Jacob, the sons of Jacob pursued them unto the borders of Seir, but they did not slay a single man from amongst them when they pursued them, for Esau's body which they carried with them excited their confusion, so they fled and the sons of Jacob turned back from them and came up to the place where their brethren were in Hebron, and they remained there on that day, and on the next day until they rested from the battle.

6 And it came to pass on the third day they assembled all the sons of Seir the Horite, and they assembled all the children of the east, a multitude of people like the sand of the sea, and they went and came down to Egypt to fight with Joseph and his brethren, in order to deliver their brethren.

7 And Joseph and all the sons of Jacob heard that the sons of Esau and the children of the east had come upon them to battle in order to deliver their brethren.

8 And Joseph and his brethren and the strong men of Egypt went forth and fought in the city of Rameses,

and Joseph and his brethren dealt out a tremendous blow amongst the sons of Esau and the children of the east.

9 And they slew of them six hundred thousand men, and they slew amongst them all the mighty men of the children of Seir the Horite; there were only a few of them left, and they slew also a great many of the children of the east, and of the children of Esau; and Eliphaz the son of Esau, and the children of the east all fled before Joseph and his brethren.

10 And Joseph and his brethren pursued them until they came unto Succoth, and they yet slew of them in Succoth thirty men, and the rest escaped and they fled each to his city.

11 And Joseph and his brethren and the mighty men of Egypt turned back from them with joy and cheerfulness of heart, for they had smitten all their enemies.

12 And Zepho the son of Eliphaz and his men were still slaves in Egypt to the sons of Jacob, and their pains increased.

13 And when the sons of Esau and the sons of Seir returned to their land, the sons of Seir saw that they had all fallen into the hands of the sons of Jacob, and the people of Egypt, on account of the battle of the sons of Esau.

14 And the sons of Seir said unto the sons of Esau, You have seen andtherefore you know that this camp was on your account, and not one mighty man or an adept in war remaineth.

15 Now therefore go forth from our land, go from us to the land of Canaan to the land of the dwelling of your fathers; wherefore shall your children inherit the effects of our children in latter days?

16 And the children of Esau would not listen to the children of Seir, and the children of Seir considered to make war with them.

17 And the children of Esau sent secretly to Angeas king of Africa, the same is Dinhabah, saying,

18 Send unto us some of thy men and let them come unto us, and we will fight together with the children of Seir the Horite, for they have resolved to fight with us to drive us away from the land.

19 And Angeas king of Dinhabah did so, for he was in those days friendly to the children of Esau, and Angeas sent five hundred valiant infantry to the children of Esau, and eight hundred cavalry.

20 And the children of Seir sent unto the children of the east and unto the children of Midian, saying, You have seen what the children of Esau have done unto us, upon whose account

we are almost all destroyed, in their battle with the sons of Jacob.

21 Now therefore come unto us and assist us, and we will fight them together, and we will drive them from the land and be avenged of the cause of our brethren who died for their sakes in their battle with their brethren the sons of Jacob.

22 And all the children of the east listened to the children of Seir, and they came unto them about eight hundred men with drawn swords, and the children of Esau fought with the children of Seir at that time in the wilderness of Paran.

23 And the children of Seir prevailed then over the sons of Esau, and the children of Seir slew on that day of the children of Esau in that battle about two hundred men of the people of Angeas king of Dinhabah.

24 And on the second day the children of Esau came again to fight a second time with the children of Seir, and the battle was sore upon the children of Esau this second time, and it troubled them greatly on account of the children of Seir.

25 And when the children of Esau saw that the children of Seir were more powerful than they were, some men of the children of Esau turned and assisted the children of Seir their enemies.

26 And there fell yet of the people of the children of Esau in the second battle fifty-eight men of the people at Angeas king of Dinhabah.

27 And on the third day the children of Esau heard that some of their brethren had turned from them to fight against them in the second battle; and the children of Esau mourned when they heard this thing.

28 And they said, What shall we do unto our brethren who turned from us to assist the children of Seir our enemies? and the children of Esau again sent to Angeas king of Dinhabah, saying,

29 Send unto us again other men that with them we may fight with the children of Seir, for they have already twice been heavier than we were.

30 And Angeas again sent to the children of Esau about six hundred valiant men, and they came to assist the children of Esau.

31 And in ten days' time the children of Esau again waged war with the children of Seir in the wilderness of Paran, and the battle was very severe upon the children of Seir, and the children of Esau prevailed at this time over the children of Seir, and the children of Seir were smitten before the children of Esau, and the children of Esau slew from them about two thousand men.

32 And all the mighty men of the children of Seir died in this battle,

and there only remained their young children that were left in their cities.

33 And all Midian and the children of the east betook themselves to flight from the battle, and they left the children of Seir and fled when they saw that the battle was severe upon them, and the children of Esau pursued all the children of the east until they reached their land.

34 And the children of Esau slew yet of them about two hundred and fifty men and from the people of the children of Esau there fell in that battle about thirty men, but this evil came upon them through their brethren turning from them to assist the children of Seir the Horite, and the children of Esau again heard of the evil doings of their brethren, and they again mourned on account of this thing.

35 And it came to pass after the battle, the children of Esau turned back and came home unto Seir, and the children of Esau slew those who had remained in the land of the children of Seir; they slew also their wives and little ones, they left not a soul alive except fifty young lads and damsels whom they suffered to live, and the children of Esau did not put them to death, and the lads became their slaves, and the damsels they took for wives.

36 And the children of Esau dwelt in Seir in the place of the children of

Seir, and they inherited their land and took possession of it.

37 And the children of Esau took all belonging in the land to the children of Seir, also their flocks, their bullocks and their goods, and all belonging to the children of Seir, did the children of Esau take, and the children of Esau dwelt in Seir in the place of the children of Seir unto this day, and the children of Esau divided the land into divisions to the five sons of Esau, according to their families.

38 And it came to pass in those days, that the children of Esau resolved to crown a king over them in the land of which they became possessed. And they said to each other, Not so, for he shall reign over us in our land, and we shall be under his counsel and he shall fight our battles, against our enemies, and they did so.

39 And all the children of Esau swore, saying, That none of their brethren should ever reign over them, but a strange man who is not of their brethren, for the souls of all the children of Esau were embittered every man against his son, brother and friend, on account of the evil they sustained from their brethren when they fought with the children of Seir.

40 Therefore the sons of Esau swore, saying, From that day forward they would not choose a king from

their brethren, but one from a strange land unto this day.

41 And there was a man there from the people of Angeas king of Dinhabah; his name was Bela the son of Beor, who was a very valiant man, beautiful and comely and wise in all wisdom, and a man of sense and counsel; and there was none of the people of Angeas like unto him.

42 And all the children of Esau took him and anointed him and they crowned him for a king, and they bowed down to him, and they said unto him, May the king live, may the king live.

43 And they spread out the sheet, and they brought him each man earrings of gold and silver or rings or bracelets, and they made him very rich in silver and in gold, in onyx stones and bdellium, and they made him a royal throne, and they placed a regal crown upon his head, and they built a palace for him and he dwelt therein, and he became king over all the children of Esau.

44 And the people of Angeas took their hire for their battle from the children of Esau, and they went and returned at that time to their master in Dinhabah.

45 And Bela reigned over the children of Esau thirty years, and the children of Esau dwelt in the land instead of the children of Seir, and they dwelt securely in their stead unto this day.

Jasher 58

1 And it came to pass in the thirty-second year of the Israelites going down to Egypt, that is in the seventy-first year of the life of Joseph, in that year died Pharaoh king of Egypt, and Magron his son reigned in his stead.

2 And Pharaoh commanded Joseph before his death to be a father to his son, Magron, and that Magron should be under the care of Joseph and under his counsel.

3 And all Egypt consented to this thing that Joseph should be king over them, for all the Egyptians loved Joseph as of heretofore, only Magron the son of Pharaoh sat upon, his father's throne, and he became king in those days in his father's stead.

4 Magron was forty-one years old when he began to reign, and forty years he reigned in Egypt, and all Egypt called his name Pharaoh after the name of his father, as it was their custom to do in Egypt to every king that reigned over them.

5 And it came to pass when Pharaoh reigned in his father's stead, he placed the laws of Egypt and all the affairs of government in the hand of Joseph, as his father had commanded him.

6 And Joseph became king over Egypt, for he superintended over all Egypt, and all Egypt was under his care and under his counsel, for all Egypt inclined to Joseph after the death of Pharaoh, and they loved him exceedingly to reign over them.

7 But there were some people amongst them, who did not like him, saying, No stranger shall reign over us; still the whole government of Egypt devolved in those days upon Joseph, after the death of Pharaoh, he being the regulator, doing as he liked throughout the land without any one interfering.

8 And all Egypt was under the care of Joseph, and Joseph made war with all his surrounding enemies, and he subdued them; also all the land and all the Philistines, unto the borders of Canaan, did Joseph subdue, and they were all under his power and they gave a yearly tax unto Joseph.

9 And Pharaoh king of Egypt sat upon his throne in his father's stead, but he was under the control and counsel of Joseph, as he was at first under the control of his father.

10 Neither did he reign but in the land of Egypt only, under the counsel of Joseph, but Joseph reigned over the whole country at that time, from Egypt unto the great river Perath.

11 And Joseph was successful in all his ways, and the Lord was with him, and the Lord gave Joseph additional wisdom, and honor, and glory, and love toward him in the hearts of the Egyptians and throughout the land, and Joseph reigned over the whole country forty years.

12 And all the countries of the Philistines and Canaan and Zidon, and on the other side of Jordan, brought presents unto Joseph all his days, and the whole country was in the hand of Joseph, and they brought unto him a yearly tribute as it was regulated, for Joseph had fought against all his surrounding enemies and subdued them, and the whole country was in the hand of Joseph, and Joseph sat securely upon his throne in Egypt.

13 And also all his brethren the sons of Jacob dwelt securely in the land, all the days of Joseph, and they were fruitful and multiplied exceedingly in the land, and they served the Lord all their days, as their father Jacob had commanded them.

14 And it came to pass at the end of many days and years, when the children of Esau were dwelling quietly in their land with Bela their king, that the children of Esau were fruitful and multiplied in the land, and they resolved to go and fight with the sons of Jacob and all Egypt, and to deliver their brother Zepho, the son of Eliphaz, and his men, for they

were yet in those days slaves to Joseph.

15 And the children of Esau sent unto all the children of the east, and they made peace with them, and all the children of the east came unto them to go with the children of Esau to Egypt to battle.

16 And there came also unto them of the people of Angeas, king of Dinhabah, and they also sent unto the children of Ishmael and they also came unto them.

17 And all this people assembled and came unto Seir to assist the children of Esau in their battle, and this camp was very large and heavy with people, numerous as the sand of the sea, about eight hundred thousand men, infantry and cavalry, and all these troops went down to Egypt to fight with the sons of Jacob, and they encamped by Rameses.

18 And Joseph went forth with his brethren with the mighty men of Egypt, about six hundred men, and they fought with them in the land of Rameses; and the sons of Jacob at that time again fought with the children of Esau, in the fiftieth year of the sons of Jacob going down to Egypt, that is the thirtieth year of the reign of Bela over the children of Esau in Seir.

19 And the Lord gave all the mighty men of Esau and the children of the east into the hand of Joseph and his brethren, and the people of the children of Esau and the children of the east were smitten before Joseph.

20 And of the people of Esau and the children of the east that were slain, there fell before the sons of Jacob about two hundred thousand men, and their king Bela the son of Beor fell with them in the battle, and when the children of Esau saw that their king had fallen in battle and was dead, their hands became weak in the combat.

21 And Joseph and his brethren and all Egypt were still smiting the people of the house of Esau, and all Esau's people were afraid of the sons of Jacob and fled from before them.

22 And Joseph and his brethren and all Egypt pursued them a day's journey, and they slew yet from them about three hundred men, continuing to smite them in the road; and they afterward turned back from them.

23 And Joseph and all his brethren returned to Egypt, not one man was missing from them, but of the Egyptians there fell twelve men.

24 And when Joseph returned to Egypt he ordered Zepho and his men to be additionally bound, and they bound them in irons and they increased their grief.

25 And all the people of the children of Esau, and the children of the east, returned in shame each unto his city,

for all the mighty men that were with them had fallen in battle.

26 And when the children of Esau saw that their king had died in battle they hastened and took a man from the people of the children of the east; his name was Jobab the son of Zarach, from the land of Botzrah, and they caused him to reign over them instead of Bela their king.

27 And Jobab sat upon the throne of Bela as king in his stead, and Jobab reigned in Edom over all the children of Esau ten years, and the children of Esau went no more to fight with the sons of Jacob from that day forward, for the sons of Esau knew the valor of the sons of Jacob, and they were greatly afraid of them.

28 But from that day forward the children of Esau hated the sons of Jacob, and the hatred and enmity were very strong between them all the days, unto this day.

29 And it came to pass after this, at the end of ten years, Jobab, the son of Zarach, from Botzrah, died, and the children of Esau took a man whose name was Chusham, from the land of Teman, and they made him king over them instead of Jobab, and Chusham reigned in Edom over all the children of Esau for twenty years.

30 And Joseph, king of Egypt, and his brethren, and all the children of Israel dwelt securely in Egypt in those days, together with all the children of Joseph and his brethren, having no hindrance or evil accident and the land of Egypt was at that time at rest from war in the days of Joseph and his brethren.

Jasher 59

1 And these are the names of the sons of Israel who dwelt in Egypt, who had come with Jacob, all the sons of Jacob came unto Egypt, every man with his household.

2 The children of Leah were Reuben, Simeon, Levi, Judah, Issachar and Zebulun, and their sister Dinah.

3 And the sons of Rachel were Joseph and Benjamin.

4 And the sons of Zilpah, the handmaid of Leah, were Gad and Asher.

5 And the sons of Bilhah, the handmaid of Rachel, were Dan and Naphtali.

6 And these were their offspring that were born unto them in the land of Canaan, before they came unto Egypt with their father Jacob.

7 The sons of Reuben were Chanoch, Pallu, Chetzron and Carmi.

8 And the sons of Simeon were Jemuel, Jamin, Ohad, Jachin, Zochar and Saul, the son of the Canaanitish woman.

9 And the children of Levi were Gershon, Kehath and Merari, and their sister Jochebed, who was born unto them in their going down to Egypt.

10 And the sons of Judah were Er, Onan, Shelah, Perez and Zarach.

11 And Er and Onan died in the land of Canaan; and the sons of Perez were Chezron and Chamul.

12 And the sons of Issachar were Tola, Puvah, Job and Shomron.

13 And the sons of Zebulun were Sered, Elon and Jachleel, and the son of Dan was Chushim.

14 And the sons of Naphtali were Jachzeel, Guni, Jetzer and Shilam.

15 And the sons of Gad were Ziphion, Chaggi, Shuni, Ezbon, Eri, Arodi and Areli.

16 And the children of Asher were Jimnah, Jishvah, Jishvi, Beriah and their sister Serach; and the sons of Beriah were Cheber and Malchiel.

17 And the sons of Benjamin were Bela, Becher, Ashbel, Gera, Naaman, Achi, Rosh, Mupim, Chupim and Ord.

18 And the sons of Joseph, that were born unto him in Egypt, were Manasseh and Ephraim.

19 And all the souls that went forth from the loins of Jacob, were seventy souls; these are they who came with Jacob their father unto Egypt to dwell there: and Joseph and all his brethren dwelt securely in Egypt, and they ate of the best of Egypt all the days of the life of Joseph.

20 And Joseph lived in the land of Egypt ninety-three years, and Joseph reigned over all Egypt eighty years.

21 And when the days of Joseph drew nigh that he should die, he sent and called for his brethren and all his father's household, and they all came together and sat before him.

22 And Joseph said unto his brethren and unto the whole of his father's household, Behold I die, and God will surely visit you and bring you up from this land to the land which he swore to your fathers to give unto them.

23 And it shall be when God shall visit you to bring you up from here to the land of your fathers, then bring up my bones with you from here.

24 And Joseph made the sons of Israel to swear for their seed after them, saying, God will surely visit you and you shall bring up my bones with you from here.

25 And it came to pass after this that Joseph died in that year, the seventy-first year of the Israelites going down to Egypt.

26 And Joseph was one hundred and ten years old when he died in

the land of Egypt, and all his brethren and all his servants rose up and they embalmed Joseph, as was their custom, and his brethren and all Egypt mourned over him for seventy days.

27 And they put Joseph in a coffin filled with spices and all sorts of perfume, and they buried him by the side of the river, that is Sihor, and his sons and all his brethren, and the whole of his father's household made a seven day's mourning for him.

28 And it came to pass after the death of Joseph, all the Egyptians began in those days to rule over the children of Israel, and Pharaoh, king of Egypt, who reigned in his father's stead, took all the laws of Egypt and conducted the whole government of Egypt under his counsel, and he reigned securely over his people.

Jasher 60

1 And when the year came round, being the seventy-second year from the Israelites going down to Egypt, after the death of Joseph, Zepho, the son of Eliphaz, the son of Esau, fled from Egypt, he and his men, and they went away.

2 And he came to Africa, which is Dinhabah, to Angeas king of Africa, and Angeas received them with great honor, and he made Zepho the captain of his host.

3 And Zepho found favor in the sight of Angeas and in the sight of his people, and Zepho was captain of the host to Angeas king of Africa for many days.

4 And Zepho enticed Angeas king of Africa to collect all his army to go and fight with the Egyptians, and with the sons of Jacob, and to avenge of them the cause of his brethren.

5 But Angeas would not listen to Zepho to do this thing, for Angeas knew the strength of the sons of Jacob, and what they had done to his army in their warfare with the children of Esau.

6 And Zepho was in those days very great in the sight of Angeas and in the sight of all his people, and he continually enticed them to make war against Egypt, but they would not.

7 And it came to pass in those days there was in the land of Chittim a man in the city of Puzimna, whose name was Uzu, and he became degenerately deified by the children of Chittim, and the man died and had no son, only one daughter whose name was Jania.

8 And the damsel was exceedingly beautiful, comely and intelligent, there was none seen like unto her for beauty and wisdom throughout the land.

9 And the people of Angeas king of Africa saw her and they came and praised her unto him, and Angeas sent to the children of Chittim, and

he requested to take her unto himself for a wife, and the people of Chittim consented to give her unto him for a wife.

10 And when the messengers of Angeas were going forth from the land of Chittim to take their journey, behold the messengers of Turnus king of Bibentu came unto Chittim, for Turnus king of Bibentu also sent his messengers to request Jania for him, to take unto himself for a wife, for all his men had also praised her to him, therefore he sent all his servants unto her.

11 And the servants of Turnus came to Chittim, and they asked for Jania, to be taken unto Turnus their king for a wife.

12 And the people of Chittim said unto them, We cannot give her, because Angeas king of Africa desired her to take her unto him for a wife before you came, and that we should give her unto him, and now therefore we cannot do this thing to deprive Angeas of the damsel in order to give her unto Turnus.

13 For we are greatly afraid of Angeas lest he come in battle against us and destroy us, and Turnus your master will not be able to deliver us from his hand.

14 And when the messengers of Turnus heard all the words of the children of Chittim, they turned back

to their master and told him all the words of the children of Chittim.

15 And the children of Chittim sent a memorial to Angeas, saying, Behold Turnus has sent for Jania to take her unto him for a wife, and thus have we answered him; and we heard that he has collected his whole army to go to war against thee, and he intends to pass by the road of Sardunia to fight against thy brother Lucus, and after that he will come to fight against thee.

16 And Angeas heard the words of the children of Chittim which they sent to him in the record, and his anger was kindled and he rose up and assembled his whole army and came through the islands of the sea, the road to Sardunia, unto his brother Lucus king of Sardunia.

17 And Niblos, the son of Lucus, heard that his uncle Angeas was coming, and he went out to meet him with a heavy army, and he kissed him and embraced him, and Niblos said unto Angeas, When thou askest my father after his welfare, when I shall go with thee to fight with Turnus, ask of him to make me captain of his host, and Angeas did so, and he came unto his brother and his brother came to meet him, and he asked him after his welfare.

18 And Angeas asked his brother Lucus after his welfare, and to make his son Niblos captain of his host, and Lucus did so, and Angeas and

his brother Lucus rose up and they went toward Turnus to battle, and there was with them a great army and a heavy people.

19 And he came in ships, and they came into the province of Ashtorash, and behold Turnus came toward them, for he went forth to Sardunia, and intended to destroy it and afterward to pass on from there to Angeas to fight with him.

20 And Angeas and Lucus his brother met Turnus in the valley of Canopia, and the battle was strong and mighty between them in that place.

21 And the battle was severe upon Lucus king of Sardunia, and all his army fell, and Niblos his son fell also in that battle.

22 And his uncle Angeas commanded his servants and they made a golden coffin for Niblos and they put him into it, and Angeas again waged battle toward Turnus, and Angeas was stronger than he, and he slew him, and he smote all his people with the edge of the sword, and Angeas avenged the cause of Niblos his brother's son and the cause of the army of his brother Lucus.

23 And when Turnus died, the hands of those that survived the battle became weak, and they fled from before Angeas and Lucus his brother.

24 And Angeas and his brother Lucus pursued them unto the highroad, which is between Alphanu and Romah, and they slew the whole army of Turnus with the edge of the sword.

25 And Lucus king of Sardunia commanded his servants that they should make a coffin of brass, and that they should place therein the body of his son Niblos, and they buried him in that place.

26 And they built upon it a high tower there upon the highroad, and they called its name after the name of Niblos unto this day, and they also buried Turnus king of Bibentu there in that place with Niblos.

27 And behold upon the highroad between Alphanu and Romah the grave of Niblos is on one side and the grave of Turnus on the other, and a pavement between them unto this day.

28 And when Niblos was buried, Lucus his father returned with his army to his land Sardunia, and Angeas his brother king of Africa went with his people unto the city of Bibentu, that is the city of Turnus.

29 And the inhabitants of Bibentu heard of his fame and they were greatly afraid of him, and they went forth to meet him with weeping and supplication, and the inhabitants of Bibentu entreated of Angeas not to slay them nor destroy their city; and

he did so, for Bibentu was in those days reckoned as one of the cities of the children of Chittim; therefore he did not destroy the city.

30 But from that day forward the troops of the king of Africa would go to Chittim to spoil and plunder it, and whenever they went, Zepho the captain of the host of Angeas would go with them.

31 And it was after this that Angeas turned with his army and they came to the city of Puzimna, and Angeas took thence Jania the daughter of Uzu for a wife and brought her unto his city unto Africa.

Jasher 61

1 And it came to pass at that time Pharaoh king of Egypt commanded all his people to make for him a strong palace in Egypt.

2 And he also commanded the sons of Jacob to assist the Egyptians in the building, and the Egyptians made a beautiful and elegant palace for a royal habitation, and he dwelt therein and he renewed his government and he reigned securely.

3 And Zebulun the son of Jacob died in that year, that is the seventy-second year of the going down of the Israelites to Egypt, and Zebulun died a hundred and fourteen years old, and was put into a coffin and given into the hands of his children.

4 And in the seventy-fifth year died his brother Simeon, he was a hundred and twenty years old at his death, and he was also put into a coffin and given into the hands of his children.

5 And Zepho the son of Eliphaz the son of Esau, captain of the host to Angeas king of Dinhabah, was still daily enticing Angeas to prepare for battle to fight with the sons of Jacob in Egypt, and Angeas was unwilling to do this thing, for his servants had related to him all the might of the sons of Jacob, what they had done unto them in their battle with the children of Esau.

6 And Zepho was in those days daily enticing Angeas to fight with the sons of Jacob in those days.

7 And after some time Angeas hearkened to the words of Zepho and consented to him to fight with the sons of Jacob in Egypt, and Angeas got all his people in order, a people numerous as the sand which is upon the sea shore, and he formed his resolution to go to Egypt to battle.

8 And amongst the servants of Angeas was a youth fifteen years old, Balaam the son of Beor was his name and the youth was very wise and understood the art of witchcraft.

9 And Angeas said unto Balaam, Conjure for us, I pray thee, with the witchcraft, that we may know who

will prevail in this battle to which we are now proceeding.

10 And Balaam ordered that they should bring him wax, and he made thereof the likeness of chariots and horsemen representing the army of Angeas and the army of Egypt, and he put them in the cunningly prepared waters that he had for that purpose, and he took in his hand the boughs of myrtle trees, and he exercised his cunning, and he joined them over the water, and there appeared unto him in the water the resembling images of the hosts of Angeas falling before the resembling images of the Egyptians and the sons of Jacob.

11 And Balaam told this thing to Angeas, and Angeas despaired and did not arm himself to go down to Egypt to battle, and he remained in his city.

12 And when Zepho the son of Eliphaz saw that Angeas despaired of going forth to battle with the Egyptians, Zepho fled from Angeas from Africa, and he went and came unto Chittim.

13 And all the people of Chittim received him with great honor, and they hired him to fight their battles all the days, and Zepho became exceedingly rich in those days, and the troops of the king of Africa still spread themselves in those days, and the children of Chittim assembled and went to Mount

Cuptizia on account of the troops of Angeas king of Africa, who were advancing upon them.

14 And it was one day that Zepho lost a young heifer, and he went to seek it, and he heard it lowing round about the mountain.

15 And Zepho went and he saw and behold there was a large cave at the bottom of the mountain, and there was a great stone there at the entrance of the cave, and Zepho split the stone and he came into the cave and he looked and behold, a large animal was devouring the ox; from the middle upward it resembled a man, and from the middle downward it resembled an animal, and Zepho rose up against the animal and slew it with his swords.

16 And the inhabitants of Chittim heard of this thing, and they rejoiced exceedingly, and they said, What shall we do unto this man who has slain this animal that devoured our cattle?

17 And they all assembled to consecrate one day in the year to him, and they called the name thereof Zepho after his name, and they brought unto him drink offerings year after year on that day, and they brought unto him gifts.

18 At that time Jania the daughter of Uzu wife of king Angeas became ill, and her illness was heavily felt by Angeas and his officers, and Angeas

said unto his wise men, What shall I do to Jania and how shall I heal her from her illness? And his wise men said unto him, Because the air of our country is not like the air of the land of Chittim, and our water is not like their water, therefore from this has the queen become ill.

19 For through the change of air and water she became ill, and also because in her country she drank only the water which came from Purmah, which her ancestors had brought up with bridges.

20 And Angeas commanded his servants, and they brought unto him in vessels of the waters of Purmah belonging to Chittim, and they weighed those waters with all the waters of the land of Africa, and they found those waters lighter than the waters of Africa.

21 And Angeas saw this thing, and he commanded all his officers to assemble the hewers of stone in thousands and tens of thousands, and they hewed stone without number, and the builders came and they built an exceedingly strong bridge, and they conveyed the spring of water from the land of Chittim unto Africa, and those waters were for Jania the queen and for all her concerns, to drink from and to bake, wash and bathe therewith, and also to water therewith all seed from which food can be obtained, and all fruit of the ground.

22 And the king commanded that they should bring of the soil of Chittim in large ships, and they also brought stones to build therewith, and the builders built palaces for Jania the queen, and the queen became healed of her illness.

23 And at the revolution of the year the troops of Africa continued coming to the land of Chittim to plunder as usual, and Zepho son of Eliphaz heard their report, and he gave orders concerning them and he fought with them, and they fled before him, and he delivered the land of Chittim from them.

24 And the children of Chittim saw the valor of Zepho, and the children of Chittim resolved and they made Zepho king over them, and he became king over them, and whilst he reigned they went to subdue the children of Tubal, and all the surrounding islands.

25 And their king Zepho went at their head and they made war with Tubal and the islands, and they subdued them, and when they returned from the battle they renewed his government for him, and they built for him a very large palace for his royal habitation and seat, and they made a large throne for him, and Zepho reigned over the whole land of Chittim and over the land of Italia fifty years.

Jasher 62

1 In that year, being the seventy-ninth year of the Israelites going down to Egypt, died Reuben the son of Jacob, in the land of Egypt; Reuben was a hundred and twenty-five years old when he died, and they put him into a coffin, and he was given into the hands of his children.

2 And in the eightieth year died his brother Dan; he was a hundred and twenty years at his death, and he was also put into a coffin and given into the hands of his children.

3 And in that year died Chusham king of Edom, and after him reigned Hadad the son of Bedad, for thirty-five years; and in the eighty-first year died Issachar the son of Jacob, in Egypt, and Issachar was a hundred and twenty-two years old at his death, and he was put into a coffin in Egypt, and given into the hands of his children.

4 And in the eighty-second year died Asher his brother, he was a hundred and twenty-three years old at his death, and he was placed in a coffin in Egypt, and given into the hands of his children.

5 And in the eighty-third year died Gad, he was a hundred and twenty-five years old at his death, and he was put into a coffin in Egypt, and given into the hands of his children.

6 And it came to pass in the eighty-fourth year, that is the fiftieth year of the reign of Hadad, son of Bedad, king of Edom, that Hadad assembled all the children of Esau, and he got his whole army in readiness, about four hundred thousand men, and he directed his way to the land of Moab, and he went to fight with Moab and to make them tributary to him.

7 And the children of Moab heard this thing, and they were very much afraid, and they sent to the children of Midian to assist them in fighting with Hadad, son of Bedad, king of Edom.

8 And Hadad came unto the land of Moab, and Moab and the children of Midian went out to meet him, and they placed themselves in battle array against him in the field of Moab.

9 And Hadad fought with Moab, and there fell of the children of Moab and the children of Midian many slain ones, about two hundred thousand men.

10 And the battle was very severe upon Moab, and when the children of Moab saw that the battle was sore upon them, they weakened their hands and turned their backs, and left the children of Midian to carry on the battle.

11 And the children of Midian knew not the intentions of Moab, but they strengthened themselves in battle

and fought with Hadad and all his host, and all Midian fell before him.

12 And Hadad smote all Midian with a heavy smiting, and he slew them with the edge of the sword, he left none remaining of those who came to assist Moab.

13 And when all the children of Midian had perished in battle, and the children at Moab had escaped, Hadad made all Moab at that time tributary to him, and they became under his hand, and they gave a yearly tax as it was ordered, and Hadad turned and went back to his land.

14 And at the revolution of the year, when the rest of the people of Midian that were in the land heard that all their brethren had fallen in battle with Hadad for the sake of Moab, because the children of Moab had turned their backs in battle and left Midian to fight, then five of the princes of Midian resolved with the rest of their brethren who remained in their land, to fight with Moab to avenge the cause of their brethren.

15 And the children of Midian sent to all their brethren the children of the east, and all their brethren, all the children of Keturah came to assist Midian to fight with Moab.

16 And the children of Moab heard this thing, and they were greatly afraid that all the children of the east had assembled together against them for battle, and they the children of Moab sent a memorial to the land of Edom to Hadad the son of Bedad, saying,

17 Come now unto us and assist us and we will smite Midian, for they all assembled together and have come against us with all their brethren the children of the east to battle, to avenge the cause of Midian that fell in battle.

18 And Hadad, son of Bedad, king of Edom, went forth with his whole army and went to the land of Moab to fight with Midian, and Midian and the children of the east fought with Moab in the field of Moab, and the battle was very fierce between them.

19 And Hadad smote all the children of Midian and the children of the east with the edge of the sword, and Hadad at that time delivered Moab from the hand of Midian, and those that remained of Midian and of the children of the east fled before Hadad and his army, and Hadad pursued them to their land, and smote them with a very heavy slaughter, and the slain fell in the road.

20 And Hadad delivered Moab from the hand of Midian, for all the children of Midian had fallen by the edge of the sword, and Hadad turned and went back to his land.

21 And from that day forth, the children of Midian hated the children

of Moab, because they had fallen in battle for their sake, and there was a great and mighty enmity between them all the days.

22 And all that were found of Midian in the road of the land of Moab perished by the sword of Moab, and all that were found of Moab in the road of the land of Midian, perished by the sword of Midian; thus did Midian unto Moab and Moab unto Midian for many days.

23 And it came to pass at that time that Judah the son of Jacob died in Egypt, in the eighty-sixth year of Jacob's going down to Egypt, and Judah was a hundred and twenty-nine years old at his death, and they embalmed him and put him into a coffin, and he was given into the hands of his children.

24 And in the eighty-ninth year died Naphtali, he was a hundred and thirty-two years old, and he was put into a coffin and given into the hands of his children.

25 And it came to pass in the ninety-first year of the Israelites going down to Egypt, that is in the thirtieth year of the reign of Zepho the son of Eliphaz, the son of Esau, over the children of Chittim, the children of Africa came upon the children of Chittim to plunder them as usual, but they had not come upon them for these thirteen years.

26 And they came to them in that year, and Zepho the son of Eliphaz went out to them with some of his men and smote them desperately, and the troops of Africa fled from before Zepho and the slain fell before him, and Zepho and his men pursued them, going on and smiting them until they were near unto Africa.

27 And Angeas king of Africa heard the thing which Zepho had done, and it vexed him exceedingly, and Angeas was afraid of Zepho all the days.

Jasher 63

1 And in the ninety-third year died Levi, the son of Jacob, in Egypt, and Levi was a hundred and thirty-seven years old when he died, and they put him into a coffin and he was given into the hands of his children.

2 And it came to pass after the death of Levi, when all Egypt saw that the sons of Jacob the brethren of Joseph were dead, all the Egyptians began to afflict the children of Jacob, and to embitter their lives from that day unto the day of their going forth from Egypt, and they took from their hands all the vineyards and fields which Joseph had given unto them, and all the elegant houses in which the people of Israel lived, and all the fat of Egypt, the Egyptians took all from the sons of Jacob in those days.

3 And the hand of all Egypt became more grievous in those days against the children of Israel, and the Egyptians injured the Israelites until the children of Israel were wearied of their lives on account of the Egyptians.

4 And it came to pass in those days, in the hundred and second year of Israel's going down to Egypt, that Pharaoh king of Egypt died, and Melol his son reigned in his stead, and all the mighty men of Egypt and all that generation which knew Joseph and his brethren died in those days.

5 And another generation rose up in their stead, which had not known the sons of Jacob and all the good which they had done to them, and all their might in Egypt.

6 Therefore all Egypt began from that day forth to embitter the lives of the sons of Jacob, and to afflict them with all manner of hard labor, because they had not known their ancestors who had delivered them in the days of the famine.

7 And this was also from the Lord, for the children of Israel, to benefit them in their latter days, in order that all the children of Israel might know the Lord their God.

8 And in order to know the signs and mighty wonders which the Lord would do in Egypt on account of his people Israel, in order that the children of Israel might fear the Lord God of their ancestors, and walk in all his ways, they and their seed after them all the days.

9 Melol was twenty years old when he began to reign, and he reigned ninety-four years, and all Egypt called his name Pharaoh after the name of his father, as it was their custom to do to every king who reigned over them in Egypt.

10 At that time all the troops of Angeas king of Africa went forth to spread along the land of Chittim as usual for plunder.

11 And Zepho the son of Eliphaz the son of Esau heard their report, and he went forth to meet them with his army, and he fought them there in the road.

12 And Zepho smote the troops of the king of Africa with the edge of the sword, and left none remaining of them, and not even one returned to his master in Africa.

13 And Angeas heard of this which Zepho the son of Eliphaz had done to all his troops, that he had destroyed them, and Angeas assembled all his troops, all the men of the land of Africa, a people numerous like the sand by the sea shore.

14 And Angeas sent to Lucus his brother, saying, Come to me with all thy men and help me to smite Zepho and all the children of Chittim who

have destroyed my men, and Lucus came with his whole army, a very great force, to assist Angeas his brother to fight with Zepho and the children of Chittim.

15 And Zepho and the children of Chittim heard this thing, and they were greatly afraid and a great terror fell upon their hearts.

16 And Zepho also sent a letter to the land of Edom to Hadad the son of Bedad king of Edom and to all the children of Esau, saying,

17 I have heard that Angeas king of Africa is coming to us with his brother for battle against us, and we are greatly afraid of him, for his army is very great, particularly as he comes against us with his brother and his army likewise.

18 Now therefore come you also up with me and help me, and we will fight together against Angeas and his brother Lucus, and you will save us out of their hands, but if not, know ye that we shall all die.

19 And the children of Esau sent a letter to the children of Chittim and to Zepho their king, saying, We cannot fight against Angeas and his people for a covenant of peace has been between us these many years, from the days of Bela the first king, and from the days of Joseph the son of Jacob king of Egypt, with whom we fought on the other side of Jordan when he buried his father.

20 And when Zepho heard the words of his brethren the children of Esau he refrained from them, and Zepho was greatly afraid of Angeas.

21 And Angeas and Lucus his brother arrayed all their forces, about eight hundred thousand men, against the children of Chittim.

22 And all the children of Chittim said unto Zepho, Pray for us to the God of thy ancestors, peradventure he may deliver us from the hand of Angeas and his army, for we have heard that he is a great God and that he delivers all who trust in him.

23 And Zepho heard their words, and Zepho sought the Lord and he said,

24 0 Lord God of Abraham and Isaac my ancestors, this day I know that thou art a true God, and all the gods of the nations are vain and useless.

25 Remember now this day unto me thy covenant with Abraham our father, which our ancestors related unto us, and do graciously with me this day for the sake of Abraham and Isaac our fathers, and save me and the children of Chittim from the hand of the king of Africa who comes against us for battle.

26 And the Lord hearkened to the voice of Zepho, and he had regard for him on account of Abraham and Isaac, and the Lord delivered Zepho and the children of Chittim from the hand of Angeas and his people.

27 And Zepho fought Angeas king of Africa and all his people on that day, and the Lord gave all the people of Angeas into the hands of the children of Chittim.

28 And the battle was severe upon Angeas, and Zepho smote all the men of Angeas and Lucus his brother, with the edge of the sword, and there fell from them unto the evening of that day about four hundred thousand men.

29 And when Angeas saw that all his men perished, he sent a letter to all the inhabitants of Africa to come to him, to assist him in the battle, and he wrote in the letter, saying, All who are found in Africa let them come unto me from ten years old and upward; let them all come unto me, and behold if he comes not he shall die, and all that he has, with his whole household, the king will take.

30 And all the rest of the inhabitants of Africa were terrified at the words of Angeas, and there went out of the city about three hundred thousand men and boys, from ten years upward, and they came to Angeas.

31 And at the end of ten days Angeas renewed the battle against Zepho and the children of Chittim, and the battle was very great and strong between them.

32 And from the army of Angeas and Lucus, Zepho sent many of the wounded unto his hand, about two thousand men, and Sosiphtar the captain of the host of Angeas fell in that battle.

33 And when Sosiphtar had fallen, the African troops turned their backs to flee, and they fled, and Angeas and Lucus his brother were with them.

34 And Zepho and the children of Chittim pursued them, and they smote them still heavily on the road, about two hundred men, and they pursued Azdrubal the son of Angeas who had fled with his father, and they smote twenty of his men in the road, and Azdrubal escaped from the children of Chittim, and they did not slay him.

35 And Angeas and Lucus his brother fled with the rest of their men, and they escaped and came into Africa with terror and consternation, and Angeas feared all the days lest Zepho the son of Eliphaz should go to war with him.

Jasher 64

1 And Balaam the son of Beor was at that time with Angeas in the battle, and when he saw that Zepho prevailed over Angeas, he fled from there and came to Chittim.

2 And Zepho and the children of Chittim received him with great honor, for Zepho knew Balaam's wisdom, and Zepho gave unto Balaam many gifts and he remained with him.

3 And when Zepho had returned from the war, he commanded all the children of Chittim to be numbered who had gone into battle with him, and behold not one was missed.

4 And Zepho rejoiced at this thing, and he renewed his kingdom, and he made a feast to all his subjects.

5 But Zepho remembered not the Lord and considered not that the Lord had helped him in battle, and that he had delivered him and his people from the hand of the king of Africa, but still walked in the ways of the children of Chittim and the wicked children of Esau, to serve other gods which his brethren the children of Esau had taught him; it is therefore said, From the wicked goes forth wickedness.

6 And Zepho reigned over all the children of Chittim securely, but knew not the Lord who had delivered him and all his people from the hand of the king of Africa; and the troops of Africa came no more to Chittim to plunder as usual, for they knew of the power of Zepho who had smitten them all at the edge of the sword, so Angeas was afraid of Zepho the son of Eliphaz, and of the children of Chittim all the days.

7 At that time when Zepho had returned from the war, and when Zepho had seen how he prevailed over all the people of Africa and had smitten them in battle at the edge of the sword, then Zepho advised with the children of Chittim, to go to Egypt to fight with the sons of Jacob and with Pharaoh king of Egypt.

8 For Zepho heard that the mighty men of Egypt were dead and that Joseph and his brethren the sons at Jacob were dead, and that all their children the children of Israel remained in Egypt.

9 And Zepho considered to go to fight against them and all Egypt, to avenge the cause of his brethren the children of Esau, whom Joseph with his brethren and all Egypt had smitten in the land of Canaan, when they went up to bury Jacob in Hebron.

10 And Zepho sent messengers to Hadad, son of Bedad, king of Edom, and to all his brethren the children of Esau, saying,

11 Did you not say that you would not fight against the king of Africa for he is a member of your covenant? behold I fought with him and smote him and all his people.

12 Now therefore I have resolved to fight against Egypt and the children of Jacob who are there, and I will be revenged of them for what Joseph, his brethren and ancestors did to us in the land of Canaan when they went up to bury their father in Hebron.

13 Now then if you are willing to come to me to assist me in fighting against them and Egypt, then shall

we avenge the cause of our brethren.

14 And the children of Esau hearkened to the words of Zepho, and the children of Esau gathered themselves together, a very great people, and they went to assist Zepho and the children of Chittim in battle.

15 And Zepho sent to all the children of the east and to all the children of Ishmael with words like unto these, and they gathered themselves and came to the assistance of Zepho and the children of Chittim in the war upon Egypt.

16 And all these kings, the king of Edom and the children of the east, and all the children of Ishmael, and Zepho the king of Chittim went forth and arrayed all their hosts in Hebron.

17 And the camp was very heavy, extending in length a distance of three days' journey, a people numerous as the sand upon the sea shore which can not be counted.

18 And all these kings and their hosts went down and came against all Egypt in battle, and encamped together in the valley of Pathros.

19 And all Egypt heard their report, and they also gathered themselves together, all the people of the land of Egypt, and of all the cities belonging to Egypt, about three hundred thousand men.

20 And the men of Egypt sent also to the children of Israel who were in those days in the land of Goshen, to come to them in order to go and fight with these kings.

21 And the men of Israel assembled and were about one hundred and fifty men, and they went into battle to assist the Egyptians.

22 And the men of Israel and of Egypt went forth, about three hundred thousand men and one hundred and fifty men, and they went toward these kings to battle, and they placed themselves from without the land of Goshen opposite Pathros.

23 And the Egyptians believed not in Israel to go with them in their camps together for battle, for all the Egyptians said, Perhaps the children of Israel will deliver us into the hand of the children of Esau and Ishmael, for they are their brethren.

24 And all the Egyptians said unto the children of Israel, Remain you here together in your stand and we will go and fight against the children of Esau and Ishmael, and if these kings should prevail over us, then come you altogether upon them and assist us, and the children of Israel did so.

25 And Zepho the son of Eliphaz the son of Esau king of Chittim, and Hadad the son of Bedad king of Edom, and all their camps, and all

the children of the east, and children of Ishmael, a people numerous as sand, encamped together in the valley of Pathros opposite Tachpanches.

26 And Balaam the son of Beor the Syrian was there in the camp of Zepho, for he came with the children of Chittim to the battle, and Balaam was a man highly honored in the eyes of Zepho and his men.

27 And Zepho said unto Balaam, Try by divination for us that we may know who will prevail in the battle, we or the Egyptians.

28 And Balaam rose up and tried the art of divination, and he was skillful in the knowledge of it, but he was confused and the work was destroyed in his hand.

29 And he tried it again but it did not succeed, and Balaam despaired of it and left it and did not complete it, for this was from the Lord, in order to cause Zepho and his people to fall into the hand of the children of Israel, who had trusted in the Lord, the God of their ancestors, in their war.

30 And Zepho and Hadad put their forces in battle array, and all the Egyptians went alone against them, about three hundred thousand men, and not one man of Israel was with them.

31 And all the Egyptians fought with these kings opposite Pathros and Tachpanches, and the battle was severe against the Egyptians.

32 And the kings were stronger than the Egyptians in that battle, and about one hundred and eighty men of Egypt fell on that day, and about thirty men of the forces of the kings, and all the men of Egypt fled from before the kings, so the children of Esau and Ishmael pursued the Egyptians, continuing to smite them unto the place where was the camp of the children of Israel.

33 And all the Egyptians cried unto the children of Israel, saying, Hasten to us and assist us and save us from the hand of Esau, Ishmael and the children of Chittim.

34 And the hundred and fifty men of the children of Israel ran from their station to the camps of these kings, and the children of Israel cried unto the Lord their God to deliver them.

35 And the Lord hearkened to Israel, and the Lord gave all the men of the kings into their hand, and the children of Israel fought against these kings, and the children of Israel smote about four thousand of the kings' men.

36 And the Lord threw a great consternation in the camp of the kings, so that the fear of the children of Israel fell upon them.

37 And all the hosts of the kings fled from before the children of Israel and the children of Israel pursued them

continuing to smite them unto the borders of the land of Cush.

38 And the children of Israel slew of them in the road yet two thousand men, and of the children of Israel not one fell.

39 And when the Egyptians saw that the children of Israel had fought with such few men with the kings, and that the battle was so very severe against them,

40 All the Egyptians were greatly afraid of their lives on account of the strong battle, and all Egypt fled, every man hiding himself from the arrayed forces, and they hid themselves in the road, and they left the Israelites to fight.

41 And the children of Israel inflicted a terrible blow upon the kings' men, and they returned from them after they had driven them to the border of the land of Cush.

42 And all Israel knew the thing which the men of Egypt had done to them, that they had fled from them in battle, and had left them to fight alone.

43 So the children of Israel also acted with cunning, and as the children of Israel returned from battle, they found some of the Egyptians in the road and smote them there.

44 And whilst they slew them, they said unto them these words:

45 Wherefore did you go from us and leave us, being a few people, to fight against these kings who had a great people to smite us, that you might thereby deliver your own souls?

46 And of some which the Israelites met on the road, they the children of Israel spoke to each other, saying, Smite, smite, for he is an Ishmaelite, or an Edomite, or from the children of Chittim, and they stood over him and slew him, and they knew that he was an Egyptian.

47 And the children of Israel did these things cunningly against the Egyptians, because they had deserted them in battle and had fled from them.

48 And the children of Israel slew of the men of Egypt in the road in this manner, about two hundred men.

49 And all the men of Egypt saw the evil which the children of Israel had done to them, so all Egypt feared greatly the children of Israel, for they had seen their great power, and that not one man of them had fallen.

50 So all the children of Israel returned with joy on their road to Goshen, and the rest of Egypt returned each man to his place.

Jasher 65

1 And it came to pass after these things, that all the counsellors of Pharaoh, king of Egypt, and all the

elders of Egypt assembled and came before the king and bowed down to the ground, and they sat before him.

2 And the counsellors and elders of Egypt spoke unto the king, saying,

3 Behold the people of the children of Israel is greater and mightier than we are, and thou knowest all the evil which they did to us in the road when we returned from battle.

4 And thou hast also seen their strong power, for this power is unto them from their fathers, for but a few men stood up against a people numerous as the sand, and smote them at the edge of the sword, and of themselves not one has fallen, so that if they had been numerous they would then have utterly destroyed them.

5 Now therefore give us counsel what to do with them, until we gradually destroy them from amongst us, lest they become too numerous for us in the land.

6 For if the children of Israel should increase in the land, they will become an obstacle to us, and if any war should happen to take place, they with their great strength will join our enemy against us, and fight against us, destroy us from the land and go away from it.

7 So the king answered the elders of Egypt and said unto them, This is the plan advised against Israel, from which we will not depart,

8 Behold in the land are Pithom and Rameses, cities unfortified against battle, it behooves you and us to build them, and to fortify them.

9 Now therefore go you also and act cunningly toward them, and proclaim a voice in Egypt and in Goshen at the command of the king, saying,

10 All ye men of Egypt, Goshen, Pathros and all their inhabitants! the king has commanded us to build Pithom and Rameses, and to fortify them for battle; who amongst you of all Egypt, of the children of Israel and of all the inhabitants of the cities, are willing to build with us, shall each have his wages given to him daily at the king's order; so go you first and do cunningly, and gather yourselves and come to Pithom and Rameses to build.

11 And whilst you are building, cause a proclamation of this kind to be made throughout Egypt every day at the command of the king.

12 And when some of the children of Israel shall come to build with you, you shall give them their wages daily for a few days.

13 And after they shall have built with you for their daily hire, drag yourselves away from them daily one by one in secret, and then you shall rise up and become their task-masters and officers, and you shall leave them afterward to build without wages, and should they refuse, then

force them with all your might to build.

14 And if you do this it will be well with us to strengthen our land against the children of Israel, for on account of the fatigue of the building and the work, the children of Israel will decrease, because you will deprive them from their wives day by day.

15 And all the elders of Egypt heard the counsel of the king, and the counsel seemed good in their eyes and in the eyes of the servants of Pharaoh, and in the eyes of all Egypt, and they did according to the word of the king.

16 And all the servants went away from the king, and they caused a proclamation to be made in all Egypt, in Tachpanches and in Goshen, and in all the cities which surrounded Egypt, saying,

17 You have seen what the children of Esau and Ishmael did to us, who came to war against us and wished to destroy us.

18 Now therefore the king commanded us to fortify the land, to build the cities Pithom and Rameses, and to fortify them for battle, if they should again come against us.

19 Whosoever of you from all Egypt and from the children of Israel will come to build with us, he shall have his daily wages given by the king, as his command is unto us.

20 And when Egypt and all the children of Israel heard all that the servants of Pharaoh had spoken, there came from the Egyptians, and the children of Israel to build with the servants of Pharaoh, Pithom and Rameses, but none of the children of Levi came with their brethren to build.

21 And all the servants of Pharaoh and his princes came at first with deceit to build with all Israel as daily hired laborers, and they gave to Israel their daily hire at the beginning.

22 And the servants of Pharaoh built with all Israel, and were employed in that work with Israel for a month.

23 And at the end of the month, all the servants of Pharaoh began to withdraw secretly from the people of Israel daily.

24 And Israel went on with the work at that time, but they then received their daily hire, because some of the men of Egypt were yet carrying on the work with Israel at that time; therefore the Egyptians gave Israel their hire in those days, in order that they, the Egyptians their fellow-workmen, might also take the pay for their labor.

25 And at the end of a year and four months all the Egyptians had withdrawn from the children of Israel, so that the children of Israel were left alone engaged in the work.

26 And after all the Egyptians had withdrawn from the children of Israel they returned and became oppressors and officers over them, and some of them stood over the children of Israel as task masters, to receive from them all that they gave them for the pay of their labor.

27 And the Egyptians did in this manner to the children of Israel day by day, in order to afflict in their work.

28 And all the children of Israel were alone engaged in the labor, and the Egyptians refrained from giving any pay to the children of Israel from that time forward.

29 And when some of the men of Israel refused to work on account of the wages not being given to them, then the exactors and the servants of Pharaoh oppressed them and smote them with heavy blows, and made them return by force, to labor with their brethren; thus did all the Egyptians unto the children of Israel all the days.

30 And all the children of Israel were greatly afraid of the Egyptians in this matter, and all the children of Israel returned and worked alone without pay.

31 And the children of Israel built Pithom and Rameses, and all the children of Israel did the work, some making bricks, and some building, and the children of Israel built and fortified all the land of Egypt and its walls, and the children of Israel were engaged in work for many years, until the time came when the Lord remembered them and brought them out of Egypt.

32 But the children of Levi were not employed in the work with their brethren of Israel, from the beginning unto the day of their going forth from Egypt.

33 For all the children of Levi knew that the Egyptians had spoken all these words with deceit to the Israelites, therefore the children of Levi refrained from approaching to the work with their brethren.

34 And the Egyptians did not direct their attention to make the children of Levi work afterward, since they had not been with their brethren at the beginning, therefore the Egyptians left them alone.

35 And the hands of the men of Egypt were directed with continued severity against the children of Israel in that work, and the Egyptians made the children of Israel work with rigor.

36 And the Egyptians embittered the lives of the children of Israel with hard work, in mortar and bricks, and also in all manner of work in the field.

37 And the children of Israel called Melol the king of Egypt "Meror, king of Egypt," because in his days the Egyptians had embittered their lives with all manner of work.

38 And all the work wherein the Egyptians made the children of Israel labor, they exacted with rigor, in order to afflict the children of Israel, but the more they afflicted them, the more they increased and grew, and the Egyptians were grieved because of the children of Israel.

Jasher 66

1 At that time died Hadad the son of Bedad king of Edom, and Samlah from Mesrekah, from the country of the children of the east, reigned in his place.

2 In the thirteenth year of the reign of Pharaoh king of Egypt, which was the hundred and twenty-fifth year of the Israelites going down into Egypt, Samlah had reigned over Edom eighteen years.

3 And when he reigned, he drew forth his hosts to go and fight against Zepho the son of Eliphaz and the children of Chittim, because they had made war against Angeas king of Africa, and they destroyed his whole army.

4 But he did not engage with him, for the children of Esau prevented him, saying, He was their brother, so Samlah listened to the voice of the children of Esau, and turned back with all his forces to the land of Edom, and did not proceed to fight against Zepho the son of Eliphaz.

5 And Pharaoh king of Egypt heard this thing, saying, Samlah king of Edom has resolved to fight the children of Chittim, and afterward he will come to fight against Egypt.

6 And when the Egyptians heard this matter, they increased the labor upon the children of Israel, lest the Israelites should do unto them as they did unto them in their war with the children of Esau in the days of Hadad.

7 So the Egyptians said unto the children of Israel, Hasten and do your work, and finish your task, and strengthen the land, lest the children of Esau your brethren should come to fight against us, for on your account will they come against us.

8 And the children of Israel did the work of the men of Egypt day by day, and the Egyptians afflicted the children of Israel in order to lessen them in the land.

9 But as the Egyptians increased the labor upon the children of Israel, so did the children of Israel increase and multiply, and all Egypt was filled with the children of Israel.

10 And in the hundred and twenty-fifth year of Israel's going down into Egypt, all the Egyptians saw that their counsel did not succeed against Israel, but that they increased and grew, and the land of Egypt and the land of Goshen were filled with the children of Israel.

11 So all the elders of Egypt and its wise men came before the king and

bowed down to him and sat before him.

12 And all the elders of Egypt and the wise men thereof said unto the king, May the king live forever; thou didst counsel us the counsel against the children of Israel, and we did unto them according to the word of the king.

13 But in proportion to the increase of the labor so do they increase and grow in the land, and behold the whole country is filled with them.

14 Now therefore our lord and king, the eyes of all Egypt are upon thee to give them advice with thy wisdom, by which they may prevail over Israel to destroy them, or to diminish them from the land; and the king answered them saying, Give you counsel in this matter that we may know what to do unto them.

15 And an officer, one of the king's counsellors, whose name was Job, from Mesopotamia, in the land of Uz, answered the king, saying,

16 If it please the king, let him hear the counsel of his servant; and the king said unto him, Speak.

17 And Job spoke before the king, the princes, and before all the elders of Egypt, saying,

18 Behold the counsel of the king which he advised formerly respecting the labor of the children of Israel is very good, and you must not remove from them that labor forever.

19 But this is the advice counselled by which you may lessen them, if it seems good to the king to afflict them.

20 Behold we have feared war for a long time, and we said, When Israel becomes fruitful in the land, they will drive us from the land if a war should take place.

21 If it please the king, let a royal decree go forth, and let it be written in the laws of Egypt which shall not be revoked, that every male child born to the Israelites, his blood shall be spilled upon the ground.

22 And by your doing this, when all the male children of Israel shall have died, the evil of their wars will cease; let the king do so and send for all the Hebrew midwives and order them in this matter to execute it; so the thing pleased the king and the princes, and the king did according to the word of Job.

23 And the king sent for the Hebrew midwives to be called, of which the name of one was Shephrah, and the name of the other Puah.

24 And the midwives came before the king, and stood in his presence.

25 And the king said unto them, When you do the office of a midwife to the Hebrew women, and see them upon the stools, if it be a son, then

you shall kill him, but if it be a daughter, then she shall live.

26 But if you will not do this thing, then will I burn you up and all your houses with fire.

27 But the midwives feared God and did not hearken to the king of Egypt nor to his words, and when the Hebrew women brought forth to the midwife son or daughter, then did the midwife do all that was necessary to the child and let it live; thus did the midwives all the days.

28 And this thing was told to the king, and he sent and called for the midwives and he said to them, Why have you done this thing and have saved the children alive?

29 And the midwives answered and spoke together before the king, saying,

30 Let not the king think that the Hebrew women are as the Egyptian women, for all the children of Israel are hale, and before the midwife comes to them they are delivered, and as for us thy handmaids, for many days no Hebrew woman has brought forth upon us, for all the Hebrew women are their own midwives, because they are hale.

31 And Pharaoh heard their words and believed them in this matter, and the midwives went away from the king, and God dealt well with them, and the people multiplied and waxed exceedingly.

Jasher 67

1 There was a man in the land of Egypt of the seed of Levi, whose name was Amram, the son of Kehath, the son of Levi, the son of Israel.

2 And this man went and took a wife, namely Jochebed the daughter of Levi his father's sister, and she was one hundred and twenty-six years old, and he came unto her.

3 And the woman conceived and bare a daughter, and she called her name Miriam, because in those days the Egyptians had embittered the lives of the children of Israel.

4 And she conceived again and bare a son and she called his name Aaron, for in the days of her conception, Pharaoh began to spill the blood of the male children of Israel.

5 In those days died Zepho the son of Eliphaz, son of Esau, king of Chittim, and Janeas reigned in his stead.

6 And the time that Zepho reigned over the children of Chittim was fifty years, and he died and was buried in the city of Nabna in the land of Chittim.

7 And Janeas, one of the mighty men of the children of Chittim, reigned after him and he reigned fifty years.

8 And it was after the death of the king of Chittim that Balaam the son of Beor fled from the land of Chittim, and he went and came to Egypt to Pharaoh king of Egypt.

9 And Pharaoh received him with great honor, for he had heard of his wisdom, and he gave him presents and made him for a counsellor, and aggrandized him.

10 And Balaam dwelt in Egypt, in honor with all the nobles of the king, and the nobles exalted him, because they all coveted to learn his wisdom.

11 And in the hundred and thirtieth year of Israel's going down to Egypt, Pharaoh dreamed that he was sitting upon his kingly throne, and lifted up his eyes and saw an old man standing before him, and there were scales in the hands of the old man, such scales as are used by merchants.

12 And the old man took the scales and hung them before Pharaoh.

13 And the old man took all the elders of Egypt and all its nobles and great men, and he tied them together and put them in one scale.

14 And he took a milk kid and put it into the other scale, and the kid preponderated over all.

15 And Pharaoh was astonished at this dreadful vision, why the kid should preponderate over all, and Pharaoh awoke and behold it was a dream.

16 And Pharaoh rose up early in the morning and called all his servants and related to them the dream, and the men were greatly afraid.

17 And the king said to all his wise men, Interpret I pray you the dream which I dreamed, that I may know it.

18 And Balaam the son of Beor answered the king and said unto him, This means nothing else but a great evil that will spring up against Egypt in the latter days.

19 For a son will be born to Israel who will destroy all Egypt and its inhabitants, and bring forth the Israelites from Egypt with a mighty hand.

20 Now therefore, O king, take counsel upon this matter, that you may destroy the hope of the children of Israel and their expectation, before this evil arise against Egypt.

21 And the king said unto Balaam, And what shall we do unto Israel? surely after a certain manner did we at first counsel against them and could not prevail over them.

22 Now therefore give you also advice against them by which we may prevail over them.

23 And Balaam answered the king, saying, Send now and call thy two counsellors, and we will see what

their advice is upon this matter and afterward thy servant will speak.

24 And the king sent and called his two counsellors Reuel the Midianite and Job the Uzite, and they came and sat before the king.

25 And the king said to them, Behold you have both heard the dream which I have dreamed, and the interpretation thereof; now therefore give counsel and know and see what is to be done to the children of Israel, whereby we may prevail over them, before their evil shall spring up against us.

26 And Reuel the Midianite answered the king and said, May the king live, may the king live forever.

27 If it seem good to the king, let him desist from the Hebrews and leave them, and let him not stretch forth his hand against them.

28 For these are they whom the Lord chose in days of old, and took as the lot of his inheritance from amongst all the nations of the earth and the kings of the earth; and who is there that stretched his hand against them with impunity, of whom their God was not avenged?

29 Surely thou knowest that when Abraham went down to Egypt, Pharaoh, the former king of Egypt, saw Sarah his wife, and took her for a wife, because Abraham said, She is my sister, for he was afraid, lest the men of Egypt should slay him on account of his wife.

30 And when the king of Egypt had taken Sarah then God smote him and his household with heavy plagues, until he restored unto Abraham his wife Sarah, then was he healed.

31 And Abimelech the Gerarite, king of the Philistines, God punished on account of Sarah wife of Abraham, in stopping up every womb from man to beast.

32 When their God came to Abimelech in the dream of night and terrified him in order that he might restore to Abraham Sarah whom he had taken, and afterward all the people of Gerar were punished on account of Sarah, and Abraham prayed to his God for them, and he was entreated of him, and he healed them.

33 And Abimelech feared all this evil that came upon him and his people, and he returned to Abraham his wife Sarah, and gave him with her many gifts.

34 He did so also to Isaac when he had driven him from Gerar, and God had done wonderful things to him, that all the water courses of Gerar were dried up, and their productive trees did not bring forth.

35 Until Abimelech of Gerar, and Ahuzzath one of his friends, and Pichol the captain of his host, went

to him and they bent and bowed down before him to the ground.

36 And they requested of him to supplicate for them, and he prayed to the Lord for them, and the Lord was entreated of him and he healed them.

37 Jacob also, the plain man, was delivered through his integrity from the hand of his brother Esau, and the hand of Laban the Syrian his mother's brother, who had sought his life; likewise from the hand of all the kings of Canaan who had come together against him and his children to destroy them, and the Lord delivered them out of their hands, that they turned upon them and smote them, for who had ever stretched forth his hand against them with impunity?

38 Surely Pharaoh the former, thy father's father, raised Joseph the son of Jacob above all the princes of the land of Egypt, when he saw his wisdom, for through his wisdom he rescued all the inhabitants of the land from the famine.

39 After which he ordered Jacob and his children to come down to Egypt, in order that through their virtue, the land of Egypt and the land of Goshen might be delivered from the famine.

40 Now therefore if it seem good in thine eyes, cease from destroying the children of Israel, but if it be not

thy will that they shall dwell in Egypt, send them forth from here, that they may go to the land of Canaan, the land where their ancestors sojourned.

41 And when Pharaoh heard the words of Jethro he was very angry with him, so that he rose with shame from the king's presence, and went to Midian, his land, and took Joseph's stick with him.

42 And the king said to Job the Uzite, What sayest thou Job, and what is thy advice respecting the Hebrews?

43 So Job said to the king, Behold all the inhabitants of the land are in thy power, let the king do as it seems good in his eyes.

44 And the king said unto Balaam, What dost thou say, Balaam, speak thy word that we may hear it.

45 And Balaam said to the king, Of all that the king has counselled against the Hebrews will they be delivered, and the king will not be able to prevail over them with any counsel.

46 For if thou thinkest to lessen them by the flaming fire, thou canst not prevail over them, for surely their God delivered Abraham their father from Ur of the Chaldeans; and if thou thinkest to destroy them with a sword, surely Isaac their father was delivered from it, and a ram was placed in his stead.

47 And if with hard and rigorous labor thou thinkest to lessen them, thou wilt not prevail even in this, for their father Jacob served Laban in all manner of hard work, and prospered.

48 Now therefore, O King, hear my words, for this is the counsel which is counselled against them, by which thou wilt prevail over them, and from which thou shouldst not depart.

49 If it please the king let him order all their children which shall be born from this day forward, to be thrown into the water, for by this canst thou wipe away their name, for none of them, nor of their fathers, were tried in this manner.

50 And the king heard the words of Balaam, and the thing pleased the king and the princes, and the king did according to the word of Balaam.

51 And the king ordered a proclamation to be issued and a law to be made throughout the land of Egypt, saying, Every male child born to the Hebrews from this day forward shall be thrown into the water.

52 And Pharaoh called unto all his servants, saying, Go now and seek throughout the land of Goshen where the children of Israel are, and see that every son born to the Hebrews shall be cast into the river, but every daughter you shall let live.

53 And when the children of Israel heard this thing which Pharaoh had commanded, to cast their male children into the river, some of the people separated from their wives and others adhered to them.

54 And from that day forward, when the time of delivery arrived to those women of Israel who had remained with their husbands, they went to the field to bring forth there, and they brought forth in the field, and left their children upon the field and returned home.

55 And the Lord who had sworn to their ancestors to multiply them, sent one of his ministering angels which are in heaven to wash each child in water, to anoint and swathe it and to put into its hands two smooth stones from one of which it sucked milk and from the other honey, and he caused its hair to grow to its knees, by which it might cover itself; to comfort it and to cleave to it, through his compassion for it.

56 And when God had compassion over them and had desired to multiply them upon the face of the land, he ordered his earth to receive them to be preserved therein till the time of their growing up, after which the earth opened its mouth and vomited them forth and they sprouted forth from the city like the herb of the earth, and the grass of the forest, and they returned each to his family and to his father's house, and they remained with them.

57 And the babes of the children of Israel were upon the earth like the

herb of the field, through God's grace to them.

58 And when all the Egyptians saw this thing, they went forth, each to his field with his yoke of oxen and his ploughshare, and they ploughed it up as one ploughs the earth at seed time.

59 And when they ploughed they were unable to hurt the infants of the children of Israel, so the people increased and waxed exceedingly.

60 And Pharaoh ordered his officers daily to go to Goshen to seek for the babes of the children of Israel.

61 And when they had sought and found one, they took it from its mother's bosom by force, and threw it into the river, but the female child they left with its mother; thus did the Egyptians do to the Israelites all the days.

Jasher 68

1 And it was at that time the spirit of God was upon Miriam the daughter of Amram the sister of Aaron, and she went forth and prophesied about the house, saying, Behold a son will be born unto us from my father and mother this time, and he will save Israel from the hands of Egypt.

2 And when Amram heard the words of his daughter, he went and took his wife back to the house, after he had driven her away at the time when Pharaoh ordered every male child of the house of Jacob to be thrown into the water.

3 So Amram took Jochebed his wife, three years after he had driven her away, and he came to her and she conceived.

4 And at the end of seven months from her conception she brought forth a son, and the whole house was filled with great light as of the light of the sun and moon at the time of their shining.

5 And when the woman saw the child that it was good and pleasing to the sight, she hid it for three months in an inner room.

6 In those days the Egyptians conspired to destroy all the Hebrews there.

7 And the Egyptian women went to Goshen where the children of Israel were, and they carried their young ones upon their shoulders, their babes who could not yet speak.

8 And in those days, when the women of the children of Israel brought forth, each woman had hidden her son from before the Egyptians, that the Egyptians might not know of their bringing forth, and might not destroy them from the land.

9 And the Egyptian women came to Goshen and their children who could not speak were upon their shoulders, and when an Egyptian woman came

into the house of a Hebrew woman her babe began to cry.

10 And when it cried the child that was in the inner room answered it, so the Egyptian women went and told it at the house of Pharaoh.

11 And Pharaoh sent his officers to take the children and slay them; thus did the Egyptians to the Hebrew women all the days.

12 And it was at that time, about three months from Jochebed's concealment of her son, that the thing was known in Pharaoh's house.

13 And the woman hastened to take away her son before the officers came, and she took for him an ark of bulrushes, and daubed it with slime and with pitch, and put the child therein, and she laid it in the flags by the river's brink.

14 And his sister Miriam stood afar off to know what would be done to him, and what would become of her words.

15 And God sent forth at that time a terrible heat in the land of Egypt, which burned up the flesh of man like the sun in his circuit, and it greatly oppressed the Egyptians.

16 And all the Egyptians went down to bathe in the river, on account of the consuming heat which burned up their flesh.

17 And Bathia, the daughter of Pharaoh, went also to bathe in the river, owing to the consuming heat, and her maidens walked at the river side, and all the women of Egypt as well.

18 And Bathia lifted up her eyes to the river, and she saw the ark upon the water, and sent her maid to fetch it.

19 And she opened it and saw the child, and behold the babe wept, and she had compassion on him, and she said, This is one of the Hebrew children.

20 And all the women of Egypt walking on the river side desired to give him suck, but he would not suck, for this thing was from the Lord, in order to restore him to his mother's breast.

21 And Miriam his sister was at that time amongst the Egyptian women at the river side, and she saw this thing and she said to Pharaoh's daughter, Shall I go and fetch a nurse of the Hebrew women, that she may nurse the child for thee?

22 And Pharaoh's daughter said to her, Go, and the young woman went and called the child's mother.

23 And Pharaoh's daughter said to Jochebed, Take this child away and suckle it for me, and I will pay thee thy wages, two bits of silver daily; and the woman took the child and nursed it.

24 And at the end of two years, when the child grew up, she brought him to the daughter of Pharaoh, and he was unto her as a son, and she called his name Moses, for she said, Because I drew him out of the water.

25 And Amram his father called his name Chabar, for he said, It was for him that he associated with his wife whom he had turned away.

26 And Jochebed his mother called his name Jekuthiel, Because, she said, I have hoped for him to the Almighty, and God restored him unto me.

27 And Miriam his sister called him Jered, for she descended after him to the river to know what his end would be.

28 And Aaron his brother called his name Abi Zanuch, saying, My father left my mother and returned to her on his account.

29 And Kehath the father of Amram called his name Abigdor, because on his account did God repair the breach of the house of Jacob, that they could no longer throw their male children into the water.

30 And their nurse called him Abi Socho, saying, In his tabernacle was he hidden for three months, on account of the children of Ham.

31 And all Israel called his name Shemaiah, son of Nethanel, for they said, In his days has God heard their cries and rescued them from their oppressors.

32 And Moses was in Pharaoh's house, and was unto Bathia, Pharaoh's daughter, as a son, and Moses grew up amongst the king's children.

Jasher 69

1 And the king of Edom died in those days, in the eighteenth year of his reign, and was buried in his temple which he had built for himself as his royal residence in the land of Edom.

2 And the children of Esau sent to Pethor, which is upon the river, and they fetched from there a young man of beautiful eyes and comely aspect, whose name was Saul, and they made him king over them in the place of Samlah.

3 And Saul reigned over all the children of Esau in the land of Edom for forty years.

4 And when Pharaoh king of Egypt saw that the counsel which Balaam had advised respecting the children of Israel did not succeed, but that still they were fruitful, multiplied and increased throughout the land of Egypt,

5 Then Pharaoh commanded in those days that a proclamation should be issued throughout Egypt to the children of Israel, saying, No man shall diminish any thing of his daily labor.

6 And the man who shall be found deficient in his labor which he performs daily, whether in mortar or in bricks, then his youngest son shall be put in their place.

7 And the labor of Egypt strengthened upon the children of Israel in those days, and behold if one brick was deficient in any man's daily labor, the Egyptians took his youngest boy by force from his mother, and put him into the building in the place of the brick which his father had left wanting.

8 And the men of Egypt did so to all the children of Israel day by day, all the days for a long period.

9 But the tribe of Levi did not at that time work with the Israelites their brethren, from the beginning, for the children of Levi knew the cunning of the Egyptians which they exercised at first toward the Israelites.

Jasher 70

1 And in the third year from the birth of Moses, Pharaoh was sitting at a banquet, when Alparanith the queen was sitting at his right and Bathia at his left, and the lad Moses was lying upon her bosom, and Balaam the son of Beor with his two sons, and all the princes of the kingdom were sitting at table in the king's presence.

2 And the lad stretched forth his hand upon the king's head, and took the crown from the king's head and placed it on his own head.

3 And when the king and princes saw the work which the boy had done, the king and princes were terrified, and one man to his neighbor expressed astonishment.

4 And the king said unto the princes who were before him at table, What speak you and what say you, O ye princes, in this matter, and what is to be the judgment against the boy on account of this act?

5 And Balaam the son of Beor the magician answered before the king and princes, and he said, Remember now, O my lord and king, the dream which thou didst dream many days since, and that which thy servant interpreted unto thee.

6 Now therefore this is a child from the Hebrew children, in whom is the spirit of God, and let not my lord the king imagine that this youngster did this thing without knowledge.

7 For he is a Hebrew boy, and wisdom and understanding are with him, although he is yet a child, and with wisdom has he done this and chosen unto himself the kingdom of Egypt.

8 For this is the manner of all the Hebrews to deceive kings and their nobles, to do all these things cunningly, in order to make the kings of the earth and their men tremble.

9 Surely thou knowest that Abraham their father acted thus, who deceived the army of Nimrod king of Babel,

and Abimelech king of Gerar, and that he possessed himself of the land of the children of Heth and all the kingdoms of Canaan.

10 And that he descended into Egypt and said of Sarah his wife, she is my sister, in order to mislead Egypt and her king.

11 His son Isaac also did so when he went to Gerar and dwelt there, and his strength prevailed over the army of Abimelech king of the Philistines.

12 He also thought of making the kingdom of the Philistines stumble, in saying that Rebecca his wife was his sister.

13 Jacob also dealt treacherously with his brother, and took from his hand his birthright and his blessing.

14 He went then to Padan-aram to the house of Laban his mother's brother, and cunningly obtained from him his daughter, his cattle, and all belonging to him, and fled away and returned to the land of Canaan to his father.

15 His sons sold their brother Joseph, who went down into Egypt and became a slave, and was placed in the prison house for twelve years.

16 Until the former Pharaoh dreamed dreams, and withdrew him from the prison house, and magnified him above all the princes in Egypt on account of his interpreting his dreams to him.

17 And when God caused a famine throughout the land he sent for and brought his father and all his brothers, and the whole of his father's household, and supported them without price or reward, and bought the Egyptians for slaves.

18 Now therefore my lord king behold this child has risen up in their stead in Egypt, to do according to their deeds and to trifle with every king, prince and judge.

19 If it please the king, let us now spill his blood upon the ground, lest he grow up and take away the government from thy hand, and the hope of Egypt perish after he shall have reigned.

20 And Balaam said to the king, Let us moreover call for all the judges of Egypt and the wise men thereof, and let us know if the judgment of death is due to this boy as thou didst say, and then we will slay him.

21 And Pharaoh sent and called for all the wise men of Egypt and they came before the king, and an angel of the Lord came amongst them, and he was like one of the wise men of Egypt.

22 And the king said to the wise men, Surely you have heard what this Hebrew boy who is in the house has done, and thus has Balaam judged in the matter.

23 Now judge you also and see what is due to the boy for the act he has committed.

24 And the angel, who seemed like one of the wise men of Pharaoh, answered and said as follows, before all the wise men of Egypt and before the king and the princes:

25 If it please the king let the king send for men who shall bring before him an onyx stone and a coal of fire, and place them before the child, and if the child shall stretch forth his hand and take the onyx stone, then shall we know that with wisdom has the youth done all that he has done, and we must slay him.

26 But if he stretch forth his hand upon the coal, then shall we know that it was not with knowledge that he did this thing, and he shall live.

27 And the thing seemed good in the eyes of the king and the princes, so the king did according to the word of the angel of the Lord.

28 And the king ordered the onyx stone and coal to be brought and placed before Moses.

29 And they placed the boy before them, and the lad endeavored to stretch forth his hand to the onyx stone, but the angel of the Lord took his hand and placed it upon the coal, and the coal became extinguished in his hand, and he lifted it up and put it into his mouth, and burned part of his lips and part of his tongue, and

he became heavy in mouth and tongue.

30 And when the king and princes saw this, they knew that Moses had not acted with wisdom in taking off the crown from the king's head.

31 So the king and princes refrained from slaying the child, so Moses remained in Pharaoh's house, growing up, and the Lord was with him.

32 And whilst the boy was in the king's house, he was robed in purple and he grew amongst the children of the king.

33 And when Moses grew up in the king's house, Bathia the daughter of Pharaoh considered him as a son, and all the household of Pharaoh honored him, and all the men of Egypt were afraid of him.

34 And he daily went forth and came into the land of Goshen, where his brethren the children of Israel were, and Moses saw them daily in shortness of breath and hard labor.

35 And Moses asked them, saying, Wherefore is this labor meted out unto you day by day?

36 And they told him all that had befallen them, and all the injunctions which Pharaoh had put upon them before his birth.

37 And they told him all the counsels which Balaam the son of Beor had counselled against them, and what

he had also counselled against him in order to slay him when he had taken the king's crown from off his head.

38 And when Moses heard these things his anger was kindled against Balaam, and he sought to kill him, and he was in ambush for him day by day.

39 And Balaam was afraid of Moses, and he and his two sons rose up and went forth from Egypt, and they fled and delivered their souls and betook themselves to the land of Cush to Kikianus, king of Cush.

40 And Moses was in the king's house going out and coming in, the Lord gave him favor in the eyes of Pharaoh, and in the eyes of all his servants, and in the eyes of all the people of Egypt, and they loved Moses exceedingly.

41 And the day arrived when Moses went to Goshen to see his brethren, that he saw the children of Israel in their burdens and hard labor, and Moses was grieved on their account.

42 And Moses returned to Egypt and came to the house of Pharaoh, and came before the king, and Moses bowed down before the king.

43 And Moses said unto Pharaoh, I pray thee my lord, I have come to seek a small request from thee, turn not away my face empty; and Pharaoh said unto him, Speak.

44 And Moses said unto Pharaoh, Let there be given unto thy servants the children of Israel who are in Goshen, one day to rest therein from their labor.

45 And the king answered Moses and said, Behold I have lifted up thy face in this thing to grant thy request.

46 And Pharaoh ordered a proclamation to be issued throughout Egypt and Goshen, saying,

47 To you, all the children of Israel, thus says the king, for six days you shall do your work and labor, but on the seventh day you shall rest, and shall not preform any work, thus shall you do all the days, as the king and Moses the son of Bathia have commanded.

48 And Moses rejoiced at this thing which the king had granted to him, and all the children of Israel did as Moses ordered them.

49 For this thing was from the Lord to the children of Israel, for the Lord had begun to remember the children of Israel to save them for the sake of their fathers.

50 And the Lord was with Moses and his fame went throughout Egypt.

51 And Moses became great in the eyes of all the Egyptians, and in the eyes of all the children of Israel, seeking good for his people Israel and speaking words of peace regarding them to the king.

Jasher 71

1 And when Moses was eighteen years old, he desired to see his father and mother and he went to them to Goshen, and when Moses had come near Goshen, he came to the place where the children of Israel were engaged in work, and he observed their burdens, and he saw an Egyptian smiting one of his Hebrew brethren.

2 And when the man who was beaten saw Moses he ran to him for help, for the man Moses was greatly respected in the house of Pharaoh, and he said to him, My lord attend to me, this Egyptian came to my house in the night, bound me, and came to my wife in my presence, and now he seeks to take my life away.

3 And when Moses heard this wicked thing, his anger was kindled against the Egyptian, and he turned this way and the other, and when he saw there was no man there he smote the Egyptian and hid him in the sand, and delivered the Hebrew from the hand of him that smote him.

4 And the Hebrew went to his house, and Moses returned to his home, and went forth and came back to the king's house.

5 And when the man had returned home, he thought of repudiating his wife, for it was not right in the house of Jacob, for any man to come to his wife after she had been defiled.

6 And the woman went and told her brothers, and the woman's brothers sought to slay him, and he fled to his house and escaped.

7 And on the second day Moses went forth to his brethren, and saw, and behold two men were quarreling, and he said to the wicked one, Why dost thou smite thy neighbor?

8 And he answered him and said to him, Who has set thee for a prince and judge over us? dost thou think to slay me as thou didst slay the Egyptian? and Moses was afraid and he said, Surely the thing is known?

9 And Pharaoh heard of this affair, and he ordered Moses to be slain, so God sent his angel, and he appeared unto Pharaoh in the likeness of a captain of the guard.

10 And the angel of the Lord took the sword from the hand of the captain of the guard, and took his head off with it, for the likeness of the captain of the guard was turned into the likeness of Moses.

11 And the angel of the Lord took hold of the right hand of Moses, and brought him forth from Egypt, and placed him from without the borders of Egypt, a distance of forty days' journey.

12 And Aaron his brother alone remained in the land of Egypt, and he prophesied to the children of Israel, saying,

13 Thus says the Lord God of your ancestors, Throw away, each man, the abominations of his eyes, and do not defile yourselves with the idols of Egypt.

14 And the children of Israel rebelled and would not hearken to Aaron at that time.

15 And the Lord thought to destroy them, were it not that the Lord remembered the covenant which he had made with Abraham, Isaac and Jacob.

16 In those days the hand of Pharaoh continued to be severe against the children of Israel, and he crushed and oppressed them until the time when God sent forth his word and took notice of them.

Jasher 72

1 And it was in those days that there was a great war between the children of Cush and the children of the east and Aram, and they rebelled against the king of Cush in whose hands they were.

2 So Kikianus king of Cush went forth with all the children of Cush, a people numerous as the sand, and he went to fight against Aram and the children of the east, to bring them under subjection.

3 And when Kikianus went out, he left Balaam the magician, with his two sons, to guard the city, and the lowest sort of the people of the land.

4 So Kikianus went forth to Aram and the children of the east, and he fought against them and smote them, and they all fell down wounded before Kikianus and his people.

5 And he took many of them captives and he brought them under subjection as at first, and he encamped upon their land to take tribute from them as usual.

6 And Balaam the son of Beor, when the king of Cush had left him to guard the city and the poor of the city, he rose up and advised with the people of the land to rebel against king Kikianus, not to let him enter the city when he should come home.

7 And the people of the land hearkened to him, and they swore to him and made him king over them, and his two sons for captains of the army.

8 So they rose up and raised the walls of the city at the two corners, and they built an exceeding strong building.

9 And at the third corner they dug ditches without number, between the city and the river which surrounded the whole land of Cush, and they made the waters of the river burst forth there.

10 At the fourth corner they collected numerous serpents by their incantations and enchantments, and they fortified the city and dwelt

therein, and no one went out or in before them.

11 And Kikianus fought against Aram and the children of the east and he subdued them as before, and they gave him their usual tribute, and he went and returned to his land.

12 And when Kikianus the king of Cush approached his city and all the captains of the forces with him, they lifted up their eyes and saw that the walls of the city were built up and greatly elevated, so the men were astonished at this.

13 And they said one to the other, It is because they saw that we were delayed, in battle, and were greatly afraid of us, therefore have they done this thing and raised the city walls and fortified them so that the kings of Canaan might not come in battle against them.

14 So the king and the troops approached the city door and they looked up and behold, all the gates of the city were closed, and they called out to the sentinels, saying, Open unto us, that we may enter the city.

15 But the sentinels refused to open to them by the order of Balaam the magician, their king, they suffered them not to enter their city.

16 So they raised a battle with them opposite the city gate, and one hundred and thirty men of the army at Kikianus fell on that day.

17 And on the next day they continued to fight and they fought at the side of the river; they endeavored to pass but were not able, so some of them sank in the pits and died.

18 So the king ordered them to cut down trees to make rafts, upon which they might pass to them, and they did so.

19 And when they came to the place of the ditches, the waters revolved by mills, and two hundred men upon ten rafts were drowned.

20 And on the third day they came to fight at the side where the serpents were, but they could not approach there, for the serpents slew of them one hundred and seventy men, and they ceased fighting against Cush, and they besieged Cush for nine years, no person came out or in.

21 At that time that the war and the siege were against Cush, Moses fled from Egypt from Pharaoh who sought to kill him for having slain the Egyptian.

22 And Moses was eighteen years old when he fled from Egypt from the presence of Pharaoh, and he fled and escaped to the camp of Kikianus, which at that time was besieging Cush.

23 And Moses was nine years in the camp of Kikianus king of Cush, all the time that they were besieging

Cush, and Moses went out and came in with them.

24 And the king and princes and all the fighting men loved Moses, for he was great and worthy, his stature was like a noble lion, his face was like the sun, and his strength was like that of a lion, and he was counsellor to the king.

25 And at the end of nine years, Kikianus was seized with a mortal disease, and his illness prevailed over him, and he died on the seventh day.

26 So his servants embalmed him and carried him and buried him opposite the city gate to the north of the land of Egypt.

27 And they built over him an elegant strong and high building, and they placed great stones below.

28 And the king's scribes engraved upon those stones all the might of their king Kikianus, and all his battles which he had fought, behold they are written there at this day.

29 Now after the death of Kikianus king of Cush it grieved his men and troops greatly on account of the war.

30 So they said one to the other, Give us counsel what we are to do at this time, as we have resided in the wilderness nine years away from our homes.

31 If we say we will fight against the city many of us will fall wounded or killed, and if we remain here in the siege we shall also die.

32 For now all the kings of Aram and of the children of the east will hear that our king is dead, and they will attack us suddenly in a hostile manner, and they will fight against us and leave no remnant of us.

33 Now therefore let us go and make a king over us, and let us remain in the siege until the city is delivered up to us.

34 And they wished to choose on that day a man for king from the army of Kikianus, and they found no object of their choice like Moses to reign over them.

35 And they hastened and stripped off each man his garments and cast them upon the ground, and they made a great heap and placed Moses thereon.

36 And they rose up and blew with trumpets and called out before him, and said, May the king live, may the king live!

37 And all the people and nobles swore unto him to give him for a wife Adoniah the queen, the Cushite, wife of Kikianus, and they made Moses king over them on that day.

38 And all the people of Cush issued a proclamation on that day, saying, Every man must give something to Moses of what is in his possession.

39 And they spread out a sheet upon the heap, and every man cast into it something of what he had, one a gold earring and the other a coin.

40 Also of onyx stones, bdellium, pearls and marble did the children of Cush cast unto Moses upon the heap, also silver and gold in great abundance.

41 And Moses took all the silver and gold, all the vessels, and the bdellium and onyx stones, which all the children of Cush had given to him, and he placed them amongst his treasures.

42 And Moses reigned over the children of Cush on that day, in the place of Kikianus king of Cush.

Jasher 73

1 In the fifty-fifth year of the reign of Pharaoh king of Egypt, that is in the hundred and fifty-seventh year of the Israelites going down into Egypt, reigned Moses in Cush.

2 Moses was twenty-seven years old when he began to reign over Cush, and forty years did he reign.

3 And the Lord granted Moses favor and grace in the eyes of all the children of Cush, and the children of Cush loved him exceedingly, so Moses was favored by the Lord and by men.

4 And in the seventh day of his reign, all the children of Cush assembled and came before Moses and bowed down to him to the ground.

5 And all the children spoke together in the presence of the king, saying, Give us counsel that we may see what is to be done to this city.

6 For it is now nine years that we have been besieging round about the city, and have not seen our children and our wives.

7 So the king answered them, saying, If you will hearken to my voice in all that I shall command you, then will the Lord give the city into our hands and we shall subdue it.

8 For if we fight with them as in the former battle which we had with them before the death of Kikianus, many of us will fall down wounded as before.

9 Now therefore behold here is counsel for you in this matter; if you will hearken to my voice, then will the city be delivered into our hands.

10 So all the forces answered the king, saying, All that our lord shall command that will we do.

11 And Moses said unto them, Pass through and proclaim a voice in the whole camp unto all the people, saying,

12 Thus says the king, Go into the forest and bring with you of the young ones of the stork, each man a young one in his hand.

13 And any person transgressing the word of the king, who shall not bring his young one, he shall die, and the king will take all belonging to him.

14 And when you shall bring them they shall be in your keeping, you shall rear them until they grow up, and you shall teach them to dart upon, as is the way of the young ones of the hawk.

15 So all the children of Cush heard the words of Moses, and they rose up and caused a proclamation to be issued throughout the camp, saying,

16 Unto you, all the children of Cush, the king's order is, that you go all together to the forest, and catch there the young storks each man his young one in his hand, and you shall bring them home.

17 And any person violating the order of the king shall die, and the king will take all that belongs to him.

18 And all the people did so, and they went out to the wood and they climbed the fir trees and caught, each man a young one in his hand, all the young of the storks, and they brought them into the desert and reared them by order of the king, and they taught them to dart upon, similar to the young hawks.

19 And after the young storks were reared, the king ordered them to be hungered for three days, and all the people did so.

20 And on the third day, the king said unto them, strengthen yourselves and become valiant men, and put on each man his armor and gird on his sword upon him, and ride each man his horse and take each his young stork in his hand.

21 And we will rise up and fight against the city at the place where the serpents are; and all the people did as the king had ordered.

22 And they took each man his young one in his hand, and they went away, and when they came to the place of the serpents the king said to them, Send forth each man his young stork upon the serpents.

23 And they sent forth each man his young stork at the king's order, and the young storks ran upon the serpents and they devoured them all and destroyed them out of that place.

24 And when the king and people had seen that all the serpents were destroyed in that place, all the people set up a great shout.

25 And they approached and fought against the city and took it and subdued it, and they entered the city.

26 And there died on that day one thousand and one hundred men of the people of the city, all that inhabited the city, but of the people besieging not one died.

27 So all the children of Cush went each to his home, to his wife and children and to all belonging to him.

28 And Balaam the magician, when he saw that the city was taken, he opened the gate and he and his two sons and eight brothers fled and returned to Egypt to Pharaoh king of Egypt.

29 They are the sorcerers and magicians who are mentioned in the book of the law, standing against Moses when the Lord brought the plagues upon Egypt.

30 So Moses took the city by his wisdom, and the children of Cush placed him on the throne instead of Kikianus king of Cush.

31 And they placed the royal crown upon his head, and they gave him for a wife Adoniah the Cushite queen, wife of Kikianus.

32 And Moses feared the Lord God of his fathers, so that he came not to her, nor did he turn his eyes to her.

33 For Moses remembered how Abraham had made his servant Eliezer swear, saying unto him, Thou shalt not take a woman from the daughters of Canaan for my son Isaac.

34 Also what Isaac did when Jacob had fled from his brother, when he commanded him, saying, Thou shalt not take a wife from the daughters of Canaan, nor make alliance with any of the children of Ham.

35 For the Lord our God gave Ham the son of Noah, and his children and all his seed, as slaves to the children of Shem and to the children of Japheth, and unto their seed after them for slaves, forever.

36 Therefore Moses turned not his heart nor his eyes to the wife of Kikianus all the days that he reigned over Cush.

37 And Moses feared the Lord his God all his life, and Moses walked before the Lord in truth, with all his heart and soul, he turned not from the right way all the days of his life; he declined not from the way either to the right or to the left, in which Abraham, Isaac and Jacob had walked.

38 And Moses strengthened himself in the kingdom of the children of Cush, and he guided the children of Cush with his usual wisdom, and Moses prospered in his kingdom.

39 And at that time Aram and the children of the east heard that Kikianus king of Cush had died, so Aram and the children of the east rebelled against Cush in those days.

40 And Moses gathered all the children of Cush, a people very mighty, about thirty thousand men, and he went forth to fight with Aram and the children of the east.

41 And they went at first to the children of the east, and when the children of the east heard their report, they went to meet them, and engaged in battle with them.

42 And the war was severe against the children of the east, so the Lord gave all the children of the east into the hand of Moses, and about three hundred men fell down slain.

43 And all the children of the east turned back and retreated, so Moses and the children of Cush followed them and subdued them, and put a tax upon them, as was their custom.

44 So Moses and all the people with him passed from there to the land of Aram for battle.

45 And the people of Aram also went to meet them, and they fought against them, and the Lord delivered them into the hand of Moses, and many of the men of Aram fell down wounded.

46 And Aram also were subdued by Moses and the people of Cush, and also gave their usual tax.

47 And Moses brought Aram and the children of the east under subjection to the children of Cush, and Moses and all the people who were with him, turned to the land of Cush.

48 And Moses strengthened himself in the kingdom of the children of Cush, and the Lord was with him, and all the children of Cush were afraid of him.

Jasher 74

1 In the end of years died Saul king of Edom, and Baal Chanan the son of Achbor reigned in his place.

2 In the sixteenth year of the reign of Moses over Cush, Baal Chanan the son of Achbor reigned in the land of Edom over all the children of Edom for thirty-eight years.

3 In his days Moab rebelled against the power of Edom, having been under Edom since the days of Hadad the son of Bedad, who smote them and Midian, and brought Moab under subjection to Edom.

4 And when Baal Chanan the son of Achbor reigned over Edom, all the children of Moab withdrew their allegiance from Edom.

5 And Angeas king of Africa died in those days, and Azrubal his son reigned in his stead.

6 And in those days died Janeas king of the children of Chittim, and they buried him in his temple which he had built for himself in the plain of Canopia for a residence, and Latinus reigned in his stead.

7 In the twenty-second year of the reign of Moses over the children of Cush, Latinus reigned over the children of Chittim forty-five years.

8 And he also built for himself a great and mighty tower, and he built therein an elegant temple for his residence, to conduct his government, as was the custom.

9 In the third year of his reign he caused a proclamation to be made to all his skilful men, who made many ships for him.

10 And Latinus assembled all his forces, and they came in ships, and went therein to fight with Azdrubal son of Angeas king of Africa, and they came to Africa and engaged in battle with Azdrubal and his army.

11 And Latinus prevailed over Azdrubal, and Latinus took from Azdrubal the aqueduct which his father had brought from the children of Chittim, when he took Janiah the daughter of Uzi for a wife, so Latinus overthrew the bridge of the aqueduct, and smote the whole army of Azdrubal a severe blow.

12 And the remaining strong men of Azdrubal strengthened themselves, and their hearts were filled with envy, and they courted death, and again engaged in battle with Latinus king of Chittim.

13 And the battle was severe upon all the men of Africa, and they all fell wounded before Latinus and his people, and Azdrubal the king also fell in that battle.

14 And the king Azdrubal had a very beautiful daughter, whose name was Ushpezena, and all the men of Africa embroidered her likeness on their garments, on account of her great beauty and comely appearance.

15 And the men of Latinus saw Ushpezena, the daughter of Azdrubal, and praised her unto Latinus their king.

16 And Latinus ordered her to be brought to him, and Latinus took Ushpezena for a wife, and he turned back on his way to Chittim.

17 And it was after the death of Azdrubal son of Angeas, when Latinus had turned back to his land from the battle, that all the inhabitants of Africa rose up and took Anibal the son of Angeas, the younger brother of Azdrubal, and made him king instead at his brother over the whole land at Africa.

18 And when he reigned, he resolved to go to Chittim to fight with the children of Chittim, to avenge the cause of Azdrubal his brother, and the cause of the inhabitants of Africa, and he did so.

19 And he made many ships, and he came therein with his whole army, and he went to Chittim.

20 So Anibal fought with the children of Chittim, and the children of Chittim fell wounded before Anibal and his army, and Anibal avenged his brother's cause.

21 And Anibal continued the war for eighteen years with the children of Chittim, and Anibal dwelt in the land of Chittim and encamped there for a long time.

22 And Anibal smote the children of Chittim very severely, and he slew their great men and princes, and of the rest of the people he smote about eighty thousand men.

23 And at the end of days and years, Anibal returned to his land of Africa, and he reigned securely in the place of Azdrubal his brother.

Jasher 75

1 At that time, in the hundred and eightieth year of the Israelites going down into Egypt, there went forth from Egypt valiant men, thirty thousand on foot, from the children of Israel, who were all of the tribe of Joseph, of the children of Ephraim the son of Joseph.

2 For they said the period was completed which the Lord had appointed to the children of Israel in the times of old, which he had spoken to Abraham.

3 And these men girded themselves, and they put each man his sword at his side, and every man his armor upon him, and they trusted to their strength, and they went out together from Egypt with a mighty hand.

4 But they brought no provision for the road, only silver and gold, not even bread for that day did they bring in their hands, for they thought of getting their provision for pay from the Philistines, and if not they would take it by force.

5 And these men were very mighty and valiant men, one man could pursue a thousand and two could rout ten thousand, so they trusted to their strength and went together as they were.

6 And they directed their course toward the land of Gath, and they went down and found the shepherds of Gath feeding the cattle of the children of Gath.

7 And they said to the shepherds, Give us some of the sheep for pay, that we may eat, for we are hungry, for we have eaten no bread this day.

8 And the shepherds said, Are they our sheep or cattle that we should give them to you even for pay? so the children of Ephraim approached to take them by force.

9 And the shepherds of Gath shouted over them that their cry was heard at a distance, so all the children of Gath went out to them.

10 And when the children of Gath saw the evil doings of the children of Ephraim, they returned and assembled the men of Gath, and they put on each man his armor, and came forth to the children of Ephraim for battle.

11 And they engaged with them in the valley of Gath, and the battle was severe, and they smote from each other a great many on that day.

12 And on the second day the children of Gath sent to all the cities of the Philistines that they should come to their help, saying,

13 Come up unto us and help us, that we may smite the children of Ephraim who have come forth from Egypt to take our cattle, and to fight against us without cause.

14 Now the souls of the children of Ephraim were exhausted with hunger and thirst, for they had eaten no bread for three days. And forty thousand men went forth from the cities of the Philistines to the assistance of the men of Gath.

15 And these men were engaged in battle with the children of Ephraim, and the Lord delivered the children of Ephraim into the hands of the Philistines.

16 And they smote all the children of Ephraim, all who had gone forth from Egypt, none were remaining but ten men who had run away from the engagement.

17 For this evil was from the Lord against the children of Ephraim, for they transgressed the word of the Lord in going forth from Egypt, before the period had arrived which the Lord in the days of old had appointed to Israel.

18 And of the Philistines also there fell a great many, about twenty thousand men, and their brethren carried them and buried them in their cities.

19 And the slain of the children of Ephraim remained forsaken in the valley of Gath for many days and years, and were not brought to burial, and the valley was filled with men's bones.

20 And the men who had escaped from the battle came to Egypt, and told all the children of Israel all that had befallen them.

21 And their father Ephraim mourned over them for many days, and his brethren came to console him.

22 And he came unto his wife and she bare a son, and he called his name Beriah, for she was unfortunate in his house.

Jasher 76

1 And Moses the son of Amram was still king in the land of Cush in those days, and he prospered in his kingdom, and he conducted the government of the children of Cush in justice, in righteousness, and integrity.

2 And all the children of Cush loved Moses all the days that he reigned over them, and all the inhabitants of the land of Cush were greatly afraid of him.

3 And in the fortieth year of the reign of Moses over Cush, Moses was sitting on the royal throne whilst Adoniah the queen was before him, and all the nobles were sitting around him.

4 And Adoniah the queen said before the king and the princes, What is this thing which you, the children of Cush, have done for this long time?

5 Surely you know that for forty years that this man has reigned over Cush he has not approached me, nor has he served the gods of the children of Cush.

6 Now therefore hear, O ye children of Cush, and let this man no more reign over you as he is not of our flesh.

7 Behold Menacrus my son is grown up, let him reign over you, for it is better for you to serve the son of your lord, than to serve a stranger, slave of the king of Egypt.

8 And all the people and nobles of the children of Cush heard the words which Adoniah the queen had spoken in their ears.

9 And all the people were preparing until the evening, and in the morning they rose up early and made Menacrus, son of Kikianus, king over them.

10 And all the children of Cush were afraid to stretch forth their hand against Moses, for the Lord was with Moses, and the children of Cush remembered the oath which they swore unto Moses, therefore they did no harm to him.

11 But the children of Cush gave many presents to Moses, and sent him from them with great honor.

12 So Moses went forth from the land of Cush, and went home and ceased to reign over Cush, and Moses was sixty-six years old when he went out of the land of Cush, for the thing was from the Lord, for the period had arrived which he had appointed in the days of old, to bring forth Israel from the affliction of the children of Ham.

13 So Moses went to Midian, for he was afraid to return to Egypt on account of Pharaoh, and he went and sat at a well of water in Midian.

14 And the seven daughters of Reuel the Midianite went out to feed their father's flock.

15 And they came to the well and drew water to water their father's flock.

16 So the shepherds of Midian came and drove them away, and Moses rose up and helped them and watered the flock.

17 And they came home to their father Reuel, and told him what Moses did for them.

18 And they said, An Egyptian man has delivered us from the hands of the shepherds, he drew up water for us and watered the flock.

19 And Reuel said to his daughters, And where is he? wherefore have you left the man?

20 And Reuel sent for him and fetched him and brought him home, and he ate bread with him.

21 And Moses related to Reuel that he had fled from Egypt and that he reigned forty years over Cush, and that they afterward had taken the government from him, and had sent him away in peace with honor and with presents.

22 And when Reuel had heard the words of Moses, Reuel said within himself, I will put this man into the prison house, whereby I shall conciliate the children of Cush, for he has fled from them.

23 And they took and put him into the prison house, and Moses was in prison ten years, and whilst Moses was in the prison house, Zipporah the daughter of Reuel took pity over him, and supported him with bread and water all the time.

24 And all the children of Israel were yet in the land of Egypt serving the Egyptians in all manner of hard work, and the hand of Egypt continued in severity over the children of Israel in those days.

25 At that time the Lord smote Pharaoh king of Egypt, and he afflicted with the plague of leprosy from the sole of his foot to the crown of his head; owing to the cruel treatment of the children of Israel was this plague at that time from the Lord upon Pharaoh king of Egypt.

26 For the Lord had hearkened to the prayer of his people the children of Israel, and their cry reached him on account of their hard work.

27 Still his anger did not turn from them, and the hand of Pharaoh was still stretched out against the children of Israel, and Pharaoh hardened his neck before the Lord, and he increased his yoke over the children of Israel, and embittered their lives with all manner of hard work.

28 And when the Lord had inflicted the plague upon Pharaoh king of Egypt, he asked his wise men and sorcerers to cure him.

29 And his wise men and sorcerers said unto him, That if the blood of little children were put into the wounds he would be healed.

30 And Pharaoh hearkened to them, and sent his ministers to Goshen to the children of Israel to take their little children.

31 And Pharaoh's ministers went and took the infants of the children of Israel from the bosoms of their mothers by force, and they brought them to Pharaoh daily, a child each

day, and the physicians killed them and applied them to the plague; thus did they all the days.

32 And the number of the children which Pharaoh slew was three hundred and seventy-five.

33 But the Lord hearkened not to the physicians of the king of Egypt, and the plague went on increasing mightily.

34 And Pharaoh was ten years afflicted with that plague, still the heart of Pharaoh was more hardened against the children of Israel.

35 And at the end of ten years the Lord continued to afflict Pharaoh with destructive plagues.

36 And the Lord smote him with a bad tumor and sickness at the stomach, and that plague turned to a severe boil.

37 At that time the two ministers of Pharaoh came from the land of Goshen where all the children of Israel were, and went to the house of Pharaoh and said to him, We have seen the children of Israel slacken in their work and negligent in their labor.

38 And when Pharaoh heard the words of his ministers, his anger was kindled against the children of Israel exceedingly, for he was greatly grieved at his bodily pain.

39 And he answered and said, Now that the children of Israel know that I am ill, they turn and scoff at us, now therefore harness my chariot for me, and I will betake myself to Goshen and will see the scoff of the children of Israel with which they are deriding me; so his servants harnessed the chariot for him.

40 And they took and made him ride upon a horse, for he was not able to ride of himself;

41 And he took with him ten horsemen and ten footmen, and went to the children of Israel to Goshen.

42 And when they had come to the border of Egypt, the king's horse passed into a narrow place, elevated in the hollow part of the vineyard, fenced on both sides, the low, plain country being on the other side.

43 And the horses ran rapidly in that place and pressed each other, and the other horses pressed the king's horse.

44 And the king's horse fell into the low plain whilst the king was riding upon it, and when he fell the chariot turned over the king's face and the horse lay upon the king, and the king cried out, for his flesh was very sore.

45 And the flesh of the king was torn from him, and his bones were broken and he could not ride, for this thing was from the Lord to him, for the Lord had heard the cries of his

people the children of Israel and their affliction.

46 And his servants carried him upon their shoulders, a little at a time, and they brought him back to Egypt, and the horsemen who were with him came also back to Egypt.

47 And they placed him in his bed, and the king knew that his end was come to die, so Aparanith the queen his wife came and cried before the king, and the king wept a great weeping with her.

48 And all his nobles and servants came on that day and saw the king in that affliction, and wept a great weeping with him.

49 And the princes of the king and all his counselors advised the king to cause one to reign in his stead in the land, whomsoever he should choose from his sons.

50 And the king had three sons and two daughters which Aparanith the queen his wife had borne to him, besides the king's children of concubines.

51 And these were their names, the firstborn Othri, the second Adikam, and the third Morion, and their sisters, the name of the elder Bathia and of the other Acuzi.

52 And Othri the first born of the king was an idiot, precipitate and hurried in his words.

53 But Adikam was a cunning and wise man and knowing in all the wisdom of Egypt, but of unseemly aspect, thick in flesh, and very short in stature; his height was one cubit.

54 And when the king saw Adikam his son intelligent and wise in all things, the king resolved that he should be king in his stead after his death.

55 And he took for him a wife Gedudah daughter of Abilot, and he was ten years old, and she bare unto him four sons.

56 And he afterward went and took three wives and begat eight sons and three daughters.

57 And the disorder greatly prevailed over the king, and his flesh stank like the flesh of a carcass cast upon the field in summer time, during the heat of the sun.

58 And when the king saw that his sickness had greatly strengthened itself over him, he ordered his son Adikam to be brought to him, and they made him king over the land in his place.

59 And at the end of three years, the king died, in shame, disgrace, and disgust, and his servants carried him and buried him in the sepulcher of the kings of Egypt in Zoan Mizraim.

60 But they embalmed him not as was usual with kings, for his flesh was putrid, and they could not

approach to embalm him on account of the stench, so they buried him in haste.

61 For this evil was from the Lord to him, for the Lord had requited him evil for the evil which in his days he had done to Israel.

62 And he died with terror and with shame, and his son Adikam reigned in his place.

Jasher 77

1 Adikam was twenty years old when he reigned over Egypt, he reigned four years.

2 In the two hundred and sixth year of Israel's going down to Egypt did Adikam reign over Egypt, but he continued not so long in his reign over Egypt as his fathers had continued their reigns.

3 For Melol his father reigned ninety-four years in Egypt, but he was ten years sick and died, for he had been wicked before the Lord.

4 And all the Egyptians called the name of Adikam Pharaoh like the name of his fathers, as was their custom to do in Egypt.

5 And all the wise men of Pharaoh called the name of Adikam Ahuz, for short is called Ahuz in the Egyptian language.

6 And Adikam was exceedingly ugly, and he was a cubit and a span and he had a great beard which reached to the soles of his feet.

7 And Pharaoh sat upon his father's throne to reign over Egypt, and he conducted the government of Egypt in his wisdom.

8 And whilst he reigned he exceeded his father and all the preceding kings in wickedness, and he increased his yoke over the children of Israel.

9 And he went with his servants to Goshen to the children of Israel, and he strengthened the labor over them and he said unto them, Complete your work, each day's task, and let not your hands slacken from our work from this day forward as you did in the days of my father.

10 And he placed officers over them from amongst the children of Israel, and over these officers he placed taskmasters from amongst his servants.

11 And he placed over them a measure of bricks for them to do according to that number, day by day, and he turned back and went to Egypt.

12 At that time the task-masters of Pharaoh ordered the officers of the children of Israel according to the command of Pharaoh, saying,

13 Thus says Pharaoh, Do your work each day, and finish your task, and observe the daily measure of bricks; diminish not anything.

14 And it shall come to pass that if you are deficient in your daily bricks, I will put your young children in their stead.

15 And the task-masters of Egypt did so in those days as Pharaoh had ordered them.

16 And whenever any deficiency was found in the children of Israel's measure of their daily bricks, the task-masters of Pharaoh would go to the wives of the children of Israel and take infants of the children of Israel to the number of bricks deficient, they would take them by force from their mother's laps, and put them in the building instead of the bricks;

17 Whilst their fathers and mothers were crying over them and weeping when they heard the weeping voices of their infants in the wall of the building.

18 And the task-masters prevailed over Israel, that the Israelites should place their children in the building, so that a man placed his son in the wall and put mortar over him, whilst his eyes wept over him, and his tears ran down upon his child.

19 And the task-masters of Egypt did so to the babes of Israel for many days, and no one pitied or had compassion over the babes of the children of Israel.

20 And the number of all the children killed in the building was two hundred and seventy, some whom they had built upon instead of the bricks which had been left deficient by their fathers, and some whom they had drawn out dead from the building.

21 And the labor imposed upon the children of Israel in the days of Adikam exceeded in hardship that which they performed in the days of his father.

22 And the children of Israel sighed every day on account of their heavy work, for they had said to themselves, Behold when Pharaoh shall die, his son will rise up and lighten our work!

23 But they increased the latter work more than the former, and the children of Israel sighed at this and their cry ascended to God on account of their labor.

24 And God heard the voice of the children of Israel and their cry, in those days, and God remembered to them his covenant which he had made with Abraham, Isaac and Jacob.

25 And God saw the burden of the children of Israel, and their heavy work in those days, and he determined to deliver them.

26 And Moses the son of Amram was still confined in the dungeon in those days, in the house of Reuel the Midianite, and Zipporah the

daughter of Reuel did support him with food secretly day by day.

27 And Moses was confined in the dungeon in the house of Reuel for ten years.

28 And at the end of ten years which was the first year of the reign of Pharaoh over Egypt, in the place of his father,

29 Zipporah said to her father Reuel, No person inquires or seeks after the Hebrew man, whom thou didst bind in prison now ten years.

30 Now therefore, if it seem good in thy sight, let us send and see whether he is living or dead, but her father knew not that she had supported him.

31 And Reuel her father answered and said to her, Has ever such a thing happened that a man should be shut up in a prison without food for ten years, and that he should live?

32 And Zipporah answered her father, saying, Surely thou hast heard that the God of the Hebrews is great and awful, and does wonders for them at all times.

33 He it was who delivered Abraham from Ur of the Chaldeans, and Isaac from the sword of his father, and Jacob from the angel of the Lord who wrestled with him at the ford of Jabbuk.

34 Also with this man has he done many things, he delivered him from the river in Egypt and from the sword of Pharaoh, and from the children of Cush, so also can he deliver him from famine and make him live.

35 And the thing seemed good in the sight of Reuel, and he did according to the word of his daughter, and sent to the dungeon to ascertain what became of Moses.

36 And he saw, and behold the man Moses was living in the dungeon, standing upon his feet, praising and praying to the God of his ancestors.

37 And Reuel commanded Moses to be brought out of the dungeon, so they shaved him and he changed his prison garments and ate bread.

38 And afterward Moses went into the garden of Reuel which was behind the house, and he there prayed to the Lord his God, who had done mighty wonders for him.

39 And it was that whilst he prayed he looked opposite to him, and behold a sapphire stick was placed in the ground, which was planted in the midst of the garden.

40 And he approached the stick and he looked, and behold the name of the Lord God of hosts was engraved thereon, written and developed upon the stick.

41 And he read it and stretched forth his hand and he plucked it like a

forest tree from the thicket, and the stick was in his hand.

42 And this is the stick with which all the works of our God were performed, after he had created heaven and earth, and all the host of them, seas, rivers and all their fishes.

43 And when God had driven Adam from the garden of Eden, he took the stick in his hand and went and tilled the ground from which he was taken.

44 And the stick came down to Noah and was given to Shem and his descendants, until it came into the hand of Abraham the Hebrew.

45 And when Abraham had given all he had to his son Isaac, he also gave to him this stick.

46 And when Jacob had fled to Padan-aram, he took it into his hand, and when he returned to his father he had not left it behind him.

47 Also when he went down to Egypt he took it into his hand and gave it to Joseph, one portion above his brethren, for Jacob had taken it by force from his brother Esau.

48 And after the death of Joseph, the nobles of Egypt came into the house of Joseph, and the stick came into the hand of Reuel the Midianite, and when he went out of Egypt, he took it in his hand and planted it in his garden.

49 And all the mighty men of the Kinites tried to pluck it when they endeavored to get Zipporah his daughter, but they were unsuccessful.

50 So that stick remained planted in the garden of Reuel, until he came who had a right to it and took it.

51 And when Reuel saw the stick in the hand of Moses, he wondered at it, and he gave him his daughter Zipporah for a wife.

Jasher 78

1 At that time died Baal Channan son of Achbor, king of Edom, and was buried in his house in the land of Edom.

2 And after his death the children of Esau sent to the land of Edom, and took from there a man who was in Edom, whose name was Hadad, and they made him king over them in the place of Baal Channan, their king.

3 And Hadad reigned over the children of Edom forty-eight years.

4 And when he reigned he resolved to fight against the children of Moab, to bring them under the power of the children of Esau as they were before, but he was not able, because the children of Moab heard this thing, and they rose up and hastened to elect a king over them from amongst their brethren.

5 And they afterward gathered together a great people, and sent to

the children of Ammon their brethren for help to fight against Hadad king of Edom.

6 And Hadad heard the thing which the children of Moab had done, and was greatly afraid of them, and refrained from fighting against them.

7 In those days Moses, the son of Amram, in Midian, took Zipporah, the daughter of Reuel the Midianite, for a wife.

8 And Zipporah walked in the ways of the daughters of Jacob, she was nothing short of the righteousness of Sarah, Rebecca, Rachel and Leah.

9 And Zipporah conceived and bare a son and he called his name Gershom, for he said, I was a stranger in a foreign land; but he circumcised not his foreskin, at the command of Reuel his father-in-law.

10 And she conceived again and bare a son, but circumcised his foreskin, and called his name Eliezer, for Moses said, Because the God of my fathers was my help, and delivered me from the sword of Pharaoh.

11 And Pharaoh king of Egypt greatly increased the labor of the children of Israel in those days, and continued to make his yoke heavier upon the children of Israel.

12 And he ordered a proclamation to be made in Egypt, saying, Give no more straw to the people to make

bricks with, let them go and gather themselves straw as they can find it.

13 Also the tale of bricks which they shall make let them give each day, and diminish nothing from them, for they are idle in their work.

14 And the children of Israel heard this, and they mourned and sighed, and they cried unto the Lord on account of the bitterness of their souls.

15 And the Lord heard the cries of the children of Israel, and saw the oppression with which the Egyptians oppressed them.

16 And the Lord was jealous of his people and his inheritance, and heard their voice, and he resolved to take them out of the affliction of Egypt, to give them the land of Canaan for a possession.

Jasher 79

1 And in those days Moses was feeding the flock of Reuel the Midianite his father-in-law, beyond the wilderness of Sin, and the stick which he took from his father-in-law was in his hand.

2 And it came to pass one day that a kid of goats strayed from the flock, and Moses pursued it and it came to the mountain of God to Horeb.

3 And when he came to Horeb, the Lord appeared there unto him in the bush, and he found the bush burning

with fire, but the fire had no power over the bush to consume it.

4 And Moses was greatly astonished at this sight, wherefore the bush was not consumed, and he approached to see this mighty thing, and the Lord called unto Moses out of the fire and commanded him to go down to Egypt, to Pharaoh king of Egypt, to send the children of Israel from his service.

5 And the Lord said unto Moses, Go, return to Egypt, for all those men who sought thy life are dead, and thou shalt speak unto Pharaoh to send forth the children of Israel from his land.

6 And the Lord showed him to do signs and wonders in Egypt before the eyes of Pharaoh and the eyes of his subjects, in order that they might believe that the Lord had sent him.

7 And Moses hearkened to all that the Lord had commanded him, and he returned to his father-in-law and told him the thing, and Reuel said to him, Go in peace.

8 And Moses rose up to go to Egypt, and he took his wife and sons with him, and he was at an inn in the road, and an angel of God came down, and sought an occasion against him.

9 And he wished to kill him on account of his first born son, because he had not circumcised him, and had transgressed the covenant which the Lord had made with Abraham.

10 For Moses had hearkened to the words of his father-in-law which he had spoken to him, not to circumcise his first born son, therefore he circumcised him not.

11 And Zipporah saw the angel of the Lord seeking an occasion against Moses, and she knew that this thing was owing to his not having circumcised her son Gershom.

12 And Zipporah hastened and took of the sharp rock stones that were there, and she circumcised her son, and delivered her husband and her son from the hand of the angel of the Lord.

13 And Aaron the son of Amram, the brother of Moses, was in Egypt walking at the river side on that day.

14 And the Lord appeared to him in that place, and he said to him, Go now toward Moses in the wilderness, and he went and met him in the mountain of God, and he kissed him.

15 And Aaron lifted up his eyes, and saw Zipporah the wife of Moses and her children, and he said unto Moses, Who are these unto thee?

16 And Moses said unto him, They are my wife and sons, which God gave to me in Midian; and the thing grieved Aaron on account of the woman and her children.

17 And Aaron said to Moses, Send away the woman and her children that they may go to her father's house, and Moses hearkened to the words of Aaron, and did so.

18 And Zipporah returned with her children, and they went to the house of Reuel, and remained there until the time arrived when the Lord had visited his people, and brought them forth from Egypt from the hand at Pharaoh.

19 And Moses and Aaron came to Egypt to the community of the children of Israel, and they spoke to them all the words of the Lord, and the people rejoiced an exceeding great rejoicing.

20 And Moses and Aaron rose up early on the next day, and they went to the house of Pharaoh, and they took in their hands the stick of God.

21 And when they came to the king's gate, two young lions were confined there with iron instruments, and no person went out or came in from before them, unless those whom the king ordered to come, when the conjurors came and withdrew the lions by their incantations, and this brought them to the king.

22 And Moses hastened and lifted up the stick upon the lions, and he loosed them, and Moses and Aaron came into the king's house.

23 The lions also came with them in joy, and they followed them and rejoiced as a dog rejoices over his master when he comes from the field.

24 And when Pharaoh saw this thing he was astonished at it, and he was greatly terrified at the report, for their appearance was like the appearance of the children of God.

25 And Pharaoh said to Moses, What do you require? and they answered him, saying, The Lord God of the Hebrews has sent us to thee, to say, Send forth my people that they may serve me.

26 And when Pharaoh heard their words he was greatly terrified before them, and he said to them, Go today and come back to me tomorrow, and they did according to the word of the king.

27 And when they had gone Pharaoh sent for Balaam the magician and to Jannes and Jambres his sons, and to all the magicians and conjurors and counsellors which belonged to the king, and they all came and sat before the king.

28 And the king told them all the words which Moses and his brother Aaron had spoken to him, and the magicians said to the king, But how came the men to thee, on account of the lions which were confined at the gate?

29 And the king said, Because they lifted up their rod against the lions

and loosed them, and came to me, and the lions also rejoiced at them as a dog rejoices to meet his master.

30 And Balaam the son of Beor the magician answered the king, saying, These are none else than magicians like ourselves.

31 Now therefore send for them, and let them come and we will try them, and the king did so.

32 And in the morning Pharaoh sent for Moses and Aaron to come before the king, and they took the rod of God, and came to the king and spoke to him, saying,

33 Thus said the Lord God of the Hebrews, Send my people that they may serve me.

34 And the king said to them, But who will believe you that you are the messengers of God and that you come to me by his order?

35 Now therefore give a wonder or sign in this matter, and then the words which you speak will be believed.

36 And Aaron hastened and threw the rod out of his hand before Pharaoh and before his servants, and the rod turned into a serpent.

37 And the sorcerers saw this and they cast each man his rod upon the ground and they became serpents.

38 And the serpent of Aaron's rod lifted up its head and opened its mouth to swallow the rods of the magicians.

39 And Balaam the magician answered and said, This thing has been from the days of old, that a serpent should swallow its fellow, and that living things devour each other.

40 Now therefore restore it to a rod as it was at first, and we will also restore our rods as they were at first, and if thy rod shall swallow our rods, then shall we know that the spirit of God is in thee, and if not, thou art only an artificer like unto ourselves.

41 And Aaron hastened and stretched forth his hand and caught hold of the serpent's tail and it became a rod in his hand, and the sorcerers did the like with their rods, and they got hold, each man of the tail of his serpent, and they became rods as at first.

42 And when they were restored to rods, the rod of Aaron swallowed up their rods.

43 And when the king saw this thing, he ordered the book of records that related to the kings of Egypt, to be brought, and they brought the book of records, the chronicles of the kings of Egypt, in which all the idols of Egypt were inscribed, for they thought of finding therein the name of Jehovah, but they found it not.

44 And Pharaoh said to Moses and Aaron, Behold I have not found the

name of your God written in this book, and his name I know not.

45 And the counsellors and wise men answered the king, We have heard that the God of the Hebrews is a son of the wise, the son of ancient kings.

46 And Pharaoh turned to Moses and Aaron and said to them, I know not the Lord whom you have declared, neither will I send his people.

47 And they answered and said to the king, The Lord God of Gods is his name, and he proclaimed his name over us from the days of our ancestors, and sent us, saying, Go to Pharaoh and say unto him, Send my people that they may serve me.

48 Now therefore send us, that we may take a journey for three days in the wilderness, and there may sacrifice to him, for from the days of our going down to Egypt, he has not taken from our hands either burnt offering, oblation or sacrifice, and if thou wilt not send us, his anger will be kindled against thee, and he will smite Egypt either with the plague or with the sword.

49 And Pharaoh said to them, Tell me now his power and his might; and they said to him, He created the heaven and the earth, the seas and all their fishes, he formed the light, created the darkness, caused rain upon the earth and watered it, and made the herbage and grass to sprout, he created man and beast and the animals of the forest, the birds of the air and the fish of the sea, and by his mouth they live and die.

50 Surely he created thee in thy mother's womb, and put into thee the breath of life, and reared thee and placed thee upon the royal throne of Egypt, and he will take thy breath and soul from thee, and return thee to the ground whence thou wast taken.

51 And the anger of the king was kindled at their words, and he said to them, But who amongst all the Gods of nations can do this? my river is mine own, and I have made it for myself.

52 And he drove them from him, and he ordered the labor upon Israel to be more severe than it was yesterday and before.

53 And Moses and Aaron went out from the king's presence, and they saw the children of Israel in an evil condition for the task-masters had made their labor exceedingly heavy.

54 And Moses returned to the Lord and said, Why hast thou ill treated thy people? for since I came to speak to Pharaoh what thou didst send me for, he has exceedingly ill used the children of Israel.

55 And the Lord said to Moses, Behold thou wilt see that with an

outstretched hand and heavy plagues, Pharaoh will send the children of Israel from his land.

56 And Moses and Aaron dwelt amongst their brethren the children of Israel in Egypt.

57 And as for the children of Israel the Egyptians embittered their lives, with the heavy work which they imposed upon them.

Jasher 79

1 And in those days Moses was feeding the flock of Reuel the Midianite his father-in-law, beyond the wilderness of Sin, and the stick which he took from his father-in-law was in his hand.

2 And it came to pass one day that a kid of goats strayed from the flock, and Moses pursued it and it came to the mountain of God to Horeb.

3 And when he came to Horeb, the Lord appeared there unto him in the bush, and he found the bush burning with fire, but the fire had no power over the bush to consume it.

4 And Moses was greatly astonished at this sight, wherefore the bush was not consumed, and he approached to see this mighty thing, and the Lord called unto Moses out of the fire and commanded him to go down to Egypt, to Pharaoh king of Egypt, to send the children of Israel from his service.

5 And the Lord said unto Moses, Go, return to Egypt, for all those men who sought thy life are dead, and thou shalt speak unto Pharaoh to send forth the children of Israel from his land.

6 And the Lord showed him to do signs and wonders in Egypt before the eyes of Pharaoh and the eyes of his subjects, in order that they might believe that the Lord had sent him.

7 And Moses hearkened to all that the Lord had commanded him, and he returned to his father-in-law and told him the thing, and Reuel said to him, Go in peace.

8 And Moses rose up to go to Egypt, and he took his wife and sons with him, and he was at an inn in the road, and an angel of God came down, and sought an occasion against him.

9 And he wished to kill him on account of his first born son, because he had not circumcised him, and had transgressed the covenant which the Lord had made with Abraham.

10 For Moses had hearkened to the words of his father-in-law which he had spoken to him, not to circumcise his first born son, therefore he circumcised him not.

11 And Zipporah saw the angel of the Lord seeking an occasion against Moses, and she knew that this thing was owing to his not

having circumcised her son Gershom.

12 And Zipporah hastened and took of the sharp rock stones that were there, and she circumcised her son, and delivered her husband and her son from the hand of the angel of the Lord.

13 And Aaron the son of Amram, the brother of Moses, was in Egypt walking at the river side on that day.

14 And the Lord appeared to him in that place, and he said to him, Go now toward Moses in the wilderness, and he went and met him in the mountain of God, and he kissed him.

15 And Aaron lifted up his eyes, and saw Zipporah the wife of Moses and her children, and he said unto Moses, Who are these unto thee?

16 And Moses said unto him, They are my wife and sons, which God gave to me in Midian; and the thing grieved Aaron on account of the woman and her children.

17 And Aaron said to Moses, Send away the woman and her children that they may go to her father's house, and Moses hearkened to the words of Aaron, and did so.

18 And Zipporah returned with her children, and they went to the house of Reuel, and remained there until the time arrived when the Lord had visited his people, and brought them forth from Egypt from the hand at Pharaoh.

19 And Moses and Aaron came to Egypt to the community of the children of Israel, and they spoke to them all the words of the Lord, and the people rejoiced an exceeding great rejoicing.

20 And Moses and Aaron rose up early on the next day, and they went to the house of Pharaoh, and they took in their hands the stick of God.

21 And when they came to the king's gate, two young lions were confined there with iron instruments, and no person went out or came in from before them, unless those whom the king ordered to come, when the conjurors came and withdrew the lions by their incantations, and this brought them to the king.

22 And Moses hastened and lifted up the stick upon the lions, and he loosed them, and Moses and Aaron came into the king's house.

23 The lions also came with them in joy, and they followed them and rejoiced as a dog rejoices over his master when he comes from the field.

24 And when Pharaoh saw this thing he was astonished at it, and he was greatly terrified at the report, for their appearance was like the appearance of the children of God.

25 And Pharaoh said to Moses, What do you require? and they answered him, saying, The Lord God of the Hebrews has sent us to thee, to say, Send forth my people that they may serve me.

26 And when Pharaoh heard their words he was greatly terrified before them, and he said to them, Go today and come back to me tomorrow, and they did according to the word of the king.

27 And when they had gone Pharaoh sent for Balaam the magician and to Jannes and Jambres his sons, and to all the magicians and conjurors and counsellors which belonged to the king, and they all came and sat before the king.

28 And the king told them all the words which Moses and his brother Aaron had spoken to him, and the magicians said to the king, But how came the men to thee, on account of the lions which were confined at the gate?

29 And the king said, Because they lifted up their rod against the lions and loosed them, and came to me, and the lions also rejoiced at them as a dog rejoices to meet his master.

30 And Balaam the son of Beor the magician answered the king, saying, These are none else than magicians like ourselves.

31 Now therefore send for them, and let them come and we will try them, and the king did so.

32 And in the morning Pharaoh sent for Moses and Aaron to come before the king, and they took the rod of God, and came to the king and spoke to him, saying,

33 Thus said the Lord God of the Hebrews, Send my people that they may serve me.

34 And the king said to them, But who will believe you that you are the messengers of God and that you come to me by his order?

35 Now therefore give a wonder or sign in this matter, and then the words which you speak will be believed.

36 And Aaron hastened and threw the rod out of his hand before Pharaoh and before his servants, and the rod turned into a serpent.

37 And the sorcerers saw this and they cast each man his rod upon the ground and they became serpents.

38 And the serpent of Aaron's rod lifted up its head and opened its mouth to swallow the rods of the magicians.

39 And Balaam the magician answered and said, This thing has been from the days of old, that a serpent should swallow its fellow, and that living things devour each other.

40 Now therefore restore it to a rod as it was at first, and we will also restore our rods as they were at first, and if thy rod shall swallow our rods, then shall we know that the spirit of God is in thee, and if not, thou art only an artificer like unto ourselves.

41 And Aaron hastened and stretched forth his hand and caught hold of the serpent's tail and it became a rod in his hand, and the sorcerers did the like with their rods, and they got hold, each man of the tail of his serpent, and they became rods as at first.

42 And when they were restored to rods, the rod of Aaron swallowed up their rods.

43 And when the king saw this thing, he ordered the book of records that related to the kings of Egypt, to be brought, and they brought the book of records, the chronicles of the kings of Egypt, in which all the idols of Egypt were inscribed, for they thought of finding therein the name of Jehovah, but they found it not.

44 And Pharaoh said to Moses and Aaron, Behold I have not found the name of your God written in this book, and his name I know not.

45 And the counsellors and wise men answered the king, We have heard that the God of the Hebrews is a son of the wise, the son of ancient kings.

46 And Pharaoh turned to Moses and Aaron and said to them, I know not the Lord whom you have declared, neither will I send his people.

47 And they answered and said to the king, The Lord God of Gods is his name, and he proclaimed his name over us from the days of our ancestors, and sent us, saying, Go to Pharaoh and say unto him, Send my people that they may serve me.

48 Now therefore send us, that we may take a journey for three days in the wilderness, and there may sacrifice to him, for from the days of our going down to Egypt, he has not taken from our hands either burnt offering, oblation or sacrifice, and if thou wilt not send us, his anger will be kindled against thee, and he will smite Egypt either with the plague or with the sword.

49 And Pharaoh said to them, Tell me now his power and his might; and they said to him, He created the heaven and the earth, the seas and all their fishes, he formed the light, created the darkness, caused rain upon the earth and watered it, and made the herbage and grass to sprout, he created man and beast and the animals of the forest, the birds of the air and the fish of the sea, and by his mouth they live and die.

50 Surely he created thee in thy mother's womb, and put into thee the

breath of life, and reared thee and placed thee upon the royal throne of Egypt, and he will take thy breath and soul from thee, and return thee to the ground whence thou wast taken.

51 And the anger of the king was kindled at their words, and he said to them, But who amongst all the Gods of nations can do this? my river is mine own, and I have made it for myself.

52 And he drove them from him, and he ordered the labor upon Israel to be more severe than it was yesterday and before.

53 And Moses and Aaron went out from the king's presence, and they saw the children of Israel in an evil condition for the task-masters had made their labor exceedingly heavy.

54 And Moses returned to the Lord and said, Why hast thou ill treated thy people? for since I came to speak to Pharaoh what thou didst send me for, he has exceedingly ill used the children of Israel.

55 And the Lord said to Moses, Behold thou wilt see that with an outstretched hand and heavy plagues, Pharaoh will send the children of Israel from his land.

56 And Moses and Aaron dwelt amongst their brethren the children of Israel in Egypt.

57 And as for the children of Israel the Egyptians embittered their lives, with the heavy work which they imposed upon them.

Jasher 81

1 And the children of Israel journeyed from Rameses to Succoth, about six hundred thousand men on foot, besides the little ones and their wives.

2 Also a mixed multitude went up with them, and flocks and herds, even much cattle.

3 And the sojourning of the children of Israel, who dwelt in the land of Egypt in hard labor, was two hundred and ten years.

4 And at the end of two hundred and ten years, the Lord brought forth the children of Israel from Egypt with a strong hand.

5 And the children of Israel traveled from Egypt and from Goshen and from Rameses, and encamped in Succoth on the fifteenth day of the first month.

6 And the Egyptians buried all their first born whom the Lord had smitten, and all the Egyptians buried their slain for three days.

7 And the children of Israel traveled from Succoth and encamped in Ethom, at the end of the wilderness.

8 And on the third day after the Egyptians had buried their first born,

many men rose up from Egypt and went after Israel to make them return to Egypt, for they repented that they had sent the Israelites away from their servitude.

9 And one man said to his neighbor, Surely Moses and Aaron spoke to Pharaoh, saying, We will go a three days' journey in the wilderness and sacrifice to the Lord our God.

10 Now therefore let us rise up early in the morning and cause them to return, and it shall be that if they return with us to Egypt to their masters, then shall we know that there is faith in them, but if they will not return, then will we fight with them, and make them come back with great power and a strong hand.

11 And all the nobles of Pharaoh rose up in the morning, and with them about seven hundred thousand men, and they went forth from Egypt on that day, and came to the place where the children of Israel were.

12 And all the Egyptians saw and behold Moses and Aaron and all the children of Israel were sitting before Pi-hahiroth, eating and drinking and celebrating the feast of the Lord.

13 And all the Egyptians said to the children of Israel, Surely you said, We will go a journey for three days in the wilderness and sacrifice to our God and return.

14 Now therefore this day makes five days since you went, why do you not return to your masters?

15 And Moses and Aaron answered them, saying, Because the Lord our God has testified in us, saying, You shall no more return to Egypt, but we will betake ourselves to a land flowing with milk and honey, as the Lord our God had sworn to our ancestors to give to us.

16 And when the nobles of Egypt saw that the children of Israel did not hearken to them, to return to Egypt, they girded themselves to fight with Israel.

17 And the Lord strengthened the hearts of the children of Israel over the Egyptians, that they gave them a severe beating, and the battle was sore upon the Egyptians, and all the Egyptians fled from before the children of Israel, for many of them perished by the hand of Israel.

18 And the nobles of Pharaoh went to Egypt and told Pharaoh, saying, The children of Israel have fled, and will no more return to Egypt, and in this manner did Moses and Aaron speak to us.

19 And Pharaoh heard this thing, and his heart and the hearts of all his subjects were turned against Israel, and they repented that they had sent Israel; and all the Egyptians advised Pharaoh to pursue the children of

Israel to make them come back to their burdens.

20 And they said each man to his brother, What is this which we have done, that we have sent Israel from our servitude?

21 And the Lord strengthened the hearts of all the Egyptians to pursue the Israelites, for the Lord desired to overthrow the Egyptians in the Red Sea.

22 And Pharaoh rose up and harnessed his chariot, and he ordered all the Egyptians to assemble, not one man was left excepting the little ones and the women.

23 And all the Egyptians went forth with Pharaoh to pursue the children of Israel, and the camp of Egypt was an exceedingly large and heavy camp, about ten hundred thousand men.

24 And the whole of this camp went and pursued the children of Israel to bring them back to Egypt, and they reached them encamping by the Red Sea.

25 And the children of Israel lifted up their eyes, and beheld all the Egyptians pursuing them, and the children of Israel were greatly terrified at them, and the children of Israel cried to the Lord.

26 And on account of the Egyptians, the children of Israel divided themselves into four divisions, and they were divided in their opinions, for they were afraid of the Egyptians, and Moses spoke to each of them.

27 The first division was of the children of Reuben, Simeon, and Issachar, and they resolved to cast themselves into the sea, for they were exceedingly afraid of the Egyptians.

28 And Moses said to them, Fear not, stand still and see the salvation of the Lord which He will effect this day for you.

29 The second division was of the children of Zebulun, Benjamin and Naphtali, and they resolved to go back to Egypt with the Egyptians.

30 And Moses said to them, Fear not, for as you have seen the Egyptians this day, so shall you see them no more for ever.

31 The third division was of the children of Judah and Joseph, and they resolved to go to meet the Egyptians to fight with them.

32 And Moses said to them, Stand in your places, for the Lord will fight for you, and you shall remain silent.

33 And the fourth division was of the children of Levi, Gad, and Asher, and they resolved to go into the midst of the Egyptians to confound them, and Moses said to them, Remain in your stations and fear not,

only call unto the Lord that he may save you out of their hands.

34 After this Moses rose up from amidst the people, and he prayed to the Lord and said,

35 O Lord God of the whole earth, save now thy people whom thou didst bring forth from Egypt, and let not the Egyptians boast that power and might are theirs.

36 So the Lord said to Moses, Why dost thou cry unto me? speak to the children of Israel that they shall proceed, and do thou stretch out thy rod upon the sea and divide it, and the children of Israel shall pass through it.

37 And Moses did so, and he lifted up his rod upon the sea and divided it.

38 And the waters of the sea were divided into twelve parts, and the children of Israel passed through on foot, with shoes, as a man would pass through a prepared road.

39 And the Lord manifested to the children of Israel his wonders in Egypt and in the sea by the hand of Moses and Aaron.

40 And when the children of Israel had entered the sea, the Egyptians came after them, and the waters of the sea resumed upon them, and they all sank in the water, and not one man was left excepting Pharaoh, who gave thanks to the Lord and believed in him, therefore the Lord did not cause him to perish at that time with the Egyptians.

41 And the Lord ordered an angel to take him from amongst the Egyptians, who cast him upon the land of Ninevah and he reigned over it for a long time.

42 And on that day the Lord saved Israel from the hand of Egypt, and all the children of Israel saw that the Egyptians had perished, and they beheld the great hand of the Lord, in what he had performed in Egypt and in the sea.

43 Then sang Moses and the children of Israel this song unto the Lord, on the day when the Lord caused the Egyptians to fall before them.

44 And all Israel sang in concert, saying, I will sing to the Lord for He is greatly exalted, the horse and his rider has he cast into the sea; behold it is written in the book of the law of God.

45 After this the children of Israel proceeded on their journey, and encamped in Marah, and the Lord gave to the children of Israel statutes and judgments in that place in Marah, and the Lord commanded the children of Israel to walk in all his ways and to serve him.

46 And they journeyed from Marah and came to Elim, and in Elim were twelve springs of water and seventy

date trees, and the children encamped there by the waters.

47 And they journeyed from Elim and came to the wilderness of Sin, on the fifteenth day of the second month after their departure from Egypt.

48 At that time the Lord gave the manna to the children of Israel to eat, and the Lord caused food to rain from heaven for the children of Israel day by day.

49 And the children of Israel ate the manna for forty years, all the days that they were in the wilderness, until they came to the land of Canaan to possess it.

50 And they proceeded from the wilderness of Sin and encamped in Alush.

51 And they proceeded from Alush and encamped in Rephidim.

52 And when the children of Israel were in Rephidim, Amalek the son of Eliphaz, the son of Esau, the brother of Zepho, came to fight with Israel.

53 And he brought with him eight hundred and one thousand men, magicians and conjurers, and he prepared for battle with Israel in Rephidim.

54 And they carried on a great and severe battle against Israel, and the Lord delivered Amalek and his people into the hands of Moses and the children of Israel, and into the hand of Joshua, the son of Nun, the Ephrathite, the servant of Moses.

55 And the children of Israel smote Amalek and his people at the edge of the sword, but the battle was very sore upon the children of Israel.

56 And the Lord said to Moses, Write this thing as a memorial for thee in a book, and place it in the hand of Joshua, the son of Nun, thy servant, and thou shalt command the children of Israel, saying, When thou shalt come to the land of Canaan, thou shalt utterly efface the remembrance of Amalek from under heaven.

57 And Moses did so, and he took the book and wrote upon it these words, saying,

58 Remember what Amalek has done to thee in the road when thou wentest forth from Egypt.

59 Who met thee in the road and smote thy rear, even those that were feeble behind thee when thou wast faint and weary.

60 Therefore it shall be when the Lord thy God shall have given thee rest from all thine enemies round about in the land which the Lord thy God giveth thee for an inheritance, to possess it, that thou shalt blot out the remembrance of Amalek from under heaven, thou shalt not forget it.

61 And the king who shall have pity on Amalek, or upon his memory or

upon his seed, behold I will require it of him, and I will cut him off from amongst his people.

62 And Moses wrote all these things in a book, and he enjoined the children of Israel respecting all these matters.

Jasher 82

1 And the children of Israel proceeded from Rephidim and they encamped in the wilderness of Sinai, in the third month from their going forth from Egypt.

2 At that time came Reuel the Midianite, the father-in-law of Moses, with Zipporah his daughter and her two sons, for he had heard of the wonders of the Lord which he had done to Israel, that he had delivered them from the hand of Egypt.

3 And Reuel came to Moses to the wilderness where he was encamped, where was the mountain of God.

4 And Moses went forth to meet his father-in-law with great honor, and all Israel was with him.

5 And Reuel and his children remained amongst the Israelites for many days, and Reuel knew the Lord from that day forward.

6 And in the third month from the children of Israel's departure from Egypt, on the sixth day thereof, the Lord gave to Israel the ten commandments on Mount Sinai.

7 And all Israel heard all these commandments, and all Israel rejoiced exceedingly in the Lord on that day.

8 And the glory of the Lord rested upon Mount Sinai, and he called to Moses, and Moses came in the midst of a cloud and ascended the mountain.

9 And Moses was upon the mount forty days and forty nights; he ate no bread and drank no water, and the Lord instructed him in the statutes and judgments in order to teach the children of Israel.

10 And the Lord wrote the ten commandments which he had commanded the children of Israel upon two tablets of stone, which he gave to Moses to command the children of Israel.

11 And at the end of forty days and forty nights, when the Lord had finished speaking to Moses on Mount Sinai, then the Lord gave to Moses the tablets of stone, written with the finger of God.

12 And when the children of Israel saw that Moses tarried to come down from the mount, they gathered round Aaron, and said, As for this man Moses we know not what has become of him.

13 Now therefore rise up, make unto us a god who shall go before us, so that thou shalt not die.

14 And Aaron was greatly afraid of the people, and he ordered them to bring him gold and he made it into a molten calf for the people.

15 And the Lord said to Moses, before he had come down from the mount, Get thee down, for thy people whom thou didst bring forth from Egypt have corrupted themselves.

16 They have made to themselves a molten calf, and have bowed down to it, now therefore leave me, that I may consume them from off the earth, for they are a stiffnecked people.

17 And Moses besought the countenance of the Lord, and he prayed to the Lord for the people on account of the calf which they had made, and he afterward descended from the mount and in his hands were the two tablets of stone, which God had given him to command the Israelites.

18 And when Moses approached the camp and saw the calf which the people had made, the anger of Moses was kindled and he broke the tablets under the mount.

19 And Moses came to the camp and he took the calf and burned it with fire, and ground it till it became fine dust, and strewed it upon the water and gave it to the Israelites to drink.

20 And there died of the people by the swords of each other about three thousand men who had made the calf.

21 And on the morrow Moses said to the people, I will go up to the Lord, peradventure I may make atonement for your sins which you have sinned to the Lord.

22 And Moses again went up to the Lord, and he remained with the Lord forty days and forty nights.

23 And during the forty days did Moses entreat the Lord in behalf of the children of Israel, and the Lord hearkened to the prayer of Moses, and the Lord was entreated of him in behalf of Israel.

24 Then spake the Lord to Moses to hew two stone tablets and to bring them up to the Lord, who would write upon them the ten commandments.

25 Now Moses did so, and he came down and hewed the two tablets and went up to Mount Sinai to the Lord, and the Lord wrote the ten commandments upon the tablets.

26 And Moses remained yet with the Lord forty days and forty nights, and the Lord instructed him in statutes and judgments to impart to Israel.

27 And the Lord commanded him respecting the children of Israel that they should make a sanctuary for the Lord, that his name might rest therein, and the Lord showed him the likeness of the sanctuary and the likeness of all its vessels.

28 And at the end of the forty days, Moses came down from the mount and the two tablets were in his hand.

29 And Moses came to the children of Israel and spoke to them all the words of the Lord, and he taught them laws, statutes and judgments which the Lord had taught him.

30 And Moses told the children of Israel the word of the Lord, that a sanctuary should be made for him, to dwell amongst the children of Israel.

31 And the people rejoiced greatly at all the good which the Lord had spoken to them, through Moses, and they said, We will do all that the Lord has spoken to thee.

32 And the people rose up like one man and they made generous offerings to the sanctuary of the Lord, and each man brought the offering of the Lord for the work of the sanctuary, and for all its service.

33 And all the children of Israel brought each man of all that was found in his possession for the work of the sanctuary of the Lord, gold, silver and brass, and every thing that was serviceable for the sanctuary.

34 And all the wise men who were practiced in work came and made the sanctuary of the Lord, according to all that the Lord had commanded, every man in the work in which he had been practiced; and all the wise men in heart made the sanctuary, and its furniture and all the vessels for the holy service, as the Lord had commanded Moses.

35 And the work of the sanctuary of the tabernacle was completed at the end of five months, and the children of Israel did all that the Lord had commanded Moses.

36 And they brought the sanctuary and all its furniture to Moses; like unto the representation which the Lord had shown to Moses, so did the children of Israel.

37 And Moses saw the work, and behold they did it as the Lord had commanded him, so Moses blessed them.

Jasher 83

1 And in the twelfth month, in the twenty-third day of the month, Moses took Aaron and his sons, and he dressed them in their garments, and anointed them and did unto them as the Lord had commanded him, and Moses brought up all the offerings which the Lord had on that day commanded him.

2 Moses afterward took Aaron and his sons and said to them, For seven days shall you remain at the door of the tabernacle, for thus am I commanded.

3 And Aaron and his sons did all that the Lord had commanded them through Moses, and they remained for seven days at the door of the tabernacle.

4 And on the eighth day, being the first day of the first month, in the second year from the Israelites' departure from Egypt, Moses erected the sanctuary, and Moses put up all the furniture of the tabernacle and all the furniture of the sanctuary, and he did all that the Lord had commanded him.

5 And Moses called to Aaron and his sons, and they brought the burnt offering and the sin offering for themselves and the children of Israel, as the Lord had commanded Moses.

6 On that day the two sons of Aaron, Nadab and Abihu, took strange fire and brought it before the Lord who had not commanded them, and a fire went forth from before the Lord, and consumed them, and they died before the Lord on that day.

7 Then on the day when Moses had completed to erect the sanctuary, the princes of the children of Israel began to bring their offerings before the Lord for the dedication of the altar.

8 And they brought up their offerings each prince for one day, a prince each day for twelve days.

9 And all the offerings which they brought, each man in his day, one silver charger weighing one hundred and thirty shekels, one silver bowl of seventy shekels after the shekel of the sanctuary, both of them full of fine flour, mingled with oil for a meat offering.

10 One spoon, weighing ten shekels of gold, full of incense.

11 One young bullock, one ram, one lamb of the first year for a burnt offering.

12 And one kid of the goats for a sin offering.

13 And for a sacrifice of peace offering, two oxen, five rams, five he-goats, five lambs of a year old.

14 Thus did the twelve princes of Israel day by day, each man in his day.

15 And it was after this, in the thirteenth day of the month, that Moses commanded the children of Israel to observe the Passover.

16 And the children of Israel kept the Passover in its season in the fourteenth day of the month, as the Lord had commanded Moses, so did the children of Israel.

17 And in the second month, on the first day thereof, the Lord spoke unto Moses, saying,

18 Number the heads of all the males of the children of Israel from twenty years old and upward, thou and thy brother Aaron and the twelve princes of Israel.

19 And Moses did so, and Aaron came with the twelve princes of Israel, and they numbered the

children of Israel in the wilderness of Sinai.

20 And the numbers of the children of Israel by the houses of their fathers, from twenty years old and upward, were six hundred and three thousand, five hundred and fifty.

21 But the children of Levi were not numbered amongst their brethren the children of Israel.

22 And the number of all the males of the children of Israel from one month old and upward, was twenty-two thousand, two hundred and seventy-three.

23 And the number of the children of Levi from one month old and above, was twenty-two thousand.

24 And Moses placed the priests and the Levites each man to his service and to his burden to serve the sanctuary of the tabernacle, as the Lord had commanded Moses.

25 And on the twentieth day of the month, the cloud was taken away from the tabernacle of testimony.

26 At that time the children of Israel continued their journey from the wilderness of Sinai, and they took a journey of three days, and the cloud rested upon the wilderness of Paran; there the anger of the Lord was kindled against Israel, for they had provoked the Lord in asking him for meat, that they might eat.

27 And the Lord hearkened to their voice, and gave them meat which they ate for one month.

28 But after this the anger of the Lord was kindled against them, and he smote them with a great slaughter, and they were buried there in that place.

29 And the children of Israel called that place Kebroth Hattaavah, because there they buried the people that lusted flesh.

30 And they departed from Kebroth Hattaavah and pitched in Hazeroth, which is in the wilderness of Paran.

31 And whilst the children of Israel were in Hazeroth, the anger of the Lord was kindled against Miriam on account of Moses, and she became leprous, white as snow.

32 And she was confined without the camp for seven days, until she had been received again after her leprosy.

33 The children of Israel afterward departed from Hazeroth, and pitched in the end of the wilderness of Paran.

34 At that time, the Lord spoke to Moses to send twelve men from the children of Israel, one man to a tribe, to go and explore the land of Canaan.

35 And Moses sent the twelve men, and they came to the land of Canaan to search and examine it, and they

explored the whole land from the wilderness of Sin to Rechob as thou comest to Chamoth.

36 And at the end of forty days they came to Moses and Aaron, and they brought him word as it was in their hearts, and ten of the men brought up an evil report to the children of Israel, of the land which they had explored, saying, It is better for us to return to Egypt than to go to this land, a land that consumes its inhabitants.

37 But Joshua the son of Nun, and Caleb the son of Jephuneh, who were of those that explored the land, said, The land is exceedingly good.

38 If the Lord delight in us, then he will bring us to this land and give it to us, for it is a land flowing with milk and honey.

39 But the children of Israel would not hearken to them, and they hearkened to the words of the ten men who had brought up an evil report of the land.

40 And the Lord heard the murmurings of the children of Israel and he was angry and swore, saying,

41 Surely not one man of this wicked generation shall see the land from twenty years old and upward excepting Caleb the son of Jephuneh and Joshua the son of Nun.

42 But surely this wicked generation shall perish in this wilderness, and their children shall come to the land and they shall possess it; so the anger of the Lord was kindled against Israel, and he made them wander in the wilderness for forty years until the end of that wicked generation, because they did not follow the Lord.

43 And the people dwelt in the wilderness of Paran a long time, and they afterward proceeded to the wilderness by the way of the Red Sea.

Jasher 84

1 At that time Korah the son of Jetzer the son of Kehath the son of Levi, took many men of the children of Israel, and they rose up and quarreled with Moses and Aaron and the whole congregation.

2 And the Lord was angry with them, and the earth opened its mouth, and swallowed them up, with their houses and all belonging to them, and all the men belonging to Korah.

3 And after this God made the people go round by the way of Mount Seir for a long time.

4 At that time the Lord said unto Moses, Provoke not a war against the children of Esau, for I will not give to you of any thing belonging to them, as much as the sole of the foot could tread upon, for I have given

Mount Seir for an inheritance to Esau.

5 Therefore did the children of Esau fight against the children of Seir in former times, and the Lord had delivered the children of Seir into the hands of the children of Esau, and destroyed them from before them, and the children of Esau dwelt in their stead unto this day.

6 Therefore the Lord said to the children of Israel, Fight not against the children of Esau your brethren, for nothing in their land belongs to you, but you may buy food of them for money and eat it, and you may buy water of them for money and drink it.

7 And the children of Israel did according to the word of the Lord.

8 And the children of Israel went about the wilderness, going round by the way of Mount Sinai for a long time, and touched not the children of Esau, and they continued in that district for nineteen years.

9 At that time died Latinus king of the children of Chittim, in the forty-fifth year of his reign, which is the fourteenth year of the children of Israel's departure from Egypt.

10 And they buried him in his place which he had built for himself in the land of Chittim, and Abimnas reigned in his place for thirty-eight years.

11 And the children of Israel passed the boundary of the children of Esau in those days, at the end of nineteen years, and they came and passed the road of the wilderness of Moab.

12 And the Lord said to Moses, besiege not Moab, and do not fight against them, for I will give you nothing of their land.

13 And the children of Israel passed the road of the wilderness of Moab for nineteen years, and they did not fight against them.

14 And in the thirty-sixth year of the children of Israel's departing from Egypt the Lord smote the heart of Sihon, king of the Amorites, and he waged war, and went forth to fight against the children of Moab.

15 And Sihon sent messengers to Beor the son of Janeas, the son of Balaam, counsellor to the king of Egypt, and to Balaam his son, to curse Moab, in order that it might be delivered into the hand of Sihon.

16 And the messengers went and brought Beor the son of Janeas, and Balaam his son, from Pethor in Mesopotamia, so Beor and Balaam his son came to the city of Sihon and they cursed Moab and their king in the presence of Sihon king of the Amorites.

17 So Sihon went out with his whole army, and he went to Moab and fought against them, and he subdued them, and the Lord

delivered them into his hands, and Sihon slew the king of Moab.

18 And Sihon took all the cities of Moab in the battle; he also took Heshbon from them, for Heshbon was one of the cities of Moab, and Sihon placed his princes and his nobles in Heshbon, and Heshbon belonged to Sihon in those days.

19 Therefore the parable speakers Beor and Balaam his son uttered these words, saying, Come unto Heshbon, the city of Sihon will be built and established.

20 Woe unto thee Moab! thou art lost, O people of Kemosh! behold it is written upon the book of the law of God.

21 And when Sihon had conquered Moab, he placed guards in the cities which he had taken from Moab, and a considerable number of the children of Moab fell in battle into the hand of Sihon, and he made a great capture of them, sons and daughters, and he slew their king; so Sihon turned back to his own land.

22 And Sihon gave numerous presents of silver and gold to Beor and Balaam his son, and he dismissed them, and they went to Mesopotamia to their home and country.

23 At that time all the children of Israel passed from the road of the wilderness of Moab, and returned and surrounded the wilderness of Edom.

24 So the whole congregation came to the wilderness of Sin in the first month of the fortieth year from their departure from Egypt, and the children of Israel dwelt there in Kadesh, of the wilderness of Sin, and Miriam died there and she was buried there.

25 At that time Moses sent messengers to Hadad king of Edom, saying, Thus says thy brother Israel, Let me pass I pray thee through thy land, we will not pass through field or vineyard, we will not drink the water of the well; we will walk in the king's road.

26 And Edom said to him, Thou shalt not pass through my country, and Edom went forth to meet the children of Israel with a mighty people.

27 And the children of Esau refused to let the children of Israel pass through their land, so the Israelites removed from them and fought not against them.

28 For before this the Lord had commanded the children of Israel, saying, You shall not fight against the children of Esau, therefore the Israelites removed from them and did not fight against them.

29 So the children of Israel departed from Kadesh, and all the people came to Mount Hor.

30 At that time the Lord said to Moses, Tell thy brother Aaron that he shall die there, for he shall not come to the land which I have given to the children of Israel.

31 And Aaron went up, at the command of the Lord, to Mount Hor, in the fortieth year, in the fifth month, in the first day of the month.

32 And Aaron was one hundred and twenty-three years old when he died in Mount Hor

Jasher 85

1 And king Arad the Canaanite, who dwelt in the south, heard that the Israelites had come by the way of the spies, and he arranged his forces to fight against the Israelites.

2 And the children of Israel were greatly afraid of him, for he had a great and heavy army, so the children of Israel resolved to return to Egypt.

3 And the children of Israel turned back about the distance of three days' journey unto Maserath Beni Jaakon, for they were greatly afraid on account of the king Arad.

4 And the children of Israel would not get back to their places, so they remained in Beni Jaakon for thirty days.

5 And when the children of Levi saw that the children of Israel would not turn back, they were jealous for the sake of the Lord, and they rose up

and fought against the Israelites their brethren, and slew of them a great body, and forced them to turn back to their place, Mount Hor.

6 And when they returned, king Arad was still arranging his host for battle against the Israelites.

7 And Israel vowed a vow, saying, If thou wilt deliver this people into my hand, then I will utterly destroy their cities.

8 And the Lord hearkened to the voice of Israel, and he delivered the Canaanites into their hand, and he utterly destroyed them and their cities, and he called the name of the place Hormah.

9 And the children of Israel journeyed from Mount Hor and pitched in Oboth, and they journeyed from Oboth and they pitched at Ije-abarim, in the border of Moab.

10 And the children of Israel sent to Moab, saying, Let us pass now through thy land into our place, but the children of Moab would not suffer the children of Israel to pass through their land, for the children of Moab were greatly afraid lest the children of Israel should do unto them as Sihon king of the Amorites had done to them, who had taken their land and had slain many of them.

11 Therefore Moab would not suffer the Israelites to pass through his land, and the Lord commanded the children of Israel, saying, That they

should not fight against Moab, so the Israelites removed from Moab.

12 And the children of Israel journeyed from the border of Moab, and they came to the other side of Arnon, the border of Moab, between Moab and the Amorites, and they pitched in the border of Sihon, king of the Amorites, in the wilderness of Kedemoth.

13 And the children of Israel sent messengers to Sihon, king of the Amorites, saying,

14 Let us pass through thy land, we will not turn into the fields or into the vineyards, we will go along by the king's highway until we shall have passed thy border, but Sihon would not suffer the Israelites to pass.

15 So Sihon collected all the people of the Amorites and went forth into the wilderness to meet the children of Israel, and he fought against Israel in Jahaz.

16 And the Lord delivered Sihon king of the Amorites into the hand of the children of Israel, and Israel smote all the people of Sihon with the edge of the sword and avenged the cause of Moab.

17 And the children of Israel took possession of the land of Sihon from Aram unto Jabuk, unto the children of Ammon, and they took all the spoil of the cities.

18 And Israel took all these cities, and Israel dwelt in all the cities of the Amorites.

19 And all the children of Israel resolved to fight against the children of Ammon, to take their land also.

20 So the Lord said to the children of Israel, Do not besiege the children of Ammon, neither stir up battle against them, for I will give nothing to you of their land, and the children of Israel hearkened to the word of the Lord, and did not fight against the children of Ammon.

21 And the children of Israel turned and went up by the way of Bashan to the land of Og, king of Bashan, and Og the king of Bashan went out to meet the Israelites in battle, and he had with him many valiant men, and a very strong force from the people of the Amorites.

22 And Og king of Bashan was a very powerful man, but Naaron his son was exceedingly powerful, even stronger than he was.

23 And Og said in his heart, Behold now the whole camp of Israel takes up a space of three parsa, now will I smite them at once without sword or spear.

24 And Og went up Mount Jahaz, and took therefrom one large stone, the length of which was three parsa, and he placed it on his head, and resolved to throw it upon the camp of

the children of Israel, to smite all the Israelites with that stone.

25 And the angel of the Lord came and pierced the stone upon the head of Og, and the stone fell upon the neck of Og that Og fell to the earth on account of the weight of the stone upon his neck.

26 At that time the Lord said to the children of Israel, Be not afraid of him, for I have given him and all his people and all his land into your hand, and you shall do to him as you did to Sihon.

27 And Moses went down to him with a small number of the children of Israel, and Moses smote Og with a stick at the ankles of his feet and slew him.

28 The children of Israel afterward pursued the children of Og and all his people, and they beat and destroyed them till there was no remnant left of them.

29 Moses afterward sent some of the children of Israel to spy out Jaazer, for Jaazer was a very famous city.

30 And the spies went to Jaazer and explored it, and the spies trusted in the Lord, and they fought against the men of Jaazer.

31 And these men took Jaazer and its villages, and the Lord delivered them into their hand, and they drove out the Amorites who had been there.

32 And the children of Israel took the land of the two kings of the Amorites, sixty cities which were on the other side of Jordan, from the brook of Arnon unto Mount Herman.

33 And the children of Israel journeyed and came into the plain of Moab which is on this side of Jordan, by Jericho.

34 And the children of Moab heard all the evil which the children of Israel had done to the two kings of the Amorites, to Sihon and Og, so all the men of Moab were greatly afraid of the Israelites.

35 And the elders of Moab said, Behold the two kings of the Amorites, Sihon and Og, who were more powerful than all the kings of the earth, could not stand against the children of Israel, how then can we stand before them?

36 Surely they sent us a message before now to pass through our land on their way, and we would not suffer them, now they will turn upon us with their heavy swords and destroy us; and Moab was distressed on account of the children of Israel, and they were greatly afraid of them, and they counselled together what was to be done to the children of Israel.

37 And the elders of Moab resolved and took one of their men, Balak the son of Zippor the Moabite, and made

him king over them at that time, and Balak was a very wise man.

38 And the elders of Moab rose up and sent to the children of Midian to make peace with them, for a great battle and enmity had been in those days between Moab and Midian, from the days of Hadad the son of Bedad king of Edom, who smote Midian in the field of Moab, unto these days.

39 And the children of Moab sent to the children of Midian, and they made peace with them, and the elders of Midian came to the land of Moab to make peace in behalf of the children of Midian.

40 And the elders of Moab counselled with the elders of Midian what to do in order to save their lives from Israel.

41 And all the children of Moab said to the elders of Midian, Now therefore the children of Israel lick up all that are round about us, as the ox licks up the grass of the field, for thus did they do to the two kings of the Amorites who are stronger than we are.

42 And the elders of Midian said to Moab, We have heard that at the time when Sihon king of the Amorites fought against you, when he prevailed over you and took your land, he had sent to Beor the son of Janeas and to Balaam his son from Mesopotamia, and they came and

cursed you; therefore did the hand of Sihon prevail over you, that he took your land.

43 Now therefore send you also to Balaam his son, for he still remains in his land, and give him his hire, that he may come and curse all the people of whom you are afraid; so the elders of Moab heard this thing, and it pleased them to send to Balaam the son of Beor.

44 So Balak the son of Zippor king of Moab sent messengers to Balaam, saying,

45 Behold there is a people come out from Egypt, behold they cover the face of the earth, and they abide over against me.

46 Now therefore come and curse this people for me, for they are too mighty for me, peradventure I shall prevail to fight against them, and drive them out, for I heard that he whom thou blessest is blessed, and whom thou cursest is cursed.

47 So the messengers of Balak went to Balaam and brought Balaam to curse the people to fight against Moab.

48 And Balaam came to Balak to curse Israel, and the Lord said to Balaam, Curse not this people for it is blessed.

49 And Balak urged Balaam day by day to curse Israel, but Balaam hearkened not to Balak on account

of the word of the Lord which he had spoken to Balaam.

50 And when Balak saw that Balaam would not accede to his wish, he rose up and went home, and Balaam also returned to his land and he went from there to Midian.

51 And the children of Israel journeyed from the plain of Moab, and pitched by Jordan from Beth-jesimoth even unto Abel-shittim, at the end of the plains of Moab.

52 And when the children of Israel abode in the plain of Shittim, they began to commit whoredom with the daughters of Moab.

53 And the children of Israel approached Moab, and the children of Moab pitched their tents opposite to the camp of the children of Israel.

54 And the children of Moab were afraid of the children of Israel, and the children of Moab took all their daughters and their wives of beautiful aspect and comely appearance, and dressed them in gold and silver and costly garments.

55 And the children of Moab seated those women at the door of their tents, in order that the children of Israel might see them and turn to them, and not fight against Moab.

56 And all the children of Moab did this thing to the children of Israel, and every man placed his wife and daughter at the door of his tent, and all the children of Israel saw the act of the children of Moab, and the children of Israel turned to the daughters of Moab and coveted them, and they went to them.

57 And it came to pass that when a Hebrew came to the door of the tent of Moab, and saw a daughter of Moab and desired her in his heart, and spoke with her at the door of the tent that which he desired, whilst they were speaking together the men of the tent would come out and speak to the Hebrew like unto these words:

58 Surely you know that we are brethren, we are all the descendants of Lot and the descendants of Abraham his brother, wherefore then will you not remain with us, and wherefore will you not eat our bread and our sacrifice?

59 And when the children of Moab had thus overwhelmed him with their speeches, and enticed him by their flattering words, they seated him in the tent and cooked and sacrificed for him, and he ate of their sacrifice and of their bread.

60 They then gave him wine and he drank and became intoxicated, and they placed before him a beautiful damsel, and he did with her as he liked, for he knew not what he was doing, as he had drunk plentifully of wine.

61 Thus did the children of Moab to Israel in that place, in the plain of Shittim, and the anger of the Lord was kindled against Israel on account of this matter, and he sent a pestilence amongst them, and there died of the Israelites twenty-four thousand men.

62 Now there was a man of the children of Simeon whose name was Zimri, the son of Salu, who connected himself with the Midianite Cosbi, the daughter of Zur, king of Midian, in the sight of all the children of Israel.

63 And Phineas the son of Elazer, the son of Aaron the priest, saw this wicked thing which Zimri had done, and he took a spear and rose up and went after them, and pierced them both and slew them, and the pestilence ceased from the children of Israel.

Jasher 86

1 At that time after the pestilence, the Lord said to Moses, and to Elazer the son of Aaron the priest, saying,

2 Number the heads of the whole community of the children of Israel, from twenty years old and upward, all that went forth in the army.

3 And Moses and Elazer numbered the children of Israel after their families, and the number of all Israel was seven hundred thousand, seven hundred and thirty.

4 And the number of the children of Levi, from one month old and upward, was twenty-three thousand, and amongst these there was not a man of those numbered by Moses and Aaron in the wilderness of Sinai.

5 For the Lord had told them that they would die in the wilderness, so they all died, and not one had been left of them excepting Caleb the son of Jephuneh, and Joshua the son of Nun.

6 And it was after this that the Lord said to Moses, Say unto the children of Israel to avenge upon Midian the cause of their brethren the children of Israel.

7 And Moses did so, and the children of Israel chose from amongst them twelve thousand men, being one thousand to a tribe, and they went to Midian.

8 And the children of Israel warred against Midian, and they slew every male, also the five princes of Midian, and Balaam the son of Beor did they slay with the sword.

9 And the children of Israel took the wives of Midian captive, with their little ones and their cattle, and all belonging to them.

10 And they took all the spoil and all the prey, and they brought it to Moses and to Elazer to the plains of Moab.

11 And Moses and Elazer and all the princes of the congregation went forth to meet them with joy.

12 And they divided all the spoil of Midian, and the children of Israel had been revenged upon Midian for the cause of their brethren the children of Israel.

Jasher 87

1 At that time the Lord said to Moses, Behold thy days are approaching to an end, take now Joshua the son of Nun thy servant and place him in the tabernacle, and I will command him, and Moses did so.

2 And the Lord appeared in the tabernacle in a pillar of cloud, and the pillar of cloud stood at the entrance of the tabernacle.

3 And the Lord commanded Joshua the son of Nun and said unto him, Be strong and courageous, for thou shalt bring the children of Israel to the land which I swore to give them, and I will be with thee.

4 And Moses said to Joshua, Be strong and courageous, for thou wilt make the children of Israel inherit the land, and the Lord will be with thee, he will not leave thee nor forsake thee, be not afraid nor disheartened.

5 And Moses called to all the children of Israel and said to them, You have seen all the good which the Lord your God has done for you in the wilderness.

6 Now therefore observe all the words of this law, and walk in the way of the Lord your God, turn not from the way which the Lord has commanded you, either to the right or to the left.

7 And Moses taught the children of Israel statutes and judgments and laws to do in the land as the Lord had commanded him.

8 And he taught them the way of the Lord and his laws; behold they are written upon the book of the law of God which he gave to the children of Israel by the hand of Moses.

9 And Moses finished commanding the children of Israel, and the Lord said to him, saying, Go up to the Mount Abarim and die there, and be gathered unto thy people as Aaron thy brother was gathered.

10 And Moses went up as the Lord had commanded him, and he died there in the land of Moab by the order of the Lord, in the fortieth year from the Israelites going forth from the land of Egypt.

11 And the children of Israel wept for Moses in the plains of Moab for thirty days, and the days of weeping and mourning for Moses were completed.

Jasher 88

1 And it was after the death of Moses that the Lord said to Joshua the son of Nun, saying,

2 Rise up and pass the Jordan to the land which I have given to the children of Israel, and thou shalt make the children of Israel inherit the land.

3 Every place upon which the sole of your feet shall tread shall belong to you, from the wilderness of Lebanon unto the great river the river of Perath shall be your boundary.

4 No man shall stand up against thee all the days of thy life; as I was with Moses, so will I be with thee, only be strong and of good courage to observe all the law which Moses commanded thee, turn not from the way either to the right or to the left, in order that thou mayest prosper in all that thou doest.

5 And Joshua commanded the officers of Israel, saying, Pass through the camp and command the people, saying, Prepare for yourselves provisions, for in three days more you will pass the Jordan to possess the land.

6 And the officers of the children of Israel did so, and they commanded the people and they did all that Joshua had commanded.

7 And Joshua sent two men to spy out the land of Jericho, and the men went and spied out Jericho.

8 And at the end of seven days they came to Joshua in the camp and said to him, The Lord has delivered the whole land into our hand, and the inhabitants thereof are melted with fear because of us.

9 And it came to pass after that, that Joshua rose up in the morning and all Israel with him, and they journeyed from Shittim, and Joshua and all Israel with him passed the Jordan; and Joshua was eighty-two years old when he passed the Jordan with Israel.

10 And the people went up from Jordan on the tenth day of the first month, and they encamped in Gilgal at the eastern corner of Jericho.

11 And the children of Israel kept the Passover in Gilgal, in the plains of Jericho, on the fourteenth day at the month, as it is written in the law of Moses.

12 And the manna ceased at that time on the morrow of the Passover, and there was no more manna for the children of Israel, and they ate of the produce of the land of Canaan.

13 And Jericho was entirely closed against the children of Israel, no one came out or went in.

14 And it was in the second month, on the first day of the month, that the

Lord said to Joshua, Rise up, behold I have given Jericho into thy hand with all the people thereof; and all your fighting men shall go round the city, once each day, thus shall you do for six days.

15 And the priests shall blow upon trumpets, and when you shall hear the sound of the trumpet, all the people shall give a great shouting, that the walls of the city shall fall down; all the people shall go up every man against his opponent.

16 And Joshua did so according to all that the Lord had commanded him.

17 And on the seventh day they went round the city seven times, and the priests blew upon trumpets.

18 And at the seventh round, Joshua said to the people, Shout, for the Lord has delivered the whole city into our hands.

19 Only the city and all that it contains shall be accursed to the Lord, and keep yourselves from the accursed thing, lest you make the camp of Israel accursed and trouble it.

20 But all the silver and gold and brass and iron shall be consecrated to the Lord, they shall come into the treasury of the Lord.

21 And the people blew upon trumpets and made a great shouting, and the walls of Jericho fell down,

and all the people went up, every man straight before him, and they took the city and utterly destroyed all that was in it, both man and woman, young and old, ox and sheep and ass, with the edge of the sword.

22 And they burned the whole city with fire; only the vessels of silver and gold, and brass and iron, they put into the treasury of the Lord.

23 And Joshua swore at that time, saying, Cursed be the man who builds Jericho; he shall lay the foundation thereof in his first-born, and in his youngest son shall he set up the gates thereof.

24 And Achan the son of Carmi, the son of Zabdi, the son of Zerah, son of Judah, dealt treacherously in the accursed thing, and he took of the accursed thing and hid it in the tent, and the anger of the Lord was kindled against Israel.

25 And it was after this when the children of Israel had returned from burning Jericho, Joshua sent men to spy out also Ai, and to fight against it.

26 And the men went up and spied out Ai, and they returned and said, Let not all the people go up with thee to Ai, only let about three thousand men go up and smite the city, for the men thereof are but few.

27 And Joshua did so, and there went up with him of the children of Israel about three thousand men,

and they fought against the men of Ai.

28 And the battle was severe against Israel, and the men of Ai smote thirty-six men of Israel, and the children of Israel fled from before the men of Ai.

29 And when Joshua saw this thing, he tore his garments and fell upon his face to the ground before the Lord, he, with the elders of Israel, and they put dust upon their heads.

30 And Joshua said, Why O Lord didst thou bring this people over the Jordan? what shall I say after the Israelites have turned their backs against their enemies?

31 Now therefore all the Canaanites, inhabitants of the land, will hear this thing, and surround us and cut off our name.

32 And the Lord said to Joshua, Why dost thou fall upon thy face? rise, get thee off, for the Israelites have sinned, and taken of the accursed thing; I will no more be with them unless they destroy the accursed thing from amongst them.

33 And Joshua rose up and assembled the people, and brought the Urim by the order of the Lord, and the tribe of Judah was taken, and Achan the son of Carmi was taken.

34 And Joshua said to Achan, Tell me my son, what hast thou done,

and Achan said, I saw amongst the spoil a goodly garment of Shinar and two hundred shekels of silver, and a wedge of gold of fifty shekels weight; I coveted them and took them, and behold they are all hid in the earth in the midst of the tent.

35 And Joshua sent men who went and took them from the tent of Achan, and they brought them to Joshua.

36 And Joshua took Achan and these utensils, and his sons and daughters and all belonging to him, and they brought them into the valley of Achor.

37 And Joshua burned them there with fire, and all the Israelites stoned Achan with stones, and they raised over him a heap of stones, therefore did he call that place the valley of Achor, so the Lord's anger was appeased, and Joshua afterward came to the city and fought against it.

38 And the Lord said to Joshua, Fear not, neither be thou dismayed, behold I have given into thy hand Ai, her king and her people, and thou shalt do unto them as thou didst to Jericho and her king, only the spoil thereof and the cattle thereof shall you take for a prey for yourselves; lay an ambush for the city behind it.

39 So Joshua did according to the word of the Lord, and he chose from amongst the sons of war thirty

thousand valiant men, and he sent them, and they lay in ambush for the city.

40 And he commanded them, saying, When you shall see us we will flee before them with cunning, and they will pursue us, you shall then rise out of the ambush and take the city, and they did so.

41 And Joshua fought, and the men of the city went out toward Israel, not knowing that they were lying in ambush for them behind the city.

42 And Joshua and all the Israelites feigned themselves wearied out before them, and they fled by the way of the wilderness with cunning.

43 And the men of Ai gathered all the people who were in the city to pursue the Israelites, and they went out and were drawn away from the city, not one remained, and they left the city open and pursued the Israelites.

44 And those who were lying in ambush rose up out of their places, and hastened to come to the city and took it and set it on fire, and the men of Ai turned back, and behold the smoke of the city ascended to the skies, and they had no means of retreating either one way or the other.

45 And all the men of Ai were in the midst of Israel, some on this side and some on that side, and they smote them so that not one of them remained.

46 And the children of Israel took Melosh king of Ai alive, and they brought him to Joshua, and Joshua hanged him on a tree and he died.

47 And the children of Israel returned to the city after having burned it, and they smote all those that were in it with the edge of the sword.

48 And the number of those that had fallen of the men of Ai, both man and woman, was twelve thousand; only the cattle and the spoil of the city they took to themselves, according to the word of the Lord to Joshua.

49 And all the kings on this side Jordan, all the kings of Canaan, heard of the evil which the children of Israel had done to Jericho and to Ai, and they gathered themselves together to fight against Israel.

50 Only the inhabitants of Gibeon were greatly afraid of fighting against the Israelites lest they should perish, so they acted cunningly, and they came to Joshua and to all Israel, and said unto them, We have come from a distant land, now therefore make a covenant with us.

51 And the inhabitants of Gibeon over-reached the children of Israel, and the children of Israel made a covenant with them, and they made peace with them, and the princes of the congregation swore unto them, but afterward the children of Israel

knew that they were neighbors to them and were dwelling amongst them.

52 But the children of Israel slew them not; for they had sworn to them by the Lord, and they became hewers of wood and drawers of water.

53 And Joshua said to them, Why did you deceive me, to do this thing to us? and they answered him, saying, Because it was told to thy servants all that you had done to all the kings of the Amorites, and we were greatly afraid of our lives, and we did this thing.

54 And Joshua appointed them on that day to hew wood and to draw water, and he divided them for slaves to all the tribes of Israel.

55 And when Adonizedek king of Jerusalem heard all that the children of Israel had done to Jericho and to Ai, he sent to Hoham king of Hebron and to Piram king at Jarmuth, and to Japhia king of Lachish and to Deber king of Eglon, saying,

56 Come up to me and help me, that we may smite the children of Israel and the inhabitants of Gibeon who have made peace with the children of Israel.

57 And they gathered themselves together and the five kings of the Amorites went up with all their camps, a mighty people numerous as the sand of the sea shore.

58 And all these kings came and encamped before Gibeon, and they began to fight against the inhabitants of Gibeon, and all the men of Gibeon sent to Joshua, saying, Come up quickly to us and help us, for all the kings of the Amorites have gathered together to fight against us.

59 And Joshua and all the fighting people went up from Gilgal, and Joshua came suddenly to them, and smote these five kings with a great slaughter.

60 And the Lord confounded them before the children at Israel, who smote them with a terrible slaughter in Gibeon, and pursued them along the way that goes up to Beth Horon unto Makkedah, and they fled from before the children of Israel.

61 And whilst they were fleeing, the Lord sent upon them hailstones from heaven, and more of them died by the hailstones, than by the slaughter of the children of Israel.

62 And the children of Israel pursued them, and they still smote them in the road, going on and smiting them.

63 And when they were smiting, the day was declining toward evening, and Joshua said in the sight of all the people, Sun, stand thou still upon Gibeon, and thou moon in the valley of Ajalon, until the nation shall have revenged itself upon its enemies.

64 And the Lord hearkened to the voice of Joshua, and the sun stood

still in the midst of the heavens, and it stood still six and thirty moments, and the moon also stood still and hastened not to go down a whole day.

65 And there was no day like that, before it or after it, that the Lord hearkened to the voice of a man, for the Lord fought for Israel.

Jasher 89

1 Then spoke Joshua this song, on the day that the Lord had given the Amorites into the hand of Joshua and the children of Israel, and he said in the sight of all Israel,

2 Thou hast done mighty things, O Lord, thou hast performed great deeds; who is like unto thee? my lips shall sing to thy name.

3 My goodness and my fortress, my high tower, I will sing a new song unto thee, with thanksgiving will I sing to thee, thou art the strength of my salvation.

4 All the kings of the earth shall praise thee, the princes of the world shall sing to thee, the children of Israel shall rejoice in thy salvation, they shall sing and praise thy power.

5 To thee, O Lord, did we confide; we said thou art our God, for thou wast our shelter and strong tower against our enemies.

6 To thee we cried and were not ashamed, in thee we trusted and were delivered; when we cried unto thee, thou didst hear our voice, thou didst deliver our souls from the sword, thou didst show unto us thy grace, thou didst give unto us thy salvation, thou didst rejoice our hearts with thy strength.

7 Thou didst go forth for our salvation, with thine arm thou didst redeem thy people; thou didst answer us from the heavens of thy holiness, thou didst save us from ten thousands of people.

8 The sun and moon stood still in heaven, and thou didst stand in thy wrath against our oppressors and didst command thy judgments over them.

9 All the princes of the earth stood up, the kings of the nations had gathered themselves together, they were not moved at thy presence, they desired thy battles.

10 Thou didst rise against them in thine anger, and didst bring down thy wrath upon them; thou didst destroy them in thine anger, and cut them off in thine heart.

11 Nations have been consumed with thy fury, kingdoms have declined because of thy wrath, thou didst wound kings in the day of thine anger.

12 Thou didst pour out thy fury upon them, thy wrathful anger took hold of them; thou didst turn their iniquity upon them, and didst cut them off in their wickedness.

13 They did spread a trap, they fell therein, in the net they hid, their foot was caught.

14 Thine hand was ready for all thine enemies who said, Through their sword they possessed the land, through their arm they dwelt in the city; thou didst fill their faces with shame, thou didst bring their horns down to the ground, thou didst terrify them in thy wrath, and didst destroy them in thine anger.

15 The earth trembled and shook at the sound of thy storm over them, thou didst not withhold their souls from death, and didst bring down their lives to the grave.

16 Thou didst pursue them in thy storm, thou didst consume them in thy whirlwind, thou didst turn their rain into hail, they fell in deep pits so that they could not rise.

17 Their carcasses were like rubbish cast out in the middle of the streets.

18 They were consumed and destroyed in thine anger, thou didst save thy people with thy might.

19 Therefore our hearts rejoice in thee, our souls exalt in thy salvation.

20 Our tongues shall relate thy might, we will sing and praise thy wondrous works.

21 For thou didst save us from our enemies, thou didst deliver us from those who rose up against us, thou didst destroy them from before us and depress them beneath our feet.

22 Thus shall all thine enemies perish O Lord, and the wicked shall be like chaff driven by the wind, and thy beloved shall be like trees planted by the waters.

23 So Joshua and all Israel with him returned to the camp in Gilgal, after having smitten all the kings, so that not a remnant was left of them.

24 And the five kings fled alone on foot from battle, and hid themselves in a cave, and Joshua sought for them in the field of battle, and did not find them.

25 And it was afterward told to Joshua, saying, The kings are found and behold they are hidden in a cave.

26 And Joshua said, Appoint men to be at the mouth of the cave, to guard them, lest they take themselves away; and the children of Israel did so.

27 And Joshua called to all Israel and said to the officers of battle, Place your feet upon the necks of these kings, and Joshua said, So shall the Lord do to all your enemies.

28 And Joshua commanded afterward that they should slay the kings and cast them into the cave, and to put great stones at the mouth of the cave.

29 And Joshua went afterward with all the people that were with him on that day to Makkedah, and he smote it with the edge of the sword.

30 And he utterly destroyed the souls and all belonging to the city, and he did to the king and people thereof as he had done to Jericho.

31 And he passed from there to Libnah and he fought against it, and the Lord delivered it into his hand, and Joshua smote it with the edge of the sword, and all the souls thereof, and he did to it and to the king thereof as he had done to Jericho.

32 And from there he passed on to Lachish to fight against it, and Horam king of Gaza went up to assist the men of Lachish, and Joshua smote him and his people until there was none left to him.

33 And Joshua took Lachish and all the people thereof, and he did to it as he had done to Libnah.

34 And Joshua passed from there to Eglon, and he took that also, and he smote it and all the people thereof with the edge of the sword.

35 And from there he passed to Hebron and fought against it and took it and utterly destroyed it, and he returned from there with all Israel to Debir and fought against it and smote it with the edge of the sword.

36 And he destroyed every soul in it, he left none remaining, and he did to it and the king thereof as he had done to Jericho.

37 And Joshua smote all the kings of the Amorites from Kadesh-barnea to Azah, and he took their country at once, for the Lord had fought for Israel.

38 And Joshua with all Israel came to the camp to Gilgal.

39 When at that time Jabin king of Chazor heard all that Joshua had done to the kings of the Amorites, Jabin sent to Jobat king of Midian, and to Laban king of Shimron, to Jephal king of Achshaph, and to all the kings of the Amorites, saying,

40 Come quickly to us and help us, that we may smite the children of Israel, before they come upon us and do unto us as they have done to the other kings of the Amorites.

41 And all these kings hearkened to the words of Jabin, king of Chazor, and they went forth with all their camps, seventeen kings, and their people were as numerous as the sand on the sea shore, together with horses and chariots innumerable, and they came and pitched together at the waters of Merom, and they were met together to fight against Israel.

42 And the Lord said to Joshua, Fear them not, for tomorrow about this time I will deliver them up all slain before you, thou shalt hough their

horses and burn their chariots with fire.

43 And Joshua with all the men of war came suddenly upon them and smote them, and they fell into their hands, for the Lord had delivered them into the hands of the children of Israel.

44 So the children of Israel pursued all these kings with their camps, and smote them until there was none left of them, and Joshua did to them as the Lord had spoken to him.

45 And Joshua returned at that time to Chazor and smote it with the sword and destroyed every soul in it and burned it with fire, and from Chazor, Joshua passed to Shimron and smote it and utterly destroyed it.

46 From there he passed to Achshaph and he did to it as he had done to Shimron.

47 From there he passed to Adulam and he smote all the people in it, and he did to Adulam as he had done to Achshaph and to Shimron.

48 And he passed from them to all the cities of the kings which he had smitten, and he smote all the people that were left of them and he utterly destroyed them.

49 Only their booty and cattle the Israelites took to themselves as a prey, but every human being they smote, they suffered not a soul to live.

50 As the Lord had commanded Moses so did Joshua and all Israel, they failed not in anything.

51 So Joshua and all the children of Israel smote the whole land of Canaan as the Lord had commanded them, and smote all their kings, being thirty and one kings, and the children of Israel took their whole country.

52 Besides the kingdoms of Sihon and Og which are on the other side Jordan, of which Moses had smitten many cities, and Moses gave them to the Reubenites and the Gadites and to half the tribe of Manasseh.

53 And Joshua smote all the kings that were on this side Jordan to the west, and gave them for an inheritance to the nine tribes and to the half tribe of Israel.

54 For five years did Joshua carry on the war with these kings, and he gave their cities to the Israelites, and the land became tranquil from battle throughout the cities of the Amorites and the Canaanites.

Jasher 90

1 At that time in the fifth year after the children of Israel had passed over Jordan, after the children of Israel had rested from their war with the Canaanites, at that time great and severe battles arose between Edom and the children of Chittim, and the children of Chittim fought against Edom.

2 And Abianus king of Chittim went forth in that year, that is in the thirty-first year of his reign, and a great force with him of the mighty men of the children of Chittim, and he went to Seir to fight against the children of Esau.

3 And Hadad the king of Edom heard of his report, and he went forth to meet him with a heavy people and strong force, and engaged in battle with him in the field of Edom.

4 And the hand of Chittim prevailed over the children of Esau, and the children of Chittim slew of the children of Esau, two and twenty thousand men, and all the children of Esau fled from before them.

5 And the children of Chittim pursued them and they reached Hadad king of Edom, who was running before them and they caught him alive, and brought him to Abianus king of Chittim.

6 And Abianus ordered him to be slain, and Hadad king of Edom died in the forty-eighth year of his reign.

7 And the children of Chittim continued their pursuit of Edom, and they smote them with a great slaughter and Edom became subject to the children of Chittim.

8 And the children of Chittim ruled over Edom, and Edom became under the hand of the children of Chittim and became one kingdom from that day.

9 And from that time they could no more lift up their heads, and their kingdom became one with the children of Chittim.

10 And Abianus placed officers in Edom and all the children of Edom became subject and tributary to Abianus, and Abianus turned back to his own land, Chittim.

11 And when he returned he renewed his government and built for himself a spacious and fortified palace for a royal residence, and reigned securely over the children of Chittim and over Edom.

12 In those days, after the children of Israel had driven away all the Canaanites and the Amorites, Joshua was old and advanced in years.

13 And the Lord said to Joshua, Thou art old, advanced in life, and a great part of the land remains to be possessed.

14 Now therefore divide this land for an inheritance to the nine tribes and to the half tribe of Manasseh, and Joshua rose up and did as the Lord had spoken to him.

15 And he divided the whole land to the tribes of Israel as an inheritance according to their divisions.

16 But to the tribe at Levi he gave no inheritance, the offerings of the Lord are their inheritance as the Lord had

spoken of them by the hand of Moses.

17 And Joshua gave Mount Hebron to Caleb the son of Jephuneh, one portion above his brethren, as the Lord had spoken through Moses.

18 Therefore Hebron became an inheritance to Caleb and his children unto this day.

19 And Joshua divided the whole land by lots to all Israel for an inheritance, as the Lord had commanded him.

20 And the children of Israel gave cities to the Levites from their own inheritance, and suburbs for their cattle, and property, as the Lord had commanded Moses so did the children of Israel, and they divided the land by lot whether great or small.

21 And they went to inherit the land according to their boundaries, and the children of Israel gave to Joshua the son of Nun an inheritance amongst them.

22 By the word of the Lord did they give to him the city which he required, Timnath-serach in Mount Ephraim, and he built the city and dwelt therein.

23 These are the inheritances which Elazer the priest and Joshua the son of Nun and the heads of the fathers of the tribes portioned out to the children of Israel by lot in Shiloh,

before the Lord, at the door of the tabernacle, and they left off dividing the land.

24 And the Lord gave the land to the Israelites, and they possessed it as the Lord had spoken to them, and as the Lord had sworn to their ancestors.

25 And the Lord gave to the Israelites rest from all their enemies around them, and no man stood up against them, and the Lord delivered all their enemies into their hands, and not one thing failed of all the good which the Lord had spoken to the children of Israel, yea the Lord performed every thing.

26 And Joshua called to all the children of Israel and he blessed them, and commanded them to serve the Lord, and he afterward sent them away, and they went each man to his city, and each man to his inheritance.

27 And the children of Israel served the Lord all the days of Joshua, and the Lord gave them rest from all around them, and they dwelt securely in their cities.

28 And it came to pass in those days, that Abianus king of Chittim died, in the thirty-eighth year of his reign, that is the seventh year of his reign over Edom, and they buried him in his place which he had built for himself, and Latinus reigned in his stead fifty years.

29 And during his reign he brought forth an army, and he went and fought against the inhabitants of Britannia and Kernania, the children of Elisha son of Javan, and he prevailed over them and made them tributary.

30 He then heard that Edom had revolted from under the hand of Chittim, and Latinus went to them and smote them and subdued them, and placed them under the hand of the children of Chittim, and Edom became one kingdom with the children of Chittim all the days.

31 And for many years there was no king in Edom, and their government was with the children of Chittim and their king.

32 And it was in the twenty-sixth year after the children of Israel had passed the Jordan, that is the sixty-sixth year after the children of Israel had departed from Egypt, that Joshua was old, advanced in years, being one hundred and eight years old in those days.

33 And Joshua called to all Israel, to their elders, their judges and officers, after the Lord had given to all the Israelites rest from all their enemies round about, and Joshua said to the elders of Israel, and to their judges, Behold I am old, advanced in years, and you have seen what the Lord has done to all the nations whom he has driven away from before you, for it is the Lord who has fought for you.

34 Now therefore strengthen yourselves to keep and to do all the words of the law of Moses, not to deviate from it to the right or to the left, and not to come amongst those nations who are left in the land; neither shall you make mention of the name of their gods, but you shall cleave to the Lord your God, as you have done to this day.

35 And Joshua greatly exhorted the children of Israel to serve the Lord all their days.

36 And all the Israelites said, We will serve the Lord our God all our days, we and our children, and our children's children, and our seed for ever.

37 And Joshua made a covenant with the people on that day, and he sent away the children of Israel, and they went each man to his inheritance and to his city.

38 And it was in those days, when the children of Israel were dwelling securely in their cities, that they buried the coffins of the tribes of their ancestors, which they had brought up from Egypt, each man in the inheritance of his children, the twelve sons of Jacob did the children of Israel bury, each man in the possession of his children.

39 And these are the names of the cities wherein they buried the twelve sons of Jacob, whom the children of Israel had brought up from Egypt.

40 And they buried Reuben and Gad on this side Jordan, in Romia, which Moses had given to their children.

41 And Simeon and Levi they buried in the city Mauda, which he had given to the children of Simeon, and the suburb of the city was for the children of Levi.

42 And Judah they buried in the city of Benjamin opposite Bethlehem.

43 And the bones of Issachar and Zebulun they buried in Zidon, in the portion which fell to their children.

44 And Dan was buried in the city of his children in Eshtael, and Naphtali and Asher they buried in Kadesh-naphtali, each man in his place which he had given to his children.

45 And the bones of Joseph they buried in Shechem, in the part of the field which Jacob had purchased from Hamor, and which became to Joseph for an inheritance.

46 And they buried Benjamin in Jerusalem opposite the Jebusite, which was given to the children of Benjamin; the children of Israel buried their fathers each man in the city of his children.

47 And at the end of two years, Joshua the son of Nun died, one hundred and ten years old, and the time which Joshua judged Israel was twenty-eight years, and Israel served the Lord all the days of his life.

48 And the other affairs of Joshua and his battles and his reproofs with which he reproved Israel, and all which he had commanded them, and the names of the cities which the children of Israel possessed in his days, behold they are written in the book of the words of Joshua to the children of Israel, and in the book of the wars of the Lord, which Moses and Joshua and the children of Israel had written.

49 And the children of Israel buried Joshua in the border of his inheritance, in Timnath-serach, which was given to him in Mount Ephraim.

50 And Elazer the son of Aaron died in those days, and they buried him in a hill belonging to Phineas his son, which was given him in Mount Ephraim.

Jasher 91

1 At that time, after the death of Joshua, the children of the Canaanites were still in the land, and the Israelites resolved to drive them out.

2 And the children of Israel asked of the Lord, saying, Who shall first go up for us to the Canaanites to fight against them? and the Lord said, Judah shall go up.

3 And the children of Judah said to Simeon, Go up with us into our lot, and we will fight against the Canaanites and we likewise will go

up with you, in your lot, so the children of Simeon went with the children of Judah.

4 And the children of Judah went up and fought against the Canaanites, so the Lord delivered the Canaanites into the hands of the children of Judah, and they smote them in Bezek, ten thousand men.

5 And they fought with Adonibezek in Bezek, and he fled from before them, and they pursued him and caught him, and they took hold of him and cut off his thumbs and great toes.

6 And Adonibezek said, Three score and ten kings having their thumbs and great toes cut off, gathered their meat under my table, as I have done, so God has requited me, and they brought him to Jerusalem and he died there.

7 And the children of Simeon went with the children of Judah, and they smote the Canaanites with the edge of the sword.

8 And the Lord was with the children of Judah, and they possessed the mountain, and the children of Joseph went up to Bethel, the same is Luz, and the Lord was with them.

9 And the children of Joseph spied out Bethel, and the watchmen saw a man going forth from the city, and they caught him and said unto him, Show us now the entrance of the city and we will show kindness to thee.

10 And that man showed them the entrance of the city, and the children of Joseph came and smote the City with the edge of the sword.

11 And the man with his family they sent away, and he went to the Hittites and he built a city, and he called the name thereof Luz, so all the Israelites dwelt in their cities, and the children at Israel dwelt in their cities, and the children of Israel served the Lord all the days of Joshua, and all the days of the elders, who had lengthened their days after Joshua, and saw the great work of the Lord, which he had performed for Israel.

12 And the elders judged Israel after the death of Joshua for seventeen years.

13 And all the elders also fought the battles of Israel against the Canaanites and the Lord drove the Canaanites from before the children of Israel, in order to place the Israelites in their land.

14 And he accomplished all the words which he had spoken to Abraham, Isaac, and Jacob, and the oath which he had sworn, to give to them and to their children, the land of the Canaanites.

15 And the Lord gave to the children of Israel the whole land of Canaan, as he had sworn to their ancestors, and the Lord gave them rest from

those around them, and the children of Israel dwelt securely in their cities.

16 Blessed be the Lord for ever, amen, and amen.

17 Strengthen yourselves, and let the hearts of all you that trust in the Lord be of good courage.

THE END

THE BOOK OF JUBILEES

Jubilees 1

1. And it came to pass in the first year of the exodus of the children of Israel out of Egypt, in the third month, on the sixteenth day of the month, [2450 Anno Mundi] that God spake to Moses, saying: 'Come up to Me on the Mount, and I will give thee two tables of stone of the law and of the commandment, which I have written, that thou mayst teach them.'

2. And Moses went up into the mount of God, and the glory of the Lord abode on Mount Sinai, and a cloud overshadowed it six days.

3. And He called to Moses on the seventh day out of the midst of the cloud, and the appearance of the glory of the Lord was like a flaming fire on the top of the mount.

4. And Moses was on the Mount forty days and forty nights, and God taught him the earlier and the later history of the division of all the days of the law and of the testimony.

5. And He said: 'Incline thine heart to every word which I shall speak to thee on this mount, and write them in a book in order that their generations may see how I have not forsaken them for all the evil which they have wrought in transgressing the covenant which I establish between

Me and thee for their generations this day on Mount Sinai.

6. And thus it will come to pass when all these things come upon them, that they will recognise that I am more righteous than they in all their judgments and in all their actions, and they will recognise that I have been truly with them.

7. And do thou write for thyself all these words which I declare unto, thee this day, for I know their rebellion and their stiff neck, before I bring them into the land of which I sware to their fathers, to Abraham and to Isaac and to Jacob, saying: ' Unto your seed will I give a land flowing with milk and honey.

8. And they will eat and be satisfied, and they will turn to strange gods, to (gods) which cannot deliver them from aught of their tribulation: and this witness shall be heard for a witness against them. For they will forget all My commandments, (even) all that I command them, and they will walk after the Gentiles, and after their uncleanness, and after their shame, and will serve their gods, and these will prove unto them an offence and a tribulation and an affliction and a snare.

9. And many will perish and they will be taken captive, and will fall into the hands of the enemy, because they have forsaken My ordinances and My commandments, and the festivals of My covenant, and My sabbaths, and My holy place which I

have hallowed for Myself in their midst, and My tabernacle, and My sanctuary, which I have hallowed for Myself in the midst of the land, that I should set my name upon it, and that it should dwell (there).

10. And they will make to themselves high places and groves and graven images, and they will worship, each his own (graven image), so as to go astray, and they will sacrifice their children to demons, and to all the works of the error of their hearts.

11. And I will send witnesses unto them, that I may witness against them, but they will not hear, and will slay the witnesses also, and they will persecute those who seek the law, and they will abrogate and change everything so as to work evil before My eyes.

12. And I will hide My face from them, and I will deliver them into the hand of the Gentiles for captivity, and for a prey, and for devouring, and I will remove them from the midst of the land, and I will scatter them amongst the Gentiles.

13. And they will forget all My law and all My commandments and all My judgments, and will go astray as to new moons, and sabbaths, and festivals, and jubilees, and ordinances.

14. And after this they will turn to Me from amongst the Gentiles with all their heart and with all their soul and with all their strength, and I will

gather them from amongst all the Gentiles, and they will seek me, so that I shall be found of them, when they seek me with all their heart and with all their soul.

15. And I will disclose to them abounding peace with righteousness, and I will remove them the plant of uprightness, with all My heart and with all My soul, and they shall be for a blessing and not for a curse, and they shall be the head and not the tail.

16, And I will build My sanctuary in their midst, and I will dwell with them, and I will be their God and they shall be My people in truth and righteousness.

17. And I will not forsake them nor fail them; for I am the Lord their God.'

18. And Moses fell on his face and prayed and said, 'O Lord my God, do not forsake Thy people and Thy inheritance, so that they should wander in the error of their hearts, and do not deliver them into the hands of their enemies, the Gentiles, lest they should rule over them and cause them to sin against Thee.

19. Let thy mercy, O Lord, be lifted up upon Thy people, and create in them an upright spirit, and let not the spirit of Beliar rule over them to accuse them before Thee, and to ensnare them from all the paths of righteousness, so that they may perish from before Thy face.

20. But they are Thy people and Thy inheritance, which thou hast delivered with thy great power from the hands of the Egyptians: create in them a clean heart and a holy spirit, and let them not be ensnared in their sins from henceforth until eternity.'

21. And the Lord said unto Moses: 'I know their contrariness and their thoughts and their stiffneckedness, and they will not be obedient till they confess their own sin and the sin of their fathers.

22. And after this they will turn to Me in all uprightness and with all (their) heart and with all (their) soul, and I will circumcise the foreskin of their heart and the foreskin of the heart of their seed, and I will create in them a holy spirit, and I will cleanse them so that they shall not turn away from Me from that day unto eternity.

23. And their souls will cleave to Me and to all My commandments, and they will fulfil My commandments, and I will be their Father and they shall be My children.

24. And they all shall be called children of the living God, and every angel and every spirit shall know, yea, they shall know that these are My children, and that I am their Father in uprightness and righteousness, and that I love them.

25. And do thou write down for thyself all these words which I declare unto thee on this mountain, the first and the last, which shall come to pass in all the divisions of the days in the law and in the testimony and in the weeks and the jubilees unto eternity, until I descend and dwell with them throughout eternity.'

26. And He said to the angel of the presence: Write for Moses from the beginning of creation till My sanctuary has been built among them for all eternity.

27, And the Lord will appear to the eyes of all, and all shall know that I am the God of Israel and the Father of all the children of Jacob, and King on Mount Zion for all eternity. And Zion and Jerusalem shall be holy.'

28. And the angel of the presence who went before the camp of Israel took the tables of the divisions of the years -from the time of the creation- of the law and of the testimony of the weeks of the jubilees, according to the individual years, according to all the number of the jubilees [according, to the individual years], from the day of the [new] creation when the heavens and the earth shall be renewed and all their creation according to the powers of the heaven, and according to all the creation of the earth, until the sanctuary of the Lord shall be made in Jerusalem on Mount Zion, and all the luminaries be renewed for healing and for peace and for blessing for all the elect of Israel, and that thus it may be from that day and unto all the days of the earth.

Jubilees 2

1. And the angel of the presence spake to Moses according to the word of the Lord, saying: Write the complete history of the creation, how in six days the Lord God finished all His works and all that He created, and kept Sabbath on the seventh day and hallowed it for all ages, and appointed it as a sign for all His works.

2. For on the first day He created the heavens which are above and the earth and the waters and all the spirits which serve before him -the angels of the presence, and the angels of sanctification, and the angels [of the spirit of fire and the angels] of the spirit of the winds, and the angels of the spirit of the clouds, and of darkness, and of snow and of hail and of hoar frost, and the angels of the voices and of the thunder and of the lightning, and the angels of the spirits of cold and of heat, and of winter and of spring and of autumn and of summer and of all the spirits of his creatures which are in the heavens and on the earth, (He created) the abysses and the darkness, eventide <and night>, and the light, dawn and day, which He hath prepared in the knowledge of his heart.

3. And thereupon we saw His works, and praised Him, and lauded before Him on account of all His works; for seven great works did He create on the first day.

4. And on the second day He created the firmament in the midst of the waters, and the waters were divided on that day -half of them went up above and half of them went down below the firmament (that was) in the midst over the face of the whole earth. And this was the only work (God) created on the second day.

5. And on the third day He commanded the waters to pass from off the face of the whole earth into one place, and the dry land to appear.

6. And the waters did so as He commanded them, and they retired from off the face of the earth into one place outside of this firmament, and the dry land appeared.

7. And on that day He created for them all the seas according to their separate gathering-places, and all the rivers, and the gatherings of the waters in the mountains and on all the earth, and all the lakes, and all the dew of the earth, and the seed which is sown, and all sprouting things, and fruit-bearing trees, and trees of the wood, and the garden of Eden, in Eden and all *plants after their kind*.

8. These four great works God created on the third day. And on the fourth day He created the sun and the moon and the stars, and set them in the firmament of the heaven, to give light upon all the earth, and to

rule over the day and the night, and divide the light from the darkness.

9. And God appointed the sun to be a great sign on the earth for days and for sabbaths and for months and for feasts and for years and for sabbaths of years and for jubilees and for all seasons of the years.

10. And it divideth the light from the darkness [and] for prosperity, that all things may prosper which shoot and grow on the earth.

11. These three kinds He made on the fourth day. And on the fifth day He created great sea monsters in the depths of the waters, for these were the first things of flesh that were created by his hands, the fish and everything that moves in the waters, and everything that flies, the birds and all their kind.

12. And the sun rose above them to prosper (them), and above everything that was on the earth, everything that shoots out of the earth, and all fruit-bearing trees, and all flesh.

13. These three kinds He created on the fifth day. And on the sixth day He created all the animals of the earth, and all cattle, and everything that moves on the earth.

14. And after all this He created man, a man and a woman created He them, and gave him dominion over all that is upon the earth, and in the seas, and over everything that

flies, and over beasts and over cattle, and over everything that moves on the earth, and over the whole earth, and over all this He gave him dominion.

15. And these four kinds He created on the sixth day. And there were altogether two and twenty kinds.

16. And He finished all his work on the sixth day -all that is in the heavens and on the earth, and in the seas and in the abysses, and in the light and in the darkness, and in everything.

17. And He gave us a great sign, the Sabbath day, that we should work six days, but keep Sabbath on the seventh day from all work.

18. And all the angels of the presence, and all the angels of sanctification, these two great classes -He hath bidden us to keep the Sabbath with Him in heaven and on earth.

19. And He said unto us: 'Behold, I will separate unto Myself a people from among all the peoples, and these shall keep the Sabbath day, and I will sanctify them unto Myself as My people, and will bless them; as I have sanctified the Sabbath day and do sanctify (it) unto Myself, even so will I bless them, and they shall be My people and I will be their God.

20. And I have chosen the seed of Jacob from amongst all that I have seen, and have written him down as

My first-born son,and have sanctified him unto Myself for ever and ever; and I will teach them the Sabbath day, that they may keep Sabbath thereon from all work.

21. And thus He created therein a sign in accordance with which they should keep Sabbath with us on the seventh day, to eat and to drink, and to bless Him who has created all things as He has blessed and sanctified unto Himself a peculiar people above all peoples, and that they should keep Sabbath together with us.

22. And He caused His commands to ascend as a sweet savour acceptable before Him all the days . . .

23. There (were) two and twenty heads of mankind from Adam to Jacob, and two and twenty kinds of work were made until the seventh day; this is blessed and holy; and the former also is blessed and holy; and this one serves with that one for sanctification and blessing.

24. And to this (Jacob and his seed) it was granted that they should always be the blessed and holy ones of the first testimony and law, even as He had sanctified and blessed the Sabbath day on the seventh day.

25. He created heaven and earth and everything that He created in six days, and God made the seventh day holy, for all His works; therefore He commanded on its behalf that,

whoever does any work thereon shall die, and that he who defiles it shall surely die.

26. Wherefore do thou command the children of Israel to observe this day that they may keep it holy and not do thereon any work, and not to defile it, as it is holier than all other days.

27. And whoever profanes it shall surely die, and whoever does thereon any work shall surely die eternally, that the children of Israel may observe this day throughout their generations, and not be rooted out of the land; for it is a holy day and a blessed day.

28. And every one who observes it and keeps Sabbath thereon from all his work, will be holy and blessed throughout all days like unto us.

29. Declare and say to the children of Israel the law of this day both that they should keep Sabbath thereon, and that they should not forsake it in the error of their hearts; (and) that it is not lawful to do any work thereon which is unseemly, to do thereon their own pleasure, and that they should not prepare thereon anything to be eaten or drunk, and (that it is not lawful) to draw water, or bring in or take out thereon through their gates any burden, which they had not prepared for themselves on the sixth day in their dwellings.

30. And they shall not bring in nor take out from house to house on that day; for that day is more holy and

blessed than any jubilee day of the jubilees; on this we kept Sabbath in the heavens before it was made known to any flesh to keep Sabbath thereon on the earth.

31. And the Creator of all things blessed it, but he did not sanctify all peoples and nations to keep Sabbath thereon, but Israel alone: them alone he permitted to eat and drink and to keep Sabbath thereon on the earth.

32. And the Creator of all things blessed this day which He had created for blessing and holiness and glory above all days.

33. This law and testimony was given to the children of Israel as a law for ever unto their generations.

Jubilees 3

1. And on the six days of the second week we brought, according to the word of God, unto Adam all the beasts, and all the cattle, and all the birds, and everything that moves on the earth, and everything that moves in the water, according to their kinds, and according to their types: the beasts on the first day; the cattle on the second day; the birds on the third day; and all that which moves on the earth on the fourth day; and that which moves in the water on the fifth day.

2. And Adam named them all by their respective names, and as he called them, so was their name.

3. And on these five days Adam saw all these, male and female, according to every kind that was on the earth, but he was alone and found no helpmeet for him.

4. And the Lord said unto us: 'It is not good that the man should be alone: let us make a helpmeet for him.'

5. And the Lord our God caused a deep sleep to fall upon him, and he slept, and He took for the woman one rib from amongst his ribs, and this rib was the origin of the woman from amongst his ribs, and He built up the flesh in its stead, and built the woman.

6. And He awaked Adam out of his sleep and on awaking he rose on the sixth day, and He brought her to him, and he knew her, and said unto her: 'This is now bone of my bones and flesh of my flesh; she shall be called [my] wife; because she was taken from her husband.'

7. Therefore shall man and wife be one and therefore shall a man leave his father and his mother, and cleave unto his wife, and they shall be one flesh.

8. In the first week was Adam created, and the rib -his wife: in the second week He showed her unto him: and for this reason the commandment was given to keep in their defilement, for a male seven days, and for a female twice seven days.

9. And after Adam had completed forty days in the land

where he had been created, we brought him into the garden of Eden to till and keep it, but his wife they brought in on the eightieth day, and after this she entered into the garden of Eden.

10. And for this reason the commandment is written on the heavenly tablets in regard to her that gives birth: 'if she bears a male, she shall remain in her uncleanness seven days according to the first week of days, and thirty and three days shall she remain in the blood of her purifying, and she shall not touch any hallowed thing, nor enter into the sanctuary, until she accomplishes these days which (are enjoined) in the case of a male child.

11. But in the case of a female child she shall remain in her uncleanness two weeks of days, according to the first two weeks, and sixty-six days in the blood of her purification, and they will be in all eighty days.'

12. And when she had completed these eighty days we brought her into the garden of Eden, for it is holier than all the earth besides and every tree that is planted in it is holy.

13. Therefore, there was ordained regarding her who bears a male or a female child the statute of those days that she should touch no hallowed thing, nor enter into the sanctuary until these days for the male or female child are accomplished.

14. This is the law and testimony which was written down for Israel, in order that they should observe (it) all the days.

15. And in the first week of the first jubilee, [1-7 A.M.] Adam and his wife were in the garden of Eden for seven years tilling and keeping it, and we gave him work and we instructed him to do everything that is suitable for tillage.

16. And he tilled (the garden), and was naked and knew it not, and was not ashamed, and he protected the garden from the birds and beasts and cattle, and gathered its fruit, and eat, and put aside the residue for himself and for his wife [and put aside that which was being kept].

17. And after the completion of the seven years, which he had completed there, seven years exactly, [8 A.M.] and in the second month, on the seventeenth day (of the month), the serpent came and approached the woman, and the serpent said to the woman, 'Hath God commanded you, saying, Ye shall not eat of every tree of the garden?'

18. And she said to it, 'Of all the fruit of the trees of the garden God hath said unto us, Eat; but of the fruit of the tree which is in the midst of the garden God hath said unto us, Ye shall not eat thereof, neither shall ye touch it, lest ye die.'

19. And the serpent said unto the woman, 'Ye shall not surely die: for God doth know that on the day ye

shall eat thereof, your eyes will be opened, and ye will be as gods, and ye will know good and evil.

20. And the woman saw the tree that it was agreeable and pleasant to the eye, and that its fruit was good for food, and she took thereof and eat.

21. And when she had first covered her shame with figleaves, she gave thereof to Adam and he eat, and his eyes were opened, and he saw that he was naked.

22. And he took figleaves and sewed (them) together, and made an apron for himself, and ,covered his shame.

23. And God cursed the serpent, and was wroth with it for ever . . .

24. And He was wroth with the woman, because she harkened to the voice of the serpent, and did eat; and He said unto her: 'I will greatly multiply thy sorrow and thy pains: in sorrow thou shalt bring forth children, and thy return shall be unto thy husband, and he will rule over thee.'

25. And to Adam also he said, ' Because thou hast harkened unto the voice of thy wife, and hast eaten of the tree of which I commanded thee that thou shouldst not eat thereof, cursed be the ground for thy sake: thorns and thistles shall it bring forth to thee, and thou shalt eat thy bread in the sweat of thy face, till thou returnest to the earth from whence thou wast taken; for earth thou art, and unto earth shalt thou return.'

26. And He made for them coats of skin, and clothed them, and sent them forth from the Garden of Eden.

27. And on that day on which Adam went forth from the Garden, he offered as a sweet savour an offering, frankincense, galbanum, and stacte, and spices in the morning with the rising of the sun from the day when he covered his shame.

28. And on that day was closed the mouth of all beasts, and of cattle, and of birds, and of whatever walks, and of whatever moves, so that they could no longer speak: for they had all spoken one with another with one lip and with one tongue.

29. And He sent out of the Garden of Eden all flesh that was in the Garden of Eden, and all flesh was scattered according to its kinds, and according to its types unto the places which had been created for them.

30. And to Adam alone did He give (the wherewithal) to cover his shame, of all the beasts and cattle.

31. On this account, it is prescribed on the heavenly tablets as touching all those who know the judgment of the law, that they should cover their shame, and should not uncover themselves as the Gentiles uncover themselves.

32. And on the new moon of the fourth month, Adam and his wife went forth from the Garden of Eden, and they dwelt in the land of Elda in the land of their creation.

33.   And Adam called the name of his wife Eve.

34.   And they had no son till the first jubilee, [8 A.M.] and after this he knew her.

35.   Now he tilled the land as he had been instructed in the Garden of Eden.

Jubilees 4

1.   And in the third week in the second jubilee [64-70 A.M.] she gave birth to Cain, and in the fourth [71-77 A.M.] she gave birth to Abel, and in the fifth [78-84 A.M.] she gave birth to her daughter Âwân.

2.   And in the first (year) of the third jubilee [99-105 A.M.], Cain slew Abel because (God) accepted the sacrifice of Abel, and did not accept the offering of Cain.

3.   And he slew him in the field: and his blood cried from the ground to heaven, complaining because he had slain him.

4.   And the Lord reproved Cain because of Abel, because he had slain him, and he made him a fugitive on the earth because of the blood of his brother, and he cursed him upon the earth.

5.   And on this account it is written on the heavenly tables, 'Cursed is ,he who smites his neighbour treacherously, and let all who have seen and heard say, So be it; and the man who has seen and not declared (it), let him be accursed as the other.'

6.   And for this reason we announce when we come before the Lord our God all the sin which is committed in heaven and on earth, and in light and in darkness, and everywhere.

7.   And Adam and his wife mourned for Abel four weeks of years, [99-127 A.M] and in the fourth year of the fifth week [130 A.M.] they became joyful, and Adam knew his wife again, and she bare him a son, and he called his name Seth; for he said 'GOD has raised up a second seed unto us on the earth instead of Abel; for Cain slew him.'

8.   And in the sixth week [134-40 A.M.] he begat his daughter Azûrâ.

9.   And Cain took Âwân his sister to be his wife and she bare him Enoch at the close of the fourth jubilee. [190-196 A.M.] And in the first year of the first week of the fifth jubilee, [197 A.M.] houses were built on the earth, and Cain built a city, and called its name after the name of his son Enoch.

10.   And Adam knew Eve his wife and she bare yet nine sons.

11.   And in the fifth week of the fifth jubilee [225-31 A.M.] Seth took Azûrâ his sister to be his wife, and in the fourth (year of the sixth week) [235 A.M.] she bare him Enos.

12.   He began to call on the name of the Lord on the earth.

13.   And in the seventh jubilee in the third week [309-15 A.M.] Enos took Nôâm his sister to be his wife,

and she bare him a son in the third year of the fifth week, and he called his name Kenan.

14.   And at the close of the eighth jubilee [325, 386-3992 A.M.] Kenan took Mûalêlêth his sister to be his wife, and she bare him a son in the ninth jubilee, in the first week in the third year of this week, [395 A.M] and he called his name Mahalalel.

15.   And in the second week of the tenth jubilee [449-55 A.M.] Mahalalel took unto him to wife DinaH, the daughter of Barakiel the daughter of his father's brother, and she bare him a son in the third week in the sixth year, [461 A.M.] and he called his name Jared, for in his days the angels of the Lord descended on the earth, those who are named the Watchers, that they should instruct the children of men, and that they should do judgment and uprightness on the earth.

16.   And in the eleventh jubilee [512-18 A.M.] Jared took to himself a wife, and her name was Baraka, the daughter of Râsûjâl, a daughter of his father's brother, in the fourth week of this jubilee, [522 A.M.] and she bare him a son in the fifth week, in the fourth year of the jubilee, and he called his name Enoch.

17.   And he was the first among men that are born on earth who learnt writing and knowledge and wisdom and who wrote down the signs of heaven according to the order of their months in a book, that men might know the seasons of the years according to the order of their separate months.

18.   And he was the first to write a testimony and he testified to the sons of men among the generations of the earth, and recounted the weeks of the jubilees, and made known to them the days of the years, and set in order the months and recounted the Sabbaths of the years as we made (them), known to him.

19.   And what was and what will be he saw in a vision of his sleep, as it will happen to the children of men throughout their generations until the day of judgment; he saw and understood everything, and wrote his testimony, and placed the testimony on earth for all the children of men and for their generations.

20.   And in the twelfth jubilee, [582-88] in the seventh week thereof, he took to himself a wife, and her name was Edna, the daughter of Danel, the daughter of his father's brother, and in the sixth year in this week [587 A.M.] she bare him a son and he called his name Methuselah.

21.   And he was moreover with the angels of God these six jubilees of years, and they showed him everything which is on earth and in the heavens, the rule of the sun, and he wrote down everything.

22.   And he testified to the Watchers, who had sinned with the daughters of men; for these had begun to unite themselves, so as to be defiled, with the daughters of

men, and Enoch testified against (them) all.

23. And he was taken from amongst the children of men, and we conducted him into the Garden of Eden in majesty and honour, and behold there he writes down the condemnation and judgment of the world, and all the wickedness of the children of men.

24. And on account of it (God) brought the waters of the flood upon all the land of Eden; for there he was set as a sign and that he should testify against all the children of men, that he should recount all the deeds of the generations until the day of condemnation.

25. And he burnt the incense of the sanctuary, (even) sweet spices acceptable before the Lord on the Mount.

26. For the Lord has four places on the earth, the Garden of Eden, and the Mount of the East, and this mountain on which thou art this day, Mount Sinai, and Mount Zion (which) will be sanctified in the new creation for a sanctification of the earth; through it will the earth be sanctified from all (its) guilt and its uncleanness through- out the generations of the world.

27. And in the fourteenth jubilee [652 A.M.] Methuselah took unto himself a wife, Edna the daughter of Azrial, the daughter of his father's brother, in the third week, in the first year of this week, [701-7 A.M.] and

he begat a son and called his name Lamech.

28. And in the fifteenth jubilee in the third week Lamech took to himself a wife, and her name was Betenos the daughter of Baraki'il, the daughter of his father's brother, and in this week she bare him a son and he called his name Noah, saying, 'This one will comfort me for my trouble and all my work, and for the ground which the Lord hath cursed.'

29. And at the close of the nineteenth jubilee, in the seventh week in the sixth year [930 A.M.] thereof, Adam died, and all his sons buried him in the land of his creation, and he was the first to be buried in the earth.

30. And he lacked seventy years of one thousand years; for one thousand years are as one day in the testimony of the heavens and therefore was it written concerning the tree of knowledge: 'On the day that ye eat thereof ye shall die.' For this reason he did not complete the years of this day; for he died during it.

31. At the close of this jubilee Cain was killed after him in the same year; for his house fell upon him and he died in the midst of his house, and he was killed by its stones; for with a stone he had killed Abel, and by a stone was he killed in righteous judgment.

32. For this reason it was ordained on the heavenly tablets: With the instrument with which a

man kills his neighbour with the same shall he be killed; after the manner that he wounded him, in like manner shall they deal with him.'

33.   And in the twenty-fifth [1205 A.M.] jubilee Noah took to himself a wife, and her name was `Emzârâ, the daughter of Râkê'êl, the daughter of his father's brother, in the first year in the fifth week [1207 A.M.]: and in the third year thereof she bare him Shem, in the fifth year thereof [1209 A.M.] she bare him Ham, and in the first year in the sixth week [1212 A.M.] she bare him Japheth.

Jubilees 5

1.   And it came to pass when the children of men began to multiply on the face of the earth and daughters were born unto them, that the angels of God saw them on a certain year of this jubilee, that they were beautiful to look upon; and they took themselves wives of all whom they chose, and they bare unto them sons and they were giants.

2.   And lawlessness increased on the earth and all flesh corrupted its way, alike men and cattle and beasts and birds and everything that walks on the earth -all of them corrupted their ways and their orders, and they began to devour each other, and lawlessness increased on the earth and every imagination of the thoughts of all men (was) thus evil continually.

3.   And God looked upon the earth, and behold it was corrupt, and all flesh had corrupted its orders, and all that were upon the earth had wrought all manner of evil before His eyes.

4.   And He said that He would destroy man and all flesh upon the face of the earth which He had created.

5.   But Noah found grace before the eyes of the Lord.

6.   And against the angels whom He had sent upon the earth, He was exceedingly wroth, and He gave commandment to root them out of all their dominion, and He bade us to bind them in the depths of the earth, and behold they are bound in the midst of them, and are (kept) separate.

7.   And against their sons went forth a command from before His face that they should be smitten with the sword, and be removed from under heaven.

8.   And He said 'My spirit shall not always abide on man; for they also are flesh and their days shall be one hundred and twenty years'.

9.   And He sent His sword into their midst that each should slay his neighbour, and they began to slay each other till they all fell by the sword and were destroyed from the earth.

10.   And their fathers were witnesses (of their destruction), and after this they were bound in the depths of the earth for ever, until the day of the great condemnation, when

judgment is executed on all those who have corrupted their ways and their works before the Lord.

11. And He destroyed all from their places, and there was not left one of them whom He judged not according to all their wickedness.

12. And he made for all his works a new and righteous nature, so that they should not sin in their whole nature for ever, but should be all righteous each in his kind alway.

13. And the judgment of all is ordained and written on the heavenly tablets in righteousness -even (the judgment of) all who depart from the path which is ordained for them to walk in; and if they walk not therein, judgment is written down for every creature and for every kind.

14. And there is nothing in heaven or on earth, or in light or in darkness, or in Sheol or in the depth, or in the place of darkness (which is not judged); and all their judgments are ordained and written and engraved.

15. In regard to all He will judge,the great according to his greatness, and the small according to his smallness, and each according to his way.

16. And He is not one who will regard the person (of any), nor is He one who will receive gifts, if He says that He will execute judgment on each: if one gave everything that is on the earth, He will not regard the gifts or the person (of any), nor accept anything at his hands, for He is a righteous judge.

17. [And of the children of Israel it has been written and ordained: If they turn to him in righteousness He will forgive all their transgressions and pardon all their sins.

18. It is written and ordained that He will show mercy to all who turn from all their guilt once each year.]

19. And as for all those who corrupted their ways and their thoughts before the flood, no man's person was accepted save that of Noah alone; for his person was accepted in behalf of his sons, whom (God) saved from the waters of the flood on his account; for his heart was righteous in all his ways, according as it was commanded regarding him, and he had not departed from aught that was ordained for him.

20. And the Lord said that he would destroy everything which was upon the earth, both men and cattle, and

21. beasts, and fowls of the air, and that which moveth on the earth. And He commanded Noah to make him an ark, that he might save himself from the waters of the flood.

22. And Noah made the ark in all respects as He commanded him, in the twenty-seventh jubilee of years, in the fifth week in the fifth year (on the new moon of the first month). [1307 A.M.]

23.   And he entered in the sixth (year) thereof, [1308 A.M.] in the second month, on the new moon of the second month, till the sixteenth; and he entered, and all that we brought to him, into the ark, and the Lord closed it from without on the seventeenth evening.

24.   And the Lord opened seven flood-gates of heaven, And the mouths of the fountains of the great deep, seven mouths in number.

25.   And the flood-gates began to pour down water from the heaven forty days and forty nights, And the fountains of the deep also sent up waters, until the whole world was full of water.

26.   And the waters increased upon the earth: Fifteen cubits did the waters rise above all the high mountains, And the ark was lift up above the earth,
And it moved upon the face of the waters.

27.   And the water prevailed on the face of the earth five months - one hundred and fifty days.

28.   And the ark went and rested on the top of Lubar, one of the mountains of Ararat.

29.   And (on the new moon) in the fourth month the fountains of the great deep were closed and the flood-gates of heaven were restrained; and on the new moon of the seventh month all the mouths of the abysses of the earth were opened, and the water began to descend into the deep below.

30.   And on the new moon of the tenth month the tops of the mountains were seen, and on the new moon of the first month the earth became visible.

31.   And the waters disappeared from above the earth in the fifth week in the seventh year [1309 A.M.] thereof, and on the seventeenth day in the second month the earth was dry.

32.   And on the twenty-seventh thereof he opened the ark, and sent forth from it beasts, and cattle, and birds, and every moving thing.

Jubilees 6

1.   And on the new moon of the third month he went forth from the ark, and built an altar on that mountain.

2.   And he made atonement for the earth, and took a kid and made atonement by its blood for all the guilt of the earth; for everything that had been on it had been destroyed, save those that were in the ark with Noah.

3.   And he placed the fat thereof on the altar, and he took an ox, and a goat, and a sheep and kids, and salt, and a turtle-dove, and the young of a dove, and placed a burnt sacrifice on the altar, and poured thereon an offering mingled with oil, and sprinkled wine and strewed frankincense over everything, and

caused a goodly savour to arise, acceptable before the Lord.

4.   And the Lord smelt the goodly savour, and He made a covenant with him that there should not be any more a flood to destroy the earth; that all the days of the earth seed-time and harvest should never cease; cold and heat, and summer and winter, and day and night should not change their order, nor cease for ever.

5.   'And you, increase ye and multiply upon the earth, and become many upon it, and be a blessing upon it. The fear of you and the dread of you I will inspire in everything that is on earth and in the sea.

6.   And behold I have given unto you all beasts, and all winged things, and everything that moves on the earth, and the fish in the waters, and all things for food; as the green herbs, I have given you all things to eat.

7.   But flesh, with the life thereof, with the blood, ye shall not eat; for the life of all flesh is in the blood, lest your blood of your lives be required. At the hand of every man, at the hand of every (beast) will I require the blood of man.

8.   Whoso sheddeth man's blood by man shall his blood be shed, for in the image of God made He man.

9.   And you, increase ye, and multiply on the earth.'

10.   And Noah and his sons swore that they would not eat any blood that was in any flesh, and he made a covenant before the Lord God for ever throughout all the generations of the earth in this month.

11.   On this account He spake to thee that thou shouldst make a covenant with the children of Israel in this month upon the mountain with an oath, and that thou shouldst sprinkle blood upon them because of all the words of the covenant, which the Lord made with them for ever.

12.   And this testimony is written concerning you that you should observe it continually, so that you should not eat on any day any blood of beasts or birds or cattle during all the days of the earth, and the man who eats the blood of beast or of cattle or of birds during all the days of the earth, he and his seed shall be rooted out of the land.

13.   And do thou command the children of Israel to eat no blood, so that their names and their seed may be before the Lord our God continually.

14.   And for this law there is no limit of days, for it is for ever. They shall observe it throughout their generations, so that they may continue supplicating on your behalf with blood before the altar; every day and at the time of morning and evening they shall seek forgiveness on your behalf perpetually before the Lord that they may keep it and not be rooted out.

15.   And He gave to Noah and his sons a sign that there should not again be a flood on the earth.

16.   He set His bow in the cloud for a sign of the eternal covenant that there should not again be a flood on the earth to destroy it all the days of the earth.

17.   For this reason it is ordained and written on the heavenly tablets, that they should celebrate the feast of weeks in this month once a year, to renew the covenant every year.

18.   And this whole festival was celebrated in heaven from the day of creation till the days of Noah -twenty-six jubilees and five weeks of years [1309-1659 A.M.]: and Noah and his sons observed it for seven jubilees and one week of years, till the day of Noah's death, and from the day of Noah's death his sons did away with (it) until the days of Abraham, and they eat blood.

19.   But Abraham observed it, and Isaac and Jacob and his children observed it up to thy days, and in thy days the children of Israel forgot it until ye celebrated it anew on this mountain.

20.   And do thou command the children of Israel to observe this festival in all their generations for a commandment unto them: one day in the year in this month they shall celebrate the festival.

21.   For it is the feast of weeks and the feast of first fruits: this feast is twofold and of a double nature:

according to what is written and engraven concerning it, celebrate it.

22.   For I have written in the book of the first law, in that which I have written for thee, that thou shouldst celebrate it in its season, one day in the year, and I explained to thee its sacrifices that the children of Israel should remember and should celebrate it throughout their generations in this month, one day in every year.

23.   And on the new moon of the first month, and on the new moon of the fourth month, and on the new moon of the seventh month, and on the new moon of the tenth month are the days of remembrance, and the days of the seasons in the four divisions of the year. These are written and ordained as a testimony for ever.

24.   And Noah ordained them for himself as feasts for the generations for ever, so that they have become thereby a memorial unto him.

25.   And on the new moon of the first month he was bidden to make for himself an ark, and on that (day) the earth became dry and he opened (the ark) and saw the earth.

26.   And on the new moon of the fourth month the mouths of the depths of the abyss beneath were closed. And on the new moon of the seventh month all the mouths of the abysses of the earth were opened, and the waters began to descend into them.

27. And on the new moon of the tenth month the tops of the mountains were seen, and Noah was glad.

28. And on this account he ordained them for himself as feasts for a memorial for ever, and thus are they ordained.

29. And they placed them on the heavenly tablets, each had thirteen weeks; from one to another (passed) their memorial, from the first to the second, and from the second to the third, and from the third to the fourth.

30. And all the days of the commandment will be two and fifty weeks of days, and (these will make) the entire year complete. Thus it is engraven and ordained on the heavenly tablets.

31. And there is no neglecting (this commandment) for a single year or from year to year.

32. And command thou the children of Israel that they observe the years according to this reckoning- three hundred and sixty-four days, and (these) will constitute a complete year, and they will not disturb its time from its days and from its feasts; for everything will fall out in them according to their testimony, and they will not leave out any day nor disturb any feasts.

33. But if they do neglect and do not observe them according to His commandment, then they will disturb all their seasons and the years will be dislodged from this (order), [and they will disturb the seasons and the years will be dislodged] and they will neglect their ordinances.

34. And all the children of Israel will forget and will not find the path of the years, and will forget the new moons, and seasons, and sabbaths and they will go wrong as to all the order of the years.

35. For I know and from henceforth will I declare it unto thee, and it is not of my own devising; for the book (lies) written before me, and on the heavenly tablets the division of days is ordained, lest they forget the feasts of the covenant and walk according to the feasts of the Gentiles after their error and after their ignorance.

36. For there will be those who will assuredly make observations of the moon -how (it) disturbs the seasons and comes in from year to year ten days too soon.

37. For this reason the years will come upon them when they will disturb (the order), and make an abominable (day) the day of testimony, and an unclean day a feast day, and they will confound all the days, the holy with the unclean, and the unclean day with the holy; for they will go wrong as to the months and sabbaths and feasts and jubilees.

38. For this reason I command and testify to thee that thou mayst testify to them; for after thy death thy children will disturb (them), so that they will not make the year three hundred and sixty-four days only,

and for this reason they will go wrong as to the new moons and seasons and sabbaths and festivals, and they will eat all kinds of blood with all kinds of flesh.

Jubilees 7

1. And in the seventh week in the first year [1317 A.M.] thereof, in this jubilee, Noah planted vines on the mountain on which the ark had rested, named Lubar, one of the Ararat Mountains, and they produced fruit in the fourth year, [1320 A.M.] and he guarded their fruit, and gathered it in this year in the seventh month.

2. And he made wine therefrom and put it into a vessel, and kept it until the fifth year, [1321 A.M.] until the first day, on the new moon of the first month.

3. And he celebrated with joy the day of this feast, and he made a burnt sacrifice unto the Lord, one young ox and one ram, and seven sheep, each a year old, and a kid of the goats, that he might make atonement thereby for himself and his sons.

4. And he prepared the kid first, and placed some of its blood on the flesh that was on the altar which he had made, and all the fat he laid on the altar where he made the burnt sacrifice, and the ox and the ram and the sheep, and he laid all their flesh upon the altar.

5. And he placed all their offerings mingled with oil upon it, and afterwards he sprinkled wine on the fire which he had previously made on the altar, and he placed incense on the altar and caused a sweet savour to ascend acceptable before the Lord his God.

6. And he rejoiced and drank of this wine, he and his children with joy.

7. And it was evening, and he went into his tent, and being drunken he lay down and slept, and was uncovered in his tent as he slept.

8. And Ham saw Noah his father naked, and went forth and told his two brethren without.

9. And Shem took his garment and arose, he and Japheth, and they placed the garment on their shoulders and went backward and covered the shame of their father, and their faces were backward.

10. And Noah awoke from his sleep and knew all that his younger son had done unto him, and he cursed his son and said: 'Cursed be Canaan; an enslaved servant shall he be unto his brethren.'

11. And he blessed Shem, and said: 'Blessed be the Lord God of Shem, and Canaan shall be his servant.

12. God shall enlarge Japheth, and God shall dwell in the dwelling of Shem, and Canaan shall be his servant.'

13. And Ham knew that his father had cursed his younger son, and he was displeased that he had cursed

his son. and he parted from his father, he and his sons with him, Cush and Mizraim and Put and Canaan.

14.   And he built for himself a city and called its name after the name of his wife Ne'elatama'uk.

15.   And Japheth saw it, and became envious of his brother, and he too built for himself a city, and he called its name after the name of his wife 'Adataneses.

16.   And Shem dwelt with his father Noah, and he built a city close to his father on the mountain, and he too called its name after the name of his wife Sedeqetelebab.

17.   And behold these three cities are near Mount Lubar; Sedeqetelebab fronting the mountain on its east; and Na'eltama'uk on the south; 'Adatan'eses towards the west.

18.   And these are the sons of Shem: Elam, and Asshur, and Arpachshad -this (son) was born two years after the flood- and Lud, and Aram.

19.   The sons of Japheth: Gomer and Magog and Madai and Javan, Tubal and Meshech and Tiras: these are the sons of Noah.

20.   And in the twenty-eighth jubilee [1324-1372 A.M.] Noah began to enjoin upon his sons' sons the ordinances and commandments, and all the judgments that he knew, and he exhorted his sons to observe righteousness, and to cover the shame of their flesh, and to bless their Creator, and honour father and mother, and love their neighbour, and guard their souls from fornication and uncleanness and all iniquity.

21.   For owing to these three things came the flood upon the earth, namely, owing to the fornication wherein the Watchers against the law of their ordinances went a whoring after the daughters of men, and took themselves wives of all which they chose: and they made the beginning of uncleanness.

22.   And they begat sons the Naphidim, and they were all unlike, and they devoured one another: and the Giants slew the Naphil, and the Naphil slew the Eljo, and the Eljo mankind, and one man another.

23.   And every one sold himself to work iniquity and to shed much blood, and the earth was filled with iniquity.

24.   And after this they sinned against the beasts and birds, and all that moves and walks on the earth: and much blood was shed on the earth, and every imagination and desire of men imagined vanity and evil continually.

25.   And the Lord destroyed everything from off the face of the earth; because of the wickedness of their deeds, and because of the blood which they had shed in the midst of the earth He destroyed everything.

26.   'And we were left, I and you, my sons, and everything that entered with us into the ark, and behold I see your works before me that ye do not walk in righteousness: for in the path of destruction ye have begun to walk, and ye are parting one from another, and are envious one of another, and (so it comes) that ye are not in harmony, my sons, each with his brother.

27.   For I see, and behold the demons have begun (their) seductions against you and against your children and now I fear on your behalf, that after my death ye will shed the blood of men upon the earth, and that ye, too, will be destroyed from the face of the earth.

28.   For whoso sheddeth man's blood, and whoso eateth the blood of any flesh, shall all be destroyed from the earth.

29.   And there shall not be left any man that eateth blood, or that sheddeth the blood of man on the earth, Nor shall there be left to him any seed or descendants living under heaven; For into Sheol shall they go, And into the place of condemnation shall they descend, And into the darkness of the deep shall they all be removed by a violent death.

30.   There shall be no blood seen upon you of all the blood there shall be all the days in which ye have killed any beasts or cattle or whatever flies upon the earth, and work ye a good work to your souls by covering that which has been shed on the face of the earth.

31.   And ye shall not be like him who eats with blood, but guard yourselves that none may eat blood before you: cover the blood, for thus have I been commanded to testify to you and your children, together with all flesh.

32.   And suffer not the soul to be eaten with the flesh, that your blood, which is your life, may not be required at the hand of any flesh that sheds (it) on the earth.

33.   For the earth will not be clean from the blood which has been shed upon it; for (only) through the blood of him that shed it will the earth be purified throughout all its generations.

34.   And now, my children, harken: work judgment and righteousness that ye maybe planted in righteousness over the face of the whole earth, and your glory lifted up before my God, who saved me from the waters of the flood.

35.   And behold, ye will go and build for yourselves cities, and plant in them all the plants that are upon the earth, and moreover all fruit-bearing trees.

36.   For three years the fruit of everything that is eaten will not be gathered: and in the fourth year its fruit will be accounted holy [and they will offer the first-fruits], acceptable before the Most High God, who created heaven and earth and all things. Let them offer in abundance

the first of the wine and oil (as) first-fruits on the altar of the Lord, who receives it, and what is left let the servants of the house of the Lord eat before the altar which receives (it).

37. And in the fifth year make ye the release so that ye release it in righteousness and uprightness, and ye shall be righteous, and all that you plant shall prosper.

38. For thus did Enoch, the father of your father command Methuselah, his son, and Methuselah his son Lamech, and Lamech commanded me all the things which his fathers commanded him.

39. And I also will give you commandment, my sons, as Enoch commanded his son in the first jubilees: whilst still living, the seventh in his generation, he commanded and testified to his son and to his son's sons until the day of his death.'

Jubilees 8

1. In the twenty-ninth jubilee, in the first week, [1373 A.M.] in the beginning thereof Arpachshad took to himself a wife and her name was Rasu'eja, the daughter of Susan, the daughter of Elam, and she bare him a son in the third year in this week, [1375 A.M.] and he called his name Kainam.

2. And the son grew, and his father taught him writing, and he went to seek for himself a place where he might seize for himself a city.

3. And he found a writing which former (generations) had carved on the rock, and he read what was thereon, and he transcribed it and sinned owing to it; for it contained the teaching of the Watchers in accordance with which they used to observe the omens of the sun and moon and stars in all the signs of heaven.

4. And he wrote it down and said nothing regarding it; for he was afraid to speak to Noah about it lest he should be angry with him on account of it.

5. And in the thirtieth jubilee, [1429 A.M.] in the second week, in the first year thereof, he took to himself a wife, and her name was Melka, the daughter of Madai, the son of Japheth, and in the fourth year [1432 A.M.] he begat a son, and called his name Shelah; for he said: 'Truly I have been sent.'

6. [And in the fourth year he was born], and Shelah grew up and took to himself a wife, and her name was Mu'ak, the daughter of Kesed, his father's brother, in the one and thirtieth jubilee, in the fifth week, in the first year [1499 A.M.] thereof.

7. And she bare him a son in the fifth year [1503 A.M.] thereof, and he called his name Eber: and he took unto himself a wife, and her name was 'Azûrâd, the daughter of Nebrod, in the thirty-second jubilee, in the seventh week, in the third year thereof. [1564 A.M.]

8.　　And in the sixth year [1567 A.M.] thereof, she bare him son, and he called his name Peleg; for in the days when he was born the children of Noah began to divide the earth amongst themselves: for this reason he called his name Peleg.

9.　　And they divided (it) secretly amongst themselves, and told it to Noah.

10.　　And it came to pass in the beginning of the thirty-third jubilee [1569 A.M.] that they divided the earth into three parts, for Shem and Ham and Japheth, according to the inheritance of each, in the first year in the first week, when one of us who had been sent, was with them.

11.　　And he called his sons, and they drew nigh to him, they and their children, and he divided the earth into the lots, which his three sons were to take in possession, and they reached forth their hands, and took the writing out of the bosom of Noah, their father.

12.　　And there came forth on the writing as Shem's lot the middle of the earth which he should take as an inheritance for himself and for his sons for the generations of eternity, from the middle of the mountain range of Rafa, from the mouth of the water from the river Tina, and his portion goes towards the west through the midst of this river, and it extends till it reaches the water of the abysses, out of which this river goes forth and pours its waters into the sea Me'at, and this river flows into the great sea. And all that is towards the north is Japheth's, and all that is towards the south belongs to Shem.

13.　　And it extends till it reaches Karaso: this is in the bosom of the tongue which looks towards the south.

14.　　And his portion extends along the great sea, and it extends in a straight line till it reaches the west of the tongue which looks towards the south: for this sea is named the tongue of the Egyptian Sea.

15.　　And it turns from here towards the south towards the mouth of the great sea on the shore of (its) waters, and it extends to the west to 'Afra, and it extends till it reaches the waters of the river Gihon, and to the south of the waters of Gihon, to the banks of this river.

16.　　And it extends towards the east, till it reaches the Garden of Eden, to the south thereof, [to the south] and from the east of the whole land of Eden and of the whole east, it turns to the east and proceeds till it reaches the east of the mountain named Rafa, and it descends to the bank of the mouth of the river Tina.

17.　　This portion came forth by lot for Shem and his sons, that they should possess it for ever unto his generations for evermore.

18.　　And Noah rejoiced that this portion came forth for Shem and for his sons, and he remembered all that he had spoken with his mouth in prophecy; for he had said: 'Blessed be the Lord God of Shem And may the Lord dwell in the dwelling of Shem.'

19. And he knew that the Garden of Eden is the holy of holies, and the dwelling of the Lord, and Mount Sinai the centre of the desert, and Mount Zion -the centre of the navel of the earth: these three were created as holy places facing each other.

20. And he blessed the God of gods, who had put the word of the Lord into his mouth, and the Lord for evermore.

21. And he knew that a blessed portion and a blessing had come to Shem and his sons unto the generations for ever -the whole land of Eden and the whole land of the Red Sea, and the whole land of the east and India, and on the Red Sea and the mountains thereof, and all the land of Bashan, and all the land of Lebanon and the islands of Kaftur, and all the mountains of Sanir and 'Amana, and the mountains of Asshur in the north, and all the land of Elam, Asshur, and Babel, and Susan and Ma'edai, and all the mountains of Ararat, and all the region beyond the sea, which is beyond the mountains of Asshur towards the north, a blessed and spacious land, and all that is in it is very good.

22. And for Ham came forth the second portion, beyond the Gihon towards the south to the right of the Garden, and it extends towards the south and it extends to all the mountains of fire, and it extends towards the west to the sea of 'Atel

and it extends towards the west till it reaches the sea of Ma'uk -that (sea) into which everything which is not destroyed descends.

23. And it goes forth towards the north to the limits of Gadir, and it goes forth to the coast of the waters of the sea to the waters of the great sea till it draws near to the river Gihon, and goes along the river Gihon till it reaches the right of the Garden of Eden.

24. And this is the land which came forth for Ham as the portion which he was to occupy for ever for himself and his sons unto their generations for ever.

25. And for Japheth came forth the third portion beyond the river Tina to the north of the outflow of its waters, and it extends north- easterly to the whole region of Gog, and to all the country east thereof.

26. And it extends northerly to the north, and it extends to the mountains of Qelt towards the north, and towards the sea of Ma'uk, and it goes forth to the east of Gadir as far as the region of the waters of the sea.

27. And it extends until it approaches the west of Fara and it returns towards 'Aferag, and it extends easterly to the waters of the sea of Me'at.

28. And it extends to the region of the river Tina in a north-easterly direction until it approaches the boundary of its waters towards the

mountain Rafa, and it turns round towards the north.

29.   This is the land which came forth for Japheth and his sons as the portion of his inheritance which he should possess for himself and his sons, for their generations for ever; five great islands, and a great land in the north.

30.   But it is cold, and the land of Ham is hot, and the land of Shem is neither hot nor cold, but it is of blended cold and heat.

Jubilees 9

1.   And Ham divided amongst his sons, and the first portion came forth for Cush towards the east, and to the west of him for Mizraim, and to the west of him for Put, and to the west of him [and to the west thereof] on the sea for Canaan.

2.   And Shem also divided amongst his sons, and the first portion came forth for Ham and his sons, to the east of the river Tigris till it approachcs the east, the whole land of India, and on the Red Sea on its coast, and the waters of Dedan, and all the mountains of Mebri and Ela, and all the land of Susan and all that is on the side of Pharnak to the Red Sea and the river Tina.

3.   And for Asshur came forth the second Portion, all the land of Asshur and Nineveh and Shinar and to the border of India, and it ascends and skirts the river.

4.   And for Arpachshad came forth the third portion, all the land of the region of the Chaldees to the east of the Euphrates, bordering on the Red Sea, and all the waters of the desert close to the tongue of the sea which looks towards Egypt, all the land of Lebanon and Sanir and 'Amana to the border of the Euphrates.

5.   And for Aram there came forth the fourth portion, all the land of Mesopotamia between the Tigris and the Euphrates to the north of the Chaldees to the border of the mountains of Asshur and the land of 'Arara.

6.   And there came forth for Lud the fifth portion, the mountains of Asshur and all appertaining to them till it reaches the Great Sea, and till it reaches the east of Asshur his brother.

7.   And Japheth also divided the land of his inheritance amongst his sons.

8.   And the first portion came forth for Gomer to the east from the north side to the river Tina; and in the north there came forth for Magog all the inner portions of the north until it reaches to the sea of Me'at.

9.   And for Madai came forth as his portion that he should posses from the west of his two brothers to the islands, and to the coasts of the islands.

10.   And for Javan came forth the fourth portion every island and the

islands which are towards the border of Lud.

11.   And for Tubal there came forth the fifth portion in the midst of the tongue which approaches towards the border of the portion of Lud to the second tongue, to the region beyond the second tongue unto the third tongue.

12.   And for Meshech came forth the sixth portion, all the region beyond the third tongue till it approaches the east of Gadir.

13.   And for Tiras there came forth the seventh portion, four great islands in the midst of the sea, which reach to the portion of Ham [and the islands of Kamaturi came out by lot for the sons of Arpachshad as his inheritance].

14.   And thus the sons of Noah divided unto their sons in the presence of Noah their father, and he bound them all by an oath, imprecating a curse on every one that sought to seize the portion which had not fallen (to him) by his lot.

15.   And they all said, 'So be it; so be it ' for themselves and their sons for ever throughout their generations till the day of judgment, on which the Lord God shall judge them with a sword and with fire for all the unclean wickedness of their errors, wherewith they have filled the earth with transgression and uncleanness and fornication and sin.

Jubilees 10

1.   And in the third week of this jubilee the unclean demons began to lead astray the children of the sons of Noah, and to make to err and destroy them.

2.   And the sons of Noah came to Noah their father, and they told him concerning the demons which were leading astray and blinding and slaying his sons' sons.

3.   And he prayed before the Lord his God, and said:

'God of the spirits of all flesh, who hast shown mercy unto me
And hast saved me and my sons from the waters of the flood,
And hast not caused me to perish as Thou didst the sons of perdition;

For Thy grace has been great towards   me,
And great has been Thy mercy to my soul;

Let Thy grace be lift up upon my sons,
And let not wicked spirits rule over them
Lest they should destroy them from the earth.

4.   But do Thou bless me and my sons, that we may increase and Multiply and replenish the earth.

5.   And Thou knowest how Thy Watchers, the fathers of these spirits, acted in my day: and as for these spirits which are living,

imprison them and hold them fast in the place of condemnation, and let them not bring destruction on the sons of thy servant, my God; for these are malignant, and created in order to destroy.

6.   And let them not rule over the spirits of the living; for Thou alone canst exercise dominion over them. And let them not have power over the sons of the righteous from henceforth and for evermore.'

7.   And the Lord our God bade us to bind all.

8.   And the chief of the spirits, Mastêmâ, came and said: 'Lord, Creator, let some of them remain before me, and let them harken to my voice, and do all that I shall say unto them; for if some of them are not left to me, I shall not be able to execute the power of my will on the sons of men; for these are for corruption and leading astray before my judgment, for great is the wickedness of the sons of men.'

9.   And He said: Let the tenth part of them remain before him, and let nine parts descend into the place of condemnation.'

10.   And one of us He commanded that we should teach Noah all their medicines; for He knew that they would not walk in uprightness, nor strive in righteousness.

11.   And we did according to all His words: all the malignant evil ones we bound in the place of condemnation and a tenth part of them we left that they might be subject before Satan on the earth.

12.   And we explained to Noah all the medicines of their diseases, together with their seductions, how he might heal them with herbs of the earth.

13.   And Noah wrote down all things in a book as we instructed him concerning every kind of medicine. Thus the evil spirits were precluded from (hurting) the sons of Noah.

14.   And he gave all that he had written to Shem, his eldest son; for he loved him exceedingly above all his sons.

15.   And Noah slept with his fathers, and was buried on Mount Lubar in the land of Ararat.

16.   Nine hundred and fifty years he completed in his life, nineteen jubilees and two weeks and five years. [1659 A.M.]

17.   And in his life on earth he excelled the children of men save Enoch because of the righteousness, wherein he was perfect. For Enoch's office was ordained for a testimony to the generations of the world, so that he should recount all the deeds of generation unto generation, till the day of judgment.

18.   And in the three and thirtieth jubilee, in the first year in the second week, Peleg took to himself a wife, whose name was Lomna the daughter of Sina'ar, and she bare him a son in the fourth year of this week, and he called his name Reu;

for he said: 'Behold the children of men have become evil through the wicked purpose of building for themselves a city and a tower in the land of Shinar.'

19.   For they departed from the land of Ararat eastward to Shinar; for in his days they built the city and the tower, saying, 'Go to, let us ascend thereby into heaven.'

20.   And they began to build, and in the fourth week they made brick with fire, and the bricks served them for stone, and the clay with which they cemented them together was asphalt which comes out of the sea, and out of the fountains of water in the land of Shinar.

21.   And they built it: forty and three years [1645-1688 A.M.] were they building it; its breadth was 203 bricks, and the height (of a brick) was the third of one; its height amounted to 5433 cubits and 2 palms, and (the extent of one wall was) thirteen stades (and of the other thirty stades).

22.   And the Lord our God said unto us: Behold, they are one people, and (this) they begin to do, and now nothing will be withholden from them. Go to, let us go down and confound their language, that they may not understand one another's speech, and they may be dispersed into cities and nations, and one purpose will no longer abide with them till the day of judgment.'

23.   And the Lord descended, and we descended with him to see the city and the tower which the children of men had built.

24.   And he confounded their language, and they no longer understood one another's speech, and they ceased then to build the city and the tower.

25.   For this reason the whole land of Shinar is called Babel, because the Lord did there confound all the language of the children of men, and from thence they were dispersed into their cities, each according to his language and his nation.

26.   And the Lord sent a mighty wind against the tower and overthrew it upon the earth, and behold it was between Asshur and Babylon in the land of Shinar, and they called its name 'Overthrow'.

27.   In the fourth week in the first year [1688 A.M.] in the beginning thereof in the four and thirtieth jubilee, were they dispersed from the land of Shinar.

28.   And Ham and his sons went into the land which he was to occupy, which he acquired as his portion in the land of the south.

29.   And Canaan saw the land of Lebanon to the river of Egypt, that it was very good, and he went not into the land of his inheritance to the west (that is to) the sea, and he dwelt in the land of Lebanon, eastward and westward from the border of Jordan and from the border of the sea.

30.   And Ham, his father, and Cush and Mizraim his brothers said unto him: 'Thou hast settled in a land which is not thine, and which did not fall to us by lot: do not do so; for if thou dost do so, thou and thy sons will fall in the land and (be) accursed through sedition; for by sedition ye have settled, and by sedition will thy children fall, and thou shalt be rooted out for ever.

31.   Dwell not in the dwelling of Shem; for to Shem and to his sons did it come by their lot.

32.   Cursed art thou, and cursed shalt thou be beyond all the sons of Noah, by the curse by which we bound ourselves by an oath in the presence of the holy judge, and in the presence of Noah our father.'

33.   But he did not harken unto them, and dwelt in the land of Lebanon from Hamath to the entering of Egypt, he and his sons until this day.

34.   And for this reason that land is named Canaan.

35.   And Japheth and his sons went towards the sea and dwelt in the land of their portion, and Madai saw the land of the sea and it did not please him, and he begged a (portion) from Ham and Asshur and Arpachshad, his wife's brother, and he dwelt in the land of Media, near to his wife's brother until this day.

36.   And he called his dwelling-place, and the dwelling-place of his sons, Media, after the name of their father Madai.

Jubilees 11

1.   And in the thirty-fifth jubilee, in the third week, in the first year [1681 A.M.] thereof, Reu took to himself a wife, and her name was 'Ôrâ, the daughter of 'Ûr, the son of Kesed, and she bare him a son, and he called his name Sêrôh, in the seventh year of this week in this jubilee. [1687 A.M.]

2.   And the sons of Noah began to war on each other, to take captive and to slay each other, and to shed the blood of men on the earth, and to eat blood, and to build strong cities, and walls, and towers, and individuals (began) to exalt themselves above the nation, and to found the beginnings of kingdoms, and to go to war people against people, and nation against nation, and city against city, and all (began) to do evil, and to acquire arms, and to teach their sons war, and they began to capture cities, and to sell male and female slaves.

3.   And 'Ûr, the son of Kesed, built the city of 'Ara of the Chaldees, and called its name after his own name and the name of his father. And they made for themselves molten images, and they worshipped each the idol, the molten image which they had made for themselves, and they began to make graven images and unclean simulacra, and malignant spirits assisted and seduced (them) into committing transgression and uncleanness.

4.   And the prince Mastêmâ exerted himself to do all this, and he sent forth other spirits, those which were put under his hand, to do all manner of wrong and sin, and all manner of transgression, to corrupt and destroy, and to shed blood upon the earth.

5.   For this reason he called the name of Sêrôh, Serug, for every one turned to do all manner of sin and transgression.

6.   And he grew up, and dwelt in Ur of the Chaldees, near to the father of his wife's mother, and he worshipped idols, and he took to himself a wife in the thirty-sixth jubilee, in the fifth week, in the first year thereof, [1744 A.M.] and her name was Melka, the daughter of Kaber, the daughter of his father's brother.

7.   And she bare him Nahor, in the first year of this week, and he grew and dwelt in Ur of the Chaldees, and his father taught him the researches of the Chaldees to divine and augur, according to the signs of heaven.

8.   And in the thirty-seventh jubilee in the sixth week, in the first year thereof, [1800 A.M.] he took to himself a wife, and her name was 'Ijaska, the daughter of Nestag of the Chaldees.

9.   And she bare him Terah in the seventh year of this week. [1806 A.M.]

10.   And the prince Mastêmâ sent ravens and birds to devour the seed which was sown in the land, in order to destroy the land, and rob the children of men of their labours. Before they could plough in the seed, the ravens picked (it) from the surface of the ground.

11.   And for this reason he called his name Terah because the ravens and the birds reduced them to destitution and devoured their seed.

12.   And the years began to be barren, owing to the birds, and they devoured all the fruit of the trees from the trees: it was only with great effort that they could save a little of all the fruit of the earth in their days.

13.   And in this thirty-ninth jubilee, in the second week in the first year, [1870 A.M.] Terah took to himself a wife, and her name was 'Edna, the daughter of 'Abram, the daughter of his father's sister. And in the seventh year of this week [1876 A.M.] she bare him a son, and he called his name Abram, by the name of the father of his mother;

14.   for he had died before his daughter had conceived a son.

15.   And the child began to understand the errors of the earth that all went astray after graven images and after uncleanness, and his father taught him writing, and he was two weeks of years old, [1890 A.M.] and he separated himself from his father, that he might not worship idols with him.

16.   And he began to pray to the Creator of all things that He might save him from the errors of the

children of men, and that his portion should not fall into error after uncleanness and vileness.

17.   And the seed time came for the sowing of seed upon the land, and they all went forth together to protect their seed against the ravens, and Abram went forth with those that went, and the child was a lad of fourteen years.

18.   And a cloud of ravens came to devour the seed, and Abram ran to meet them before they settled on the ground, and cried to them before they settled on the ground to devour the seed, and said, ' Descend not: return to the place whence ye came,' and they proceeded to turn back.

19.   And he caused the clouds of ravens to turn back that day seventy times, and of all the ravens throughout all the land where Abram was there settled there not so much as one.

20.   And all who were with him throughout all the land saw him cry out, and all the ravens turn back, and his name became great in all the land of the Chaldees.

21.   And there came to him this year all those that wished to sow, and he went with them until the time of sowing ceased: and they sowed their land, and that year they brought enough grain home and eat and were satisfied.

22.   And in the first year of the fifth week [1891 A.M.] Abram taught those who made implements for oxen, the artificers in wood, and they made a vessel above the ground, facing the frame of the plough, in order to put the seed thereon, and the seed fell down therefrom upon the share of the plough, and was hidden in the earth, and they no longer feared the ravens.

23.   And after this manner they made (vessels) above the ground on all the frames of the ploughs, and they sowed and tilled all the land, according as Abram commanded them, and they no longer feared the birds.

Jubilees 12

1.   And it came to pass in the sixth week, in the seventh year thereof, [1904 A.M.] that Abram said to Terah his father, saying, 'Father!'

2.   And he said, 'Behold, here am I, my son.' And he said,

'What help and profit have we from those idols which thou dost worship, And before which thou dost bow thyself?

3.   For there is no spirit in them, For they are dumb forms, and a misleading   of   the   heart. Worship them not:

4.   Worship the God of heaven, Who causes the rain and the dew to descend   on   the   earth And does everything upon the earth,

And has created everything by His word,
And all life is from before His face.

5.   Why do ye worship things that have no spirit in them? For they are the work of (men's) hands,

And on your shoulders do ye bear them,
And ye have no help from them,

But they are a great cause of shame to those who make them, And a misleading of the heart to those who worship them: Worship them not.'

6.   And his father said unto him, I also know it, my son, but what shall I do with a people who have made me to serve before them?

7.   And if I tell them the truth, they will slay me; for their soul cleaves to them to worship them and honour them.

8.   Keep silent, my son, lest they slay thee.' And these words he spake to his two brothers, and they were angry with him and he kept silent.

9.   And in the fortieth jubilee, in the second week, in the seventh year thereof, [1925 A.M.] Abram took to himself a wife, and her name was Sarai, the daughter of his father, and she became his wife.

10.   And Haran, his brother, took to himself a wife in the third year of the third week, [1928 A.M.] and she bare him a son in the seventh year of this week, [1932 A.M.] and he called his name Lot.

11.   And Nahor, his brother, took to himself a wife.

12.   And in the sixtieth year of the life of Abram, that is, in the fourth week, in the fourth year thereof, [1936 A.M.] Abram arose by night, and burned the house of the idols, and he burned all that was in the house and no man knew it.

13.   And they arose in the night and sought to save their gods from the midst of the fire.

14.   And Haran hasted to save them, but the fire flamed over him, and he was burnt in the fire, and he died in Ur of the Chaldees before Terah his father, and they buried him in Ur of the Chaldees.

15.   And Terah went forth from Ur of the Chaldees, he and his sons, to go into the land of Lebanon and into the land of Canaan, and he dwelt in the land of Haran, and Abram dwelt with Terah his father in Haran two weeks of years.

16.   And in the sixth week, in the fifth year thereof, [1951 A.M.] Abram sat up throughout the night on the new moon of the seventh month to observe the stars from the evening to the morning, in order to see what would be the character of the year with regard to the rains, and he was alone as he sat and observed.

17.   And a word came into his heart and he said: All the signs of the stars, and the signs of the moon and of the sun are all in the hand of the Lord. Why do I search (them) out?

18.   If He desires, He causes it to rain, morning and evening; And if He desires, He withholds it, And all things are in his hand.'

19.   And he prayed that night and said,
'My God, God Most High, Thou alone art my God,
And Thee and Thy dominion have I chosen.
And Thou hast created all things, And all things that are the work of thy hands.

20.   Deliver me from the hands of evil spirits who have dominion over the thoughts of men's hearts, And let them not lead me astray from Thee, my God.

And stablish Thou me and my seed for ever
That we go not astray from henceforth and for evermore.'

21.   And he said, 'Shall I return unto Ur of the Chaldees who seek my face that I may return to them, am I to remain here in this place? The right path before Thee prosper it in the hands of Thy servant that he may fulfil (it) and that I may not walk in the deceitfulness of my heart, O my God.'

22.   And he made an end of speaking and praying, and behold the word of the Lord was sent to him through me, saying: 'Get thee up from thy country, and from thy kindred and from the house of thy father unto a land which I will show thee, and I shall make thee a great and numerous nation.

23.   And I will bless thee And I will make thy name great, And thou shalt be blessed in the earth,
And in Thee shall all families of the earth be blessed,
And I will bless them that bless thee, And curse them that curse thee.

24.   And I will be a God to thee and thy son, and to thy son's son, and to all thy seed: fear not, from henceforth and unto all generations of the earth I am thy God.'

25.   And the Lord God said: 'Open his mouth and his ears, that he may hear and speak with his mouth, with the language which has been revealed'; for it had ceased from the mouths of all the children of men from the day of the overthrow (of Babel).

26.   And I opened his mouth, and his ears and his lips, and I began to speak with him in Hebrew in the tongue of the creation.

27.   And he took the books of his fathers, and these were written in Hebrew, and he transcribed them, and he began from henceforth to study them, and I made known to him that which he could not (understand), and he studied them during the six rainy months.

28.   And it came to pass in the seventh year of the sixth week [1953 A.M.] that he spoke to his father and informed him, that he would leave

Haran to go into the land of Canaan to see it and return to him.

29.   And Terah his father said unto him; Go in peace:

May the eternal God make thy path straight.
And the Lord [(be) with thee, and] protect thee from all evil,
And grant unto thee grace, mercy and favour before those who see thee,
And may none of the children of men have power over thee to harm thee;
Go in peace.

30.   And if thou seest a land pleasant to thy eyes to dwell in, then arise and take me to thee and take Lot with thee, the son of Haran thy brother as thine own son: the Lord be with thee.

31.   And Nahor thy brother leave with me till thou returnest in peace, and we go with thee all together.'

Jubilees 13

1.   And Abram journeyed from Haran, and he took Sarai, his wife, and Lot, his brother Haran's son, to the land of Canaan, and he came into Asshur, and proceeded to Shechem, and dwelt near a lofty oak.

2.   And he saw, and, behold, the land was very pleasant from the entering of Hamath to the lofty oak.

3.   And the Lord said to him: 'To thee and to thy seed will I give this land.'

4.   And he built an altar there, and he offered thereon a burnt sacrifice to the Lord, who had appeared to him.

5.   And he removed from thence unto the mountain . . . Bethel on the west and Ai on the east, and pitched his tent there.

6.   And he saw and behold, the land was very wide and good, and everything grew thereon -vines and figs and pomegranates, oaks and ilexes, and terebinths and oil trees, and cedars and cypresses and date trees, and all trees of the field, and there was water on the mountains.

7.   And he blessed the Lord who had led him out of Ur of the Chaldees, and had brought him to this land.

8.   And it came to pass in the first year, in the seventh week, on the new moon of the first month, 1954 A.M.] that he built an altar on this mountain, and called on the name of the Lord: 'Thou, the eternal God, art my God.'

9.   And he offered on the altar a burnt sacrifice unto the Lord that He should be with him and not forsake him all the days of his life.

10.   And he removed from thence and went towards the south, and he came to Hebron and Hebron was built at that time, and he dwelt there two years, and he went (thence) into the land of the south, to Bealoth, and there was a famine in the land.

11. And Abram went into Egypt in the third year of the week, and he dwelt in Egypt five years before his wife was torn away from him.

12. Now Tanais in Egypt was at that time built- seven years after Hebron.

13. And it came to pass when Pharaoh seized Sarai, the wife of Abram that the Lord plagued Pharaoh and his house with great plagues because of Sarai, Abram's wife.

14. And Abram was very glorious by reason of possessions in sheep, and cattle, and asses, and horses, and camels, and menservants, and maidservants, and in silver and gold exceedingly. And Lot also his brother's son, was wealthy.

15. And Pharaoh gave back Sarai, the wife of Abram, and he sent him out of the land of Egypt, and he journeyed to the place where he had pitched his tent at the beginning, to the place of the altar, with Ai on the east, and Bethel on the west, and he blessed the Lord his God who had brought him back in peace.

16. And it came to pass in the forty-first jubilee in the third year of the first week, [1963 A.M.] that he returned to this place and offered thereon a burnt sacrifice, and called on the name of the Lord, and said: 'Thou, the most high God, art my God for ever and ever.'

17. And in the fourth year of this week [1964 A.M.] Lot parted from him, and Lot dwelt in Sodom, and the men of Sodom were sinners exceedingly.

18. And it grieved him in his heart that his brother's son had parted from him; for he had no children.

19. In that year when Lot was taken captive, the Lord said unto Abram, after that Lot had parted from him, in the fourth year of this week: 'Lift up thine eyes from the place where thou art dwelling, northward and southward, and westward and eastward.

20. For all the land which thou seest I will give to thee and to thy seed for ever, and I will make thy seed as the sand of the sea: though a man may number the dust of the earth, yet thy seed shall not be numbered.

21. Arise, walk (through the land) in the length of it and the breadth of it, and see it all; for to thy seed will I give it.' And Abram went to Hebron, and dwelt there.

22. And in this year came Chedorlaomer, king of Elam, and Amraphel, king of Shinar, and Arioch king of Sellasar, and Tergal, king of nations, and slew the king of Gomorrah, and the king of Sodom fled, and many fell through wounds in the vale of Siddim, by the Salt Sea.

23. And they took captive Sodom and Adam and Zeboim, and they took captive Lot also, the son of Abram's brother, and all his possessions, and they went to Dan.

24.	And one who had escaped came and told Abram that his brother's son had been taken captive and (Abram) armed his household servants . . .

25.	. . . . for Abram, and for his seed, a tenth of the first fruits to the Lord, and the Lord ordained it as an ordinance for ever that they should give it to the priests who served before Him, that they should possess it for ever.

26.	And to this law there is no limit of days; for He hath ordained it for the generations for ever that they should give to the Lord the tenth of everything, of the seed and of the wine and of the oil and of the cattle and of the sheep.

27.	And He gave (it) unto His priests to eat and to drink with joy before Him.

28.	And the king of Sodom came to him and bowed himself before him, and said: 'Our Lord Abram, give unto us the souls which thou hast rescued, but let the booty be thine.'

29.	And Abram said unto him: 'I lift up my hands to the Most High God, that from a thread to a shoe-latchet I shall not take aught that is thine lest thou shouldst say, I have made Abram rich; save only what the young men have eaten, and the portion of the men who went with me -Aner, Eschol, and Mamre. These shall take their portion.'

Jubilees 14

1.	After these things, in the fourth year of this week, on the new moon of the third month, the word of the Lord came to Abram in a dream, saying: 'Fear not, Abram; I am thy defender, and thy reward will be exceeding great.'

2.	And he said: 'Lord, Lord, what wilt thou give me, seeing I go hence childless, and the son of Maseq, the son of my handmaid, is the Dammasek Eliezer: he will be my heir, and to me thou hast given no seed.'

3.	And he said unto him: 'This (man) will not be thy heir, but one that will come out of thine own bowels; he will be thine heir.'

4.	And He brought him forth abroad, and said unto him: 'Look toward heaven and number the stars if thou art able to number them.'

5.	And he looked toward heaven, and beheld the stars. And He said unto him: 'So shall thy seed be.'

6.	And he believed in the Lord, and it was counted to him for righteousness.

7.	And He said unto him: 'I am the Lord that brought thee out of Ur of the Chaldees, to give thee the land of the Canaanites to possess it for ever; and I will be God unto thee and to thy seed after thee.'

8.   And he said: 'Lord, Lord, whereby shall I know that I shall inherit (it)?'

9.   And He said unto him: 'Take Me an heifer of three years, and a goat of three years, and a sheep of three years, and a turtle-dove, and a pigeon.'

10.   And he took all these in the middle of the month and he dwelt at the oak of Mamre, which is near Hebron.

11.   And he built there an altar, and sacrificed all these; and he poured their blood upon the altar, and divided them in the midst, and laid them over against each other; but the birds divided he not.

12.   And birds came down upon the pieces, and Abram drove them away, and did not suffer the birds to touch them.

13.   And it came to pass, when the sun had set, that an ecstasy fell upon Abram, and lo ! an horror of great darkness fell upon him, and it was said unto Abram: 'Know of a surety that thy seed shall be a stranger in a land (that is) not theirs, and they shall bring them into bondage, and afflict them four hundred years.

14.   And the nation also to whom they will be in bondage will I judge, and after that they shall come forth thence with much substance.

15.   And thou shalt go to thy fathers in peace, and be buried in a good old age.

16.   But in the fourth generation they shall return hither; for the iniquity of the Amorites is not yet full.'

17.   And he awoke from his sleep, and he arose, and the sun had set; and there was a flame, and behold ! a furnace was smoking, and a flame of fire passed between the pieces.

18.   And on that day the Lord made a covenant with Abram, saying: 'To thy seed will I give this land, from the river of Egypt unto the great river, the river Euphrates, the Kenites, the Kenizzites, the Kadmonites, the Perizzites, and the Rephaim, the Phakorites, and the Hivites, and the Amorites, and the Canaanites, and the Girgashites, and the Jebusites.

19.   And the day passed, and Abram offered the pieces, and the birds, and their fruit offerings, and their drink offerings, and the fire devoured them.

20.   And on that day we made a covenant with Abram, according as we had covenanted with Noah in this month; and Abram renewed the festival and ordinance for himself for ever.

21.   And Abram rejoiced, and made all these things known to Sarai his wife; and he believed that he would have seed, but she did not bear.

22.   And Sarai advised her husband Abram, and said unto him: 'Go in unto Hagar, my Egyptian maid: it may be that I shall build up seed unto thee by her.'

23.   And Abram harkened unto the voice of Sarai his wife, and said unto her, 'Do (so).' And Sarai took Hagar, her maid, the Egyptian, and gave her to Abram, her husband, to be his wife.

24.   And he went in unto her, and she conceived and bare him a son, and he called his name Ishmael, in the fifth year of this week [1965 A.M.]; and this was the eighty-sixth year in the life of Abram.

Jubilees 15

1.   And in the fifth year of the fourth week of this jubilee, [1979 A.M.] in the third month, in the middle of the month, Abram celebrated the feast of the first-fruits of the grain harvest.

2.   And he offered new offerings on the altar, the first-fruits of the produce, unto the Lord, an heifer and a goat and a sheep on the altar as a burnt sacrifice unto the Lord; their fruit offerings and their drink offerings he offered upon the altar with frankincense.

3.   And the Lord appeared to Abram, and said unto him: 'I am God Almighty; approve thyself before me and be thou perfect.

4.   And I will make My covenant between Me and thee, and I will multiply thee exceedingly.'

5.   And Abram fell on his face, and God talked with him, and said:

6.   'Behold my ordinance is with thee,

And thou shalt be the father of many nations.

7.   Neither shall thy name any more be called Abram, But thy name from henceforth, even for ever, shall be Abraham. For the father of many nations have I made thee.

8.   And I will make thee very great, And I will make thee into nations, And kings shall come forth from thee.

9.   And I shall establish My covenant between Me and thee, and thy seed after thee, throughout their generations, for an eternal covenant, so that I may be a God unto thee, and to thy seed after thee.

10.   <And I will give to thee and to thy seed after thee> the land where thou hast been a sojourner, the land of Canaan, that thou mayst possess it for ever, and I will be their God.'

11.   And the Lord said unto Abraham: 'And as for thee, do thou keep my covenant, thou and thy seed after thee: and circumcise ye every male among you, and circumcise your foreskins, and it shall be a token of an eternal covenant between Me and you.

12.   And the child on the eighth day ye shall circumcise, every male throughout your generations, him that is born in the house, or whom ye have bought with money from any stranger, whom ye have acquired who is not of thy seed.

13.   He that is born in thy house shall surely be circumcised, and those whom thou hast bought with money shall be circumcised, and My covenant shall be in your flesh for an eternal ordinance.

14.   And the uncircumcised male who is not circumcised in the flesh of his foreskin on the eighth day, that soul shall be cut off from his people, for he has broken My covenant.'

15.   And God said unto Abraham: 'As for Sarai thy wife, her name shall no more be called Sarai, but Sarah shall be her name.

16.   And I will bless her, and give thee a son by her, and I will bless him, and he shall become a nation, and kings of nations shall proceed from him.'

17.   And Abraham fell on his face, and rejoiced, and said in his heart: 'Shall a son be born to him that is a hundred years old, and shall Sarah, who is ninety years old, bring forth?'

18.   And Abraham said unto God: 'O that Ishmael might live before thee!'

19.   And God said: 'Yea, and Sarah also shall bear thee a son, and thou shalt call his name Isaac, and I will establish My covenant with him, an everlasting covenant, and for his seed after him.

20.   And as for Ishmael also have I heard thee, and behold I will bless him, and make him great, and multiply him exceedingly, and he shall beget twelve princes, and I will make him a great nation.

21.   But My covenant will I establish with Isaac, whom Sarah shall bear to thee, in these days, in the next year.'

22.   And He left off speaking with him, and God went up from Abraham.

23.   And Abraham did according as God had said unto him, and he took Ishmael his son, and all that were born in his house, and whom he had bought with his money, every male in his house, and circumcised the flesh of their foreskin.

24.   And on the selfsame day was Abraham circumcised, and all the men of his house, <and those born in the house>, and all those, whom he had bought with money from the children of the stranger, were circumcised with him.

25.   This law is for all the generations for ever, and there is no circumcision of the days, and no omission of one day out of the eight days; for it is an eternal ordinance, ordained and written on the heavenly tablets.

26.   And every one that is born, the flesh of whose foreskin is not circumcised on the eighth day, belongs not to the children of the covenant which the Lord made with Abraham, but to the children of destruction; nor is there, moreover, any sign on him that he is the Lord's, but (he is destined) to be destroyed and slain from the earth, and to be

rooted out of the earth, for he has broken the covenant of the Lord our God.

27.   For all the angels of the presence and all the angels of sanctification have been so created from the day of their creation, and before the angels of the presence and the angels of sanctification He hath sanctified Israel, that they should be with Him and with His holy angels.

28.   And do thou command the children of Israel and let them observe the sign of this covenant for their generations as an eternal ordinance, and they will not be rooted out of the land.

29.   For the command is ordained for a covenant, that they should observe it for ever among all the children of Israel.

30.   For Ishmael and his sons and his brothers and Esau, the Lord did not cause to approach Him, and he chose them not because they are the children of Abraham, because He knew them, but He chose Israel to be His people.

31.   And He sanctified it, and gathered it from amongst all the children of men; for there are many nations and many peoples, and all are His, and over all hath He placed spirits in authority to lead them astray from Him.

32.   But over Israel He did not appoint any angel or spirit, for He alone is their ruler, and He will preserve them and require them at the hand of His angels and His spirits, and at the hand of all His powers in order that He may preserve them and bless them, and that they may be His and He may be theirs from henceforth for ever.

33.   And now I announce unto thee that the children of Israel will not keep true to this ordinance, and they will not circumcise their sons according to all this law; for in the flesh of their circumcision they will omit this circumcision of their sons, and all of them, sons of Beliar, will leave their sons uncircumcised as they were born.

34.   And there will be great wrath from the Lord against the children of Israel. because they have forsaken His covenant and turned aside from His word, and provoked and blasphemed, inasmuch as they do not observe the ordinance of this law; for they have treated their members like the Gentiles, so that they may be removed and rooted out of the land. And there will no more be pardon or forgiveness unto them [so that there should be forgiveness and pardon] for all the sin of this eternal error.

Jubilees 16

1.   And on the new moon of the fourth month we appeared unto Abraham, at the oak of Mamre, and we talked with him, and we announced to him that a son would be given to him by Sarah his wife.

776

2.   And Sarah laughed, for she heard that we had spoken these words with Abraham, and we admonished her, and she became afraid, and denied that she had laughed on account of the words.

3.   And we told her the name of her son, as his name is ordained and written in the heavenly tablets (i.e.) Isaac,

4.   And (that) when we returned to her at a set time, she would have conceived a son.

5.   And in this month the Lord executed his judgments on Sodom, and Gomorrah, and Zeboim, and all the region of the Jordan, and He burned them with fire and brimstone, and destroyed them until this day, even as [lo] I have declared unto thee all their works, that they are wicked and sinners exceedingly, and that they defile themselves and commit fornication in their flesh, and work uncleanness on the earth.

6.   And, in like manner, God will execute judgment on the places where they have done according to the uncleanness of the Sodomites, like unto the judgment of Sodom.

7.   But Lot we saved; for God remembered Abraham, and sent him out from the midst of the overthrow.

8.   And he and his daughters committed sin upon the earth, such as had not been on the earth since the days of Adam till his time; for the man lay with his daughters.

9.   And, behold, it was commanded and engraven concerning all his seed, on the heavenly tablets, to remove them and root them out, and to execute judgment upon them like the judgment of Sodom, and to leave no seed of the man on earth on the day of condemnation.

10.   And in this month Abraham moved from Hebron, and departed and dwelt between Kadesh and Shur in the mountains of Gerar.

11.   And in the middle of the fifth month he moved from thence, and dwelt at the Well of the Oath.

12.   And in the middle of the sixth month the Lord visited Sarah and did unto her as He had spoken and she conceived.

13.   And she bare a son in the third month, and in the middle of the month, at the time of which the Lord had spoken to Abraham, on the festival of the first fruits of the harvest, Isaac was born.

14.   And Abraham circumcised his son on the eighth day: he was the first that was circumcised according to the covenant which is ordained for ever.

15.   And in the sixth year of the fourth week we came to Abraham, to the Well of the Oath, and we appeared unto him [as we had told Sarah that we should return to her, and she would have conceived a son.

16.   And we returned in the seventh month, and found Sarah with child before us] and we blessed him, and we announced to him all the things which had been decreed concerning him, that he should not die till he should beget six sons more, and should see (them) before he died; but (that) in Isaac should his name and seed be called:

17.   And (that) all the seed of his sons should be Gentiles, and be reckoned with the Gentiles; but from the sons of Isaac one should become a holy seed, and should not be reckoned among the Gentiles.

18.   For he should become the portion of the Most High, and all his seed had fallen into the possession of God, that it should be unto the Lord a people for (His) possession above all nations and that it should become a kingdom and priests and a holy nation.

19.   And we went our way, and we announced to Sarah all that we had told him, and they both rejoiced with exceeding great joy.

20.   And he built there an altar to the Lord who had delivered him, and who was making him rejoice in the land of his sojourning, and he celebrated a festival of joy in this month seven days, near the altar which he had built at the Well of the Oath.

21.   And he built booths for himself and for his servants on this festival, and he was the first to celebrate the feast of tabernacles on the earth.

22.   And during these seven days he brought each day to the altar a burnt offering to the Lord, two oxen, two rams, seven sheep, one he-goat, for a sin offering, that he might atone thereby for himself and for his seed.

23.   And, as a thank-offering, seven rams, seven kids, seven sheep, and seven he-goats, and their fruit offerings and their drink offerings; and he burnt all the fat thereof on the altar, a chosen offering unto the Lord for a sweet smelling savour.

24.   And morning and evening he burnt fragrant substances, frankincense and galbanum, and stackte, and nard, and myrrh, and spice, and costum; all these seven he offered, crushed, mixed together in equal parts (and) pure.

25.   And he celebrated this feast during seven days, rejoicing with all his heart and with all his soul, he and all those who were in his house, and there was no stranger with him, nor any that was uncircumcised.

26.   And he blessed his Creator who had created him in his generation, for He had created him according to His good pleasure; for He knew and perceived that from him would arise the plant of righteousness for the eternal generations, and from him a holy seed, so that it should become like Him who had made all things.

27.   And he blessed and rejoiced, and he called the name of this

festival the festival of the Lord, a joy acceptable to the Most High God.

28. And we blessed him for ever, and all his seed after him throughout all the generations of the earth, because he celebrated this festival in its season, according to the testimony of the heavenly tablets.

29. For this reason it is ordained on the heavenly tablets concerning Israel, that they shall celebrate the feast of tabernacles seven days with joy, in the seventh month, acceptable before the Lord -a statute for ever throughout their generations every year.

30. And to this there is no limit of days; for it is ordained for ever regarding Israel that they should celebrate it and dwell in booths, and set wreaths upon their heads, and take leafy boughs, and willows from the brook.

31. And Abraham took branches of palm trees, and the fruit of goodly trees, and every day going round the altar with the branches seven times [a day] in the morning, he praised and gave thanks to his God for all things in joy.

Jubilees 17

1. And in the first year of the fifth week Isaac was weaned in this jubilee, [1982 A.M.] and Abraham made a great banquet in the third month, on the day his son Isaac was weaned.

2. And Ishmael, the son of Hagar, the Egyptian, was before the face of Abraham, his father, in his place, and Abraham rejoiced and blessed God because he had seen his sons and had not died childless.

3. And he remembered the words which He had spoken to him on the day on which Lot had parted from him, and he rejoiced because the Lord had given him seed upon the earth to inherit the earth, and he blessed with all his mouth the Creator of all things.

4. And Sarah saw Ishmael playing and dancing, and Abraham rejoicing with great joy, and she became jealous of Ishmael and said to Abraham, 'Cast out this bondwoman and her son; for the son of this bondwoman will not be heir with my son, Isaac.'

5. And the thing was grievous in Abraham's sight, because of his maidservant and because of his son, that he should drive them from him.

6. And God said to Abraham 'Let it not be grievous in thy sight, because of the child and because of the bondwoman; in all that Sarah hath said unto thee, harken to her words and do (them); for in Isaac shall thy name and seed be called.

7. But as for the son of this bondwoman I will make him a great nation, because he is of thy seed.'

8. And Abraham rose up early in the morning, and took bread and a bottle of water, and placed them on

the shoulders of Hagar and the child, and sent her away.

9.   And she departed and wandered in the wilderness of Beersheba, and the water in the bottle was spent, and the child thirsted, and was not able to go on, and fell down.

10.   And his mother took him and cast him under an olive tree, and went and sat her down over against him, at the distance of a bow-shot; for she said, 'Let me not see the death of my child,' and as she sat she wept.

11.   And an angel of God, one of the holy ones, said unto her, 'Why weepest thou, Hagar? Arise take the child, and hold him in thine hand; for God hath heard thy voice, and hath seen the child.'

12.   And she opened her eyes, and she saw a well of water, and she went and filled her bottle with water, and she gave her child to drink, and she arose and went towards the wilderness of Paran.

13.   And the child grew and became an archer, and God was with him, and his mother took him a wife from among the daughters of Egypt.

14.   And she bare him a son, and he called his name Nebaioth; for she said, 'The Lord was nigh to me when I called upon him.'

15.   And it came to pass in the seventh week, in the first year thereof, [2003 A.M.] in the first month in this jubilee, on the twelfth of this month, there were voices in heaven regarding Abraham, that he was faithful in all that He told him, and that he loved the Lord, and that in every affliction he was faithful.

16.   And the prince Mastêmâ came and said before God, 'Behold, Abraham loves Isaac his son, and he delights in him above all things else; bid him offer him as a burnt-offering on the altar, and Thou wilt see if he will do this command, and Thou wilt know if he is faithful in everything wherein Thou dost try him.

17.   And the Lord knew that Abraham was faithful in all his afflictions; for He had tried him through his country and with famine, and had tried him with the wealth of kings, and had tried him again through his wife, when she was torn (from him), and with circumcision; and had tried him through Ishmael and Hagar, his maid-servant, when he sent them away.

18.   And in everything wherein He had tried him, he was found faithful, and his soul was not impatient, and he was not slow to act; for he was faithful and a lover of the Lord.

Jubilees 18

1.   And God said to him, 'Abraham, Abraham'; and he said, Behold, (here) am I.'

2.   And he said, Take thy beloved son whom thou lovest, (even) Isaac, and go unto the high country, and

offer him on one of the mountains which I will point out unto thee.'

3. And he rose early in the morning and saddled his ass, and took his two young men with him, and Isaac his son, and clave the wood of the burnt offering, and he went to the place on the third day, and he saw the place afar off.

4. And he came to a well of water, and he said to his young men, 'Abide ye here with the ass, and I and the lad shall go (yonder), and when we have worshipped we shall come again to you.'

5. And he took the wood of the burnt-offering and laid it on Isaac his son, and he took in his hand the fire and the knife, and they went both of them together to that place.

6. And Isaac said to his father, 'Father;' and he said, 'Here am I, my son.' And he said unto him, 'Behold the fire, and the knife, and the wood; but where is the sheep for the burnt-offering, father?'

7. And he said, 'God will provide for himself a sheep for a burnt-offering, my son.' And he drew near to the place of the mount of God.

8. And he built an altar, and he placed the wood on the altar, and bound Isaac his son, and placed him on the wood which was upon the altar, and stretched forth his hand to take the knife to slay Isaac his son.

9. And I stood before him, and before the prince Mastêmâ, and the Lord said, 'Bid him not to lay his hand on the lad, nor to do anything to him, for I have shown that he fears the Lord.'

10. And I called to him from heaven, and said unto him: 'Abraham, Abraham;' and he was terrified and said: 'Behold, (here) am I.'

11. And I said unto him: 'Lay not thy hand upon the lad, neither do thou anything to him; for now I have shown that thou fearest the Lord, and hast not withheld thy son, thy first-born son, from me.'

12. And the prince Mastêmâ was put to shame; and Abraham lifted up his eyes and looked, and, behold a ram caught . . . by his horns, and Abraham went and took the ram and offered it for a burnt-offering in the stead of his son.

13. And Abraham called that place 'The Lord hath seen', so that it is said *in the mount* the Lord hath seen: that is Mount Sion.

14. And the Lord called Abraham by his name a second time from heaven, as he caused us to appear to speak to him in the name of the Lord.

15. And he said: 'By Myself have I sworn, saith the Lord,Because thou hast done this thing, And hast not withheld thy son, thy beloved son, from Me, That in blessing I will bless thee,And in multiplying I will multiply thy seed As the stars of heaven, And as the sand which is on the seashore.And

thy seed shall inherit the cities of its enemies,

16.   And in thy seed shall all nations of the earth be blessed; Because thou hast obeyed My voice,
And I have shown to all that thou art faithful unto Me in all that I have said unto thee: Go in peace.'

17.   And Abraham went to his young men, and they arose and went together to Beersheba, and Abraham [2010 A.M.] dwelt by the Well of the Oath.

18.   And he celebrated this festival every year, seven days with joy, and he called it the festival of the Lord according to the seven days during which he went and returned in peace.

19.   And accordingly has it been ordained and written on the heavenly tablets regarding Israel and its seed that they should observe this festival seven days with the joy of festival.

Jubilees 19

1.   And in the first year of the first week in the forty-second jubilee, Abraham returned and dwelt opposite Hebron, that is Kirjath Arba, two weeks of years.

2.   And in the first year of the third week of this jubilee the days of the life of Sarah were accomplished, and she died in Hebron.

3.   And Abraham went to mourn over her and bury her, and we tried him [to see] if his spirit were patient and he were not indignant in the words of his mouth; and he was found patient in this, and was not disturbed.

4.   For in patience of spirit he conversed with the children of Heth, to the intent that they should give him a place in which to bury his dead.

5.   And the Lord gave him grace before all who saw him, and he besought in gentleness the sons of Heth, and they gave him the land of the double cave over against Mamre, that is Hebron, for four hundred pieces of silver.

6.   And they besought him saying, We shall give it to thee for nothing; but he would not take it from their hands for nothing, for he gave the price of the place, the money in full, and he bowed down before them twice, and after this he buried his dead in the double cave.

7.   And all the days of the life of Sarah were one hundred and twenty-seven years, that is, two jubilees and four weeks and one year: these are the days of the years of the life of Sarah.

8.   This is the tenth trial wherewith Abraham was tried, and he was found faithful, patient in spirit.

9.   And he said not a single word regarding the rumour in the land how that God had said that He would give it to him and to his seed after him, and he begged a place there to bury his dead; for he was found faithful,

and was recorded on the heavenly tablets as the friend of God.

10.　And in the fourth year thereof he took a wife for his son Isaac and her name was Rebecca [2020 A.M.] [the daughter of Bethuel, the son of Nahor, the brother of Abraham] the sister of Laban and daughter of Bethuel; and Bethuel was the son of Melca, who was the wife of Nahor, the brother of Abraham.

11.　And Abraham took to himself a third wife, and her name was Keturah, from among the daughters of his household servants, for Hagar had died before Sarah. And she bare him six sons, Zimram, and Jokshan, and Medan, and Midian, and Ishbak, and Shuah, in the two weeks of years.

12.　And in the sixth week, in the second year thereof, Rebecca bare to Isaac two sons, Jacob and Esau,

13.　and [2046 A.M.] Jacob was a smooth and upright man, and Esau was fierce, a man of the field, and hairy, and Jacob dwelt in tents.

14.　And the youths grew, and Jacob learned to write; but Esau did not learn, for he was a man of the field and a hunter, and he learnt war, and all his deeds were fierce.

15.　And Abraham loved Jacob, but Isaac loved Esau.

16.　And Abraham saw the deeds of Esau, and he knew that in Jacob should his name and seed be called; and he called Rebecca and gave commandment regarding Jacob, for he knew that she (too) loved Jacob much more than Esau.

17.　And he said unto her:

My daughter, watch over my son Jacob,
For he shall be in my stead on the earth,
And for a blessing in the midst of the children of men,
And for the glory of the whole seed of Shem.

18.　For I know that the Lord will choose him to be a people for possession unto Himself, above all peoples that are upon the face of the earth.

19.　And behold, Isaac my son loves Esau more than Jacob, but I see that thou truly lovest Jacob.

20.　Add still further to thy kindness to him,
And let thine eyes be upon him in love;
For he shall be a blessing unto us on the earth from henceforth unto all generations of the earth.

21.　Let thy hands be strong
And let thy heart rejoice in thy son Jacob;
For I have loved him far beyond all my sons.

He shall be blessed for ever,
And his seed shall fill the whole earth.

22.　If a man can number the sand of the earth,
His seed also shall be numbered.

23.   And all the blessings wherewith the Lord hath blessed me and my seed shall belong to Jacob and his seed alway.

24.   And in his seed shall my name be blessed, and the name of my fathers, Shem, and Noab, and Enoch, and Mahalalel, and Enos, and Seth, and Adam.

25.   And these shall serve

To lay the foundations of the heaven,
And to strengthen the earth,
And to renew all the luminaries which are in the firmament.

26.   And he called Jacob before the eyes of Rebecca his mother, and kissed him, and blessed him, and said:

27.   'Jacob, my beloved son, whom my soul loveth, may God bless thee from above the firmament, and may He give thee all the blessings wherewith He blessed Adam, and Enoch, and Noah, and Shem; and all the things of which He told me, and all the things which He promised to give me, may he cause to cleave to thee and to thy seed for ever, according to the days of heaven above the earth.

28.   And the Spirits of Mastêmâ shall not rule over thee or over thy seed to turn thee from the Lord, who is thy God from henceforth for ever.

29.   And may the Lord God be a father to thee and thou the first-born son, and to the people alway.

30.   Go in peace, my son.' And they both went forth together from Abraham.

31.   And Rebecca loved Jacob, with all her heart and with all her soul, very much more than Esau; but Isaac loved Esau much more than Jacob.

Jubilees 20

1.   And in the forty-second jubilee, in the first year of the seventh week, Abraham called Ishmael, [2052 (2045?) A.M.] and his twelve sons, and Isaac and his two sons, and the six sons of Keturah, and their sons.

2.   And he commanded them that they should observe the way of the Lord; that they should work righteousness, and love each his neighbour, and act on this manner amongst all men; that they should each so walk with regard to them as to do judgment and righteousness on the earth.

3.   That they should circumcise their sons, according to the covenant which He had made with them, and not deviate to the right hand or the left of all the paths which the Lord had commanded us; and that we should keep ourselves from all fornication and uncleanness, [and renounce from amongst us all fornication and uncleanness].

4.   And if any woman or maid commit fornication amongst you, burn her with fire and let them not commit fornication with her after their

eyes and their heart; and let them not take to themselves wives from the daughters of Canaan; for the seed of Canaan will be rooted out of the land.

5.   And he told them of the judgment of the giants, and the judgment of the Sodomites, how they had been judged on account of their wickedness, and had died on account of their fornication, and uncleanness, and mutual corruption through fornication.

6.   'And guard yourselves from all fornication and uncleanness, And from all pollution of sin,

Lest ye make our name a curse, And your whole life a hissing,

And all your sons to be destroyed by the   sword, And ye become accursed like Sodom, And all your remnant as the sons of Gomorrah.

7.   I implore you, my sons, love the   God   of   heaven And   cleave   ye   to   all   His commandments.

And walk not after their idols, and after their uncleannesses,

8.   And make not for yourselves molten or graven gods;

For   they   are   vanity, And there is no spirit in them;

For they are work of (men's) hands, And all who trust in them, trust in nothing.

9.   Serve them not, nor worship them, But serve ye the most high God, and worship   Him   continually: And   hope   for   His   countenance always, And   work   uprightness   and righteousness before Him,

That He may have pleasure in you and   grant   you   His   mercy, And send rain upon you morning and evening,

And bless all your works which ye have   wrought   upon   the   earth, And bless thy bread and thy water,

And bless the fruit of thy womb and the   fruit   of   thy   land, And the herds of thy cattle, and the flocks of thy sheep.

10.   And ye will be for a blessing on   the   earth, And all nations of the earth will desire you,

And bless your sons in my name, That they may be blessed as I am.

11.   And he gave to Ishmael and to his sons, and to the sons of Keturah, gifts, and sent them away from Isaac his son, and he gave everything to Isaac his son.

12.   And Ishmael and his sons, and the sons of Keturah and their sons, went together and dwelt from

Paran to the entering in of Babylon in all the land which is towards the East facing the desert.

13.   And these mingled with each other, and their name was called Arabs, and Ishmaelites.

Jubilees 21

1.   And in the sixth year of the seventh week of this jubilee Abraham called Isaac his son, and [2057 (2050?) A.M.] commanded him: saying, 'I am become old, and know not the day of my death, and am full of my days.

2.   And behold, I am one hundred and seventy-five years old, and throughout all the days of my life I have remembered the Lord, and sought with all my heart to do His will, and to walk uprightly in all His ways.

3.   My soul has hated idols, <and I have despised those that served them, and I have given my heart and spirit> that I might observe to do the will of Him who created me.

4.   For He is the living God, and He is holy and faithful, and He is righteous beyond all, and there is with Him no accepting of (men's) persons and no accepting of gifts; for God is righteous, and executeth judgment on all those who transgress His commandments and despise His covenant.

5.   And do thou, my son, observe His commandments and His ordinances and His judgments, and walk not after the abominations and after the graven images and after the molten images.

6.   And eat no blood at all of animals or cattle, or of any bird which flies in the heaven.

7.   And if thou dost slay a victim as an acceptable peace offering, slay ye it, and pour out its blood upon the altar, and all the fat of the offering offer on the altar with fine flour and the meat offering mingled with oil, with its drink offering -offer them all together on the altar of burnt offering; it is a sweet savour before the Lord.

8.   And thou wilt offer the fat of the sacrifice of thank offerings on the fire which is upon the altar, and the fat which is on the belly, and all the fat on the inwards and the two kidneys, and all the fat that is upon them, and upon the loins and liver thou shalt remove, together with the kidneys.

9.   And offer all these for a sweet savour acceptable before the Lord, with its meat-offering and with its drink- offering, for a sweet savour, the bread of the offering unto the Lord.

10.   And eat its meat on that day and on the second day, and let not the sun on the second day go down upon it till it is eaten, and let nothing be left over for the third day; for it is not acceptable [for it is not approved] and let it no longer be eaten, and all who eat thereof will bring sin upon themselves; for thus I have found it

written in the books of my forefathers, and in the words of Enoch, and in the words of Noah.

11. And on all thy oblations thou shalt strew salt, and let not the salt of the covenant be lacking in all thy oblations before the Lord.

12. And as regards the wood of the sacrifices, beware lest thou bring (other) wood for the altar in addition to these: cypress, bay, almond, fir, pine, cedar, savin, fig, olive, myrrh, laurel, aspalathus.

13. And of these kinds of wood lay upon the altar under the sacrifice, such as have been tested as to their appearance, and do not lay (thereon) any split or dark wood, (but) hard and clean, without fault, a sound and new growth; and do not lay (thereon) old wood, [for its fragrance is gone] for there is no longer fragrance in it as before.

14. Besides these kinds of wood there is none other that thou shalt place (on the altar), for the fragrance is dispersed, and the smell of its fragrance goes not up to heaven.

15. Observe this commandment and do it, my son, that thou mayst be upright in all thy deeds.

16. And at all times be clean in thy body, and wash thyself with water before thou approachest to offer on the altar, and wash thy hands and thy feet before thou drawest near to the altar; and when thou art done sacrificing, wash again thy hands and thy feet.

17. And let no blood appear upon you nor upon your clothes; be on thy guard, my son, against blood, be on thy guard exceedingly; cover it with dust.

18. And do not eat any blood for it is the soul; eat no blood whatever.

19. And take no gifts for the blood of man, lest it be shed with impunity, without judgment; for it is the blood that is shed that causes the earth to sin, and the earth cannot be cleansed from the blood of man save by the blood of him who shed it.

20. And take no present or gift for the blood of man: blood for blood, that thou mayest be accepted before the Lord, the Most High God; for He is the defence of the good: and that thou mayest be preserved from all evil, and that He may save thee from every kind of death.

21. I see, my son,
That all the works of the children of men are sin and wickedness,
And all their deeds are uncleanness and an abomination and a pollution,
And there is no righteousness with them.

22. Beware, lest thou shouldest walk in their ways
And tread in their paths,
And sin a sin unto death before the Most High God.

Else He will [hide His face from thee
And] give thee back into the hands of thy transgression,
And root thee out of the land, and thy seed likewise from under heaven,

And thy name and thy seed shall perish from the whole earth.

23.　Turn away from all their deeds and all their uncleanness, And observe the ordinance of the Most High God, And do His will and be upright in all things.

24.　And He will bless thee in all thy deeds, And will raise up from thee a plant of righteousness through all the earth, throughout all generations of the earth, And my name and thy name shall not be forgotten under heaven for ever.

25.　Go, my son in peace. May the Most High God, my God and thy God, strengthen thee to do His will, And may He bless all thy seed and the residue of thy seed for the generations for ever, with all righteous blessings, That thou mayest be a blessing on all the earth.'

26.　And he went out from him rejoicing.

Jubilees 22

1.　And it came to pass in the first week in the forty-fourth jubilee, in the second year, that is, the year in which Abraham died, that Isaac and Ishmael came from the Well of the Oath to celebrate the feast of weeks -that is, the feast of the first fruits of the harvest-to Abraham, their father, and Abraham rejoiced because his two sons had come.

2.　For Isaac had many possessions in Beersheba, and Isaac was wont to go and see his possessions and to return to his father.

3.　And in those days Ishmael came to see his father, and they both came together, and Isaac offered a sacrifice for a burnt offering, and presented it on the altar of his father which he had made in Hebron.

4.　And he offered a thank offering and made a feast of joy before Ishmael, his brother: and Rebecca made new cakes from the new grain, and gave them to Jacob, her son, to take them to Abraham, his father, from the first fruits of the land, that he might eat and bless the Creator of all things before he died.

5.　And Isaac, too, sent by the hand of Jacob to Abraham a best thank offering, that he might eat and drink.

6.　And he eat and drank, and blessed the Most High God,

Who hath created heaven and earth, Who hath made all the fat things of the earth, And given them to the children of men That they might eat and drink and bless their Creator.

7.　'And now I give thanks unto Thee, my God, because thou hast caused me to see this day: behold, I am one hundred three score and fifteen years, an old man and full of days, and all my days have been unto me peace.

8.   The sword of the adversary has not overcome me in all that Thou hast given me and my children all the days of my life until this day.

9.   My God, may Thy mercy and Thy peace be upon Thy servant, and upon the seed of his sons, that they may be to Thee a chosen nation and an inheritance from amongst all the nations of the earth from henceforth unto all the days of the generations of the earth, unto all the ages.'

10.   And he called Jacob and said: 'My son Jacob, may the God of all bless thee and strengthen thee to do righteousness, and His will before Him, and may He choose thee and thy seed that ye may become a people for His inheritance according to His will alway.

11.   And do thou, my son, Jacob, draw near and kiss me.' And he drew near and kissed him, and he said:

'Blessed be my son Jacob And all the sons of God Most High, unto all the ages:

May God give unto thee a seed of righteousness;
And some of thy sons may He sanctify in the midst of the whole earth;

May nations serve thee,
And all the nations bow themselves before thy seed.

12.   Be strong in the presence of men,
And exercise authority over all the seed of Seth.

Then thy ways and the ways of thy sons will be justified,
So that they shall become a holy nation.

13.   May the Most High God give thee all the blessings
Wherewith He has blessed me

And wherewith He blessed Noah and Adam;
May they rest on the sacred head of thy seed from generation to generation for ever.

14.   And may He cleanse thee from all unrighteousness and impurity,
That thou mayest be forgiven all the transgressions; which thou hast committed ignorantly.

And may He strengthen thee,
And bless thee.
And mayest thou inherit the whole earth,

15.   And may He renew His covenant with thee.
That thou mayest be to Him a nation for His inheritance for all the ages,
And that He may be to thee and to thy seed a God in truth and

righteousness throughout all the days of the earth.

16.   And do thou, my son Jacob, remember my words, And observe the commandments of Abraham, thy father:

Separate thyself from the nations, And eat not with them:

And do not according to their works, And become not their associate;

For their works are unclean, And all their ways are a Pollution and an abomination and uncleanness.

17.   They offer their sacrifices to the   dead And they worship evil spirits,

And they eat over the graves, And all their works are vanity and nothingness.

18.   They have no heart to understand And their eyes do not see what their works are,

And how they err in saying to a piece of wood: 'Thou art my God,' And to a stone: 'Thou art my Lord and thou art my deliverer.' [And they have no heart.]

19.   And as for thee, my son Jacob, May the Most High God help thee And the God of heaven bless thee And remove thee from their uncleanness and from all their error.

20.   Be thou ware, my son Jacob, of taking a wife from any seed of the daughters of Canaan;

For all his seed is to be rooted out of the earth.

21.   For, owing to the transgression of Ham, Canaan erred, And all his seed shall be destroyed from off the earth and all the residue thereof, And none springing from him shall be saved on the day of judgment.

22.   And as for all the worshippers of idols and the profane (b) There shall be no hope for them in the land of the living; (c) And there shall be no remembrance of them on the earth; (c) For they shall descend into Sheol, (d) And into the place of condemnation shall they go,

As the children of Sodom were taken away from the earth So will all those who worship idols be taken away.

23.   Fear not, my son Jacob, And be not dismayed, O son of Abraham:

May the Most High God preserve thee from destruction, And from all the paths of error may he deliver thee.

24.   This house have I built for myself that I might put my name upon it in the earth: [it is given to

thee and to thy seed for ever], and it will be named the house of Abraham; it is given to thee and to thy seed for ever; for thou wilt build my house and establish my name before God for ever: thy seed and thy name will stand throughout all generations of the earth.'

25.   And he ceased commanding him and blessing him.

26.   And the two lay together on one bed, and Jacob slept in the bosom of Abraham, his father's father and he kissed him seven times, and his affection and his heart rejoiced over him.

27.   And he blessed him with all his heart and said: 'The Most High God, the God of all, and Creator of all, who brought me forth from Ur of the Chaldees that he might give me this land to inherit it for ever, and that I might establish a holy seed-blessed be the Most High for ever.'

28.   And he blessed Jacob and said: 'My son, over whom with all my heart and my affection I rejoice, may Thy grace and Thy mercy be lift up upon him and upon his seed alway.

29.   And do not forsake him, nor set him at nought from henceforth unto the days of eternity, and may Thine eyes be opened upon him and upon his seed, that Thou mayst preserve him, and bless him, and mayest sanctify him as a nation for Thine inheritance;

30.   And bless him with all Thy blessings from henceforth unto all the days of eternity, and renew Thy

covenant and Thy grace with him and with his seed according to all Thy good pleasure unto all the generations of the earth.'

Jubilees 23

1.   And he placed two fingers of Jacob on his eyes, and he blessed the God of gods, and he covered his face and stretched out his feet and slept the sleep of eternity, and was gathered to his fathers.

2.   And notwithstanding all this Jacob was lying in his bosom, and knew not that Abraham, his father's father, was dead.

3.   And Jacob awoke from his sleep, and behold Abraham was cold as ice, and he said 'Father, father'; but there was none that spake, and he knew that he was dead.

4.   And he arose from his bosom and ran and told Rebecca, his mother; and Rebecca went to Isaac in the night, and told him; and they went together, and Jacob with them, and a lamp was in his hand, and when they had gone in they found Abraham lying dead.

5.   And Isaac fell on the face of his father and wept and kissed him.

6.   And the voices were heard in the house of Abraham, and Ishmael his son arose, and went to Abraham his father, and wept over Abraham his father, he and all the house of Abraham, and they wept with a great weeping.

7.　And his sons Isaac and Ishmael buried him in the double cave, near Sarah his wife, and they wept for him forty days, all the men of his house, and Isaac and Ishmael, and all their sons, and all the sons of Keturah in their places; and the days of weeping for Abraham were ended.

8.　And he lived three jubilees and four weeks of years, one hundred and seventy-five years, and completed the days of his life, being old and full of days.

9.　For the days of the forefathers, of their life, were nineteen jubilees; and after the Flood they began to grow less than nineteen jubilees, and to decrease in jubilees, and to grow old quickly, and to be full of their days by reason of manifold tribulation and the wickedness of their ways, with the exception of Abraham.

10.　For Abraham was perfect in all his deeds with the Lord, and well-pleasing in righteousness all the days of his life; and behold, he did not complete four jubilees in his life, when he had grown old by reason of the wickedness, and was full of his days.

11.　And all the generations which shall arise from this time until the day of the great judgment shall grow old quickly, before they complete two jubilees, and their knowledge shall forsake them by reason of their old age Land all their know- ledge shall vanish away].

12.　And in those days, if a man live a jubilee and a-half of years, they shall say regarding him: 'He has lived long, and the greater part of his days are pain and sorrow and tribulation, and there is no peace:

13.　For calamity follows on calamity, and wound on wound, and tribulation on tribulation, and evil tidings on evil tidings, and illness on illness, and all evil judgments such as these, one with another, illness and overthrow, and snow and frost and ice, and fever, and chills, and torpor, and famine, and death, and sword, and captivity, and all kinds of calamities and pains.'

14.　And all these shall come on an evil generation, which transgresses on the earth: their works are uncleanness and fornication, and pollution and abominations.

15.　Then they shall say: 'The days of the forefathers were many (even), unto a thousand years, and were good; but behold, the days of our life, if a man has lived many, are three score years and ten, and, if he is strong, four score years, and those evil, and there is no peace in the days of this evil generation.'

16.　And in that generation the sons shall convict their fathers and their elders of sin and unrighteousness, and of the words of their mouth and the great wickednesses which they perpetrate, and concerning their forsaking the covenant which the Lord made between them and Him, that they should observe and do all His commandments and His ordinances and all His laws, without departing either to the right hand or the left.

17.   For all have done evil, and every mouth speaks iniquity and all their works are an uncleanness and an abomination, and all their ways are pollution, uncleanness and destruction.

18.   Behold the earth shall be destroyed on account of all their works, and there shall be no seed of the vine, and no oil; for their works are altogether faithless, and they shall all perish together, beasts and cattle and birds, and all the fish of the sea, on account of the children of men.

19.   And they shall strive one with another, the young with the old, and the old with the young, the poor with the rich, the lowly with the great, and the beggar with the prince, on account of the law and the covenant; for they have forgotten commandment, and covenant, and feasts, and months, and Sabbaths, and jubilees, and all judgments.

20.   And they shall stand <with bows and> swords and war to turn them back into the way; but they shall not return until much blood has been shed on the earth, one by another.

21.   And those who have escaped shall not return from their wickedness to the way of righteousness, but they shall all exalt themselves to deceit and wealth, that they may each take all that is his neighbour's, and they shall name the great name, but not in truth and not in righteousness, and they shall defile the holy of holies with their uncleanness and the corruption of their pollution.

22.   And a great punishment shall befall the deeds of this generation from the Lord, and He will give them over to the sword and to judgment and to captivity, and to be plundered and devoured.

23.   And He will wake up against them the sinners of the Gentiles, who have neither mercy nor compassion, and who shall respect the person of none, neither old nor young, nor any one, for they are more wicked and strong to do evil than all the children of men.

And they shall use violence against Israel and transgression against Jacob,
And much blood shall be shed upon the   earth,
And there shall be none to gather and none to bury.

24.   In those days they shall cry aloud,
And call and pray that they may be saved from the hand of the sinners, the   Gentiles;
But none shall be saved.

25.   And the heads of the children shall be white with grey hair,
And a child of three weeks shall appear old like a man of one hundred   years,

And their stature shall be destroyed by tribulation and oppression.

26.   And in those days the children shall begin to study the laws, And to seek the commandments, And to return to the path of righteousness.

27.   And the days shall begin to grow many and increase amongst those children of men Till their days draw nigh to one thousand years. And to a greater number of years than (before) was the number of the days.

28.   And there shall be no old man Nor one who is <not> satisfied with his days, For all shall be (as) children and youths.

29.   And all their days they shall complete and live in peace and in joy, And there shall be no Satan nor any evil destroyer; For all their days shall be days of blessing and healing.

30.   And at that time the Lord will heal His servants, And they shall rise up and see great peace, And drive out their adversaries.

And the righteous shall see and be thankful, And rejoice with joy for ever and ever, And shall see all their judgments and all their curses on their enemies.

31.   And their bones shall rest in the   earth, And their spirits shall have much joy, And they shall know that it is the Lord who executes judgment, And shows mercy to hundreds and thousands and to all that love Him

32.   And do thou, Moses, write down these words; for thus are they written, and they record (them) on the heavenly tablets for a testimony for the generations for ever.

Jubilees 24

1.   And it came to pass after the death of Abraham, that the Lord blessed Isaac his son, and he arose from Hebron and went and dwelt at the Well of the Vision in the first year of the third week [2073 A.M.] of this jubilee, seven years.

2.   And in the first year of the fourth week a famine began in the land, [2080 A.M.] besides the first famine, which had been in the days of Abraham.

3.   And Jacob sod lentil pottage, and Esau came from the field hungry. And he said to Jacob his brother: 'Give me of this red pottage.' And Jacob said to him: 'Sell to me thy [primogeniture, this] birthright and I will give thee bread, and also some of this lentil pottage.'

4.   And Esau said in his heart: 'I shall die; of what profit to me is this birthright?

5.   'And he said to Jacob: 'I give it to thee.' And Jacob said: 'Swear to me, this day,' and he sware unto him.

6.   And Jacob gave his brother Esau bread and pottage, and he eat till he was satisfied, and Esau despised his birthright; for this reason was Esau's name called Edom, on account of the red pottage which Jacob gave him for his birthright.

7.   And Jacob became the elder, and Esau was brought down from his dignity.

8.   And the famine was over the land, and Isaac departed to go down into Egypt in the second year of this week, and went to the king of the Philistines to Gerar, unto Abimelech.

9.   And the Lord appeared unto him and said unto him: 'Go not down into Egypt; dwell in the land that I shall tell thee of, and sojourn in this land, and I will be with thee and bless thee.

10.   For to thee and to thy seed will I give all this land, and I will establish My oath which I sware unto Abraham thy father, and I will multiply thy seed as the stars of heaven, and will give unto thy seed all this land.

11.   And in thy seed shall all the nations of the earth be blessed, because thy father obeyed My voice, and kept My charge and My commandments, and My laws, and My ordinances, and My covenant;

and now obey My voice and dwell in this land.'

12.   And he dwelt in Gelar three weeks of years.

13.   And Abimelech charged concerning him, [2080-2101 A.M.] and concerning all that was his, saying: 'Any man that shall touch him or aught that is his shall surely die.'

14.   And Isaac waxed strong among the Philistines, and he got many possessions, oxen and sheep and camels and asses and a great household.

15.   And he sowed in the land of the Philistines and brought in a hundred-fold, and Isaac became exceedingly great, and the Philistines envied him.

16.   Now all the wells which the servants of Abraham had dug during the life of Abraham, the Philistines had stopped them after the death of Abraham, and filled them with earth.

17.   And Abimelech said unto Isaac: 'Go from us, for thou art much mightier than we', and Isaac departed thence in the first year of the seventh week, and sojourned in the valleys of Gerar.

18.   And they digged again the wells of water which the servants of Abraham, his father, had digged, and which the Philistines had closed after the death of Abraham his father, and he called their names as Abraham his father had named them.

19.   And the servants of Isaac dug a well in the valley, and found living

water, and the shepherds of Gerar strove with the shepherds of Isaac, saying: 'The water is ours'; and Isaac called the name of the well 'Perversity', because they had been perverse with us.

20.   And they dug a second well, and they strove for that also, and he called its name 'Enmity'. And he arose from thence and they digged another well, and for that they strove not, and he called the name of it 'Room', and Isaac said: 'Now the Lord hath made room for us, and we have increased in the land.'

21.   And he went up from thence to the Well of the Oath in the first year of the first week in the [2108 A.M.] forty-fourth jubilee.

22.   And the Lord appeared to him that night, on the new moon of the first month, and said unto him: 'I am the God of Abraham thy father; fear not, for I am with thee, and shall bless thee and shall surely multiply thy seed as the sand of the earth, for the sake of Abraham my servant.'

23.   And he built an altar there, which Abraham his father had first built, and he called upon the name of the Lord, and he offered sacrifice to the God of Abraham his father.

24.   And they digged a well and they found living water.

25.   And the servants of Isaac digged another well and did not find water, and they went and told Isaac that they had not found water, and Isaac said: 'I have sworn this day to the Philistines and this thing has been announced to us.'

26.   And he called the name of that place the Well of the Oath; for there he had sworn to Abimelech and Ahuzzath his friend and Phicol the prefect Or his host.

27.   And Isaac knew that day that under constraint he had sworn to them to make peace with them.

28.   And Isaac on that day cursed the Philistines and said: 'Cursed be the Philistines unto the day of wrath and indignation from the midst of all nations; may God make them a derision and a curse and an object of wrath and indignation in the hands of the sinners the Gentiles and in the hands of the Kittim.

29.   And whoever escapes the sword of the enemy and the Kittim, may the righteous nation root out in judgment from under heaven; for they shall be the enemies and foes of my children throughout their generations upon the earth.

30.   And no remnant shall be left to   them,
Nor one that shall be saved on the day of the wrath of judgment;
For destruction and rooting out and expulsion from the earth is the whole seed of the Philistines (reserved), And there shall no longer be left for these Caphtorim a name or a seed on the earth.

31.   For though he ascend unto heaven,
Thence shall he be brought down,

And though he make himself strong on earth,
Thence shall he be dragged forth,

And though he hide himself amongst the nations,
Even from thence shall he be rooted out;

And though he descend into Sheol,
There also shall his condemnation be great,
And there also he shall have no peace.

32.   And if he go into captivity,
By the hands of those that seek his life shall they slay him on the way,
And neither name nor seed shall be left to him on all the earth;
For into eternal malediction shall he depart.'

33.   And thus is it written and engraved concerning him on the heavenly tablets, to do unto him on the day of judgment, so that he may be rooted out of the earth.

Jubilees 25

1.   And in the second year of this week in this jubilee, Rebecca called Jacob her son, and spake unto [2109 A.M.] him, saying: 'My son, do not take thee a wife of the daughters of Canaan, as Esau, thy brother, who took him two wives of the daughters of Canaan, and they have embittered my soul with all their unclean deeds: for all their deeds are fornication and lust, and there is no righteousness with them, for (their deeds) are evil.

2.   And I, my son, love thee exceedingly, and my heart and my affection bless thee every hour of the day and watch of the night.

3.   And now, my son, hearken to my voice, and do the will of thy mother, and do not take thee a wife of the daughters of this land, but only of the house of my father, and of my father's kindred. Thou shalt take thee a wife of the house of my father, and the Most High God will bless thee, and thy children shall be a righteous generation and a holy seed.'

4.   And then spake Jacob to Rebecca, his mother, and said unto her: 'Behold, mother, I am nine weeks of years old, and I neither know nor have I touched any woman, nor have I betrothed myself to any, nor even think of taking me a wife of the daughters of Canaan.

5.   For I remember, mother, the words of Abraham, our father, for he commanded me not to take a wife of the daughters of Canaan, but to take me a wife from the seed of my father's house and from my kindred.

6.   I have heard before that daughters have been born to Laban, thy brother, and I have set my heart on them to take a wife from amongst them.

7.   And for this reason I have guarded myself in my spirit against sinning or being corrupted in all my ways throughout all the days of my life; for with regard to lust and fornication, Abraham, my father, gave me many commands.

8.   And, despite all that he has commanded me, these two and twenty years my brother has striven with me, and spoken frequently to me and said: 'My brother, take to wife a sister of my two wives'; but I refuse to do as he has done.

9.   I swear before thee, mother, that all the days of my life I will not take me a wife from the daughters of the seed of Canaan, and I will not act wickedly as my brother has done.

10.   Fear not, mother; be assured that I shall do thy will and walk in uprightness, and not corrupt my ways for ever.'

11.   And thereupon she lifted up her face to heaven and extended the fingers of her hands, and opened her mouth and blessed the Most High God, who had created the heaven and the earth, and she gave Him thanks and praise.

12.   And she said: 'Blessed be the Lord God, and may His holy name be blessed for ever and ever, who has given me Jacob as a pure son and a holy seed; for he is Thine, and Thine shall his seed be continually and throughout all the generations for evermore.

13.   Bless him, O Lord, and place in my mouth the blessing of righteousness, that I may bless him.'

14.   And at that hour, when the spirit of righteousness descended into her mouth, she placed both her hands on the head of Jacob, and said:

15.   Blessed art thou, Lord of righteousness and God of the ages
And may He bless thee beyond all the generations of men.

May He give thee, my Son, the path of   righteousness,
And reveal righteousness to thy seed.

16.   And may He make thy sons many   during   thy   life,
And may they arise according to the number of the months of the year.
And may their sons become many and great beyond the stars of heaven,
And their numbers be more than the sand of the sea.

17.   And may He give them this goodly land -as He said He would give it to Abraham and to his seed after   him   alway-
And may they hold it as a possession for ever.

18.   And may I see (born) unto thee, my son, blessed children during   my   life,
And a blessed and holy seed may all thy seed be.

19.   And as thou hast refreshed thy mother's spirit during her life, The womb of her that bare thee blesses thee thus,

[My affection] and my breasts bless thee
And my mouth and my tongue praise thee greatly.

20.   Increase and spread over the earth,
And may thy seed be perfect in the joy of heaven and earth for ever;

And may thy seed rejoice,
And on the great day of peace may it have peace.

21.   And may thy name and thy seed endure to all the ages,
And may the Most High God be their God,

And may the God of righteousness dwell with them,
And by them may His sanctuary be built unto all the ages.

22.   Blessed be he that blesseth thee,
And all flesh that curseth thee falsely, may it be cursed.'

23.   And she kissed him, and said to him;
'May the Lord of the world love thee
As the heart of thy mother and her affection rejoice in thee and bless thee.'
And she ceased from blessing.

Jubiless 26

1.   And in the seventh year of this week Isaac called Esau, his elder Son, and said unto him: ' I am [2114 A.M.] old, my son, and behold my eyes are dim in seeing, and I know not the day of my death.

2.   And now take thy hunting weapons thy quiver and thy bow, and go out to the field, and hunt and catch me (venison), my son, and make me savoury meat, such as my soul loveth, and bring it to me that I may eat, and that my soul may bless thee before I die.'

3.   But Rebecca heard Isaac speaking to Esau.

4.   And Esau went forth early to the field to hunt and catch and bring home to his father.

5.   And Rebecca called Jacob, her son, and said unto him: 'Behold, I heard Isaac, thy father, speak unto Esau, thy brother, saying: "Hunt for me, and make me savoury meat, and bring (it) to me that

6.   I may eat and bless thee before the Lord before I die." And now, my son, obey my voice in that which I command thee: Go to thy flock and fetch me two good kids of the goats, and I will make them savoury meat for thy father, such as he loves, and thou shalt bring (it) to thy father that he may eat and bless thee before the Lord before he die, and that thou mayst be blessed.'

7.   And Jacob said to Rebecca his mother: 'Mother, I shall not withhold anything which my father would eat, and which would please him: only I fear, my mother, that he will recognise my voice and wish to touch me.

8.   And thou knowest that I am smooth, and Esau, my brother, is hairy, and I shall appear before his eyes as an evildoer, and shall do a deed which he had not commanded me, and he will be wroth with me,

and I shall bring upon myself a curse, and not a blessing.'

9. And Rebecca, his mother, said unto him: 'Upon me be thy curse, my son, only obey my voice.'

10. And Jacob obeyed the voice of Rebecca, his mother, and went and fetched two good and fat kids of the goats, and brought them to his mother, and his mother made them ~savoury meat~ such as he loved.

11. And Rebecca took the goodly rainment of Esau, her elder son, which was with her in the house, and she clothed Jacob, her younger son, (with them), and she put the skins of the kids upon his hands and on the exposed parts of his neck.

12. And she gave the meat and the bread which she had prepared into the hand of her son Jacob.

13. And Jacob went in to his father and said: 'I am thy son: I have done according as thou badest me: arise and sit and eat of that which I have caught, father, that thy soul may bless me.'

14. And Isaac said to his son: 'How hast thou found so quickly, my son?

15. 'And Jacob said: 'Because <the Lord> thy God caused me to find.'

16. And Isaac said unto him: Come near, that I may feel thee, my son, if thou art my son Esau or not.'

17. And Jacob went near to Isaac, his father, and he felt him and said:

'The voice is Jacob's voice, but the hands are the hands of Esau,'

18. and he discerned him not, because it was a dispensation from heaven to remove his power of perception and Isaac discerned not, for his hands were hairy as his brother Esau's, so that he blessed him.

19. And he said: 'Art thou my son Esau? ' and he said: 'I am thy son': and he said, 'Bring near to me that I may eat of that which thou hast caught, my son, that my soul may bless thee.'

20. And he brought near to him, and he did eat, and he brought him wine and he drank.

21. And Isaac, his father, said unto him: 'Come near and kiss me, my son.

22. And he came near and kissed him. And he smelled the smell of his raiment, and he blessed him and said: 'Behold, the smell of my son is as the smell of a <full> field which the Lord hath blessed.

23. And may the Lord give thee of the dew of heaven And of the dew of the earth, and plenty of corn and oil:

Let nations serve thee, And peoples bow down to thee.

24. Be lord over thy brethren, And let thy mother's sons bow down to thee;

And may all the blessings wherewith the Lord hath blessed me and blessed Abraham, my father; Be imparted to thee and to thy seed for ever:

Cursed be he that curseth thee, And blessed be he that blesseth thee.'

25. And it came to pass as soon as Isaac had made an end of blessing his son Jacob, and Jacob had gone forth from Isaac his father he hid himself and Esau, his brother, came in from his hunting.

26. And he also made savoury meat, and brought (it) to his father, and said unto his father: 'Let my father arise, and eat of my venison that thy soul may bless me.'

27. And Isaac, his father, said unto him: 'Who art thou? 'And he said unto him: 'I am thy first born, thy son Esau: I have done as thou hast commanded me.'

28. And Isaac was very greatly astonished, and said: 'Who is he that hath hunted and caught and brought (it) to me, and I have eaten of all before thou camest, and have blessed him: (and) he shall be blessed, and all his seed for ever.'

29. And it came to pass when Esau heard the words of his father Isaac that he cried with an exceeding great and bitter cry, and said unto his father: 'Bless me, (even) me also, father.'

30. And he said unto him: 'Thy brother came with guile, and hath taken away thy blessing.' And he said: 'Now I know why his name is named Jacob: behold, he hath supplanted me these two times: he took away my birth-right, and now he hath taken away my blessing.'

31. And he said: 'Hast thou not reserved a blessing for me, father?' and Isaac answered and said unto Esau:

'Behold, I have made him thy lord, And all his brethren have I given to him for servants, And with plenty of corn and wine and oil have I strengthened him:

And what now shall I do for thee, my son?'

32. And Esau said to Isaac, his father:
'Hast thou but one blessing, O father?
Bless me, (even) me also, father: '

33. And Esau lifted up his voice and wept. And Isaac answered and said unto him:

'Behold, far from the dew of the earth shall be thy dwelling, And far from the dew of heaven from above.

34. And by thy sword wilt thou live, And thou wilt serve thy brother.

And it shall come to pass when thou becomest great,

And dost shake his yoke from off thy neck,
Thou shalt sin a complete sin unto death,
And thy seed shall be rooted out from under heaven.'

35.   And Esau kept threatening Jacob because of the blessing wherewith his father blessed him, and he: said in his heart: 'May the days of mourning for my father now come, so that I may slay my brother Jacob.'

Jubilees 27

1.   And the words of Esau, her elder son, were told to Rebecca in a dream, and Rebecca sent and called Jacob her younger son,

2.   and said unto him: 'Behold Esau thy brother will take vengeance on thee so as to kill thee.

3.   Now, therefore, my son, obey my voice, and arise and flee thou to Laban, my brother, to Haran, and tarry with him a few days until thy brother's anger turns away, and he remove his anger from thee, and forget all that thou hast done; then I will send and fetch thee from thence.'

4.   And Jacob said: 'I am not afraid; if he wishes to kill me, I will kill him.'

5.   But she said unto him: 'Let me not be bereft of both my sons on one day.'

6.   And Jacob said to Rebecca his mother: 'Behold, thou knowest that my father has become old, and does not see because his eyes are dull, and if I leave him it will be evil in his eyes, because I leave him and go away from you, and my father will be angry, and will curse me. I will not go; when he sends me, then only will I go.'

7.   And Rebecca said to Jacob: 'I will go in and speak to him, and he will send thee away.'

8.   And Rebecca went in and said to Isaac: 'I loathe my life because of the two daughters of Heth, whom Esau has taken him as wives; and if Jacob take a wife from among the daughters of the land such as these, for what purpose do I further live, for the daughters of Canaan are evil.'

9.   And Isaac called Jacob and blessed him, and admonished him and said unto him: 'Do not take thee a wife of any of the daughters of Canaan;

10.   arise and go to Mesopotamia, to the house of Bethuel, thy mother's father, and take thee a wife from thence of the daughters of Laban, thy mother's brother.

11.   And God Almighty bless thee and increase and multiply thee that thou mayest become a company of nations, and give thee the blessings of my father Abraham, to thee and to thy seed after thee, that thou mayest inherit the land of thy sojournings and all the land which God gave to Abraham: go, my son, in peace.'

12.   And Isaac sent Jacob away, and he went to Mesopotamia, to Laban the son of Bethuel the Syrian, the brother of Rebecca, Jacob's mother.

13.   And it came to pass after Jacob had arisen to go to Mesopotamia that the spirit of Rebecca was grieved after her son, and she wept.

14.   And Isaac said to Rebecca: 'My sister, weep not on account of Jacob, my son; for he goeth in peace, and in peace will he return.

15.   The Most High God will preserve him from all evil, and will be with him; for He will not forsake him all his days;

16.   For I know that his ways will be prospered in all things wherever he goes, until he return in peace to us, and we see him in peace.

17.   Fear not on his account, my sister, for he is on the upright path and he is a perfect man: and he is faithful and will not perish. Weep not.'

18.   And Isaac comforted Rebecca on account of her son Jacob, and blessed him.

19.   And Jacob went from the Well of the Oath to go to Haran on the first year of the second week in the forty-fourth jubilee, and he came to Luz on the mountains, that is, Bethel, on the new moon of the first month of this week, [2115 A.M.] and he came to the place at even and turned from the way to the west of the road that night: and he slept there; for the sun had set.

20.   And he took one of the stones of that place and laid <it at his head> under the tree, and he was journeying alone, and he slept.

21.   And he dreamt that night, and behold a ladder set up on the earth, and the top of it reached to heaven, and behold, the angels of the Lord ascended and descended on it: and behold, the Lord stood upon it.

22.   And he spake to Jacob and said: 'I am the Lord God of Abraham, thy father, and the God of Isaac; the land whereon thou art sleeping, to thee will I give it, and to thy seed after thee.

23.   And thy seed shall be as the dust of the earth, and thou shalt increase to the west and to the east, to the north and the south, and in thee and in thy seed shall all the families of the nations be blessed.

24.   And behold, I will be with thee, and will keep thee whithersoever thou goest, and I will bring thee again into this land in peace; for I will not leave thee until I do everything that I told thee of.'

25.   And Jacob awoke from his sleep, and said, 'Truly this place is the house of the Lord, and I knew it not.' And he was afraid and said: 'Dreadful is this place which is none other than the house of God, and this is the gate of heaven.'

26.   And Jacob arose early in the morning, and took the stone which

he had put under his head and set it up as a pillar for a sign, and he poured oil upon the top of it. And he called the name of that place Bethel; but the name of the place was Luz at the first.

27.   And Jacob vowed a vow unto the Lord, saying: 'If the Lord will be with me, and will keep me in this way that I go, and give me bread to eat and raiment to put on, so that I come again to my father's house in peace, then shall the Lord be my God, and this stone which I have set up as a pillar for a sign in this place, shall be the Lord's house, and of all that thou givest me, I shall give the tenth to thee, my God.'

Jubilees 28

1.   And he went on his journey, and came to the land of the east, to Laban, the brother of Rebecca, and he was with him, and served him for Rachel his daughter one week.

2.   And in the first year of the third week [2122 A.M.] he said unto him: 'Give me my wife, for whom I have served thee seven years '; and Laban said unto Jacob: 'I will give thee thy wife.'

3.   And Laban made a feast, and took Leah his elder daughter, and gave (her) to Jacob as a wife, and gave her Zilpah his handmaid for an hand- maid; and Jacob did not know, for he thought that she was Rachel.

4.   And he went in unto her, and behold, she was Leah; and Jacob was angry with Laban, and said unto him: 'Why hast thou dealt thus with me? Did not I serve thee for Rachel and not for Leah? Why hast thou wronged me?

5.   Take thy daughter, and I will go; for thou hast done evil to me.' For Jacob loved Rachel more than Leah; for Leah's eyes were weak, but her form was very handsome; but Rachel had beautiful eyes and a beautiful and very handsome form.

6.   And Laban said to Jacob: 'It is not so done in our country, to give the younger before the elder.' And it is not right to do this; for thus it is ordained and written in the heavenly tablets, that no one should give his younger daughter before the elder; but the elder, one gives first and after her the younger -and the man who does so, they set down guilt against him in heaven, and none is righteous that does this thing, for this deed is evil before the Lord.

7.   And command thou the children of Israel that they do not this thing; let them neither take nor give the younger before they have given the elder, for it is very wicked.

8.   And Laban said to Jacob: 'Let the seven days of the feast of this one pass by, and I shall give thee Rachel, that thou mayst serve me another seven years, that thou mayst pasture my sheep as thou didst in the former week.'

9.   And on the day when the seven days of the feast of Leah had passed, Laban gave Rachel to Jacob, that he might serve him

another seven years, and he gave to Rachel Bilhah, the sister of Zilpah, as a handmaid.

10. And he served yet other seven years for Rachel, for Leah had been given to him for nothing.

11. And the Lord opened the womb of Leah, and she conceived and bare Jacob a son, and he called his name Reuben, on the fourteenth day of the ninth month, in the first year of the third week. [2122 A.M.]

12. But the womb of Rachel was closed, for the Lord saw that Leah was hated and Rachel loved.

13. And again Jacob went in unto Leah, and she conceived, and bare Jacob a second son, and he called his name Simeon, on the twenty-first of the tenth month, and in the third year of this week. [2124 A.M.]

14. And again Jacob went in unto Leah, and she conceived, and bare him a third son, and he called his name Levi, in the new moon of the first month in the sixth year of this week. [2127 A.M.]

15. And again Jacob went in unto her, and she conceived, and bare him a fourth son, and he called his name Judah, on the fifteenth of the third month, in the first year of the fourth week. [2129 A.M.]

16. And on account of all this Rachel envied Leah, for she did not bear, and she said to Jacob: 'Give me children'; and Jacob said: 'Have I withheld from thee the fruits of thy womb? Have I forsaken thee?'

17. And when Rachel saw that Leah had borne four sons to Jacob, Reuben and Simeon and Levi and Judah, she said unto him: 'Go in unto Bilhah my handmaid, and she will conceive, and bear a son unto me.' (And she gave (him) Bilhah her handmaid to wife).

18. And he went in unto her, and she conceived, and bare him a son, and he called his name Dan, on the ninth of the sixth month, in the sixth year of the third week. [2127 A.M.]

19. And Jacob went in again unto Bilhah a second time, and she conceived, and bare Jacob another son, and Rachel called his name Napthali, on the fifth of the seventh month, in the second year of the fourth week. [2130 A.M.]

20. And when Leah saw that she had become sterile and did not bear, she envied Rachel, and she also gave her handmaid Zilpah to Jacob to wife, and she conceived, and bare a son, and Leah called his name Gad, on the twelfth of the eighth month, in the third year of the fourth week. [2131 A.M.]

21. And he went in again unto her, and she conceived, and bare him a second son, and Leah called his name Asher, on the second of the eleventh month, in the fifth year of the fourth week. [2133 A.M.]

22. And Jacob went in unto Leah, and she conceived, and bare a son, and she called his name Issachar, on the fourth of the fifth month, in the

fourth year of the fourth week,[2132 A.M.] and she gave him to a nurse.

23.   And Jacob went in again unto her, and she conceived, and bare two (children), a son and a daughter, and she called the name of the son Zabulon, and the name of the daughter Dinah, in the seventh of the seventh month, in the sixth year of the fourth week. [2134 A.M.]

24.   And the Lord was gracious to Rachel, and opened her womb, and she conceived, and bare a son, and she called his name Joseph, on the new moon of the fourth month, in the sixth year in this fourth week. [2134 A.M.]

25.   And in the days when Joseph was born, Jacob said to Laban: 'Give me my wives and sons, and let me go to my father Isaac, and let me make me an house; for I have completed the years in which I have served thee for thy two daughters, and I will go to the house of my father.'

26.   And Laban said to Jacob: 'Tarry with me for thy wages, and pasture my flock for me again, and take thy wages.'

27.   And they agreed with one another that he should give him as his wages those of the lambs and kids which were born black and spotted and white, (these) were to be his wages.

28.   And all the sheep brought forth spotted and speckled and black, variously marked, and they brought forth again lambs like

themselves, and all that were spotted were Jacob's and those which were not were Laban's.

29.   And Jacob's possessions multiplied exceedingly, and he possessed oxen and sheep and asses and camels, and menservants and maid-servants.

30.   And Laban and his sons envied Jacob, and Laban took back his sheep from him, and he observed him with evil intent.

Jubilees 29

1.   And it came to pass when Rachel had borne Joseph, that Laban went to shear his sheep; for they were distant from him a three days' journey.

2.   And Jacob saw that Laban was going to shear his sheep, and Jacob called Leah and Rachel, and spake kindly unto them that they should come with him to the land of Canaan.

3.   For he told them how he had seen everything in a dream, even all that He had spoken unto him that he should return to his father's house, and they said: 'To every place whither thou goest we will go with thee.'

4.   And Jacob blessed the God of Isaac his father, and the God of Abraham his father's father, and he arose and mounted his wives and his children, and took all his possessions and crossed the river, and came to the land of Gilead, and

Jacob hid his intention from Laban and told him not.

5. And in the seventh year of the fourth week Jacob turned (his face) toward Gilead in the first month, on the twenty-first thereof. [2135 A.M.] And Laban pursued after him and overtook Jacob in the mountain of Gilead in the third month, on the thirteenth thereof.

6. And the Lord did not suffer him to injure Jacob; for he appeared to him in a dream by night. And Laban spake to Jacob.

7. And on the fifteenth of those days Jacob made a feast for Laban, and for all who came with him, and Jacob sware to Laban that day, and Laban also to Jacob, that neither should cross the mountain of Gilead to the other with evil purpose.

8. And he made there a heap for a witness; wherefore the name of that place is called: 'The Heap of Witness,' after this heap.

9. But before they used to call the land of Gilead the land of the Rephaim; for it was the land of the Rephaim, and the Rephaim were born (there), giants whose height was ten, nine, eight down to seven cubits.

10. And their habitation was from the land of the children of Ammon to Mount Hermon, and the seats of their kingdom were Karnaim and Ashtaroth, and Edrei, and Misur, and Beon.

11. And the Lord destroyed them because of the evil of their deeds; for they were very malignant, and the Amorites dwelt in their stead, wicked and sinful, and there is no people to-day which has wrought to the full all their sins, and they have no longer length of life on the earth.

12. And Jacob sent away Laban, and he departed into Mesopotamia, the land of the East, and Jacob returned to the land of Gilead.

13. And he passed over the Jabbok in the ninth month, on the eleventh thereof. And on that day Esau, his brother, came to him, and he was reconciled to him, and departed from him unto the land of Seir, but Jacob dwelt in tents.

14. And in the first year of the fifth week in this jubilee [2136 A.M.] he crossed the Jordan, and dwelt beyond the Jordan, and he pastured his sheep from the sea of the heap unto Bethshan, and unto Dothan and unto the forest of Akrabbim.

15. And he sent to his father Isaac of all his substance, clothing, and food, and meat, and drink, and milk, and butter, and cheese, and some dates of the valley.

16. And to his mother Rebecca also four times a year, between the times of the months, between ploughing and reaping, and between autumn and the rain (season) and between winter and spring, to the tower of Abraham.

17. For Isaac had returned from the Well of the Oath and gone up to

the tower of his father Abraham, and he dwelt there apart from his son Esau.

18.   For in the days when Jacob went to Mesopotamia, Esau took to himself a wife Mahalath, the daughter of Ishmael, and he gathered together all the flocks of his father and his wives, and went Up and dwelt on Mount Seir, and left Isaac his father at the Well of the Oath alone.

19.   And Isaac went up from the Well of the Oath and dwelt in the tower of Abraham his father on the mountains of Hebron,

20.   And thither Jacob sent all that he did send to his father and his mother from time to time, all they needed, and they blessed Jacob with all their heart and with all their soul.

Jubilees 30

1.   And in the first year of the sixth week [2143 A.M.] he went up to Salem, to the east of Shechem, in peace, in the fourth month.

2.   And there they carried off Dinah, the daughter of Jacob, into the house of Shechem, the son of Hamor, the Hivite, the prince of the land, and he lay with her and defiled her, and she was a little girl, a child of twelve years.

3.   And he besought his father and her brothers that she might be given to him to wife. And Jacob and his sons were wroth because of the men of Shechem; for they had defiled Dinah, their sister, and they spake to them with evil intent and dealt deceitfully with them and beguiled them.

4.   And Simeon and Levi came unexpectedly to Shechem and executed judgment on all the men of Shechem, and slew all the men whom they found in it, and left not a single one remaining in it: they slew all in torments because they had dishonoured their sister Dinah.

5.   And thus let it not again be done from henceforth that a daughter of Israel be defiled; for judgment is ordained in heaven against them that they should destroy with the sword all the men of the Shechemites because they had wrought shame in Israel.

6.   And the Lord delivered them into the hands of the sons of Jacob that they might exterminate them with the sword and execute judgment upon them, and that it might not thus again be done in Israel that a virgin of Israel should be defiled.

7.   And if there is any man who wishes in Israel to give his daughter or his sister to any man who is of the seed of the Gentiles he shall surely die, and they shall stone him with stones; for he hath wrought shame in Israel; and they shall burn the woman with fire, because she has dishonoured the name of the house of her father, and she shall be rooted out of Israel.

8.   And let not an adulteress and no uncleanness be found in Israel throughout all the days of the generations of the earth; for Israel is holy unto the Lord, and every man who has defiled (it) shall surely die: they shall stone him with stones.

9.   For thus has it been ordained and written in the heavenly tablets regarding all the seed of Israel: he who defileth (it) shall surely die, and he shall be stoned with stones.

10.   And to this law there is no limit of days, and no remission, nor any atonement: but the man who has defiled his daughter shall be rooted out in the midst of all Israel, because he has given of his seed to Moloch, and wrought impiously so as to defile it.

11.   And do thou, Moses, command the children of Israel and exhort them not to give their daughters to the Gentiles, and not to take for their sons any of the daughters of the Gentiles, for this is abominable before the Lord.

12.   For this reason I have written for thee in the words of the Law all the deeds of the Shechemites, which they wrought against Dinah, and how the sons of Jacob spake, saying: 'We will not give our daughter to a man who is uncircumcised; for that were a reproach unto us.'

13.   And it is a reproach to Israel, to those who live, and to those that take the daughters of the Gentiles; for this is unclean and abominable to Israel.

14.   And Israel will not be free from this uncleanness if it has a wife of the daughters of the Gentiles, or has given any of its daughters to a man who is of any of the Gentiles.

15.   For there will be plague upon plague, and curse upon curse, and every judgment and plague and curse will come *upon him*: if he do this thing, or hide his eyes from those who commit uncleanness, or those who defile the sanctuary of the Lord, or those who profane His holy name, (then) will the whole nation together be judged for all the uncleanness and profanation of this man.

16.   And there will be no respect of persons [and no consideration of persons] and no receiving at his hands of fruits and offerings and burnt-offerings and fat, nor the fragrance of sweet savour, so as to accept it: and so fare every man or woman in Israel who defiles the sanctuary.

17.   For this reason I have commanded thee, saying: 'Testify this testimony to Israel: see how the Shechemites fared and their sons: how they were delivered into the hands of two sons of Jacob, and they slew them under tortures, and it was (reckoned) unto them for righteousness, and it is written down to them for righteousness.

18.   And the seed of Levi was chosen for the priesthood, and to be Levites, that they might minister before the Lord, as we, continually, and that Levi and his sons may be

blessed for ever; for he was zealous to execute righteousness and judgment and vengeance on all those who arose against Israel.

19.   And so they inscribe as a testimony in his favour on the heavenly tablets blessing and righteousness before the God of all:

20.   And we remember the righteousness which the man fulfilled during his life, at all periods of the year; until a thousand generations they will record it, and it will come to him and to his descendants after him, and he has been recorded on the heavenly tablets as a friend and a righteous man.

21.   All this account I have written for thee, and have commanded thee to say to the children of Israel, that they should not commit sin nor transgress the ordinances nor break the covenant which has been ordained for them, (but) that they should fulfil it and be recorded as friends.

22.   But if they transgress and work uncleanness in every way, they will be recorded on the heavenly tablets as adversaries, and they will be destroyed out of the book of life, and they will be recorded in the book of those who will be destroyed and with those who will be rooted out of the earth.

23.   And on the day when the sons of Jacob slew Shechem a writing was recorded in their favour in heaven that they had executed righteousness and uprightness and vengeance on the sinners, and it was written for a blessing.

24.   And they brought Dinah, their sister, out of the house of Shechem, and they took captive everything that was in Shechem, their sheep and their oxen and their asses, and all their wealth, and all their flocks, and brought them all to Jacob their father.

25.   And he reproached them because they had put the city to the sword for he feared those who dwelt in the land, the Canaanites and the Perizzites.

26.   And the dread of the Lord was upon all the cities which are around about Shechem, and they did not rise to pursue after the sons of Jacob; for terror had fallen upon them.

Jubilees 31

1.   And on the new moon of the month Jacob spake to all the people of his house. saying: 'Purify yourselves and change your garments, and let us arise and go up to Bethel, where I vowed a vow to Him on the day when I fled from the face of Esau my brother, because he has been with me and brought me into this land in peace, and put ye away the strange gods that arc among you.'

2.   And they gave up the strange gods and that which was in their ears and which was on their necks and the idols which Rachel stole from Laban her father she gave wholly to

810

Jacob. And he burnt and brake them to pieces and destroyed them, and hid them under an oak which is in the land of Shechem.

3.   And he went up on the new moon of the seventh month to Bethel. And he built an altar at the place where he had slept, and he set up a pillar there, and he sent word to his father Isaac to come to him to his sacrifice, and to his mother Rebecca.

4.   And Isaac said: 'Let my son Jacob come, and let me see him before I die.'

5.   And Jacob went to his father Isaac and to his mother Rebecca, to the house of his father Abraham, and he took two of his sons with him, Levi and Judah, and he came to his father Isaac and to his mother Rebecca.

6.   And Rebecca came forth from the tower to the front of it to kiss Jacob and embrace him; for her spirit had revived when she heard: 'Behold Jacob thy son has come'; and she kissed him.

7.   And she saw his two sons, and she recognised them, and said unto him: 'Are these thy sons, my son?' and she embraced them and kissed them, and blessed them, saying: 'In you shall the seed of Abraham become illustrious, and ye shall prove a blessing on the earth.'

8.   And Jacob went in to Isaac his father, to the chamber where he lay, and his two sons were with him, and he took the hand of his father, and stooping down he kissed him,

and Isaac clung to the neck of Jacob his son, and wept upon his neck.

9.   And the darkness left the eyes of Isaac, and he saw the two sons of Jacob, Levi, and Judah, and he said: 'Are these thy sons, my son? for they are like thee.'

10.   And he said unto him that they were truly his sons: 'And thou hast truly seen that they are truly my sons'.

11.   And they came near to him, and he turned and kissed them and embraced them both together.

12.   And the spirit of prophecy came down into his mouth, and he took Levi by his right hand and Judah by his left.

13.   And he turned to Levi first, and began to bless him first, and said unto him: May the God of all, the very Lord of all the ages, bless thee and thy children throughout all the ages.

14.   And may the Lord give to thee and to thy seed greatness and great glory, and cause thee and thy seed, from among all flesh, to approach Him to serve in His sanctuary as the angels of the presence and as the holy ones. (Even) as they, shall the seed of thy sons be for glory and greatness and holiness, and may He make them great unto all the ages.

15.   And they shall be judges and princes, and chiefs of all the seed of the sons of Jacob;

They shall speak the word of the Lord in righteousness,
And they shall judge all His judgments in righteousness.

And they shall declare My ways to Jacob
And My paths to Israel.

The blessing of the Lord shall be given in their mouths
To bless all the seed of the beloved.

16. Thy mother has called thy name Levi,
And justly has she called thy name;

Thou shalt be joined to the Lord
And be the companion of all the sons of Jacob;

Let His table be thine,
And do thou and thy sons eat thereof;

And may thy table be full unto all generations,
And thy food fail not unto all the ages.

17. And let all who hate thee fall down before thee,
And let all thy adversaries be rooted out and perish;

And blessed be he that blesses thee,
And cursed be every nation that curses thee.'

18. And to Judah he said:
'May the Lord give thee strength and power

To tread down all that hate thee;
A prince shalt thou be, thou and one of thy sons, over the sons of Jacob;

May thy name and the name of thy sons go forth and traverse every land and region.
Then shall the Gentiles fear before thy face,

And all the nations shall quake
[And all the peoples shall quake].

19. In thee shall be the help of Jacob,
And in thee be found the salvation of Israel.

20. And when thou sittest on the throne of honour of thy righteousness
There shall be great peace for all the seed of the sons of the beloved;

Blessed be he that blesseth thee,
And all that hate thee and afflict thee and curse thee
Shall be rooted out and destroyed from the earth and be accursed.'

21. And turning he kissed him again and embraced him, and rejoiced greatly; for he had seen the sons of Jacob his son in very truth.

22. And he went forth from between his feet and fell down and bowed down to him, and he blessed them and rested there with Isaac his father that night, and they eat and drank with joy.

23. And he made the two sons of Jacob sleep, the one on his right

hand and the other on his left, and it was counted to him for righteousness.

24. And Jacob told his father everything during the night, how the Lord had shown him great mercy, and how he had prospered (him in) all his ways, and protected him from all evil.

25. And Isaac blessed the God of his father Abraham, who had not withdrawn his mercy and his righteousness from the sons of his servant Isaac.

26. And in the morning Jacob told his father Isaac the vow which he had vowed to the Lord, and the vision which he had seen, and that he had built an altar, and that everything was ready for the sacrifice to be made before the Lord as he had vowed, and that he had come to set him on an ass.

27. And Isaac said unto Jacob his son: 'I am not able to go with thee; for I am old and not able to bear the way: go, my son, in peace; for I am one hundred and sixty-five years this day; I am no longer able to journey; set thy mother (on an ass) and let her go with thee.

28. And I know, my son, that thou hast come on my account, and may this day be blessed on which thou hast seen me alive, and I also have seen thee, my son.

29. Mayest thou prosper and fulfil the vow which thou hast vowed; and put not off thy vow; for thou shalt be called to account as touching the vow; now therefore make haste to perform it, and may He be pleased who has made all things, to whom thou hast vowed the vow.'

30. And he said to Rebecca: 'Go with Jacob thy son'; and Rebecca went with Jacob her son, and Deborah with her, and they came to Bethel.

31. And Jacob remembered the prayer with which his father had blessed him and his two sons, Levi and Judah, and he rejoiced and blessed the God of his fathers, Abraham and Isaac.

32. And he said: 'Now I know that I have an eternal hope, and my sons also, before the God of all'; and thus is it ordained concerning the two; and they record it as an eternal testimony unto them on the heavenly tablets how Isaac blessed them.

Jubilees 32

1. And he abode that night at Bethel, and Levi dreamed that they had ordained and made him the priest of the Most High God, him and his sons for ever; and he awoke from his sleep and blessed the Lord.

2. And Jacob rose early in the morning, on the fourteenth of this month, and he gave a tithe of all that came with him, both of men and cattle, both of gold and every vessel and garment, yea, he gave tithes of all.

3. And in those days Rachel became pregnant with her son

Benjamin. And Jacob counted his sons from him upwards and Levi fell to the portion of the Lord, and his father clothed him in the garments of the priesthood and filled his hands.

4. And on the fifteenth of this month, he brought to the altar fourteen oxen from amongst the cattle, and twenty-eight rams, and forty-nine sheep, and seven lambs, and twenty-one kids of the goats as a burnt-offering on the altar of sacrifice, well pleasing for a sweet savour before God.

5. This was his offering, in consequence of the vow which he had vowed that he would give a tenth, with their fruit-offerings and their drink- offerings.

6. And when the fire had consumed it, he burnt incense on the fire over the fire, and for a thank-offering two oxen and four rams and four sheep, four he-goats, and two sheep of a year old, and two kids of the goats; and thus he did daily for seven days.

7. And he and all his sons and his men were eating (this) with joy there during seven days and blessing and thanking the Lord, who had delivered him out of all his tribulation and had given him his vow.

8. And he tithed all the clean animals, and made a burnt sacrifice, but the unclean animals he gave (not) to Levi his son, and he gave him all the souls of the men.

9. And Levi discharged the priestly office at Bethel before Jacob his father in preference to his ten brothers, and he was a priest there, and Jacob gave his vow: thus he tithed again the tithe to the Lord and sanctified it, and it became holy unto Him.

10. And for this reason it is ordained on the heavenly tablets as a law for the tithing again the tithe to eat before the Lord from year to year, in the place where it is chosen that His name should dwell, and to this law there is no limit of days for ever.

11. This ordinance is written that it may be fulfilled from year to year in eating the second tithe before the Lord in the place where it has been chosen, and nothing shall remain over from it from this year to the year following.

12. For in its year shall the seed be eaten till the days of the gathering of the seed of the year, and the wine till the days of the wine, and the oil till the days of its season.

13. And all that is left thereof and becomes old, let it be regarded as polluted: let it be burnt with fire, for it is unclean.

14. And thus let them eat it together in the sanctuary, and let them not suffer it to become old.

15. And all the tithes of the oxen and sheep shall be holy unto the Lord, and shall belong to his priests, which they will eat before Him from year to year; for thus is it ordained

and engraven regarding the tithe on the heavenly tablets.

16.   And on the following night, on the twenty-second day of this month, Jacob resolved to build that place, and to surround the court with a wall, and to sanctify it and make it holy for ever, for himself and his children after him.

17.   And the Lord appeared to him by night and blessed him and said unto him: 'Thy name shall not be called Jacob, but Israel shall they name thy name.'

18.   And He said unto him again: 'I am the Lord who created the heaven and the earth, and I will increase thee and multiply thee exceedingly, and kings shall come forth from thee, and they shall judge everywhere wherever the foot of the sons of men has trodden.

19.   And I will give to thy seed all the earth which is under heaven, and they shall judge all the nations according to their desires, and after that they shall get possession of the whole earth and inherit it for ever.'

20.   And He finished speaking with him, and He went up from him. and Jacob looked till He had ascended into heaven.

21.   And he saw in a vision of the night, and behold an angel descended from heaven with seven tablets in his hands, and he gave them to Jacob, and he read them and knew all that was written therein which would befall him and his sons throughout all the ages.

22.   And he showed him all that was written on the tablets, and said unto him: 'Do not build this place, and do not make it an eternal sanctuary, and do not dwell here; for this is not the place. Go to the house of Abraham thy father and dwell with Isaac thy father until the day of the death of thy father.

23.   For in Egypt thou shalt die in peace, and in this land thou shalt be buried with honour in the sepulchre of thy fathers, with Abraham and Isaac.

24.   Fear not, for as thou hast seen and read it, thus shall it all be; and do thou write down everything as thou hast seen and read.'

25.   And Jacob said: 'Lord, how can I remember all that I have read and seen? 'And he said unto him: 'I will   bring   all   things   to   thy remembrance.'

26.   And he went up from him, and he awoke from his sleep, and he remembered everything which he had read and seen, and he wrote down all the words which he had read and seen.

27.   And he celebrated there yet another day, and he sacrificed thereon according to all that he sacrificed on the former days, and called its name 'Addition,' for this day was added and the former days he called 'The Feast '.

28.   And thus it was manifested that it should be, and it is written on the heavenly tablets: wherefore it was revealed to him that he should

815

celebrate it, and add it to the seven days of the feast.

29.   And its name was called 'Addition,' because that it was recorded amongst the days of the feast days, according to the number of the days of the year.

30.   And in the night, on the twenty-third of this month, Deborah Rebecca's nurse died, and they buried her beneath the city under the oak of the river, and he called the name of this place, 'The river of Deborah,' and the oak, 'The oak of the mourning of Deborah.'

31.   And Rebecca went and returned to her house to his father Isaac, and Jacob sent by her hand rams and sheep and he-goats that she should prepare a meal for his father such as he desired.

32.   And he went after his mother till he came to the land of Kabratan, and he dwelt there.

33.   And Rachel bare a son in the night, and called his name 'Son of my sorrow '; for she suffered in giving him birth: but his father called his name Benjamin, on the eleventh of the eighth month in the first of the sixth week of this jubilee. [2143 A.M.]

34.   And Rachel died there and she was buried in the land of Ephrath, the same is Bethlehem, and Jacob built a pillar on the grave of Rachel, on the road above her grave.

Jubilees 33

1.   And Jacob went and dwelt to the south of Magdaladra'ef. And he went to his father Isaac, he and Leah his wife, on the new moon of the tenth month.

2.   And Reuben saw Bilhah, Rachel's maid, the concubine of his father, bathing in water in a secret place, and he loved her.

3.   And he hid himself at night, and he entered the house of Bilhah [at night], and he found her sleeping alone on a bed in her house.

4.   And he lay with her, and she awoke and saw, and behold Reuben was lying with her in the bed, and she uncovered the border of her covering and seized him, and cried out, and discovered that it was Reuben.

5.   And she was ashamed because of him, and released her hand from him, and he fled.

6.   And she lamented because of this thing exceedingly, and did not tell it to any one.

7.   And when Jacob returned and sought her, she said unto him: 'I am not clean for thee, for I have been defiled as regards thee; for Reuben has defiled me, and has lain with me in the night, and I was asleep, and did not discover until he uncovered my skirt and slept with me.'

8.   And Jacob was exceedingly wroth with Reuben because he had

lain with Bilhah, because he had uncovered his father's skirt.

9.   And Jacob did not approach her again because Reuben had defiled her. And as for any man who uncovers his father's skirt his deed is wicked exceedingly, for he is abominable before the Lord.

10.   For this reason it is written and ordained on the heavenly tablets that a man should not lie with his father's wife, and should not uncover his father's skirt, for this is unclean: they shall surely die together, the man who lies with his father's wife and the woman also, for they have wrought uncleanness on the earth.

11.   And there shall be nothing unclean before our God in the nation which He has chosen for Himself as a possession.

12.   And again, it is written a second time: 'Cursed be he who lieth with the wife of his father, for he hath uncovered his father's shame'; and all the holy ones of the Lord said 'So be it; so be it.'

13.   And do thou, Moses, command the children of Israel that they observe this word; for it (entails) a punishment of death; and it is unclean, and there is no atonement for ever to atone for the man who has committed this, but he is to be put to death and slain, and stoned with stones, and rooted out from the midst of the people of our God.

14.   For to no man who does so in Israel is it permitted to remain alive a single day on the earth, for he is abominable and unclean.

15.   And let them not say: to Reuben was granted life and forgiveness after he had lain with his father's concubine, and to her also though she had a husband, and her husband Jacob, his father, was still alive.

16.   For until that time there had not been revealed the ordinance and judgment and law in its completeness for all, but in thy days (it has been revealed) as a law of seasons and of days, and an everlasting law for the everlasting generations.

17.   And for this law there is no consummation of days, and no atonement for it, but they must both be rooted out in the midst of the nation: on the day whereon they committed it they shall slay them.

18.   And do thou, Moses, write (it) down for Israel that they may observe it, and do according to these words, and not commit a sin unto death; for the Lord our God is judge, who respects not persons and accepts not gifts.

19.   And tell them these words of the covenant, that they may hear and observe, and be on their guard with respect to them, and not be destroyed and rooted out of the land; for an uncleanness, and an abomination, and a contamination, and a pollution are all they who commit it on the earth before our God.

20. And there is no greater sin than the fornication which they commit on earth; for Israel is a holy nation unto the Lord its God, and a nation of inheritance, and a priestly and royal nation and for (His own) possession; and there shall no such uncleanness appear in the midst of the holy nation.

21. And in the third year of this sixth week [2145 A.M.] Jacob and all his sons went and dwelt in the house of Abraham, near Isaac his father and Rebecca his mother.

22. And these were the names of the sons of Jacob: the first-born Reuben, Simeon, Levi, Judah, Issachar, Zebulon, the sons of Leah; and the sons of Rachel, Joseph and Benjamin; and the sons of Bilhah, Dan and Naphtali; and the sons of Zilpah, Gad and Asher; and Dinah, the daughter of Leah, the only daughter of Jacob.

23. And they came and bowed themselves to Isaac and Rebecca, and when they saw them they blessed Jacob and all his sons, and Isaac rejoiced exceedingly, for he saw the sons of Jacob, his younger son and he blessed them.

Jubilees 34

1. And in the sixth year of this week of this forty-fourth jubilee [2148 A.M.] Jacob sent his sons to pasture their sheep, and his servants with them to the pastures of Shechem.

2. And the seven kings of the Amorites assembled themselves together against them, to slay them, hiding themselves under the trees, and to take their cattle as a prey.

3. And Jacob and Levi and Judah and Joseph were in the house with Isaac their father; for his spirit was sorrowful, and they could not leave him: and Benjamin was the youngest, and for this reason remained with his father.

4. And there came the king[s] of Taphu and the king[s] of 'Aresa, and the king[s] of Seragan, and the king[s] of Selo, and the king[s] of Ga'as, and the king of Bethoron, and the king of Ma'anisakir, and all those who dwell in these mountains (and) who dwell in the woods in the land of Canaan.

5. And they announced this to Jacob saying: 'Behold, the kings of the Amorites have surrounded thy sons, and plundered their herds.'

6. And he arose from his house, he and his three sons and all the servants of his father, and his own servants, and he went against them with six thousand men, who carried swords.

7. And he slew them in the pastures of Shechem, and pursued those who fled, and he slew them with the edge of the sword, and he slew 'Aresa and Taphu and Saregan and Selo and 'Amani- sakir and Ga[ga]'as, and he recovered his herds.

8. And he prevailed over them, and imposed tribute on them that they should pay him tribute, five fruit

products of their land, and he built Robel and Tamnatares.

9. And he returned in peace, and made peace with them, and they became his servants, until the day that he and his sons went down into Egypt.

10. And in the seventh year of this week [2149 A.M.] he sent Joseph to learn about the welfare of his brothers from his house to the land of Shechem, and he found them in the land of Dothan.

11. And they dealt treacherously with him, and formed a plot against him to slay him, but changing their minds, they sold him to Ishmaelite merchants, and they brought him down into Egypt, and they sold him to Potiphar, the eunuch of Pharaoh, the chief of the cooks, priest of the city of 'Elew.

12. And the sons of Jacob slaughtered a kid, and dipped the coat of Joseph in the blood, and sent (it) to Jacob their father on the tenth of the seventh month.

13. And he mourned all that night, for they had brought it to him in the evening, and he became feverish with mourning for his death, and he said: 'An evil beast hath devoured Joseph'; and all the members of his house [mourned with him that day, and they] were grieving and mourning with him all that day.

14. And his sons and his daughter rose up to comfort him, but he refused to be comforted for his son.

15. And on that day Bilhah heard that Joseph had perished, and she died mourning him, and she was living in Qafratef, and Dinah also, his daughter, died after Joseph had perished.

16. And there came these three mournings upon Israel in one month. And they buried Bilhah over against the tomb of Rachel, and Dinah also. his daughter, they buried there.

17. And he mourned for Joseph one year, and did not cease, for he said 'Let me go down to the grave mourning for my son'.

18. For this reason it is ordained for the children of Israel that they should afflict themselves on the tenth of the seventh month -on the day that the news which made him weep for Joseph came to Jacob his father- that they should make atonement for themselves thereon with a young goat on the tenth of the seventh month, once a year, for their sins; for they had grieved the affection of their father regarding Joseph his son.

19. And this day has been ordained that they should grieve thereon for their sins, and for all their transgressions and for all their errors, so that they might cleanse themselves on that day once a year.

20. And after Joseph perished, the sons of Jacob took unto themselves wives. The name of Reuben's wife is 'Ada; and the name of Simeon's wife is 'Adlba'a, a Canaanite; and the name of Levi's wife is Melka, of the daughters of

Aram, of the seed of the sons of Terah; and the name of Judah's wife, Betasu'el, a Canaanite; and the name of Issachar's wife, Hezaqa: and the name of Zabulon's wife, Ni'iman; and the name of Dan's wife, 'Egla; and the name of Naphtali's wife, Rasu'u, of Mesopotamia; and the name of Gad's wife, Maka; and the name of Asher's wife, 'Ijona; and the name of Joseph's wife, Asenath, the Egyptian; and the name of Benjamin's wife, 'Ijasaka.

21.   And Simeon repented, and took a second wife from Mesopotamia as his brothers.

Jubilees 35

1.   And in the first year of the first week of the forty-fifth jubilee [2157 A.M.] Rebecca called Jacob, her son, and commanded him regarding his father and regarding his brother, that he should honour them all the days of his life.

2.   And Jacob said: 'I will do everything as thou hast commanded me; for this thing will be honour and greatness to me, and righteousness before the Lord, that I should honour them.

3.   And thou too, mother, knowest from the time I was born until this day, all my deeds and all that is in my heart, that I always think good concerning all.

4.   And how should I not do this thing which thou hast commanded me, that I should honour my father and my brother!

5.   Tell me, mother, what perversity hast thou seen in me and I shall turn away from it, and mercy will be upon me.'

6.   And she said unto him: 'My son, I have not seen in thee all my days any perverse but (only) upright deeds. And yet I will tell thee the truth, my son: I shall die this year, and I shall not survive this year in my life; for I have seen in a dream the day of my death, that I should not live beyond a hundred and fifty-five years: and behold I have completed all the days of my life which I am to live.'

7.   And Jacob laughed at the words of his mother. because his mother had said unto him that she should die; and she was sitting opposite to him in possession of her strength, and she was not infirm in her strength; for she went in and out and saw, and her teeth were strong, and no ailment had touched her all the days of her life.

8.   And Jacob said unto her: 'Blessed am I, mother, if my days approach the days of thy life, and my strength remain with me thus as thy strength: and thou wilt not die, for thou art jesting idly with me regarding thy death.'

9.   And she went in to Isaac and said unto him: 'One petition I make unto thee: make Esau swear that he will not injure Jacob, nor pursue him with enmity; for thou knowest Esau's thoughts that they are perverse from his youth, and there is no goodness

in him; for he desires after thy death to kill him.

10.   And thou knowest all that he has done since the day Jacob his brother went to Haran until this day: how he has forsaken us with his whole heart, and has done evil to us; thy flocks he has taken to himself, and carried off all thy possessions from before thy face.

11.   And when we implored and besought him for what was our own, he did as a man who was taking pity on us.

12.   And he is bitter against thee because thou didst bless Jacob thy perfect and upright son; for there is no evil but only goodness in him, and since he came from Haran unto this day he has not robbed us of aught, for he brings us everything in its season always, and rejoices with all his heart when we take at his hands and he blesses us, and has not parted from us since he came from Haran until this day, and he remains with us continually at home honouring us.'

13.   And Isaac said unto her: 'I, too, know and see the deeds of Jacob who is with us, how that with all his heart he honours us; but I loved Esau formerly more than Jacob, because he was the firstborn; but now I love Jacob more than Esau, for he has done manifold evil deeds, and there is no righteousness in him, for all his ways are unrighteousness and violence, [and there is no righteousness around him.]

14.   And now my heart is troubled because of all his deeds, and neither he nor his seed is to be saved, for they are those who will be destroyed from the earth and who will be rooted out from under heaven, for he has forsaken the God of Abraham and gone after his wives and after their uncleanness and after their error, he and his children.

15.   And thou dost bid me make him swear that he will not slay Jacob his brother; even if he swear he will not abide by his oath, and he will not do good but evil only.

16.   But if he desires to slay Jacob, his brother, into Jacob's hands will he be given, and he will not escape from his hands, [for he will descend into his hands.]

17.   And fear thou not on account of Jacob; for the guardian of Jacob is great and powerful and honoured, and praised more than the guardian of Esau.'

18.   And Rebecca sent and called Esau and he came to her, and she said unto him: 'I have a petition, my son, to make unto thee, and do thou promise to do it, my son.'

19.   And he said: 'I will do everything that thou sayest unto me, and I will not refuse thy petition.'

20.   And she said unto him: 'I ask you that the day I die, thou wilt take me in and bury me near Sarah, thy father's mother, and that thou and Jacob will love each other and that neither will desire evil against the other, but mutual love only, and (so)

ye will prosper, my sons, and be honoured in the midst of the land, and no enemy will rejoice over you, and ye will be a blessing and a mercy in the eyes of all those that love you.'

21.   And he said: 'I will do all that thou hast told me, and I shall bury thee on the day thou diest near Sarah, my father's mother, as thou hast desired that her bones may be near thy bones.

22.   And Jacob, my brother, also, I shall love above all flesh; for I have not a brother in all the earth but him only: and this is no great merit for me if I love him; for he is my brother, and we were sown together in thy body, and together came we forth from thy womb, and if I do not love my brother, whom shall I love?

23.   And I, myself, beg thee to exhort Jacob concerning me and concerning my sons, for I know that he will assuredly be king over me and my sons, for on the day my father blessed him he made him the higher and me the lower.

24.   And I swear unto thee that I shall love him, and not desire evil against him all the days of my life but good only.'

25.   And he sware unto her regarding all this matter. And she called Jacob before the eyes of Esau, and gave him commandment according to the words which she had spoken to Esau.

26.   And he said: 'I shall do thy pleasure; believe me that no evil will proceed from me or from my sons against Esau, and I shall be first in naught save in love only.'

27.   And they eat and drank, she and her sons that night, and she died, three jubilees and one week and one year old, on that night, and her two sons, Esau and Jacob, buried her in the double cave near Sarah, their father's mother.

Jubilees 36

1.   And in the sixth year of this week [2162 A.M.] Isaac called his two sons Esau and Jacob, and they came to him, and he said unto them: 'My sons, I am going the way of my fathers, to the eternal house where my fathers are.

2.   Wherefore bury me near Abraham my father, in the double cave in the field of Ephron the Hittite, where Abraham purchased a sepulchre to bury in; in the sepulchre which I digged for myself, there bury me.

3.   And this I command you, my sons, that ye practise righteousness and uprightness on the earth, so that the Lord may bring upon you all that the Lord said that he would do to Abraham and to his seed.

4.   And love one another, my sons, your brothers as a man who loves his own soul, and let each seek in what he may benefit his brother, and act together on the earth; and let them love each other as their own souls.

5.   And concerning the question of idols, I command and admonish you to reject them and hate them, and love them not, for they are full of deception for those that worship them and for those that bow down to them.

6.   Remember ye, my sons, the Lord God of Abraham your father, and how I too worshipped Him and served Him in righteousness and in joy, that He might multiply you and increase your seed as the stars of heaven in multitude, and establish you on the earth as the plant of righteousness which will not be rooted out unto all the generations for ever.

7.   And now I shall make you swear a great oath -for there is no oath which is greater than it by the name glorious and honoured and great and splendid and wonderful and mighty, which created the heavens and the earth and all things together- that ye will fear Him and worship Him.

8.   And that each will love his brother with affection and righteousness, and that neither will desire evil against his brother from henceforth for ever all the days of your life so that ye may prosper in all your deeds and not be destroyed.

9.   And if either of you devises evil against his brother, know that from henceforth everyone that devises evil against his brother shall fall into his hand, and shall be rooted out of the land of the living, and his seed shall be destroyed from under heaven.

10.   But on the day of turbulence and execration and indignation and anger, with flaming devouring fire as He burnt Sodom, so likewise will He burn his land and his city and all that is his, and he shall be blotted out of the book of the discipline of the children of men, and not be recorded in the book of life, but in that which is appointed to destruction, and he shall depart into eternal execration; so that their condemnation may be always renewed in hate and in execration and in wrath and in torment and in indignation and in plagues and in disease for ever.

11.   I say and testify to you, my sons, according to the judgment which shall come upon the man who wishes to injure his brother.

12.   And he divided all his possessions between the two on that day and he gave the larger portion to him that was the first-born, and the tower and all that was about it, and all that Abraham possessed at the Well of the Oath.

13.   And he said: 'This larger portion I will give to the firstborn.'

14.   And Esau said, 'I have sold to Jacob and given my birthright to Jacob; to him let it be given, and I have not a single word to say regarding it, for it is his.'

15.   And Isaac said, May a blessing rest upon you, my sons, and upon your seed this day, for ye have given me rest, and my heart is

not pained concerning the birthright, lest thou shouldest work wickedness on account of it.

16.   May the Most High God bless the man that worketh righteousness, him and his seed for ever.'

17.   And he ended commanding them and blessing them, and they eat and drank together before him, and he rejoiced because there was one mind between them, and they went forth from him and rested that day and slept.

18.   And Isaac slept on his bed that day rejoicing; and he slept the eternal sleep, and died one hundred and eighty years old. He completed twenty-five weeks and five years; and his two sons Esau and Jacob buried him.

19.   And Esau went to the land of Edom, to the mountains of Seir, and dwelt there.

20.   And Jacob dwelt in the mountains of Hebron, in the tower of the land of the sojournings of his father Abraham, and he worshipped the Lord with all his heart and according to the visible commands according as He had divided the days of his generations.

21.   And Leah his wife died in the fourth year of the second week of the forty-fifth jubilee, [2167 A.M.] and he buried her in the double cave near Rebecca his mother to the left of the grave of Sarah, his father's mother

22.   and all her sons and his sons came to mourn over Leah his wife

with him and to comfort him regarding her, for he was lamenting her for he loved her exceedingly after Rachel her sister died;

23.   for she was perfect and upright in all her ways and honoured Jacob,and all the days that she lived with him he did not hear from her mouth a harsh word, for she was gentle and peaceable and upright and honourable.

24.   And he remembered all her deeds which she had done during her life and he lamented her exceedingly; for he loved her with all his heart and with all his soul.

Jubilees 37

1.   And on the day that Isaac the father of Jacob and Esau died, [2162 A.M.] the sons of Esau heard that Isaac had given the portion of the elder to his younger son Jacob and they were very angry.

2.   And they strove with their father, saying 'Why has thy father given Jacob the portion of the elder and passed over thee, although thou art the elder and Jacob the younger?'

3.   And he said unto them 'Because I sold my birthright to Jacob for a small mess of lentils, and on the day my father sent me to hunt and catch and bring him something that he should eat and bless me, he came with guile and brought my father food and drink, and my father blessed him and put me under his hand.

4.　And now our father has caused us to swear, me and him, that we shall not mutually devise evil, either against his brother, and that we shall continue in love and in peace each with his brother and not make our ways corrupt.'

5.　And they said unto him, 'We shall not hearken unto thee to make peace with him; for our strength is greater than his strength, and we are more powerful than he; we shall go against him and slay him, and destroy him and his sons. And if thou wilt not go with us, we shall do hurt to thee also.

6.　And now hearken unto us: Let us send to Aram and Philistia and Moab and Ammon, and let us choose for ourselves chosen men who are ardent for battle, and let us go against him and do battle with him, and let us exterminate him from the earth before he grows strong.'

7.　And their father said unto them, 'Do not go and do not make war with him lest ye fall before him.'

8.　And they said unto him, 'This too, is exactly thy mode of action from thy youth until this day, and thou art putting thy neck under his yoke.

9.　We shall not hearken to these words.' And they sent to Aram, and to 'Aduram to the friend of their father, and they hired along with them one thousand fighting men, chosen men of war.

10.　And there came to them from Moab and from the children of Ammon, those who were hired, one thousand chosen men, and from Philistia, one thousand chosen men of war, and from Edom and from the Horites one thousand chosen fighting men, and from the Kittim mighty men of war.

11.　And they said unto their father: Go forth with them and lead them, else we shall slay thee.'

12.　And he was filled with wrath and indignation on seeing that his sons were forcing him to go before (them) to lead them against Jacob his brother.

13.　But afterward he remembered all the evil which lay hidden in his heart against Jacob his brother; and he remembered not the oath which he had sworn to his father and to his mother that he would devise no evil all his days against Jacob his brother.

14.　And notwithstanding all this, Jacob knew not that they were coming against him to battle, and he was mourning for Leah, his wife, until they approached very near to the tower with four thousand warriors and chosen men of war.

15.　And the men of Hebron sent to him saying, 'Behold thy brother has come against thee, to fight thee, with four thousand girt with the sword, and they carry shields and weapons'; for they loved Jacob more than Esau. So they told him; for Jacob was a more liberal and merciful man than Esau.

16.   But Jacob would not believe until they came very near to the tower.

17.   And he closed the gates of the tower; and he stood on the battlements and spake to his brother Esau and said, 'Noble is the comfort wherewith thou hast come to comfort me for my wife who has died. Is this the oath that thou didst swear to thy father and again to thy mother before they died? Thou hast broken the oath, and on the moment that thou didst swear to thy father wast thou condemned.'

18.   And then Esau answered and said unto him, 'Neither the children of men nor the beasts of the earth have any oath of righteousness which in swearing they have sworn (an oath valid) for ever; but every day they devise evil one against another, and how each may slay his adversary and foe.

19.   And thou dost hate me and my children for ever. And there is no observing the tie of brotherhood with thee.

20.   Hear these words which I declare unto thee,

If the boar can change its skin and make its bristles as soft as wool,
Or if it can cause horns to sprout forth on its head like the horns of a stag   or   of   a   sheep,
Then   will   I   observe   the   tie   of brotherhood   with   thee
And   if   the   breasts   separated themselves from their mother, for thou hast not been a brother to me.

21.   And if the wolves make peace with the lambs so as not to devour or do   them   violence,
And if their hearts are towards them for   good,
Then there shall be peace in my heart towards thee

22.   And if the lion becomes the friend of the ox and makes peace with   him
And if he is bound under one yoke with him and ploughs with him,
Then will I make peace with thee.

23.   And when the raven becomes white   as   the   raza,
Then know that I have loved thee
And shall make peace with thee
Thou   shalt   be   rooted   out,
And thy sons shall be rooted out,
And there shall be no peace for thee'

24.   And when Jacob saw that he was (so) evilly disposed towards him with his heart, and with all his soul as to slay him, and that he had come springing like the wild boar which comes upon the spear that pierces and kills it, and recoils not from it;

25.   then he spake to his own and to his servants that they should attack him and all his companions.

Jubilees 38

1.   And after that Judah spake to Jacob, his father, and said unto him: 'Bend thy bow, father, and send forth thy arrows and cast down the adversary and slay the enemy; and mayst thou have the power, for we shall not slay thy brother, for he is

such as thou, and he is like thee let us give him (this) honour.'

2.   Then Jacob bent his bow and sent forth the arrow and struck Esau, his brother (on his right breast) and slew him.

3.   And again he sent forth an arrow and struck 'Adoran the Aramaean, on the left breast, and drove him backward and slew him.

4.   And then went forth the sons of Jacob, they and their servants, dividing themselves into companies on the four sides of the tower.

5.   And Judah went forth in front, and Naphtali and Gad with him and fifty servants with him on the south side of the tower, and they slew all they found before them, and not one individual of them escaped.

6.   And Levi and Dan and Asher went forth on the east side of the tower, and fifty (men) with them, and they slew the fighting men of Moab and Ammon.

7.   And Reuben and Issachar and Zebulon went forth on the north side of the tower, and fifty men with them, and they slew the fighting men of the Philistines.

8.   And Simeon and Benjamin and Enoch, Reuben's son, went forth on the west side of the tower, and fifty (men) with them, and they slew of Edom and of the Horites four hundred men, stout warriors; and six hundred fled, and four of the sons of Esau fled with them, and left their father lying slain, as he had fallen on the hill which is in 'Aduram.

9.   And the sons of Jacob pursued after them to the mountains of Seir. And Jacob buried his brother on the hill which is in 'Aduram, and he returned to his house.

10.   And the sons of Jacob pressed hard upon the sons of Esau in the mountains of Seir, and bowed their necks so that they became servants of the sons of Jacob.

11.   And they sent to their father (to inquire) whether they should make peace with them or slay them.

12.   And Jacob sent word to his sons that they should make peace, and they made peace with them, and placed the yoke of servitude upon them, so that they paid tribute to Jacob and to his sons always.

13.   And they continued to pay tribute to Jacob until the day that he went down into Egypt.

14.   And the sons of Edom have not got quit of the yoke of servitude which the twelve sons of Jacob had imposed on them until this day.

15.   And these are the kings that reigned in Edom before there reigned any king over the children of Israel [until this day] in the land of Edom.

16.   And Balaq, the son of Beor, reigned in Edom, and the name of his city was Danaba.

17.   And Balaq died, and Jobab, the son of Zara of Boser, reigned in his stead.

18.   And Jobab died, and 'Asam, of the land of Teman, reigned in his stead.

19.   And 'Asam died, and 'Adath, the son of Barad, who slew Midian in the field of Moab, reigned in his stead, and the name of his city was Avith.

20.   And 'Adath died, and Salman, from 'Amaseqa, reigned in his stead.

21.   And Salman died, and Saul of Ra'aboth (by the) river, reigned in his stead.

22.   And Saul died, and Ba'elunan, the son of Achbor, reigned in his stead.

23.   And Ba'elunan, the son of Achbor died, and 'Adath reigned in his stead, and the name of his wife was Maitabith, the daughter of Matarat, the daughter of Metabedza'ab.

24.   These are the kings who reigned in the land of Edom.

Jubilees 39

1.   And Jacob dwelt in the land of his father's sojournings in the land of Canaan. These are the generations of Jacob.

2.   And Joseph was seventeen years old when they took him down into the land of Egypt, and Potiphar, an eunuch of Pharaoh, the chief cook bought him.

3.   And he set Joseph over all his house and the blessing of the Lord came upon the house of the Egyptian on account of Joseph, and the Lord prospered him in all that he did.

4.   And the Egyptian committed everything into the hands of Joseph; for he saw that the Lord was with him, and that the Lord prospered him in all that he did.

5.   And Joseph's appearance was comely [and very beautiful was his appearance], and his master's wife lifted up her eyes and saw Joseph, and she loved him and besought him to lie with her.

6.   But he did not surrender his soul, and he remembered the Lord and the words which Jacob, his father, used to read from amongst the words of Abraham, that no man should commit fornication with a woman who has a husband; that for him the punishment of death has been ordained in the heavens before the Most High God, and the sin will be recorded against him in the eternal books continually before the Lord.

7.   And Joseph remembered these words and refused to lie with her.

8.   And she besought him for a year, but he refused and would not listen.

9.   But she embraced him and held him fast in the house in order to force him to lie with her, and closed the doors of the house and held him

fast; but he left his garment in her hands and broke through the door and fled without from her presence.

10. And the woman saw that he would not lie with her, and she calumniated him in the presence of his lord, saying 'Thy Hebrew servant, whom thou lovest, sought to force me so that he might lie with me; and it came to pass when I lifted up my voice that he fled and left his garment in my hands when I held him, and he brake through the door.'

11. And the Egyptian saw the garment of Joseph and the broken door, and heard the words of his wife, and cast Joseph into prison into the place where the prisoners were kept whom the king imprisoned.

12. And he was there in the prison; and the Lord gave Joseph favour in the sight of the chief of the prison guards and compassion before him, for he saw that the Lord was with him, and that the Lord made all that he did to prosper.

13. And he committed all things into his hands, and the chief of the prison guards knew of nothing that was with him, for Joseph did every thing, and the Lord perfected it.

14. And he remained there two years. And in those days Pharaoh, king of Egypt was wroth against his two eunuchs, against the chief butler, and against the chief baker, and he put them in ward in the house of the chief cook, in the prison where Joseph was kept.

15. And the chief of the prison guards appointed Joseph to serve them; and he served before them.

16. And they both dreamed a dream, the chief butler and the chief baker, and they told it to Joseph.

17. And as he interpreted to them so it befell them, and Pharaoh restored the chief butler to his office and the (chief) baker he slew, as Joseph had interpreted to them.

18. But the chief butler forgot Joseph in the prison, although he had informed him what would befall him, and did not remember to inform Pharaoh how Joseph had told him, for he forgot.

Jubilees 40

1. And in those days Pharaoh dreamed two dreams in one night concerning a famine which was to be in all the land, and he awoke from his sleep and called all the interpreters of dreams that were in Egypt, and magicians, and told them his two dreams, and they were not able to declare (them).

2. And then the chief butler remembered Joseph and spake of him to the king, and he brought him forth from the prison, and he told his two dreams before him.

3. And he said before Pharaoh that his two dreams were one, and he said unto him: 'Seven years shall come (in which there shall be) plenty over all the land of Egypt, and after that seven years of famine, such a

famine as has not been in all the land.

4. And now let Pharaoh appoint overseers in all the land of Egypt, and let them store up food in every city throughout the days of the years of plenty, and there will be food for the seven years of famine, and the land will not perish through the famine, for it will be very severe.'

5. And the Lord gave Joseph favour and mercy in the eyes of Pharaoh, and Pharaoh said unto his servants. We shall not find such a wise and discreet man as this man, for the spirit of the Lord is with him.'

6. And he appointed him the second in all his kingdom and gave him authority over all Egypt, and caused him to ride in the second chariot of Pharaoh.

7. And he clothed him with byssus garments, and he put a gold chain upon his neck, and (a herald) proclaimed before him ' 'El 'El wa 'Abirer,' and placed a ring on his hand and made him ruler over all his house, and magnified him, and said unto him. 'Only on the throne shall I be greater than thou.'

8. And Joseph ruled over all the land of Egypt, and all the princes of Pharaoh, and all his servants, and all who did the king's business loved him, for he walked in uprightness, for he was without pride and arrogance, and he had no respect of persons, and did not accept gifts, but he judged in uprightness all the people of the land.

9. And the land of Egypt was at peace before Pharaoh because of Joseph, for the Lord was with him, and gave him favour and mercy for all his generations before all those who knew him and those who heard concerning him, and Pharaoh's kingdom was well ordered, and there was no Satan and no evil person (therein).

10. And the king called Joseph's name Sephantiphans, and gave Joseph to wife the daughter of Potiphar, the daughter of the priest of Heliopolis, the chief cook.

11. And on the day that Joseph stood before Pharaoh he was thirty years old [when he stood before Pharaoh].

12. And in that year Isaac died. And it came to pass as Joseph had said in the interpretation of his two dreams, according as he had said it, there were seven years of plenty over all the land of Egypt, and the land of Egypt abundantly produced, one measure (producing) eighteen hundred measures.

13. And Joseph gathered food into every city until they were full of corn until they could no longer count and measure it for its multitude.

Jubilees 41

1. And in the forty-fifth jubilee, in the second week, (and) in the second year, [2165 A.M.] Judah took for his first-born Er, a wife from the daughters of Aram, named Tamar.

2.   But he hated, and did not lie with her, because his mother was of the daughters of Canaan, and he wished to take him a wife of the kinsfolk of his mother, but Judah, his father, would not permit him.

3.   And this Er, the first-born of Judah, was wicked, and the Lord slew him.

4.   And Judah said unto Onan, his brother 'Go in unto thy brother's wife and perform the duty of a husband's brother unto her, and raise up seed unto thy brother.'

5.   And Onan knew that the seed would not be his, (but) his brother's only, and he went into the house of his brother's wife, and spilt the seed on the ground, and he was wicked in the eyes of the Lord, and He slew him.

6.   And Judah said unto Tamar, his daughter-in-law: 'Remain in thy father's house as a widow till Shelah my son be grown up, and I shall give thee to him to wife.'

7.   And he grew up; but Bedsu'el, the wife of Judah, did not permit her son Shelah to marry. And Bedsu'el, the wife of Judah, died [2168 A.M.] in the fifth year of this week.

8.   And in the sixth year Judah went up to shear his sheep at Timnah. [2169 A.M.] And they told Tamar: 'Behold thy father-in-law goeth up to Timnah to shear his sheep.'

9.   And she put off her widow's clothes, and put on a veil, and adorned herself, and sat in the gate adjoining the way to Timnah.

10.   And as Judah was going along he found her, and thought her to be an harlot, and he said unto her: 'Let me come in unto thee'; and she said unto him Come in,' and he went in.

11.   And she said unto him: 'Give me my hire'; and he said unto her: 'I have nothing in my hand save my ring that is on my finger, and my necklace, and my staff which is in my hand.'

12.   And she said unto him 'Give them to me until thou dost send me my hire', and he said unto her: 'I will send unto thee a kid of the goats'; and he gave them to her, *and he went in unto her*, and she conceived by him.

13.   And Judah went unto his sheep, and she went to her father's house.

14.   And Judah sent a kid of the goats by the hand of his shepherd, an Adullamite, and he found her not; and he asked the people of the place, saying: 'Where is the harlot who was here?' And they said unto him; 'There is no harlot here with us.'

15.   And he returned and informed him, and said unto him that he had not found her: 'I asked the people of the place, and they said unto me: "There is no harlot here." '

16.   And he said: 'Let her keep (them) lest we become a cause of derision.' And when she had

completed three months, it was manifest that she was with child, and they told Judah, saying: 'Behold Tamar, thy daughter-in-law, is with child by whoredom.'

17. And Judah went to the house of her father, and said unto her father and her brothers: 'Bring her forth, and let them burn her, for she hath wrought uncleanness in Israel.'

18. And it came to pass when they brought her forth to burn her that she sent to her father-in-law the ring and the necklace, and the staff, saying: 'Discern whose are these, for by him am I with child.'

19. And Judah acknowledged, and said: 'Tamar is more righteous than I am.

20. And therefore let them burn her not' And for that reason she was not given to Shelah, and he did not again approach her.

21. And after that she bare two sons, Perez [2170 A.M.] and Zerah, in the seventh year of this second week.

22. And thereupon the seven years of fruitfulness were accomplished, of which Joseph spake to Pharaoh.

23. And Judah acknowledged that the deed which he had done was evil, for he had lain with his daughter-in-law, and he esteemed it hateful in his eyes, and he acknowledged that he had transgressed and gone astray, for he had uncovered the skirt of his son,

and he began to lament and to supplicate before the Lord because of his transgression.

24. And we told him in a dream that it was forgiven him because he supplicated earnestly, and lamented, and did not again commit it.

25. And he received forgiveness because he turned from his sin and from his ignorance, for he transgressed greatly before our God; and every one that acts thus, every one who lies with his mother-in-law, let them burn him with fire that he may burn therein, for there is uncleanness and pollution upon them, with fire let them burn them.

26. And do thou command the children of Israel that there be no uncleanness amongst them, for every one who lies with his daughter-in-law or with his mother-in-law hath wrought uncleanness; with fire let them burn the man who has lain with her, and likewise the woman, and He will turn away wrath and punishment from Israel.

27. And unto Judah we said that his two sons had not lain with her, and for this reason his seed was stablished for a second generation, and would not be rooted out.

28. For in singleness of eye he had gone and sought for punishment, namely, according to the judgment of Abraham, which he had commanded his sons, Judah had sought to burn her with fire.

Jubilees 42

1.   And in the first year of the third week of the forty-fifth jubilee the famine began to come into the [2171 A.M.] land, and the rain refused to be given to the earth, for none whatever fell.

2.   And the earth grew barren, but in the land of Egypt there was food, for Joseph had gathered the seed of the land in the seven years of plenty and had preserved it.

3.   And the Egyptians came to Joseph that he might give them food, and he opened the store-houses where was the grain of the first year, and he sold it to the people of the land for gold.

4.   <Now the famine was very sore in the land of Canaan>, and Jacob heard that there was food in Egypt, and he sent his ten sons that they should procure food for him in Egypt; but Benjamin he did not send, and <the ten sons of Jacob> arrived <in Egypt> among those that went (there).

5.   And Joseph recognised them, but they did not recognise him, and he spake unto them and questioned them, and he said unto them; 'Are ye not spies and have ye not come to explore the approaches of the land? 'And he put them in ward.

6.   And after that he set them free again, and detained Simeon alone and sent off his nine brothers.

7.   And he filled their sacks with corn, and he put their gold in their sacks, and they did not know.

8.   And he commanded them to bring their younger brother, for they had told him their father was living and their younger brother.

9.   And they went up from the land of Egypt and they came to the land of Canaan; and they told their father all that had befallen them, and how the lord of the country had spoken roughly to them, and had seized Simeon till they should bring Benjamin.

10.   And Jacob said: 'Me have ye bereaved of my children! Joseph is not and Simeon also is not, and ye will take Benjamin away. On me has your wickedness come.

11.   'And he said: 'My son will not go down with you lest perchance he fall sick; for their mother gave birth to two sons, and one has perished, and this one also ye will take from me. If perchance he took a fever on the road, ye would bring down my old age with sorrow unto death.'

12.   For he saw that their money had been returned to every man in his sack, and for this reason he feared to send him.

13.   And the famine increased and became sore in the land of Canaan, and in all lands save in the land of Egypt, for many of the children of the Egyptians had stored up their seed for food from the time when they saw Joseph gathering seed together and

putting it in storehouses and preserving it for the years of famine.

14. And the people of Egypt fed themselves thereon during the first year of their famine.

15. But when Israel saw that the famine was very sore in the land, and that there was no deliverance, he said unto his sons: 'Go again, and procure food for us that we die not.'

16. And they said: 'We shall not go; unless our youngest brother go with us, we shall not go.'

17. And Israel saw that if he did not send him with them, they should all perish by reason of the famine

18. And Reuben said: 'Give him into my hand, and if I do not bring him back to thee, slay my two sons instead of his soul.'

19. And he said unto him: 'He shall not go with thee.' And Judah came near and said: 'Send him with me, and if I do not bring him back to thee, let me bear the blame before thee all the days of my life.'

20. And he sent him with them in the second year of this week on the [2172 A.m.] first day of the month, and they came to the land of Egypt with all those who went, and (they had) presents in their hands, stacte and almonds and terebinth nuts and pure honey.

21. And they went and stood before Joseph, and he saw Benjamin his brother, and he knew him, and said unto them: Is this your youngest brother?' And they said unto him: 'It

is he.' And he said The Lord be gracious to thee, my son!'

22. And he sent him into his house and he brought forth Simeon unto them and he made a feast for them, and they presented to him the gift which they had brought in their hands.

23. And they eat before him and he gave them all a portion, but the portion of Benjamin was seven times larger than that of any of theirs.

24. And they eat and drank and arose and remained with their asses.

25. And Joseph devised a plan whereby he might learn their thoughts as to whether thoughts of peace prevailed amongst them, and he said to the steward who was over his house: 'Fill all their sacks with food, and return their money unto them into their vessels, and my cup, the silver cup out of which I drink, put it in the sack of the youngest, and send them away.'

Jubilees 43

1. And he did as Joseph had told him, and filled all their sacks for them with food and put their money in their sacks, and put the cup in Benjamin's sack.

2. And early in the morning they departed, and it came to pass that, when they had gone from thence, Joseph said unto the steward of his house: 'Pursue them, run and seize them, saying, "For good ye have requited me with evil; you have

stolen from me the silver cup out of which my lord drinks." And bring back to me their youngest brother, and fetch (him) quickly before I go forth to my seat of judgment.'

3. And he ran after them and said unto them according to these words.

4. And they said unto him: 'God forbid that thy servants should do this thing, and steal from the house of thy lord any utensil, and the money also which we found in our sacks the first time, we thy servants brought back from the land of Canaan.

5. How then should we steal any utensil? Behold here are we and our sacks search, and wherever thou findest the cup in the sack of any man amongst us, let him be slain, and we and our asses will serve thy lord.'

6. And he said unto them: 'Not so, the man with whom I find, him only shall I take as a servant, and ye shall return in peace unto your house.'

7. And as he was searching in their vessels, beginning with the eldest and ending with the youngest, it was found in Benjamin's sack.

8. And they rent their garments, and laded their asses, and returned to the city and came to the house of Joseph, and they all bowed themselves on their faces to the ground before him.

9. And Joseph said unto them: 'Ye have done evil.' And they said: 'What shall we say and how shall we defend ourselves? Our lord hath discovered the transgression of his servants; behold we are the servants of our lord, and our asses also.

10. 'And Joseph said unto them: 'I too fear the Lord; as for you, go ye to your homes and let your brother be my servant, for ye have done evil. Know ye not that a man delights in his cup as I with this cup? And yet ye have stolen it from me.'

11. And Judah said: 'O my lord, let thy servant, I pray thee, speak a word in my lord's ear two brothers did thy servant's mother bear to our father: one went away and was lost, and hath not been found, and he alone is left of his mother, and thy servant our father loves him, and his life also is bound up with the life of this (lad).

12. And it will come to pass, when we go to thy servant our father, and the lad is not with us, that he will die, and we shall bring down our father with sorrow unto death.

13. Now rather let me, thy servant, abide instead of the boy as a bondsman unto my lord, and let the lad go with his brethren, for I became surety for him at the hand of thy servant our father, and if I do not bring him back, thy servant will hear the blame to our father for ever.'

14. And Joseph saw that they were all accordant in goodness one with another, and he could not

refrain himself, and he told them that he was Joseph.

15. And he conversed with them in the Hebrew tongue and fell on their neck and wept.

16. But they knew him not and they began to weep. And he said unto them: 'Weep not over me, but hasten and bring my father to me; and ye see that it is my mouth that speaketh and the eyes of my brother Benjamin see.

17. For behold this is the second year of the famine, and there are still five years without harvest or fruit of trees or ploughing.

18. Come down quickly ye and your households, so that ye perish not through the famine, and do not be grieved for your possessions, for the Lord sent me before you to set things in order that many people might live.

19. And tell my father that I am still alive, and ye, behold, ye see that the Lord has made me as a father to Pharaoh, and ruler over his house and over all the land of Egypt.

20. And tell my father of all my glory, and all the riches and glory that the Lord hath given me.'

21. And by the command of the mouth of Pharaoh he gave them chariots and provisions for the way, and he gave them all many-coloured raiment and silver.

22. And to their father he sent raiment and silver and ten asses which carried corn, and he sent them away.

23. And they went up and told their father that Joseph was alive, and was measuring out corn to all the nations of the earth, and that he was ruler over all the land of Egypt.

24. And their father did not believe it, for he was beside himself in his mind; but when he saw the wagons which Joseph had sent, the life of his spirit revived, and he said: 'It is enough for me if Joseph lives; I will go down and see him before I die.'

Jubilees 44

1. And Israel took his journey from Haran from his house on the new moon of the third month, and he went on the way of the Well of the Oath, and he offered a sacrifice to the God of his father Isaac on the seventh of this month.

2. And Jacob remembered the dream that he had seen at Bethel, and he feared to go down into Egypt.

3. And while he was thinking of sending word to Joseph to come to him, and that he would not go down, he remained there seven days, if perchance he could see a vision as to whether he should remain or go down.

4. And he celebrated the harvest festival of the first-fruits with old grain, for in all the land of Canaan there was not a handful of seed [in the land], for the famine was over all

the beasts and cattle and birds, and also over man.

5.   And on the sixteenth the Lord appeared unto him, and said unto him, 'Jacob, Jacob'; and he said, 'Here am I.' And He said unto him: 'I am the God of thy fathers, the God of Abraham and Isaac; fear not to go down into Egypt, for I will there make of thee a great nation I will go down with thee, and I will bring thee up (again), and in this land shalt thou be buried, and Joseph shall put his hands upon thy eyes.

6.   Fear not; go down into Egypt.'

7.   And his sons rose up, and his sons' sons, and they placed their father and their possessions upon wagons.

8.   And Israel rose up from the Well of the Oath on the sixteenth of this third month, and he went to the land of Egypt.

9.   And Israel sent Judah before him to his son Joseph to examine the Land of Goshen, for Joseph had told his brothers that they should come and dwell there that they might be near him.

10.   And this was the goodliest (land) in the land of Egypt, and near to him, for all (of them) and also for the cattle.

11.   And these are the names of the sons of Jacob who went into Egypt with Jacob their father.

12.   Reuben, the First-born of Israel; and these are the names of

his sons Enoch, and Pallu, and Hezron and Carmi-five.

13.   Simeon and his sons; and these are the names of his sons: Jemuel, and Jamin, and Ohad, and Jachin, and Zohar, and Shaul, the son of the Zephathite woman-seven.

14.   Levi and his sons; and these are the names of his sons: Gershon, and Kohath, and Merari-four.

15.   Judah and his sons; and these are the names of his sons: Shela, and Perez, and Zerah-four.

16.   Issachar and his sons; and these are the names of his sons: Tola, and Phua, and Jasub, and Shimron-five.

17.   Zebulon and his sons; and these are the names of his sons: Sered, and Elon, and Jahleel-four.

18.   And these are the sons of Jacob and their sons whom Leah bore to Jacob in Mesopotamia, six, and their one sister, Dinah and all the souls of the sons of Leah, and their sons, who went with Jacob their father into Egypt, were twenty-nine, and Jacob their father being with them, they were thirty.

19.   And the sons of Zilpah, Leah's handmaid, the wife of Jacob, who bore unto Jacob Gad and Ashur.

20.   And these are the names of their sons who went with him into Egypt. The sons of Gad: Ziphion, and Haggi, and Shuni, and Ezbon, <and Eri>, and Areli, and Arodi-eight.

21.   And the sons of Asher: Imnah, and Ishvah, <and Ishvi>, and Beriah, and Serah, their one sister-six.

22.   All the souls were fourteen, and all those of Leah were forty-four.

23.   And the sons of Rachel, the wife of Jacob: Joseph and Benjamin.

24.   And there were born to Joseph in Egypt before his father came into Egypt, those whom Asenath, daughter of Potiphar priest of Heliopolis bare unto him, Manasseh, and Ephraim-three.

25.   And the sons of Benjamin: Bela and Becher and Ashbel, Gera, and Naaman, and Ehi, and Rosh, and Muppim, and Huppim, and Ard-eleven.

26.   And all the souls of Rachel were fourteen.

27.   And the sons of Bilhah, the handmaid of Rachel, the wife of Jacob, whom she bare to Jacob, were Dan and Naphtali.

28.   And these are the names of their sons who went with them into Egypt. And the sons of Dan were Hushim, and Samon, and Asudi. and 'Ijaka, and Salomon-six.

29.   And they died the year in which they entered into Egypt, and there was left to Dan Hushim alone.

30.   And these are the names of the sons of Naphtali Jahziel, and Guni and Jezer, and Shallum, and 'Iv.

31.   And 'Iv, who was born after the years of famine, died in Egypt.

32.   And all the souls of Rachel were twenty-six.

33.   And all the souls of Jacob which went into Egypt were seventy souls. These are his children and his children's children, in all seventy, but five died in Egypt before Joseph, and had no children.

34.   And in the land of Canaan two sons of Judah died, Er and Onan, and they had no children, and the children of Israel buried those who perished, and they were reckoned among the seventy Gentile nations.

Jubilees 45

1.   And Israel went into the country of Egypt, into the land of Goshen, on the new moon of the fourth [2172 A.M]. month, in the second year of the third week of the forty-fifth jubilee.

2.   And Joseph went to meet his father Jacob, to the land of Goshen, and he fell on his father's neck and wept.

3.   And Israel said unto Joseph: 'Now let me die since I have seen thee, and now may the Lord God of Israel be blessed the God of Abraham and the God of Isaac who hath not withheld His mercy and His grace from His servant Jacob.

4.   It is enough for me that I have seen thy face whilst I am yet alive; yea, true is the vision which I saw at Bethel. Blessed be the Lord my God

for ever and ever, and blessed be His name.'

5.   And Joseph and his brothers eat bread before their father and drank wine, and Jacob rejoiced with exceeding great joy because he saw Joseph eating with his brothers and drinking before him, and he blessed the Creator of all things who had preserved him, and had preserved for him his twelve sons.

6.   And Joseph had given to his father and to his brothers as a gift the right of dwelling in the land of Goshen and in Rameses and all the region round about, which he ruled over before Pharaoh. And Israel and his sons dwelt in the land of Goshen, the best part of the land of Egypt and Israel was one hundred and thirty years old when he came into Egypt.

7.   And Joseph nourished his father and his brethren and also their possessions with bread as much as sufficed them for the seven years of the famine.

8.   And the land of Egypt suffered by reason of the famine, and Joseph acquired all the land of Egypt for Pharaoh in return for food, and he got possession of the people and their cattle and everything for Pharaoh.

9.   And the years of the famine were accomplished, and Joseph gave to the people in the land seed and food that they might sow (the land) in the eighth year, for the river had overflowed all the land of Egypt.

10.   For in the seven years of the famine it had (not) overflowed and had irrigated only a few places on the banks of the river, but now it overflowed and the Egyptians sowed the land, and it bore much corn that year.

11.   And this was the first year of [2178 A.M.] the fourth week of the forty-fifth jubilee.

12.   And Joseph took of the corn of the harvest the fifth part for the king and left four parts for them for food and for seed, and Joseph made it an ordinance for the land of Egypt until this day.

13.   And Israel lived in the land of Egypt seventeen years, and all the days which he lived were three jubilees, one hundred and forty-seven years, and he died in the fourth [2188 A.M.] year of the fifth week of the forty-fifth jubilee.

14.   And Israel blessed his sons before he died and told them everything that would befall them in the land of Egypt; and he made known to them what would come upon them in the last days, and blessed them and gave to Joseph two portions in the land.

15.   And he slept with his fathers, and he was buried in the double cave in the land of Canaan, near Abraham his father in the grave which he dug for himself in the double cave in the land of Hebron.

16.   And he gave all his books and the books of his fathers to Levi his son that he might preserve them and

renew them for his children until this day.

Jubilees 46

1. And it came to pass that after Jacob died the children of Israel multiplied in the land of Egypt, and they became a great nation, and they were of one accord in heart, so that brother loved brother and every man helped his brother, and they increased abundantly and multiplied exceedingly, ten [2242 A.M.] weeks of years, all the days of the life of Joseph.

2. And there was no Satan nor any evil all the days of the life of Joseph which he lived after his father Jacob, for all the Egyptians honoured the children of Israel all the days of the life of Joseph.

3. And Joseph died being a hundred and ten years old; seventeen years he lived in the land of Canaan, and ten years he was a servant, and three years in prison, and eighty years he was under the king, ruling all the land of Egypt.

4. And he died and all his brethren and all that generation.

5. And he commanded the children of Israel before he died that they should carry his bones with them when they went forth from the land of Egypt.

6. And he made them swear regarding his bones, for he knew that the Egyptians would not again bring forth and bury him in the land of Canaan, for Makamaron, king of Canaan, while dwelling in the land of Assyria, fought in the valley with the king of Egypt and slew him there, and pursued after the Egyptians to the gates of 'Ermon.

7. But he was not able to enter, for another, a new king, had become king of Egypt, and he was stronger than he, and he returned to the land of Canaan, and the gates of Egypt were closed, and none went out and none came into Egypt.

8. And Joseph died in the forty-sixth jubilee, in the sixth week, in the second year, and they buried him in the land of Egypt, and [2242 A.M.] all his brethren died after him.

9. And the king of Egypt went forth to war with the king of Canaan [2263 A.M.] in the forty-seventh jubilee, in the second week in the second year, and the children of Israel brought forth all the bones of the children of Jacob save the bones of Joseph, and they buried them in the field in the double cave in the mountain.

10. And the most (of them) returned to Egypt, but a few of them remained in the mountains of Hebron, and Amram thy father remained with them.

11. And the king of Canaan was victorious over the king of Egypt, and he closed the gates of Egypt.

12. And he devised an evil device against the children of Israel of afflicting them and he said unto the people of Egypt: 'Behold the people

of the children of Israel have increased and multiplied more than we.

13.   Come and let us deal wisely with them before they become too many, and let us afflict them with slavery before war come upon us and before they too fight against us; else they will join themselves unto our enemies and get them up out of our land, for their hearts and faces are towards the land of Canaan.'

14.   And he set over them taskmasters to afflict them with slavery; and they built strong cities for Pharaoh, Pithom, and Raamses and they built all the walls and all the fortifications which had fallen in the cities of Egypt.

15.   And they made them serve with rigour, and the more they dealt evilly with them, the more they increased and multiplied.

16.   And the people of Egypt abominated the children of Israel

Jubilees 47

1.   And in the seventh week, in the seventh year, in the forty-seventh jubilee, thy father went forth [2303 A.M.] from the land of Canaan, and thou wast born in the fourth week, in the sixth year thereof, in the [2330 A.M.] forty-eighth jubilee; this was the time of tribulation on the children of Israel.

2.   And Pharaoh, king of Egypt, issued a command regarding them that they should cast all their male

children which were born into the river.

3.   And they cast them in for seven months until the day that thou wast born

4.   And thy mother hid thee for three months, and they told regarding her. And she made an ark for thee, and covered it with pitch and asphalt, and placed it in the flags on the bank of the river, and she placed thee in it seven days, and thy mother came by night and suckled thee, and by day Miriam, thy sister, guarded thee from the birds.

5.   And in those days Tharmuth, the daughter of Pharaoh, came to bathe in the river, and she heard thy voice crying, and she told her maidens to bring thee forth, and they brought thee unto her.

6.   And she took thee out of the ark, and she had compassion on thee.

7.   And thy sister said unto her: 'Shall I go and call unto thee one of the Hebrew women to nurse and suckle this babe for thee?'

8.   And she said <unto her>: 'Go.' And she went and called thy mother Jochebed, and she gave her wages, and she nursed thee.

9.   And afterwards, when thou wast grown up, they brought thee unto the daughter of Pharaoh, and thou didst become her son, and Amram thy father taught thee writing, and after thou hadst completed three

weeks they brought thee into the royal court.

10.　And thou wast three weeks of years at court until the time [2351-] when thou didst go forth from the royal court and didst see an Egyptian smiting thy friend who was [2372 A.M.] of the children of Israel, and thou didst slay him and hide him in the sand.

11.　And on the second day thou didst and two of the children of Israel striving together, and thou didst say to him who was doing the wrong: 'Why dost thou smite thy brother?'

12.　And he was angry and indignant, and said: 'Who made thee a prince and a judge over us? Thinkest thou to kill me as thou killedst the Egyptian yesterday?' And thou didst fear and flee on account of these words.

Jubilees 48

1.　And in the sixth year of the third week of the forty-ninth jubilee thou didst depart and dwell <in [2372 A.M.] the land of Midian>, five weeks and one year. And thou didst return into Egypt in the second week in the second year in the fiftieth jubilee.

2.　And thou thyself knowest what He spake unto thee on [2410 A.M.] Mount Sinai, and what prince Mastêmâ desired to do with thee when thou wast returning into Egypt <on the way when thou didst meet him at the lodging-place>.

3.　Did he not with all his power seek to slay thee and deliver the Egyptians out of thy hand when he saw that thou wast sent to execute judgment and vengeance on the Egyptians?

4.　And I delivered thee out of his hand, and thou didst perform the signs and wonders which thou wast sent to perform in Egypt against Pharaoh, and against all his house, and against his servants and his people.

5.　And the Lord executed a great vengeance on them for Israel's sake, and smote them through (the plagues of) blood and frogs, lice and dog-flies, and malignant boils breaking forth in blains; and their cattle by death; and by hail-stones, thereby He destroyed everything that grew for them; and by locusts which devoured the residue which had been left by the hail, and by darkness; and <by the death> of the first-born of men and animals, and on all their idols the Lord took vengeance and burned them with fire.

6.　And everything was sent through thy hand, that thou shouldst declare (these things) before they were done, and thou didst speak with the king of Egypt before all his servants and before his people.

7.　And everything took place according to thy words; ten great and terrible judgments came on the land of Egypt that thou mightest execute vengeance on it for Israel.

8.   And the Lord did everything for Israel's sake, and according to His covenant, which he had ordained with Abraham that He would take vengeance on them as they had brought them by force into bondage.

9.   And the prince Mastêmâ stood up against thee, and sought to cast thee into the hands of Pharaoh, and he helped the Egyptian sorcerers,

10.   and they stood up and wrought before thee the evils indeed we permitted them to work, but the remedies we did not allow to be wrought by their hands.

11.   And the Lord smote them with malignant ulcers, and they were not able to stand, for we destroyed them so that they could not perform a single sign.

12.   And notwithstanding all (these) signs and wonders the prince Mastêmâ was not put to shame because he took courage and cried to the Egyptians to pursue after thee with all the powers of the Egyptians, with their chariots, and with their horses, and with all the hosts of the peoples of Egypt.

13.   And I stood between the Egyptians and Israel, and we delivered Israel out of his hand, and out of the hand of his people, and the Lord brought them through the midst of the sea as if it were dry land.

14.   And all the peoples whom he brought to pursue after Israel, the Lord our God cast them into the midst of the sea, into the depths of the abyss beneath the children of Israel, even as the people of Egypt had cast their children into the river He took vengeance on 1,000,000 of them, and one thousand strong and energetic men were destroyed on account of one suckling of the children of thy people which they had thrown into the river.

15.   And on the fourteenth day and on the fifteenth and on the sixteenth and on the seventeenth and on the eighteenth the prince Mastêmâ was bound and imprisoned behind the children of Israel that he might not accuse them.

16.   And on the nineteenth we let them loose that they might help the Egyptians and pursue the children of Israel.

17.   And he hardened their hearts and made them stubborn, and the device was devised by the Lord our God that He might smite the Egyptians and cast them into the sea.

18.   And on the fourteenth we bound him that he might not accuse the children of Israel on the day when they asked the Egyptians for vessels and garments, vessels of silver, and vessels of gold, and vessels of bronze, in order to despoil the Egyptians in return for the bondage in which they had forced them to serve.

19.   And we did not lead forth the children of Israel from Egypt empty handed.

Jubilees 49

1. Remember the commandment which the Lord commanded thee concerning the passover, that thou shouldst celebrate it in its season on the fourteenth of the first month, that thou shouldst kill it before it is evening, and that they should eat it by night on the evening of the fifteenth from the time of the setting of the sun.

2. For on this night -the beginning of the festival and the beginning of the joy- ye were eating the passover in Egypt, when all the powers of Mastêmâ had been let loose to slay all the first-born in the land of Egypt, from the first-born of Pharaoh to the first-born of the captive maid-servant in the mill, and to the cattle.

3. And this is the sign which the Lord gave them: Into every house on the lintels of which they saw the blood of a lamb of the first year, into (that) house they should not enter to slay, but should pass by (it), that all those should be saved that were in the house because the sign of the blood was on its lintels.

4. And the powers of the Lord did everything according as the Lord commanded them, and they passed by all the children of Israel, and the plague came not upon them to destroy from amongst them any soul either of cattle, or man, or dog.

5. And the plague was very grievous in Egypt, and there was no house in Egypt where there was not one dead, and weeping and lamentation.

6. And all Israel was eating the flesh of the paschal lamb, and drinking the wine, and was lauding, and blessing, and giving thanks to the Lord God of their fathers, and was ready to go forth from under the yoke of Egypt, and from the evil bondage.

7. And remember thou this day all the days of thy life, and observe it from year to year all the days of thy life, once a year, on its day, according to all the law thereof, and do not adjourn (it) from day to day, or from month to month.

8. For it is an eternal ordinance, and engraven on the heavenly tablets regarding all the children of Israel that they should observe it every year on its day once a year, throughout all their generations; and there is no limit of days, for this is ordained for ever.

9. And the man who is free from uncleanness, and does not come to observe it on occasion of its day, so as to bring an acceptable offering before the Lord, and to eat and to drink before the Lord on the day of its festival, that man who is clean and close at hand shall be cut off: because he offered not the oblation of the Lord in its appointed season, he shall take the guilt upon himself.

10. Let the children of Israel come and observe the passover on the day of its fixed time, on the fourteenth

day of the first month, between the evenings, from the third part of the day to the third part of the night, for two portions of the day are given to the light, and a third part to the evening.

11. This is that which the Lord commanded thee that thou shouldst observe it between the evenings.

12. And it is not permissible to slay it during any period of the light, but during the period bordering on the evening, and let them eat it at the time of the evening, until the third part of the night, and whatever is left over of all its flesh from the third part of the night and onwards, let them burn it with fire.

13. And they shall not cook it with water, nor shall they eat it raw, but roast on the fire: they shall eat it with diligence, its head with the inwards thereof and its feet they shall roast with fire, and not break any bone thereof; for of the children of Israel no bone shall be crushed.

14. For this reason the Lord commanded the children of Israel to observe the passover on the day of its fixed time, and they shall not break a bone thereof; for it is a festival day, and a day commanded, and there may be no passing over from day to day, and month to month, but on the day of its festival let it be observed.

15. And do thou command the children of Israel to observe the passover throughout their days, every year, once a year on the day of its fixed time, and it shall come for a memorial well pleasing before the Lord, and no plague shall come upon them to slay or to smite in that year in which they celebrate the passover in its season in every respect according to His command.

16. And they shall not eat it outside the sanctuary of the Lord, but before the sanctuary of the Lord, and all the people of the congregation of Israel shall celebrate it in its appointed season.

17. And every man who has come upon its day shall eat it in the sanctuary of your God before the Lord from twenty years old and upward; for thus is it written and ordained that they should eat it in the sanctuary of the Lord.

18. And when the children of Israel come into the land which they are to possess, into the land of Canaan, and set up the tabernacle of the Lord in the midst of the land in one of their tribes until the sanctuary of the Lord has been built in the land, let them come and celebrate the passover in the midst of the tabernacle of the Lord, and let them slay it before the Lord from year to year.

19. And in the days when the house has been built in the name of the Lord in the land of their inheritance, they shall go there and slay the passover in the evening, at sunset, at the third part of the day.

20. And they shall offer its blood on the threshold of the altar, and

shall place its fat on the fire which is upon the altar, and they shall eat its flesh roasted with fire in the court of the house which has been sanctified in the name of the Lord.

21.   And they may not celebrate the passover in their cities, nor in any place save before the tabernacle of the Lord, or before His house where His name hath dwelt; and they shall not go astray from the Lord.

22.   And do thou, Moses, command the children of Israel to observe the ordinances of the passover, as it was commanded unto thee; declare thou unto them every year and the day of its days, and the festival of unleavened bread, that they should eat unleavened bread seven days, (and) that they should observe its festival, and that they bring an oblation every day during those seven days of joy before the Lord on the altar of your God.

23.   For ye celebrated this festival with haste when ye went forth from Egypt till ye entered into the wilderness of Shur; for on the shore of the sea ye completed it.

Jubilees 50

1.   And after this law I made known to thee the days of the Sabbaths in the desert of Sin[ai], which is between Elim and Sinai.

2.   And I told thee of the Sabbaths of the land on Mount Sinai, and I told thee of the jubilee years in the sabbaths of years: but the year

thereof have I not told thee till ye enter the land which ye are to possess.

3.   And the land also shall keep its sabbaths while they dwell upon it, and they shall know the jubilee year.

4.   Wherefore I have ordained for thee the year-weeks and the years and the jubilees: there are forty-nine jubilees from the days of Adam until this day, [2410 A.M.] and one week and two years: and there are yet forty years to come (lit. 'distant') for learning the [2450 A.M.] commandments of the Lord, until they pass over into the land of Canaan, crossing the Jordan to the west.

5.   And the jubilees shall pass by, until Israel is cleansed from all guilt of fornication, and uncleanness, and pollution, and sin, and error, and dwells with confidence in all the land, and there shall be no more a Satan or any evil one, and the land shall be clean from that time for evermore.

6.   And behold the commandment regarding the Sabbaths -I have written (them) down for thee- and all the judgments of its laws.

7.   Six days shalt thou labour, but on the seventh day is the Sabbath of the Lord your God. In it ye shall do no manner of work, ye and your sons, and your men- servants and your maid-servants, and all your cattle and the sojourner also who is with you.

8.   And the man that does any work on it shall die: whoever desecrates that day, whoever lies with (his) wife, or whoever says he will do something on it, that he will set out on a journey thereon in regard to any buying or selling: and whoever draws water thereon which he had not prepared for himself on the sixth day, and whoever takes up any burden to carry it out of his tent or out of his house shall die.

9.   Ye shall do no work whatever on the Sabbath day save what ye have prepared for yourselves on the sixth day, so as to eat, and drink, and rest, and keep Sabbath from all work on that day, and to bless the Lord your God, who has given you a day of festival and a holy day: and a day of the holy kingdom for all Israel is this day among their days for ever.

10.   For great is the honour which the Lord has given to Israel that they should eat and drink and be satisfied on this festival day, and rest thereon from all labour which belongs to the labour of the children of men save burning frankincense and bringing oblations and sacrifices before the Lord for days and for Sabbaths.

11.   This work alone shall be done on the Sabbath-days in the sanctuary of the Lord your God; that they may atone for Israel with sacrifice continually from day to day for a memorial well-pleasing before the Lord, and that He may receive them always from day to day according as thou hast been commanded.

12.   And every man who does any work thereon, or goes a journey, or tills (his) farm, whether in his house or any other place, and whoever lights a fire, or rides on any beast, or travels by ship on the sea, and whoever strikes or kills anything, or slaughters a beast or a bird, or whoever catches an animal or a bird or a fish, or whoever fasts or makes war on the Sabbaths:

13.   The man who does any of these things on the Sabbath shall die, so that the children of Israel shall observe the Sabbaths according to the commandments regarding the Sabbaths of the land, as it is written in the tablets, which He gave into my hands that I should write out for thee the laws of the seasons, and the seasons according to the division of their days.

Herewith is completed the account of the division of the days.

Assembled by
KARAJAH YASHAR

www.ingramcontent.com/pod-product-compliance
Lightning Source LLC
Chambersburg PA
CBHW080942120626
46546CB00010B/2808